DATE DUE

AP 1 9 05			
06			

DEMCO 38-296

NEW WORKPLACES
FOR NEW WORKSTYLES

New Workplaces for New Workstyles

Marilyn Zelinsky

McGraw-Hill

New York San Francisco Washington, D.C. Auckland Bogotá
Caracas Lisbon London Madrid Mexico City Milan
Montreal New Delhi San Juan Singapore
Sydney Tokyo Toronto

1998

Library of Congress Cataloging-in-Publication Data

Zelinsky, Marilyn.
   New workplaces for new workstyles / Marilyn Zelinsky.
      p.   cm.
   Includes bibliographical references and index.
   ISBN 0-07-063324-X
   1. Office decoration—United States.   2. Interior architecture—
United States.   I. Title.
   NK2195.04Z46   1997
   725'.23'0973—dc21   97-30216
                                                       CIP

McGraw-Hill
   *A Division of The **McGraw·Hill** Companies*

1 2 3 4 5 6 7 8 9 0   KGP/KGP   9 0 3 2 1 0 9 8

ISBN 0-07-063324-X

*The sponsoring editor for this book was Wendy Lochner, the editing supervisor was Patricia V. Amoroso, and the production supervisor was
Clare B. Stanley. It was designed and set by Silvers Design.*

Printed and bound by Quebecor/Kingsport.

McGraw-Hill books are available at special quantity discounts to use as premiums and sales promotions, or for use in
corporate training programs. For more information, please write to the Director of Special Sales, McGraw-Hill, 11 West
19th Street, New York, NY 10011. Or contact your local bookstore.

To my husband, best friend, and soul mate, Steve,
and my cherished mother, Ida, with whose
unconditional love I feel I can
accomplish anything.

Contents

Foreword

"Breaking out of the box" is one of those business phrases that makes me gag. It inherently elevates "change," "difference," and "innovation" over most everything else. Since knowledge of anything is based on the contemplation of it, our hyper-world honors changes in things over contemplation which seriously undermines knowing. And, in our mesmerized-by-what's-new culture, this "breaking out of the box" means that people offering untested ideas are given as much or more credence and air-time as those engaged in the hard-work process of really understanding how their piece of the world works, and how it might work better. (A phrase I'd like to hear more of in corporate-land is, "there are no easy solutions . . . that are actually solutions" or better yet, "there are no solutions . . . just successive steps towards one." But enough of quotable-phrase wisdom, and back to crankiness.)

The phrase "we need to break out of the box" is sometimes used by corporate managers who want people to accept (even embrace) a poorly thought through innovation, . . . one which probably will make work-life harder or meaner, one that really can't be sold on its merits. So these corporate change agents dish out the intended-to-be-humiliating challenge, "aren't you willing to break out of the box?"

New Officing is a breaking out of the box, but it is an important business and design idea that has real merit, one that has gained much momentum since its first development around 1990. Now it too is in danger of becoming one of these cliché'd break-out-of-the-box innovations. It is much hyped in the design and business media as the cure for everything: "bloated real estate," "attention-to-customer deficit," "poor team interactions," and other ills. All this hype is probably too much of a burden for any innovations to actually have to deliver on, although New Officing can deliver on

much of it. And New Officing isn't even a single "it" to begin with, but a process of organizational analysis that seems to yield three basic strategies. These can be used singly or in concert based on the situation, the organization's strategy and needs, and their attitude towards their people, who are their intellectual capital.

The process is one of thoughtfully examining the organization in terms of its business strategy, projective futures, its past history of initiatives, its use of technology, and its work processes, all in the framework of its people and culture. The three strategies that seem to emerge consistently from this process are:

1. *Radically redesigning the workplace to support radically changing ways of working.* This strategy re-examines the underlying assumptions about what work is in the company and emphasizes the increased importance of both continuous learning in-the-work and team and group work.

2. *Working-from-anywhere, which broadens the range of locations considered useful as workplaces.* This broadening is only enabled by powerful, portable technology and robust networks. In work-from-anywhere, the "extra" work site most everybody has is the home. Using the home is an arrangement which is often attractive; to companies because it is (almost) "free" workspace; and to those workers whose quality of life is improved, and who are comfortable with the increasing blurring of the traditional compartmentalization of work, homelife, vacation, travel, etc.

3. *"Hoteling," which recognizes that folks using work-from-anywhere's multiple work locations may not spend enough time in any one workspace to justify "owning" one.* This would certainly be true for those who are out of the office far more than in. In hoteling, you don't "own" a workspace in the base office, but get a really good one whenever you need it. When you

are out again, it goes back into "inventory" and is distributed to others as needed, a space-saving, fluid, just-in-time resource.

Most companies and commentators call all this "alternative" something or other . . . Alternative Work Environments, Alternative Officing, etc. I call all of this New Officing because "alternative" suggests that there is a primary mode of officing, the traditional office, which really still makes the most sense. The rapidity of New Officing's adoption and the fact that every company we know of is actively exploring its use suggest to me that it will be the norm very quickly and the word "alternative" will make no sense, as in "alternative to what?"

Right now, all the hype and the hope that New Officing is an easy solution tends to undermine the thoughtful process necessary to develop the most appropriate New Officing strategy. Most would-be box-breakers/change agents/corporate innovators behave as if New Officing were a new "product" that you can buy off the shelf from a design firm, their own facilities department, or a management consultant. Or that they could go out and benchmark how other companies have "bought" and used this product and then you could go and do "it" yourself. But because it is a process (not a product), and a new one, and certainly not business-as-usual, it's important to temper hope for easy solutions with some real contemplation of your particular situation, and to supplant hype with knowledge, such as Marilyn emphasizes throughout this book.

New Officing is one of the most explosive innovations I've seen in 40 years of practice, and because it is based on thoughtful analysis, it is still really new. It has its share of zealots, hucksters, and hypesters and thankfully, some thoughtful and even innovative practitioners, observers, and analysts. But many forces are still at work in our culture that assume very simplistic approaches will magically bring great benefit. Some examples are:

- Managers' desires to be seen as innovators by their bosses and other innovators. "Box-breaking" often clouds managers' thinking about New Officing, leading to problems in its conception, its pacing, its execution, in assessment of a company's readiness-to-adopt, or even its appropriateness for the company or for the department in the first place.
- Many design firms, with little New Officing experience, have instantly declared themselves New

Officing experts, marketing it as if it were an additional "specialty," like graphics programs, construction management, or value engineering. This posture assumes New Officing is an "it," and whatever the problem is, the solution is a design. It is a process and a response to a business problem, and design is just an enabler.

- Corporate real estate folks, in perhaps their last bid to become corporate heroes, are promising a massive, portfolio-wide space reduction through New Officing. However, success in this is quite dependent on new mobile technology and substantial cultural change, neither of which real estate can normally control. More importantly, experience thus far shows that where massive space reduction is the primary goal, New Officing tends to have a high failure rate. The success rate is much higher where the goal of space reduction is strongly coupled with helping people "work smarter," in which New Officing is conceived of as an integrated system of work-enablers.
- Facilities Managers (FM), perhaps as a hedge against their work being increasingly outsourced, could be touting New Officing as a new form of facilities management. If "facilities" were to be reconceptualized as "all the locations in which work is done" and "management" was of an integrated system of work-enablers, it really could be a new discipline. But the FM folks seem to be doing little to develop the new perspectives, skills, values, and roles required to reach this vision.
- Companies continue to benchmark each other's New Officing successes (no one reports failures). Those now considering innovation interview those who were responsible for it at other companies, who tell them, "oh, it really worked here." And a half-truth becomes gospel in yet another boardroom.

This is certainly not an indictment of New Officing, since I'm one of its pioneers, remain a strong advocate, and have a substantial practice solely devoted to it. But it is intended as a strong warning that we're converting this new set of good ideas into an approved, commercial "product" long before its outcomes are fully understood; long before there is an adequate body of work to learn enough from for widespread competent copycat applications; long before there are many competent distributors of New Officing (it requires complex, cross-disciplinary analysis and actions); and long before most organizations that want to adopt New

Officing have the ability to successfully implement the integrated system of changes that it implies.

So what do we do? If New Officing were just another trend (like the hula hoop, the pet rock, and Post-modern design), we could just wait for it to go away, and we could get back to business-as-usual. But it will not go away, for it is an intelligent response to a set of interlinked trends (many of them global) that are now transforming the very nature of work and soon, settlement patterns, modes of learning, and social relationships. What we need to do is seek, welcome, read, and heed books like this one. It is a thoughtful and comprehensive work that casts Marilyn's fine journalistic eye over the practices of New Officing, and a close reading can help us make wiser decisions about supporting people's best work and doing New Officing at its best.

Michael Brill
Architect
President of the Buffalo
Organization for Social and
Technological Innovation, Inc.

Foreword

It was the summer of 1968. I had just begun my first work-study assignment during my undergraduate work at Northeastern University and was spending 6 months working for a well-known consumer products company near New York City.

One of the many lessons I quickly learned about organizational life was that rank did indeed have its privileges, in this case, in the form of job level-matched office size and decor. Under the tutelage of a seasoned employee, I learned how easy it was to deduce the job level and status of anyone by simply scanning his or her office, eyeballing the square footage, and doing a quick inventory of the thickness of the rug pile, the plushness of the upholstery, and the patina of the wood desk—even the distinction between a metal versus wooden coat-and-hat tree in the corner of the office.

It was as if every feature of the office carried an invisible label that the savvy could see and use to decide how much respect and deference to accord the inhabitant of the office. I was even taught to recognize the signs that an executive had been put out to pasture—mismatched furniture, fewer buttons on the telephone than the size of the desk would normally indicate, and so on.

Since then, I've been intrigued by the ways in which organizations use space and furnishings to connote—and confer—status and rank. I'll admit to being party to this game throughout my corporate years; by the time I left my "real" job in 1982 to start my consulting business, I had moved into progressively bigger and better offices to match my bigger and better paychecks and titles. It was quite a letdown to move into my first home office—a hastily emptied small fourth bedroom in our home, furnished with a bridge chair and card table. Spartan as it was, I never felt as comfortable in any office as I did in that one.

Having spent almost 15 years since then consulting, speaking, and writing about telecommuting and alternative officing, it has become increasingly clear to me that if the state of the practice of "officing" (a term that I first heard used by Duncan Sutherland, Jr.) were the benchmark for all the other organizational "-ing's," then we would be doing our accounting with quill pens, our manufacturing with hammer and anvil, and our marketing with sandwich boards. The bad news is that, for the most part, the office hasn't progressed nearly as much as have the activities done in the office—but the good news is that there is a growing recognition of this problem and a rapidly expanding set of solutions, research, and advice for dealing with it.

Just as it's said that a hospital is a terrible place to get well, an office is a terrible place to get office work done. The office of today is, for the most part, a descendant of the farm workplace of the 1700s and the factory workplace of the 1800s. In both cases, employers had no choice but to bring all the workers to one workplace and to require them to be there at the same time. No one would say that the 1990s office is anything like the farm or factory of old—except that we've clung to those same time–same place rules mercilessly, and only since the early 1990s have we begun to rethink the assumptions about where and how office workers do their work.

Let me make four observations about this budding transition to the alternative officing model:

1. *Task differentiation:* We're getting smarter about realizing that knowledge workers in the office don't do the same thing 8 hours a day, 5 days a week. Their jobs are broken up into heads-down, intensive, individual-contributor work, informal interactions with one or more coworkers or clients, and more formal team or group interactions. Smart organizations (with a healthy push from architects and designers) are realizing that we need to let people work where they work best, given what they need to do. The office is one place, not the only place, to do "office work."

2. *Enabling technology:* Office work is more portable than ever. We have more technology on the shelf that we know what to do with, and it continues to get better, faster, and cheaper. While it all doesn't work as well or as smoothly as the commercials during the Super Bowl might suggest, the fact is that the right combination of hardware, software, and telecommunications is opening up plenty of opportunities for decentralizing the office.

3. *Generation X and life after downsizing:* There are two demographic factors influencing the move to alternative officing. First, the influx of the VCR-skilled, Nintendo-trained, laptop-literate workers is creating a bottom-up pressure on organizations to allow more flexibility in work methods and locations. The twenty-something MBA who grew up using a computer in elementary school, a cellular phone in high school, and a laptop in college won't sit still (figuratively or literally) if told to come into the office every day.

I'm always reminded about the technological prowess of this generation when I think of my own kids. At this writing, our son Adam has just gone off for his freshman year at Yale; among the many reasons I'll miss him is that he was my resident computer consultant. After we moved him into his dorm, we picked up his computer (as did all the other freshmen). I suspect he has more computing power in his machine than existed on my entire campus when I was a college freshman in 1967. Our daughter, Lisa, now almost 14, is equally competent with the computer; both have been using one since their preschool years. I distinctly remember some fights in the back of the car over which kid was going to get to use my laptop while we were driving to visit the grandparents.

Second, one of the outcomes of downsizing is the "do-more-with-less" ethic that drives smart managers to realize the value of options like telecommuting. The employees who remain after staff cuts are freed from the boundaries of time and space of the traditional office and allowed to work in environments where they can more likely meet increasingly difficult expectations.

4. *Managerial mindsets:* Last but not least, we're seeing a slow but sure move away from the command-and-control style of management that was almost universally taught, modeled, and rewarded from the 1950s forward. Many authors have written about the alternatives; suffice it to say here that managers are starting to change from nontrusting autocrats to empowering coaches for whom having remote workers isn't so frightening a prospect. The transition isn't complete, and may never be, but we're heading in the right direction.

There's one more factor that can't be ignored, and it is perhaps the best—and worst—reason for alternative officing: the undeniable waste of space and the excessive cost of traditional office designs. The good news is that today's business climate is forcing executives to reconsider sacred cows such as the fixed space standards, permanently assigned office space, and status-linked space allocations.

The bad news is that greed is at times overtaking good design and common sense; the opportunity to save some money by using nonterritorial designs or telecommuting or the "virtual office" can lead to the temptation to save much more money by reducing office space dramatically or closing offices altogether. As the old office is shuttered, the departing employees are given their laptops, cell phones, and pagers and pushed out the door with the encouragement to "go virtual" while the controller or CFO calculates the anticipated savings.

This is the greatest challenge we face today as we consider alternative officing, and it is one of the reasons that this book is so valuable. There's nothing wrong with saving money, economizing on space, or pushing employees out into the field to have more contact with customers. But when this is done indiscriminately, and the floorplan is trimmed with a hatchet instead of a scalpel, we risk creating more problems than we solve.

In visiting alternative offices around the world, I've noticed that many companies are out to save money as the primary objective. I remember speaking to a sales rep for a Fortune 100 company; his branch office was being drastically reduced in size, and the sales reps were all told they were going "virtual." He was in his mid-fifties, and he seemed quite upset about the fact that he would be going to the office only rarely. "For 27 years, I've managed to keep my sanity working for this company—and keep my marriage together—by maintaining a clear separation between my work life and my home life. Now I have to bring my work life into my home life, and I'm not sure how my wife and I are going to deal with this."

As dysfunctional as the office can be—a fact that has been aptly highlighted by Scott Adams's *Dilbert* comic strips—we must remember that it serves several functions that can't be easily replaced. It is a focal point for organizational identity, it is a common space for shared resources and shared experiences, and it is an ideal work location for people who cannot or should not work at home or on the road.

For every person who feels more at ease and more effective working in blue jeans from home, there's another person who either needs the structure and cues of the office in order to be effective or has two preschoolers running around under foot that makes the typical office distractions pale by comparison. The role of the design and facilities professionals is to push the pendulum away from the factory-based same time–same place model toward the reasonable alternative, without letting it swing to the any time–no place extreme model.

The other main role for these professionals is to capitalize on best practices, and Marilyn's book can help identify those companies. As Marilyn points out throughout this book, it makes no sense to innovate for innovation's sake if six other organizations have painfully learned that painting the walls three shades of purple doesn't have quite the effect on productivity that was imagined. Designers and facilities professionals always have to walk the fine line between providing their best advice and complying with client wishes and preferences, however ill-founded the latter might be.

In fact, in my experience working with a company that hired a design firm to redesign its space, I saw a design evolve that was quite troubling. The designers did a good job collecting information about what the people did and what kind of collaboration space and privacy they needed, but the client seemed intent on having a free-address office that flew in the face of the established company culture. The end product was beautiful—but dysfunctional. Hardly anyone who had to work in it liked it. I wished the designers had stuck to their guns and prevailed with a more appropriate design.

I would argue that alternative officing is one case where these professionals must be a "benevolent conscience," i.e., they have to push the client to do what's right without moralizing or threatening. That is a particular challenge with alternative officing because of the dual temptations of keeping up with trends and cost-cutting greed. This is a far more complex role than consulting on which vendor's panel system to use in a more traditional office. Alternative officing initiatives can mask a range of cultural, psychological, and customer-service issues that must be put on the table—and it's the design and facility professionals' role to do so as you will realize must be done as you read and refer to this book.

Speaking of vendors, let me offer one last observation based on 15 years of watching the furniture ad furnishings industry cope with home offices, mobile offices, team offices, satellite offices, and all the rest. There is a difference between adapting designs and innovating designs. Putting wheels and a handle on a two-drawer file cabinet so it can be pulled around the office is an adaptation. Designing a complete workspace that magically folds up and disappears when it's not needed is an innovation. Wheeled file cabinets do not an alternative office make, and the vendors who will make the more significant and lasting contributions to alternative officing are the ones that depart most dramatically from their metal-bending roots.

I know this is easier said than done, and I don't want to minimize some of the truly brilliant designs that have come from the major and lesser-known firms in the last 5 years. I empathize with the vendors that have huge investments in design and production to churn out panel systems and modular desking units; a major transition for them is not easier than it was for the Big Three automobile companies to face the small-car challenge or for the big mainframe computer companies to deal with the PC revolution. But unless they really commit to that kind of a change, I'm not sure the traditional vendors in this officing field will maintain their leadership positions.

I've written this sitting in my home office, wearing a T-shirt and shorts, on a Saturday morning, looking out the window at my backyard at a clear late-summer morning. I've come a long way from my late sixties corporate-office roots, and the office itself has also come a long way as Marilyn illustrates throughout her book. The best is yet to come, however, and we will be here to track it for you. I welcome an outstanding guide and reference like this book as a vital and necessary tool to move us further along the alternative officing path.

Gil Gordon
Gil Gordon Associates
Editor of *Telecommuting Review*

Introduction

After a decade of living and working in New York City, I became fed up with noisy, dirty city life and moved out to greener suburbs. Sometime around 1990, I decided I had had enough of commuting by train every day into and out of the city, but felt I had no choice but to continue on this tiring, antiproductive path because I wanted to write for *Interiors Magazine*. Around the same time, two things happened: I was assigned to write a monthly column on home office design, and a few hardy snowstorms prevented me from taking that train ride into the city. To my surprise, I was able to work at home and hand in my articles even earlier than before. I felt like I had discovered the secret of having the best of both worlds, but I still felt sneaky, like I was doing something wrong by working better and smarter from the comfort of my home. But it was during the research for the home office design column that I learned about a trend called *alternative officing*, a subject with which I became profoundly fascinated.

When I began to work at home on a regular basis—one or two days a week—it was not the normal way to conduct business in my former company. It still isn't today, and I was among the ranks of "closet" telecommuters who didn't report these kinds of work habits to human resources or facilities. I began to wonder if there were other companies out there that embraced new and flexible work processes, and from there my natural curiosity and research grew until it ultimately turned itself into this book.

When I came to work at *Interiors* in 1990, the commercial interior design industry was in a shambles—well, more like a long and lazy slump. Downsizing was just becoming business as usual. Suddenly it started to turn around by a few degrees in 1994, then a few more degrees in 1995. Now, just about every commercial interior designer says the same thing, "I'm so busy I can't believe it! I can't BELIEVE it!" Flying here and there, never in the office for more than a few days at a time, it became customary to do many of my interviews by e-mail with designers. End users are no different. Clients in the real estate and facility departments are so busy traveling to and from various business units to find out their newest needs that it came down to doing phone interviews via car phones and e-mail at all times during the day and night. It was pretty thrilling to hear throngs of people say they were so busy after years of hearing this industry cry on each other's shoulders.

Why is everyone so busy? Most people said that just about every client has a new work process, sales model, or just general way of business that now needs the right physical environment to support those objectives. The myriad designers I've spoken with across the country report that almost every corporate client now asks them about alternative officing and how it might impact their businesses. Most companies that expanded in the 1980s signed on 10- and 15-year leases that are all up somewhere from 1995 through the year 2000, and now they are realizing it's way too much space to renew for staffs that are streamlined, mobile, and more reliant now than ever on their laptop.

WHO SHOULD READ THIS BOOK?

This is a book about planning and design written for everyone who has a keen interest in the workplace of today and tomorrow, which is a central theme and concern in almost everyone's life. Whether you are a junior designer or senior designer, a newly minted or seasoned facility or corporate real estate manager, a workplace strategist, a human resources or IT professional, you're bombarded day after day with a mountain of information about the new workplace that can be overwhelming. This book creates the framework to help you embrace and better understand the benefits and consequences of what is happening in the newly evolving contemporary workplace. The many stories and insights of design and facility professionals in this book will give you information and help in easing the transition within your workplace. In addition, the comprehensive index will make it easy and fast to find the information you are seeking, whether it be about hoteling software or about selling the idea of initiating a new workplace to the CEO or finding a survey on the number of companies with new workplace programs.

WHAT THIS BOOK WILL DO FOR YOU

As the business world changes, so does the role of many designers and facility executives. Corporate restructuring of the white-collar workforce, finding better ways to deal with bloated occupancy costs, team-based problem solving, the need and the apprehension of dissolving hierarchies, or the schizophrenic activity of the Clean Air Act of 1990, new laws and liability issues are impacting planning and management at all levels, especially in the design, facility, and real estate management community. You are the professionals increasingly being asked to define, program, design, and manage a reinvented workplace. To do so requires skills that differ from those needed years ago.

I've heard you ask the following questions about alternative office design and management during informal conversations, formal interviews, and at the many conferences and seminars I've attended on the subject, which are covered within this book:

- How can the designer, facility, and real estate professional become proactive in achieving a company's business objectives?
- How has strategic facility planning changed in the advent of the alternative work environment?
- What are the furniture solutions for the alternative office?
- What do terms like *hoteling* and *free address* really mean?
- How many people actually work in alternative workplaces?
- How do you get employees to accept new ways of working?
- How do you sell the concept of alternative officing to the CEO?
- Does alternative officing really lower occupancy costs?
- How do we plan, design, and manage a telecommuter's home office?

- How do we deal with corporate culture problems in a virtual office?
- What are the new technologies and wiring options we should know about?
- How do we analyze work patterns to determine what type of virtual office to plan?
- What are the legal issues we need to know?
- What are other companies doing in the way of alternative office design?
- Where do I get a boilerplate telecommuting and remote work policy?

There are three major themes addressed in the three parts of this book:

Part 1, Synergy, will bring into focus how the social and business climate has rendered the need to rethink the workplace. In this part, you will find definitions and a collection of surveys about alternative workplace strategies and an overview of some of the pioneering projects that made headlines and paved the way for more recent contemporary offices.

Part 2, Framework, deals with the steps involved in planning, piloting, and establishing an alternative workplace, including what you need to know about new space planning techniques for alternative offices, complicated technologies that support the new workplace, product and furniture solutions for both on-site and off-site interiors, and finally, a chapter on the evolving legal issues associated with the nontraditional workplace.

Part 3, Strategies, features case studies of companies from a variety of industries that have implemented, or are in the process of defining, their alternative office pilots and programs. Chapter 9 takes a look at companywide alternative workplace strategies, and Chap. 10 focuses on site-specific design strategies.

A FAIR VIEW OF THE NEW WORKPLACE

Although flexibility and mobility is an issue for the end user, it disturbs me that some alternative workplace experts tell designers that they are going to go out of business or facility professionals that they will lose their jobs if they don't subscribe to nontraditional business models. I'll admit that I believe that it doesn't hurt a commercial designer or a facility manager to have a basic understanding of these evolving facility and business concepts (do you need to know what a "white-space opportunity" is in strategic planning lingo? You do if you are dealing with CEOs.) Even if they aren't currently practicing them, for inevitably the need to know and answer questions will arise. And of course we continue to hear that facility professionals want to speak and understand the language of the boardroom, to understand fully the corporate objectives. Most important, however, is the need for a design and facility professional to know when *not* to pursue an alternative work environment because it doesn't fit in with the overall corporate objectives.

In fact, the percentage of people both domestically and abroad who live in new workplace environments is still small, growing and sometimes subsiding at jagged and incremental rates. The vestiges of hierarchy and tradition are still evident in many a company and will continue to be that way for years for they may not be ready, or they may not have the need to telecommute, hotel, motel, free-address, or live in a universal plan. Some say that alternative officing is sometimes a religion to many advocates. And I say we learn to respect everyone's choice of religion, perhaps educating others about our preferences, without trying to intimidate or force our predilections on someone else. The danger with embracing alternative and potentially exotic ways of working is that companies will fail to consider a company's long-term plans. When Corporate America fervently embraced management consultant Michael Hammer's concepts of reengineering, it basically blew up in many companies' faces (it ultimately resulted in massive downsizings). Why? Hammer says in his newest book on the subject that managers tend to grow too excited when they hear that there is an idea out there that is radical and promises dramatic results and improvement even if it doesn't fit within the overall strategic planning of the organization.

Nevertheless, the need to build more flexibility into the workplace is more than a mere fad—it is a very real concern of end users around the country, around the world. There are indeed pockets of end users around the country who are now shifting and exploring ways to support new work processes. Others are sifting through pertinent information about the new workplace, to determine at a later date how to integrate relevant processes. That kind of action presents new opportunities for designers to help the client understand how real estate and physical environment can affect a company's shifting business objectives. Putting an alternative workplace strategy into place is a long, arduous, and much of the time confusing process. But luckily, there are examples and models from which to learn, companies who took the plunge before alternative officing was ever fashionable. To steal a line from Brenda Laffin (I've borrowed much of her time-tested wisdom throughout the book), alternative workplace strategist at Southern California Edison, I bow down every night to the pioneers of alternative officing. I believe, however, that right now, we are *all* pioneers in crafting these new work processes, new workstyles, and new work environments, and I stand up and honor those who are in the trenches learning about and fighting for the same cause.

During the 5 years it took to research the book, and the additional year it took to write it, I became more and more of a self-appointed virtual worker. Now that I have resigned my position at *Interiors* to write full time from home, I still have two computers, a cellular phone, voice mail, and I get more done than I ever imagined by the sheer fact that I eliminated 20 hours a week of commuting time. Luckily, I am not alone in my quest for quality and balance of work and family life. Admittedly, although I am lovesick with this concept of the alternative workplace, the honeymoon is over for I have experienced both the joys and pitfalls of working outside corporate walls. I am learning even more as I "walk the talk," experiencing life firsthand as a home-based worker as research for the second book that I'm writing for McGraw-Hill about the home office. Fortunately, all of my experiences allow me to write this book with a fair eye on the subject. My views on the alternative office have matured, and they will continue to do so as I proceed to learn from myself and others about the processes of living and working in the new workplace and in this new world. My hope is that this book, with its collection of information and experiences from industry experts on the alternative office, will be a reference, an inspiration, and a tool for you to use toward your own discoveries in planning, designing, and managing the evolving contemporary workplace.

Marilyn Zelinsky Syarto
Fairfield, Connecticut
1998
E-mail:mzelinsky@aol.com

Acknowledgments

If we are going to talk about teaming and the virtual workplace, we should start here with acknowledgments. Behind every meaningful project, there is bound to be a team of dedicated colleagues, friends, and family members along for the ride, to witness the blood, sweat, and tears of the process. I dedicate this page to the following invaluable—and virtual—team that helped put this book together.

Words alone will never be enough to thank the following people. I am most grateful to my dearest friend, beacon of light, and colleague, Kristen Richards, who was a fountain of inspiration and insight; her never-ending spirit can be felt on each page. I cherish my dearest friend Lorraine Shea for her unconditional friendship, compassion, advice, love, and understanding when the book took priority over other things such as our friendship. I'm most thankful that my very patient former editor at *Interiors*, M. J. Madigan, pulled me together whenever I fell apart. Cynthia Froggatt's incredible knowledge of the subject and willingness to guide me along made a great deal of the information in this book possible. Michele Foyer gave me faith and hope in my abilities while climbing this long and winding mountain.

I'd like to give thanks to Dennis Cahill for his invaluable support and for being a fellow believer of the benefits of working "off-campus." Many thanks to Loren Arethas for introducing me to Okamura. I'm grateful to the entire *Interiors* staff for their patience and support.

I'd especially like to thank Paula Rice Jackson who gave me the opportunity to write the *Interiors'* column *HomeWork* from which the seeds of this book were sown.

Thanks from the bottom of my heart to the incredibly generous, supportive people in the design and facilities industry willing to share their valuable time and wisdom: Larry Cohen and Bob Evett of Steelcase; Ben Watson of Vitra, Ethan Anthony of Hoyle, Doran and Berry Architects for his help and insights; Alan Abrahams, who proves that along with wisdom comes a wry sense of humor and a generous heart; and Robin Morad for her willingness to share her brilliant insights on the subject. Thanks also to Jim Prendergast of Perkins & Will (for a great idea in "the day in the life of a hoteler"), Mark Gribbons of HOK, Brett Shwery of Leo A Daly, Susan Juliani Wray and Beth Owens of Haworth, and Nikki Stern of The Hillier Group for their help and support. My thanks to John Holey for his sheer brilliance. To Gil Gordon for being the most easygoing guru on the subject. And to an always entertaining Mike Brill for pioneering this subject which is so important to the world of business and design.

I'd like to express my appreciation to the National Telecommuting Advisory Council for being the best association with the most professional membership to which I've ever had the honor of belonging, and I applaud Ellen Reilly for her hard work in spreading the word in New York City on telecommuting.

To my loved family—Steve, Ida, Jean, Ronnie, Laurie and Tom, to cousin Sharon who kept me in stitches through e-mail. To my cherished friends in Connecticut—Maureen and Bob, Kevin and Sylvia, Frank and Cindy, and Jerry and Lorraine for their love and support.

My thanks to spiritual advisors and loving friends Lesley Godden and Kathryn Kimball for helping to support and center me when I needed it most.

To my sweet friend Grace who never left my side while writing this book.

I am especially grateful to Wendy Lochner at McGraw-Hill for believing in the need for this book and realizing the value of it even before I finished the first sentence of my pitch. I'm especially thankful for her putting up with my endless stream of nervous-Nelly e-mails. My thanks to Robin Gardner of McGraw-Hill for keeping cool, calm, and collected with frazzled authors. More thanks goes to Pattie Amoroso at McGraw-Hill and Marcy Nugent for their positive comments and for making my words so much more intelligible.

I will always be grateful to the higher powers that saw me through this project to its completion.

And, I'd like to dedicate the last, but not least, acknowledgment to my long-time dear friend, Debbie Bauer, in the loving memory of her mother, Catherine Bauer.

NEW WORKPLACES
FOR NEW WORKSTYLES

Synergy

Historical Shifts in Values and Lifestyles to the Alternative
Workplace Environment

Chapter 1.

Looking Backward...
Looking Forward as
Society Heads to
New Ways of Living
and Working

It's as foolish for a society to cling to old ideas in new times as it is for a grown man to squeeze into the clothes that fit him in his youth.

Thomas Jefferson

What is *alternative officing* (AO)?

"Back when I was with Pacific Gas & Electric in the 1980s, the letters AO meant Herman Miller Action Office!" says Marina van Overbeek, workplace strategist at Cisco Systems in San Jose, California.

Many people ask about "alternative officing" with a more than subtle hint of cynicism in their voice. Others realize something really is going on here; the business of planning and designing offices has changed, and it has something to do with this term *alternative officing.* So what does it mean, for heaven's sake? Originally, the term was coined by design firm Hellmuth, Obata, and Kassabaum (HOK) in the early 1990s to describe the trend in evolving workplace planning, design, and management. Here is HOK's original definition:

AO is the label for the new approaches to how, when, and where people work.

The HOK Facilities Consulting Report, no. 1, 1994

When we coined the term, the key word was alternative, says Gary Micunius, former vice president of HOK Consulting. "Many people don't like the word *alternative* because it's no longer alternative, it's now part of the mainstream. The other thing I think people disliked about the phrase is this word *officing.*[1] Some don't like the fact that it's a verb; others think it's too much emphasis on a place."

When architects Philip J. Stone and Robert Luchetti wrote "Your Office Is Where You Are," an article for the March–April 1985 issue of the *Harvard Business Review,* on the "alternative office" (without

even mentioning the term once—it hadn't been coined by HOK as of then), the authors referred to the new workplace as a series of "activity settings." This term described an environment of multiple workspaces and has successfully prevailed in the officing industry for over a decade. In the article written before its time, Stone and Luchetti challenged managers even then to rethink the office environment and to "show how managers can gain the advantages and avoid the disadvantages of the new technologies." Stone and Luchetti didn't need to include the term "alternative officing," or any other kind of cutting-edge vocabulary; they simply discussed in black and white the limiting way in which managers look at modern office space. (It's hard enough today to get managers to understand and appreciate a new and less structured office space, so one wonders if an article in 1985 made any sort of dent in managerial thinking.)

The term *AO,* or *alternative officing,* is American, and it isn't familiar in Europe, where they prefer to talk about the "new ways of working," a term that is becoming increasingly popular here in the United States to define evolving workplaces and work processes that aren't considered quite that radical or alternative anymore. On the West Coast, the word *alternative* is still popular, but professionals use the whole phrase *alternative work environment,* or *AWE.* It's another play on words, but it all comes down to the same thing—the strategies companies use to meet their shifting business objectives. Initially people thought that alternative officing was a single strategy of handing employees a laptop and telling them they no longer had an office; today they understand that the new workplace comprises a broader array of solutions.

TODAY'S BEST DEFINITION OF THE ALTERNATIVE WORKPLACE

For the best stripped-down definition of the *alternative workplace*, credit goes to Alfonso D'Elia, AIA and president of Mancini Duffy, a design firm in New York City:

Alternative offices, most simply put, are new approaches to workspace design.

Yet another good definition comes from Gere Picasso, principal of Engel Picasso Associates, a design firm in Albuquerque, New Mexico:

Alternative worksettings is an inclusive terminology used to describe different corporate strategies which have altered the design of the workplace and how people work.[2]

For as many offices as there are, there are as many definitions of *alternative officing*. We all see the term in a little different light. Some people call it "alternate offices" or "office alternatives." Why is there such a problem defining the subject of the alternative workplace? Because it is still in its infancy, still in the formative stage. People are in a state of reaction to the much larger picture that captures many of the more complex cultural and societal issues that have evolved over the past decade.

Whichever definition or term you choose, there is no doubt that the new workplace is a volatile subject right now in just about every industry. Look in any newspaper or trade or consumer magazine over the past few years, and you'll find many articles on the subject of the alternative office. There are few comprehensive published works that pull all the parts together. And now, there's even a new *Alternative Office Journal* and accompanying trade show called alt.office devoted to the subject that made its debut August 1997.[3] Within the pages of this book you'll find a concise reference work that chronicles briefly where the workplace has been and discusses in depth where it is now and where it's going in the future.

THE ALTERNATIVE WORKPLACE: A CURIOSITY OR A CULTURAL ARCHETYPE?

What's wrong with office design and work processes as they've been set up all along, you ask. Once you look at the holistic picture of where our soci-ety came from and where it's going, it's clear that the traditional office doesn't work for many of us anymore.

The alternative office...office of the future: Whatever you call it, is it a cultural curiosity or cultural archetype? Let's begin at the beginning. We were doing pretty well working in traditional offices for 50 years. Things started to rev up in the 1980s when technology started to take over most of our lives. The alternative workplace hasn't hit us like a tidal wave, but we feel the way we work is somehow different today.

Four critical business and social developments from the late 1980s to the mid to late 1990s explain how and why the alternative workplace has evolved. What's happening around us causes us to shift gears to view our experiences differently from what we perceive is the norm in most parts of our lives based on what is evolving before our eyes in technology, real estate, legislation, job functions, and lifestyles. *Each development is contingent upon each other.* But there is an undeniable common thread of change that runs throughout each and every fact, figure, and idea.

Although we complain of being overwhelmed with information, there is not enough of it to synthesize all that's changing around us, and keep up with a world in which the rules change daily. There are four main areas of life that are shifting and, in turn, directly affect the workplace:

1. Unfolding information technologies
2. Unfolding real estate and settlement patterns[4]
3. Unfolding employment patterns
4. Unfolding social patterns

Information technology is the big umbrella under which other shifting patterns fall to create the continuum of changes. It's the catalyst that changes the job outlook, which changes the real estate and settlement patterning of our society, which changes how we socialize, live, and work.

HISTORY OF THE MECHANICAL OFFICE

The long road on which we walk to get from the traditional office to the alternative office began to form in the early to late 1800s. We can see along the way that reducing real estate portfolios is a common and major reason for exploring and implementing alternative workplace strategies, but it's the technology that allows it to happen.

Before the technology and before the office was the farm. Work in the 1900s was oriented to agriculture, and farmers worked together in family units and formed village communities. Agrarians were entrepreneurial in nature, controlled their own hours, and did not have written job descriptions, yearly reviews, or time sheets to fill out. They worked and lived in the same place, which created a very well-balanced lifestyle.

In the late 1800s, farms grew at an unprecedented pace and so did their crops and produce. By the end of the century, the steam engine enabled the farmer to ship goods overseas, and thus the farmer-entrepreneur went global. Production, packaging, and shipping of goods couldn't be done at home any longer, so the workplace moved to the city, to the factory. Farmers were now looking for a structured, well-paying job that lasted only 8 hours a day, so the factory life invited many into its fold. The industrial age was born.

As the industrial age flourished, so did the need for more efficient manufacturing means and the lawyers, financiers, and managers to run the businesses. The larger the business, the more paperwork was produced, and that meant the paper had to be separated from the factory floor. That's when the true office was born, and it has stayed virtually the same in scope and structure until now.

The following timeline tracks the major strides in technology, office design, management practice, and economy that have together become the building blocks from which the traditional workplace has evolved into what we now call the "alternative workplace."

We need to start the timeline with the first notion of the computer back in the 1800s. But it was the introduction of the typewriter that was the true point at which we began to speed up our data and communications input and output. The only other invention that so profoundly shifted the way we communicate occurred in about 1450 when Johannes Gutenberg invented movable type and introduced the first printing press to Europe. The typewriter was our first interface with the office machine.

1834 Charles Babbage, a British inventor, sketched the first plans for an engine that would work as a calculating machine with the help of a memory stored on punched cards. The punched-card idea was used by Herman Hollerith, a U.S. statistician, to calculate the results of the 1890 Census (see Ayensu 1982).

1868 The typewriter was invented and registered for patenting by Christopher Latham Sholes, Carlos Glidden, and Samuel Soule.

1874 Remington, a gun manufacturer, began to mass-produce typewriters.

1880 Sales of typewriters exploded while at the same time, management theorist Frederick Taylor took a scientific look at the way factories were run to find ways to improve and maximize efficiency by rationalizing the production process into a series of repeatable steps (see Lupton 1993).

1904 TO 1906 Frank Lloyd Wright's Larkin Building housed the Larkin Soap Company, a mail-order business that employed over 1000 women who sat in an open office landscape processing huge volumes of paper. Furniture for clerical staff designed by Wright restricted workers' movements because the chairs were attached to the desks. This furniture design was supposed to improve efficiencies. In contrast, Larkin's executives sat in chairs that glided on castors.

1910 THROUGH 1920s Taylor's work spawned the scientific management movement, which made its way into the office.

1945 The first fully electronic computer was built, called the *Électronic Numerical Integrator and Calculator* (ENIAC). The massive machine took up 1500 square feet (138 m^2) of floor space (see Ayensu 1982).

1956 The first desk-sized computer, the Burroughs E-101, was made in Philadelphia, intended for use by mathematicians and scientists. At the same time in New York, Bell Telephone Laboratories built the Leprechaun, a more economical transistorized computer that caught the interest of IBM, Philco, and General Electric. Bell Telephone also introduced, but quickly abandoned, the sight-sound visual telephone (videophone), because it was too costly and too slow (see Ayensu 1982).

1956 THROUGH 1960s ARPANET, a government project, founded the Internet, which was used for computer science and engineering projects.

1961 The term *quality control circles* was coined in Japan. A quality control circle is a group of employees who perform similar work who meet regularly to learn about and apply certain techniques to solve work problems. This was the beginning of "teaming."

1963 The Ninoflax office in Nordhorn, West Germany, is an early example of *Bürolandschaft*, or *office landscaping*, a concept of office design that promoted a relaxed, status-free arena with free-form

layouts of random desk placement, plants, lots of light, mobile furnishings, and relaxation areas. Due to corporate pressures, the offices were obsolete within 10 years after their introduction.

1966 A psychologist, Tom Marill, began to develop the modem, which he called an *automatic dialer* and which operated at 2000 bits per second (bps) (see Hafner 1996).

1967 A battery-operated cordless telephone that allowed two-way conversations was tested in the United States (see Ayensu 1982).

1969 The Defense Department's Advanced Research Projects Agency (ARPA), headed by scientist J. C. R. Licklider, built a computerized switch, called the *Interface Message Processor*, that would become known as the *ARPANET*, then as the *Internet*.

1971 Intel introduced the world's first microprocessor—a "computer on a chip"—that will completely change the face of business around the world (see Ayensu 1982) (Fig. 1.1).

1973 Len Kleinrock, ARPA, sent the first e-mail over the ARPANET (see Hafner 1996).

1973 Futurist Jack Nilles coined the word *telecommuting*.

1980 Contemporary fax machines (Group III) were manufactured using digital scanning and data compression. A document was sent from London to Toronto in minutes with Intelpost, the first public international electronic facsimile service (see Ayensu 1982).

1981 The Federal Communications Commission (FCC) decided to allocate airspace on the radio spectrum that will be used for cellular radio communications, i.e., cellular phones.

1983 The first marketable laptop computer, Model 100, was sold by Radio Shack for $799. It was designed by Bill Gates and Kazuhiko Nishi (see Gates 1995).

LATE 1980s Use of voice mail became widespread.

1989 Timothy Berners-Lee, now a professor at M.I.T., invented W3, also known as the World Wide Web (graphics portion of the Internet).

1992 Ernst & Young made news when it opened up its first hoteling office in the Sears Tower in Chicago and announced that it will save millions of dollars in real estate costs due to its new ways of working.

1993 In a move to save millions of dollars in real estate, IBM consolidated its sales force in a warehouse designed for hoteling in Cranford, New Jersey, while Jay Chiat took his ad agency virtual to reduce his real estate, work closer to the client, and make the company both fascinating to the public eye and attractive on paper to potential buyers. Both companies got lots of attention in the press, and they attributed the ability to work in new ways to technology.

1995 Haworth, a furniture manufacturer, introduced Crossings, a furniture collection, to an industry hungry for new products to support new ways of working.

1996 *Business Week*'s April 29 cover story, entitled "Office of the Future," turned out to be a catalyst for clients—especially executive and upper management—to learn more about alternative workplace solutions. The Blizzard of '96 on the East Coast and the Summer Olympics in Atlanta forced many businesses to experiment with telecommuting.

1996 Schools across the United States hooked up to the Internet for distance learning.

1996 Sony and Philips Magnavox introduced Web TV for $300 so that anyone could access the World Wide Web without a computer.

1997 A company called 8 x 8 introduced a $500 videophone unit that plugged into the television and required no extra monthly charges or phone upcharges.

UNFOLDING INFORMATION TECHNOLOGIES

For years, office work stayed the same—from the 1940s right up through the 1980s. That is, it did until technology started to infiltrate our daily lives, but it is changing so fast that it is hard to keep up with necessary investments, upgrades, wiring, understanding, and training. Cable-ready modems, ISDN, smart phones, war of the browsers, the maze of telephony—the hardware and software of technology changes daily. But it is people that drive its growth.

THE INTERNET GOES MAINSTREAM

In 1997, Microsoft announced that it was developing programs to let people check e-mail and surf the Internet while they drive, via a dashboard computer and voice commands. But in 1996, few people knew anything about the Internet. Then Mosaic, a breakthrough software program designed by Tim Berners-Lee, gave users access to the World Wide Web (one part of the Internet) with more ease.

As of mid-1996, about 35 million people over the age of 16 in the United States had accessed the Web, had been online, or had used other Internet databases between March and May, according to Intelliquest, an Austin, Texas, based research firm.[5] The same study said that 21 million nonusers indicate that they will begin using the Internet or an online service in 1997. A 1996 AT&T study reported that the Internet user population is growing at 30 percent a year.

The Internet is ubiquitous, and some say overrated. Nonetheless, it's clear that consumer use of the Internet has driven many layers of change from the way we personally communicate with friends and family to the way a company communicates with its employees through the use of an intranet. With Sony's introduction of a $300 Web TV, more people are now willing to jump into the Net.

Internet users come in all shapes, sizes, and incomes. One source, the GVU Partnership, studies who uses the Internet and why. The partnership is between I/PRO, a Web measurement and analysis company that enables marketers to understand its customers' site usage, and Georgia Tech's Graphics, Visualization and Usability (GVU) Center survey.[6] Together, they recognize the need for complementary and comprehensive research on the subject. It has so far provided six surveys since its first one in 1994. The biannual Web-based survey of more than 10,000 Web users is the only demographic profile of this community that provides international trending data back to 1994. The first GVU survey found that Web users were 95 percent male, but as of 1996, it hovered around 70 percent. In addition, Internet users have an average income of around $69,000 in the United States and over $53,000 in Europe.

THE DECLINING COST OF TECHNOLOGY

Technology got another price break in December 1996, when ministers from 128 nations declared a blueprint for the future of computers. In it was a promise to scrap tariffs on a $600 billion world market in computer-related products, which in turn will drive down the cost of technology further (Table 1.1).

PC TRAINING IN THE EXECUTIVE SUITE

There was a time not so long ago that an executive felt no urgency to learn how to use a computer.[7] That's not the case anymore. For senior executives who (a) never learned to type, (b) rely too heavily on their secretary, or (c) feel they don't need to know how to use a computer to e-mail, access data and sales, or tap into the Internet, there's help.

In 1992, Computer Associates International, Inc., the mega-software maker, and CEO Institutes, a New York executive seminar firm, joined together to develop an executive retreat, or technology "boot camp," a name by which it is better known. For a few thousand dollars ($7000 in 1996), an executive can get 4 days of one-on-one basic training, including intensive keyboard workouts. (One recent student asked if the computer's mouse was a foot pedal.)

The retreat exposes CEOs to technologies that can immediately benefit their businesses and, by demystifying information technology, bring about a clear understanding of technology's effect on the global business environment. At check-in, CEOs are issued a color notebook computer, portable printer, communications software, and a suite of office productivity software, all hooked up to a network. Each CEO is assigned a personal technology advisor to help him or her get through the obstacles to learning technology.

FEARLESS TECHNOTOTS

On the other end of the scale are those who are destined for the executive suite: children. Today they

TABLE 1.1
THE EXPENSE OF CONNECTIVITY THEN AND NOW

Technology	Old Pricing	New Pricing
Modems	$169, Supra Express 28.8, late 1995	$69.99, Supra Express 33.6, late 1997
Online services	$2.95 per hour, early 1996	$9.95 to $19.95 average unlimited usage, late 1997
Cell phone service	$29.99 average monthly fee,* 1995	$14.99 average monthly fee, 1997
Web site design	A few thousand dollars minimum for custom, early 1990s	$800–$900, NetObjects Fusion Software, 1996
Videoconferencing	$60 per minute, 1985	$2.50 per minute per site at Kinko's,† 1997

*Bell Atlantic NYNEX Mobile and AT&T Wireless quoted these prices for a 1-year contract (see Herring 1995). In addition, Bell Atlantic NYNEX Mobile introduced EZ MAX ANNUAL, a cell phone-in-a-box with the lowest monthly access of $18.99, slightly higher than other plans.

†According to 1997 videoconferencing prices at two Kinko's located in Stamford and Orange, Connecticut, the $150 per hour per site is for a standard point-to-point connection although prices vary slightly around the country. Multiple sites and custom equipment affect prices. Kinko's also has special "out-of-town families" rates at half price during the holiday season.

cut their teeth on computers, even at the tender age of 5, when they can experiment with toy laptops (Fig. 1.2). Once a guest on NBC's *Tonight Show,*[8] Microsoft's chairman and cofounder Bill Gates explained to host Jay Leno why kids are better than adults in understanding computers. A kid-at-heart himself with his fetish for M&Ms and a self-designed trampoline room in his house (described by Leno as Gates's rubber room with padded walls), Gates explained: "Adults can be good at computers, but they are a little reluctant because they are not used to being out of control. Kids are used to being out of control, so they seek out something they can control like computers."

Talk to anyone under the age of 20 and chances are that they know an impressive amount of information about computers. Why? This generation started to get their feet wet early when computers were most prevalent in high school and college. They're a fearless bunch who aren't afraid to reach into the guts of a computer or launch aimlessly into the darkness of cyberspace.

Kids are starting to learn computers at an earlier age. It's becoming as mainstream as learning the alphabet. This newest generation of technotots now works on toy laptop computers that are built for children as young as 1 to 3 years old. Increasingly

complex toy versions designed for kids up through ages 10 to 12 have lined the shelves of toy stores since the 1990s. Compaq Computer and preschool toy giant Fisher-Price teamed up to produce a line of new compu-toys that will, they hope, attract the 18 million U.S. families with kids under the age of 7 to drop $150 for computers and keyboards. There's even software for this new type of compu-toy.

To learn how to use these tools, there are summer camps across the country that take teens for a week and teach them all aspects of computer programming. Sacred Heart University in Bridgeport, Connecticut, offers just that kind of fun in the sun. For a $650 tuition fee, students aged 12 to 15 can attend intensive courses on computer programming and take a daytrip to the Computer Museum in Boston.

There will always be a place for school textbooks. But penny-pinching schools realize that computers provide the cheapest, most efficient teaching tool, especially when real-time access to rich forms of information can be found as far away as Russia and India.

Schools across the country are hooking up to the Internet for distance learning. In Connecticut, for example, community volunteers are wiring for

Figure 1.2
Kids naturally connect with computers at a young age. To keep them comfortable, there's even a market for computer furniture for kids like this Kin-der-link bentwood computer table designed by Rlaz Jurney. (Photo by Don Hamerman.)

Kids that grow up on compu-toys and with access at school to the Internet have bright futures. The hottest jobs in the highest demand for 1996, and beyond, are managers of Internet-related companies, chief technology officers, and vice presidents of multimedia content, according to a 1996 study conducted by the executive search firm Christian & Timers. And look at the newest job, the Web site designer, a fast-emerging niche for young graphic designers. It's estimated that the number of sites on the expanding Web range from 90,000 to 265,000 as nearly every business decides it needs a Web site virtually overnight. Average age of a Web site artist: early to mid 20s.

CYBERCAFÉS CREATE NEW COMMUNITIES

Cybercafés aren't as intimidating as you might think, and they've actually gone mainstream.[9] The original intention of the cybercafé was to provide an oasis of socialization for the digeratti who tend to spend their time alone in front of a computer. That was only the beginning of what has taken hold as an almost mysterious, unnerving cultural icon that keeps anxious technophobes on the other side of the street while it lures the future leaders of commerce into its confines.

Most cybercafés are still nothing more than a place to log on to the Internet for a small fee while drinking coffee at the same time (Fig. 1.3). But one prototypical phenomenon, Cybersmith, proves that

Internet access the state's 1500 public schools, grades K through 12, and 250 public libraries as part of a new federal program called ConneCT96. Any school or library that has raised up to $800 for the connection kit is eligible to participate and take advantage of the Southern New England Telephone Company's 60 hours a month of free access. To prepare for Internet access, most schools are planning media rooms or media areas in libraries or auditoriums, or they are setting aside one classroom with wires and modems.

Figure 1.3
Most cybercafés are merely computers on tables. Not at Cybersmith, a retail experience with virtual reality games and computer terminals designed to grab a kid's attention. At the Boston Cybersmith, a closer look shows two teenagers on the Internet completely unaware of their surroundings. The retailer reports that traveling business people come in to check e-mail. (Photo by Steve Syarto.)

a cybercafé can be more than a room full of computers on tables. This store/alternative office/videoarcade, the brainchild of retailer Marshall Smith and designed by Schwartz/Silver Architects in Boston, recently opened an indoor-outdoor 3500-square-foot facility in Boston (others exist in nearby Cambridge—the first one that opened in early 1995—suburban New York City, and another will open soon in Palo Alto). Intended by Smith to be the family's "future den," Cybersmith has dismissed the look of sterile, high-tech materials and instead opted for an environment swathed in woods that denotes a safe, cozy, yet still highly stimulating place.

"We had to define an aesthetic combining a cozy, denlike atmosphere with the sale of information flow," says Warren Schwartz, principal of Schwartz/Silver. Monitors encased in blond wood are built into spacious circular booths quiet for concentration, maintained by the clear plastic round domes hovering over each booth to keep ambient noise at bay.

Cybersmith accommodates kids who surf the net, business people who drop in to check e-mail if they didn't take their own computer on the road with them, and companies in need of computer training and videoconferencing. You can also take a computer training class, throw a party, or plan a special event for a group at Cybersmith.

THE NEXT TECHNOLOGY BREAKTHROUGHS

Well, we can put a man on the moon, but we are having a hard time changing computer memory to recognize the year 2000. While Silicon Alley and Valley are both busy trying to fix that programming glitch, they are also toying with some other technologies to change the way we live and work. The introductions of Web TV in 1996 and a videophone unit that plugs into the television are just the beginning.

Computer telephony is an up-and-coming technology that has long-distance phone companies in a tizzy. Turning this technology around, phone companies see the lowly phone as a potential appliance for surfing the Internet and other information technology–related activities.

Speech recognition for computers has been 20 years in the making, and once it makes it to the mainstream, it can cause all kinds of other problems such as poor recognition resulting in warped information (just look at the problems with PDA recognition of handwriting) and acoustical issues.

Wearable computers: Leo A Daly, a design firm in Santa Monica, California, made a prototype of a wearable computer belt that was presented at AOX (one of the first alternative workplace trade shows) in 1994. Wireless technology built into belts could allow the wearer to surf the Net or check e-mail while jogging, walking the dog, or standing in line at the grocer!

Ubiquitous computing: Haworth experimented with a tabletop computer during NeoCon 1996 in its showroom. The concept means that computers and sensors built into desks and walls could read your handwriting and keep track of papers on your desk. Xerox[10] and Olivetti are now experimenting with this technology. At MIT's Media Lab in Cambridge, Massachusetts, the computer researchers built a table that detects the position of hands that are located in the air above the desk surface. In theory, your hands become a mouse and relate what's on your desk to a computer. So you don't have to scan documents physically into the computer; the desk is the scanner. In addition, in a Big Brother kind of way, embedded computers in furniture keep track of people so that phone calls can be rerouted (see Verity 1996).

A few more down-to-earth predictions come from Bill Gates and are documented in his book. He says videoconferencing will become more important and that "Net meetings will explode in popularity once people realize how readily and inexpensively they can use networks to discuss and edit documents that appear on two or more screens simultaneously." He also predicts that laptops and other portable PCs will grow in popularity to assist mobile workers for docking between home and work desktop computers. Wallet PCs, he adds, will proliferate around the turn of the century and will become more popular than cell phones (see Gates 1997).

UNFOLDING REAL ESTATE AND SETTLEMENT PATTERNS

Remember once when any kind of real estate was thought to be the best long-term (and in the early 1980s short-term) investment? That all changed in the mid-1980s through the early 1990s. From the mid-1990s, real estate has struggled to stay on a road to its comeback, even though there's no hope for the boom market like the one that spun out of control in the mid-1980s.

As far as residential real estate goes, there's a real key demographic issue preventing that market from flourishing: There's no longer a huge influx of young baby-boomers into the market for homes and other property investments. Many baby-boomers are looking to relocate to cheaper areas where they can get more house for less money and slash associated costs.

There's hope stirring among real estate investors that better times are back for commercial real estate. In the late months of 1996, stocks of real estate companies, including the investment pools known as *real estate investment trusts* (REITs) were among the best picks in the stock market. Analysts say that most of the real estate mistakes made in the past few years to devalue commercial real estate are distant memories and severe learning experiences never to be repeated. But there's still another big issue looming over the real estate market—the long-term effects of technology. In theory, the Internet is becoming an enabler for cyberspace retailing, working, and communicating, thus reducing the need for physical space once necessary for such activities. The Internet may not be the downfall of all retail or office space around the world, but no doubt it has begun to impact the amount of space and the types of space consumed.

THE COMMERCIAL REAL ESTATE SEESAW

One of the most hard-hitting quotes that describes the realities of real estate concerns comes directly from the *Harvard Business Review* in an article written by Charles Handy of the London Business School:

An office that is available 168 hours a week but occupied for perhaps 20 is a luxury that organizations can ill afford.

(Handy 1995)

Another sobering statistic comes from Franklin Becker, a Cornell University professor who studies workplace strategies and coauthored the book *Workplace by Design*. Becker's figures indicate that 70 percent of desks, offices, or workstations go unoccupied at any given time on a typical workday. Factoring in weekends, vacations, and holidays, a company's overall occupancy can tumble to as low as 15 percent. Yet companies pay the real estate bills 365 days a year. Clearly, the client is making the connection between excessive real estate portfolios and the bottom line.

Rents Still High, Leases Still Long

In 1996, midtown commercial rents per square foot in Boston averaged $38, Washington cost $35,

and Manhattan a relatively low $33, according to a midyear market survey by Oncor International, a network of realtors who conduct the poll. Empty, expensive offices aren't found only in the United States. Consider renting prime office space in Bombay, India, for $450 a square foot! How about in Bogota, Colombia, for $250 a square foot! "Who would think you can pay that much in Bogota? I find Bombay amazing; in this city where people are begging in the street you find some of the most expensive square footage in the world. But then try to find a cheap hotel room in these cities!" said Claude Berube, past president of the Indian Institute of Interior Designers (IFI).[11]

In the United States, the 5- to 10-year lease still reigns. In the United Kingdom, it's not uncommon to find a 25-year lease, but in Germany and Holland, 5-year leases are common. "It's difficult to handle the 25-year leases," says Ernest Piccone, director of CRE for Tandem Computers, making a case for global AWE. "You typically get 5 years into a 25-year lease, and you find you either have too much or too little space, so what are you supposed to do?" Flexible, alternative officing is clearly the answer.

Office Sizes Shrink

The old rule of thumb for the size of private office cubicles used to be 250 square feet per white-collar employee; it's now more common for companies to go below 200 square feet per person. Most typically, cubicles for administrative staff have gone down to 80 square feet per person. Work spaces have shrunk 25 to 50 percent over the past decade in most large companies (see Coy 1997). No doubt it's cramped when you consider that the average person with arms outstretched occupies 6 square feet of space, and the average amount of technology found in the cubicle of an administrative professional is two to three times as much as what management has in their much larger offices (and which they are hardly ever in, anyway).

Shared Amenities and Executive Centers Grow in Popularity...

Furnished offices with shared amenities such as a receptionist, plus word processing and clerical help—typically called *executive suites* or *executive centers*—and leased by the hour, day, week, or month are not uncommon. Most executive centers have a variety of office sizes and suites, with or without windows, corner or aisle—you name it, it's there. But the concept has risen in popularity, and the executive suite industry went from a $1 billion industry to a $2.5 billion dollar industry in 1996, according to the Executive Suites Association in Plano, Texas. Now that executive center phone systems are more sophisticated (when the phone rings, a customized screen comes up on the computer with pertinent details of where someone in the company will be that day and when they will be back, for example), the leased shared-amenities environment is more appealing to new or small companies that need to create the appearance of a large and professionally staffed office. For instance, HQ Business Centers, ahead of its time when founded in 1966, now has 150 locations worldwide and continues to grow to keep up with demand. HQ's new tagline reads, "The Flexible Alternative to the Traditional Office." What does HQ consider a long-term lease to be? Twelve months!

Optima Offices in New York City rents office space from $10 an hour to $550 a month with Internet and e-mail access and word processing services,[12] and most other centers offer short-term leases that average a month in length with rents ranging from $500 to $2000 a month depending on the size and location of the offices. More and more centers are cropping up across the country to accommodate the sometimes temporary needs for growing ranks of entrepreneurs and virtual companies being formed. Now that corporations are more cost conscious, long-term-leasing situations are not as appealing as they once were. If a company wants to try out a new market or open a new business, they go to an executive center instead of signing a traditional long-term lease. Interestingly enough, short-term-lease executive centers have become a good business strategy for some of the more traditional industries, as well.

Whoever thought there would be a growing market for fully built offices designed for trading firms who need short-term, 3-month leases? It's happened in New York City. Austria-based Trade Point of America, Inc., a subsidiary of the BANK group of companies, started the trend by converting one floor of a Wall Street building (199 Water Street) into a temporary trading room. At about $5000 a month per trading station, tenants get uninterrupted power sources (backed up by a battery-run generator in case of blackout), fiber-optic telephone lines (copper can take over in case of damage), telephone recording devices, market information displays, and individually controlled air-conditioning units in each station so that tenants pay for only the amount they use. In this way, a tenant can request a

24-hour access to the office, and other tenants don't have to pay for an increased use of energy (see Holusha 1996).

The interior's build-out is flexible. Offices are built out of movable sound-proof walls, and all power, telephone, and data cables are overhead so there are no access floors. Overhead cabling enables reconfiguration to be achieved without interrupting other tenants. Shared spaces include a business library, conference room, and eating area. Access to the space is controlled by a changing digital code.

What about law firms—those denizens of luxury living within the mahogany-riddled interiors of trophy buildings? They are also in need of short-term space, but with interiors and amenities that help them keep up appearances while swimming with the sharks down the street. There are numerous facilities in New York City that cater to the small law firm, but one building in particular, Foxhall Realty's 805 Third Avenue, has helped small law firms manage shared space for 17 years. An 11- by 14-foot office with two windows rents for nearly $2000 a month, a larger; three-window office rents for $2300 a month. At Foxhall, a lawyer gets to share support services, reception area, law library, and conference rooms. The lesson for building developers? The need for shared facilities grows no matter how prosperous the industry (see Holusha 1996).

...While Trophy Buildings Topple

Take a look at the toll signature architecture has had on big business. In the 1970s, a typical suburban office building was 100,000 square feet, and by the 1980s, it had doubled to 200,000 square feet. In the 1990s the footage has dropped back to the 100,000-square-foot mark because companies are doing away with elaborate lobbies, reception areas, boardrooms, and massive private offices.

What has happened to some of these architectural jewels from the 1970s and 1980s?

• By 1999, the Equitable Life Assurance Company will move out of the Equitable Center in New York City, a massive 3.3-million-square-foot monument it developed for itself in the 1980s. The new space will be 500,000 square feet located at 1290 Avenue of the Americas. What will remain of the Equitable Center will be a meeting center and boardroom, both revenue producers from rentals. Equitable expects to save $30 million annually in occupancy costs over the next 16 years as a result of this move (see Deutsch 1996).

- Nestlé Food Corporation headquarters in Purchase in Westchester County built in 1986 has a two-story atrium lobby, a dining area that doubles as a 325-seat theater, and an executive wing with private baths and a mahogany-paneled boardroom with an octagonal skylight. The four-story building is faced with blue-gray granite and blue reflective glass. After a year on the market, TransAmerica Leasing leased 125,000 square feet of office space in 1993 (see Vizard 1994).
- The former American Can Company headquarters in Greenwich, Connecticut, was built in 1971. The 625,000-square-foot building sits on a 300-acre campus and has a 50,000-square-foot annex building and a guest house that sleeps 12. Witco, a chemical company, leased 250,000 square feet of the building in 1993 with the help of a financial assistance and incentive package from the state of Connecticut (see Vizard 1994). In 1996, Witco announced it would lay off 1800 people and close 15 factories in North America.
- The IBM building at 2000 Purchase Street in Purchase, New York, designed by I. M. Pei, and built in 1983, is 476,823 square feet. As a cost-cutting measure, the company moved 550 employees out of the building in May 1992 and relocated them to Armonk headquarters and other company-owned buildings in the area. The company found it cut costs at the Purchase building by 50 percent by simply shutting it down. Today, Swanke, Hayden, Connell has designed a brand-new building for the headquarters in Armonk that is significantly smaller than the original building.
- In Pittsburgh, Pennsylvania, alone, there is a lot of activity with trophy buildings, according to a report in The New York Times (see Swaney 1997). For instance, Alcoa is soon moving into a new headquarters building half the size of the one it has inhabited since 1952; Westinghouse Electric Corporation's 23-story, 420,000-square-foot headquarters building on the Monongahela River holds 450 employees (down from 1000 in the 1970s), and as of early 1997, it wanted to lease out 6 of its empty floors to other companies. Koppers Corporation, an industrial products manufacturer, occupies 15 percent of its 459,000-square-foot headquarters since it was taken over by a British concern, and the rest of the building is occupied by lawyers and other small companies. Finally, there's no trace of the Gulf Oil Corporation in its former, famous 44-story trophy headquarters, which now houses a couple of major tenants.

These icons are still being built, even in the nineties, but on a much smaller scale, like the IBM building and the Swiss Bank campus in Stamford, Connecticut, by SOM. For instance, Duracell International's new single-occupancy 310,000-square-foot, $70 million world headquarters in Bethel, Connecticut, is a self-sufficient corporate campus with its own cafeteria, sundries shop, outdoor jogging trails, media center, and fitness center. Why is it smaller? It's actually a consolidation of eight rented buildings on a 325-acre Berkshire Office Park property, relocating down to 48 acres in the same Bethel park, leaving 200,000 square feet of space behind. There is no executive dining room, parking area, or entrance, all ideas contributed by 160 employees during the planning period. And, it's a building designed so that it can be rented if Duracell ever decides to leave (see Charles 1995).

Say Good-Bye to Grand Granite Interiors

Peter Colwell, professor of finance in the University of Illinois at Champaign's College of Commerce and Business Administration, said in the article, "Right now, people are looking at marble and granite as a corporate embarrassment" (see Murphy 1995). One notable commercial designer sadly confessed recently that he believed that all the palatial corporate interiors he designed in the 1980s have unfortunately become burdensome to his clients.

Frank Farrington of Atlanta-based Farrington Design talks about a recent office he witnessed being built in Washington, D.C. The office was swathed in custom, carved wood panels on the walls and ceilings at the cost of $400 per square foot, and that was just for the millwork. Farrington said he heard the millworker for that particular project went out of business from the decrease in demand for such large quantities of luxury woodwork. That Washington, D.C., office is sure to be considered an overdesigned dinosaur on the real estate market by now.

Whereas solid red granite exteriors, expansive, expensive marble lobbies, and African mahogany walls and trim were the norm of design in the mid-1980s, we now see precast concrete, all-weather carpeting, vinyl wallcovering, and glass with steel or granite trim at one-third the cost of solid granite for corporate clients fast shedding the stigma of status buildings. Real estate executives notice more companies are designing new offices with an eye toward leaving them some day. So instead of paying the $40 to $60 a square foot per job, it's more in the neighborhood of $20 to $40—and below—a square foot on a corporate project.

Tomorrow's Offices in Yesterday's Buildings

Architectural jewels from the 1980s are not as much embarrassing as they are dysfunctional by today's technology standards (Table 1.2). But there is another train of thought in the real estate industry: "You'd expect that the newer the building, the easier it would be to renovate it for high-tech clients, right?" asks Don Erwin, senior associate of Fox & Fowle Architects. "In many ways, however, the older buildings—the ones built in the 1920s and 1930s that were passed over in the 1960s—are considered today prime real estate and are more desirable for renovations." Erwin lists reasons for the resurrection of older buildings for high-tech clients: Older buildings are overengineered. He says punching holes and openings in older buildings won't make them collapse. In newer buildings, he explains, the structures are usually quite unforgiving, the engineering is much tighter with little flexibility, and steel needs reinforcement for many changes and additions. Older buildings, he states, have larger floor plates, more vertical openings such as flues, columns, and light shafts and thicker walls which are critical areas—huge raceways—in which to run technology wiring up and down a building.

ALTERNATIVE URBAN PLANNING AND RENEWAL

There's an entire town built for telecommuters.

Telluride has a normal small-town feel to it. Residents live on streets named Oak and Spruce, and they pick up odds and ends at the Sunshine Pharmacy. But underneath it all, people here are wired differently.

Telluride became a haven for visiting skiers who never left the town, taken in by the exquisite beauty of the Colorado Rocky Mountains and laid-back lifestyle that could be had year-round. The town saw that its appeal was more to some than just a cozy ski hamlet in which to hide out one season per year; it was filling up slowly with new permanent residents that still managed to keep jobs that were located out of state. Collectively, the residents decided it needed more technology infrastructure, more bandwidth, more ways to communicate in order to live in town while working out of town via modem. Telluride soon became a local Internet hub and testbed for manufacturers looking for a place to try out new

TABLE 1.2	
WHAT COMMERCIAL TENANTS EXPECTED IN BUILDINGS THEN, AND WHAT THEY EXPECT NOW	
1950s	**1990s**
Large footprints	Small footprints
Mail chute	Bandwidth for electronic communication
Private offices on window wall	Private offices in core, workstations on perimeter
Building open 9–5	Building open 24 hours a day
Outlets per square foot	Watts per square foot
Accessibility to telephone wires in janitor's closet	Controlled, dedicated, secure telecom closet

products and services on a larger scale than in a lab. The Telluride Institute, the not-for-profit cultural organization, founded the local Internet hub in 1993 under its new program called InfoZone.[13]

Over one-third of Telluride's 1800 residents have InfoZone Internet accounts, starting with the 56Kb phone circuit connection pulled through the Colorado Supernet to the Internet during the pilot's first phase in 1993. It's now further along, acting as a testbed for Tetherless Access, Ltd's, 128-Kb+ wireless MAN system among other beta experiments involving technology intelligence.

Close by to Telluride is suburban Salt Lake City, a "high-tech corridor" full of telecommuters. Pinnacle at South Valley is a 492-unit apartment development in Salt Lake City designed with advanced telecommunications systems to accommodate telecommuters. The luxury community includes services such as high-speed modem access and Internet service along with the usual telephone and cable features. It's a single-source solution, meaning that there will be one installation, one bill, and one customer-service number for tenants to call.

"There are a lot of communities looking to attract telecommuters," says John Holey, president of Holey Associates and cofounder of @WORK, a firm consulting with areas in Southern California and in Kentucky that are looking at ways to leverage their community resources without imposing any environmental impact on the area. "To do that they need a robust solution that makes it work best for them. Telecommuters have to have the right facilities in the city, places that have fiber optics if they need to do a videoconference, or libraries and research centers that function as touch-down offices with 24-hour access."

LIVE/WORK SPACES GROW

Joining Telluride and Salt Lake City is Vail, Colorado. Vacationing skiers and snowboarders come here to relax…well, sort of. Many of the Type-A personalities vacationing on the mountaintop found they still had the urge to connect with the office, so the local Vail Association and Sprint teamed up to build its wealthy patrons a business center, called the Sprint Communications Center. The full-service business center is outfitted with videoconferencing, Internet, phone conferencing, faxes, copiers, and more capabilities than even a typical office. As one patron says about the addition of the business center in Vail since it opened in the beginning of 1997, "It makes a vacation a lot more comfortable" (see Kelly 1997).

In New York City alone, there's a growing emphasis on "live/work" apartments. These hybrid apartments tend to be in luxury buildings, with amenities such as conference rooms, technology support, secretarial services, and sometimes a party room that can be rented out for special occasions.[14]

- A work/life initiative can be found in Crescent Heights at 25 Broad Street in New York City. Crescent Heights has 345 rental apartments with separate office spaces complete with their own doors and hallways to set them apart from living spaces. The tenants can use the "business center" that includes a conference room for 30 with a copier, executive offices, and audiovisual services (see Denitto 1996). Rents at Crescent Heights will run on average $1350 for a one-bedroom apartment.
- Another work/life initiative is being built into four floors at 47 West Street. These units are also being converted into live/work spaces along with several other loft developments going in the same direction in downtown New York City.
- The Towers at 45 Wall Street are being converted into apartments under New York City's Lower Manhattan Revitalization Plan. The 28-story building has been vacant for several years and will now be transformed into 437 rental apartments, some of which have mixed-use allowances for "home-occupancy" tenants. That means the apartments will actually be commercially ventilated spaces for small-business occupancy.
- Elsewhere, an increasing number of builders in the New York region are including computer-ready home offices in their subdivisions. Models, such as the ones in Chappaqua, New York, called Hardscrabble Lake, showed a studio off the master bedroom suite set up to be a home office. In fact, architects from around the country report that the home office is one of the most frequently requested features in both new houses and in older homes (see Vizard 1995). *Custom Homes Magazine* called the home office a "hot" trend in 1995 and did so again in 1996. *Home Mechanix Magazine* reported that a new category of remodeling projects, the home office conversion, is valued in many parts of the nation (see *Home Mechanix* 1996).

BREATHING NEW LIFE INTO DOWNTOWN USA

A wired building there, a wired building here, does not necessarily spell welcome to those seeking to live and work in the same city. Can downtown USA revitalize itself to attract a population that will work and live in the same city? Urban planners agree that as self-employment grows, it behooves a city to respond to the fact that the microbusinesses operate on a different schedule and in a different physical pattern than ever before. Cities that will flourish are the cities that attract people, enabling them to live and work within close proximity in the most synergistic way possible, as opposed to cities that are antagonistic toward dwellers.

Sure enough, New York City has had its share of antagonized residents.[15] But there have been some bright spots. In the 1980s, the renovation of the South Street Seaport created such excitement for New Yorkers that mingling among the tourists on a balmy summer eve didn't bother jaded New Yorkers one bit. It was new, fresh, and a great place to travel to and hang out. A number of coop apartments on the wharf overlooking the water became available, and any young and still energetic Wall Street trader could go down to the Seaport on a Friday night and find the inevitable all-night party going on at any of the restaurants with open-air dining.

Enter the age of frugality—the 1990s—and no longer was the Seaport home to many traders let go in the 1987 blow to Wall Street's ego. But New York City in all its tenacity refused to roll up its sidewalks, tuck in its perfectly good—albeit temporarily obsolete—but empty buildings to wave goodbye, walk away, and never look back. To the rescue came a revitalization plan encouraged by tax-incentive packages to spur residential conversion and commercial renovation. After the Rudin family of developers gave new life to 55 Broad Street, turning it into a haven for new-media businesses,[16] others joined in and are fast transforming Wall Street into a 24-hour work/live village.

But looking at downtown on a broader, national scale, you can't help wondering if downtown New York City is alone in its venture for rehab. But sure enough, it's Wall Street that is on the heels of Chicago's historic Loop where the vacancy rate for older office space in the area is about 26 percent (see Sharoff 1996). But two obsolete buildings faced the welcome of conversion to residences in 1995 and 1996. The Motor Club, a 1928 building with views to the Chicago River and the Singer Building, a 1926 find near Marshall Field's historic flagship store, have been acquired by local developers who will test the viability of residential space in the Loop area. And, after Florsheim vacated its 50-year-old building in downtown Chicago in early 1997, developers are turning it into a residential condominium building called Metropolitan Place (see Schachner Chanen 1997).

CHANGING INDUSTRIAL AND RESIDENTIAL LOCATION PATTERNS—AND PARADISE LOST

The increased use of powerful computers and telecommunications systems means that businesses and people are freer to locate wherever they'll best benefit. This means regions across the country are shifting in population and economies. In 1995, the now-defunct government agency, the Office of Technology,[17] issued a report, *The Technological Reshaping of Metropolitan America*, to examine if shifts and new policies would help the economic revitalization of urban core areas. Drawing its information from corporations, technology, local governments, and academic sectors, the pertinent highlights of this study meaningful to the development and maintenance of virtual workplace programs include the following:

- The spatial form of the U.S. metro areas has changed over the past 20 years. The accepted thumbnail sketch of a metro area with burgeoning downtown skyscrapers and inner-ring factories is obsolete. Today, 57 percent of office stocks are located in the suburbs, up from 25 percent in 1970.
- The bedroom suburb is a rare part of today's landscape. In fact, approximately 55 percent of Americans live in the suburbs. In the largest 25 metros, 75 percent of the population live in the suburbs. Why the growth? Technology is connecting economic activities enabling them to locate physically farther apart, reducing the benefits of high-cost, congested urban areas.
- Buildings with large floorplates have become increasingly desirable because they can be easily reconfigured to install fiber optics. These buildings are located at the edge of metros or in suburbs where larger and cheaper land on which to build is available.

There's another settlement pattern affecting work and lifestyle. It's urban sprawl, and it's happening in places we never thought possible. Take Scottsdale, Arizona, as an example. In 1950, there were barely 2000 people living in the single square mile of the town. Today, it's mushroomed to be three times the physical size of San Francisco with 165,000 people who came there to seek peace, quiet, and clean, dry air. But more people are coming to Scottsdale yet as developers rush to build gated communities on the fringes of town. But the air is so bad sometimes that people are advised to stay indoors (see Egan 1996).

It's a case of paradise lost. In cities like Scottsdale and Phoenix (with a population of over 1 million people), there is a civic group called "Not L.A." that is trying to curtail the influx of people and development creating city sprawl. Today, Phoenix has the worst air, second only to Southern California.

Arizona is not the only state affected by exurban sprawl. It affects Seattle, Portland, Salt Lake City, Denver, and even Las Vegas as Americans turn their sights away from Southern California, seeking a new place with a new cure that can't be found in the cramped state that once promised a life of milk and honey and great tans year-round. Seattle, a city once rated as the most desirable place to live for most of the 1990s, now ranks among the top five cities with the worst traffic congestion. The state projects that the growth spurt will continue, anticipating 300,000 more people to move into Seattle and the metropolitan area in the next 4 years.

The air is bad enough, but more roads will inevitably lead to more trouble in these past paradises. It's a rule of thumb for urban planners that the number of miles traveled by cars and trucks increases by at least twice the rate of local population growth. Denver, Seattle, Portland, and Salt Lake City are contemplating or planning a small rail system to take the burden off the roads. Other measures may affect traffic congestion and spur telecommuting. For instance, Redmond, home of Microsoft, will impose a head tax that charges businesses $65 annually for every employee who works

The

Clean Air Act of 1990 continues to be a political hotbed for Corporate America.

The Clean Air Act of 1990: A Stalled Vehicle for Change

In a move to address air pollution and emission reduction throughout the country, the federal government passed the Clean Air Act Amendments of 1990 on November 15, 1990, requiring many states to revise its clean air legislation and regulatory provisions. Companies had to file plans to reduce their employees' use of automobiles. But in the beginning of 1996, the Republican-dominated Congress decided that many of the provisions of the Employee Commute Options (ECO) program should be voluntary rather than mandatory, defeating the purpose of compliance. Many companies that have put into place extensive programs are **rethinking** them or abandoning them. Simply put, people are losing their commitment to meeting air-quality standards. Or are they?

Clearing the Air: Grassroots Efforts

Sick and tired of the gridlock holding the Clean Air Act back from saving San Francisco's sooty air, a voluntary consortium of employers called the Bay Area Clean Air Partnership (BayCAP) was formed in the summer of 1996. BayCAP's goal is to coordinate voluntary efforts to keep the Bay Area's skies clean.

BayCAP has rallied 400 companies to participate, all helping to develop plans to boost activities, such as telecommuting efforts, especially during the summer season when smog is heavy.

Update on Amendments in 1997

As of mid-1997, there's been no real and concrete progress with the controversial Clean Air Act as a true catalyst for telecommunication programs. In fact, much of the nation has experienced improvements in air quality over the last decade due to a reduction in emissions from automobiles, a result of cleaner engines and fuels. There's a **reduction** in pollution despite a 32 percent increase in vehicle travel between 1986 and 1995, according to The Road Information Program (TRIP), a Washington, D.C.-based transportation research group. Therefore, most of the attention regarding the management of air quality focuses on modernizing power plants, investing in the development and improvement of the country's transportation infrastructure, and on the continuing reformulation of fuel for cars and trucks rather than on keeping people off the roads. However, there's been movement in tightened air pollution regulations.

In July 1997, President Clinton approved significantly tighter limits on smog and soot **pollution**. As a result, the Environmental Protection Agency's rules on smog-causing ozone have changed from the current 120 parts per billion to 80 parts per billion. However, there's controversy over how much mortality and damage pollution can cause to our health. In the face of this scientific uncertainty, big business is stepping in to further dispute air quality regulations. Compliance with the rules set by the EPA won't be enforced until 2007 for ozone **control** and 2008 for soot, and extensions are possible. What does this mean for the new workplace? States may have to invest more in mass transit and other measures to reduce smog and soot pollution emitted from automobiles. However, states are assured they will have flexibility in deciding how to reach the new goals over the next decade.

States such as Florida and Michigan are fighting the EPA's plan because it will cost millions of dollars to comply with the new regulations. One exception to the rule is Phoenix, Arizona, a state which has taken a serious look at its air quality issues. In May 1996, Operation Ozone was put into place as the state's governor, Fife Symington, called for an increase in the commitment to air quality. One provision of Operation Ozone included a mandate for all state agencies to implement The State of Arizona Telecommuting Program with a goal of having 15 percent of state employees in Maricopa County actively telecommuting by December 1998. Today, John Corbett of the office of the State of Arizona is working with all agencies to **implement** the state program in three phases. Currently, 53 state agencies are either implementing or expanding their telecommuting program, says Corbett. In May 1997, all remaining state agencies joined the program.

"By county ordinance, employers with 50 or more employees per site are still required to submit plans to reduce employee trips by 10 percent per year for the first 5 years, with 5 percent a year reduction for the next 5 years or until they achieve and maintain a threshold of 40 percent single occupant trip reduction, or 40 percent of their employees participating in some form of commute trip reduction," says Corbett.

However, the controversy over how states, counties, and companies will reduce pollution still brews in most of the country.

in the city. Stay tuned for an area of the country that seeks alternative ways of working as its salvation.

UNFOLDING EMPLOYMENT AND ECONOMIC PATTERNS

Downsizing hasn't stopped. Younger women want to marry and have families earlier instead of focusing on careers. Older women decide to have children and slow down their career tracks. And the workforce is dwindling as baby-boomers age and a smaller population of technologically savvy younger men and women seek flexible employment. Things are changing in Corporate America. The companies that find a way to support these changes will thrive. Those that go along as they did in the past, business as usual will fall behind.

CORPORATE AMERICA'S HEROES AND ANTIHEROES

Right before Christmas 1996, America was surprised to find humanity in Corporate America. When word got out that Kingston Technology Corp., the world's largest maker of computer memory products, based in Fountain Valley, California, gave its 523 employees $100 million in bonuses, the whole country fell in love with its founders, John Tu and David Sun, immigrants from Taiwan. The windfall came out of the sale of 80 percent of Kingston to Japan's Softbank Corporation for $1.5 billion. This was nothing new for Tu and Sun, for employees are used to being showered with surprises from their bosses. Once they paid for the funeral of an employee's mother; other times they have rewarded employees with trips to Cancun, Mexico. Employees say they'd take a bullet for Tu and Sun, two bosses who sit in cubicles just like everyone else.

On the other hand, there's Chainsaw Al, society's antihero.

If you watched television in December of 1996, you would have seen Sunbeam's new TV commercial with this jingle: "There's a new Sunbeam. It's getting brighter every day." Well, that was hardly the case for the folks back at Sunbeam's Florida-based headquarters where it was announced around the same time that 6000 employees—half the company—would be laid off in 1997 thanks to the company's infamous CEO, "Chainsaw Al" Dunlop's draconian "slash-and-burn" management tactics. Dunlop has been called by many society's only living heart donor.

Sunbeam's sunny vision on television didn't quite fool an American public familiar with downsizing. Although downsizing is painful and destructive to personal lives, the undeniable fact is that it has been critical to the survival of a changing American workplace being affected by the expansion of technology, deregulation of markets, and rising global competition due to the collapse of socialist regimes (Table 1.3).

DOWNSIZING VERSUS UPSIZING

Tired of hearing the word *downsize?* The word originally was used to describe the reduction of car sizes. An ad for Ford LTDs in a magazine read "Will down-sized cars have down-sized prices?" (see Safire 1996). Whether you're downsized, right-sized, or "happysized" according to Dilbert cartoonist Scott Adams, you're in good company. Today, the goal of downsizing is always to grow revenue by cutting expenses. That's the way it was supposed to play out. Instead, if feels as though world forces are pulling corporations back and forth and that they play good cop/bad cop in efforts to balance demands of employees—and more so, stockholders.

The more efficient and streamlined a company, the higher its productivity and sales.[18] Did anyone in the executive suite hear of a disease called *burnout?* People are doing the job of three to five people, and it's getting tiring. At first downsizing created bare-bones departments full of employees with low morale but thankful they had a job; everyone eventually got back to business until residual side effects, such as burnout and corporate anorexia, set in, which affected productivity.

So "upsizing" becomes the remedy to "corporate anorexia." The newest buzzwords have people, especially those in real estate, thinking that boom time is just around the corner once again as companies outgrow their downsized offices in need of bigger, spiffier digs. Read between the lines, but try not to wince. In fact, in May 1996 job cuts totaled 230,350, up 34 percent from the same period a year earlier, according to Challenger, Gray & Christmas, a firm that tracks job cuts (see Safire 1996). Companies who wore their mean business badges with honor (to get approval from stockholders, of course) saw a dark cloud of negative publicity descend over AT&T when it announced its layoffs in January 1996. Companies reacted to AT&T's struggle by finding a way to sugarcoat its own downsizing efforts. For example, here's a strange online news ticker Reuters report about America Online: "America Online will lay off 300 of its 5900 employees....A spokesperson for the world's largest online service provider said the job cuts do not represent a downsizing move at the company, which has seen exploding growth in recent years." The company did say that it would add about 1000 employees by the middle of 1997 in other parts of the country where customer-service locations would be developed. As fast as a company downsizes, it hires more people, many times deployed in other locations. The bottom line: Downsizing and upsizing balance each other out, meaning that companies are holding steady in the rate of employee growth.

There's still confusion about whether the economic trend is still downsizing, or now upsizing. But according to another study, the 1996 Employment Outlook Survey conducted by Manpower, the world's largest temporary agency, 21 percent of those interviewed expect hiring increases, 11 percent expect to downsize, and more neutral are the 61 percent who see no change at all in their staffing needs while 4 percent don't know what direction they will take.

TABLE 1.3
DOWNSIZING BY THE THOUSANDS

- Since 1979, more than 43 million jobs have been eliminated in the United States (see Uchitelle 1996).

- Since 1980, three-quarters of all American households have known a family member, friend, relative, or neighbor who has been laid off from a downsized company (see Lohr 1996).

- By mid-1996, downsizing was still running at an average of 39,000 layoffs a month (see Schellhardt 1996).

- According to Challenger, Gray & Christmas, an outplacement firm that also tracks downsizing in the United States, there were 47,911 layoffs in October 1996, up 62 percent from September 1996 and 16 percent more than October 1995.

- According to the same report, the total number of layoffs in 1996 (through November) was 410,208, 20 percent more than in 1995 (see Koretz 1996).

- Here are some examples of layoffs that were announced in 1996:

  AT&T, 40,000

  Sunbeam, 6000 (50 percent)

  Chase Manhattan merges with Chemical Bank, 12,000

  Tele-Communications, 2500 (6.5 percent)

  Witco, 1800 (25 percent)

Source: Based on layoff announcements reported in major newspapers. Where available, percentage figures refer to the company's total workforce being laid off at the time of announcement.

CATEGORIES OF WORKERS EMERGE, OTHERS SUBMERGE

"Things today are so complex and fast changing that the people doing the actual work need freedom of information. They need to be able to go anywhere up and down the hierarchy, across to other departments, diagonally. As soon as you do that, you change the internal power structure," said futurist Alvin Toffler in a 1996 online forum conducted by *Worth Magazine.* He went on to say that the people who were once the gatekeepers, who sat on top of each little unit, no longer control the flow of information that gave them power, and so they no longer have a function. And the plight worsens of the middle manager and many other levels of staff whose jobs are affected by new work processes and new technologies.

Middle Managers: Melting Away

Middle managers represent a surprising less than 10 percent of the U.S. workforce and is also shrinking in numbers every day. According to data collected by the American Management Association, almost three middle management positions were cut for every new one created. What that means is jobs require more technological expertise and less supervisory skills (see Courter 1996). It's no wonder middle managers so often oppose letting employees telecommute or work remote. Telecommuters fast become technology savvy and don't require much supervision, two skills middle managers continue to try to covet.

A Disappearing Breed of Worker: the Secretary

Where have all the secretaries gone? Are you usually taken by great surprise when you call someone's corporate office today and a secretary picks up the line instead of voice mail? After all, the voice mail industry has exploded in sales to $2.3 billion in 1996–1997, thanks to a 20 percent a year growth over the past few years (see Schiesel 1997).

Technology has made the secretary an anachronism in a world full of PCs. The computer and e-mail have redefined the role of a secretary whose work used to revolve around carbon paper, Dictaphones, and electric typewriters. Today, busy executives find it quicker to answer their own e-mail, and the secretary has taken on more responsibility, and has become more of an administrator for coordinating projects.

In 1974, 3.7 percent of the workforce was made up of secretaries. In 1994, 2.8 percent of the workforce was composed of secretaries, and soon, it will be an extinct field, according to the Bureau of Labor Statistics (see Herszenhorn 1995). This has far-reaching implications as to how we design office space because although we still see rows of offices with secretarial stations outside the doors, the rise of the technology-savvy baby-boomer is slowly chewing away at the need for all those carefully crafted, customized banks of mahogany workstations.

"Some senior partners at a very large law firm we are doing a project for told me that over the last 10 years, they have experienced a great decline of secretaries," says Caroline Brooks, senior designer and senior associate at Butler, Rogers, Basket in New York City, at a seminar at Interplan 1996 (a trade show). "Now there is one secretary for every three lawyers. Ten to 15 years ago, there was one or more secretaries per lawyer doing the filing and personal errands. No doubt the secretarial population is declining." What Brooks found is the evolution of a new realm of highly paid, highly trained professionals that take care of electronic data in-house in a law firm. "There's a whole generation of attorneys out there who are willing to use new technology and electronic storage only if there is someone available to get the information back to them quickly in a usable form," she notes.

The Rise of the New-Media Industry

Okay, so what exactly is the new-media industry you are hearing so much about? According to the New York New Media Association's Web site,[19] "The new-media industry has emerged from the embryonic stage to serve a wider audience...The new-media industry combines visual and audio elements like animation, video, and music with computing and communications technologies to create leading-edge films and videos, CD-ROMs, online services, and virtual reality applications." A sampling of new-media job titles include entertainment software producer, digital animator, HTML/Java coder, archivist, senior software engineer, game designer, server software engineer, 3-D artist, and Web master.

There seems to be a very fine line between what constitutes the new-media industry and the high-tech industry. After all, they both breed manic workers with high productivity levels. But look again at the real differences. New media is the multimedia side of technology—an exploration into new types of media on which to put information and entertainment. The high-tech industry—one that has been in full swing since the 1980s—is a more mature industry that makes the chips, manu-

facturers the hardware, and services the networks. High-tech folks make the computers on which new-media folks put their multimedia products. Together, these industries compose a larger field called *information technology* (IT). But separate, new-media companies and high-tech companies have different cultures, personal lifestyles, and values unique to their particular segment of the IT industry.

New media is an industry full of Internet providers, Internet content providers including newspapers and magazines—or 'zines, the lingo for electronic publications—Web page designers, and Web masters who need more technology on their desks and in a building's infrastructure than the typical white-collar worker.

In a 1996 study the accounting giant Coopers & Lybrand found that over 70,000 people work in the estimated 4200 new-media companies in the metropolitan New York area, and in New York City alone 18,000 people are working in 1350 such businesses—making new media a larger industry than the city's television or book publishing industry (Table 1.4). Those figures are expected to double through 1998. In 1995, a study conducted by the Bay Area Multimedia Partnership reported that the San Francisco metropolitan area had over 2200 new-media companies employing over 62,000 people.

"Most of the tenants at 55 Broad Street are on flextime. But they don't call it that. They call it 'working when we want to work,' and the building is responding to this culture by operating 24 hours a day," says Don Erwin, senior associate at Fox & Fowle, the architects responsible for rehabilitating the New York Information Technology Center for

TABLE 1.4
NEW-MEDIA JOBS TAKE CITIES BY STORM

City	Estimated Number of New-Media Jobs
San Francisco	59,000
Los Angeles	133,000
New York	60,000
Boston	44,000
Seattle	15,000
Austin, Texas	7,000

Source: Joyce Lain Kennedy, Careers Column, Connecticut Post, December 15, 1996.

The Big Shift in Ways to Work & Live

Traditional office [Office-Office] and home environments [home-home] no longer are the only way to work and live. Contemporary offices increasingly provide features of the home [home-Office], while today's home often incorporates aspects of the office [Office-home].

housing new-media companies, best known as 55 Broad Street (profiled in this chapter and in Chapter 11). The architects try to engage many of 55 Broad Street's tenants in conversations about the office of the future and alternative officing, but they don't know or understand these terms even though they are living it. "To them, it's quite simply the way they work. There's no intellectualization about the process; they are interested only in the technology that's sitting on the table first and foremost," adds Carl Lewis, principal. One thing is for certain, according to these two new-media experts: If it comes down to buying a better chair or a better computer, it's no contest that a new-media employee would invest in the technology over comfort. After all, what is furniture to a new-media Internaut than just a way to support a computer?

There's another trend in the new-media workplace, according to the observations of John Holey, architect of numerous new-media interiors. What he sees is the evolution of the "office-home," a kind of refuge for young hipsters whose work environment is more inviting and soothing to the soul than a cramped home atmosphere. An office-home differs from any other corporate office in that the office takes on the more physical attributes of a home (Fig. 1.4). An office-home takes on a special appeal to someone involved in working with scads of x's and o's to write code—they're looking for an environment full of comfort items that tie into real life because the home they are staring at all day and night is just a screen. The other reason? They just don't like regular offices.

"If you look at how people worked at Apple, there were all those kinds of signals going on there," Holey remembers. "One guy at Apple I remember dropped his work surfaces in his cubicle to 18 inches off the floor, put in a big Oriental rug, and worked cross-legged off the floor because he felt more comfortable working like that—and he probably could lay back and sleep if he wanted to.... We're seeing this all over the place now."

A Growing Breed of Worker: The Contracted Employee

The use of independent contract workers is expected to have grown to 35 percent of the total workforce by the year 2000, according to a Conference Board poll conducted in 1996 surveying personnel managers. "This will require a major reevaluation and enhanced flexibility in future space utilization plans," says Chip Julin III, RPA.[20] But another study done by the ISFE and Knoll says that the facility executives they surveyed in 1996 said the opposite and pointed to the direction of growing staffs that will decrease the need for contract or outsourced workers.

Nevertheless, it's cheaper for a company to hire a temporary employee, a tactic that bypasses the associated training, insurance, and real estate costs of hiring a staffer. Throughout the 1990s, temporary employment has consistently ranked as one of the fastest-growing segments of the workplace. You just have to take a look at the world's largest employer, Manpower. The temp agency provides employment to 1.5 million people in 41 countries on an annual basis.[21] The average employment of temporary workers in 1995 was more than 2.2 million a day, according to the National Association of Temporary and Staffing Services.

Thanks in large part to downsizing, there are many eager, smart people who have taken temp positions. Some workplace experts call temps "flex-staff," or, "just-in-time staff." Regardless of what they're called, temps are being sought not for administrative duties but more and more for technical and professional duties. Recently spotted is the trend for companies to hire their own downsized employees back as contract workers. According to the a survey by the American Management Association, over 200 companies that have downsized employees have brought them back on board as contract employees, the largest being Pacific Bell (see Uchitelle 1996).

Another segment of the temporary market is the high-tech "hired guns" that companies like Microsoft seek out for short stints as project managers, program managers, text editors, Web page developers and even sales representatives. High-tech specialists command big bucks—up to $30 an hour—and that should make this way of working a preferred lifestyle for many.

Keeping up with the sophisticated nature of its temporaries are the temporary agencies that place them. Resource Management, a placement agency that caters to the likes of Microsoft, even started a 401(k) program for its hired guns (see Egan 1996). The temporary placement agencies that are dispatching these hired guns are becoming more sophisticated, keeping up with their temp force of professionals.

Nadine Mockler and Laurie Young founded a placement agency for professionals in 1989, called Flexible Resources, that caters to career-minded women in their mid-thirties and mid-forties who wanted to keep one foot part-time in their industries, keeping their skills finely tuned while tending to family needs. Most of Flexible Resources' clients command high fees (see Magnell 1996).

Outsourcing as a Solution

It says something about our working patterns when Kinko's, "the new way to office," has grown to over 800 locations in the United States, Canada, Japan, and the Netherlands since it opened in 1970 in Isla Vista, California. Kinko's has single-handedly brought consumer awareness to the possibilities of affordable retail videoconferencing services and given customers the chance to rent high-end computers for desktop publishing projects. Its customers are not only the individual entrepreneur, the business traveler who is in need of a temporary satellite office, but also small- and midsize companies that rely on the 24-hour "branch office" for full-service copying, typesetting, faxing, finishing, printing, and mailing services.

The downsizing of the mid-1990s has left companies with bare-bones staffs who have had no choice but to begin focusing on core competencies. This opened up the demand for outsourcing services and projects, and downsized employees who went on to become entrepreneurs were right there to fill in Corporate America's need for small, specialty-driven outsourcing companies. The most popular functions to be outsourced are management services and computer programming. According to

a 1996 survey by Dun & Bradstreet (D&B), there are 146,000 outsourcing companies that are listed doing business with more than 1.6 million firms in the D&B information database. Though outsourcing companies tend to be small, under 20 employees, it is a frequent cushion on which midsized companies tend to fall back after downsizing.

Information technology outsourcing has been around for years. But experts see this branch of outsourcing in extreme demand starting in 1997 when new systems at lower prices will come onto the market. It makes sense to rely on specialist organizations to handle the complexities and training after the initial purchase of hardware and software.

Marketing Awe to a Shrinking Workforce

Despite the incredible demand for outsourcing, companies are looking to hire. But some cities around the country have tight labor markets. But tight labor markets mean that workplace flexibility is as good as money in the bank:

CENTURY 21 RADNOCK IS THE FIRST
FULL-SERVICE REAL ESTATE COMPANY TO
OFFER OUR AGENTS TELECOMMUTING
VIA THE INFORMATION SUPER HIGHWAY!

That's how the Century 21 Web site heading read in 1995. "Some agents are great prospectors but just don't want to be in the office atmosphere. That's OK with us!" the page continued. It was clearly a recruiting tool, not unlike other companies are using today to attract job applicants. The decline in numbers of young job seekers will get only worse as baby-boomers age.[22]

That's just one in dozens of stories about companies using workplace flexibility to attract the best talent in tight labor markets. In a city with only 3 percent unemployment, St. Paul, a big insurance company in Minneapolis, finds it easy to find new hires and retain employees. Its secret weapon: flexibility. Alternative schedules, 4-day weeks, and telecommuting are the norm for employees at St. Paul, providing they can prove it will work out well for everyone involved, including the customer first and foremost. In 1997, St. Paul rolled out this plan to all of its 9000 U.S. employees (see Shellenbarger 1996).

Far-Flung Virtual Corporations Staying Face to Face With Clients

Flattened hierarchies and newer, swifter technology are both enablers to employees who prefer to make decisions quickly, get the right information out faster, and stay on top of projects with ease. What does that really mean for the employee? It means most likely the worker will be mobile, or virtual.

It's an enticing idea that many entrepreneurs are trying: the *virtual corporation*. What does it mean? There are numerous blurry definitions to a very real direction of many companies. According to authors of the 1992 book *The Virtual Corporation*, William Davidow and Michael Malone, the word *virtual* means something different today: to recognize "formerly well defined structures beginning to lose their edges, seemingly permanent things starting to continuously change."[23] The authors also maintain that there is no single answer to what a virtual corporation looks like, although they exist, and that it's "best to talk of the virtual corporation in terms of patterns of information and relationships." One way to describe a virtual company is that it exists and communicates mostly through an electronic infrastructure.

Successful virtual employees are not a dime a dozen, as publicist Judith Lederman experienced. She hated her virtual company. The then work-at-home executive employed six other consultants who all worked from their homes, but nothing would ever get done, she says. Today, her business, JSL Publicity and Marketing, is housed in a traditional 800-square-foot office in Irvington, New York (see Kirke 1996).

Yet to others, the virtual office with its intoxicating notions of freedom has such a strong pull over some who've experienced the hindrances of a traditional office that they've turned down positions in conventional companies. Don Fenton is one such person. Fenton worked as a traditional corporate executive for years, and the last time for a company that went bankrupt because of the Canadian recession. He decided enough was enough and he'd take destiny into his own hands.

So the virtual company man he became—working for two virtual companies, Smart Sales, a software company of 20 people, and his own business, Powerhouse Marketing Communications with three virtual partners who all live in different cities including one who resides in Bermuda. Both businesses run on an electronic infrastructures with heavy e-mail and voice mail back and forth.

Face to face isn't a problem with Fenton. Smart Sales has real-time meetings once a week in a shared-amenities space in downtown Toronto. "I still call that office the 'legitimate' office versus my home office, a stigma of the past, I suppose," he says. Wherever his office is, Fenton now has more freedom and he relaxes into the fact that he can't be fired or downsized. And that's certainly one corporate benefit no virtual employee would want to give up.

UNFOLDING LIFESTYLES

Living the virtual company life gives Fenton the chance to go to the gym four times a week. How many of us struggle to find time to get any form of exercise but once a week if we not only commute but also have a family or the need to tend to other obligations?

Single. Single with children. Married. Married with children. Then, there's the care of aging relatives. Nearly everyone has a lifestyle issue that can throw a wrench into the balance of work and home. Statistics show that it costs U.S. companies $200 billion a year in stress-related absenteeism, lowered productivity, increased compensation claims, health insurance, and medical expenses (see Hales 1996).

More couples in their thirties are having children into their careers. Though more women have entered the workforce, many women who don't find corporate support with which to balance work and family tend to drop out of the workforce to care for children. More couples live in the suburbs and have long commutes to work. Increasing natural disasters and weather-related problems leave us without a way to get to corporate headquarters. More families have technology in their homes. The list goes on and on. New job outlooks and lifestyle changes go hand in hand, influencing each other, paving the way for more alternative workplace strategies.

BALANCING WORK AND FAMILY (MEN GET INTO THE ACT TOO)

Rocky Rhodes, cofounder and chief engineer of Silicon Graphics, gives us an indication of what the employee wants and needs. In an article in the *Wall Street Journal* (see Shellenbarger, 1996), writer Sue Shellenbarger interviewed Rhodes about his new way of working. It seems Rhodes worked 7-day weeks for years, immersed in his work so that he'd wake in the middle of the night to execute an idea in his lab. With the birth of his son Dustin, he assumed a "constant battle, a struggle against the ability of my work life to totally consume me and, on the other side, this blossoming family that I felt was more important."

So in 1987, he began to cut down on his hours, and in 1992, he worked at home for a while, then switched to part-time work in 1995. He now works on new features for the next generation of his company's machines. Though he could afford to retire, Rhodes wants the camaraderie of the lab. But he's now an advocate of restructuring the all-or-nothing demands of full-time jobs to ease the stress on family life.

It's the high-profile executive like Rhodes who will bring awareness to the rest of top-management corporate America about the benefits of letting employees work in alternative arrangements. But it is the ordinary worker who understands what these benefits could mean to their lifestyle.

Can't the employee just ask for an alternative work program? No. With downsizing and cutbacks, those workers who survive the cuts just want to keep their jobs, not rock the boat. Virtual office and alternative workplace programs are usually initiated by top management, not the employee base.

WOMEN IN THE WORKPLACE

Though the glass ceiling and old-boy networks still exist, women are a force of their own in the workplace, but not in quite the way everyone thinks. More than half the working population is female, yet men dominate the executive suites. Women are slowly but surely making their voices heard for if they can't get compensated as their male counterparts do, they may as well demand the intangible: flexibility in the workplace. It's an ongoing battle, but one that clearly can't be stopped.

Look at what's changed:

Age	Priorities 1980s	Priorities Late 1990s
Twenties	Career	Marriage and family, then career, own business
Thirties	Career	Balance career and family, own business
Forties	Career	Marriage and family, then career, own business

Women are going through numerous changes. In the 1980s, women in their twenties concentrated on building a career, waiting through their thirties and into their forties to marry and bear children. Because of this delay in childbirth, many women experienced infertility, in turn took fertility drugs, only to have multiple births.[24] This development has forced women with careers to leave the workforce to care for the larger-than-anticipated family because there is rarely a support system on the corporate level to allow mothers to continue working.

Women who must work or want to continue working continue to grapple with the demands of motherhood and work responsibilities. But daycare centers aren't always a panacea. One major financial institution in New York City opened up a daycare center in the heart of its headquarters in midtown. But it found that the city isn't exactly the best place to open up an on-site daycare center. Women didn't want to wake up their kids at the crack of dawn, drag them into the city on the commuter train, then drop them off, only to drag them through the commute home, says an employee in the human resources department. The shuttered daycare center was a huge room filled with fewer than five kids every day.

And women face harsh realities of abandoning breast-feeding their newborn babies once they return to work. Working environments have no provisions on the job for working, breast-feeding mothers such as private areas for women to use breast pumps. In anticipation of these obstacles, most women choose to give up breast-feeding even before they go back to work.

The number of dual-earner households has grown from 31 percent of all households in 1967 to 46.1 percent in 1993, according to the latest figures available from the Labor Department. But because of the demands on executive women, many are dropping out to pursue family responsibilities because their companies did little or nothing to support their needs.

Corporations beware, according to a poll conducted by Roper Starch Worldwide, Inc., for the Virginia Slims brand of Philip Morris USA (see Dobzynski 1995). Of the 3000 women polled, 84 percent agree that women still face restrictions in the workplace. Sheila Wellington, the president of Catalyst, a nonprofit women's research and advocacy group, wasn't surprised about the poll's results. "There was a kind of buoyant optimism 10 years ago and certainly 20 years ago," Wellington said. "But I don't think this means that women will leave the workforce. It does mean that they will be very careful about where they choose to work and how they choose to work."

Wellington's last sentence is critical to corporations nationwide. Those that cater to working women's needs will win the competition for attracting and keeping talent. Consider the situation with some of the leading law and accounting firms.

Only one-quarter of lawyers and accountants in the United States are women. And only 6.7 percent of partners in the Bix Six accounting firms and 13 percent of partners in the top 1160 law firms are female, according to the same article that quotes Bowman's Accounting Report and the National Association for Law Placement. Why the bias? Women who have to tend to sick children or pick up kids from school have serious marks against them, say female executives in the old-boy fields of accounting and law.

But some of these old boys see the bottom-line sense in having female partners and managers. As more women start their own businesses, they prefer to hire the council of a female. Only a couple of the majors, such as Arthur Andersen and Deloitte & Touche, have gone the way of flexible office hours and alternative workplace solutions. Although they did so to cut real estate, both firms hope a side benefit of contemporary work environments will retain the talent of women.

The American Institute of Certified Public Accountants seems to have caught on to this problem. In the March 31, 1996, edition of the Sunday New York Times' Help Wanted section, there was an ad for "Manager, Women & Family Issues." The ad read, "We have taken a leadership role in fostering an awareness among CPA firms, and corporations who employ CPAs, of the importance of facilitating the advancement of women CPAs and initiating programs to aid employees as they balance work and family responsibilities."

Accounting and law firms are not the only ones to make life difficult for women on all levels of management. "Why Corporate Women Drop Out" was the topic of a Business Week Online conference (October 18, 1995). Alice Lusk, a 20-year veteran of Electronic Data Systems, was the guest speaker there to speak about why she decided to leave her top-ranking position. Though she skirted the question over and over again, she subliminally made the point throughout the session that most corporate environments stifle women's growth due to patterns of old-boy management networks. As for Lusk, her future lies in finding "the right environment versus the right corporation." The right environment for most women clearly embodies the complexities of flexible management style, flexible corporate culture, and flexible physical workspace. The right environment would be termed "family-friendly."

What has become of the quest for the family-friendly environment? Most U.S. companies have not been able or willing to pay little more than lip service in encouraging a family-friendly environment. Millions of Americans, men and women, are put under great amounts of exhausting, guilt-ridden, anger-provoking stress in the race to fulfill work and family obligations. The Family and Medical Leave Act of 1993 was America's only hope that Corporate America would soften its sharp family-unfriendly edges. The Family and Medical Leave Act of 1993 that was vetoed twice by the Republican administration and passed on February 5, 1993, by President Clinton. The law states that in a company with 50 or more employees who work over 25 hours a week, employees can take up to 12 weeks of unpaid leave each year to recuperate from an illness, take care of a new child, or help a sick family member. When the employee returns to work, the employee will be given the same or similar job. Small and large companies alike had a fit when the act was passed. According to executive management, most employees would take advantage of the act, and companies would lose money hand over fist.

In the 1992 book Beyond Workplace 2000, author Joseph H. Boyett captures the true state of Corporate America's family-unfriendliness that surfaced when the act was passed:

> The doomsday predictions that employees would take leave in droves for everything from Johnny's sniffles to a worker's sprained ankle were totally unfounded. After all, most companies did little more than post a notice about the law....

Boyett goes on to say that if employees understood any of their legal rights at all, they were afraid to exercise them because they understood the unwritten and unspoken rules that there would be "unpleasant consequences."

Since little has been done to promote the act, the Public Policy Institute at Radcliffe College has stepped in to study the work-family problem. The project, called the New Economic Equation, is a series of focus groups of men and women from all around the country. As one part of the project, the institute held a two-day conference to review the findings of the focus groups and look for solutions.

According to the institute's findings, women have chosen to "downshift" in order to cope with work and family issues since the workplace and public polices have been inefficient. Unfortunately, there were few solid recommendations that came out of the two-day seminar, according to an article in Time Magazine (see Smolowe 1996). "Our best hope is CEOs with daughters," concluded panelist Marina von Neumann, former chief economist for General Motors.

Many have tried to help the situation, however. The late Felice N. Schwartz was president of Catalyst[25] when she prompted a national debate in 1989 with an article in the *Harvard Business Review* in which she asserted that it cost companies more to employ women than men. She noted that women's careers were often interrupted, or ended, when they had children, and she suggested that employers create policies to help mothers balance career and family responsibilities by giving them more flexibility in work hours and providing high-quality daycare.

An uproar began almost immediately. Her proposed alternative career track came to be called the "mommy track." Detractors voiced the fear that by raising the higher-cost issue, women would not be hired and promoted and that all women would be left with the primary responsibility for child care. Although Schwartz said her views were widely misinterpreted to mean that women are less ambitious than men, the fact remains that women with families face many obstacles in the workplace that men simply don't face. Schwartz felt instead of letting women's talents go to waste, that the group of male executives who run Corporate America to this day address those needs in a meaningful way. She believed, she said, that there should be a parent track.

Companies will face another inevitable issue involving women. Trends point to young career women marrying and having children sooner than their overachieving big corporate sisters who kept their personal lives at bay until their careers were established during their late thirties and early forties. Many of these younger career women in their early and mid-twenties see no point in putting off their personal lives only to endure the pain of finding an available man and then dealing with infertility issues. The twenty-something marriage boom has been explored in an article in *The Wall Street Journal* (see Duff 1996) that was based on interviews with numerous young women about their quest for marriage.

The consensus among all of these women was that being married is not a compromise to their careers but a boost. It's this group of women who will demand that Corporate America take notice of their work-family balancing act. This trend toward traditionalism means that companies who want to entice young talented women into their organizations must offer some kind of flexible working environment that allows for a work-family balance.

Many women who have children and maintain careers find themselves traveling with family on business trips. According to the Travel Industry Association of America, the number of business trips that included children jumped from approximately 26.6 million in 1990 to 43.4 million in 1994 (see Wilde 1995). The reason? More frequent and longer business trips mean parents, including breast-feeding mothers who won't compromise, are creating ways to spend time with their children even if that means lugging diapers, toys, baby food, strollers, and briefcase onto the airplane or rental car.

AT HOME AT WORK

It's not just the young new-media types who are opting to spend more time at the office. There's a subtrend that author Arlie Russell Hochschild wrote about in her book *The Time Bind: When Work Becomes Home and Home Becomes Work* (Metropolitan Books, 1997). She spent three years interviewing 130 respondents from an anonymous company, which she calls Amerco in the book. At Amerco, a company with family-friendly policies, fewer than 1 percent have taken advantage of the chance to work part-time, but about a third of the working parents have opted for flextime. Hochschild asks, "While working parents say they need more time at home, the main story of their lives does not center on a struggle to get it. Why? Given the hours parents are working these days, why aren't they taking advantage of an opportunity to reduce their time at work?"

Most think it's because working parents need the money and that's why they opt for longer hours. Others would say employees don't take alternative work opportunities for fear of being laid off. She asked why Amerco working parents weren't taking advantage of family-friendly policies? Hochschild found her answers through her interviews: Most people at Amerco felt more competent, skilled, and appreciated at work than they did at home—and work was a good way to get out from under the burdens and responsibilities of an overwhelming homelife. She witnessed that Amerco workers had more fun at work while they were setting up quality time "appointments" at home as they would in an office situation. Efficiency at home, says the author, has become more important than at work for Amerco workers.

How do we extricate ourselves from this workaholic syndrome that we thought had ended in the 1980s, only to show up again in the 1990s? And, of course, the bulk of the responsibility falls onto working women's shoulders. The author has no answer, but she is pointing out a serious problem in corporate America and in our society at large. Hochschild points to other nations such as Sweden, Norway, and Denmark, where parents tend to take off more time for their children, called parental leave. But in corporate America, paternity leave never left the ground. The solution in the United States may be to put the responsibility on company management to make it absolutely mandatory for working parents to take parental leave, paternity leave, and the like.

WORKPLACE FLEXIBILITY FOR NONPARENTS

The growth of companies that are family-friendly focus their flexible programs toward employees with children. What about the single person or the child-free couple who need to balance work and home? Those employees, often the ones over 30, who take the day off when pets are sick are often ostracized and ridiculed. Corporations that make life easier for working parents don't make it easy for nonparents. The conflict goes like this: The employee with kids tends to leave earlier under a flextime program, telecommutes, or is excused from meetings because he or she must attend to his or her children's needs, leaving the nonparent employee to stay later, pick up the extra work, and take on more burden of staff needs. After all, isn't it the perception in most corporate cultures that the nonparent has more free time for work activities?

Everyone—nonparents absolutely included—has needs that must be met. Some companies are responding to the tensions between parent and nonparent employees. Marriott International renamed its work-family department the work-life division to include both parents and nonparents. At Aetna, employees who ask for flextime are not discriminated against if they don't have children, but they must present a strong case that justifies the request (see Murray 1996).

THE SANDWICH GENERATION SQUEEZES WORKERS

It sounds like families are trying anything to be closer to one another and still maintain jobs. Children aside, there's another growing issue of the elderly who need caring for. Taking care of an elderly relative takes time out of the day and night, and often working men and women can't get away or are reprimanded from leaving the office to check on relatives. The General Accounting Office estimates that approximately 7.5 million older Americans with chronic disabilities live at home, and about 2 million working Americans provide significant unpaid care for the elderly. In 1995, there were 30 million Americans over the age of 65, and the American Association of Children of Aging Parents predicts that within 25 years every third American worker will be caring for an elderly parent (see Davidson 1996).

FUTURE WORKFORCE: GENERATION X AND "SCREEN-AGERS"

Age defies lifestyle needs. At Lucent, alternative office strategies are now used as a retention issue. College hires increasingly ask about what flexible work arrangements the technology company provides. They ask if Lucent has a 4-day workweek, telecommuting, or flextime. Karen Sansone, alternative work strategist, feels they are driven to request those types of workstyles because they've seen their parents work themselves to the ground, and they don't want to repeat the pattern, she concluded at a seminar for the Telecommuting Advisory Council in New York City.

True, post baby boomers don't like what they see:

Veal-Fattening Pen: Small, cramped office workstation built of fabric-covered wall disassembleable partitions and inhabited by junior staff members. Named after the small preslaughter cubicles used by the cattle industry.

This is the definition of a cubicle that is given in the book *Generation X* by Douglas Coupland.

Once Gen Xers (people in their twenties don't like this categorical label) and screen-agers hit the office landscape, it definitely won't be business as usual any longer. What are they looking for? They are far from a cynical bunch of couch potatoes. They just don't want to play the same tune as baby-boomers who waited too long to get married, have babies, then were downsized with no savings and were forced to sell the house or file for bankruptcy. Many Xers seek early marriage and family, along with technology that keeps their attention, jobs as Web site designers, 401(k) plans, flextime, and dress-up Fridays…huh?

We all know what a baby-boomer is: those born between 1946 and 1964 (see Stone 1996). But what's a Gen Xer? How about those born between 1965 through 1976? There are many overlapping timelines; some say it's the young men and women born between 1962 and 1971. Coupland says in his book it is anyone born from the late 1950s through the 1960s. Some say it's anyone under the age of 30; others say under the age of 34. No matter when a Gen Xer stops being a Gen Xer, they saw something in those over 35 that disturbed them. Nevertheless, there are about 48 million Xers in the United States that account for 30 percent of all computer sales, according to America's Research Group in Charleston, South Carolina (see Steinhauer 1996).

In the 1980s, Gen Xers witnessed their baby-boomer parents, relatives, and friends struggle as workaholics to make more money to buy more things. They've witnessed baby-boomers who missed their own baby boom, who never married, or married too late to have babies in lieu of the illustrious career that comes with business travel complete with tailored navy blue rolling pullman luggage carrier and the company credit card, neither of which keeps anyone warm at night.

Marrying at 40, having a baby at 43—that's not a Gen Xer's idea of having fun. College-bound and twenty-something, these women aren't waiting for marriage and family, but instead embracing the courting traditions of their parents and grandparents. What's happening here? A changing value system that puts marriage and family over career and accomplishment. Changing values predispose changing lifestyles and changing jobs and trickle into other areas like changing technology (to make work more flexible and remote in order to take care of family). It's a budding trend, but nevertheless one that deserves attention. A 1994 nationwide survey for the Diamond Information Center, an industry trade group, found that 47 percent of all first-time brides with diamond engagement rings were in their early to mid twenties, up from 37 percent just 10 years earlier (see Abel 1996).

"What's up with this Internet? It's boring." These are the voices of screen-agers who spent hours playing *Mario Brothers* when they were younger and who are both completely unimpressed with the NFL and NBA Web sites up on the computer. Screen-agers are the youngsters that grew up eating computers, video games, and televisions for breakfast, according to Douglas Rushkoff, a 35-year-old consultant and author who frequently helps Corporate America understand what goes on in the mind of a 17-year-old. Rushkoff suggests that screen-agers are better at multitasking because they have spent so much time learning *Nintendo*. Does this suggest that screen-agers won't have the capacity to

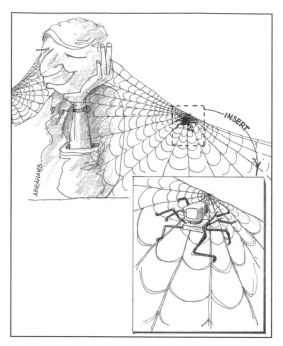

In the Web

focus and concentrate on their jobs? No, says Rushkoff. What it means, from the mind of one screen-ager consultant, is that they are better at pattern analysis and more apt at maintaining community with colleagues since they spent hours networking on the computer (see Gabriel 1996).

The one thing screen-agers won't put up with is wasting time. It's too frustrating for them to sit still. Commuting to a job may be intolerable for screen-agers, much less sitting in an office for 8 hours 5 days a week.

COMMUTING: THE BIGGEST TIME-WASTER

September 12, 1995

To Our Customers:

Yesterday, a small animal was electrocuted on the overhead wires west of Rye. The heat generated by this incident broke cautionary support brackets causing a wire to fall. When the 3:54 train from New Haven passed through this area, its pantographs became entangled in the wires, pulling them down on all four tracks....Severe overcrowding and extensive delays continued throughout the evening....We very much regret the delay and discomfort you experienced. Metro-North Railroad

The commuting patterns of employees came under scrutiny when the Clean Air Act Amendments of 1990 took hold. It seemed that companies located in cities didn't put much emphasis on the Clean Air Act and its implications since most employees came to and from work using mass transit (except in Southern California where there is barely any mass-transit infrastructure built). Commuting by mass transit may not make the air worse, but it does other damage mostly in the area of productivity.

One of Alvin Toffler's most famous quotes is: "Commuting is the single most antiproductive thing we do." Sure enough, strikes, fried squirrels, pedestrian accidents, track floods, fires, and switch problems tend to plague just about every commuter railroad across the country. One of the more considerate railroads, Metro North, the commuter train service that transports commuters in and out of New York City from Connecticut and Westchester County, spends time and money printing up apology notices for its customers every time there's a delay on the railroad. Delays, some unavoidable, others due to human carelessness, have caused passengers countless problems with missed meetings and downtime at work not to mention the mental stress of being helplessly stuck on an immobile train. Think of all the empty office space when a severe snowstorm prevents a commuter service from making the rush hour trip into the city.

Consider these commutes from places that beg for telecenters or zoning for telecommuter home offices: a man who spends 7 hours a day on seven trains from East Hampton, Long Island, to Manhattan (see Keating 1992); a woman who spends 2 hours door to door one way from Milford, Pennsylvania, to midtown Manhattan because the living is safe, clean, and affordable; and an entire community in Moreno Valley, California, that travels 4 hours a day—220 miles total into and out of Ventura County to their jobs. The people who do this moved to Moreno Valley to give their families a home in a newer and affordable suburb (see Downs 1991).

For millions of employed women with families, living in the suburbs means commuting to work in the city or over a few towns to get to the office. And as we know, the suburbs are pushing farther and farther out from the city because they offer affordable housing, but the results are long commutes, congested highways, and delayed train and bus rides that cut into the workday. Commuting is a thorn in the side not only of women but also of men.

TELECOMMUTING: RELIEF AFTER NATURAL DISASTERS

Remember the earthquake of 1994 that hit the West Coast, the Blizzard and flooding problems of 1996 that hit the East Coast, the 1996 Summer Olympics in Atlanta, and record cold temperatures that hit the Midwest the winter of 1996? Telecommuting became an immediate solution for many.

Thousands of people became telecommuters by default from Washington to Philadelphia to New York as walls of snow prevented people from getting to work during the Blizzard of '96. Companies like Bankers Trust in New York City, Wyeth-Ayerst Laboratories in Philadelphia, and law firm Mezzulo & McCandlish encouraged workers to telecommute though most were not set up to do so.

Those in the New York tristate region who decided to brave the snow to get into work relied heavily on commuter trains to transport them to and from the city from outlying areas in New Jersey, Connecticut, and Long Island. Instead, commuters endured the most hellish commuting week in decades, spending hours on lame-duck Metro North and Long Island Railroad trains that were more like cattle cars or standing elbow to elbow for hours in waiting rooms. This unending chaos convinced commuters that staying home to work the rest of the week was the best decision.

This unexpected wave of telecommuting was not without its glitches. Phone lines clogged while other workers were left without fax machines, necessary files, and phone numbers. Still others found stress in having to simultaneously work and mind their children because of canceled school. Early Monday morning of the storm, the number of calls was 90 percent higher than normal. Between 10:00 and 2:00 p.m., however, the number of calls dropped to 11 percent below usual, but those calls were much longer than normal, according to Eric W. Rabe, a spokesperson for Bell Atlantic. But the one gain from the messy storm may be that many workers who otherwise would never have telecommuted were able to taste the productivity benefits that the virtual office offers.

DOWNSHIFTERS HEADING FOR THE HILLS

For those who can't tolerate running after the American Dream on a commuter train or on stretches of bumper-to-bumper highway, appreciate the downshifter.

Downshifting hit home in Hollywood, of all places. Fans of the wildly popular medical NBC TV drama E.R. remember when actress Sherry Stringfield broke her contract, leaving fame, fortune, and her plum role as Dr. Susan Lewis to move to New York City and be with her boyfriend. The decision wasn't difficult for Stringfield—all she wanted was to have a normal, relaxed life (in New York City, of all places) and leave behind the high-paying but grueling days and nights. But her decision hit a nerve, inspiring envy among an American public, and Stringfield turned into every modern-day, career-stressed female's newest heroine. Careers can have strange effects on people's behaviors. Having problems remembering things? Many Americans as young as 35 years old feel the additional stress of memory loss. Complaints of diminished memory and concentration are attributed mostly to work and personal stress, according to a Pharmaton Natural Health Product survey of internists and family practitioners across the country. An anonymous writer at *Fast Company* magazine even gave this memory-less affliction a name when it applies to working women of the 1990s. It's fittingly called *Galzheimers* (see Spy 1996).

There are others who can no longer put up with such stress that inflexible Corporate American companies inflict upon them and have chosen another path of employment. They are called *downshifters*. Since the early 1990s, a revolt of sorts has taken place. A nationwide study on consumption trends commissioned the Merck Family Fund in the summer of 1995 showed that 28 percent of an 800-person focus group and telephone sample said they had downshifted and voluntarily cut back on their income and expenses to better reflect changes in lifestyle priorities. The survey also said that 82 percent of Americans agree with the statement "We buy and consume more than we need." Who is cutting back? Parents who desire a reduction in work hours to spend more time with kids. It's a trend going more mainstream with the increased numbers of Americans following spiritual growth paths. As more people practice Buddhism, read about Taoism, or reestablish ties with their church or temple, priorities of a different nature become increasingly clear. Suddenly, it's no longer a matter of making more and more money but of having a better quality of life that doesn't necessarily mean more money.

According to Juliet Schor, author of *The Overworked American*, of 1000 people surveyed nationwide in 1995, 28 percent made a "voluntary lifestyle change." Those who downshifted took reductions in income, moved to less stressful jobs, rejected promotions, or sought temporary or part-time work, she explains in an article in *Time* (see Smolowe 1996) .

Downshifting is not a passing phase. The Trends Research Institute of Rhinebeck, New York, says Voluntary Simplicity is a top 10 trend of 1990s and predicts that by the millennium, 15 percent of the 77 million baby-boomer generation will become part of an evolving market that prefers simple, durable, low-priced products that lack status and glamour (see Goldberg 1995).

What does this mean to the development of the virtual office? It means working at the corporate office for 12 to 15 hours a day (with the exception of the home-based worker, who tends to overwork) is no longer the norm or the desire of an increasing number of Americans. It means workers are willing to accept the responsibilities of their debt but not at the expense of quality time with their family, friends, and creative self.

SUMMARY

For most of us, trying to fit into the traditional workplace is like trying to put on clothes that we've outgrown and are too tight—constricting. We need a new wardrobe to go with all the changes in our life, a new workplace to support our evolving lifestyle.

Not since the 1700s has there been so much change in America. The overlying reason has great implications in all other aspects of our life, ultimately resulting in the increase in alternative workplaces to support the changes. Technology has changed the way America does business. Changes in business create fluctuations in real estate and urban planning, all of which affect lifestyle. Reverse the pattern, and you will find that new lifestyle needs require shifts in real estate and urban planning, which affect the job outlook across the country. The changes have just begun, and so has the conversion to new workplaces for new workstyles, new lifestyles. Consider this: Of 1184 adults recently surveyed by the BrainWaves Group in San Mateo, California, 95 percent say they are walking a tightrope in balancing work and family, and it's getting worse, a statistic which corroborates author Arlie Russell Hochschild's findings.

Southern California Edison stresses this point in much of its alternative officing materials: "Companies that embrace alternative officing are sending a loud message. They're making it clear that they're interested in their employees' welfare, that they're seeking a competitive edge, and that they aren't afraid to rethink their work practices for changing conditions."

Defining the New Workplace

Offices are not information factories; they are extensions of the mind.

Duncan Sutherland

Almost all facility and human resource professionals are familiar with the terms and concepts of *telecommuting, flexible schedules,* and *shared space.* But the same group may be less likely to be as familiar with the meaning of the terms *free address, activity setting,* or *group address.* Such are the findings of a 1995 survey of FM professionals conducted by Haworth and the International Facility Management Association (IFMA), a project initiated to get a better handle on the state and use of alternative workplace strategies.

This chapter has a ready-to-refer-to section on definition of terms for you and your client. In addition, each section discusses the concept's strengths and weaknesses, along with some mini

case studies of companies that practice these ideas so that you can get a sense of what the nontraditional workplace looks and feels like. You'll find in this chapter and in the case studies in Part 3 of this book that the alternative workplace doesn't necessarily look very different from the traditional office. It's *how* the space is used that counts more. And you don't even have to throw out the panel systems in which your company invested millions of dollars over the years.

Many factions have invested time and money in surveys to get an even better measure on the definition, scope, and use of the alternative office. However, the surveys have left us a little confused—

Figure 2.1
Some people think the alternative workplace is an outlandish idea. This scene in New York City is probably someone's vision of what an alternative work environment looks like with all the necessary amenities! (Photo by Kristen Richards.)

Figure 2.2
Do some people take the virtual office a little too far?
(Steelcase.)

Figure 2.3
The evolution of the mobile office starts here. Remember when a mobile office meant a temporary office in a trailer? Times have changed.
(Speed Space.)

how many people, how many companies, are really and truly working in alternative offices? At the end of the chapter is a listing of companies in the United States and abroad that have embraced alternative workplace strategies that may affect only small pockets of people or may be rolled out to affect thousands of employees companywide.

Before reading this chapter, heed this warning: You won't find a solution in this book or anywhere in this world that is already tailored specifically to just your set of needs. Don't look to Company X's solution to fit like a glove with your organizational needs. Planning and designing an alternative workplace can be complicated to implement and manage in a healthy, productive way that's appropriate to the company's business objectives and the corporate culture.

Keep in mind that there is a broad range of interpretations and understandings that people have of an alternative workplace solution (Figs. 2.1 and 2.2).[1] For example, to some clients, an alternative workplace may be defined simply as this: "Alternative officing means I will have a conferencing area in my office." That vision comes from a CEO of a small grooming products company on the West Coast.

Some employees aren't familiar with the new workplace terminology: "Hoteling means I get to sleep at the office" (name withheld upon request, employee of large telecommunications company).

Figure 2.4
Today's mobile office can be located in a car where 30 to 40 percent of a road warrior's work is done.
(Jotto.)

Table 2.1

OLD WORDS, NEW MEANINGS FOR ALTERNATIVE WORKPLACES

Word	Old Meaning	New Meaning
Mobile office	Temporary office in a trailer	Office in a briefcase
Home office	Corporate headquarters	Office in a home
Notebook	Three-ring binder	Laptop computer
Housekeeping	Hotel service	Hoteling service
Mouse	Cat's favorite toy	Computer's favorite toy
Touchdown	Football terminology	Hoteling terminology
Hearth	Fireplace	Area for casual employee gatherings
Home base	Baseball terminology	Designated lockers in office
Web	A spider's home	A mouse-potato's home
Caves	Holes in mountains	Places for solitary work
Commons	Center of town, the "green"	Teaming area at office
Living room	Center of house	Informal space for office meetings and gatherings
Road warrior	Motorcycle gang member	Mobile worker

Others are cynical about the whole issue: "Hoteling is a system by which cubicles are assigned to the employees as they show up each day. Nobody gets a permanent workspace, and therefore no unproductive homey feelings develop" (Scott Adams, author of *The Dilbert Principal*).

This is where the designer, the voice of reason, can step in and educate the client with words such as these:"Alternative officing is a mindset. It's really a chance for a company to reevaluate its work process and to think about what's good for them,"

says Brett Shwery, director of interior design at Leo A Daly in Santa Monica, California.

The alternative workplace has a new language to describe its various settings and components. However, some of the new words are really words already familiar to us, which can be confusing at times. Some are humorous, but the list in Table 2.1 is evidence that our language has changed in subtle ways in response to evolving contemporary work patterns and environments. (See also Figs. 2.3 through 2.5.)

Figure 2.5
Today's "living room" is more than just a room in your house. Joyce LaValle, CEO of carpet manufacturer Prince Street Technologies, manifested her desire for family spirit into a physical space the company calls the "living room." Adjacent to the open plan offices, the living room was designed by Nancy Cartledge, AIA, Thompson Ventulett, Stainback & Associates, for spontaneous and comfortable meetings. The seating is from Metro's Archipelago line. (Photo by Brian Gassel/TVS & Associates.)

Figure 2.6
Alternative work environments are sometimes called "Red Carpet Clubs" because they resemble the structure of an airport lounge. Take, for example, this United Airline Red Carpet Lounge in the London Heathrow Airport. Studios designed the 16,000-square-foot space with personal work cubicles outfitted with voice, data, and fax, more private spaces with onyx partitions, and open spaces for gathering together.
(Studios.)

THE LANGUAGE OF ALTERNATIVE WORKPLACES

Each of the following concepts are tools that companies use to reach a business objective. There are usually three common business objectives that alternative workplace strategies help companies to meet, but all three objectives generally work hand in hand:

Tools Needed to Reduce Real Estate Costs

Hoteling
Telecommuting

Shared offices
Satellite offices

Tools Needed to Increase Sales and Revenue

Hoteling
Mobile office
Virtual office

Tools Needed to Increase Team Interaction to Reduce R&D Cycle Time

Universal planning
Teaming rooms
Caves and commons

Figure 2.7
The "caves and commons" concept is clearly shown here through the use of Personal Harbors by Steelcase. Caves and commons allows a team to cluster in a relatively small footprint, forming both private and communal work areas. For privacy, several Personal Harbors in a circle act like a 48-square-foot phone booth with all the amenities of a private office and can be closed off by a sliding door. When it's time to come out of your booth for teamwork, reconfigurable and lightweight Activity Products tables by Steelcase offer plug-in capabilities. (Steelcase.)

A fourth, and limited, application of an alternative workplace program is the need to use the office as a tool of talent recruitment and retention.

Some of these spatial workplace strategies and flexible arrangements work hand in hand. For example, you can telecommute and hotel at the same time if your company has asked that you give up your dedicated space on the basis that you work at home more than you work in the office. You can telecommute and share an office[2] You can telecommute from a telecenter. Here you can see that telecommuting in itself is an extremely flexible component of the alternative workplace.

The language of the alternative workplace[3] has its own definitions, and there are a lot of different definitions floating around. The following are broad explanations with a few mini-case studies to give you a better idea of what each concept means.

ACTIVITY SETTINGS AND THE RED CARPET CLUB

What They Mean

An office with a variety of work settings designed to support diverse individual or group activities on an as-needed basis. It's called the "Red Carpet Club" sometimes because it is modeled after the way an airline club works in which there are a range of set-

tings, including an area to store luggage, soft-seating arrangements with phones and data hookups, work surfaces, carrels, a place to have coffee, a place to watch TV, and more (Fig. 2.6).

Strengths

- Increases amount of people housed without increasing space.
- Fosters team interaction.
- Provides users with a choice of settings that best-accommodates tasks.

Drawbacks

- Employees may feel confused about what spaces are used for what task.
- Personal storage areas may be necessary.
- Investments in expensive portable technology may be needed.

CAVES AND COMMONS

What They Mean

Like *group address*, this arrangement groups private work areas around a larger communal team space (Fig. 2.7).

Strengths

- Balances private and team work.
- Makes sharing information easy.

Figure 2.8

This floor plan is a free-address plan for the interior of one department in a major telecommunications company in New York City.
(HOK.)

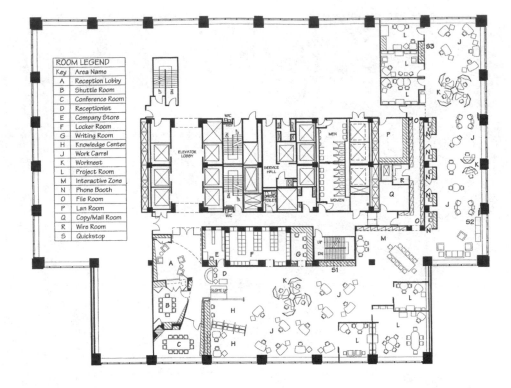

ROOM LEGEND	
Key	Area Name
A	Reception Lobby
B	Shuttle Room
C	Conference Room
D	Receptionist
E	Company Store
F	Locker Room
G	Writing Room
H	Knowledge Center
J	Work Carrel
K	Worknest
L	Project Room
M	Interactive Zone
N	Phone Booth
O	File Room
P	Lan Room
Q	Copy/Mail Room
R	Wire Room
S	Quickstop

Drawbacks

- Cramped and inflexible quarters if not designed properly for changing teams.

COCKPIT OFFICE

What It Means

Small offices that provide acoustic privacy for uninterrupted "heads-down" work and telephone calls. Sometimes called a "super-phone booth" or a "kiosk."

Strengths

- Great way to leverage space.
- Gives employees acoustical and visual privacy.

Drawbacks

- Employees tend to hide out in these little offices.
- Sometimes the offices are too cramped for teams of two.
- Employees may not use these spaces if they perceive them to be hideouts; culturally the spaces may be looked at as places to "goof off."

FREE ADDRESS

What It Means

Companies in Japan began to use this term to describe any nondedicated desk that was available for anyone to use at any time without reserving it first. Individuals don't have a permanent, assigned desk (Fig. 2.8).

Strengths

- Unassigned space gets maximum use, resulting in real estate savings.

Drawbacks

- Confusion and anxiety may result for some employees. Some companies report that employees show up at 7:00 a.m. or earlier just to get the first pick of a desk.
- Substantial investment in new technology and training is required.
- Personal storage areas need to be built.

HEARTH OR OASIS

What They Mean

Language to describe a place in which employees gather informally. Could be a café, coffee bar, or "living room." Tools to support work in a hearth would be a bulletin board, copier, fax, mail area, library, and supply cabinets (Fig. 2.9).

Strengths

- Can draw introverted employees out of workspace.

Hoteling in the twenty-first century
(Alan A. Abrahams)

Figure 2.9
The "hearth" at the MCI Boston Rally Center (opened in 1995), designed by Hoyle, Doran & Berry (HDB) Architects, is off the café area, much like a den is off the kitchen in a house. Ethan Anthony at HDB describes the hearth as an informal, flexible seating area for multipurpose uses. Within the hearth are rolling easels for presentations and informal room dividers. There is a podium and retractable projection screen for larger gatherings.
(Photo by Steve Syarto.)

- Encourages chance encounters.
- Gives employees sense of place and well-being.
- Keeps employees in the office longer if food is provided.
- Fosters communication and friendship among employees.

Drawbacks

- Introverted employees may shy away from these areas.
- Extroverted employees may never leave these areas.

HOTELING

What It Means

You don't have a permanent desk or office. Instead, you call up a reservationist or use company-provided software to reserve from an array of temporary spaces the one in which you work when you come to the office. You can stay there from a few hours to a few days, but you are not allowed to permanently move into the space. Your personal stuff is stored in a locker, bin, basket, or pedestal, which you roll with you to your space.

Strengths

- Leverages amount of real estate per person.
- Lets employees focus more on customer rather than on office.

Drawbacks

- Psychological issues include feeling a lack of belonging to the company culture, alienation, and no place to call home.
- This arrangement is not good for people who work on paper-intensive projects.

A VISUAL MINI-CASE STUDY IN HOTELING: DELOITTE & TOUCHE, CHICAGO-PERKINS & WILL

A day in the life of a hoteling office is depicted in Figs. 2.10 through 2.18.

HOT-DESKING

What It Means

Another way of saying "unassigned" or "free address." It's a term mostly used in the United Kingdom, even though it originates as an old U.S. Navy term that describes bunks kept warm by constant use by numerous sailors during different times of the day or night.

JUST-IN-TIME (JIT) OFFICES

What It Means

Andersen Consulting coined the term to mean basically the same as "hoteling," where no one has permanently assigned offices or spaces but rather are assigned to spaces on a temporary basis through a reservation system.

Fig. 2.10

Fig. 2.11

Fig. 2.12

Fig. 2.13

Fig. 2.14

Fig. 2.15

Fig. 2.16

Fig. 2.17

Fig. 2.18

Figure 2.19

The 5-mile-high office, a concept for the business traveler that the McDonnell Douglas Corporation explored in 1993. Today, carriers such as American Airlines and Delta are testing systems that will allow passengers to plug directly into a plane's electrical system. (McDonnell Douglas.)

Figure 2.20

KPMG Peat Marwick's Radnor, Pennsylvania, offices, designed by Thomas McHugh, AIA, opened in 1994. It's known as a "hoteling office," but it also has clusters of short-term "moteling" workstations—sometimes also called "heads-down" areas—in the atrium. Moteling workstations are composed simply of a work surface, computer, and telephone for employees who need to spend only a few hours at the office, between airport travel, to make quick calls or pick up files. Moteling areas are available without the need to call in for a reservation. (Photo by Tom Crane.)

MOBILE OFFICES

What It Means

You work from your briefcase, car, airplane, hotel room, or street while you're on the road (Fig. 2.19).

Strengths

Flexibility; road warriors seem to always have the most updated technology, and they seem to be more organized.

Drawbacks

* Lack of belonging, no place to call home
* Accidental loss of technology while on road
* Investment in technology necessary
* Possibility that there is no immediate help desk available

MOTELING AND TOUCHDOWN SPACES

What They Mean

Moteling means you are assigned—on the spot—to a small touchdown space (panel system or counter-like area with connectivity) from which to work. Employees who need a space for an hour or two, who are between appointments, can make use of the space. Usually moteling is part of a hoteling strategy (Fig. 2.20).

MINI-CASE STUDY

HOTELING AT DELOITTE TOUCHE: A DAY IN THE LIFE OF A HOTELING OFFICE, 1997 (opposite page)

Figure 2.10
A day in the life of a hoteling office. The daily cycle of setting up a hoteling office for consultants at the Chicago office of Deloitte & Touche Consulting Group, designed by Perkins & Will (1996), begins in the morning when the concierge's voice mailbox is checked for last-minute reservations. A work order is printed out that

lists office locations to be taken down and set up for the next morning.

Figure 2.11
The facility assistant then collects all the magnetic nameplates to set up reserved offices.

Figure 2.12
The facility assistant collects the number of personal and project tubs a consultant has

requested to be located in their reserved office location.

Figure 2.13
The assistant proceeds to the office location, stores the previous tenant's materials back into their tubs, and then inserts tomorrow's hoteling consultant's tubs into the lateral file drawers.

Figure 2.14
White-board surfaces

are cleaned off.

Figure 2.15
The "survival kit" is replenished to include stapler, Post-it notes, pad of paper, tape dispenser, formatted 3.5-inch diskettes, plus an orientation manual outlining the features of the workspace and office.

Figure 2.16
Then the assistant

installs the new consultant's nameplate on the office location.

Figure 2.17
Everything is set for the consultant the next morning when he arrives at the elevator lobby to check in at the interactive computerized directory called Time and Place, developed by Facility Innovations. The directory displays his officing location on a

map of the facility that easily guides him to his workspace.

Figure 2.18
The consultant's reserved hotel office is fresh, clean, neat, and outfitted with all the amenities necessary to get a good day's work done.
(Photos by Michelle Litvin.)

NONTERRITORIAL OFFICES

What It Means

The term was originated by MIT researcher Thomas Allen (co-author of *Managing the Reinvented Workplace*) to mean the same thing as "free address"; individuals don't have permanently assigned spaces, and reservations are made in advance.

Strengths

- Accommodates staff increases without increases in space or facilities.

Drawbacks

- People will always complain about lack of storage.
- Scheduling conflicts may occur, although they may be alleviated by an automatic reservation system.

SATELLITE OFFICES AND TELECENTERS

What They Mean

Satellite offices have been part of the traditional office, known better as a "branch" office. Satellite offices become part of an alternative workplace strategy if the company closes down larger offices in favor of smaller offices located closer to employees who live far away from the main campus.

Strengths

- Accommodates employees who live too far away to commute to headquarters but who don't, or can't, work at home.
- Gives employees all the services and amenities found at headquarters but on a smaller scale.
- Can be shared by a couple of companies to maximize space.

Drawbacks

- Satellite offices and telecenters can become the closet cousins of headquarters, perhaps forgotten and dismissed as an important company location.
- Employees may miss out on the culture at headquarters.
- If a company does not own its own telecenter but rents or leases space out of it, there could be a problem if there is financial trouble with the owner of the building or center.

MINI-CASE STUDY/ TELECENTERS
FEDERAL INTERAGENCY TELECOMMUTING CENTERS, 1994 TO THE PRESENT

Where better to test out alternative workplaces than in the metropolitan Washington, D.C., area? Take, for instance, the daily crush of traffic that bottlenecks at the intersection of Routes 5 and 301 in Waldorf, making the morning and afternoon peak hour rush a harrowing 90-minute or longer one-way nightmare for the estimated 39,000 commuters that drive in and out of the surrounding communities on a daily basis. With no room to build another road or railroad to ease traffic, the government turned its sights toward alternative solutions.

According to General Services Administration (GSA) estimates, there were more than 5000 federal civil servants commuting each day from Charles, Calvert, and St. Mary's counties that could ultimately support an alternative work center, a move that could significantly ease traffic congestion. Congress would hear testimonies on the benefits of telecommuting to the community in 1992, and by 1994, a congressional appropriation of $6 million led to the opening of six centers around the Washington, D.C., area that would allow some of those commuters to bypass the commute and would serve as a 2-year study on how best and most efficiently to operate a telecenter.

In April 1994, the Waldorf InTeleWorkCenter, a 2225-square-foot learning laboratory on telecommuting centers operated by the Charles County Community College in Maryland opened, with 14 workstations accommodating 30 to 50 teleworkers each week (Fig. 2.21). The fear many people have about opening telecenters is that their economic viability is tentative. Too many have opened in the United States, especially in the greater Los Angeles area in response to the major 1994 Northridge earthquake, only to close shortly afterward when roads reopened or because the centers were misplaced, mismarketed, and lacked resources. To make sure that wouldn't be the case, great care was taken in where the InTeleWorkNet was located.

The location is adjacent to the busy Route 301 and Route 5 corridors but below the jammed intersection so that workers can ease right into the parking lot. The center is located strategically to maximize accessibility to residents who live nearby or who need low-cost, in-county mass transit. In addition, the center is in the town center, creating a campuslike setting with accessibility to diverse retail and recreation outlets and medical services.

Workers spend 1 to 2 days each week at the telecenter, which is outfitted with upscale Herman Miller Ethospace interiors, Equa and Ergon 2 chairs, Relay furniture and mobile pedestal "puppies," and opaque screens and Scooter stands for laptops. The

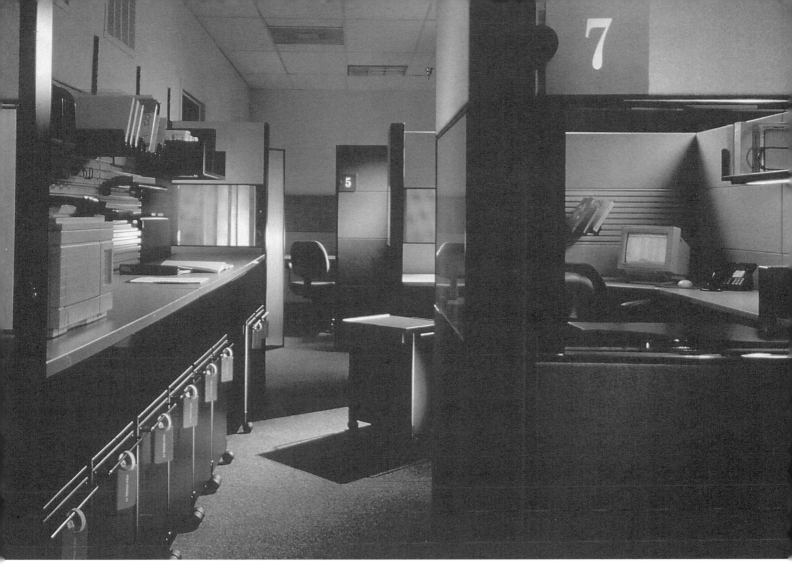

Figure 2.21
One government employee wanted to bring her dog to work with her when she telecommuted to the Waldorf InTeleWorkCenter. (Nick Merrick@Hedrich Blessing.)

videoconferencing room even has a custom Eames table.

Cindy Donn, formerly an evolutionary workplaces specialist with Herman Miller's Advanced Applications Group, helped design the Waldorf InTeleWorkNet Center. "We designed workstations that are accessible to a lot of different-sized people performing different tasks," says Donn in a Herman Miller–published case study on the project. "Since none of the workstations are permanently assigned, I selected furniture that can be easily adjusted by the individual user without assistance." Walking through the Waldorf telecenter to understand why all the different furniture components were chosen gives the visitor an appreciation for the complexity that goes into making a space so flexible. In fact, when the center was opened, a handful of the Herman Miller translucent screens were stored in the kitchen area, only to be discovered by employees who grab them and utilize them constantly.

In July 1995, the Charles County Community College gave an interim report on the Waldorf InTeleWorkNet pilot. At that point, the telecenter accommodated 56 users from 8 federal agencies, and commitments from 5 other agencies meant that the center would expand. According to Eric Blum, director of InTeleWorkNet, this particular telecenter was utilized at 112 percent, and participating agencies could rent space in the telecenter in 1994 for $8 a square foot versus the sometimes $80 a square foot in a prime downtown Washington, D.C., building.

The telecenter's future initiatives call for a 23-workstation center in Calvert County and an 18-workstation center in St. Mary's County to be operational by the end of fiscal year 1996. Blum is happy to report that the program is growing, the Waldorf center has grown from 14 to 27 workstations, and the operation has expanded into the storefront next to the original space to accommodate growth. And in October 1996, legislation was passed to allow these centers to market services to the private sector, further ensuring the success of this particular telework program.

Provisions in the Waldorf TeleWorkNet Telecenter

Phone system with voice mail
Typewriter
Fax
Copiers
Shredder
Mailing equipment
Scanners
Video, VCR, and teleconferencing
Collating machine
Bike racks and lockers
ADA ramps and elevators
Cabling
Refrigerator
Internet access
Computers
Multimedia workstations
Dedicated printers
Microwave
Coffee maker
Wellness facility
Software packages
Center file server
Security system
Workstation furniture
Plotter
Modems
Reference guides
Software manuals

At the same time, the GSA Interagency Telecommuting Pilot Project initiated the Fredericksburg Regional Telecommuting Centers to showcase how local, state, and federal governments can cooperate to run a successful telecenter operation. The Fredericksburg Regional Telecommuting Center has two locations in the Fredericksburg region: One is a 5000-square-foot space with 30 workstations located at Jackson Station in the Four Mile Fork area of Spotsylvania County, and the other one is a 3000-square-foot space with 20 workstations located in the Aquia area of Stafford County (Fig. 2.22).

SHARED OFFICES, DESK SHARING, AND SHARED-ASSIGNEDS

What They Mean

The Cornell University International Workplace Studies Program coined *shared assigned* to mean that two or more employees that work the same or different times are assigned one desk, office, or workstation.

Strengths

- Real estate savings.
- Forced communication between teams of workers.

Drawbacks

- Animosity among cohabitants if they don't like one another.
- Hygiene issues.
- Cramped quarters.
- Lost paperwork due to confusion.

TEAMING AREAS, TEAM SUITES, GROUP ADDRESSES

What They Mean

These are highly collaborative areas that groups or teams of people call their home for a short to long

Figure 2.22
The Fredericksburg Regional Tele-Centers are outfitted with top-notch amenities and Steelcase Personal Harbors. (Fredericksburg Regional Telecommuting Centers.)

period of time. IBM came up with the term *group address* term to describe when a group or team is assigned a space for a specified period of time.

Strengths

• Fosters communication within teams.

Drawbacks

• Spaces tend to be cramped with too little private space.
• Teams may acquire new members, which may create space shortages.

MINI-CASE STUDY
ON TEAMING: ALCOA

Until the late 1980s, Alcoa (Aluminum Company of America) was fairly typical of any large manufacturing company. The largest aluminum company in the world, the company was highly profitable in only 2 out of every 10 years. In 1987, Alcoa celebrated its 100th-year anniversary, and with that birthday, it appointed a chairman, Paul O'Neill, from outside the company and outside the industry. The appointment shook up many employees at Alcoa.

O'Neill had come from International Paper and was on Alcoa's board for a year. In 1991, O'Neill eliminated the presidency and the layer of group vice presidents that reported to the president. With that unprecedented move, O'Neill shifted responsibility out from under the cushioned layers of the upper executive kingdom and onto the 22 business unit managers in the field. The mandate O'Neill gave to the business unit managers was to benchmark their most critical processes with the top companies in the world regardless from which industry they came, and then work on closing any gaps—all within a 2-year period.

"In the early 1990s the Soviet Union collapsed, and the Russians began dumping aluminum on the world markets to attract currency," says Ronald Hoffman, executive vice president, human resources, at Alcoa.[4] "Metal prices were driven to their lowest level in history, but Alcoa was the only company in the world industry in aluminum to make a profit in every quarter in 1992 and 1993." By 1993, Alcoa had downsized 40 percent of the corporate jobs, and morale was at rock-bottom despite great profit. At the same time, teaming was emphasized as a way to take on more initiative and risk, so employees wouldn't spiral down into a complete depression.

To support teaming efforts, Alcoa decided it needed to focus on using physical setting. The company fully occupied its headquarters building—a 31-story, 442,500-square-foot building that was built for Alcoa in 1952. In the 1990s, the building was riddled with private offices and formal conference rooms, which were occupied only 50 percent due to downsizing.

Instead of hanging on to an oversized building, Alcoa purchased property on the Allegheny River in downtown Pittsburgh, and hired the Design Alliance, an architectural firm, to work on the design of the new building. Alcoa is set to relocate to the new $40 million, 6-story, 235,200-square-foot building in mid to late 1998 while the old building is up for sale with a 1997 price tag of $18 million. "In the meantime, we took the ideas for a design for the more open environment that we're going to create over there and completely remodeled the top floor of our existing building and relocated those of us on the executive committee in this floor, including the chairman," says Hoffman of the move to the upper floor that happened in 1994.

Though there are rumors milling about Corporate America that the Alcoa executives will have private offices along with the much publicized "common areas" promised on the executive floor in the new building, at least in the old building, nine of them, including O'Neill, are working temporarily in open cubicles. The long-term, temporary, revamped executive floor of the old building is where the executives walk their talk to benefit not only themselves but the employees as well. In addition, the executives are using the space as a testbed for products to be specified in the new building. There is even a "communications center" with televisions, fax machines, publications, and tables for serendipitous meetings. "It's like being at home in your own kitchen and sitting around the table," says O'Neill in a *Business Week* article (see Hamilton 1996). O'Neill's long-term, temporary, L-shaped workstation is anchored on the other side by his secretary's panel system.

For the rest of the company, it seems teaming isn't as easy a feat to accomplish, says Hoffman. "It's not natural for people to volunteer to leave their homeroom or their comfort zone," he says. Through a series of meetings, it was decided it was in the company's best interest that, for example, all lawyers shouldn't be grouped together in one spot, but instead they should sit wherever they find their major responsibilities lie. So the labor lawyer will sit with the industrial relations group, and the

Walk

into Milliken's offices in LaGrange, Georgia, and you'll find lots of large oil paintings on the

Teaming Saves Milliken

walls and carpeting everywhere. Tarnished, but elegant, a variety of trophies that employees have won for various events line the hallways. You'll also find that all the executives work out in the open.

"I hate the open office," says an executive who works for Milliken, a carpet manufacturer, who preferred to remain nameless. "I turn off my beeper and disappear across the street to the factory, to a restaurant, or home so I can get some work done." Although he isn't a fan of the open plan, he admits that he'll never go to work for a company that offers him a private office.

He's already talked to lots of people who have left Milliken who work in private offices, and he says they hate it: Their biggest complaint is that they aren't able to communicate with anyone else in the office.

Milliken's culture has experienced teaming since the 1960s when Roger Milliken, the illustrious owner of the company, adopted it as a strategy before the concept or term ever became fashionable. Milliken believed in instant communication between employees that would never be possible in private offices. That thinking worked to the company's advantage when a tragic fire damaged much of Milliken's manufacturing facilities in 1995. Had it not been using the team-based, open-plan workstyle, the company would never have been able to react to their clients' or business unit losses so quickly. "Instead of sitting in private offices waiting to hear about what Mr. Milliken wanted to do to get back on their feet, everyone pulled together quickly with plans for their own," the executive remembers. "We immediately knew what each business unit's losses and problems were, and we were all able to pitch in to get everyone up and ruining, back on track."

And although hierarchy isn't as visible at Milliken because of the open plan, there may be some desks along the wall that may be partitioned off with more file cabinets than others around the space. Or perhaps there's a desk that's slightly larger than the other desks in the open room. Nonetheless, despite who has more file cabinets or whose desk is slightly larger, the bottom line is that the culture who teams together, rebounds together faster should disaster strike.

Disadvantages of Telecommuting

None: 33 percent

Isolation: 31 percent

Lose visibility in office: 22 percent

Manager resists telecommuting: 17 percent

Requires self-discipline: 17 percent

Trouble with technology: 15 percent

Hinders teamwork, coworkers resist telecommuting: 13 percent

Thorough planning for supplies and managerial help: 12 percent

Some jobs can't be done at home: 7 percent

Need adjustment period: 3 percent

Source: Bell Atlantic–sponsored Manager-Employee Relationships and Telecommuting Report, N. Lamar Reinsch, Jr., Georgetown School of Business, Georgetown University, 1995.

financial communications person should probably sit with the investor relations group.

About 550 employees will use movable furniture in open spaces with nooks and crannies in which they can go to for quiet and privacy.

Alcoa's new building will have other elements built in by which to have chance encounters, according to Hoffman. There will be no elevators, only escalators, a design element typically used in today's contemporary interiors for floor-to-floor and employee-to-employee access.

TELECOMMUTING

What It Means

Futurist Jack Nilles coined the term in 1973 to describe a strategy in which employees work at home. It's more of a policy, but it does have ramifications on space design. Telecommuters typically work from home 1 or more days a week on a consistent basis. This strategy is perhaps the most widely publicized of all alternative workplace programs.

Strengths

- Flexibility.
- Saves commuting time.
- Improved productivity.
- Improved morale.
- Savings in real estate if company asks that you give up permanent space for the option of telecommuting.

Drawbacks

- It does not always save on real estate.
- Employees may feel out of sight, out of mind.
- Managers have a hard time managing remote employees.
- Labor and property law issues are still fuzzy.
- Zoning issues differ town to town.
- Tax issues are fuzzy.
- Companies don't always ensure that a telecommuter's home office is set up ergonomically correct.
- Employees may resent that the corporation has placed its real estate burden onto them without any monetary help to run a household (heat, electricity).

MINI-CASE STUDY/TELECOMMUTING
GTE 1980s TO THE PRESENT

Francine Reilly, Ed.D. and practice leader of the organization effectiveness department at GTE Service Corporation in Stamford, Connecticut, revisits[5] the days when GTE's telecommuting program was just a gleam in one employee's eyes. Telecommuting at the major telecommunications company started out of the blue when one of the managers in her department came to her one day and said she was getting married. "Great!" Reilly said until she realized the manager wanted to move 120 miles away from the Stamford, Connecticut, GTE campus to be with her husband.

New

York City can't seem to make up its mind about telecommuting.

There is a small, but fiercely loyal group of people in New York

Telecommuting in the Big Apple

City bound by the efforts of the International Telework Association (formerly known as the New York Chapter of the Telecommuting Advisory Council) to bring awareness to the general public about the benefits of telecommuting. Former chapter president Ellen Reilly feels the association has made inroads into the hallowed hallways of

Corporate America, especially in a city where the vying for the top floor corner office overlooking the East River is a sacred cow. As of 1997, the chapter boasted 60 corporate members, and Reilly dismisses the notion that New York City is behind the times compared to Southern California's fierce embrace of the flexible workplace, which includes telecommuting. "New York City is cautious to practice telecommuting, but I don't think we are against it. We approach it differently than the West Coast, but each coast has a different reason for pursuing telecommuting and other forms of alternative work," she explains.

A quick read through a January 1995 *Crain's New York* indicates that New Yorkers have turned up their noses at the mere thought of telecommuting. In one article, the reporter, Sharon McDonnell, writes, "Experts say New Yorkers aren't motivated to telecommute because of their distinctive commuting habits. Also impeding the spread of telecommuting is New York's status as a headquarters city" (see McDonnel 1995).

But jump to the present when we can see the shift in New York City's attitude toward alternative workplace strategies. "The growing success of these businesses with such concepts as telecommuting and hoteling....will hold down the growth of the commercial office market over the next four years....Some degree of telecommuting or hoteling is expected by most New York companies," according to an article in a November 1996 issue of *Crain's New York* (see Denitto 1996). According to this article, the trend is clearly to fit employees into less than 200 square feet, per private office, down from 250 square feet, which has been the norm for years. Top managers, says the article, are reducing their offices to 800 square feet down from 1100. That's still quite a large office for today's reduction standards, and an interesting reduction percentage in a city where prime real estate rents for about $50 a square foot.

"At the time, GTE was downsizing, and I knew that if she left, we'd never be able to replace her," Reilly says of her department, which is responsible for college recruiting for GTE. "In an act of desperation, I asked her what we needed to do to keep her, and she came up with this new idea called telecommuting."

That was in the mid-1980s when the term was not very familiar to Corporate America, much less Reilly. But she liked the idea and set up her employee with the little technology available at the time, and another phone line in the house. "I said, let's put the lines in first, then I'll tell my boss about it," remembers Reilly. "He went crazy when I told him."

Reilly assured her boss the woman was a valued employee, and if it didn't work out, she'd pull the plug herself on the whole telecommuting arrangement. It took no more than 6 weeks to iron out the bugs. By that time, another employee approached Reilly about telecommuting, then another, and another, and soon there were nine people coming and going at all times of the day and night.

"My boss said to me I'd regret the day I started this," Reilly says. "But it had already been 4 years of this arrangement in my department, and although it looked like total chaos, I told him not to touch a thing. I said I didn't know why, but since starting the telecommuting, I was getting more productivity out of this gang than we ever did when we worked traditional hours." So her boss just let it be.

Some time later, a group of GTE employees contacted Reilly to learn more about her department's experiments with flexible work arrangements. Word spread to even more departments in the company. "You know, trying to do things in a large organization is like pushing water up a hill," says Reilly. So although there was interest in implementing more pilot telecommuting programs around the country, the detail work was enormous, and the process of implementing pilots got bogged down.

In 1994, the department of transportation in Dallas, Texas, asked GTE if it would participate in an experiment to see if traffic and air pollution could be diminished through a company telecommuting program where employees would work at home 1 day a week. A new pilot was born with 120 volunteers—surprisingly, mostly men, says Reilly.

The Dallas pilot ran for 6 months, after which a formal policy was written for that group, and most employees began a program to telecommute three times a week. In 1995, Reilly's group decided to go around the company and "sermonize" about telecommuting, pressing for other GTE companies to get on the bandwagon. In mid-1996, the CEO of GTE sent a letter out to GTE headquarters giving the green light to telecommuting, giving employees the right to ask permission of a supervisor to telecommute 1 to 3 days a week. Through 1996 and into 1997, GTE phased in a telecommuting program with 50 volunteers to iron out all the wrinkles. And in 1997, the company rolled out a telecommuting program to the entire company throughout the United States.

Virtual Offices and Virtual Workplaces

What They Mean

These terms have numerous meanings.[6] It's under the alternative workplace umbrella, regarded as the "no-office office." Employees of a virtual office work through an electronic infrastructure, i.e., voice mail, e-mail, and videoconferencing, on which a company functions. A virtual corporation will be one that comes together via informal networks of independent contractors and bits and pieces of other companies to create solutions for a market niche, then dissolve after needs are met, never to appear again in precisely the same way.

Strengths

Employees have freedom while the company is unencumbered by real estate costs—often using short-term office and business facility rentals (by the hour, day, or week), hotel rentals, or airport lounges for meetings.

Drawbacks

- Lack of culture means isolation between employees, and there is little or no face-to-face time with colleagues.
- Productivity may be lower because of isolation and undisciplined work environment.

TEMPORAL OFFICES

What It Means

This term best describes a dedicated managerial office that can be transformed into a conference room when the "private work" is hidden away.

Strengths

- It provides great leverage of space that is empty much of the time, offering extra conference space.
- It is easy to convert an office. Many times in a traditional office arrangement, employees use the managers' offices for meetings.

Drawbacks

- Managers now can't lock their doors and may feel their territory is being invaded when they are away.
- Security can be an issue.

UNITEL

What It Means

London-based Morgan Lovel, office planning and design consultants, originally used this term to describe this new office environment, which is a cross between a university as a place to learn and share knowledge and a hotel as a place of temporary residence with shared facilities and amenities. This arrangement is an expanded version of the Red Carpet Club and activity settings.

UNIVERSAL WORKSTATIONS OR UNIVERSAL OPEN PLANS

What They Mean

One size fits all. It means employees work in a generic floorplate with fixed construction.

Strengths

- Facilitates quick interaction between employees.
- Biggest strength: People move, offices don't, reducing reconfiguration costs and problems.
- Helps organizations who cannot predict their staffing into the future.
- Helps a company keep programming from becoming obsolete.

Drawbacks

Employees have no privacy and may feel overstimulated and distracted. Employees may resent being taken out of private offices and placed in a universal plan.

MINI-CASE STUDY/VIRTUAL OFFICE
VERIFONE, 1981 TO THE PRESENT

Although there are no statistics on how many virtual companies of this nature operate in the United States, one of the most well-known, extreme, and self-described "virtual companies" is VeriFone. Since 1981, VeriFone has been a global provider of secure electronic payment systems now used in over 100 countries. Existing in a virtual world works well for them, with a 60 percent share in the North American market (see Taylor 1996).

VeriFone, a wholly-owned subsidiary of Hewlett-Packard since 1997, employs over 2500 people, one-third of whom are on the road daily, including CEO Hatim Tyabji, who has been known to log 400,000 miles in a year to visit customers and to direct overseas production. Executives live where they choose—Tyabji lives in Northern California, his CIO lives in Santa Fe, and his HR director lives in Dallas. There are no secretaries, no paper—only an electronic infrastructure that keeps business going.[7]

"People will tell you, 'I'd love to set my own hours,' but most people are happier when you tell them to be in by 8:00 in the morning and leave at

5:00 in the afternoon," says Tyabji about the way he discovers who will survive the culture of VeriFone's 24-hour-day virtual company in an interview done in *Fast Company Magazine* (see Taylor 1996). From those who embrace Tyabji's culture of freedom, he also expects tremendous accountability for sales.

Exactly how many offices can a virtual company have before it's not considered virtual anymore? VeriFone likes to say it's made up of a "decentralized network of locations." According to a Harvard Business School case study written by doctoral candidate Hossam Galal in 1994, Tyabji likes to refer to its corporate model as a "blueberry pancake," where "all berries are the same size; all locations are created equal." Tyabji's least favorite term, according to Galal, is "headquarters," and he frowns on any companies that house 70 percent of its employees in a single location while calling themselves a global company. VeriFone does have an unassuming headquarters located in Redwood City, California. It has locations in India, Taiwan, and Hawaii to serve its global clients.

One of its most rural, out-of-the-way offices is a software quality test center in an abandoned sugarcane field in Laupahoehoe, Hawaii—25 miles from the nearest town. VeriFone chose Hawaii because of time-zone differences—while east-coast programmers sleep, software is tested on the company network from Hawaii, and by the dawn of the next day, tests are completed within a 24-hour cycle. But why a rural setting? William Pape, VeriFone's senior vice-president and chief information officer, says employees like the calm, cheaper lifestyle and besides that, technology makes it possible to do business out of any location.

What kind of technology is needed to run a rural virtual office? For each worker, a computer with a modem, standard phone line, fax, LAN, printer,

PBX, and perhaps videoconferencing for larger village offices of more than five people, says Pape.

Pape has written much on how to take a company virtual. He understands the concept first-hand since he helped found and grow VeriFone from five employees to over 2500. Pape's first rule of thumb in creating a virtual company is to make the use of e-mail mandatory, conveying the message of "use the net or die." Even though the company is virtual and no one is breathing down an employee's back, the pressure to sell seems intense, which means the faster one e-mails, the better the chance of getting the job done.

But it's not so easy to hire people who intuitively understand the structure—or nonstructure—of a virtual company. So how does VeriFone recruit? Pape has identified several characteristics that define the successful virtual workers. First, a virtual worker has strong communication skills even when it means they have to communicate in a nonverbal, written way over the computer screen or phone. He also suggests seeking out employees who have had low turnover rates in their job histories, which translates into company loyalty, a rare thing today. But VeriFone has a strong philosophy it requires everyone who comes to work for the company to buy into, so it's an important element of its recruiting strategies.

Though employees don't go to a corporate campus office on a daily basis to be confronted with the company's culture, there is very much a corporate culture identified through VeriFone's business philosophy. VeriFone is quite serious about the philosophy by which the company is run. It has published a 64-page brochure, entitled "The VeriFone Philosophy," written in several different languages for all its global customers to read. What are the elements of VeriFone's philosophy? It's committed to building an excellent company, meeting customers'

More New Language from the United Kingdom

The language of the changing workplace continues to evolve, and the newest words come from DEGW, a well-known strategic workplace planning and consulting company founded by architect Francis Duffy and in partnership with John Worthington and Luigi Giffone. Its offices are based in London, New York City, and in numerous other locations worldwide. Its clients include Andersen Worldwide and Lend Lease Corporation. DEGW is also known for its part in developing with Steelcase the Workplace Envisioning software of strategic briefing exercises.

In DEGW's latest forthcoming book on the subject of the new workplace, appropriately named *New Environments for Working* (written by Duffy, Andrew Laing, and Denise Jaunzens, to be published by CRC/Spon, October 1997), the team introduces terminology to further explain the new workplace phenomena.

The *den*, the *club*, the *hive*, and the *cell* represent the four domains in which we work. Aptly named, the *den* is for teamwork, the *club* involves a variety of activity settings (like a gentleman's club, explains Laing), the *hive* represents the warren of cubicles used now in universal planning, and the *cell* is the private office for those whose tasks have high autonomy and low interaction, such as lawyers.

needs, recognizing the importance of each employee, promoting a team spirit, accountability for all actions, fostering open communications, strengthening global ties, and living an ethical life.

Living this philosophy is the glue that keeps VeriFone employees together, working together on the same track on a daily basis. But technology is no doubt VeriFone's information lifeline for its management and employees. However, that doesn't mean everyone is outfitted or upgraded with the newest technological gadget to hit the market every quarter. Pape explains in the Harvard Business School case study, "If you're just using e-mail, there's no reason to have a Pentium. You don't need a Ferrari to drive to the supermarket. You don't need the latest wireless device to enter the information age: You can do it with today's technology."

Regardless of this well thought-out network that keeps VeriFone going, Pape says that every year the company reevaluates whether a virtual operation still makes economic sense, or whether another model would be more beneficial.

WAR OF THE SURVEYS

Almost every client we have has a telecommuting pilot going on," says Karen Lalli, strategic facility planner at the Hillier Group in Princeton.

A large majority of our clients are now sharing desks, reducing sizes of workstations and offices, going into open plan," says Lou Switzer, CEO of the Switzer Group in New York City.

Since 1993, there hasn't been one client who hasn't asked about alternative workplace environments," says Ted Hammer, CEO of HLW in New York City.

Many companies have more telecommuters than the number of pilot programs would indicate because of 'guerrilla telecommuters.'"[8] Charles Grantham, Institute for the Study of Distributed Work.

So how do comments like that translate into numbers of companies or people actually working in alternative workplaces, you might ask. Well, take a look at a survey or two.

OH, WHAT A TANGLED WEB OF SURVEYS WE'VE WOVEN...

During the Steelcase BTV interactive videoconference on May 22, 1996, the audience, which was scattered all over the country and was watching from a variety of dealerships and theaters, was asked to fax in to a poll consisting of three questions (the number of audience participants is not available but probably consisted of a few hundred end-users).

- Question 1: Is your company currently practicing any form of alternative officing?

  71 percent of the audience members said yes, 17 percent said no.

- Question 2: At your site, what is the most prevalent style of alternative officing your company is currently practicing?

  55 percent teaming or collaborative

  1 percent nonterritorial

  21 percent telecommuting

  4 percent satellite

  0 percent virtual

- Question 3: As an FM, are you currently leading or supporting the AO strategy in your company?

  23 percent leading

  37 percent supporting

That's just one example of a survey on alternative workplaces.

In 1996, *Business Week* published a popularized article on the office of the future. The article, read with extreme interest by professionals around the world, quoted a statistic from the 1995 IFMA survey that said 83 percent of companies in the United States are embracing forms of alternative officing. The article didn't go the next step—it didn't take into consideration one important part of the study: Of the 83 percent of companies reporting that their facilities were participating in some level of alternative officing, 53 percent cited flexible work schedules as an alternative workplace strategy in present use. Flextime is an older work process strategy that came out of human resources (HR), and it has little to do with strategic facility planning issues (see Hamilton 1996).

The lesson from the *Business Week* article is that surveys quoted should be taken with a grain of salt. There are handfuls of surveys on alternative workplaces, and most contradict each other based on the methodology used to arrive at the figures.

Take, for instance, these examples: In 1994, there are 43.2 million home-based workers in the United States, according to Link, a research firm. No, wait, there will be 4 million telecommuters in 1996, the Department of Transportation said in 1993. But there really are 7.8 million corporate employees who telecommute, said Link in 1994. However, another study found that there were 6.6 million telecommuters in 1994, said research firm Find/SVP....

Information on who is telecommuting or what companies have telecommuting and alternative workplace programs is sketchy at best, contrived to some, contested by many, and exalted by others. Nevertheless, the one thing everyone seems to agree on is that people, no matter who, what, where, when, why, and how, are working differently today, which has everyone clamoring for details. In response to this hunger has been a slew of association meetings, seminars, symposiums and trade shows, and articles on the subject that all report on studies and surveys done by countless organizations. So how do you wade through the numbers?

Here's a look at some recent studies that have tried to get a handle on the broad subject of alternative officing and how findings compare. Note that telecommuting strategies are tracked more often due to specific organizations dedicated to the promotion of telecommuting.

TELECOMMUTING SURVEYS

Olsten, a major staffing services company, released its 1996 report, *Managing Today's Automated Workplace*, in which it surveyed 300 U.S. companies for the following findings:

- Nearly two in three companies (62 percent) in the United States encourage telecommuting arrangements with employees, up from 49 percent last year and 39 percent in 1993.
- Overall employee participation in telecommuting programs remains low with only 7 percent of workers taking advantage of the programs.
- 42 percent of companies have formal telecommuting programs under way.

Another telecommuting survey: In 1997, consultants KMPG Peat Marwick interviewed 106 human resource executives in the largest U.S. companies and found that nearly one in four companies have employees who regularly telecommute either part- or full-time. That translates into about only 26 companies out of 106.

And, Telecommute America, an organization formed in 1995 to promote telecommuting, commissioned FIND/SVP, a New York–based market research company, to conduct a survey that resulted in findings that more than 11 million people reported working as telecommuters in 1997, compared to 8 million in 1995. The survey also projects that there will be 14 million home-based workers by the year 2000.

As you can see, no two surveys come up with the same results.

Tracking Different Types of Telecommuters

62 percent of the Fortune 1000 firms surveyed have at least 50 work-at-home employees.

38 percent of the Fortune 1000 firms surveyed have no work-at-home employees.

89 percent of the telecommuters are "casual, after-hours workers."

11 percent are daytime, home-based telecommuters.

Source: Forrester Research, Inc., Network Strategy Service, *Making Work at Home Work*, by David Goodtree, Jay Batson, and Maureen Kloempken. Vol. 9, No. 6, April 1995.

INTERNATIONAL NUMBERS AND ALTERNATIVE WORKPLACES

In the United States, most business (and consumer) trends start on either the West or East Coast, but overseas, most office design and contract furniture trends start in Western Europe—Italy for the most part. Telecommuting, in its various forms including the telecenter, has been under way both in the United States and abroad for several decades. Various records say that the first formal telecenter was established along the Marne Valley in France in 1981, and Pacific-Bell opened the first U.S. telecenter in 1985. But outside the United States, new work environment experiments tend to be a little more creative and free-flowing than in the United States. Consider these findings (see U.S. GSA 1994):

- The Bank of Montreal initiated its first "floating office" in 1991. Employees worked anywhere they chose to work—branch office, client site, at home—remaining accessible by phone or pager.
- In Japan, telecenters take a twist—one center in Shiki, just outside of Tokyo, caters solely to women in clerical and secretarial jobs. Another center, called the "creative office," combines telecommuting with a resortlike atmosphere to help employees rediscover the joy in work while being productive.
- The Credit Suisse Bank in Switzerland opened a telecenter in 1986 to accommodate computer specialist shortages.
- "Office trains" were the rage in 1986 where managers worked in designated cars during their 80-minute train ride to and from Stockholm.

Figure 2.23
The new workplace thrives overseas. The Swedish telecommunications company Telia switched its customer support department over to a nonterritorial office. The department of 116 employees has 70 workstations. Associated real estate and equipment costs were reduced by 25 percent. Computer screens can be adjusted up and down by the flexible metal arm from which they hang. (Telia/Hag.)

Asking a Japanese employee to telecommute, however, is considered an insult and embarrassment to his or her neighbors. In addition, crowded housing conditions in Japan don't support the extra room needed to work at home. Although economic troubles and a bloated white-collar workforce is leading Japan to emerge a more flexible, efficient Western-like model, the Japanese are finding it hard to adapt to new work processes and new work environments; they already work in tight workspaces side-by-side every day, and it's tough to change that kind of work culture, which is pervasive throughout the country.

Nevertheless, the new workplace is alive and thriving abroad (Fig. 2.23). According to government statistics as late as 1995, out of 27 million U.K. workers, 2½ million are unemployed, 1.2 million telework, 6 million are employed part-time, and 1½ million are temps, making for a diverse amount of workspace needs to support the cross sections of population. Again, most housing is smaller by U.S. standards, but workers are enthusiastic to telecommute for the same reason we want to try telecommuting in the United States.

THE HAWORTH-IFMA SURVEY ON ALTERNATIVE WORKPLACE USAGE

The first survey of its kind, Haworth joined forces with IFMA to determine what companies, if any, were aware of, using, or considering alternative workplace. What they found was promising: The alternative workplace is not just a pie-in-the-sky idea that academicians study, but a set of strategies Corporate America is willing to seriously consider to handle numerous business objectives.

IFMA conducted three 90-minute focus groups of members familiar with the use of alternative officing to gather information and ideas from which the actual survey questionnaire was written. The survey was sent out to 4000 IFMA professionals.

The bottom line of Haworth's study: Most FMs (94 percent) surveyed expect the use of alternative workplaces to increase by the year 2000. The most likely group to use alternative workplaces is medium-sized organizations with 1000 to 2499 employees. The least likely group is large organizations with over 8500 employees (see charts on pages 51 and 52).

KNOLL-ISFE SURVEY ON ALTERNATIVE WORKPLACE USAGE

At the same time Haworth and IFMA's research hit the street in 1995, Knoll was doing its own legwork on the subject, and in 1996, it teamed up with ISFE to further investigate the state of alternative workplace.

The surveying started in 1995 when Knoll handpicked 20 progressive North American companies in which workplace process could be explored. The companies included telecommunications, banking, insurance, and manufacturing. Christine Barber, director of workplace research at Knoll, headed the study. She visited each company and conducted personal interviews and field studies that began to measure the changes in the work environment that the companies anticipated to happen within the next 5 years. She "invaded" these companies, talk-

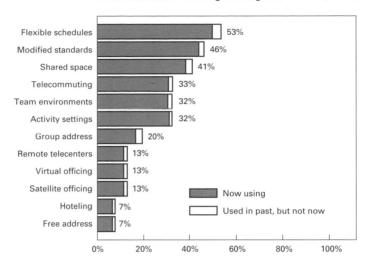

**Percent Who Have Used
These Alternative Officing Strategies (Haworth/IFMA)**

Flexible schedules	53%
Modified standards	46%
Shared space	41%
Telecommuting	33%
Team environments	32%
Activity settings	32%
Group address	20%
Remote telecenters	13%
Virtual officing	13%
Satellite officing	13%
Hoteling	7%
Free address	7%

Now using
Used in past, but not now

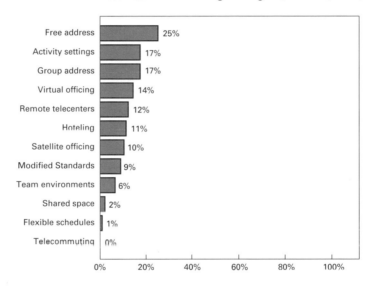

**Percent Who Have Never Heard of
These Alternative Officing Strategies (Haworth/IFMA)**

Free address	25%
Activity settings	17%
Group address	17%
Virtual officing	14%
Remote telecenters	12%
Hoteling	11%
Satellite officing	10%
Modified Standards	9%
Team environments	6%
Shared space	2%
Flexible schedules	1%
Telecommuting	0%

ing to CRE executives and vice presidents of facilities to learn about how their organizations are changing, how they deployed workers, and the technology they were using to do so and wanted to use in the future.

Barber identified three key issues in the 1995 survey:

- Emerging organizations due to mergers mean careers are no longer stable and the "30-year tenure" is gone.
- Technology: Although the 1995 research found that only 2 percent of the group surveyed could be defined as mobile workers—road warriors—new technology starts to paint a different picture of how many more in types and numbers of untethered employees could emerge.

- New work processes demand new spaces to support activities. The space no longer could support and reinforce hierarchy since there was tremendous pressure to reduce CRE.

It was in 1996 that Knoll, the International Society of Facilities Executives, and *Facilities Design & Management Magazine* collaborated to take the 1995 study even further. The 1996 survey reflected the perspectives of 33 ISFE member companies to find out how changes in the workforce, work patterns, office practices, and technology use will affect how facility professionals manage the workplace of tomorrow. (Majority of respondents were companies with between 100–999 and 1000–4999 white-collar employees.)

What Barber emphasizes is that although a number of companies are initiating and experimenting

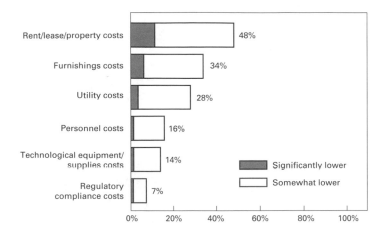

**Alternative Officing Strategies
Decreased Costs in These Areas (Haworth/IFMA)**

- Rent/lease/property costs — 48%
- Furnishings costs — 34%
- Utility costs — 28%
- Personnel costs — 16%
- Technological equipment/supplies costs — 14%
- Regulatory compliance costs — 7%

Legend: ▓ Significantly lower ☐ Somewhat lower

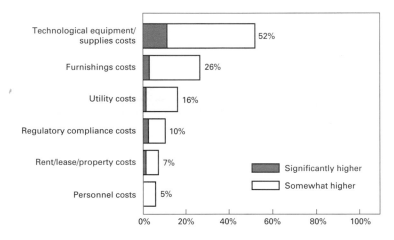

**Alternative Officing Strategies
Increased Costs in These Areas (Haworth/IFMA)**

- Technological equipment/supplies costs — 52%
- Furnishings costs — 26%
- Utility costs — 16%
- Regulatory compliance costs — 10%
- Rent/lease/property costs — 7%
- Personnel costs — 5%

Legend: ▓ Significantly higher ☐ Somewhat higher

with different forms of alternative officing, she says what counts is the number of people within each company participating in such programs. From her experiences, only small percentages of employees within each company work in any type of alternative environment.

For example, the study found that universal plan and team space was by far the most popular type of alternative office. Universal plan was used by 74 percent of the respondents by about 47 percent of the employees in the company. However, Barber notes that although 56 percent of the surveyed companies have a telecommuting program, only about 8 percent of the employees in each company participate in a telecommuting program. Further down the scale, the survey results show that although free address is practiced by 23 percent of the responding companies, that type of program only involves about 6 percent of the employees. Hoteling is within 10 percent of the companies that responded, but in each com-

pany, an average of only 3 percent of the employees participate.[9] Although the survey showed small percentages of employees participating in alternative workplace programs now, respondents said that in the next 5 years, telecommuting, free-address, and hoteling programs will take on more importance within the company (see charts on pages 53 and 54).

BREAKING OUT OF THE OFFICE: COMPANIES PRACTICING THE ALTERNATIVE WORKPLACE

It's true that AT&T in the United States, Nortel in Canada, and British Telecom in the United Kingdom are notorious advocates of alternative officing. But if anyone thinks that alternative workplace solutions are useful as a trend just for telecommunications companies, think again. It's just as popular with advertising agencies, accounting, banking and insurance consultants, and high-tech companies

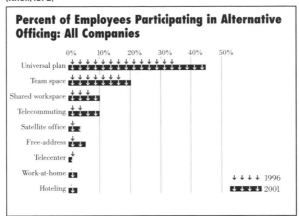

(Knoll/ISFE)

Percent of Employees Participating in Alternative Officing: All Companies

Universal plan
Team space
Shared workspace
Telecommuting
Satellite office
Free-address
Telecenter
Work-at-home
Hoteling

↓ ↓ ↓ 1996
2001

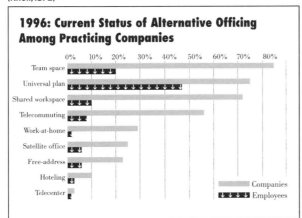

(Knoll/ISFE)

1996: Current Status of Alternative Officing Among Practicing Companies

Team space
Universal plan
Shared workspace
Telecommuting
Work-at-home
Satellite office
Free-address
Hoteling
Telecenter

Companies
Employees

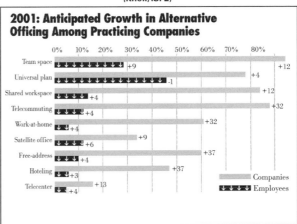

(Knoll/ISFE)

2001: Anticipated Growth in Alternative Officing Among Practicing Companies

Team space +9 / +4 / +12
Universal plan -1 / +4
Shared workspace +4 / +12
Telecommuting +4 / +32
Work-at-home +4 / +32
Satellite office +6 / +9
Free-address +4 / +37
Hoteling +3 / +37
Telecenter +4 / +13

Companies
Employees

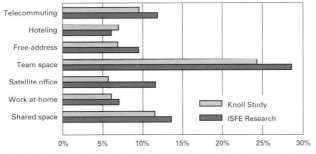

Trend Comparison: Alternative Officing Projections

Telecommuting
Hoteling
Free-address
Team space
Satellite office
Work-at-home
Shared space

Knoll Study
ISFE Research

Results of a proprietary Knoll study conducted in 1995 concerning trends in alternative officing reflect five-year projections similar to those for employees at ISFE companies.

and sales-oriented telecommunications companies representing a hefty total of the knowledge worker workforce.

To the many managers who consider themselves purists, trying to wiggle out of learning new things because "the other guys don't do it": Get out from behind the smoke screen because the other guys *do* do it. Table 2.2 is a list, albeit partial, of companies in the United States and abroad that have embraced some form(s) of alternative and flexible officing—from teaming to hoteling to telecommuting—in the past few years. Some companies have folded alternative workplace programs into little pockets of people around the company, or they've rolled out initiatives companywide, as you will see in Part 3 of this book where the case studies are located. Just remember that not every company has a success story, probably due to poor planning or the loss of a champion with vision. So some business units may have altogether abandoned or altered their flexible officing policies. Others say their new workplace initiatives are flourishing, and top-down, the company couldn't be happier with the way new workplace arrangements and policies

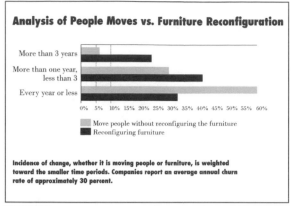

Analysis of People Moves vs. Furniture Reconfiguration

More than 3 years

More than one year, less than 3

Every year or less

0% 5% 10% 15% 20% 25% 30% 35% 40% 45% 50% 55% 60%

⬜ Move people without reconfiguring the furniture
⬛ Reconfiguring furniture

Incidence of change, whether it is moving people or furniture, is weighted toward the smaller time periods. Companies report an average annual churn rate of approximately 30 percent.

(Knoll/ISFE)

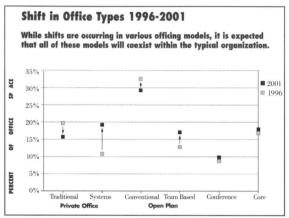

Shift in Office Types 1996-2001

While shifts are occurring in various officing models, it is expected that all of these models will coexist within the typical organization.

SPACE | OF OFFICE | PERCENT (y-axis: 0% to 35%)

⬛ 2001
⬜ 1996

Traditional | Systems | Conventional | Team Based | Conference | Core

Private Office | **Open Plan**

(Knoll/ISFE)

Change in Square Feet Per Employee

	Three years ago	In five years	% Change
Executive	267	250	- 6%
Manager	156	141	- 10%
Professional	116	102	- 12%
Technical	92	86	- 7%
Clerical	73	70	- 4%

From a percentage standpoint, managers and professional workers are facing the greatest decline in the allocation of workspace.

(Knoll/ISFE)

affect employee morale (note that nontelecommuters tend to balk at these programs because they tend to do more administrative work when employees are out of the office), productivity (however, note that productivity increases are self-reported by telecommuters who want the program to continue and not be abandoned because of *lower* productivity levels), and the bottom line.

SUMMARY

The alternative workplace has evoked a special language full of terms that may be confusing. Designers, CRE professionals, executive management, and staff all have to be communicating on the same wavelength during an alternative workplace initiative. So it's best to come to a clear understanding of what each term and name for types of work settings mean.

Part of the educational process is to keep all parties abreast of new information and to help everyone decipher why an activity setting differs from a universal plan, for example. Or why telecommuting, although part of an alternative workplace strategy, by definition can be combined with hoteling for a holistic and beneficial alternative workplace

TABLE 2.2

PARTIAL LISTING OF DOMESTIC AND INTERNATIONAL COMPANIES PRACTICING NEW WORK-PLACE STRATEGIES

Europe

Allied Dunbar: telework

American Express Travel Services: telework

Anderson consulting: hoteling

Asda: telework

Barclay's Bank: telecommuting

British Telecom: telework

Burger King: telework

Canary Wharf: telecommuting

Catalyst 400: telework

Coopers & Lybrand: Right Space program—activity settings, mobile office

Data Exchange Computers: hot desking, telework

Digital Equipment Corporation: nonterritorial

Ernst & Young: telework, hoteling

Hewlett-Packard: hot desking

Hoskyns: hot desking

IBM: telework, mobile office

Llyods TSB: flexible work program, telework

Lombard North Central: telework

National Westminster Bank: hoteling

Ogilvy & Mather: telecommuting

Oticon (Denmark): free address

Private Patient's Plan: telework

Prudential Assurance: telework

The Royal Bank of Scotland: videoconferencing

Skandia Life: telework

Smith Kline Beecham: telework

Sol (Helsinki): activity settings

Telia: free-address

Tektronix UK: telework

Unisys UK: telework

United States and North America

Aetna: telecommute, virtual office, shared worksettings, universal planning

Alcoa: some teaming

Amdahl: hoteling, telecommuting, universal planning

American Express: telecenter, telecommuting, hoteling, team settings

Ameritech: telecommuting

Apple: teaming

Arthur Andersen: J.I.T.

AT&T: telecommuting, virtual office, drop-in centers, hoteling, free-address, shared work

Autodesk: nonterritorial, telecommuting

Avery Dennison: teaming

Axiom: nonterritorial .

Bankers Trust: telecommuting, drop-in space

Bell Atlantic: telecommuting

Burger King: telecommuting

Boston Market: teaming

Caesar's Palace: teaming

Citibank: telecommuting, telework, universal planning, hoteling, teaming

Chubb: telecommuting

Cigna: telecommuting, teaming

Cisco: hoteling

Compaq: virtual office, telecommuting

Con Edison: telecommuting

Coopers & Lybrand: hoteling

Data Products: telecommuting

Deloitte & Touche: hoteling

Dow: teaming, caves and commons

Dun & Bradstreet: telecommuting, virtual office

Dupont: teaming, caves and commons

Fallon McElligott Advertising: free-address

Fritolay: team settings

Government Agencies: GSA, IRS, U.S. Postal Service: telecommuting

GTE: telecommuting

Haworth: teaming

Herman Miller: telecommuting

Hewlett Packard: universal planning

Hoffmann-La Roche: universal planning

Home Savings of America Bank:

IBM: hoteling, mobile and virtual office

In Focus Systems: caves and commons

Intel: universal planning

Kodak: some telecommuting and hoteling

KPMG Peat Marwick: hoteling

Lucent: telecommuting, variety of other new worksettings

MCI: virtual office, hoteling

McGraw-Hill: telecommuting

Mercedes-Benz: videoconferencing

Mobile: universal planning

NCR: hoteling, work at home

Nissan: teaming

NYNEX: free address, telecommuting

O+O Software: deskless office

Pacific Bell: telecommuting, satelite office, virtual office

PanEnergy: teaming

The Port Authority of New York: hoteling

Price Waterhouse: hoteling

Procter & Gamble: teaming

Prudential: telecommuting, universal planning, team settings, hoteling

Pfizer: universal planning

76 Products: open plan

Shell: teaming

Southern California Edison: work at home, hoteling, Red Carpet, telecenters, remote work

Sprint: telecommuting

Steelcase: teaming, telecommuting

Sun Microsystems: telecommuting, variety of alternative workplace settings

Tandem: remote work, hoteling

TBWA/Chiat/Day: free-address, telecommuting, virtual office

The Travelers: telework

VeriFone: virtual office

Xerox: hoteling

---

strategy. But benchmarking other alternative workplace efforts is relatively new, and results need to be taken with a grain of salt.

Even more confusing are the myriad surveys and polls, about alternative workplace. However, as we will see in Chap. 4, executive management almost always wants to see hard numbers resulting from other companies' alternative workplace efforts. Most surveys in the past decade have focused on telecommuting as it became popularized through the press especially as AT&T and other telecommunication companies embraced the strategy (Table 2.3).

TABLE 2.3

TERMS AND DEFINITIONS ASSOCIATED WITH THE NEW WORKPLACE

Term	Definition
alternative officing	nontraditional workplace settings
alternative workplace environment (AWE)	nontraditional workplace settings; same meaning as above but the term is more frequently used on the West Coast
activity settings	variety of informal and balanced work settings to fit diverse group and individual needs
Bürolandschaft	open plan developed in Germany in the 1960s
caves & commons	environment that integrates settings for individual work and team work
cellular office	European term to describe a traditional long corridor on both sides lined with enclosed private offices
club	combination shared group and individual settings
cockpit office	small hard-walled office for private work
combi-office	Scandinavian term for activity settings
cordless office	European term meaning office with wireless technology, freeing workers from desks
den	teaming area
drop-in	unassigned desk/office space used for small amounts of time (a few hours); same as moteling
fractal office	German term simplified to mean teaming areas
free address	space without assigned desks or offices, no reservations needed
group address	where team/department sits but without assigned desks or offices
hearth	casual area in office for informal gatherings; can include coffee-bar setting, soft seating
hive	European term meaning a floor full of cubicles
hoffice	blurring of the lines between home and office
home office	workplace in the home
hoteling	nondedicated desks/offices reserved for short-term use by employees
hot desking	unassigned desk/office space; U.S. Navy term
just-in-time	offices assigned to employees on a temporary basis
lean concept	European term for nonterritorial office
mobile office	working remote away from corporate campus in car, hotel, or airplane with aid of technology
moteling	unassigned desk/office space used for small amounts of time (a few hours); same as drop-in
nonterritorial	workspace without assigned desks or offices, no reservations needed
oasis	same as hearth
Red Carpet	office area with unassigned desks/offices, sometimes with higher grade amenities than hoteling
satellite office	fully equipped company-owned office away from corporate campus to accommodate workers that live far away
shared workstation	desk/office shared by two or more employees at different intervals during day or week
team suite/setting	same as group address; area dedicated to one team but filled with unassigned desks/offices
telecenter	third-party owned remote work location that offers fully equipped workspace for telecommuters from a variety of companies
telecommute	working from home office one or more days per week
telecottage	European term for satellite office designed for teleworkers that allows them to get out of the house (in Europe, there's even a niche telecottage for women only!)
telework	European term for remote work done via computer/modem; same as telecommuting
temporal office	private office that doubles as manager's office and conference space
touch down space	same as moteling; drop in
Unitel	European term for activity settings
universal plan	one-size-fits-all standard offices or workstations; people, not walls, move, does away with hierarchical space allocations
war room	conference room assigned long-term to team working on project
virtual office	a workplace that is disassociated from a specific time or place, i. e., being equipped with technology in order to work anytime, anyplace

Source: compilation from various articles and books on the subject of the new workplace.

Pioneering Alternative Workplace Projects

It ain't easy being green.
Kermit the Frog

Early 1980s Digital Electronics Corporation, Espoo, Finland

1987 Xerox PARC, Palo Alto, California, teaming

1987 to the present Andersen Consulting, San Francisco, JIT

1992 to the present Ernst & Young, Chicago, Illinois, hoteling

1992 to the present Chiat/Day, Los Angeles, New York, Dallas, free address

1992 American Express Field Sales Offices, nationwide, virtual office

1993 to the present IBM Cranford, New Jersey, hoteling

This chapter is dedicated to the pioneering companies that set out to explore alternative workplace solutions before most buzzwords were even coined in the early 1990s. These companies took risks— with their employees and stockholders—to carve out unorthodox work settings that left many observers scratching their heads and gave yet others the inspiration to do so with their own organizations. They went on the assumption that new work processes and new work environments could salvage poor customer relations, foster internal communication, and reduce bloated real estate portfolios. These pioneers had faith that the benefits of alternative officing would overcome any unseen, but inevitable obstacles that were bound to accompany change.

Here are the pioneers that many corporations studied after 1993 when the call for alternative

workplace strategies began to become louder. There is an entire book that can be written about the early adopters of telecommuting alone (that's only one aspect of the new workplace), including AT&T, Pacific Bell, the federal government, and Smart Valley, Inc. There are certainly other alternative office pioneers than those listed here to which companies look for inspiration. For example, in the early 1970s, Dutch architect Herman Hertzberger developed the Centraal Beheer insurance company headquarters in Apeldoorn, Holland, which, when completed in 1972, was a massive building that wove together office clusters linked by raised walkways, common spaces for social interaction, and a street-scape type of atmosphere. More recently, when Tandem began research for its Business Center program, it looked to Hewlett-Packard and Amdahl for their hoteling initiatives and Oracle for the way its field offices shared workstations. When MCI and Hoyle, Doran & Berry Architects began work on the telecommunication company's Boston Rally Center (a hoteling space), it took a look at IBM's Cranford, New Jersey, and Xerox's New England offices, both of which embrace hoteling programs. At Southern California Edison, the team responsible for initiating its alternative officing programs looked to the Ernst & Young model for guidance. Below are profiles of the projects and experiences that many companies have used as jumping-off points; from them we can begin to learn what about alternative officing works, what doesn't, and why.

The following profiles start with the earliest alternative office project and many track the companies'

Figure 3.1
Pioneers DEC in Finland
experimented in
comfortable, but open,
work settings in 1980.
(DEC.)

efforts through to the present day. Here you will see how alternative workplace strategies are fluid, morphing, and evolving situations as each company sees its needs unfolding year after year, sometimes month by month.

THE FIRST GENERATION: DIGITAL EQUIPMENT CORPORATION, ESPOO, FINLAND, EARLY 1980S

Back in the early 1980s, Digital Equipment Corporation Finland took a first stab at what would later be known as alternative officing. "It's the original nonterritorial office says William Sims, CFM, Ph.D., author and alternative officing expert based at Cornell University.[1] The main idea in this experimental office was that the office was supposed to be more like home, a more comfortable environment in which to work (Fig. 3.1). The employees selected the furniture, including recliners, and put computers on mobile tables that could be moved around within a fixed zone. At the time, everyone was scratching their heads about what to do with desktop computers so they could be mobile and not chained to a wall plug.[2] One employee had the answer. While having his car serviced one day, he looked up and saw the flexible wiring system with which the mechanics worked on cars. The idea became a spiral drop-down wiring system attached to the computers so that they could be moved within a fixed zone and not tethered to the desk nearest

the wall outlet. For privacy, employees chose an enclosed bubble chair and a private phone booth. "This environment has gone through at least three or four generations of offices over the years," says Sims. Now, it is dismantled.

DESIGNING FOR COLLABORATION: XEROX PARC IN PALO ALTO, 1987

The architect must be able to design formal tools for informal collaborations and informal tools for formal collaborations.
                                                        Michael Schrage

It was only under 3000 square feet but a powerhouse of a project for Osburn Design of San Francisco. The design team was charged to establish a prototype "Colab" (Collaborative Laboratory) for computer-supported group meetings at Xerox Palo Alto Research Center (PARC) (Figs. 3.2 through 3.4). The user group was a team of high-level artificial intelligence researchers in the Intelligent Systems Laboratory. At that time the Colab was one of Xerox PARC's many experimental projects to study collaboration and supporting technology[3] led by John Seely Brown, who today is vice president and chief scientist at Xerox. There were other such experiments, as well, that have not received the kind of publicity that came from Xerox PARC's efforts. The project grew out of the group's belief that professional people wanted to have the same kind of access to computers in their meetings as they have in the privacy of their offices. The Colab

project's objective was pure and simple: Create an environment to simplify product design and in-house communication. One stringent design criterion from the engineers: no mahogany—just flexibility.

The Colab was more than a design experiment; in fact, we can see where and how the noteworthy, free-thinking ideas that came out of the experiment are used today. The Colab room was a comfortable place for engineers and computer scientists to both test and use new communicating computer and software systems to support collaborative writing and other group activities. In addition, inconspicuous video cameras would document meetings so that psychologists could study how behavior is

changed by having computer support at meetings (see Tetlow 1987).

What was so different about this teaming environment in 1987 from any other group or training work setting in existence at that time? Probably the acceptance of computer collaboration was the first and foremost difference. Timing was right. The Colab became more than just a training or meeting room. "At Xerox PARC, the notion of personal computing gives way to interpersonal computing. The computer becomes the medium for shared space," says Schrage in *Shared Minds: The New Technologies of Collaboration*. The analogy of collaborative processes that Schrage makes is that of doctors who traditionally collaborate in an ad hoc way

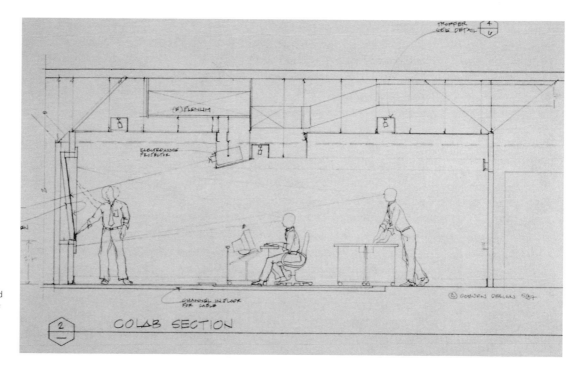

Figure 3.3
The Osburn design team envisioned the spatial and furniture requirements of electronic collaboration for Xerox PARC.
(Steve Osburn.)

Figure 3.4

Finally, a physical
manifestation of an
environment at Xerox
PARC for perfect
electronic teaming.
(Photo by Floyd A.
Johnson.)

usually standing around the x-ray board to discuss and diagnose a patient's film.

With the computer as the collaborative medium, there comes new territory. There are new patterns of thinking, new patterns of speech both internal and external, both audible and inaudible. There are more complexities in this kind of collaboration than meets the eye, and the design of such a space has to support all the tangible and intangible elements to the group. Where do you begin?

They started from scratch: After all, what kinds of products, furnishings, and physical elements were available in 1987 to support such a venture? Not much. The Osburns built a customized environment (these were the days before training desks with plug-in capability large enough to support a monitor). The mobile desks that the firm's principals, Joan and Steven Osburn, designed were angled and made out of insulated, sound-attenuating board finished in maple and Wilsonart laminate. Each desk, or *station* as it was called, had its own keyboard, room for two persons, and a pop-up CRT that rose from the back of the desk. A podium, called an *electern* (electrified lectern) had an adjustable-height keyboard, mouse pad, and projection controls (see Tetlow 1987). Cabling for all this was still run from the wall.

BIRTH OF THE ELECTRONIC WHITEBOARD

Collaborative meetings took place outside the confines of the Colab room. Whiteboards near the coffeepot were used most frequently, as evidenced by the multicolored scrawls overlapping other scribbles and sketches. This was the beginning of the electronic whiteboard.

The Colab provided a blackboard-sized, touch-sensitive screen for the group, which they called a *liveboard*, that displayed an image of approximately a million pixels. Brown noted that the liveboard at the front of the room, not the individual computer screen, became the dominant medium of use in these meetings.

To further the whiteboard concept, each person in a meeting was given a smaller, "computational" whiteboard—a personal whiteboard at that—networked together to promote shared, synchronized viewing and access. The Colab engineers coined the phrase WYSIWIS (shorthand for *what you see is what I see*), pronounced "whizzy whiz."

It was here that the limitations of the whiteboard were discovered. Whiteboards have limited storage capacity and must be erased at some point to keep the meeting going. Nevertheless, it was as good as any collaborative tool yet, and it had numerous applications.[4]

THE PORTABLE MEETING

Even today traditional meetings take place where one person keeps one set of personalized notes, another participant walks off with a separate set of ideas, and so on, which obliterates the truly collaborative process. It was Seely Brown's idea back then that the portable office would allow—through use of a liveboard—a universal set of notes initiated in one meeting to be reused in its original form in another meeting at a second location without the need for manual copying (see Olson 1989). This was not only an advantage for wildly creative ideas but for traditional means as well. He saw that the same information in certain types of meetings—financial and legal, for example—were so often repeated that it would be worthwhile to create the computerized collaboration tools that would support this kind of work.

But what happens outside of a meeting room, wondered Brown. It was at the System Sciences Laboratory at Xerox PARC where we see one of the first semihearths. Here by design, employees shared ideas on floor-to-ceiling whiteboards surrounded by soft seating that could be found everywhere. "Many visitors…are surprised by the number of floor-to-ceiling whiteboards, each in its own corner with comfortable seats or couches around them. This is not by accident or just a sign of opulence. These areas were explicitly designed to foster small collaborative teams working in semiprivate areas" (see Olson 1996).

But what interested Brown most was this notion of the coffee, lounge, and cafeteria areas where he believed most creative, informal, and relaxed collaboration happens, most often documented on coffee-stained napkins, scraps of pulverized or crumpled paper pulled from one's pockets, or a word or two written on the side of a dollar bill to later be pulled out to jog the memory. His idea was to create a seamless working environment where there would be a tool to transport ideas from one physical location to the next without losing the original intended interpretation through manual copying. That, he said, could even mean surfacing tabletops with interactive flat display screens that could be taken intact—without the inevitable ketchup stain—to the next location (see Olson 1989).

Steve Osburn of Osburn Design reported: "What we were doing in 1983 for Xerox PARC was a precursor for what was to come. It was way beyond what we as an industry were doing in office design elsewhere—it was all very inspirational. During the design process for Colabs, the environment for creating the design was very open, and they were very interested in hearing whatever we had to say. There wasn't a commander deciding it would be this way or that way—it was a very open and expansive sort of experience. This spoiled us a little bit. We did three to four of these rooms for Xerox in different parts of the country that they used for collaborating between software engineers, business people, and equipment engineers. It was clear that lots of other companies were interested in this collaborative, interactive design." After Xerox PARC, the Osburns designed a second Xerox Colab in Webster, New York, 1989 and 1990.

Today, Brown has become an even stronger advocate of experimentation. He believes that all people and all corporations should partake in robust forms of learning. "But the real challenge today is unlearning, which is much harder," he told *Fast Company Magazine* (February/March 1997). "The new world of business behaves differently from the world in which we grew up. Before any of us can learn new things, we have to make our current assumptions explicit and find ways to challenge them."

BEFORE HOTELING: ANDERSEN CHECKS INTO JUST-IN-TIME OFFICES IN SAN FRANCISCO, 1987

In the 1980s, Andersen Consulting was a fast-growing, image-conscious management consulting firm. Most offices have the old vestiges of power in the form of a mahogany door (see box, "How a Set of Doors Became an Andersen Icon"). Right about then, the company decided to break through that mold and strive for a more high-tech image. Trophy office space was becoming more and more difficult to find; at the same time, technology advances made it viable for consultants to stay out of the office and nearer to their clients while communicating with home base.

As anticipated, no one at Andersen wanted to give up their office space. In fact, consultants were demanding larger offices. Ironically, no one was ever in their offices, and desk drawers were relegated to holding out-of-season clothing such as snowboots left in the office over the summertime. Partners began to wonder why the company was paying top dollar to store employees' stuff. Something had to give.

Andersen borrowed a term from its manufacturing clients, translated it from factory floor to office space, and the *just-in-time* (JIT) office concept was born. The JIT office was modeled on just-in-time manufacturing in which inventories are kept low and parts arrive only when needed so that there is no chance of wasted merchandise or materials. Translated into white-collar speak, the JIT office is an inventory of workspaces that accommodates an employee on an as-need basis so that there is no chance of wasted space. The JIT office began as a trial run in the San Francisco office in 1987. Andersen told employees they could call and check into one of 13 offices, but a few partners would retain dedicated offices. It made sense to many, especially to one consultant who said he would go through periods of work where he would go to "headquarters" only once a year. San Francisco halved their square footage to less than 80 square feet per person. The money saved immediately went into technology investments (see Groves 1995). The concept grew fast and furiously throughout the years.

ANDERSEN CONSULTING TODAY

Andersen Consulting and Arthur Andersen[5] are two business units under the umbrella organization of Andersen Worldwide[6] which was formed in 1989. Andersen Worldwide employs over 82,000 people in more than 360 total locations in 74 countries.

At Andersen Consulting the JIT concept is still very much in process across the board. The company, however, continues to create public awareness of its alternative workplace strategies as they are developing. In contrast, Arthur Andersen is a bit more reticent in publicizing its strategies. Between 1994 and 1996, SOM and DEGW implemented a Global Real Estate Management Strategy for Arthur Andersen's Chicago office relocation that incorporates the use of activity settings and mobile storage units throughout the Washington Street space.

In this section, four of Andersen Consulting's offices offer glimpses into the physical manifestations of the company's JIT philosophy.

ANDERSEN CONSULTING IN EUROPE

Today, Andersen Consulting continues its hoteling strategies as far away as Europe and Czechoslovakia. Andersen's European Technology Center in Sophia Antipolis, France, designed by STUDIOS, reflects the dynamic nature of consulting work by making movement of employees within one location, or between multiple locations, a primary project objective. To help Andersen determine their officing needs, STUDIOS conducted detailed program studies including key department analysis and user group discussions. The results showed a need for flexible consultant offices that could be used for variable lengths of time and could accommodate significant organizational change. Hoteling and just-in-time work environments met those needs. STUDIOS worked with Andersen to develop standards for groups and processes. This included developing modular offices, creating workstations with docking capabilities and LAN accessibility, and incorporating phone systems linked to individuals rather than desk locations.

In 1996, Eva Jiricna Architects designed the Andersen Consulting office in Czechoslovakia. Reaching out as a global management firm with over 150 offices in 47 countries, Andersen opened headquarters in Prague, Czechoslovakia, taking the notion of hoteling to Eastern Europe.

Designed by Eva Jiricna Architects Limited in London, the Prague office staff of 100 employees occupies three 4500-square-foot floors. Five partners plus a handful of other staffers have enclosed offices while the rest of the project consultants or managers work in an open area in this hoteling environment, called "hot-desking" overseas (see Cohen 1996).

How a Set of Doors Became an Andersen Icon

It's ironic that such a progressive company as Arthur Andersen is known for its mahogany-paneled doors originally designed and installed in the Chicago offices in 1941. Vilas Johnson, Arthur Andersen's son-in-law, was the Chicago office manager during the mid-1940s, and it was his responsibility to handle the interior design of the space. He designed the deeply carved mahogany panels after doors he saw in England, eschewing the idea that the doors had to mimic the popular glass designs of other accounting firms. "These are the doors to a firm of professionals," Johnson once said.

Johnson died in the early 1980s, but his legacy was set in place with mahogany doors installed in every Arthur Andersen (and Andersen Consulting) office throughout the world. The original doors are permanently displayed at the Arthur Andersen Center for Professional Education. Today, the new image that Andersen Worldwide is seeking means that slowly, but surely, the heavy wood panel doors are being replaced by glass.

ANDERSEN CONSULTING'S RED CARPET CLUB IN NEW YORK CITY, GHK, 1995

In early 1993, Andersen Consulting's New York office began to investigate the concept of JIT offices to minimize rentable footage requirements. In the request for purchase (RFP), the partners required that a hoteling scenario be put in place for its sixth and seventh floors (totaling 58,000 square feet). One of the partners in New York came from the San Francisco office and saw the benefits it could have on the bottom line and productivity. That September, GHK was awarded the project.

It would have been easier if Andersen were going through only a physical change. But that particular office was going through several concurrent initiatives. The physical facility was being reconfigured, the secretaries' job functions were evolving into administrative assistants, and facilities in the upstate New York area were closing down and the influx of people were scheduled to be reassigned to work from the Manhattan office.

To begin the process of transforming the Manhattan location into corporate's own tried-and-true version of a just-in-time office, GHK put into action its preliminary plans of "bed checks" and focus groups. The bed checks took place over a 6-week period to see who was in at what times during the day or week. Some managers from various business units were in 6 to 8 days a year, but they had a dedicated office. "Some partners told us they never left their desks except to go to the restroom or get coffee," remembers Robert Heizler, R.A. and vice president of GHK who managed the project. To

get the proper levels and indications of office usage, the GHK team conducted discreet but unannounced bed checks. Focus groups took about 9 months to complete (typically focus groups take about 3 months to complete) because of the complexities of forming horizontal and vertically oriented groups that involved a cross section of partners through to the administrative assistants in each of the five business units, many of whom come in only on a once-monthly basis in the first place.

Each floor was 27,000 square feet of usable square footage on which 120 people would fit according to a traditional program. It was clear there was a totally inefficient use of space now that upstate New York staff would soon be assigned to the Manhattan location. After the hoteling scenario, each floor was programmed to accommodate 335 people. The staff was concerned that this large number would be overcrowding if everyone suddenly decided to come into the office at once. At one point, there were over 500 people assigned to the seventh floor while the floor below was under construction. That turn of events proved to people that there would not be any worry of overcrowding.

ANDERSEN CONSULTING'S SEMI-STATUS-FREE ENVIRONMENT

The New York office became the Red Carpet Club because it describes a place containing a variety of workspaces suited to various tasks, not unlike the designated spaces found within airline clubs. In this environment, spaces are *status-free*, meaning a person chooses the space most appropriate to the task at hand, regardless of his or her personnel level. GHK created the types of spaces for this project that are described in Figs. 3.5 through 3.10.

The Meeting Office

Designed as an office for Equity Partners and used by more senior people who are responsible for multiple projects. The offices have glass fronts for high visibility and can be used to conference when the partner is out of the office (Fig. 3.5 and Fig. 3.6).

The Retreat Office

Designed for individual "heads-down" work with room to spread out. The retreat office can accom-

Figure 3.5
The partner offices at Andersen Consulting in New York City have a unique desk that can be used for normal face-to-face meetings. (Photo by Peter Paige.)

Figure 3.6
Or the specially
crafted table can
easily swing to a
vertical position to
be used as an in-
house conference
table that seats a
handful of people
for teaming.
(Photo by Peter
Paige.)

modate a meeting of two persons, and it has a minimal interruption factor (Fig. 3.7). Retreat offices
look permanent, but they must be reserved to use.

The Huddle Room

Designed for informal private discussions, interviews, annual reviews, small-group work, and in-
house networking in a more casual lounge set-up
(Fig. 3.8).

The Locker Room

Designed to house an individual's personal files and
materials and also has areas for short-term work
such as reading e-mail (Fig. 3.9).

The Project Team Room

Designed for intensive group work, proposal development, and project management and supplied
with all resource and technological amenities.

Figure 3.7
These retreat offices are
popular in the New York
Andersen consulting
office because they are
quiet with lots of room to
spread out.
(Photo by Peter Paige.)

Figure 3.8
Whenever the pocket doors are closed to the numerous Andersen Consulting office's huddle room, it's an unspoken rule that no one dares open them out of consideration.

The Quick Stop

Designed to centralize equipment such as faxes, printers, and desktop copiers. The quick stop provides whiteboard, tack board, and tucked away bench seating for quick and quiet conversations and networking right off the main corridors.

On the Beach

To house consultants "on the beach" describes consultants who are between projects and need a place to sit. GHK designed a galley-like area with carrels in which at any given time a crowd of young consultants can be seen sitting at built-in tables, working on self-educational materials and learning company practices.

The Study

The special language used to describe space spawned by alternative officing can illicit responses no one could have imagined. Take, for instance, the term *lounge* and all the perceptions it can create for employees.

At first, when designers created this space, they called it "the lounge," but that is no longer true since it was perceived—by its name only—to be a "goof-off" area. The space, now used without hesitation, was renamed "the study" (Fig. 3.10). It is a soft-seating area designed with carrels and phones for staff interaction, knowledge sharing, research materials, and self-study for staffers unassigned to a project at a particular time. The space is also

Figure 3.9
Many people at Andersen in New York can be found in this drop-in space reading the newspaper while waiting for a fax to come through. (Photo by Peter Paige.)

designed as a break-out area as work going on in project rooms can spill out into the area.

The Kiosk

Another space designed for short duration in which an individual can complete private tasks and phone work was originally called the "phone booth." After some perception problems on the part of the employees (no one wants to be cooped up in a booth), the spaces were renamed "kiosks."

ANDERSEN CONSULTING IN NORTHBROOK, ILLINOIS, THE ENVIRONMENTS GROUP, 1995

In November 1995, The Environments Group completed the Andersen Consulting Technology Park facility in Northbrook, Illinois. The Technology Park relocated from downtown Chicago to Northbrook and now houses 1500 employees. The primary focus of this environment is for staff to develop quickly Andersen Consulting's technology and business integration capabilities for its clients worldwide.

The goal of this facility was simple: to create flexibility, effectiveness, and collaborative environment for all employees, as evidenced by the original con-

ceptual (not final) drawings created by the Environments Group to give Andersen an idea of the variety of settings possible (Fig. 3.11).

The project took 1 year to complete and consists of 320,000 square feet of completely renovated space in a series of buildings constructed in the mid-1970s and serves now as a working laboratory showcasing Andersen's latest thinking on the ideal work environment. Office areas are spatially and technologically flexible, offering a variety of alternative officing configurations including teaming solutions, hoteling, and JIT workstations for their mobile workforce.

ACCOUNTING GIANT ERNST & YOUNG'S USE OF HOTELING AS AN EFFICIENCY STRATEGY FOR CHICAGO, 1992

It happened in 1992, but people still talk about the project's catalytic brilliance. It was even the first hoteling environment to use an electronic reservation system. The first of many accounting and consulting firms to jump on the hoteling bandwagon, Ernst & Young has since taken its show on the road espousing the story to the skeptics about how alternative workplace strategies yielded major occupancy savings.

Figure 3.11

The Environments Group
designed the Andersen
Consulting Technology
Park to include several
types of interactive
spaces, like the ones
illustrated. Final
workplace solutions vary
from those shown.
(Environments Group.)

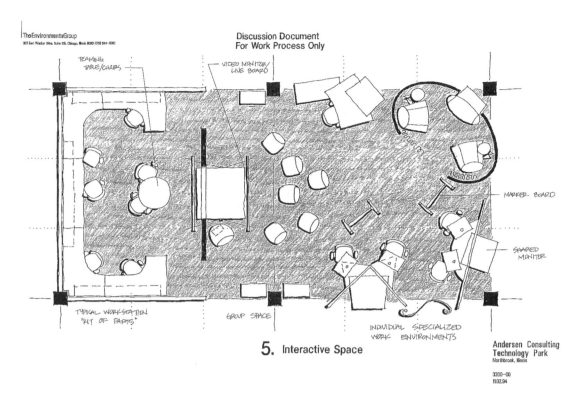

TheEnvironmentsGroup

Discussion Document
For Work Process Only

TEAMING TABLE/CHAIRS

VIDEO MONITOR/ LIVE BOARD

MARKER BOARD

SHARED MONITOR

TYPICAL WORKSTATION "KIT OF PARTS"

GROUP SPACE

INDIVIDUAL SPECIALIZED WORK ENVIRONMENTS

5. Interactive Space

Andersen Consulting
Technology Park
Northbrook, Illinois

3200-00
11.02.94

In 1989, Arthur Young and Ernst & Whinney merged, and in 1991 came the inevitable consolidation of three different facilities in Chicago that totaled 21 floors. The move of 1350 employees and 18,000 boxes of files from 21 floors down to 7 floors in the Sears Tower became instead of a chore, a chance to explore alternative ways of using space. One requirement for relocation was that the annual occupancy costs after the move couldn't be higher than the annual occupancy costs before the move, said Larry Ebert, director of real estate services for Ernst & Young.

Sverdrup, along with consultant Michael Brill of BOSTI, worked on the Chicago project which included the design of an interior space and technology infrastructure. After a study on the then-current patterns of periodic residency, it was established that 43 percent of consultants were "out-long" (for extended periods of time), 21 percent were "out-often" (for short periods of time), and 36 percent were "in" most of the time. It became clear that hoteling would be the strategy used to achieve the project's financial objectives. One of its main goals not only for Chicago but for all other Ernst & Young offices was to be able to grow without having to take more space—a managing partner's dream come true.

In 1992, Ernst & Young opened the first computerized hoteling office in 350,000 square feet of space that was, and still is, driven by a new and sophisticated voice and data infrastructure but overlaid by a physical environment that looked similar in furniture and finishes to a traditional setting.

At the time, the Chicago office employed 1350 employees including 500 accountants who weren't in the office at least 60 percent of the time. The rest of the employees had 100 offices from which to reserve whenever and if ever they came in to the office. If too many accountants decide to show up at the same time, there are "touchdown" spaces—or carrels—sprinkled throughout the space to accommodate overflow (see Schellhardt 1992). Most important was that hoteling offices should be indistinguishable in quality and size from the permanently occupied offices, according to Sverdrup's recommendations.

Since the Chicago office opened its hoteling facility, there have been two management changes. The mandate stays the same: Keep real estate costs low. And the partners still have 150-square-foot offices compared to the 225-square-foot offices from years ago before hoteling (managers and senior managers work in 96-square-foot offices, and other miscellaneous private offices remain at 75 square feet).

Sverdrup handled the interior logistics and suggested the use of hoteling to save in occupancy costs and to reach company objectives. Sverdrup's proposal to hotel the staff included the following goals, recommendations, and possible problems that would support the company's strategic plans:

Goals

- Increase space efficiency.
- Utilize excess space more effectively.
- Increase office density.
- Provide functional workspace.
- Improve support for periodic residents when they are in and out of the office.
- Increase sense of "belonging" and "place."
  - Support communications between coworkers.
  - Everyone who needs an office gets one when they need it.

Recommendations

- Limit hoteling to professionals who are "out-long."
- Hoteling participants receive locker, which becomes a permanent address and "place."
- Hoteling offices should look and feel no different than designated space; no "second-class" workspaces allowed.
- Set up war rooms for intensive periodic group work.
- Implement universal planning and limited workstation standards for flexibility.
- Adopt procedures to support hoteling and resources committed.
- Manager and senior manager offices should be 96 square feet.

Possible Problems

- Staff members don't make reservations or follow assigned space designations.
- Hotelers start to move into an office and maintain one even when they're out.
- Calculations are off, and hotelers are in or out longer or shorter than anticipated.
- Hotelers can't predict when they need to come in.
- Staff locator system is not maintained.

In addition to the above issues, Sverdrup identified the kinds of administrative and technology investments necessary if Enrst & Young wanted to hotel:

- Implementation and support mechanisms
- Hoteling staff
- Reservations system
- Electronic locator system and directory
- Capability to move belongings
- High-performance workstations
  - Supplies

- Name tags
- Scheduled mail delivery
- Computers with LAN accessibility
- Telephone extensions
- Ergonomic furniture
- Systems to encourage people to stay out of office
  - Laptops with modems
  - Mail delivery
  - Voice mail
  - E-mail
  - Aggressive scheduling
  - Car phones
  - Management site visits

"An important part of the job was to make sure that all of the necessary technology would fit physically and logically into the space," says Bill Gay, Sverdrup's special systems integrator on the project. "In addition, because Ernst & Young has a very traditional decor, we had to ensure that the integration of all this technology into the building was invisible."

ERNST & YOUNG TODAY

"In mid-1992, we started with 7 million square feet of space; 400,000 of that was subleased—so we were actually occupying 6.6 million net square feet. Today, we have 6 million square feet of space—but we are now out of 1 million of it. We have a million square feet subleased—so now we are a major landlord. About 500,000 square feet is still on the market. So, we occupy 4.5 million square feet net—a 30 percent reduction from when we started in 1992. In 1997, our annual occupancy costs will be reduced about $30 million.

"We saw a quick ramp up once we started these initiatives. By 1994, we had already saved $20 million in occupancy costs. Our firm merged in 1989, and in the period of 1990 to 1992, we entered into

TABLE 3.1

ERNST & YOUNG'S STORY AT A GLANCE

1992	1997
6.6 million square feet net occupied by E&Y	4.5 million square feet net occupied by E&Y
20,000 employees	23,000 employees
230 rentable square feet per person (includes circulation, conference, and reception)	195 rentable square feet per person (includes circulation, conference, and reception)

Figure 3.12
GHK also designed the
Ernst & Young offices in
Virginia. It may be
traditional in its
aesthetics, but it is a
hoteling office.
(Photo by Jim Tetra.)

15- to 20-year leases so I have a portfolio that turns over big in the year 2002 to 2004," says Ebert.

Its business transformation consulting practice is now the fastest-growing segment of Ernst & Young's $6 billion international organization. It now has a total of 8500 employees, and it's divided into seven groups of services:

- Business reengineering and measurement
- Business change implementation
- Knowledge and information management
- Process and IT outsourcing
- Systems development and integration
- SAP implementation
- Technology enablement

ERNST & YOUNG'S VIENNA, VIRGINIA, OFFICE, 1996

Vienna, Virginia, is an up-and-coming suburban town in which Ernst & Young opened an office in 1990, designed by GHK. But by 1994, they ran out of space, and GHK was called back on the project to do a feasibility study for a hoteling scenario, or to decide if the company should take on another floor. They were already located on two floors, and the main goal was to maintain current real estate costs, so it looked like hoteling, combined with universal planning, would be the workable strategy (Table 3.1).

Hoteling had since become a national initiative for Ernst & Young, so it wasn't a difficult buy-in process. GHK also had a track record with the Ernst & Young

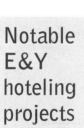

Notable E&Y hoteling projects

1992,
Chicago Sears Tower,
Sverdrup

1993,
New York: Mekus
Johnson

1993,
Cleveland: Mekus
Johnson

1993,
Washington, D.C.,
GHK

1994,
Vienna, Virginia,
GHK

Figure 3.13
A war room with walls of
whiteboard in the Ernst
& Young, Vienna,
Virginia, offices.
(Photo by Jim Tetra.)

Figure 3.14

There's still lots of space for hotelers and nonhotelers to spread out in the Ernst & Young offices in Vienna. (Photo by Jim Tetra.)

office it designed in 1994 in Washington, D.C., in which two downtown locations totaling 221,000 square feet were consolidated into a single space of 131,000 square feet through the use of hoteling.

The Vienna renovated facility uses two universal workspace standards of a 160-square-foot private office for partners, directors, and senior managers and a 42-square-foot open workspace for managers, staff, and administrative support. At the onset of the Vienna project, the facility provided 208 rentable square feet per person. The renovated facility provides 169 rentable square feet per nonhoteler and 152 rentable square feet per hoteler with ratios of 8:1, a 28 percent reduction of space (Figs. 3.12 through 3.14).

THE LEGACY OF CHIAT/DAY: TIMELINE OF AN AD AGENCY BRASH, YOUNG, VIRTUAL, AND UP FOR SALE, 1993 TO PRESENT

IBM's Cranford, New Jersey, hoteling facility may have been severely criticized by alternative office skeptics (see "A Humble Office" later in this chapter), but TBWA/Chiat/Day's virtual offices have

been, for the most part, unfairly raked over the coals in recent years. Usually when people think about the most drastic of alternative offices, they tend to think of Chiat/Day, now known after a merger in 1995 with TBWA as TBWA/Chiat/Day. This advertising agency, known for its creative advertising campaigns for Apple Computer (most notably the Super Bowl half-time 1984 commercial), Energizer Bunny, U.B.U. for Reebok, and recent dreamlike Nissan ads, the agency was able to create an incredible media splash in the early 1990s when it unveiled its first alternative offices (Chiat/Day call them "virtual offices") in New York City and Venice, California. Thanks to its past chairman, the illustrious Jay Chiat, who decided to take the agency virtual, both the Los Angeles and New York City offices made the news and were critiqued so often, that as of today, the agency has ceased tours to the curious. It's tough to get a glimpse of the historical New York City space that surprisingly looks the same in 1997 as it did when it opened in 1994.

The attention Chiat/Day received for its controversial office designs brought the idea of the alternative office into the mainstream. According to many designers and facility professionals, clients say that the thought of working in an environment that looks and acts like Chiat/Day scares most people into avoiding any discussion about the alternative workplace. Having to carry cell phones into the restroom or to crawl into a relic carnival tilt-a-whirl in order to make a private call can be degrading and ridiculous after the thrill has worn off, they anxiously say. But, an alternative office can look and act any way the company wants it to look and act. Chiat/Day is not necessarily a blueprint for success for any other company. Chiat/Day, like any other office—alternative or traditional—tweaks its office space once in a while to accommodate internal change. And although the rumors are hot and heavy that TBWA/Chiat/Day has completely abandoned their crazy quilt offices, you'll see here that's not the case. TBWA/Chiat/Day's new Dallas offices, designed by Washington, D.C.–based firm Greenwell Goetz Architects, decided to go alternative. At this point, TBWA/Chiat/Day in Toronto, however, has stayed traditional.

Though we'd all agree that Chiat/Day is one of the most heavily promoted alternative offices in the country, this book would not be complete without an overview about what makes its facilities tick. To begin, let's take a look at the history of Chiat/Day's alternative officing efforts.

CHIAT/DAY IN THE 1980S

Chiat/Day made its mark on the world with its ad campaigns for Apple Computer and Nike—and then lost both accounts in 1986, nearly devastating the company. A couple of months later, the Nissan account saved the day, and it continues to be a client of TBWA/Chiat/Day. Even back in the 1980s, the average age of a Chiat/Day employee was 31 (see Birnbach 1988). In 1981, a New York office opened on lower Madison Avenue in an attempt to avoid the traditional midtown Madison Avenue location where competitors were housed. In January 1988, Chiat/Day relocated its LA headquarters to Venice Beach, an old three-story warehouse that the agency leased from Antioch College—55,000 square feet of space which Frank Gehry designed.

CHIAT/DAY IN 1993

Voted by *Advertising Age* as the "Agency of the Decade," Chiat/Day had worldwide billings totaling $1.1 billion in mid-1992. Jay Chiat realized that there's a new way to work. What sounded like Chiat's sincere

idea to empower employees by drastically streamlining offices sounded to others like an attention-getting ploy to attract a buyer for the agency.

Chiat/Day has never been an orthodox company, like many creative ad agencies. In its 28 years, employees have never had titles printed on their business cards. Hierarchy has always been a foreign term. "We've always been zigging when everyone is zagging," said Julia Leach, the former project manager for the New York City virtual office, in an article in *Incentive Magazine* in October 1993.

So the redesign of the Venice, California, and the Manhattan offices began. The Venice project was awarded to Paul Lubowicki and Susan Lanier, Lubowicki/Lanier Architects, who studied university and airport spaces before designing the signature interiors.

The New York office moved from Fifth Avenue to 180 Maiden Lane downtown in an extremely windy point in the heart of Wall Street. That project was awarded to iconoclast, architect, and product designer Gaetano Pesce.

CHIAT/DAY IN 1995

February 1995 marked the merger between advertising agencies TBWA and Chiat/Day to make one $2 billion agency called TBWA/Chiat/Day. The question was how the two agencies would successfully merge different corporate cultures. Chiat/Day's virtual offices were the opposite of ultratraditional TBWA. TBWA had occupied the "same barren gray and white office on Madison Avenue for the past 18 years," commented reporter Ylonda Gault in her *Crain's New York* article. Bill Tragos, chairman of TBWA/Chiat/Day, did not know how to use a laptop, a shocking discovery by Chiat/Day's young cyberpunks.

On April 17, 1995, an article in *The Wall Street Journal* claimed that Jay Chiat had encouraged his agency to create a "chaotic environment and a flagrant arrogance that prompted clients to walk out the door despite superior work." Reports said that employees of Chiat/Day questioned why Chiat stripped them of office space and shoved them out the door without getting any feedback from the trenches about the move. To answer that question, you only have to read the same *Wall Street Journal* article that goes on to say that Chiat conceded that he felt that "great work is more important than the feelings of the person involved."

Chiat/Day decided to expand its New York City offices by taking up the 37th floor (the original colorful and alternative office concept was built on the 38th floor). To help Chiat/Day stand out from the plain glass facade of its 180 Maiden Lane address, Pesce wanted to move four windows on each floor in by 10 feet and build two terraces. The company that handled the building's leasing company rejected Pesce's idea.

JAY CHIAT SPEAKS OUT

There are two schools of thought on the virtual offices Jay Chiat created. One school says Chiat's drive to be eccentric turned the agency upside down while the other school of thought says Chiat isn't given nearly enough credit for the brilliant way he restructured the agency and brought to the public an acute awareness of innovative office design integrated with new work processes.

Jay Chiat, along with Gaetano Pesce and a host of other alternative workplace experts, was part of a panel discussion at the Van Allen Institute's 1996 seminar in New York City on the future of work. Seemingly more mellow than his earlier years while heading up the agency, Chiat was able to openly discuss why he brought Chiat/Day virtual. Here's an excerpt of the panel discussion:

The reason we did the office—and I didn't know what the word *virtual* meant at the time—was really to restage the agency. I was skiing at the time when I started to think about what we should actually do and I struck on how I actually work and what I actually do. We did work for Apple starting in 1981 so we have all these Macintoshes in the office. My typical day would be spent partially in the office, and I'd plug into my network to see my messages, e-mail—then I'd leave the office to find someone or go on client meetings—my office wasn't a real office because in 1976 we tore down walls and shared with everyone else—so we didn't really have to give up all that much—but when I left, my office space would remain empty—that was my pattern almost every day. It didn't seem to be a very efficient use of space. And I looked in my files, and the last piece of relevant information was dated March of 1986! Somehow I survived and got through all of this without referring once to my files.

So I went around to other people's cubicles, opened their files, and everybody else had even more obsolete material than I had in my drawers, and it proved to me that all this material was pretty invaluable and that it was just personal security. You know, people were thinking if I have this piece of information in my hands and you don't, then I have the upper hand. And that didn't seem to make any sense to me either. So I started to question people to give me logical reasons as to why eliminating offices altogether would be a stupid idea. I got a lot of reasons, but none of them were logical; they were all emotional. People would say, "I need my office. How can I make that phone call if I don't have one?" You don't have to go into an office to make a phone call. You don't even have to go into an office to plug in your computer to get your messages from network. I've done it in Eastern Europe!

So we looked at what the office really means. What a lot of people think we've done is hoteling. But we, as an agency, really had to interact. So it occurred to me that perhaps if we made the office a resource instead of just a space to store stuff, it would be more valuable. So we then began to observe how we work—meetings with clients that are a bit more formal with a conference table and rear-screen projection, creative meetings where we tack things on the wall, so we set out to design meeting rooms. So if you think about it, eliminating all the space that is taken up by private offices, you have a lot more room for meetings. So we have living rooms, places to go for tacking things on the wall, places with elaborate conference tables. Then we asked what else we need, and we need information. We need a library. So we set up an electronic library. So what do you do if you don't have an office to go into and put all your stuff? Well, in a university environment, students don't have an office, professors don't care where you work, you come in, you get an assignment, you work with someone in the library, in your dorm room, then you return it, and then you get marked. And that sounded like a really good business model because I was really tired of working with all these business people that I kept having to tell what to do. I thought it would be great to work with intelligent people who you could give an assignment, give them parameters, then they'd go off, do the research, and come back with the completed assignment. I told people to come back in two weeks, we'd rate the assignment, and that would determine your bonus or raise. And that was very scary because we had people who made entire careers out of sailing through the day and doing nothing while they kept getting promoted.

This new concept of the office changed the way we looked at people, and in the end, the result was a group of people who were now able to operate independently, and people who were now capable of taking control of their own personal freedom that I don't think you can get from working in a traditional hierarchical environment.

Our management always met and discussed their issues. But our new way of working was based on three things. Every partner was given an account to handle. We first asked ourselves how good the creative materials turned out; second, were our client relationships tight and solid, and third, how profitable was the account. Other partners voted on each other's accounts, and every person on the staff knew fully what he or she was supposed to do.

The physical structure brought about all these changes. It was amazing how uptight everyone was about not having a private office so we took everyone to *The New York Times* offices to show them how they get a paper published without working in any private offices. The New York TBWA/Chiat/Day office is really very tranquil even with all the color. You have to be there for about 15 to 20 minutes, and then the design all starts to make sense.

Many offices are structured to answer to people's status and egos. My personal lifestyle was lavish enough that I didn't have any of those needs. I didn't need a great office. I figured if I didn't have an office, no one else could complain about not having an office. Once you get over that, you can be productive.

We used some of the best architects around, and our instructions were always, hey, this isn't a shrine, it's a work environment.

TBWA/CHIAT/DAY TODAY

It was a rumor for a while, but it's true that TBWA/Chiat/Day is moving out of its infamous Frank Gehry binocular building it had built for $16 million and moved into in 1992.[7] The agency started its scouting for a bigger and better location for its West Coast office, confirmed by *ADWEEK*'s September 30, 1996, issue. The office has grown to 400 staffers, and even with its virtual office set-up, it's too small to handle the expanding ranks.

A Virtual Tour Through the New York City Office

No doubt the New York City office was meant to be a jazzier version of a virtual office in comparison to the Venice office. However, there are those who believe these two offices look alike. That assessment is rather strange since Lubowicki/Lanier and Pesce had two entirely visions when designing the interiors. Lubowicki/Lanier's theme for the Venice office

was that of relaxation and flexibility noted by the more muted colors and use of natural elements. Gaetano Pesce's philosophy is that workplaces look dull and that the office should be more shocking and inspiring, doused in clashing colors. That was his objective for the New York City Chiat/Day office, although the low-intensity lighting and the views to the river create a peaceful and tranquil setting that obliterates much of the chaotic "dream factory" effect Pesce was aiming for in his choice of colors, furnishings, and skewed angles of walls.

Nevertheless, in 1997, the New York City TBWA/Chiat/Day office looks the same as it did when it opened its doors in 1993. The only difference from when Jay Chiat was at the agency is that CEO Bill Tragos's office is furnished with Gaetano Pesce furniture, but it is arranged in a traditional way (there are even a couple of traditional leather club chairs in the office), there's no evidence of a computer or any other technology in the large private office, and his secretary sits right smack outside of his door at a brightly colored plastic and rubber desk.

A guest approaching the reception desk off the elevator immediately realizes that the environment is relatively quiet except for passers-by with cell phones stuck to their ears, but even they are speaking low as they move about the office. Right off the reception desk is a waiting area for guests that is no more than 5 feet away from a few people working from mobile wire workstations.

Figure 3.15
TBWA/Chiat/Day lockers are shaped like human faces. (TBWA/Chiat/Day.)

Figure 3.16
An example of a privacy chamber at the New York TBWA/Chiat/Day office. Employees call this structure the "outhouse," and they say almost no one uses it because it's too dark inside. (TBWA/Chiat/Day.)

Figure 3.17
The project rooms at TBWA/Chiat/Day are getting crowded at the New York office. They are popular since they are located on the windows overlooking the harbor—and they have doors. (TBWA/Chiat/Day.)

The New York office had a total of 225 people in 1996. About 10 percent of the staff is over 30 years of age, but most are in their upper twenties. (One employee who turned 28 that year said he was getting too old to work there.)

There's lots of brilliant color and comfortable lighting, but the locker area is much too dark and doesn't look very utilized by the staff. In fact, a few doors—each one molded into the profile of a human face—were broken off their hinges and empty inside. It looked more like any other average storage area in which employees store their miscellaneous and never-to-be-seen again "junk." The real work is stored in the project rooms in ready-to-retrieve piles.

No one has an assigned desk, so the office has a couple of "runners" whose job it is to track down an employee, usually by phoning them on the cell phone. Runners keep tabs on who walked which way at what time during the day. Runners keep an eye out for staffers, but they generally pick up on someone's preferences and habits, and they generally migrate to the same place—one person may

like the window seat on the 37th floor better than the darker nook-and-cranny area on the 38th floor—when they come into the office.

The most surprising part of touring the New York City office is that it can captivate even the biggest alternative office skeptic. The vibrant colors, the subdued voices, the soft rubber floors, and the views to the harbor can grow on you after walking around the space when you realize that the space isn't as garish as the press has made it out to be.

Although many people thought that TBWA/ Chiat/Day would abandon its virtual offices with the departure of Jay Chiat, it in fact has just opened a teaming environment in Toronto and a hoteling environment in Dallas. And, in addition, Laurie Coots, the firm's chief operating office based in Los Angeles, was recently charged to implement the new operating philosophy she refers to as "resource architecture" rather than the term it made famous, "the virtual office." Today, Coots speaks all over the world on the topic of workplace innovation (Figs. 3.15 through 3.17).

Figure 3.18
The Dallas office of
TBWA/Chiat/Day looks
more user-friendly than
the first two alternative
offices.
(Photo by David
Patterson Photography.)

The Newest of TBWA/Chiat/Day's AWE: Dallas by Greenwell Goetz Architects, Washington, D.C., 1996

The design criteria for TBWA/Chiat/Day's Dallas office was that it should not be like the New York City or Venice, California, offices for which the agency became famous. Why? The problem was cited by the TBWA/Chiat/Day facilities team that those two offices looked too much alike. But the Dallas office still wanted to follow suit and be virtual. So the design team of Greenwell Goetz suggested an office that embraced the flavor of the city in which it was located. "They said that if you looked at the two pictures of those offices, you wouldn't know whether you were in Los Angeles or New York City's offices," says Alfred H. Gooden, III, the senior project architect for the Dallas office. "Programmatically, things were to be in the same spirit of other Chiat/Day offices, but that there were no real rules. I asked to see photos of other offices, and facilities didn't allow it. They didn't want me to be influenced by what was already out there." After

hearing the concerns of the agency's facility department, the design team of Greenwell Goetz suggested an office design that embraced the flavor of the city in which it was located.

The Dallas hub of Chiat/Day included a staff of 28, and when the merger happened, additional TBWA personnel meant employees would total 36. The original space that was built for Chiat/Day in the early 1990s had the standard of 2 persons to one 8-foot by 8-foot dry-wall surround office with a traditional furniture including an L-shaped 30- by 60-inch desk with a 42-inch return, a wall unit, and file cabinets. The lease was up, and the merger was in place, and it was prime time to move.

New space that houses the merged company of TBWA/Chiat/Day is reduced in size from the old space of 9800 square feet down to 7500 square feet, but with the hoteling program, more employees fit into the smaller space. Because it is a hoteling office, the current staff of 36 could easily and comfortably expand to a staff of 52 or more.

Figure 3.19

It's perfectly normal to lie on the padding in the Dallas TBWA/Chiat/Day office to get some work done, especially since there are voice and data hookups on the wall. (Photos by David Patterson Photography.)

Figure 3.20

The Dallas location of TBWA/Chiat/Day is set up for hoteling. (Photo by David Patterson Photography.)

Although the Dallas office has a western saloon and looks different than either the New York or Venice office, it operates in much the same way. Employees work where they feel like working, whether that means lying down on a snake's head to think about the words to an ad or plugging into one of the desks. The "body" of the rattlesnake is the spine on which are built 26 workstations (18 workstations back to back), 4 of which are purposely oversized to accommodate graphic computers and too large to be moved. The bar's drink rail is wired for a laptop plug. The wagon wheel has a banquet of conversation space in the middle, but spokes create six stations on the outside of the wheel, which are mostly used for drop-in guests. There's a corral with four desks that are slightly larger—6 feet wide instead of 5 feet wide—also used for guests who need more work surface. Even the managing director and office manager work where they want to and aren't chained to a dedicated office or desk.

The overscaled wagon wheel is a conversation pit, and there are voice and data outlets in the middle so that people can casually lounge there while plugging in to work.

Chiat/Day is known for the strange private areas it manages to carve out for its employees. In Los Angeles there's the office balcony and the famous twirl-a-gig unit from which people make private calls. In New York, the oversized padded chair that overlooks the southern tip of Manhattan is the favored private space from which to make a call. In Dallas, they have opted for small "phone rooms" with walls.

As for storage, Gooden decided to avoid replicating the locker set-up that the New York City office built. "The lockers in New York, though highly stylized, were impractical," says Gooden. They were all painted different colors, but there was no way to identify which locker was yours because you couldn't put your name on it since it would destroy the integrity of the design. So you had to remember which locker was yours."

In the Dallas office, employees use Herman Miller's Puppies for mobile storage. Each employee has a chance to personalize his or her puppy with a choice of laminates and magnet letters that spell out his or her name so that no one forgets which file cabinet is his or hers. "In this office, you know that the red puppy with the green stripe is yours, and that has worked out well so far," says Gooden.

Greenwell Goetz also worked on TBWA/Chiat/Day's Virginia office in the spring of 1997—another office designed in the virtual spirit that was Jay Chiat's personal vision (Figs. 3.18 through 3.20).

Problems With New York and Venice Avoided, Successes Replicated

"In the beginning stages of this project, we talked about things that didn't work well in the New York City and Venice offices," says Gooden. "In particular were the problems with the odd meeting rooms that were designed in both offices." For example, a meeting room in New York City consists of a stair in the middle of a reception area—like a stoop in a rowhouse or a bleacher. "But there's no way you can have a concentrated meeting if people are zooming past you. They found that even though it's good to have an open table without walls for quick meetings, there are times you need concentrated meetings with four walls and a door," says Gooden from Greenwell Goetz.

The desks in New York and Venice were 40 inches wide, and only 3 feet deep. Even though the company was trying to be more laptop dependent, there were still many desktop models and lots of printouts. Gooden specified 60-inch-wide desks as the appropriate width on which to work.

In addition, says Gooden, desks on both coasts were made from particle-board plywood, which is not a good surface on which to work. "Clothing would get stuck to the edges, and the color was creating a disturbing mottled effect, but it was used since it was inexpensive," says Gooden. "There's medium-density fiber board (paper fiber) that is also a plywood but one which is homogeneous in color. We sponge painted it and smoothed it down so that no one ruins their clothing."

Gooden relays one of the funniest stories he heard about the New York City office in which there was one wall full of glued-on videocassette tapes. Employees who wheeled their mobile workstations to be next to that wall realized their computers weren't working. The problem, it turned out, was that no one demagnetized the VHS tapes before applying them to the wall, and that affected the way the computers worked. To fix the problem, all the VHS tapes were taken off the wall, demagnetized, and then reinstalled on the wall on which they still hang today.

AMERICAN EXPRESS AND THE VIRTUAL OFFICE, 1992

The rumors about the sale of American Express were flying in late 1996, so much so that it caused the stock to rise, hitting an all time high of 60 ⅜ in December. First it was rumored that the purchaser would be Citicorp; the second rumor was a General Electric buy. Nevertheless, the core business of American Express, its credit card business, remains a force to be reckoned with, even for its own sales divisions. But one division in particular—Travel Related Services (TRS)—remade itself into a virtual business unit[8] that would be attractive to any potential buyer of Amex.

Amex's field sales force calls on approximately 1 million local mom-and-pop retail stores and restaurants nationwide to sell and maintain American Express services. In 1992, Richard Tiani[9] was responsible for significantly increasing the productivity of the American Express field sales force by tearing down and rebuilding the sales-call process, introducing technology, and then establishing a virtual office environment in 1993.

The King of Credit Cards since the 1950s, American Express admittedly began to take its standing for granted. That is, it did so until competitor Visa sought a makeover from working-class card to preferred credit card. Visa began to air a series of slick, attention-grabbing television commercials featuring trendy restaurants and stores that bucked the tradition of accepting American Express, opting instead for the "other card." Visa was not American Express's only concern. In the early 1980s, the Discovery credit card made its debut.

It was 1992, the year that American Express began its in-house makeover that turned into something more like full-body plastic surgery. American Express began a three-stage process to reshape the field sales force to increase the productivity of its 325-person sales team. At the start, however, the initiative had nothing to do with reducing real estate occupancy costs but everything to do with increasing revenue.

Tiani became a human arrow, pointing American Express in the direction the sales force ultimately had to go before it lost its customer base to ambitious competitors. Benchmarking, along with merchant and employee surveys, revealed the numerous hidden inefficiencies of the sales team's work process. It became evident that consumer and customer perceptions, plus revenues, were at stake.

So American Express took a look at its 325 salespeople across the United States. They benchmarked the sales force by measuring their results with competitor results. Though Amex was not considered number 1 with customers, it still wasn't doing poorly, but they knew their standing and revenues could be better.

The sales force took 1 month to measure all processes and behaviors such as the number of sales calls made, the number of closes, the quality of sales calls, and the number of marketing and sales programs generated. Merchants and in-house salespeople gladly participated in the survey, and they were measured against each other to discover discrepancies in perception and satisfaction. Sales managers evaluated why the precall process, the preparation for the sales call, and postsales call results were weak.

There was a belief that the sales force was not as productive as they could be. And there were solid reasons to confirm that assumption. For instance, over the years, account loads became unwieldy; One salesperson carried a hefty load of 3000 accounts. Each salesperson should have only been responsible for 200 to 250 accounts, so that area clearly needed realignment.

"We were about a B+," says Tiani. "Client surveys told us a lot. For instance, customers would say, "When our salesperson comes in, he can't answer all the questions, and it takes too long to get back to us."" The salesperson would call the customer back 2 days later with the answer from management. But the process broke down when the salesperson would request a meeting a week later to follow up on the information. It was a long cycle period that left the customer time to wonder about American Express's efficiencies.

The process to upgrade its services was threefold:

- Phase 1: After gathering general information from all the regions, Tiani chose to restructure the Atlanta and Philadelphia offices first. Again, more observations exercises honed in on the nonproductive activities of each salesperson. It was at this point Tiani discovered the right technology needs for the sales teams. New technology was offered to each salesperson such as car phone, laptop, centralized voice mail, 7-day-a-week help desk open from 7 a.m. to 6 p.m., and e-mail. Salespeople became acquainted with the technology with a mandatory 2-day training session.
- Phase 2: The next step was identifying real estate issues and leases. Establishing the need for virtual offices began to take form.
- Phase 3: Solutions were established for problems employees encountered from working out of the virtual office. The program rolled out across country.

The sales force, and especially sales team management, hesitated to be away from the office because of concerns of access (Table 3.2).

Management support was established in a variety of ways, including a 2-day monthly meeting in a local hotel. Every Monday morning there is a 2-hour conference call to get the week started. Managers call in midweek to talk and "take the pulse of things." A buddy system was also established for employees. Managers asked salespeople to reacquaint themselves with someone they may have worked with or had met at a function and use each other as sounding boards, much the same way coworkers do who physically work in the same office.

There were design issues involved. Tiani admitted that helping employees establish an efficient private work area at home has been one of the most difficult issues with which he has had to grapple. "Some people have marginal set-ups at home, some have excellent home offices," he said. "We do ask them that they choose an area where they can leave out their current work and information, but not a dining table or kitchen."

To help employees deal with the task of setting up a home office, Amex offered to each a training program. Each employee went through a 3- to 4-hour training program with a startup kit that discussed the advantages and disadvantages of using each room in the house as a home office. This booklet was meant to help employees make the best choice of where in the house to establish a home office. The problem management encountered was employees in cities who lived in studio apartments. So they included in the guide a section on how to set up and work out of a closet.

Employees were given a one-time allowance of $1000 with which to purchase any items from stationery stores that they needed to set up a home office including furniture and file cabinets. "The correct amount is really $800, but $1000 sounds

TABLE 3.2

VIRTUAL OFFICE CONCERNS OF AMEX FIELD SALES DIVISION

Access Concerns	%	Solution
To remote computer system	60	Powerbooks
To support	30	Powerbooks, e-mail
To public domain info	30	Powerbooks
Office support equipment	25	Supply equipment for home office
Social interaction	15	Weekly calls and/or monthly meetings
Private work area	15	Set up home office

better to the employee," said Tiani. "That $200 went a long way with employees." Employees kept the purchases they made with the allowance. About 20 to 25 percent of the virtual workers with larger accounts have copiers in their home offices, and a few district offices are available for large administrative support projects with a promise of a 2-day turnaround. Others use local copy services. Tiani said the most frequently asked question by the employee was whether Amex would pay for electricity and air-conditioning. It turned out the employee was responsible to pay for those incurred costs. Amex did, however, put in a second phone line under the company's name, and Amex received the bill so the employee did not have to see it.

Paying the electricity bill turned out to be a minor issue compared to what Tiani soon discovered after launching the two pilot programs. According to Tiani, the biggest problem they had was getting sales managers out of their offices and into the field calling on prospects with the sales force. Managers said they felt obligated to be behind their desks at headquarters to receive calls from superiors. Managers felt they could respond to superiors' questions and requests only if they had immediate access to file drawers near the office filled with hard copies of data and reports. The simple solution: A memo from senior management that made it mandatory to be out in the field and that insisted that they rely on voice mail for messaging. It was the simple wave of a management wand that made it okay for employees to relax the traditional and limiting rules of Corporate America.

As far as liability and insurance were concerned, Tiani said the company established the fact that a home owner's insurance policy covered everything, and so far, there have not been any problems.

In addition to the required package, American Express developed a proprietary software, called TeamMate, to help employees stay connected to information via a Powerbook.

Results of the Amex's Field Sales Division's Virtual Office as of 1996-1997

- Signing up a new account: Average up 43 percent, 4.2 to 6+ calls per day
- Account development: Average up 40 percent, 2.5 to 3.5 per day
- Sales management in field: Average up from 2.5 to 4 days per week
- Sales administration: 110 employees down to 55 support staff

- Customer satisfaction: Totals up 28 percent
- Employee satisfaction: Totals up 26 percent
- Profitability: Totals up 10 percent
- Productivity: Up 15 to 40 percent depending on region
- Revenues: Totals up 8 percent to $40 million
- Process cycle time: Reduced 30 percent
- Cost reductions (overhead and real estate): Reduced 15 to 30 percent depending on region

There are over 500 people (up from 325 in 1992) in the division with a staff of 60 in headquarters, up from 45 in 1992, 205 that work from virtual offices, and 55 support staff that work in permanent "brick-and-mortar offices." Sales reps work out of their home office about 15 percent of the week during prime time, 9:00 a.m. to 4:30 p.m., and 80 percent of the workweek they are out on customer and prospect calls. There are four regional offices, down from seven. There are 27 district offices, down from 35. There are zero satellite offices, down from 44. As leases expire, offices will close. The goal is to keep three to five offices open across the country in metropolitan areas such as New York and Los Angeles.

"Be 110 percent convinced you're doing the right thing, or else the company management and employees will push you back hard," advises Tiani. "Also, be aware that you're affecting people's lives, so do the right thing for the people involved."

A HUMBLE OFFICE THAT DUCKS BIG BLUE'S TREND: IBM CRANFORD, NEW JERSEY, 1993

Visitors to IBM's 24-hour Cranford, New Jersey, offices are often surprised. Most expect to see desks filled—but only 20 people, if that, are typically there. Perhaps to the public, the fact that few people can be found at Cranford at any given time is somehow viewed as a failed alternative workplace project. To IBM, keeping people out of the office is exactly what the low-budget space was always intended to do. And that's quite a different way for IBM to do business.

IBM has been as American as any corporate icon can get where shirts were always white and ink was always black, and there was always a piece of original late-nineteenth-century art that could be found on an office wall. Employed there for life, no one expected that after its heyday in 1983, IBM would soon be coined a "Corporate Dinosaur" by the media, the personal computer race would leave IBM

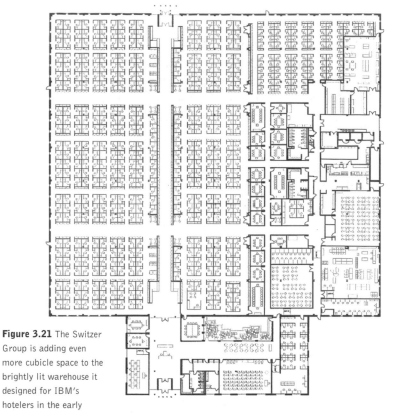

Figure 3.21 The Switzer Group is adding even more cubicle space to the brightly lit warehouse it designed for IBM's hotelers in the early 1990s. (Peter Paige.)

behind in a heap at the starting gate, and the company operations would almost come to a crashing halt. What happened? Simply put, IBM was too big, too set in its ways, too hierarchical—full of gatekeepers who made it nearly impossible for anyone to make a quick, informed decision before it was passed through layers of red tape, task forces, committee meetings, and reams of memos. Not only that, its customers hated the arrogant and cold relationships its reps kept with them. To create more of a black hole full of red ink, IBM measured how well a sales division did by the amount of revenue it generated, not taking into account costs or profitability. IBM became a classic case of an industrial age company that needed to get itself nimble, and downright nicer, to its customers.

Enter Louis V. Gerstner, Jr., as chairman. Cranford, whether he knew it or not, quickly became part of the plan he had to put into forward gear in order to make IBM a growth company once again: Get cozy

Figure 3.22
The entrance to the IBM-Cranford, New Jersey, space is unadorned. (The Switzer Group.)

Fast Facts about the Cranford, New Jersey, IBM Facility:

222 nondedicated desks

100,000 square feet

$10 a square foot

200 dedicated administrative employees plus 500 customer service personnel equals 700 employees

with the customer, listen and learn their needs, and help them achieve their goals. Then came the corporate mandate: Cut all real estate by half.

IBM's Cranford facility, designed by the Switzer Group, is one of Big Blue's first messages to the public and to its customer that indeed, it has come of age. It's one of the most talked about work settings in the short history of the alternative office. Why? Because a giant traditional corporation embraced an unconventional idea as part of a strat-

egy to get them out of a deep and frightening slump in the New Jersey–New York territory while hoping to make a mark with Gerstner.

In 1993, IBM's stock was at a low of $43—and the New Jersey–New York territory, one of the biggest, most important territories, shuddered with disbelief. Big Blue decided to check its consolidated sales staff into a 100,000-square-foot whitewashed warehouse building with open ceiling ductwork and asked them to give up permanent desks and offices in favor of an emerging concept called "hoteling."

IBM Cranford elicited all kinds of emotional responses from the design and general business community. During one alternative office presentation to the New Jersey chapter of the Telecommuting Advisory Board in 1995, the IBM slides came up on screen and the audience was audibly affected by what they saw. "That's ridiculous," "sterile," and "people probably don't like going there to work," were some of the responses. That same year, Michael Brill wrote a scathing commentary on the aesthetics of the Cranford facility in *Interiors Magazine* (May 1995), calling the space an "oppressive collection of cells."

Others applauded the space: "After one year, the experiment has worked even better than was expected," wrote Rance Crain (see Crain 1995), who said his own company was going the way of IBM Cranford in that salespeople are equipped with technology for on-the-road business and that they aren't about to sign any long-term leases. There were reports that New Jersey IBM employees said the adjustment to the space was substantially less traumatic and upsetting to them because they were far too busy with clients to even make it into the office. Instead of taking time in the office, IBM reps are taking time to get to know their clients better, even traveling to trade shows with them. Because few people actually go into the space, the ratio of employees to desks which had started at 4:1 as originally planned, eventually increased to 8:1.

The bottom line: Cranford worked for IBM in 1993, and it works for IBM in 1997. Why? It's not rocket science. IBM customers want instant ideas and instant consultations and advice on how technology can be used to make their companies more efficient. They want more than just a salesperson who can supply proposals on the table at once because they are unwilling or unable to let the rep go back to the office to write up bids, gather materials, and return with package in hand. IBM ThinkPads, mobile phones, and beepers allow the "consultants" to conduct up-to-the-minute business, plugging in for prices, delivery dates, and proprietary research.

Before Cranford, employees were scattered in four different New Jersey locations and one New York City address on Madison Avenue, generating a total local portfolio of 400,000 square feet. Duke Mitchell, general manager for the New York–New Jersey territory at that time, was charged to cut its sales staff by 50 percent and then consolidate the

rest into one smaller space with cheaper rent. Mitchell found that space in a warehouse off the Garden State Parkway once owned by Universal Corrugated Box Machinery Company, a move that sent shock waves to a public that grew up with the image of IBM's fortresses.

Work on the no-frills offices began. Mitchell chose to work with the Switzer Group because they knew IBM better than most design firms having worked on numerous projects for Big Blue for over 20 years. The two issues that Mitchell and the Switzer Group had to deal with: a tight budget[10] and short period of time until move-in because leases were up. In 9 months, IBM-Cranford was done from soup to nuts but not without its problems. A severe snowstorm made part of the warehouse roof collapse and threatened the move-in date.

"I believe what Duke wanted to accomplish for IBM was right on the nose. He had a job to do, and he did it beautifully. He brought all the staff in, told them what he was trying to accomplish and why, he gave them orientation, and because of his leadership, the employees bought in on it. Everyone. Their office was the least of their cares anyway," said Neville Lewis, consultant to the Switzer Group on the IBM project. "I learned a lot from Duke Mitchell because he made me understand the pressure he was under to get something done like this project."

Today, the Cranford facility has about an 8:1 ratio, according to Andre'a Cheatham, segment manager for IBM's Workplace Mobility program. "There was too much empty space given over to the mobile staff area, so we decided to maximize the real estate and bring in more staff function area" (Figs. 3.21 through 3.23).

IBM TODAY

IBM is now the darling of Wall Street once again, at its nine-year high of 145 per share mid-November 1996, hovering at 106 in mid-1997. Its revenues per employee are up 60 percent over four years ago. Why? Gerstner still walks his talk by visiting customers weekly, regaining a client's trust, and expecting the company to follow in his footsteps right up to the client's front door. The company continues to rely on its new-found talent for listening to its customers, forgetting about the bells and whistles or cutthroat pricing that other companies use to get attention. IBM customers

The

Cranford, New Jersey, facility wasn't the first IBM office of its

BOSTI in the early 1990s, was able to evaluate **evolving** workplace environments and the effect those models could have on its workforce. The following **experimental work-style** processes took place in

time" with customers became critical. For 2 years, IBM tracked employees' work patterns to determine what new work processes and technology were necessary. As a result, the IBM Hakozaki project employed a **"group-address"** model for 2300 of the 5000 marketing employees. Generically configured workstations were set up to which employees could wheel personal files.

IBM Canada, 1991

In 1991, Canada faced the same issues with which the United Kingdom had grappled. An additional problem was commutation time to see customers between Toronto and Ottowa, a stretch of territory where the major chunk of IBM business was located. A drive of 45 minutes was not uncommon for an employee who had to come into the downtown base office only to log onto the system, then drive back out to the customer's office in the suburb. This kind of chaotic and exhausting work process that the customer service rep endured became unacceptable. A 30-person pilot, called **"Flexiplace,"** was implemented. Modems allowed customer-service reps to work at home or at the client's office.

History of Early IBM Alternative Offices That Led to Cranford

kind, however, although it became the most visible one (besides the Armonk headquarters activity) that still endures close scrutiny by the business community. IBM in Japan, the United Kingdom, and Canada were all early developers of **new models** of working. IBM, working with both the Cornell Consortium since 1989, under the direction of Frank Becker, and Michael Brill of

the late 1980s and early 1991 and have clearly influenced IBM's perspective in the United States, starting with the Cranford facility.

IBM Japan, 1986

In 1986, IBM in Japan faced two issues: Plans were under way for the consolidation into a new downtown Tokyo building for 5000 employees, and the need for employees to increase their "face

IBM United Kingdom, 1989

In 1989, IBM United Kingdom was faced with a serious financial scenario due to a weak economy. They turned to Japan's experiments to see if **alternative officing** could help. About 20 to 30 people experimented by working at home or sharing offices.

---

report that they always have a name to contact for problems. However customer-conscious IBM is, it's still streamlined and back to basics, continuing to focus on informal, no-frills work environments.

The new Armonk headquarters, designed by Swanke Hayden Connell Architects, is smaller and less of a symbol of conspicuous consumption.

IBM Workplace Mobility Program-Norfolk, VA/Gensler 1996, 1997

In April 1992, IBM implemented a program called Workplace Mobility. In January 1993, 58 marketing and services employees from the Norfolk office went mobile in an effort to reduce 58,000 square feet down to 26,000 square feet—a 40 percent reduction of space based on people using technol-

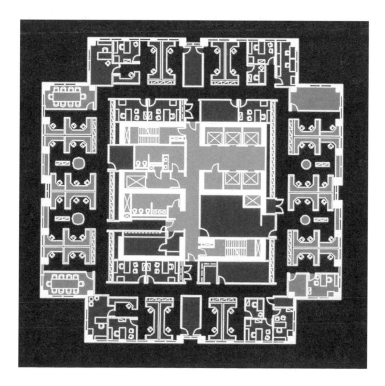

Figure 3.24
The floor plan of IBM's Norfolk, Virginia, office shows the amount of space to be used by fixed staff in black and the space to be used by mobile workers in grey. (Gensler.)

We often shake our heads at the way the government handles a project,

The U.S. Federal Government... on the Cutting Edge? 1990s

any project. But as slow and anti-quated as we tend to think the government is, this behemoth of a corporation has committed itself to telecommuting, telework centers, and the likes of other alternative workplace solutions. (Applaud these efforts for if they implement **unusual** solutions for their internal affairs, maybe then they can find the strength to break the tired molds and initiate—from start to finish—fresh solutions for the country's problems.)

Alternative workplace strategies are not alien to the government. The following agencies have conducted telecommuting studies in the past decade (dates indicate when results of pilots were published):

1988 Southern California Association of Governments
1990 State of California
1990 San Diego County
1991 Arizona Energy Office (in conjunction with AT&T)
1992 Washington State Energy Office
1992 City of Los Angeles
1993 Los Angeles County and more...

Source: Smart Valley Inc. 1994 Guide.

Since 1990, federal employees have been able to work at home or at a **convenient** satellite office for part of the week.[11] About 1000 people from 15 agencies participated under the federal Flexible Workplace Pilot Project, also known as "Flexiplace." In 1992, the nation's first Federal Alternative Worksite Center was proposed to open in Hagerstown, Maryland. The pilot program would house up to 200 employees.

Federal Flexiplace Project Through to 1997

Although the government had had experience with telecommuting initiatives, it wanted to further explore union-related issues of pay, leave, workers' comp, safety, liability, privacy, and equipment and related costs for telecommuters. It was also **interested** in learning the effects of telecommuting options on efforts to attract and retain employees in critical positions while reducing space costs. The Department of Labor sponsored two telework pilot studies under the Flexiplace programs. The first projects had been implemented earlier in January 1990, were concluded in 1993, and involved 13 federal agencies. Under the U.S. Office of Personnel Management, 700 employees had been divided into a work-at-home program, satellite work center program, and a disabled workers program.

The Department of Labor's first project involving 400 field employees began in 1993 and ended in 1996. The second one involving 200 employees in national offices began in 1994 and also ended in 1996. Both pilots were initiated in partnership with AFGE Local 12 for the national office employees and the National Council of Field Labor Locals for field offices.

Today, Flexiplace coordinators are stationed in each of the regional cities to help monitor the ongoing program. A permanent Flexiplace program was put in place in 1997 for the Department of Labor.

Though very little equipment was purchased during the pilot programs, most employees used personal computers from home and their own phone lines. In the permanent program, government-owned property, including computers, software, and other telecommunications equipment may be used by **employees** in their home offices in order to carry out their jobs, said Guest. In addition, government-appropriated funds may pay for telephone installation and basic service in a home office if it is used solely for government business.

The government has certainly come a long way.

---

ogy. At that time, the company began to develop its FlexiMOVE hoteling reservation software product that IBM now sells to outside companies in a separate marketing effort.

After Norfolk, four additional pilots were underway. "We threw standards away," says Andre'a Cheatham, segment manager of the Workplace Mobility Program who now consults with business units and outside customers on process, design, and alliances that rise out of the program. Norfolk, the first pilot, was reduced to half a floor under the Workplace Mobility program. Gensler Associates helped them to further condense the floor down to 7000 square feet to meet the most minimum requirements of an office.

At first, Norfolk had a 2:1 ratio, but it slowly began to rise to 4:1, then 8:1, and now it's 12:1, said David Insigna of Gensler. "Cutting down the space makes it look fuller and gives them a better sense of community."

Since Norfolk, Gensler has gone on to do 11 sites for IBM in the mid-Atlantic region and in the Midwest as a result of the Workplace Mobility program, and they are all a little different from one another, said Insigna. "As a further result of this work, we are looking at jointly exploring the potential of sharing leads with them from our design vantage, and they will share leads with us when a client of theirs needs alternative office planning and design," he added (Figs. 3.24 through 3.26).

SUMMARY

As computers began to proliferate in the workplace, so did new workplace environment experimentation begin to unfold. One of the first interiors that innocently pointed to the future happened in the early 1980s overseas in Finland where Digital Equipment Corporation engineers worked in a

Figure 3.25
IBM employees cue up
here to find a spot using
the company's own
hoteling software called
FlexiMove.
(Gensler.)

Figure 3.26
Workstations at the
Norfolk IBM office have
no built-in storage to
discourage squatting.
(Gensler.)

relaxing, nonterritorial space full of soft seating and reclining chairs. Following the discovery of DEC and its untraditional use of office space came Andersen Worldwide and its coined term, the "just-

in-time office." At the same time, a spate of other companies were experimenting with telecommuting, one alternative workplace strategy. And although many people still oversimplify the *alterna-*

A number of private companies have been early adopters of telecom-

AT&T Before the Trivestature of 1991 and 1992

muter pilot programs. They include (dates indicate when results of pilots were published):

1990 Blue Cross/Blue Shield
1990 Pacific Bell
1990 US West
1990 Traveler's Insurance
1991 Bell Atlantic
1992 Southern New England Telephone
1993 Sears
1993 Hughes Ground Systems Group
and more...

Source: SmartValley, Inc., 1994 Guide.

But AT&T has always been in the vanguard of telecommuting and the alternative office as a workplace strategy, and the company has used it as a sales tool to promote its own services to the outside world. In 1991, the company launched a virtual office program that consisted of giving a few thousand marketing representatives Safari workstations and cellular phones and asking them to call ahead and reserve an office for the day if they needed to come back to the office—the beginning of hoteling. To manage these efforts and AT&T's growing telecommuting program, it launched the Alternative Officing Services Integration Team (AOSIT) in 1992. AOSIT was really an integrated team that included:

- Real estate
- Corporate information services
- Environment and safety
- Customer education and training
- Procurement
- Human resources
- Tax policy
- AT&T School of Business
- Employee commute options
- Corporate services
- Economic analysis
- Bell Labs

Since then, AT&T has become a force behind the Telecommuting Advisory Council, a national grassroots organization that has grown over the years to include education on alternative workplace strategies.

Why AT&T Became Pioneers of Change

Before the 1980s, AT&T had a distinct reputation in the public's eye. The company aimed to be likable and hired an organization of low-key people from its executives down to its doddering telephone repairers. When phone service became deregulated in the early 1980s (AT&T was involved in an antitrust suit brought against it by the U.S. Department of Justice), AT&T woke up and realized it had to become a whole different organization with a focus on marketing its products and services.

In 1992, AT&T proceeded to wean 250,000 workers from office dependency. By 1993, it had 21,000 employees telecommuting from home and 5000 more salespeople out on the road—road warriors working from laptops and cellular phones. In 1994, the company had 35,000 employees telecommuting at least 1 day a week and 12,000 in virtual offices. By taking a total of 20 percent of employees and putting them into home offices or virtual offices, AT&T said it saved $80 million in real estate costs (see Noble 1995). In 1996, AT&T announced it would be laying off mostly managers.

To date, in spite of all AT&T's corporate issues (its leadership has floundered and it has lost shares in the long-distance market), the company continues to actively support telecommuting. It's involved with "Telecommute America!," a public/private effort launched in 1995 to promote telework. And, in June 1997, AT&T provided a $3000 grant to the International Telework Association to launch a chapter in Salt Lake City.

tive *workplace environment* to mean simply that of telecommuting, the new workplace is a much bigger and holistic idea than just the work-at-home component. Many who began with telecommuting expanded programs into other forms of new work processes and new work settings. Throughout the late 1980s into the early 1990s, pioneers featured in this chapter and others—who have dearly paid their own dues, learned from their mistakes, taken the heat of critical commentary, and endured the wrath of irate employees—have become the wiser through it all and have given the rest of us the courage to continue seeking new work processes and new work settings to bring our businesses gallantly into the twenty-first century.

2

Framework

Buying into the New Workplace

Chapter

4

Face it: It's easier to read about and contemplate an idea, like alternative officing, than to actually do it and change a company's entire culture.

The greatest discovery of my time is that human beings can alter their lives by altering their attitudes.

William James

Achieving buy-in to the new workplace is critical. It's a function that must be paid attention to across the board through strategic facility planning, space planning, design and management, and it hits designers, facility, and CRE professionals on many levels. The entire scope of space planning, for example, has evolved into a more holistic process. A number of responsive activities are described in this chapter.

Space planning is clearly more important today than ever before. One end-user said recently that she feared designers may be somewhat disappointed when they hear clients say that the most important role of any design firm in this day and age is space planning. It sounds less creative, less glamorous than most design projects from the 1980s; nevertheless, end-users are continuously being charged with reducing occupancy costs. Suddenly, the designer's greatest challenge is to plan not only aesthetic but creative, efficient interiors that support a company's range of business objectives that go beyond the scope of cutting operational costs. Today, the word *creative* takes on a whole different meaning and includes dynamics that were never thought before to be important to the planning, design, and management of a facility.

This is easier said than done. "Eighty percent of the effort is in getting people to change, 10 percent in persuading the chief executive that it's a good idea, and 10 percent is choosing the correct equipment," says Richard Nissen, managing director of The Virtual Office temporary office complex in London, talking about planning, designing, and managing the alternative workplace.

Juggling these precise issues when involved in an alternative workplace project is an art. "Seeking alternative ways to design an office to house and support employees and address corporate guidelines is not just an architectural solution," says Logan Need, associate at Farrington Group, an Atlanta-based design firm whose roster of clients includes Tandem and Amdahl, both companies that advocate the alternative workplace. While the designer tries to sell an alternative workplace to a client, the space has to be strategically planned. At the same time the space is being planned, the designer needs to work with the client to do two things: Retain the "champion," (an upper-management executive who believes in alternative workplace and walks the talk), and help the client achieve employee buy-in through a variety of processes such as focus groups and communications vehicles.

While all of this is going on the design side, there's a flurry of activity and demanding detail work on the client end. The team or department in charge of alternative workplace is also selling the program to in-house clients such as business units and other departments around the country, and around the world. While working to keep the champion on the straight and narrow, the alternative workplace point person(s) are keeping buy-in momentum up with all the other levels of management and, most importantly, with employees.

Unfortunately, an alternative workplace program can fail for a variety of reasons, but most of them have to do with the failure to achieve buy-in at any and all levels of the corporation. Here are some other reasons for failure:

- A company says it will reengineer its work processes but never does it.
- A company dives head first into reengineering when it doesn't fit the business objectives.
- A company tries to reengineer without an executive management champion.
- A company dips its toe into the waters of an alternative workplace but is really afraid of all the changes it incurs, so the program is abandoned.
- An alternative workplace program is not implemented quickly enough, or the process drags on past 12 months, which causes momentum to deteriorate.
- A company fails to take into consideration the most important part of an alternative workplace program: the needs, physical and emotional, of the employees doing the work.
- A company fails to take into consideration the employees' perception of an alternative workplace.

Perhaps the last point here is the most important one. A Daniel Yankelovich Group survey from 1993 found that through the 1970s and early 1980s, employees believed that CEOs did an adequate job of balancing employee interests with shareholder interests. The pendulum has swung in the opposite direction, and now it's a common belief that CEOs are mostly concerned with shareholder interests over employee interests. That shift in perception has caused employees to mistrust the company on many levels. And when they hear words relating to the alternative workplace, they fear for their jobs.

Christine Barber of Knoll, an in-house consultant who travels the country to talk to end users about the alternative workplace, tells this story: "I was in Charlotte, North Carolina, visiting a company that was intending to take down the partitions for teaming. But just taking down those partitions made the employees believe they were losing their jobs; there was a lot of fear in that company."

To that end, in this chapter, we will dissect the "search and discovery" steps of selling, initiating, planning, and programming, then rolling out an alternative workplace. All of this—planning, programming, selling an alternative workplace to upper management, selling an alternative workplace to business units, selling an alternative workplace to employees by understanding corporate culture—goes hand in hand as it never did before in the design and facility profession.

"Ultimately, we have discovered that the success of the alternative office project depends on three things: client commitment and strength of the client team to persevere through difficulties; architectural vision and the ability of the designer to produce a complete and convincing vision; and the power of the right tools to accurately assess the organization's needs, and thus, to fully understand the organization," says Ethan Anthony, vice president of Hoyle, Doran & Berry, architects and designers of the MCI Boston Rally Center and other alternative workplace environments.

To achieve all of Anthony's criteria, and most important the overall client buy-in for alternative workplace at all levels of management and employees, it's vital to understand the basics in the following areas:

- Who is making the decision on alternative workplace projects
- The designer's role in educating the client on the alternative workplace
- The facility professional's new role to educate in-house clients on alternative workplace
- The necessity for the client to form an internal task force
- The right ways to sell the alternative workplace idea to senior management
- Finding and keeping a champion for top-down buy-in
- Picking and initiating a pilot
- The cost-benefit analysis as a selling tool
- The productivity issue as a selling tool
- Understanding the touchy issue of corporate culture
- Including change management processes in the program
- Training employees to work differently and to use new technology
- Understanding issues of productivity (how it can be increased, decreased)
- How to gingerly roll out pilots to all business units (rather than forcing it down their throats)
- Finding new sources and new businesses that have sprung up in the advent of alternative workplace strategizing

It doesn't matter how exotic or simple a new alternative workplace project is, it's usually more complex and full of emotional decisions than traditional projects. The first step to begin the complicated procedure is to find out from the very first meeting who on the client side is making the physical facility decisions. This person usually differs from the designated champion (senior-management figurehead who works—or plans to work—in an alternative workplace to set an example for the rest of the company and to spur top-down buy-in). Margo Grant Walsh,[1] vice chairman of Gensler's board of directors and the managing principal of the New York office, deciphers the three types of facility management roles, emphasizing that it helps a great deal to know from the start of an alternative workplace—or any interior project—what role the facility manager plays and how he or she can best help you get through the process.

"There are three distinct kinds of facility management roles. We do lots of law firms, so you deal directly with partners, and you deal with partner money. They become the ultimate decision makers, but they use their facility staff to implement these decisions and carry out the project. Then, there's the more traditional conservative businesses such as insurance, banking, consulting groups who are all very organized in their structure, and the facility manager comes in very early and often becomes involved with the selection of a design firm. Then, there's the last one which is the most interesting—and volatile—the personality businesses such as publishing, media, investment banking. There are lots of stars, and stars have lots of demands and desires that are technology driven, and they want it yesterday or today. Ultimately, the facility professional is held responsible by their senior management," explains Grant.

Bob Evett, of Steelcase's advanced solutions team, breaks down the client categories even further. He says the hierarchical client is still out there and is still fixed on asset utilization. Those are the clients that decide to send employees home as a strategy for space cost savings. Evett's experience with clients leads him to see the following:

- The "as-is" clients still allocate space based on status and rank.
- The "redefiners" are the clients who are at the opposite side of the scale from the as-is clients. Redefiners say that no one gets space, and space will be allocated based on what the employee does. Evett says many clients think they are redefiners or they would like to be perceived as rede-

finers, but it's the smallest group. Most clients are really...

- "Refiners"—clients who realize that their business has changed, and they question why buildings and interiors are still being designed as they were 15 years ago. This is the fastest-growing group of the clients who can be found in the middle of the scale between as-is and redefiners. Refiners aren't ready to make the jump to totally redefine work and physical environment, but they are willing to work a little at a time to refine the work processes. Usually, refiners have a significant real estate portfolio that is more like "an aircraft carrier that takes longer to turn around," explains Evett.

Evett is used to clients asking about the alternative workplace. "Alternative officing is a great topic," he says. "When people say to me, 'let's talk about alternative officing,' I will ask them to tell me what their current officing strategy is first—they don't usually have one, so we have to start from the beginning."

He then asks a client to define flexibility in terms of what it means for their company. No two clients define flexibility quite the same way, Evett has observed. Usually, they aren't even sure if they are trying to enhance work performance, create space that will drive competitive advantage, or leverage real estate on other ways to meet business objectives.

Clients, he finds, rarely think about integrating physical space with work process, technology, organizational development, and design. Evett has even met with clients where facilities and real estate have never come together as a group, yet both departments are charged with work process reengineering.

"The first step then is to create that integration and determine who is responsible for officing strategies, a passionate integrator that will drive the process," Evett says. "They may come from HR, MIS, CRE, wherever." Unfortunately, Evett says, this passionate integrator won't be the driver of change. That has to come from the vice president and CEO level. That's where the buy-in process begins.

STEP 1: SELLING THE ALTERNATIVE WORKPLACE IDEA TO UPPER MANAGEMENT

"If you wake up a CEO at 3 o'clock in the morning and say, quick, tell me what three things will make your company more profitable—telecommuting isn't going to be one of those things," warns consultant Gil Gordon. "But what will get their attention is that if the company has to be reengineered to grow its productivity and revenue, telecommuting is one tool—so use alternative workplace strategies as programs that can piggyback a reengineering effort."

In Evett's experiences, it's rare to find a CEO that doesn't realize that space matters. It's just a matter of getting the CEO's attention for 5 or 10 minutes.

Andersen Worldwide, parent of Andersen Consulting, began educating top management on the new workplace in the early 1990s. Andersen is well known for its pioneering in hoteling in just about every location around the world. A difficult bunch, senior managers believe they are highly paid, work 24 hours a day, and should at least get a private office. What Jim Nixon, head of global real estate initiatives, has done over time is educate this top-management group, and help them accept and understand through examples and benchmarking why this benefits the company. As a result, Nixon has established Global Real Estate Management Strategy standards to reduce occupancy costs and property expenditures and create the most flexible and best use of space[2] whether it's an office in Tokyo, Paris, or Chicago.

Andersen Worldwide's business unit, Arthur Andersen, is a follower of the Global Real Estate Management Strategy. Today, Arthur Andersen has 100,000 employees in 76 countries occupying 381 offices. When Andersen developed its global strategy in 1993, it established four major goals for real estate management. First, the proper allocation of the firms' capital resources was a top priority at the time, said Richard Measelle, the former, and recently retired, worldwide managing partner of Arthur Andersen, at an executive forum hosted by *Forbes* Magazine and the American Society of Interior Designers in June 1997. A second goal, said Measelle, was the reduction of occupancy costs as a percentage of revenue, the third goal was to identify solutions for emerging business processes, and the fourth was "to have a mindfulness of business criteria in all facilities decisions."

To deal with the challenge of knowing where the company's capital was being allocated and where additional needs would arise, Andersen developed a worldwide lease database to track lease commitments and expirations. This strategy would also help to sell alternative workplace programs to upper management in various regions. In addition, time utilization studies helped to identify underutilized space and the degree of interaction between employees that was taking place in each location. Today, "Each new office space request now results in a local approval generation, which is presented to our local and global management before proceeding with any lease that involves more than 10,000 square feet," said Measelle. "As a result of the implementation of our global real estate management strategy, and after analyzing our people work patterns, many of the trends and workplaces in general have been adopted in our worldwide offices in the past four years." The company now works in mostly open plans, nonterritorial space, team setting, and remote work all based on a reduced focus on hierarchy.

Measelle's advice to the design community: "All your design efforts in creating new workspaces for business need to speak to the language of the practitioner. In other words, first and foremost, it is important to understand the business goals of the individual firms that you serve, and then to translate these goals into the kind of space that will drive their businesses in that direction. The solutions that you recommend also have to reinforce the value of the company when they are viewed by others." For Arthur Andersen's facilities, says Measelle, the company must "mirror the firms's image as a world-class businesslike and efficient service provider for our clients. Our clients would receive the wrong message if we didn't strike the right balance between too expensive, grand-museum looks and bare-bone warehouse kinds of operations. We have found that open plans work for our kind of firm…it tells our clients that we are innovative, yet efficient," said Measelle. Arthur Andersen seems to have achieved buy-in not only internally, but also with their external clients. And client approval is exactly what senior management likes to hear about.

Ultimately, when you get senior management's attention, they will quickly want to know what other companies in their field are doing in the way of alternative workplace. Facility professionals will have to prove the case for alternative workplace with benchmarks, other company experiences. Be forewarned: "When dealing with senior management, choose case studies very carefully. What seems relevant to you doesn't always work for the client. We showed a publisher studies from a consulting firm. They weren't interested in conceptual, theoretical similarities. They said, 'Why are you talking to us about consultants when we're publishers?'"said Lisa Cole, associate with HLW, New York, at a Telecommuting Advisory Council Chapter seminar in 1996.

Benchmarking alternative workplace projects in terms of space standards and productivity measures may be difficult right now since the whole issue is rather new and still evolving, but there are still ways to gather information on other best practices. As of late 1996, however, the International Development Research Council (IDRS) decided to take the bull by the horns and launched a new competition called "Best Practices" awards to identify and promote success stories of American companies that are meeting the challenges facing CRE executives. The winners of the 1966 Best Practices awards were Eastman Kodak, Johnson Controls, CLW Realty Group, and BankAmerica. Kodak slashed its occupancy costs by $100 million, BankAmerica (which won two awards) reduced construction costs by $120 million, while Johnson Controls and CLW Realty won for their comprehensive database and servicing to clients, respectively. BankAmerica's second award, interestingly enough, focused on the alternative workplace. Its "Workplace Alternatives" program involved the teaming of the CRE group with HR and technology to design work environments to promote flexibility, enhance employee performance, and provide cost-effective and efficient workspace. In future years, it will be easier to find benchmarking studies to include in presentations of the alternative workplace to senior management (more on benchmarking later).

But once upper management hears that five other companies in the industry are doing alternative workplaces, they may believe then that it's a competitive advantage to be given serious consideration.

The concept of the alternative workplace did catch more and more of senior management's attention in 1996 thanks to a *Business Week* cover story "The Office of the Future." Although the article was brief (the complexities of initiating, implementing, and managing an alternative workplace were left to the imagination), and prompted a few opposing letters to the editor ("Your article is unrealistic," began one letter from a disgruntled reader in Ohio), it was nevertheless upbeat with quotes from high-profile CEOs and stories about Proctor & Gamble, Alcoa, and Mobile's efforts to restructure their physical environments to support new work processes. A few facility and design professionals reported that it prompted a rash of executives to go into meetings waving the *Business Week* issue around the table, insisting that their companies needed to work in alternative offices. "The *Business Week* article caught people's eyes, and that's exactly what I needed!" says a grateful Lynne Lewicki, director of integrated workplace strategies at CIGNA CRE.

What caught other CEOs' eyes was the attitude of Alcoa's CEO, Paul O'Neill. Alcoa's new headquarters won't be ready until 1998, but in the meantime, senior management, including O'Neill, work in panel systems that are located around numerous common areas. O'Neill espoused the joys of working like that, saying he is particularly fond of sitting in the kitchen where he and his staff settle into "huddle" meetings because it reminds him of sitting around his own kitchen table at home.

Sometimes, the simplest way to capture an executive's attention about the alternative workplace is to ask him or her to reach back into a storehouse of memories and try to remember when he or she felt most energized, connected with people, working toward a common goal, and having a good time doing it. Many times the answer will be camping trips with the family, working in community settings, or in O'Neill's case, sitting around his kitchen table at home discussing issues in a most comfortable, unencumbered setting. Usually, the executive will have a sign of recognition that yes, there is a better way to work and communicate. And then, he or she will quickly revert back to business and say—"Well, who else is doing this alternative workplace thing I hear so much about?" Finding the answer to that question usually falls into the hands of the CRE, who in turn, hands over the question to a design firm.

Regardless of where upper management hears about the alternative workplace, most clients look to the design professionals to educate them on the subject of alternative officing. "Invariably, the question of alternative officing pops up when we sit down with a client to do a relocation or new headquarters," says Carl Lewis, principal of Fox & Fowle Architects in New York City. "Senior management *always* asks about the impact of alternative officing on the company."

One alternative workplace advocate, Brett Shwery, the director of interior design at Leo A Daly in Santa Monica, California, says, "When we go on interviews to get new projects, we bring up alternative officing. It's a huge flag, and people are so excited about listening and hearing about it," says Shwery.

But in 1996, he tried to help two clients see how alternative officing would benefit their work process and flow problems, but without much success. "I won't become dispirited in this process. I'm going to keep going into clients' offices and working with them to figure out what's right for them. It's a good opportunity for companies who are really looking for ways to work better, and that's what our job is all about, making people feel more comfortable in the way they work. I'll continue to offer all those solutions. But I won't go in there thinking I have to sell hoteling in every case cause it won't work everywhere," says a determined Shwery.

Only advocates of alternative workplace solutions can deal with the long struggle of sermonizing to those clients who will listen while knowing when to pull back when it isn't right for the client, either. "We are very careful to tell clients that alternative officing may not be for them," says Cary Johnson of The Environments Group. "We are working with a client who has to make a recommendation to senior management about whether an alternative officing pilot study should be conducted. We recognized that based on all gathered information involving cultural feedback, they may not be ready to go forward, and they should revisit the idea in a year or two." Johnson became aware of the conflict when he sat in on a visioning session with a pilot group recommended by facilities. After an afternoon of discussing all the aspects of alternative officing including how that strategy can support work process, save space, and more, a manager in the group raised his hand and said, "Well, where will my office be?"

It was at that moment Johnson knew this particular department's corporate culture would not be able to buy into alternative officing.

FINDING, AND KEEPING, A CHAMPION

Luckily, Alcoa found a champion in Paul O'Neill. From the beginning, he saw the need for better communication and was willing to set an example for others in which they could see the benefits of working in an open plan. We hope he will find it in his heart to persevere as a champion of the alternative workplace when the new headquarters opens, because his employees will be waiting and watching to see if he continues to work in an open plan or if he reverts back to the plush executive setting from which he came. If O'Neill fails to continue his champion position, employees will resent it, morale will spiral downward, and any alternative workplace program at Alcoa will be unsuccessful.

The importance of having a champion is unquestionable for the success of an alternative workplace. Unfortunately, there is the syndrome of NIMBY (not in my back yard!) when it comes to executive management and alternative workplace. In other words, executive managers or CEOs may read or hear about alternative officing and think an alternative workplace program will benefit their company. They are gung-ho at the beginning of an alternative

workplace program, they think all their employees should be working in an open plan, or they should convert to hoteling, or private offices should shrink down by 50 percent...until it comes down to the CEO's office. They think it's okay for everyone else, but not for the CEO. So the rest of the company is told they will work in downsized offices, cubicles, from home or on the road, but the CEO, and most of the executive staff, will maintain large offices. This will not fly with employees who feel they are losing their choice and personal freedoms and being treated like children working in a classroom setting.

Most executives tend to lack true understanding of employee behavior—it's the equivalent of academicians removed from the "real world" and stuck in the proverbial ivory tower. In fact, a 1996 survey conducted by Louis Harris & Associates and Coopers & Lybrand said that 75 of 100 CEOs of America's largest companies don't believe that employees intentionally circumvent corporate policies when they are considered a nuisance. In an alternative workplace, senior management must take off their blinders if the program is to work and achieve corporate business objectives.

The same survey said that companies found to have the strongest internal control are more likely to experience rapid growth, success in reaching overall corporate objectives, and an increase in return on equity. "An organization cannot win this triple crown until senior executives take personal responsibility for internal control and realize that relegating it to lawyers, compliance staff, internal auditors, and chief financial officers is inadequate," says William C. Jennings, a leader for In-Control Services practice, a risk management service at Coopers & Lybrand, and author of the article about the survey (see Jennings 1996).

There are true champions in the world of alternative workplace. Duke Mitchell, former general manager of the Cranford, New Jersey, office of IBM, once worked in an open cubicle, Jim Hackett, CEO of Steelcase, works in a 48-square-foot Personal Harbor, so far Paul O'Neill still works in a panel system, many partners of accounting firms work in downsized offices, and CEOs of Benevia, Autodesk, Prince Street Technologies, BBDO West, and others sit in cubicles, as well. The list is long, but the list of failure stories of champions that jumped ship is even longer.

At one computer company, a vice president of a division refuses to sit out in the open—he remains the only one that sits in a private office, and it

Figure 4.1

A diagram shows the complexity, but necessity, of garnering the strength of a cross-functional team to get an alternative workplace project off the ground.
(Port Strategic Consulting, copyright 1996.)

The Corporate Team

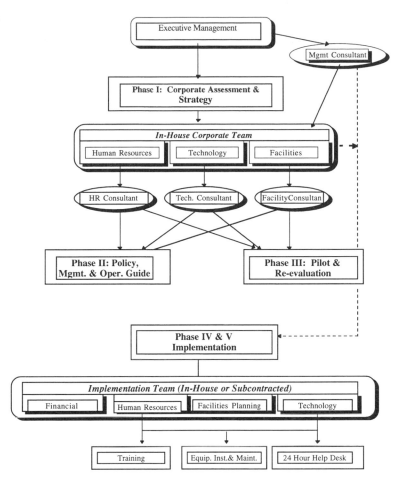

doesn't make the company's CEO or alternative workplace team very happy. There is an alternative workplace team campaign going on to push him out of his private office so he can be a positive example of the alternative workplace to employees who are exhibiting more than a little resentment.

But for those who find it frustrating to talk to a CEO about the new workplace, take heart. James Hackett, CEO of Steelcase, has seen another side of the seemingly hard-hearted CEO. Since building its famous Leadership Community in Grand Rapids, Michigan, Hackett has toured a stream of CEOs through the caves and commons executive work area where Hackett himself sits in a 48-square-foot Personal Harbor (see Chap. 10 for a full case study). "As you dive into the emotions of CEOs, you have to remember that they are making tradeoffs all the time, and when the story is made clear to them, it's easier for them to make a decision like the one we are talking about with the Leadership Community," he says. He doesn't advocate that every company copy the Leadership Community's layout, but they

could learn from the underlying philosophies that led to its birth. "Usually CEOs are embarrassed when they see where I work, and there is a tendency toward reductiveness....They say, 'Jim, you know, my office isn't as big as you think,' or 'Jim, I don't have as many walnut panels in my office as I used to.' I tell them not to apologize for it because it's the way business was organized in America for a long time, but I tell them to role-play with me through a typical day in their working life to understand their work processes and work environment." It's the CEOs like Hackett who will help pave the way for fellow CEOs' willingness to own the new workplace.

STEP 2: FORMING THE CROSS-FUNCTIONAL ALTERNATIVE WORKPLACE TEAM

Once upper management gives CRE the green light on pursuing an alternative work environment, the next step is to pull together a variety of depart-

Design,

facility, and CRE managers will be happy to hear that corporate strategic planning has once again emerged as the management tool

Visioning and Strategic Planning Make a Comeback

of the moment in which strategic facility planning can play an important role if positioned the right way. In fact, corporations that have been conservative in nature are turning to restructuring their operations and renovating facilities in an effort to be a "best-in-class" company on all fronts.

After a decade of downsizing, corporations have **bled** the loyalty out of employees, many of whom continue to expect the hatchet to fall every Friday. Although cutting staff is still a fact of life, it isn't happening with such an intense vengeance anymore because there's barely any

more fat to eliminate. Instead, Corporate America has let the blades dull a little bit and have instead turned to an old friend, strategic planning.

Exactly what is strategic planning, and where does the design and facility professional fit into the picture? In the 1960s, when Harvard professors Ken Andrews and C. Roland Christensen coined the term and the process, strategic planning was a way to link the functions and operations of a company to the way it stood up to its competitors. It quickly became a strategy that companies used, paying far too much attention to simple market share gains. Today, strategic planning has **evolved** into the more holistic, simple way that a company grows itself by identifying, visualizing, shaping, and building new markets. *Strategic planning lets*

managers identify new opportunities to grow into rather than identifying which departments to eliminate. The danger behind strategic planning is that a company may become too committed or enthusiastic in its pursuit of a vision that may never come to pass. So the necessary ingredient that has to be folded into strategic planning is that of flexibility to accommodate midstream shifts—in management techniques, in technology infrastructure, in work processes, and in the physical work settings in which a company navigates this course of growth.

Strategic planning as a corporate tool lost its luster in 1983 when word got out to the business world that new General Electric chairman Jack Welch slashed the corporate strategic planning department of 200 senior staffers because they spent too much time cranking out what he termed as meaningless vinyl-bound reports full of details that never were acted upon. Welch was anxious to focus instead on competitive posi-

tioning and developing future markets. Scores of companies followed suit in the shedding of their central corporate strategic planning departments. Today, planning has changed its course at GE, and those responsibilities fall within each business unit, which presents plans (without vinyl binders) to Welch during day-long planning sessions held each summer.

An article in *Business Week* (see Byrne 1996) emphasizes the fact that the nature and scope of strategic planning have dramatically changed since Harvard professors Ken Andrews and C. Roland Christensen coined the term and process. Although there is still lingo attached to the concept (see "The Rhetoric of Strategic Planning"), a new generation of strategy **gurus** has redefined the nature, scope, and the process's reason for being. "For decades, strategists spent much of their time figuring out how to position products and businesses within an industry. Instead,...strategy should be

ments that will make it happen. Again, it's easier said than done because historically, most corporate departments have kept to themselves, working in a vacuum, believing that nothing they did related to anything initiated by the department down the hall. In the mid-1990s, it became frighteningly apparent that projects—however large or small— needed to be implemented faster, cheaper, smarter, and with more innovation than ever before. So the *strategic alliance* was born, becoming the new in-house buzzword, and one that includes the outside design consultant, as well. Today, all types of specialties and disciplines from engineering to architecture to CRE to HR are coming together more and more quickly as cross-functional teams, luckily, as a way to grease the wheel of the alternative workplace.[3]

The CRE and the collaborating design firm will now begin to partner with in-house departments and develop a cross-functional team or task force that will carry the pilot, and ultimately the rest of the program will roll out through the company from start to finish. HR may already be part of the initial team that helped sell the idea to upper management. And note that in many cases, a company

will have already established a team that sells the program to upper management. Either way, a cross-functional team is critical to the success of an alternative workplace pilot and program.

What is a cross-functional team? It takes a representative from each of the departments in Fig. 4.1.

A NEW REASON FOR BENCHMARKING

If the contrived lingo of strategic planning makes you roll your eyes, the mere mention of the word *benchmarking* probably sends shivers up and down your spine. It was the hot topic when total quality management (TQM) was the rage in the 1980s. Benchmarking isn't passé (nor should it ever be), and it is very much a part of the whole strategic planning process, but it's shifted in its purpose. Benchmarking has changed since the early 1980s when companies began to focus on operational improvement as they embraced TQM taught by management efficiency guru Edwards Deming. Instead of benchmarking findings being used as a measure of how to chop operations, benchmarking studies are exchanges of information between competitors to help one another learn about best prac-

about changing industry rules or creating tomorrow's industries," says reporter John Byrne in the article.

Michael Hammer, an efficiency and productivity expert (described as the modern-day Frederick Taylor) who led the reengineering revolution in the late 1980s when he coined the term and then wrote the book on the subject, *Reengineering the Corporation* (1990), has written a second book to redefine his original thoughts that celebrated downsizing and cost cutting. His new book, *Beyond Reengineering* (see Hammer 1996), talks about the consequences of reengineering and with that, the aftermath. Admitting he was wrong, Hammer disclaims his earlier directives for business improvement by saying that perhaps companies who embraced reengineering did so in a rash way and had "transformed their organizations to the point where they were scarcely recognizable." (It's been said unofficially that 95 percent of all reengineering programs fail because they are initiated for the wrong reasons.) Unfortunately, says Hammer, he chose to include the word *radical* in his definition of reengineering[4] and that is what, unfortunately, "captured and excited the imagination of managers around the world." It's the same danger anyone involved in the initiation of an alternative workplace must heed, for inevitably, some form of it will come up as part of a company's overall strategic plan.

So again, where does the designer and facility professional enter the realm of the strategic plan? "Organizations must include design considerations in their strategic planning. Attempting to reengineer an organization without adjusting the physical work environment invites failure," said Marilyn Burroughs with the Weihe Partnership and Ronald Gunn, a management consulting with the TQS Group, in an article they wrote about shifting work environments for *The Futurist* (see Burroughs 1996). Years ago, facilities and real estate registered barely a blip on the executive management's radar screen. Today, more and more facility and CRE managers are proving that real estate and the workplace can indeed support organizational change and increase productivity, which lead to increased revenue and shareholder value. In the white paper, *An Agile Approach to Facility Design* (1995) written by Rodger Messer and John Glagola of HOK, the authors explain the facility's role within the overall corporate strategic plan: "Make an enterprise assessment to set the corporate resource assets and requirements, and devise a strategic scenario plan through a nonlinear scenario and strategic planning process that anticipates driving forces and their possible impacts on the business (for example, see box on "Sun Microsystems CRE Methodology")."

One conservative company that included a strategic facility plan (SFP) in its overall corporate strategic planning efforts is Mobil. The Fairfax, Virginia, headquarters's new program, called *Fairfax Workplace 2000*, is Mobil's program to reduce costs and create a workplace based on need rather than on entitlement.

This massive 4-year project involves 2600 people, 850,000 square feet over 32 floors, and will entail 4500 moves and 1000 miles of layed cable.[5] Its intent is to save Mobil $27 million annually, reducing churn (churn—a thorn in every facility manager's side—is the relocation of an employee or a group of employees resulting in a changed office environment and usually lots of headaches) and paper filing capacity and reducing the number of office standards as the company moves toward more universal planning. Mobil's overall goal with this project is to become more nimble and flexible as its business rapidly changes—clearly part of the overall strategic plan for the company.

tices of leading companies that excel in their growth and development in bringing world-class products and services to market.

But benchmarking is something that executives almost always deem critical when discussing and making a strategic management decision about shifting workplace environments and work processes. What benchmarking does entail is lots of research, phone calls, and networking with competitors and people close to your competitors. The purpose is to share information in order to fill in the matrixes and present the findings to upper management along with adaptable solutions and processes that fit well with your company.

There are two processes of benchmarking, says Beth Harmon-Vaughan, IIDA, HNTB in Kansas City.[8] One type is the *operations benchmarking process* with its goal of improving a specific process, improving operations, and lowering operating costs. The second type is *strategic benchmarking*, which "takes this to the next level where the studies are used to educate corporate and institutional executives as well as to help make informed decisions," she said in a seminar she gave at World Workplace 1996 about forecasting and shifting work processes.

Though both types of benchmarking processes are used frequently by facility managers, it is the second type, strategic benchmarking, that identifies the

The Rhetoric of Strategic Planning

- *Strategic intent:* The tangible goal that denotes the competitive position a company hopes to build over the next decade
- *Coevolution:* The concept of working with direct competitors to build new businesses, markets, and industries
- *White-space opportunity:* Areas of growth that typically go unnoticed because they don't quite fit with the skills of the company as it exists
- *Business ecosystem:* The webs of microsystems of competitive, yet cooperative, companies that exist in a coevolution
- *Core competencies:* What a company already does well in terms of processes, not product or service
- *Process-centered organization:* A company that recognizes and concentrates on their processes
- *Value migration:* A strategy process by studying where stock market value is migrating in an industry that usually reflects shifting customer priorities[6]

Sun

Microsystems in Mountain View, California, could change your life. In 1995, a computer programming language developed by Sun, called *Java*, didn't even exist. Now it does, and it will probably change the way the

Sun Microsystems CRE Methodology Integrates into Corporate Strategic Planning

entire computer industry does business. Its Java Station, a "thin client," stripped-down PC for accessing the Internet only, confuses most of us today, but it's a device we may not be able to live without tomorrow.[7] While Java **percolates**, waiting to change two decades' worth of computer wisdom, Sun is busy inside its own walls—drywall and virtual—shifting its own work processes in order to keep up with its own rapid pace of new market penetration, diversity in enterprisewide sales and services, plus a diversity in its acquisitions all the while **controlling** occupancy costs through an extensive AWE program that has been experimental since 1996 and will begin companywide implementation of sales offices in 1997.

Old Sun Design Standards Obsolete Due to Business Changes

Ann Bamesberger, Sun's manager of research and planning, hypothesized that Sun employees could potentially tire of the confines of standards-based environments like Sun's prior corporate model. Instead, they might begin "to vote with their feet," walking down the street to other companies where they may find the freedom and creativity they sought within a workspace. For a company like Sun that places its entire future growth and success on technological innovation, it's unacceptable to lose the best talent to a situation that can be easily fixed. "At the moment, we are much more concerned about the **productivity** side which we think will dwarf the cost side by the time we get into some of our research showing us that people at Sun really do want more customized environments. At the rate of Sun's explosive growth, it can't afford the lost time and creativity caused by employee turnover, says Bamesberger.

Sun is clearly a powerhouse in the technology industry. The young $5.9 billion computing

environment company founded in 1982 by Scott McNealy runs on the philosophy that technology shouldn't be limited because of the size, model, and age of a PC workstation. It means that Sun refuses to design and develop independent computing solutions for every customer, but instead concentrates on its **core** set of competencies, which includes its SPARC microprocessor design, Solaris software, and of course its most recent crown jewel, Java. Java is the most recent development that clearly expresses what Sun is all about. It's a language that will be built into every piece of software that will run across every computer platform—one language, one platform—and that means you won't have to constantly upgrade your PC.

But, at the same time, Sun has fierce competitors, yet it continues to stay in the black, averaging a 15 to 20 percent growth over the last several years, with a strong balance sheet with nearly $1 billion cash in the bank. Why? It has a reputation of being lean and mean, an image Sun intends on keeping strong. Not much of that philosophy has changed—it still lets its business alliances broaden market **penetration** to bring new technologies and services to market quicker. But the way Sun does business has shifted. No longer does it primarily sell stand-alone workstations, nor do Sun salespeople and technicians do business only in the confines of

a local geography. Today Sun's business crosses geographical boundaries, increasing the use of its partners and integrators—sure to grow larger with Java—and the company on a whole has developed competencies to make complex sales and become a full-service resource for its customers.

The Alternative Workplace Integrates with Sun's System's Approach to Sales

Though much of Sun's products are intangible, the need for real space remains inevitable.

Sun's AWE sales office implementation program, led by Bamesberger, comes at a prime time when many of the company's field sales offices' leases expire. This creates the inherent and practical opportunity for Sun's business units, totaling 15,000 employees worldwide, to migrate into a smarter, more **supportive**, and less costly work environment that Bamesberger speculates will combine central, satellite, and residential home offices. She's been working to put all the pieces of the **puzzle** in place for a seamless transition since early 1995. To that end, Sun Microsystems has designed a methodology for selling AWE to in-house clients with a focus on supporting the overall corporate strategic plan, by supporting worker effectiveness.

Bamesberger has provided the framework—a methodology, called the *Strategic Choice*—that

implications that a facility has on long-term business goals. For instance, Harmon-Vaughan says this type of benchmarking is important to have on hand for companies who expect to retain the best industry talent, for those bright stars in the labor pool often have expectations of what a work environment should be like, whether they seek out and place importance on flexibility, a private office, or the ability to work at home or they want a facility that offers the best technological infrastructure in town.

Benchmarking results also poise a company to make a better decision about real estate investments. If a company is going to increase staff but hesitates to invest in space, a report on how other companies have handled the situation will help corporate

decide whether they really do need to lease more space, or perhaps they should look toward alternative workplace scenarios to handle the growth.

Harmon-Vaughn suggests the following key elements needed to benchmark:

Step 1: Determine a specific area in the company that needs innovation or improvement.

Step 2: Understand the area's process in detail.

Step 3: Find benchmarking partners with which to share information.

Step 4: Interview people and research as many sources as your imagination can come up with.

Step 5: Analyze and focus on results that are relevant to step 1.

allows each business to get involved with the strategic design choices it has in reengineering its physical workplace to accommodate Sun's significantly shifted business model. However, it's her job to lead those businesses a few steps back to think about what in the physical environment can help them to achieve success. "People get involved primarily by talking amongst themselves and to us about what the setbacks and behaviors are that prevent them from achieving their business mission," says Bamesberger at a speech she gave at World Workplace '96. "We believe that we have put in place a **methodology** with which we can isolate the success factors that lead to output."

What Bamesberger has done is identify a three-pronged approach to implementing and measuring the impact of an alternative workplace:

1. Identify desired business outcomes.
2. Identify key success factors that lead to desired business outcomes.
3. Determine organizational, physical, and technological features needed to achieve 1, and by inference, 2.

Bamesberger believes that finally, someone—namely, Sun—can truly measure productivity as it results from an alternative, new workplace design. Her **matrix** will include all the company's identified success factors that Sun's businesses need to accomplish in order to make money and retain customers—such as customer interaction, innovation, and in-house collaboration—and they will be documentable and **measurable** based on the features chosen to enable those success factors.

To help the field offices talk to Bamesberger about strategic design choices, her team has created a systems approach to AWE that builds what she calls *scenarios*. What are scenarios? AWE scenarios are made from different feature choices within different components that make up the physical environment (see "Basic Methodology of Sun's Strategic Choice Program"). There are different features in a technology component, different features in a physical component, different features in an organizational component (management and organizational practices). So Bamesberger will present choices—or scenarios—by feature. "If someone realizes that a particular scenario makes sense to them because it optimizes for certain success factors, then they have bought into the fact that real estate is trying to help them achieve their business **mission**," she explains. "Then, they are able to buy into associated costs."

So far, real estate has developed three categories of scenarios—traditional, flexible, and virtual—under which a total of 12 different scenarios for different sales activities have been thought out. Using a scale to score the hypothesized impact the scenarios will have on key success factors, the traditional schemes have so far scored approximately 100, flexible schemes score approximately 150, and the virtual schemes score approximately 200 on the impact scale. Within each scenario there are three different components that have attached to it different ways of implementing, training, and costing it out. "What we did was link each one of the success factors to each one of the feature choices, which is then embedded into the scenarios," she says about the seemingly complex program. "We have three live experiments going on throughout the company now based on a reverse engineering of this formula in order to better evaluate these metrics." In 1997, Sun will have solidified the outcomes of each scenario and was in a position to roll it out across the company.

In summary, the traditional work environment clearly no longer works for Sun's new business model. Instead, real estate is working to provide work environments that support a **mosaic** of geographic, industry, customer, and partner organizations that make up a rich blend of individual and collaborative work activities in a variety of locations, all aimed at enterprisewide selling and service. The alternative work settings will contribute to the holistic ventures of Sun, supporting these strategic planning activities while responsibly controlling costs associated with occupancy and technology.

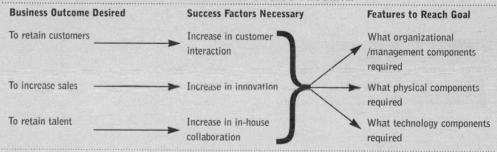

BASIC METHODOLOGY OF SUN'S STRATEGIC CHOICE PROGRAM

Business Outcome Desired	Success Factors Necessary	Features to Reach Goal
To retain customers	Increase in customer interaction	What organizational /management components required
To increase sales	Increase in innovation	What physical components required
To retain talent	Increase in in-house collaboration	What technology components required

Step 6: Present your findings to obtain support for possible shifts in work process or environment.
Step 7: Create the action plan.
Step 8: Monitor and adjust for benchmarking as an ongoing process.[9]

STEP 3: GUESSING GAMES—KNOWING THE NEW RULES OF STRATEGIC FACILITY PLANNING IN THE NEW WORKPLACE

Benchmarking is the beginning to strategic facility planning. According to an industry-related online bulletin board, one designer wrote in a question about data supporting space standards for the alternative office, most specifically for the likes of hoteling and free-address spaces. The response: "There is very little on space standards for the alternative office so if you are looking for a formula, I have no good news for you! Start off with benchmarking and focus groups, but it is not for the faint-hearted or people who find interaction tedious." Clearly, there is untreaded territory when it comes to strategic facility planning and the new workplace.

"Has strategic facility planning changed in the last 5 years? Everything has changed in the last 5 years!" says Joseph E. Valencic, CFM. "The most significant change is how closely we monitor the SFP and the long-range facility plan."

Designers agree that strategic facility planning has changed. "Ten to 15 years ago, designers went into a project to make an analysis, and we counted file drawers and counted pencil drawers and gave the client a quantitative rather than a qualitative solution," says Frank Farrington of Farrington Design Group in Atlanta. "There was very little interest from the corporate side and very little prospecting done by designers until we said, wait a minute, are we helping them operate effectively?"

Planning and designing an alternative workplace—no matter what shape or form it takes—now require design professionals to understand more and more about the clients' businesses in order to offer informed advice on how to align their facilities practices with their business goals and targets. "To implement a successful alternative officing solution, it's necessary to understand how people are really working, as opposed to what we used to ask while programming: How big is the space, what's missing in it, what do you have now, what else do you need, and again, how big is the space?" says Danny Colvin, associate at SOM in New York with a specialty in strategic planning and alternative workplaces.

And clients need help in this area. Here's a true story about a major company that decided to adopt an alternative office strategy. It seems a veteran manager (who will remain unnamed) from Coopers & Lybrand who worked in New York City was asked to reduce real estate costs and adopt a hoteling program for a group of consultants who were moving to new suburban offices. One day, out of curiosity, the manager's wife asked him what formula he used to determine the reduction of desks and office space for his consultants. Knowing her husband and his love of mathematical equations, she anticipated a complex response, a formula full of ratios and other mathematical equations from this numbers-crunching man. Instead, he just shrugged his shoulders and said, "I don't know, I just *guessed!*"

The timing of the planning and programming phase has changed, and it's confusing to both designer and client on many levels. Steelcase's Evett had a conversation with a design principal who was clearly frustrated and in the middle of a competitive situation for a large alternative workplace project. The competing design firm told the client they could develop an alternative workplace strategy for them in 5 days. The fast-track client liked the idea, but Evett and the design principal saw trouble ahead. Perhaps the competing design firm took a cavalier approach to please the client. Maybe the design firm knew the client intimately enough to come up with a quick response. But it takes anywhere from 6 weeks to 6 months (depending on the size of the company or affected department) to understand the client's business objectives, work processes, technology needs, and corporate culture before designing an appropriate alternative workplace. The shortest time frame for an alternative workplace project in this book is the plan by the Consulting and Audit arm of the Canadian government that clocked in at 46 working days to implement a hoteling plan for over 40 people from start to finish, including furniture, technology purchases, and construction.[10]

Have the processes of planning and programming changed in the advent of alternative workplace strategies? Or do executives like the Coopers & Lybrand manager guess the numbers and strategy because they just don't know how else to do it?

For Karen Lalli, a strategic facility planner with the Hillier Group in Princeton, New Jersey, her clients are asking for more design research to be included in the planning stage. "Architecture firms historically did a lot of design research, especially in England, where a space planning firm like DEGW has been practicing this sort of thing for decades," she explains. "There, you analyze, analyze, analyze before you build, but here, we build so we can get product to market tomorrow so we don't have the chance to analyze quite as much." Things are changing, says Lalli, because now clients don't want to pour money into something as fixed as a building, so they are more willing to initiate studies and research, especially in areas where there will be alternative workplace strategies.

During a seminar at an annual IFMA conference in 1992, Peter Kimmel of Peter Kimmel & Associates, Bethesda, Maryland, said that in the 1980s, the SFP was prepared by rote, presented to upper management, then filed away until it was time to adjust the numbers for the next year. The problem, he observed, is "that the 1980s SFP was designed to guide us through situations where the major variable is planned growth," he said. "What we have now, is…*unanticipated* change. In the 1980s, most SFPs had few, if any, portions that dealt with change." Kimmel suggested that today's SFP should address what they think will happen in the first section and what they think could happen in numerous scenarios in the second section.

Designers will argue that their clients' short timeline and desire to keep costs down prevent them from doing anything but generate a formulaic approach to SFPs and space planning. Look at where that approach has left many facilities today—full of inflexible offices, immobile furniture, wasted empty or underutilized space, not enough conference rooms, the list goes on. Time spent really getting to know a client and the company is time well spent. "Planning before AWE involved a conversation with the client that went something like this· I'm the design consultant. If you've got 20,000 square feet and this many people on the floor, you must need two conference rooms. And what's the average size— 10 to 12 people per meeting? Well, then let's do one room that sits 10 and two other smaller rooms to balance out the floor," says Nancy Levy from IA.

Typically, a traditional facilities planning team consisted of the facilities programmer who identifies the organizational needs. The real estate, architectural, design, and engineering professionals would then define and recommend how the physical space should be situated. Then the financial people would give the proposal an eagle-eye view from the bottom-line perspective. Depending on the number of sites the client owned or leased, it could take from 3 months to a year to project a facilities plan for the company's objectives.

To achieve this, the facilities planner would gather the organization's history and analyze the organization's business objectives and business plans as a context for decision making during the planning process. Then came a current situation analysis that took into account space inventory, standards and furniture inventory, and real estate policies.

There are subtle changes in the strategic facilities planning process for a virtual workplace that dramatically impact the way a company and its employees work. In the book, *Workplace by Design* by Frank Becker and Fritz Steele, the authors talk about traditional and new ways of strategic facilities planning for reinvented workplaces. They say the traditional approach is action oriented. An expert-based definition of goals leads to expert-based planning and design, which leads to the implementation of an environment of fair quality and mixed employee commitment. Today what's necessary is what the authors call the "organizational ecology approach." The facilities planning team reviews the company's mission, sets goals, defines themes, and takes into account behavioral objectives that are learned directly from member—that is employee—involvement. That step leads to communicating the initial planning and design scheme to employees with their feedback. Then, implement the plan, still using member involvement, to arrive at a high-quality environment with high employee commitment and buy-in.

HLW SHOWS BAYER THE BENEFITS OF MOVING AWAY FROM A TRADITIONAL PLAN

In 1994, Bayer, the makers of popular products such as Bayer Aspirin and Alka-Seltzer, moved from Pittsburgh to a 150,000-square-foot headquarters and research complex designed by HLW in Morris township, New Jersey.

Bayer already had a set of standards, which HLW's programming team of Leda Pierce and Lisa Cole set out to help the company reduce in size. In the beginning, the CEO's office was a traditional 400-square-foot large space, while other standards ran high at 300 square feet for 10 of the top-management offices, 150 square feet for midlevel managerial offices, and 80 down to 64 square feet for administrative workstations.

HLW created a presentation suggesting the benefits of reducing square footage, even if it was as little as 25 square feet. Though the programming team was hoping to get down to two standards, Bayer agreed to stay at four standards.

What's interesting about HLW's approach is found in the presentation pamphlet that showed six planning options to accommodate Bayer's programmatic requirements. The presentation broke down like this:

Plan 1: A traditional layout using the division's existing standards would result in a primarily closed space.

Plan 2: *Beginnings*: Office and workstation sizes would be reduced, resulting in space savings that could be used to create a pool of common, shared-activity areas to support team interaction. Flexibility to move people around would remain low.

Plan 3: *Looking ahead*: This would integrate a higher level of flexibility by combining two open workstation standards into one size. Space savings could be transferred into team space.

Plan 4: *Breaking barriers*: Flexibility would be high as private offices were converted into partitioned workstations to let more light into the workspace. The standard of a 225-square-foot office would be reduced to 150 square feet, and the remainder of larger standard office space would be transformed into a shared conference room.

Plan 5: *Share and share alike*: This plan would reduce the square feet per person further but would increase team space. 300-square-foot offices would be reduced to 225 square feet, and 150-square-foot offices would reduce to 112 square feet. Cost and time of churn would be sharply reduced since people move, not walls, which results in little disruption.

Plan 6: *Let's work together*: Drastic reductions of sizes of standard workspaces would create a large 5000-square-foot team space.

Bayer didn't want to give up private offices completely because it wanted to retain them to use as an employee recruiting tool. To satisfy both the need to recruit with private offices and the desire to create more teaming spaces, the client chose to combine a hybrid of these listed schemes. What HLW learned from the process was that its conceptual study for

Bayer proved to be an invaluable tool in helping upper management visualize new ways of working, which helped to facilitate a decision.

OBTAIN EMPLOYEES' FEEDBACK EARLY

The most important point to keep in mind during the facilities strategic planning phase, say the authors of *Workplace by Design,* is to "collect information directly from the users of the workplace, as well as drawing on internal and outside experts."

Management, human resources, technology, facility planners, and designers have traditionally avoided talking directly to employees. It's not always easy to get a client to agree to the obvious path that employees' feedback is necessary during planning stages. Heck, it's difficult for a designer to want to hear what the employees want to say—after all, *they* aren't paying the bills, management is. Instead, they feel the employees need to be force-fed plans whether they like it, want it, can live with it, or not.

Becker and Steele discuss one of their own client experiences. An executive realized their existing standard open-plan layout had turned into a "rabbit warren-like maze" and had become dysfunctional. But the executive quickly decided the problem was the furniture and focused on which new system to purchase instead of a thoughtful analysis of what was really going wrong in the use and allocation of space and how that related to its ailing corporate culture. "*Jumping to furniture as the solution avoids these bigger questions that don't have easy answers,*" the authors warn.

Though furniture is a quick and easy fix in the client's mind, it's narrow-minded and short-sighted. What's needed is a comprehensive process of data collection and summary analysis that will ultimately define specifically how an environment will support the way employees work. The areas to be analyzed do not differ too much from the traditional way of strategic facilities planning, but it is the way in which the data are gathered and analyzed that makes the difference. Teams still need to determine the number of people that must be accommodated on-site (off-site accommodation comes later).

WORK PROCESS SURVEYS: THE HILLIER GROUP'S APPROACH WITH OKIDATA

Employees might find themselves a little paralyzed, or just plain startled, when designers ask them to explain how they get their work done. They just aren't used to being asked such questions but rather, resign themselves to the fact that management and a faceless designer decides for them how they do their jobs and what tools they will need without any consultation whatsoever.

When The Hillier Group was awarded the project of designing a new Mount Laurel, New Jersey–based corporate facility for Okidata, the computer company that provides a wide family of printers and fax equipment founded in 1972,[12] the designer and client began the project with the mutual goal of balancing corporate goals and employee needs. The Hillier Group conducted a research study with employees using an Appropriate Officing[13] Work Process Survey designed to ascertain the paces that employees went through on a daily and weekly basis in order to get their jobs done. The results of that study would determine much of the physical aspects of the new environment. In addition, the survey would create a rating matrix designed to pinpoint which elements employees feel are most important to an individual workspace and a team workspace—helpful information when weighing budget outlays.

A two-page questionnaire was handed out to all 300 office employees at Okidata, and 262 surveys were collected 2 weeks later. No one was required to put his or her name on the survey, which made employees a little more comfortable in answering the questions. A random sample of 110 survey responses were put into the computer and analyzed, the results of which are tabulated and shown in the pie charts in Figs. 4.2 through 4.6.

Typical types of questions that are often asked on work process surveys are designed to determine what is required to make employees productive. The Hillier Group divided its survey for Okidata into six sections of questions:

- Function
- Specific work habits (meetings, teamwork, contemplative work)
- Communication and information (staff interaction, what information needs to be accessed)
- Technology and information (what technology do they use now, what could they use)
- Individual workspace (the largest section inquiring about how they would rate specifics such as amount and size of space, chairs, privacy, and lighting)
- Group workspace (how important various shared spaces are to the employee)

Design and facility professionals should rest assured that based on the qualitative comments gathered from the surveys, employees did not request the sun and the moon, but rather simple and useful things such as a chalkboard, laptop, e-mail, new software, perhaps a fax and copier locat-

Figure 4.2 (left)
Okidata staff had a chance to think about what kind of work they practiced daily. Their answers gave the Hillier Group the clues that would ultimately result in a universal plan workstation that could be customlike depending on the type of work the individual was most apt to practice during the day.
(The Hillier Group.)

Figure 4.3 (right)
The results showed that interaction among the Okidata staff is very important to the corporate culture, so that meant workstations would be smaller to accommodate the need for more conferencing spaces.
(The Hillier Group.)

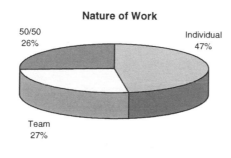

Nature of Work

50/50 26%
Individual 47%
Team 27%

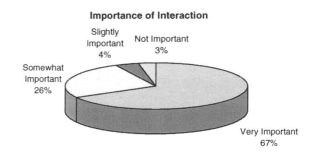

Importance of Interaction

Slightly Important 4%
Not Important 3%
Somewhat Important 26%
Very Important 67%

Figure 4.4

A small percentage of the Okidata staff did not meet with others during the week while most did collaborate. The results of this question gave The Hillier Group a better clue as to how many and how big conferencing spaces should be. (The Hillier Group.)

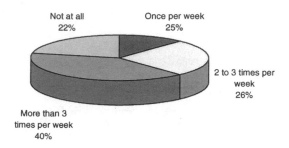

Teamwork: No. of Times per Week

Not at all
22%

Once per week
25%

2 to 3 times per week
26%

More than 3 times per week
40%

Figure 4.5

The answers to this question also helped The Hillier Group to determine how many rooms and what amenities the Okidata team spaces needed based on how long they anticipate using the conferencing rooms. (The Hillier Group.)

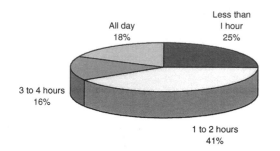

Teamwork: Duration of Meetings

All day
18%

Less than 1 hour
25%

3 to 4 hours
16%

1 to 2 hours
41%

Figure 4.6

Gensler facilitators had each Avery Dennison participant fill this easy worksheet out to give them a flavor of what the workshop would be all about. This type of questionnaire can be used in any work process survey. The simpler and the quicker, the better. (Gensler.)

ed closer to the office. Many of the Okidata employees (including supervisors and managers) already telecommute one or more days a week. At the corporate office, they were largely dissatisfied with the high noise levels and lack of work surface, inadequate storage, and drastic swings in uncontrolled temperatures. *The biggest, most critical, yet simple lesson that designers, facility managers, department supervisors, and executive management can gain from the Okidata work process survey results is that asking users for input on their workspace needs leads to positive, intelligent, productivity-enhancing design solutions. It's absolutely unnecessary to be afraid of what those responses will be. The process will only make everyone happier in the long run.*

But, as most surveys warn employees: Completion of this questionnaire does not guarantee all or certain amenities will be met.

The Alternative Workplace Gives Some Facility Professionals Churning Stomachs

Today's average U.S. company's churn rate runs 35 percent, according to IFMA studies, but some companies report up to 85 percent, says Karen Lalli,

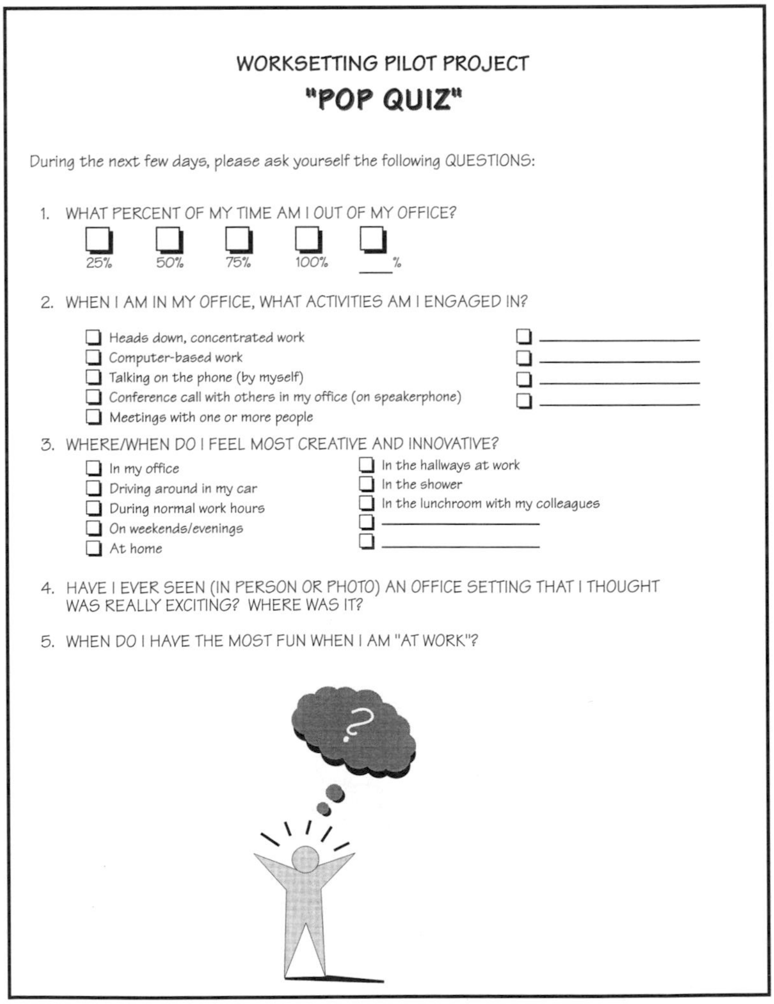

WORKSETTING PILOT PROJECT
"POP QUIZ"

During the next few days, please ask yourself the following QUESTIONS:

1. WHAT PERCENT OF MY TIME AM I OUT OF MY OFFICE?

   ☐ 25%   ☐ 50%   ☐ 75%   ☐ 100%   ☐ ____ %

2. WHEN I AM IN MY OFFICE, WHAT ACTIVITIES AM I ENGAGED IN?

   ☐ Heads down, concentrated work   ☐ _____
   ☐ Computer-based work   ☐ _____
   ☐ Talking on the phone (by myself)   ☐ _____
   ☐ Conference call with others in my office (on speakerphone)   ☐ _____
   ☐ Meetings with one or more people

3. WHERE/WHEN DO I FEEL MOST CREATIVE AND INNOVATIVE?

   ☐ In my office   ☐ In the hallways at work
   ☐ Driving around in my car   ☐ In the shower
   ☐ During normal work hours   ☐ In the lunchroom with my colleagues
   ☐ On weekends/evenings   ☐ _____
   ☐ At home   ☐ _____

4. HAVE I EVER SEEN (IN PERSON OR PHOTO) AN OFFICE SETTING THAT I THOUGHT WAS REALLY EXCITING? WHERE WAS IT?

5. WHEN DO I HAVE THE MOST FUN WHEN I AM "AT WORK"?

Hillier's facility planner. For Lalli, the best method to accommodate churn at any level is universal planning so that when it comes time to change workspace, the person moves, not the walls or partitions.

"Alternative officing is the ultimate churn," says Lalli. "That can be a nightmare to some people, moving people around all the time. They are used to having departments move, but now you have people moving on a daily or hourly basis, and they don't want to deal with it or comprehend it."[14]

Based on the results of the work process survey and interviews with upper-level management at Okidata, universal planning was proposed for the new facilities except for the customer support staff who could work in a smaller workstation.

The results also showed the following observations: Employees were either paper intensive, equipment intensive, or meeting intensive. Although most employees were paper equipment, or meeting intensive at different times during a day or week, one stood out more than the next depending upon each employee. For example, the engineering staff needed two and three computer terminals in their workspace (equipment intensive) while finance and purchasing needed more files (paper intensive), and human resources had more one-on-one meetings every day (meeting intensive). By defining workstation types as functional options, the opportunity for variations within departments was created. This allows for greater individualization in terms of responding to employee needs while still maintaining some degree of standardization.

Work Setting Designs Based on the Work Process Survey Results

The simple workstations proposed by The Hillier Group are all the same size (9 feet, 8 inches, long by 6 feet, 4 inches, wide) but are able to satisfy three different work functions depending upon the components provided within the workstation shell:

- *The paper-intensive space:* The only difference in the paper-intensive workstations is the extra two-drawer lateral file.
- *The equipment-intensive space:* This workstation does not have that extra file, but it does have another laminate shelf below the back surface to clear off the top shelf for more computer monitor space.
- *The meeting-intensive space:* This workstation forgoes the file and the extra shelf, making room for a small teardrop table on casters (36 inches in diameter) and a guest chair in the corner of the space.

STEP 4: SELLING THE ALTERNATIVE WORKPLACE TO MIDMANAGEMENT AND EMPLOYEES

Sometimes it's tough to sell an alternative workplace strategy to a client, but once you've succeeded, employee buy-in is the next big hurdle, and it's understandable as to why this is so. "While millions are energized by the prospects of a collegial, informated workplace and the notion of sequential careers, other millions are hostile to what they perceive as a further loss of personal freedom and the subjugation of their individuality and independence to standards and expectations set by others," says David Pearce Snyder, the lifestyles editor of *The Futurist* (see Snyder 1996). The whole process of buy-in from the top down is full of intangible complexities, but it's a process that absolutely must take place.

THE ELUSIVE ISSUE OF CORPORATE CULTURE

Frederick Taylor, inventor of Work Study and Scientific Management, called people—workers—"units of production" and preached his belief that they should be organized for maximum efficiency. Units of production, however, have feelings, thoughts, ideas, beliefs, and emotions that all tie together to form a web within a company of nonverbal cues called a *corporate culture*.

There is not one definition for the term *corporate culture*, for within a company are layers of unspoken cultures hidden behind departments, staffs, and relationships between colleagues and managers. For example, how do you describe the corporate culture of the new media industry? You can start to get the gist of an industry with grand, sweeping generalizations by saying workers have a different mindset, they are young, burn the midnight oil at work for the sheer act of learning, creating, and producing, and they have nose rings and spiked hair dyed red and green. It may be true that many employees in new-media companies are young, but every new-media company has a different mix of personalities, nationalities, visions, and creative energies. Therefore, you can't assume an industry's culture is by definition homogeneous.

A time-worn company's corporate culture takes on a different tone than in a new company. If you are planning and designing an alternative workspace for a client, you will be changing and dismantling a corporate culture that has been carefully built over time. Understand the corporate culture

Avery Dennison's Beta Site:
Employee Work Process Workshops
As an Interactive Buy-in Process

Now that employees are becoming more involved in planning their own spaces in progressive companies, one of the most innovative ways to help them interact with the cross-functional teams is to conduct work sessions to establish project goals.

That's what Avery Dennison did. When Avery, Dennison, and K&M merged together in 1994 to form Avery Dennison, manufacturers of office supplies, it became apparent that the total of 300 employees would need to find a new way of working as they consolidated all the offices into one headquarters. The company had to face one problem head on: What was the future of storage, binder, and filing products, and would these products be irrelevant in the future? In came Gensler Associates to develop a strategic facilities plan for the 70,000-square-foot headquarters in Diamond Bar, California. Gensler was asked to justify Diamond Bar as the headquarters (HQ) location, develop occupancy strategies for their strategic business units, and explore alternative officing opportunities. After the SFP study, Avery's senior management authorized a pilot project to test some of the office-of-the-future ideas suggested during the SFP study.

The beta project's main goal was to enhance Avery's product innovation process. One marketing and two office product development groups (for a total of 25 participants) were selected to colocate in a new work environment to test out assumptions and ideas. Gensler began to take the employees on a highly interactive research and design journey like they had never been on before.

These two product development groups were critical to the company's growth because any time a new product idea came up, these two groups were the start of that new product's pipeline. Teams simultaneously worked on different projects, so constant interaction between these groups was critical, but in fact, they worked 20 minutes apart from each other in different locations, always traveling back and forth by car to meet with each other. Not only were they exhausted from traveling back and forth, they were working in inefficient, unorganized ways, unable to overcome the

restrictions put upon them in their work environments. To make matters worse, each person worked in private offices that lined long hallways that were single and double loaded.

It was clear that colocation would be the answer for these groups and that the beta site would be highly interactive and collaborative. The beta site would be set up in 6000 square feet. And the research began.

After a kick-off orientation meeting with the participants available to explain what was happening, individual interviews with selected staff were conducted to learn more about work patterns and functions, communication linkages, adjacency requirements, and technical requirements. It was at this point the Gensler team gave each participant a "pop quiz" (see Fig.4.6 on page 104) to get the juices flowing, to get them to think about working habits, something they had never been asked to do before. "It was actually fun for them, but they usually don't think about how they work," says Beth Comsky, vice president of Gensler in Santa Monica, California, and the person who was responsible for the predesign and work process analysis for the project. The next step was to schedule a half-day workshop with all participants to further explore ideas, options, ideal space configurations, and cultural issues.

THE HALF-DAY SPACE DESIGN WORKSHOP AT AVERY DENNISON

The workshop was held on August 15, 1995, at a Steelcase showroom and facilitated by a

three-person Gensler team (Figs. 4.7 through 4.10). The goals:

- Test their cultural readiness to change.
- Decide if they could leave private offices.
- Find out if everyone needed a dedicated space.

Figure 4.7
Although they weren't used to doing so at Avery Dennison, groups worked together to come up with their ideal work setting.
(Gensler.)

The Gensler team admittedly and purposely "pushed them far" over the edge when giving them ideas and direction for their new workspaces during the kick-off orientation meeting. Gensler wanted participants to be ready to willingly experiment during the workshop.

The group was broken down into four teams of six to seven people. Each team was given "tools" for design—various sized and colored paper shapes to denote types of spaces (individual, open teaming, enclosed teaming, etc.). The participants were given 45 minutes to conceptually lay out the space, allocating and configuring the elements on a square foam-core board that represented floor space. Groups were responsible for making determinations about relative adjacencies of private and open space, staff locations, amounts of collaborative space and what types desired, location of administrative staff, and location of support areas (supplies, fax, copier, printers, and mail slots).

Figure 4.8
Each group at the Avery Dennison workshop had to explain to the rest of the participants why they felt their work setting was ideal.
(Gensler.)

Each of the four teams had to describe their team's workspace concept to the entire group. Then, Gensler presented planning options that bridged the gap between the participants' visions and realistic expectations. The design directions were now in place for the participants to vote on a design direction for the beta site.

What they voted unanimously on:

- Since speaker phones are used frequently, they would continue to use private offices.
- They would compromise by reducing the size of private offices from what they were used to (10 by 10 and 10 by 12) to cockpit size offices (7 feet, 6 inches, by 9 feet).
- They decided they did need to have dedicated offices.
- But, they decided to compromise the design of the offices by working in enclosed cubicles with glass fronts for a more visual connection and to entice more communication between coworkers.
- They wanted a "town center" with movable furniture for people to team in ad hoc ways.

The lesson? "If you ask the employees to make a cultural shift, you have to involve them 100 percent," says Comsky.

Avery Dennison Workshop and Beta Site Snapshot:

- Manufacturers of self-adhesive materials used for making labels and other office products
- Three-way merger: 1994
- Employees in United States: 300
- HQ: Diamond Bar, California 70,000 square feet
- Beta site participants: 25 employees
- Beta site size: 6000 square feet
- Gensler workshop facilitators: Randi Impey, project principal; Ingrid Lindberg, project designer; Beth Comsky, pre-design/work process analyst

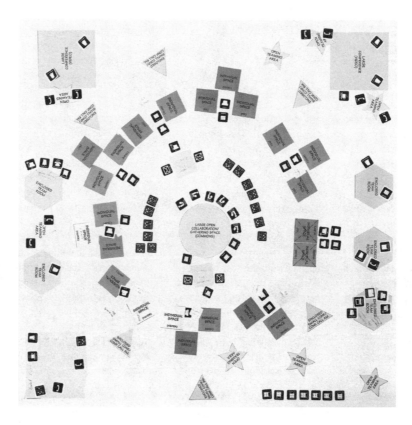

Figure 4.9
Here's a sample of one group's ideal work setting that turned out to look like a pinwheel. (Gensler.)

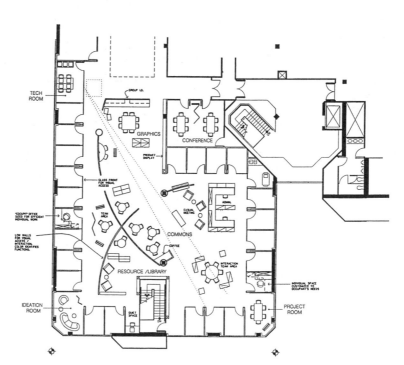

Figure 4.10
Here is the final work setting that resulted from the Avery Dennison planning workshop. (Gensler.)

"Whenever

I talk to a group of people in the facilities profession, they are very interested in hearing how I got people to really listen to me at Cisco," says Marina van

Cisco's War Story: Selling Alternative Workplaces to Resistant Employees

Overbeek, workplace strategist. "People always tell me they have a hard time getting management to **listen** to them about alternative officing, but it can be the employees that cause the most problem!"

During the initial phases of Cisco's New Workplace initiative in 1996, van Overbeek chose to work with the New York City office on a pilot project. She's particularly proud of the work she has done with the computer maker's New York City field office that housed 50 people when the project began, and was projected to mushroom to 200 to 300 people in 1 to 2 years' time. "There, we have a team of people working on this initiative who were made up of people most opposed to the virtual, alternative office," she says. "Over the year, that negative energy has been turned around to be the most creative team in the world, and they've come up with some wonderful **alternatives to the alternatives!**"

Van Overbeek wasn't as cheerful about the experience at first. Planning New York wasn't fun in the beginning, and she has her battle scars—mostly from the employees—to prove it. "We are very straightforward at Cisco, we never mince words, so I have no problem sharing this war story," she starts.

The New York City location was chosen to convert a hoteling environment because it is a very visible, successful location that others in the organization look to for inspiration. (The alternative office would also save $7 million over the five-year lease Cisco had for the space, van Overbeek projected.) So van Overbeek and her team—which included by design the corporate comptroller from Cisco—went to talk to the New York management team, who upon hearing this idea, became skittish and did not favor participating in the conversion plans. After several hours of meeting, the management team was finally convinced, thanks to the comptroller's **urging**, and they acquiesced, admitting the idea of being able to grow in staff but not have to move was an attractive offer and made sense to pursue.

"So, we congratulated ourselves and left New York City to begin planning," says van Overbeek. "The next step was to come back and meet with the 60 associates." Van Overbeek organized her slide presentation, brought with her John Duvivier of Bottom/Duvivier in San Francisco, rented a hotel conference room, and began the show. "They were absolutely livid!" she remembers. "We had this incredibly emotional 3 hours of torture. They screamed and yelled at me. I can look calm, but inside I thought they were going to kill me!"

New York was clearly not ready for change, which was confusing since they weren't even in private offices to begin with, says van Overbeek. The standard at Cisco was a 6 by 8 cubicle, but in New York, space had become so tight, they were doubling up in cubes and "sitting every which way." Most employees used their cubicles about 30 percent of the day, if that much.

"The whole scene was so illogical, but I calmly continued telling them what we were planning to do with Cisco worldwide," says van Overbeek. "At one point they were screaming so loudly I said, okay, I hear you, we will stop, we won't force this down your throats." That's when the management team finally came into the meeting and told them that the new workplace was a commitment and instead of **screaming** and yelling, why not compromise by working together as a team to develop the office space.

Van Overbeek requested that the management pull together a team with the "most boisterous people and a few supporters sprinkled in." She recognized that the loud protesters are usually the ones with the most social power and pull, and she had better work on their **concerns** if the project was to be successful.

One month after that memorable meeting, the planning began. The whole team was ready to work, rolled up their sleeves, and spent an afternoon out of the office discussing what the office could look like. What they came up with was the beginnings of a very **egalitarian** plan designed with an emphasis on teaming.

During one of the meetings about workstation mock-ups, one of the more negative, outspoken members of the team looked uncomfortable to van Overbeek. "I asked what was bothering him, and he said he thought it would always be crowded in the office, and he couldn't see how this space could possibly work for 300 people," she says. Although van Overbeek had explained to him time and time again how the plan would work, the explanation just didn't click for some reason. Finally, she tried speaking of past experiences, rather than the future. "I told him there will never be 300 people in the office at once...that never *has* happened, therefore, it never *will* happen," she says. It was at that point the man looked at her with such clarity of understanding and said, "Oh, now I understand!"

"The biggest **lesson** I learned is the importance of putting the most critical employees together on a team," she advises. "If you don't get them involved creatively, they will only get involved in a negative way. Eventually they will either quit their job or take the positive thinkers and turn them around." Thanks to van Overbeek's **tenacity**, after all the yelling and screaming, the tears and the threats, the New York City Cisco office is happily working in what they call the New Workplace.

---

before tampering with its physical setting, or you and your client will be sorry. If you fail to do so, you will dismantle a corporate culture, destroying with it the upward curve of productivity resulting in a group of people who are now disoriented, disloyal, and who could care less about the newness of the physical environment or, much more fatal, the successes of the company.

CIGNA'S CULTURE CLUB

After insurance giant Cigna's call center in Bethlehem, Pennsylvania, changed into an alternative workplace environment focused on open plans and teaming, it had to deal with some culture issues right away. There was too much noise from people talking outside people's cubicles, others would hang over the 53-inch-high panels, disturbing people on

It's

not Paris. It's not Greenwich Village. But the café—an enhanced, expanded version of the

The Corporate Coffee Klatch Catches on

traditional corporate coffee pot and kitchenette area—is a tool that companies such as MCI in Boston and New York City offices of Bloomberg News, Steelcase, and Comedy Central can use to bring employees together to schmooze, to work, and to foster and spread a positive corporate culture.

But wasn't hanging out around the watercooler once a thorn in managers' sides? Getting caught by your frowning boss in the kitchen while pouring coffee wasn't much fun. Remember back in the 1980s when many corporations with kitchens gave employees free soda and coffee, but the employees had to dart in and out of the area quickly? It was a meeting place of sorts, a small galley-style area where a secretary was bound to casually bump into an executive snagging a soda or two. But in the manager's mind, employees hanging around the kitchen weren't working. They were slacking off, gossiping, getting paid for wasting time, and using the kitchen as an excuse to get away from work. What about those who escaped to the outside the building to buy coffee? How much time that took, and the furor of the boss looking for an employee who had just stepped out to go across the street for a steaming cup of coffee and some fresh air. But, oh how things have changed.

Slowly but surely, companies are setting up new kitchens in the form of coffee bars, food tables, canteens, cafés, and nonalcoholic bars as the new employee watering hole. Companies, such as Comedy Central, call in java masters like Starbucks to set up concession coffee stands within corporate walls. It's all part of today's new workplace.

Why has the contemporary watercooler turned into a coffee bar? Companies have begun to recognize the drawbacks of technology on the corporate culture—employees become mouse potatoes, and they don't get up out of their office chairs to go to the watercooler anymore now that they can efficiently e-mail the guy down the hall! Now companies have to give employees a reason to schmooze, to come out from their offices and cubicles.

At Comedy Central, the coffee bar happened quite accidentally when it filled in unwanted, unplanned space. With a few tables and a Starbucks concession, a well-used 900-square-foot coffee bar was born. But other companies are consciously incorporating into the main street design of their environments well-thought-out, modern-day watercoolers.

But not everyone gets what it's all about. In a letter to the editor of *Fast Company Magazine* (April/May 1996), one Cleveland Heights, Ohio–based reader says in a tirade over the content of the premier issue, but especially over an article on Michael Bloomberg, "There's this guy named Mike who gives his workers free food and makes them work long hours. He has a spiral staircase in his office. How can this help me? Maybe I'm just not hip enough." Maybe this reader is not hip enough to understand that free food is a powerful tool that can be used to build a company's corporate culture while breeding loyalty.

Media mogul Michael Bloomberg explains of his company's New York City headquarters' food court, "I want people to be well fed and satisfied. I want them to be able to grab a cup of coffee with a colleague and hash things out. But most of all I want them to stay here. I don't want them leaving." The formula is simple: Make employees interact and share information. The cacophony brimming over at Bloomberg's is not for everyone, he warns. It is Bloomberg's own way of capturing in physical form his unique entrepreneurial spirit and sharing it with the young hires who are hungry for his spin on the media business (see Hass 1996).

Whatever the reason for a company's installing a coffee bar or café, the employee may now get a complimentary cup of coffee. On the downside, it seems the escape hatch has closed, and jaunts to the corner coffee cart are now just about needless.

the computer. At first they wanted to replace the panels with higher versions. "I suggested they implement a team of champions, and they formed one and call it the Culture Club," says Lynne Kelley-Lewicki, director, integrated workplace strategies, CRE. "It's a group of people, not management, and they started with a list of what needed to change." Now what the Culture Club says, goes. They set the rules of etiquette in the office. "They established the culture in the office—the aisles will be treated like a library zone. And they set up designated areas where people can talk," says Kelley-Lewicki. "Coming up with the ideas had no monetary impact, it was simple to initiate, and people listened."

CORPORATE CULTURE: A PERSPECTIVE ON AGE AND GENDER

Sally Helgesen, author of *The Female Advantage: Women's Ways of Leadership* and *The Web of Inclusion: A New Architecture for Building Great Organizations,* has spent much of her journalistic career examining how women's leadership styles can transform an organization. She believes the model of workplace corporate culture and environment is based on age and gender issues that grew strong in the 1940s and hasn't changed much until the mid-1990s. "One of the reasons office space has evolved this way is that in the traditional industrial mode, the woman's sphere was staying in the home, making the house homelike. A man's sphere was in the office world, and he charged himself to making it most unhomelike, yet, efficient. Most offices were primarily staffed by women; remember scenes from the 1940s where 200 female secretaries sat typing in a big room while one guy sat up above them barking orders? By making the office as unhomelike as possible, men were saying to women, 'Hey, you aren't at home—you're in an environment that you don't control and one which has different values, and we are enforcing that by making this as unlike your home as possible.' So the early offices had no serenity, women had no control or flexibility over their environments. This heritage is strong and it pervades corporate cultures which in turn keep office environments stagnant. But I think the advent of people going back and forth from home offices to corporate offices will break this heritage down. It's inevitable."

WHERE ALTERNATIVE WORKPLACES WON'T FLY

Not everyone is willing to listen to ideas about the alternative workplace. Insurance and accounting firms may seem like the toughest industries to nudge into alternative officing, but because of how they've changed the way they do business, they are more willing to try it than other industries. The entertainment industry is actually more reluctant, which is surprising to most, since they have new-media spin-offs, but not shocking to those who know how the industry works.

"You have to get away from this notion of insurance companies being conservative and entertainment companies being forward. The one factor that divides the two of them is ego," says Michael Beckson of Beckson Design Associates in Los Angeles, a design firm who has many entertainment clients. "Power and money drive Hollywood. Although the industry is full of brilliant, creative people, and they like forward-looking aesthetics, the culture is steeped in power and intimidation. Whoever comes in to take a meeting needs to understand how powerful that person is. And that's why offices are so big and glamorous in that industry."

DEALING WITH QUESTIONS OF PRODUCTIVITY

Measuring how a work environment or work process impacts the productivity of a white-collar knowledge worker has been a thorn in the industry's side for years (see box on "Motorola Productivity Methodology"). Now, the issue is used as a smokescreen behind which managers hide when they don't want to face the work process changes that the new workplace brings to bear.

It's a common misconception that people and communication fall apart when they work off-site. "Our experience (even to our own surprise) is that communication has actually improved because employees are so sensitized to the fact that they are mobile," says John Frank in his article "IBM's Workplace Mobility Program" in *The Total Quality Review.* "Employees are communicating more clearly, concisely, and frequently than ever before."

Too many managers—upper and middle—still fail to buy into Frank's first-hand experience, however.

Unfortunately, there is no good quantitative research so far on the effects of alternative workplace and productivity. There are soft and often self-reported figures that have been documented by companies with small telecommuting pilots. But the more holistic view of an alternative workplace and productivity stems from the answers to the questions that may take 5 years to track: What are the long-term implications of alternative workplace on staff. If a company hotels, takes away physical space and sends people home to work, what happens to the morale of a sales force over time? Has the company retained these employees, or have they left to go work for another company? Can the remote workers effectively communicate with each other (but define what *effective communication* really is)?

Gathering meaningful quantitative research on the effects of an alternative workplace on productivity takes years and requires a complex follow-through. That's why no one is taking on the task. In addition, each company has different corporate values, all of which relate to the many underlying levels of productivity. The people or organization that decides to take on such daunting long-term research will no doubt be heroes.

Until the heavily funded and very patient white-knights-in-shining-armor appear to do this kind of research, there are practical ways to measure productivity for soft numbers. If you don't already have a desktop fax modem, scanner, or much less, an assistant, think about how much time it takes to copy, then fax, a document. Say you need to fax a couple of pages of a magazine article to a client. You get up from the desk and walk down the hall to the copier. One of the following occurs: (a) the copier is out of paper and there is none to be found, (b) the copier is jammed or broken, and you don't know how to fix it, or if you do, it takes another 5 to 10 minutes to do so, (c) the copier is available right away, in which case you jump on it, then jam it with paper yourself, or (d) the copier is in heavy use, and there's a line of people who need to copy piles of receipts for their expense statements. On the bright side, you may bang into some coworkers and have a juicy conversation you wouldn't have had otherwise.

So, somewhere between 10 and 20 minutes later, you have your four-page copy to be faxed to your client. The fax is either near the copier or far, far away from the copier. You get to the fax machine, and it is (a) out of paper, (b) jammed, (c) available but then you jam it, (d) or your client's fax line is busy or they are out of paper, or (e) in heavy use. On the bright side, you may have another important conversation with a coworker, or even better, see some interesting faxed documents left at the machine which you would never have seen otherwise.

Somewhere between a half-hour and 45 minutes, you have successfully completed the fax to your client. (Your client may call and ask you to refax because he or she had a toner problem, in which case you only have to wait at the fax machine again!) Think how much easier, faster, and more productive you would be if you had a document scanner and fax modem at your desk, a process that would take all of 15 minutes tops. Common sense to you. But not so to a top executive who never has to go through this time-wasting procedure.

One design firm developed proprietary software to gather work patterns from employees, then have that information translated into statistical data to present to the CEO and board of a large company that said he wanted to reinvent the working environment. One pattern discovered through employee interviews was the inordinate amount of time spent waiting in line at the fax machine on a daily basis. But the designer could not just walk right into the president and say, "I think everyone needs a fax modem because they spend way too much time in line at the fax machine." Though it is sheer common sense to see that people waste time waiting for machines, the only way to convince a president is through the use of statistics that prove the need for change. In probability, the president rarely if ever has to fax or copy information down the hall at a group machine—instead, he or she relies on a secretary or has a personal fax and copier. (Remember how we shook our heads in pity over how surprised former President George Bush was to discover that grocery stores now have scanners at the checkout counters?)

In this case, the designer did win the case, and fax modems were installed for all. Scanners are now also being installed because the case was successfully made through statistics that people were waiting in line for too long to copy a document. In cases like this, however, benchmarking for productivity is rarely done, and perhaps it is something the designer should push the client to do as a follow-up.

Cynthia Froggatt, a change management facilitator with more than a dozen years of experience consulting on new work directions and strategic facility planning with clients such as Prudential, Mercedes-Benz, AT&T, *The New York Times*, NBC, and Dun & Bradstreet, has held scores of corporate focus groups and has heard the same objections to alternative workplace strategies time and time again. "Issues of productivity are bogus objections," Froggatt says. "People harp and harp on this performance appraisal issue, but I think it's a smokescreen to hide behind to avoid change. Managers know that no one has cracked the code to figuring out knowledge worker productivity, so they say 'aha, let's kill the idea of remote work!'" Froggatt's tactic: Whenever a manager questions how he or she is going to measure productivity of an employee who works off-site, she simply asks him or her how he or she evaluates productivity now, and why would it be any different if the employee works at home a day or two a week? A manager cannot argue with this logic.

Productivity is such a constant point of contention among managers during Froggatt's focus groups that she has divided managers into four levels of what she terms "resistors." Froggatt also maintains that most resistance is "inappropriate" and can be easily changed given the right tools.

- *Level 1:* This is the easiest level of resistance to overcome: managers who misunderstand the general concept of telecommuting. They think it means that every single employee will work at home 5 days a week. Once they learn that telecommuting is a flexible concept and may mean a group of employees can work at home 1 or more days a week, the problem is solved, and this level of resistance is dissolved.

- *Level 2:* This group of managers doesn't understand how their employees work. "Most managers don't even think about how their staff works," says Froggatt.

- *Level 3:* This group of managers simply doesn't trust their employees to work at home and can't see how they will begin to measure the productivity of off-site employees. "This is a popular objection," says Froggatt. "Managers say that things come up at the last minute, and they need to be able to grab an employee by the arm and bring that person into a meeting. 'They always have to be in the office!' So I ask them, well, how many times do they walk out of their offices now and look for an employee who isn't there and who is at another meeting, on vacation, sick, or simply not available for a variety of other legitimate reasons? Managers say, 'Oh, you're right.'"

- *Level 4*: This last group of managers is a "thorny" one, says Froggatt. She describes this person as someone who doesn't believe that the work-family issue is legitimate, a hurdle to which no one has yet to confess. "There are a lot of people, especially in management, who use their jobs to hide from their families," says Froggatt. "So, you say work-family balance, and inside they are thinking, 'Hmmm, I don't want to go home…my kids are on drugs, my elderly mother is moving in with us…why would I or anyone else want to go home? I want to be at the office with everyone else!' Even if this is not a conscious thought, this manager is feeling shaky inside about the notion of alternative officing and doesn't know why." Froggatt says it's often too hard to get these types of people to discuss their family and home life, especially during a focus group where that line of questioning is too personal and intrusive. "You have to somehow get them to see if what they are objecting to are their own problems," she says. Give them a questionnaire that they can rip up so no one will see it. It's a simple tool to help them peel away the objections and in turn help themselves clear up their own issues. Some may finally admit to themselves that they are workaholics, or that they equate showing up for work with productivity, and they don't want to be measured by results. "Alternative officing often brings up the demons we all face at the office and at home," Froggatt observes.

THE NEW WORKPLACE REQUIRES CHANGE MANAGEMENT PROGRAMS

Employees are known to resist change; that's nothing new. No matter how hard upper management wants to believe that office design fully drives employee behavior, they are wrong. Space design is only one component of what drives employee behavior in a company. The rest of the components are complex, but they can be handled through *change management* programs. Management looking for enthusiasm, acceptance, and commitment from employees for an alternative workplace initiative better put a change management program in to place from the start, whether it's for a pilot or a full-blown companywide initiative. It's easier said than done, however.

Change management programs aren't new, either, in light of total-quality-management initiatives. It's just that they aren't executed very well. The scenario is a common one: Company leaders talk about their vision for reengineering, managers then scurry to benchmark, gathering follow-up plans for process improvements, and finally, subordinates are expected to be wide-eyed and bushy-tailed, carrying out orders on those plans with unwavering support and eagerness. Much to everyone's surprise, results fall short, and an unwritten cultural code means that employees look at any future strategies for change as merely a whim coming down from the executive floor, the "flavor of the month" strategy that the CEO must have learned on his trip to Japan.

Unfortunately, the alternative workplace is often looked at by employees as the "flavor of the month." Yet companies with an alternative work-

Methodology for Productivity Measurement from the Late 1980s: Motorola				
	In the late 1980s, Gene Redman, a former (now retired) contract furniture representative for a Steelcase dealer called Walsh Brothers, worked with client Motorola on a methodology that would distinguish how a chair would impact a worker's productivity. Today, the methodology has been refined, and named "workplace performance."[15] The methodology explained below by Redman is a simplification of a very involved workplace performance process.	Redman says to assume, for argument's sake, that a highly trained technical employee makes $20 an hour (it can be much higher than this). Perhaps this employee is extremely uncomfortable in his or her work environment, chair (insert any interior component), and gets up to stretch or take two extra trips a day to the water fountain, restroom, smoke breaks, or to chat with a friend (not necessarily about work), which involves a second employee taken away from work.	It was estimated that employees use 7½ minutes during each of these two trips equaling 15 minutes of lost productivity (and it usually then takes 15 additional minutes to settle down and fully focus on work again). The 15 minutes is one quarter of an hour per day. One quarter of an hour of an employee's hourly rate is $5.00, multiplied by 5 days per week is $25. Multiply that by 26 weeks for a total of $650. Redman surmises that the purchase of a proper	$600 (at least) chair will keep an employee comfortable and reduce the total of $650 of lost time and productivity. In that case, a chair pays for itself in 1 year. A simple formula like this can be adapted to an alternative workplace scenario. For example, $650 worth of the right home office furniture for a full-time, 5-days-a-week at-home telecommuter will pay for itself in 1 year.

place initiative need change management programs to help guide employee buy-in, but it's important to see why traditional change management initiatives have failed in the past.

In an article in the Harvard Business Review (see Strebel 1996) on change management, Paul Strebel, professor and director of the change program for international managers at IMD,[16] the underlying reason most change management programs fail to succeed is that managers and employees view change differently. "Both groups know that vision and leadership drive successful change, but far too few leaders recognize the ways in which individuals commit to change to bring it about," says Strebel.

Strebel explains that upper management sees change as opportunity for new business ventures while employees, including middle managers, see change in quite the opposite light. Some see change as an annoyance to business as usual; others simply fear change for the chaos it can bring into their working and personal lives. Strebel urges senior management to recognize something called the "personal compact." The personal compact is a complex web of stated and implied agreements between employee and company that forge and define relationships. Usually, senior management is unaware of these employee personal compacts that can quite literally make or break any kind of change initiative, including an alternative workplace.

The personal compact has three dimensions: formal (job description); psychological (trust and dependence between employee and employer); and the most elusive part of the personal compact, the social dimension (employee observation and interpretation of whether or not the company practices what it preaches). Frequently, upper management embarks on change while employees are kept in the dark, often finding out about change through the grapevine, which fuels fear, resentment, and misunderstanding. The result is often a form of mutiny in an effort to squash any beneficial change for the company and the employee. The alternative workplace is quite susceptible to this backlash if change management efforts are handled improperly.

That's where change management experts like Laura Compabasso come in. Compabasso, a change management consultant with Progressive Strategies in Los Angeles, California, says the alternative workplace is like an earthquake—"It shifts the ground underneath you; it changes everything you thought about the way you work."

Compabasso helps employees ease their way into alternative workplace. "It's usually the little details that can reduce a lot of stress such as getting policies written up front, getting procedures down pat for booking conference rooms, and making sure everyone understands how to go about getting their share of privacy in an alternative office," she says.

She's also seen quite a bit of crying.

"If people are at the point where they are crying at work, it means they feel helpless and sad," she says. "When I come on to the project, they are usually at the point of disbelief and think 'how did this happen to us?' They feel sadness. So I come in and tell them there are things we can't change, but here are things we can change, and that's what we focus on, so they feel at least they get a shot at trying to change things."

Compabasso sees a lot of problems when a company goes into open plan or universal plan when they were used to being in private offices. People start to feel exposed, vulnerable, and stripped of individuality. "The alternative workplace is dangerous when companies dive right into it without really thinking about their employees' reactions. Managers fail to see that everyone is different and that we all have different needs," she says. "We have introverts and extroverts, and there are even exhibitionists, and not everyone is comfortable together in one big open plan."

Part therapist, part missionary, change management consultants like Compabasso teach clients how to think differently so that they can manage their employees on an ongoing basis. To break through the wall of personal compacts, one change management consulting company, another change management firm, Kaisen in Toronto, developed an assessment tool called the capability snapshot. This assessment tool provides a clear picture of an organization's perceived strengths and weaknesses from the perspective of both managers and employees. The company developed the snapshot in order to help its corporate clients understand how they should implement flexibility within an organization that is used to traditional linear work processes.

Just how easy is it for a company to transition from traditional into alternative workplace? According to one designer, Brett Shwery of Leo A Daly, the more established a company, the easier it is to transition into an alternative workplace. That's a surprising statement. Why? Traditional and established companies are already used to working in one way, and they already know their culture well. "A new company has a harder time working itself into an alternative office," Shwery says. "Typically in a new venture, employees are coming into the firm at a time of explosive growth from all different backgrounds from all over the country. They come from working in all different kinds of offices. There's no real culture yet, just a lot of different cultures coming together. They need time to understand each other as a company, and as fellow employees. It's easier to give them a traditional office environment that they are able to change into a more flexible one once they get to know themselves."

THE NECESSITY FOR CORPORATE COMMUNICATIONS PROGRAMS

Compabasso says that companies that do well in their bottom line have a really high percentage of employees who feel well respected in the company. Though it seems like common sense, there are too many companies that keep employees in the dark about new workplace plans and that can do an extreme amount of damage to morale. Compabasso remembers one particular client who handled the whole alternative workplace move rather poorly. The company decided to bring people into open plans, out of their private offices. But employees weren't told about this open-plan strategy until a matter of days before the move. "The employees were baffled. They expected to move into new private offices," she says. "They felt wounded—I had people telling me they had worked there for 10 years, and they felt so disrespected. It was awful." Because of the debacle, employees were compensated with more amenities, such as a technical library. The lesson is that open, direct, and constant communication is vital to employee buy-in for the alternative workplace.

There are a variety of ways to communicate the increments of progress of a conversion to alternative officing so that all the employees are kept up to speed and in the loop. "We were hot and heavy into alternative officing pilots, adjusting and evaluating every step of the way. By time we get the next group

out, we've already adjusted from the prior group's experiences," says Brenda Laffin, Southern California Edison at an Interplan 1996 seminar. "What I'm glad we haven't done yet is print up all this great literature because I'd hate to spend all this money to print something, then reprint it when something changes. So we do most of our training and presentations with low-budget color prints or power point before we actually go out and publish everything in final form."

The American Bible Society in New York City, a multimedia publishing company, has embraced teaming for its newly renovated headquarters. This is a story of initiating bottom-up buy-in and participation. The American Bible Society has town hall meetings that are mandatory for all 350 employees, led by the president who is championing the teaming effort. The monthly meetings last for about 1½ hours, enough time to disseminate information. What the publisher knows from these town meetings is that they don't want to telecommute, even though that was a potential strategy.

TRAINING FOR ALTERNATIVE WORKPLACE CHANGES

"The most consistent theme found in the initial research for implementing a mobile workforce is that projects fail or succeed in proportion to the amount of mandatory user education," says John. F. Frank, business leader for IBM's Workforce Mobility unit, as he wrote about the process in an article for *The Total Quality Review* (see Frank 1995).

To teach employees about its new Workforce Mobility program (the mandatory program to reduce occupancy costs and increase productivity through worker mobility and technology that was rolled out to IBM in the early 1990s), IBM initiated an online mobility news service for employees that included an e-mail box for questions. Town meetings followed where a local implementation team gave an overview of the roll-out process.

AT&T's School of Business to the Rescue

The AT&T Virtual Workplace Educational Series was designed to help business leaders, project teams, managers, and employees to better understand the issues, opportunities, and challenges associated with the alternative workplace. The series is layered in three tiers. The first tier explores the concept of the virtual workplace including telecommuting. It's designed for anyone interested in exploring an alternative workplace.

The second tier is the design and implementation of an alternative workplace for project managers and project teams involved already in preparing an alternative workplace. Courses include "defining and designing the virtual workplace," "the business case," and "implementing the virtual workplace."

The third tier is strictly for managers and employees. The courses explore the operation of an alternative workplace, and prepare managers and employees to effectively manage changes and work processes.

The

special language used to describe space spawned by alternative officing can illicit responses no

Be Careful What You Name "Alternative Work Settings"

one could have imagined, in part because of a corporate culture's nonverbal **cues**. Though it may sound hokey to even name an area, whatever name is chosen does have an effect on the way in which it's used...or not used by employees.

Take for instance the perceptions employees have about the term *lounge*. In the New York City offices of Andersen Consulting, GHK designed a space with soft seating, carrels, and phones they coined "the lounge." But it's no longer called "the lounge" because it was perceived to be a "goof-off" area. The space, now used without hesita-

tion, was renamed "the study."

Another type of space in the GHK–Andersen Consulting installation in New York City, originally called the "phone booth" is now termed "kiosk" for similar reasons—one reason was that no one wanted to be cooped up in a "booth," and the other reason was the **perception** that phone booths were supposed to be used to make personal calls.

The same thing happened in downtown New York City in the Deloitte & Touche offices designed by The Hillier Group. A large area with soft seating that looks like an airport lounge, and is appropriately called "the airport lounge," has gone unused by employees. There are probably several reasons for this. First of all, consultants spend way too much time in airport lounges and don't have the inclination to do so when they are in the office.

Second, the perception of what takes place in an airline lounge is not one of hard work but soft work—reading, having a cocktail, etc. The third issue might be that there isn't a coffee bar in the space, an amenity that might draw people into the area for quick encounters with colleagues or ad hoc meetings.

At TBWA/Chiat/Day in New York City, a wooden "phone booth" that was supposed to be used for private calls was dubbed by employees as the "outhouse" and subsequently goes unused by staff because of its **connotation**. And Laurie Coots of TBWA/Chiat/Day warns that naming a space an "individual study carrell has a whole lot of baggage attached to those words."

At the NYNEX installation in New York City, Rick Folke, design director of HOK, has observed quite a number of idiosyncracies of employees who work in this free-addressing environment. HOK provided phone booths for people to use for private conversations, but no one is using them. Instead,

people will take their phones into project rooms, shut the door, and make a private call in there, says Folke. "Maybe they aren't using them because if they go into the booths, others will think they are calling their boyfriends or girlfriends, and it's culturally frowned upon to do that," says Folke.

On the other hand, in the NYNEX space there's a soft-seating space called "the living room" next to the phone booths, and people use it often for impromptu meetings. Similarly, the term "living room" hasn't deterred anyone from using the space for quick meetings and coffee breaks at the Prince Street Technologies headquarters outside of Atlanta. Perhaps the term *living room* is accepted by employees because living rooms at home can be spaces in which to get into some very deep conversations on important topics (think of cocktail parties where so much information is passed back and forth), so therefore, a type of collaborative work is being accomplished in that **context**.

The first day of the Workforce Mobility program, training began with the deployment of a laptop. While the employees were in class learning laptop software, a team was collecting existing desktop technology and assets. Once new equipment was distributed, employees trained, and business processes overhauled, it was then time for the employees to cut the apron ties and vacate their permanent desks or offices. The second day of training, telephones were removed from the desks, and as Frank says in his article, sometimes the desks were removed during the second day of training.

Telecommuting expert and consultant Gil Gordon realized the need for a training tool for virtual office workers and their managers. He visited three companies, Steelcase, Fleishman, and Ernst & Young, to find out how they trained employees to work in alternative workplace environments. The purpose of the video is to "show you how to do a virtual office the right way the first time. How to avoid making mistakes that can lead to serious consequences such as breakdown in communication, confusion, fallen morale, decreases in productivity and performance, and eventually customer dissatisfaction."

In the video, Gordon offers six steps in training the alternative workplace employee and manager:

- Managers should acknowledge concerns and know they are legitimate.
- Employees should manage and deliver results.
- Communicate effectively in monthly face-to-face meetings.
- Employees should establish boundaries so the home office doesn't become a 24-hour office.
- Employees should maintain a separate workspace.
- Teams need to schedule productive time together.

STEP 5: ROLLING OUT ALTERNATIVE WORKPLACE MODELS TO ALL BUSINESS UNITS

When a pilot is up and running, smooth and in transition for the moment, and it has become a pilot that other division or business units (BUs) are looking at for their own potential impacts, the pilot has then become a model for the company. Implementing models in a variety of areas in the company comes with its own set of problems.

Just

when it looked like the design industry was ready to crawl into a hole, shrivel up, and be listed in

A New Dawn, a New Role for the Designer

history books as an extinct occupation, the bottom of Corporate America fell out (again). Sure, there was not a lot of building going on, but there was a lot of corporate moving, morphing, and scrambling as companies took a hatchet to employees and budgets. If one manager and chief bottle washer talked to the other, they echoed in the empty space. They needed the designer to design scaled-down offices for bare-to-the-bone staffs. They needed their facility planner to strategize them out of this mess. Though some have realized this more than others, there are executives who make it their life mission to follow every management trend that comes along, including the one called "reducing real estate portfolios and occupancy costs."

So design and facility professionals can embrace these new workplace strategies as an opportunity, or they can fear it as the end of the world as they know it. But embracing these new opportunities takes the vision of both a designer and a client.

Design firms that look at alternative workplace strategies as opportunity for new business have created divisions and forged different directions. Those design firms have true believers of alternative workplace solutions spearheading these efforts. After all, there had to be some way to find new opportunity. With the demise, for the most part, of the trophy building and with the overabundance of new office space—in New York City alone only 8 million square feet of office space was built in the 1990s versus 53 million square feet built in the 1980s (see Gross 1996)—design firms turned to renovation work, often involving the restructuring of a floorplan to hold double the amount of people it was originally built to accommodate.

"I think architects need to become part of the business team that is making the decisions. I'm not going to hire an architect and say to him or her, here, go put a team together and figure out what it is I need as a client. I'm an architect within my company, and I can articulate what it is that's going on in my business; then I can have a meaningful dialogue with an architect who I will hire from the outside. And I need an architect who can write, and I need an architect who can analyze numbers, and I need an architect who can look at it from my perspective—we have a business to run, we have a real estate to run, and it changes every day. I'd like a list of architects out there with that vision who can get the information, help keep our information together, and get us into the future as our plans change," said Tina Facos-Casolo, program manager, tech support, RE/site operations, IBM, at a seminar talk about the virtual office held by the AIA in 1995. What Facos-Casolo says goes for any design firm, as well.

Sometimes, a business-unit manager will hear that there's an alternative workplace initiative (telecommuting, hoteling, etc.) in the company, want to implement the program in his or her unit, call up the point-person for alternative workplace, and want to hear more about alternative workplace for his or her department. The smart alternative workplace point-person will tell the manager right away and up front during the initial phone call all the negative issues and potential problems of an alternative workplace. If the manager says, "Oh, okay, forget about it, it sounds like it wouldn't work in my department," then that business unit is clearly not ready to switch over to an alternative workplace. If the manager says, "Oh, okay, I see there are many issues about an alternative workplace I don't like, but we still need to work differently, perhaps cut down on real estate, so please come talk to me," then there's a good chance an alternative workplace pilot will be born.

The most perplexing question companies have to ask themselves when it comes to rolling out pilots is whether or not to first dispose of real estate and then send people virtual, or first send people virtual and then dispose of real estate, or do you do it simultaneously? That's the question Dan Accrocco, senior project manager for NCR's CRE division, asks based on his experience implementing a company-wide, nationwide alternative workplace program.

Accrocco's senior management thought it would be more important to first get people to work remotely so they could learn to be productive with new equipment. It was expected that by June 1996, everyone would have had their training, equipment, and home office set up regardless of the status of the unit's real estate lease.

That mandate caused a lot of problems for CRE. NCR sold their Birmingham facility but had no replacement plan. They were left with a bunch of irate people in Birmingham who were left without an office, without communications, and without equipment. In St. Louis, NCR disposed of property for a smaller hub, but the employees received their training right on top of the move. It meant that employees left a permanent desk and office to work in a home office and hoteling environment without warming up to the new work process. As a result, they went out into the field "a little green," says Accrocco.

In Atlanta, all aspects of scheduling from real estate disposal to training for remote work turned out well for NCR. Those employees were virtual before the facility was restacked, which gave them both a home office and a core office with which to

A little thought on an alternative workplace and design fee structure...

Traditionally, space planning is based on a square-foot price, says designer Marilyn Farrow at a 1996 IFMA conference. "That's

Fee Structure for Planning and Designing the Alternative Workplace

not necessarily the best thing if what you're after is a hoteling environment where I will have 50 square feet per person, not 250."

Farrow suggested that pehaps in planning an alternative office, the designer's fee structure should be changed and be built on a head count. "If I can accommodate the functional needs of 300 people in a small space, maybe our contracts and our RFPs should be focused on head counts instead of square footage," she says.

Firms Walk Their Alternative Workplace Talk

Design is almost always a balance of collaborative, face-to-face client and individual heads-down work. So it's easy for designers, real estate, and contract furniture manufacturers to embrace and understand the new workplace. It helps to walk a mile in their client's shoes. A small, but growing sampling of firms that live in nontraditional work-

places are highlighted below:

• Herman Miller announced that 30 employees will work from home in 1996 to experiment with telecommuting in order to reduce occupancy costs, retain talent, and increase productivity. (It now has a company-wide telecommuting program.)

• The Switzer Group cut back on its office space, and CEO Lou Switzer reduced his office by 50 percent when the design firm moved from Broadway to Fifth Avenue in New York City.

• Steelcase continues to experiment with all kinds of alternative officing including its Leadership Community, profiled in this book.

• Haworth redesigned its corporate showroom to incorporate all kinds of alternative work settings for visiting clients as well as employees.

• The Corcoran Group in New York City asked two low-produc-

ing agents to work from home, and today, the two are among the real estate broker firm's top producers (see Denitto 1996).

• Prudential MLBKaye International Realty also has 25 of its 100 agents working from home, offering some of its highest achievers a 10 percent increase in commission as an incentive to do so (Denitto 1996).

• The Houston office of HOK has launched a living laboratory that incorporates alternative officing concepts such as nonterritorial and remote work. The 1900 square feet of space houses the Consulting Group. "HOK's officing lab offers clients who haven't done their own pilot a place to come and kick the tires," says Steven Parshall, SVP and director of Houston's HOK Consulting Group (Fig. 4.11).

make a smooth, slower transition into remote work. Accrocco believes a grace period for employees who are going virtual is necessary in order for them to understand the environmental changes going on in the company and within their own lives.

NEW SPECIALISTS IN THE NEW WORKPLACE

A handful of design firms are hiring away management consultants and folding them into staff positions in order to help the firms speak the same language as their clients in presenting new space strategies as they relate to business objectives.

The STUDIOS design firm in San Francisco hired a former McKenzie management consultant who also happens to be trained as an architect. "We are attracting clients who want to approach projects more strategically," says Erik Sueberkrop of STUDIOS. "It's not easy to convince a client to let a design firm in on the upper-level management meetings. They aren't used to that, and that's why we hired someone from McKenzie because her word helps us a lot on that kind of level."

It was sheer luck that STUDIOS found a management consultant–architect. Other firms have tried the collaboration route and found that management consulting firms aren't interested in partnering with a design firm. Design firms find that management consultants are really scratching the surface when they do research for clients on this kind of officing. "They come in very early and do much more in-depth studies of how people work, follow them around, and make recommendations to improve productivity and work analysis," says Alfonso S. D'Elia, AIA, president of Mancini Duffy. "Management consultants charge a lot of money right up front, so working with a design firm doesn't interest them. There's not enough money in it for them, our billing rates are much lower than theirs, and there's liability in what we do, there's no liability in what they do."

Aware of the need to diversify, Mancini Duffy developed its own in-house management consultant department instead of relying on outside management consultants. Mancini Duffy launched the Mancini Duffy WRG (WRG stands for Workplace Research Group). Douglas Nicholson, president of Workspace Research Group, collaborates with Mancini Duffy WRG.

"Several years ago we felt the need to align ourselves with someone whose specialty is something different than interior design and architecture," says D'Elia. "What WRG brings to the table are behaviorists, social scientists, people who study work habits.

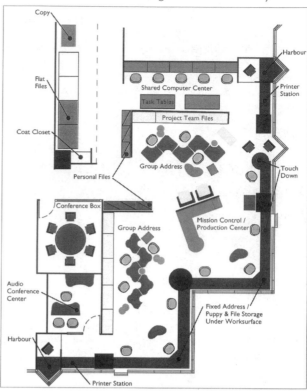

Figure 4.11
HOK's Houston office practices alternative officing in its newly designed "officing lab" of activity settings. (HOK.)

By forming a group we felt that we were servicing our clients at a much different level, getting in there earlier, and developing an alternative office."

Another consulting firm, @WORK, takes the alternative workplace and all its implications and brings it beyond the realm of the corporation out into the community. @WORK was established in 1995 to not only investigate the alternative workplace but to investigate how the changing nature of the workplace is having a significant impact on communities and their infrastructures. The group was founded by five principals: Franklin Becker (director, International Workplace Studies Program, and professor, Cornell University); John Holey (president of Holey Associates); Michael Joroff (director of development, MIT Department of Architecture); Steve PonTell (director of LaJolla Institute and formerly director of the Center for the New West); and Van Romine (director of the Institute for Telework, Center for the New West). This group of vastly experienced professionals is involved in fascinating projects that have far-reaching implications above and beyond the scope of the changes that occur within the walls of a workplace.

@WORK consultants, relying upon the depth of its experience, is currently working on projects including Marriott International on a virtual work project for traveling executives (short-term shared-office amenities aimed at retired executives) and a national workplace strategy for the district offices of the Internal Revenue Service. The Marriott project could allow a population of baby-boomers to continue working as consultants well past retirement in environments that partially parody the corporate office and the home office, a new level of comfort and efficiency that has not been before explored. As for the IRS project, we can only cross our fingers that pushing the IRS into new work patterns will force the home office taxation laws to change for the better.

As for @WORK's urban planning projects, John Holey comments, "We are discussing workplace-of-the-future issues on a whole other level, bringing it into the community, starting dialogues on how communities can begin to structure themselves to accommodate the changing nature of how people work, and that includes policy and infrastructure changes."

NEW ROLES FOR THE FACILITY PROFESSIONAL

"One minute facility professionals are being told to outsource, the next minute they are told to do alternative officing," says Heidi Schwartz, editor-in-chief of *Today's Facility Manager*, about the way facility professionals are handed down charges from upper

Brett

Shwery, director of design at Leo A Daly in Santa Monica, California, is an alternative work-

One Designer Shares the Frustrations of Educating Clients on Alternative Workplace

place advocate, and he spends a lot of time **educating** clients on the benefits of alternative officing. Recently, the behavior of two of Shwery's clients—both companies with work flow and process problems made worse by barrier walls between employees—made him realize that executive management has to be treated with kid gloves when it comes to **pitching** the alternative workplace.

Client 1: One family-owned business of 100 employees was used to working in a "chopped-up floor plan with a rabbit warren of cubicles," making office communication next to impossible. Over time, employees had naturally

become territorial over their office domain. From top down (except for the owner), this company felt it was ready for an alternative workplace. In fact, the CFO brought copies of *Business Week's* cover story, "The Office of the Future" for everyone in pre-planning meetings.

It looked like a good start to an alternative workplace until team meetings to discuss square footage for staff levels started to bog down the process. "It was downright **laborious**," says Shwery. "They started to say, 'Well, Sally has been here for 15 years, but Anne has been here 8 years, and both are secretaries, and in the new plan they wouldn't be in offices, and I don't know, she'll probably quit.' They ended up agreeing to open plan for everyone but they were still **arguing** over who gets another 5 square feet."

What the exercise did for the

company was to really open up their eyes to how they run the company. In most of the meetings, executives didn't want to answer questions in front of their colleagues. "I'd get a lot of **chuckles**," says Shwery, as a nervous response to a question they would rather not answer. "I'd say things like 'Well, the way I see your job function is that you and your secretary should be in the same office.' They'd look at me with their eyes roving back and forth to the other executives who were all looking at each other," remembers Shwery.

Shwery remembers asking them if they would consider "temporal space." Their president was in the office so little, he asked if they could use the usually empty office for meetings. "They **panicked**," says Shwery. "I was thinking to myself if I were the president of that company and there were 400 square feet of real estate that could be used by five other employees that were really working hard for me, I'd turn it into the conference room. I tried to convey that kind of thinking to them. And a lot of them nodded their head and said, 'The guy is

making sense—he's not stupid.'"

Unfortunately the president nixed the notion of alternative officing. Because the company wouldn't accept any alternative officing solutions, instead it moved to another larger facility. "It's **expensive** to move from the cost of new facilities down to the cost of reprinting of packaging, letterhead, and business cards, all because their culture was inflexible and unable to look at processes from which they would benefit," says Shwery.

Client 2: In another project, Shwery spoke to the CEO and CFO about their concept of alternative officing. "To me, an alternative workplace is **anything different** from an office with a door and a secretary sitting out front," says Shwery. "Their concept of an alternative workplace was about getting a conference area in the CEO's office." Another executive couldn't wait to see what alternative workplace Shwery would come up with for the company while another executive only wanted to know how close he could locate his secretary to his office door.

---

management. "They have no choice but to be reactionary. They are listening to upper management's joke, waiting to hear the punchline, when they realize they have to provide that punchline…or else."

The term *facility management* came into existence around 1979, but its function has been around forever. For far too long, the facilities department was considered a nuisance group, a service provider, and that's all. No longer is a facility manager solely called upon to adjust the temperature in someone's office. Today's FMs are professionals with backgrounds in engineering, architecture, design, finance, purchasing, or administration.

Because of the hasty mandates from the executive suite given to facilities professionals, progressive FMs have been able to shove one foot firmly in the door to become more closely aligned with senior management than ever before, increasing their professional recognition and becoming more visible to decision makers to help them see the difference facilities can make within the company. Unfortunately, it's not a bed of roses. At the same

time CRE struggles to improve their business acumen, companies continue to see the downsizing of facilities management staff just as executive management sees the importance of facilities to productivity and the bottom line.

In a book written by Citicorp's Stephen Binder, he says, "The facility management function exists in an organization to contribute to the bottom line profitability of each business unit through increased efficiency and reduced costs in operations, space rental, and ongoing fixed costs" (see Binder 1989). But in less than 10 years, the facility management function is evolving to become much more than that of policing fixed costs. It is now becoming a tool for companies to use to reach their corporate objectives that go way beyond reducing operational costs. The facility management can support the retention and attraction of talented labor, the initiation of in-house collaboration, and communication, and it can be the means that allows employees to work closer and more efficiently with their customers.

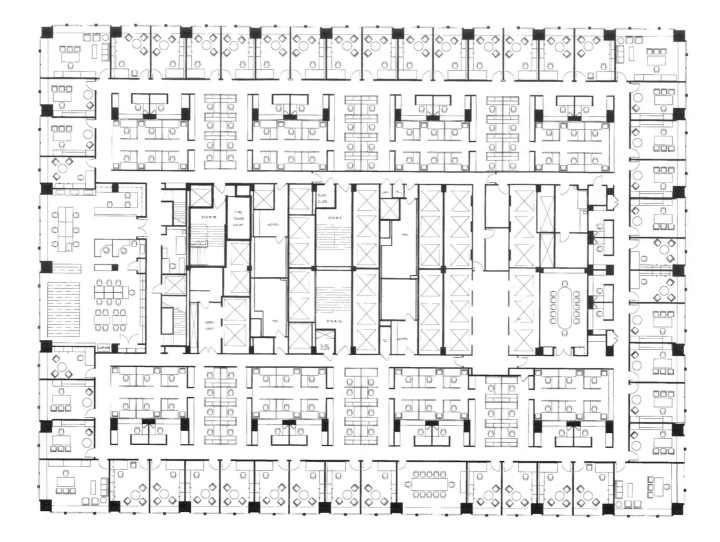

Figure 4.12
This is a floor plan Mancini Duffy planned and built for a major consulting company in the mid-1980s. The perimeter locations, except for the two conference areas, represent dedicated, private offices. (Mancini Duffy.)

Many facility and real estate professionals are seeing the benefits of understanding their own company's business processes and overall objectives. "I was intrigued by IBM's process behind its Workplace Mobility program," says Bruce Lanyon, real estate manager for Amdahl, talking about the time he spent with IBM when Amdahl was implementing its own alternative workplace program. "All the people I met with from that program were from operations....There wasn't one facility person. It really drove home the fact that if a facilities person is not involved on the cutting edge of workplace transformation, you will get left behind because someone else in the organization will pick up on this and go and do it."

In fact, there is a real estate and facilities side to the Workplace Mobility program. Tina Facos-Casolo, program manager, tech support, RE/site operations, is very much a part of the cross-functional Workplace Mobility program team. "I'm a strategist," she says of her position as in-house architect and project manager. "I've been through

the downsizing, so I don't sit around waiting for things to happen. I become involved."

The real estate team today is also looking at how to maximize the buildings IBM already has a commitment to as a long-term tenant or owner. An IBM employee since the early 1980s, Facos-Casolo, an architect, has seen her organization go through its ups and downs, changing its strategy for the better. "I remember when junior designers helped IBM executives pick out art for their offices," she says. "We don't buy art anymore, we don't buy new furniture, but what we do is revamp the way we look at space."

One more thing that Facos-Casolo is hoping to get involved with is a home office furniture policy. IBM has been taking product from the corporate office home, or going to superstores to make their purchases, a concern for Facos-Casolo. For architect Facos-Casolo, her roles prove that there is no diminishing the value of what real estate services bring to an organization. Today, about 20,000 of IBM's 118,000 U.S. employees work from

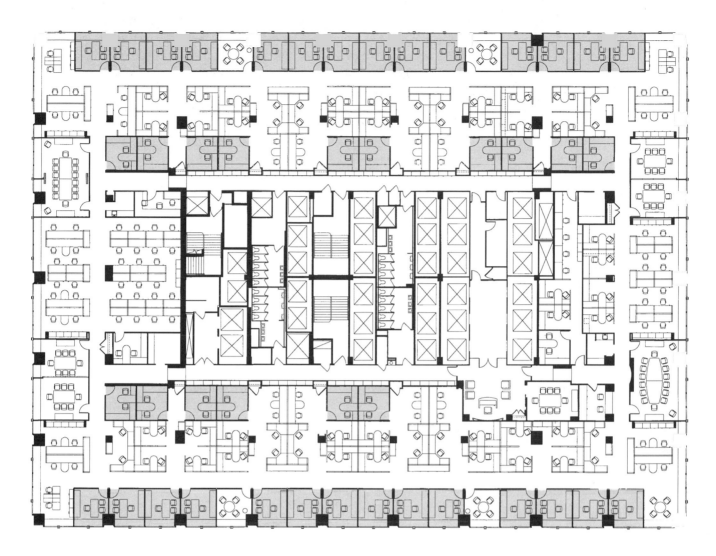

Figure 4.13.

Fifteen years later, the client (who asked to remain anonymous) asked Mancini Duffy to reengineer the same space but to fit in 40 percent more people than the original floor plan called for. Mancini Duffy applied to the new space the same budget it used 15 years earlier, resulting in more conference and teaming areas, and included a raised floor everywhere for optimum flexibility. The gray in the new workspace illustrates the decrease of dedicated, private offices. The design firm uses the two plans in comparison as a powerful selling tool for the alternative workplace. (Mancini Duffy.)

home, from customer sites, or in other remote sites.

USING BEFORE AND AFTER FLOOR PLANS TO SELL THE NEW WORKPLACE CONCEPT

Although this major professional services firm did not want its name mentioned in print, the floor plan from the early 1980s compared to the floor plan from the mid-1990s, both designed by Mancini Duffy, prove to be a powerful tool in selling the concept of the alternative office to prospective clients.

When Mancini Duffy designed the space in the early 1980s, it was considered to be a state-of-the-art workplace for the 158 people on the 36,000-square-foot floor. All private offices were placed around the perimeter with secretarial workstations located outside each door, large conference rooms had windows, a ceremonial conference room graced the area nearest to the elevator lobby, and there was a library, albeit a very hushed one, with panels. There were also two moderate-sized conference rooms.

Fifteen years later, the space was deemed by the client as inefficient. This client was no stranger to the way of alternative officing strategies because it had applied the concepts elsewhere in the country. This particular client culturally changed the way they worked by combining audit and tax together, which is like combining oil and water. Before it may be one floor was audit, one floor was tax, now there are combined teams on all floors. The staff had increased over the years by 40 percent, and they were bursting at the seams. The client didn't want to leave the floor, or the building, but it recognized the need to depart from past office planning approaches, workstyles and attitudes...and they needed to do it *fast*.

The client did, however, agree to do construction, and this floor would serve as the prototype for subsequent floors in the building that would be renovated during the next several years.

As part of the flattening of spatial hierarchy, partner offices were reduced in size, workspace footprints were decreased, and corner offices were eliminated to allow for more shared communal areas such as team rooms, libraries, and open meeting spaces. The result was a 40 percent increase in staff population and a 28 percent decrease in construction dollars spent per staff member.

The space was planned for future flexibility both in technology integration and infrastructure design. A raised floor is used, and the ceiling lighting, HVAC, and sprinklers are integrated so that these elements do not have to be relocated if planning changes occur and only have to be adjusted through the ceiling.

SUMMARY

Making an alternative workplace concept work is a complex process. It may seem that teaming can be achieved by merely tearing people out of their private offices and dumping them together in a big open space, or by eliminating panels altogether to give auditory and visual access to everyone on the floor—but that thinking is wrong. Putting people in a room and expecting them to be one big happy communicating, product-producing, cycle-reducing family is a shortsighted way to approach an alternative workplace. It simply won't work. Nor will throwing laptops at employees without any training or counseling, telling them they have to work at home or on the road and will no longer have their own corporate office to go to.

It was once easy to plan and program a space, then move the employees in to designated offices and cubicles. Employees resigned themselves to such environments. But since everything from work process to technology to interior environments has changed, a century's worth of work habits and a decade and a half of strategic space planning methods have to change, too.

If senior management is sold on the fact that the company should go in the direction of an alternative workplace, the failure to employ a champion to lead the change top down and to put a change management program in place to help deal with technology and corporate culture issues will ensure that the alternative workplace will not work. However, achieving buy-in is never as simple as it seems with the rampant emotions and demands from upper management down the line to administrative staff. Fortunately, designers and facility professionals now come together more easily, partnering along with an in-house teams of professionals to lead the way to a successful transition into an alternative workplace with buy-in top down and bottom up.

Making Sense of Alternative Workplace Technology Investments

It's unanimous. Anyone who has ever implemented an alternative workplace program stresses the need for more technology. A key ingredient to make an alternative workplace program work is having the right technology infrastructure and investment. But it's one of the most difficult pieces to get right, say the experts who've been there. Most alternative workplace experts say implementing the real estate piece of an alternative workplace program is a piece of cake compared to the technology piece of the puzzle.

Why?

First of all, technology has its own language that only the IT department knows how to interpret. Second, technology changes so fast it's hard to keep up with the updates. Third, you never really know what part of the technology puzzle will be missing until the alternative workplace program is under way.

Budgeting for technology needs is a necessary strain for alternative workplace programs, especially when it can cost about $10,000 a year in computer hardware, software, and peripheral components alone to support one remote worker,[1] and that's not including the cost of cabling at the main office. It becomes apparent after drawing up budgets for alternative workplace technology that real estate savings become a secondary, or more likely a moot, point of an alternative workplace project. Productivity and competitive gains subsequently move up the ladder to become the primary motivator of alternative work processes.

Technology is indeed an alternative workplace enabler. For instance, in the past, analog phone lines and modem technology limited the scope of telecommuting. Those who needed only to check e-mail or transfer small files could do so, but older technology couldn't allow large file transfers required by service representatives, computer programmers, engineers, or graphic artists. Now, high-speed, high-performance digital network services and access equipment allow workers to connect to corporate networks at speeds of 128 kb/s and above. That means more types of workers can telecommute and work at remote sites.

New technologies also improve productivity. However, there's the question of how much the computer has done for productivity. Many think computers have lowered a worker's productivity. But consider this: Employees can spend an average of 30 minutes a day standing at a remote fax machine while photocopying takes up to 24 minutes a day, and printing takes 21 minutes a day.[2] Think of what fax-modem software and scanners can do for enhanced productivity.

In this chapter, you'll find an overview of critical technologies that clients have invested in to make their alternative workplace programs run efficiently. Make no mistake, there is a definite architecture to technology necessary for an alternative workplace. But that doesn't make choosing platforms to work together easy since few of the necessary products are produced by one vendor. Although most end users rely on IT departments, there are also consultants to whom you can go to for more help.[3] Don't be fooled. Dealing with technology—any kind of technology—can be a hair-raising, frustrating experience given the inherent complexities and foreign-like language descriptives. But technology is a gift to the alternative workplace. Even after reviewing this chapter, the best piece of advice anyone can give a designer and client driving an alternative workplace program is this: Become best friends with the IT department.

There's an inevitable fear of technology—most people tend to mistrust technology, the perception that saving data in bits doesn't equal saving data in concrete, hard-copy form.

If you've ever doubted the reliability of sending information over the computer, consider this scene: On August 5, 1996, during morning rush hour on the New Haven Metro North commuter rail line in the New York metropolitan area, a cargo door blew open on a passing Amtrak train carrying mail, scattering quite a few packages and envelopes across— and under—the tracks for about a quarter of a mile up and down the line. Regular commuter trains had to reduce speed so that the rush of wheels wouldn't "run over any mail or blow it farther away," according to one conductor announcing the delay over the loudspeaker. Doesn't e-mail sound pretty good right about now? Okay, okay, so America Online crashed 2 days later for 19 straight hours, which meant nearly 6 million customers couldn't send or receive e-mail until the next day. But at least that mail was retrieved uncrushed and unscathed. And, remember the Federal Express cargo plane which crashed and burned its contents on July 31, 1997?

Though we still use trains and planes to transport paper mail, technology becomes smarter and more mainstream seemingly by the hour. Just remember how confounded we were when someone mentioned the word *fax* in the early 1980s, but now it's a part of our daily lives.

The following technology issues necessary for alternative workplace will be covered in this chapter: computing platforms, communication and interfacing products, and cabling platforms. *Remember that a basic understanding of technology is better than no understanding at all.*

COMPUTING PLATFORMS

The first questions you have to ask yourself are:

- What kind of notebooks should you deploy to remote and mobile workers?
- Should telecommuters have notebooks or desktop PCs at home?
- What kind of notebooks (or PCs) will be best?
- Should telecommuters take home company PCs already in inventory?
- Should the company buy or lease notebooks?

- What peripherals are necessary for home-based workers?

One of the most important things any alternative workplace expert will tell you is to consider a notebook with adequate power supply—easier said than done. However, a tip from Toshiba: It's come out with lines especially designed for mobile workers with power supply built into the system (unlike the competition that relies on separate and heavy batteries), and a lithium-ion battery will last 3 hours. Toshiba already has a reported reliable 24-hour technical support help desk.

ASSET MANAGEMENT PROGRAMS

It's common for companies to track computers they give to on-site or remote employees. However, in 1996, only 12 percent of 200 U.S. companies surveyed (each averaged 8500 desktop PCs in their ownership) by Comdisco for the first annual asset management index said they *effectively* track and manage distributed computers. According to the study, it can cost $60,000 each over a 5-year life to procure, maintain, and support one PC. So organizations that don't employ sound asset management practices, at least for expensive technology assets, are wasting money. And although most companies don't care to retrieve furniture back from home-based workers when they leave the company, equipment is almost always retrieved or the value is taken out of a final paycheck.

SPECIALIZED IN-HOUSE OR VENDOR SUPPORT SERVICES

The biggest complaint that NCR still hears from its virtual workers is the problem of adequate help desk support. Salespeople are incapacitated if they have a proposal and they have to access information right away from a remote location and that information is not available. They can't be told by the help desk that they will get a call back in 48 hours or that they have to be put on hold indefinitely.

NCR has a Hot Spare program where it keeps in inventory a large quantity of Toshibas that can be dispatched for 24-hour delivery for anyone with outstanding and unfixable problems.

COMMUNICATION INTERFACING PRODUCTS

This is just about as confounding as figuring out computer platforms. But the right interfacing products will make or break an alternative workplace program if remote work is part of the strategy.

Hewlett-Packard found out the hard way in the late 1980s when its field sales departments tried in earnest to become early adopters of alternative officing. HP rolled out the Red Carpet Club, an environment of shared spaces and touchdown areas for employees who infrequently came to the office. The goal was to give the sales group more face-to-face time with customers, using mobility as a competitive advantage, according to Kit Tuveson, an employee with HP for 30 years who is now corporate facility operations and engineering manager. "But we came to the realization that with our quasi-cell phones and no software to speak of, efficient mobility became increasingly difficult. The Red Carpet Club didn't last long because our technological infrastructure was not thought through or robust enough to manage mobility issues."

TRAINING FOR NEW TECHNOLOGY

You can't just throw a notebook at a newly anointed remote or virtual employee and expect the alternative workplace program to work. And although working virtual makes employees become more technology-savvy because they have to troubleshoot computer and software glitches on their own when help desks aren't so helpful, training is absolutely critical nevertheless. No alternative workplace manager should ever assume that an employee knows how to intuitively troubleshoot or work a computer and its software from the start.

At Southern California Edison, there is a technology training laboratory set up like a home office with all the necessary equipment to take remote workers through the paces of technology troubleshooting. At American Express, Yee Jao, former head of the Hearth program (a department that has now folded), says she used to throw a computer down on the floor, watch it break, and make employees who were going to be telecommuting for the first time fix the broken computer before they were deployed to their home offices.

Before TBWA/Chiat/Day went virtual in the early 1990s, its technological infrastructure was in need of a tune-up. "Once virtual was announced, we learned we had 6 months to identify, choose, test, and implement new desktop equipment, applications, and networking," says Janine Davis, MIS director. Though everyone worked on a Macintosh, desktop equipment ranged from a Mac Plus to a Quadra 950, typical of companies who purchase ad hoc technology. And although Chiat/Day had T1

connections throughout its North American offices, the Los Angeles office was the only one wired for LocalTalk. Due to hardware limitations, the company was stuck with older versions of productivity applications, says Davis, which she says was quite a bit to tackle in a short span of 6 months.

"No question that most people needed to learn a whole new way of working, especially considering that the personal computer in our environment was no longer personal," says Davis. "We had intensive training prior to and directly after the move in. We instituted a new training program which requires employees to take certain core classes. If they don't meet their goals, it's reflected on their yearly review."

Here's how Davis streamlined and upgraded the ad agency for its virtual debut:

Goals

- Improve communication and collaboration without getting up to go over to a physical desk.
- Reduce paper flow.
- Increase mobility, and keep consistency of equipment for seamless integration.
- Keep information centralized so that equipment could be accounted for.

Tools to Meet Goals

- Meeting Maker group calendar and scheduling system.
- Oxygen, a groupware tool developed in conjunction with the Art Technology Group in Boston.
- Paging options through e-mail or switchboard.
- MarkUp to allow documents to be saved in a non-modifiable format for routed proofing.
- Optix, a scanner for paper documents.
- ARA, or Apple Talk Remote Access, with more incoming lines to increase volume of remote network access.
- Touchbase, an electronic business card index.
- GlobalFax, fax-modem capability.

NEW WORKPLACE TECHNOLOGIES BASICS

Listed below in alphabetical order are briefs on the pertinent technologies that both the designer and end user will need to have some understanding of when putting all the pieces of the puzzle together for the new workplace:

Asymmetric digital subscriber line (ADSL)
Cabling
Category 5 cable
Digital simultaneous voice data (DSVD)
Fiber optics
Frame relay
Hoteling reservation software
Intranets
Internet
Integrated services digital network (ISDN)
Local area network (LAN) and wide area network (WAN)
Switched 56
T-1 lines
Telephony including wireless
Videoconferencing

ADSL

ISDN jokes aside, there's now even a joke about the ADSL. According to technology guru Nick Sullivan of *Home Office Computing Magazine* fame, the *asymmetric digital subscriber line* (ADSL) is like the Edsel: "ADSL sounds so much like Edsel that I couldn't help but think that they didn't run any focus groups to test consumer response," he said in one of his humor columns (see Sullivan 1997).

In fact, the ADSL is the next step to the ISDN because it is a technology that allows high-speed video, data, and voice communications over regular phone lines. ADSL enthusiasts hope it will not only put an end to the ISDN controversy for the phone companies who can't seem to understand or install the technology but will also cure the confusion for consumers and businesses. In addition, experts say the ADSL has taken over the race to run fiber optics to the home. In other words, the ADSL is simple and convenient to install (whereas the ISDN is not) because it can be plugged into the wall (with a little splitting of lines, however) and used through a switch. And you don't need a new phone for the ADSL.

The ADSL can download at 1.5 million bps, but it can't upload that fast. In fact, it can upload at only 16,000 to 500,000 bps. This means you can play interactive movies while making a regular phone call without any interruption. The ADSL can still cost about $1000 to $2000 to install, but some people predict it will be substantially lower, to about $500, in a few years.

The implications the ADSL has for telework is that it will allow a telecommuter to videoconference with the same type of quality as a large corporation's videoconferencing room has in its infrastructure.

CABLING PLATFORMS—OUT OF SIGHT, OUT OF MIND

No matter how large or small a new telephone or computer system, the cabling network is critical, but its unglamorous complexities are often misunderstood, overlooked, and underexpensed. The rule of thumb for wiring cost is that it will often amount to 10 to 20 percent of a new voice-data system. But it can go as high as 50 percent of a system for large companies.

Cabling experts say to look ahead and wire everything in sight with high capacity so that all work surfaces can handle phone, fax, modem, voice mail, PC, and LAN. In fact, most alternative workplaces adhere to this school of thinking. Shortcuts, poor planning, and penny-pinching can lead to huge costs (even exceeding the initial cost of the installation) down the line for adding, moving, and changing cabling. Interestingly enough, the worry is gone about cable separation (so that cables don't interfere with each other when housed in a panel system raceway), and now, the concern is more about surge suppression in buildings with heavy-duty technology.

CATEGORY 5 CABLE

Category 5 wiring is a twisted-pair cabling that can speed data along at 100 to 150 Mbytes/s faster and is cheaper than fiber-optic cable. Since new *asynchronous transfer mode* (ATM) hardware can process 2.5 bps, telecommunications specialists need to use the fastest cabling available. Unfortunately, category 5 is very sensitive, and if it gets pulled with an exertion of more than 35 pounds (which is really like a soft tug), the "twisted pair" will untwist, causing data transmission to be interrupted. It could take hours to find the weak cable. Experts say category 5 cable needs to be laid, not pulled, into a raceway, and not weighted down.

DIGITAL SIMULTANEOUS VOICE DATA

With *digital simultaneous voice data* (DSVD), it is possible to share information, including graphics, across a network. It is inexpensive because it requires no

Figure 5.1

Fiber optics routed and
organized through an
interconnect tray.
(Arends)

change to the existing telephone system. Phone companies won't have to modify their switches or increase your phone bill. The DSVD network works as long as the instruments at both ends of a conversation are equipped with appropriate modems and software. The interim step for using the phone companies' network docs require special telephone lines and switches. That technology is called *integrated services digital network* (ISDN).

FIBER OPTICS

In 1986, Ameritech, the phone service company, installed the nation's first fiber-optic hub to link long-distance companies to their customers. Fiber optics was the answer to the exploding telecom infrastructure on which massive information highways were to be built. The hair-thin wires that transmit data as pulses of light through glass or plastic tubing at unthinkable speeds panicked everyone in the 1990s: "Uh-oh, does our building even have fiber optics? We better get some!" Fiber optics was the indisputable net that captured new commercial tenants (see Deutsch 1993). Joining in on the fiber-optic mania were the contract furniture manufacturers building bigger, wider raceways billed to accommodate "hard-to-manage" fiber optics that can be laid in and routed around wide-radius corners without crimping problems that interrupt connections (Fig. 5.1).

The country is already wired with copper, millions and millions of miles of copper wiring, and the phone companies don't intend to spend money to rip it out and replace it with expensive fiber optics. It's been estimated that phone companies have already spent more than $60 billion to install existing copper networks. Copper cable sends voices and data as electrical signals and converts it to sound waves at the receiving end. Light travels faster—therefore, the huge interest in fiber optics. New York Telephone, however, says it costs no more than $7000 to convert a building to fiber optics.

A fiber-optic cable is about a half inch in diameter and has about 72 pairs of glass strands that can carry over 48,000 concurrent conversations. A copper cable is about $3\frac{1}{2}$ inches wide, holds 3600 pairs of copper wires, each of which carries one conversation.

Teleport Communications Group, a Staten Island, New York–based cable giant, has been weaving fiber-optic cable networks around U.S. cities for the past few years. Teleport bills itself as "the other phone company," providing both local and long-distance service to business customers on its network.

FRAME RELAY

Telecommuters who are heavy users of the phone and data transport (over 3 hours a day) should use *frame relay*. It's a fast-packet-switching technology that works by breaking data streams into variable-length packets, then routing them across a carrier's network over predetermined and dedicated connections. Frame relay is priced as a flat fee and is distance insensitive[4] (Table 5.1)

TABLE 5.1

COST PER LINE, PER MONTH, FOR HOME OFFICE AND CENTRAL SITE NETWORK HOOKUP

Analog	SW56	ISDN	Frame Relay
$12–$30	$30–$75	$22–$50	$125

Source: Network Services: Central Site Access Line Options, *Ascend Telecommuting Guide,* Ascend Communications, Inc., Alameda, CA, 1996.

HOTELING SOFTWARE

When you see a hoteling scheme, you usually see a hoteling reservation terminal set up in the front lobby (Fig. 5.2). Some companies use elaborate software packages especially designed for hoteling; others, like Price Waterhouse's Dallas office, rely on a human being, called a *concierge,* who uses Lotus Notes and a CAD program to reserve cubicles.

Back in 1993, Tandem couldn't find a vendor with the appropriate phone forwarding (a.k.a. call forwarding) software—which is part of a hoteling software package—until it worked with Desk/Flex. These two companies worked together on Tandem's proprietary RSVP system for the Tandem Business Centers. Although these systems were troublesome at first, clients have pushed the vendors to fix the bugs and streamline the systems, which has prompted Tandem and Desk/Flex to create intuitive templates and icons that can be learned easily and implemented often over the Internet or on their company's intranet. Prices are based on the specific configuration.

Many companies feel they need to put a mapping of the office floor plan on the screen, but Tom LaBelle of Desk/Flex doesn't recommend it: "Our customers have felt shrinking an office blueprint to fit a 15-inch monitor would make it too hard for users to read."

Desk/Flex

In 1993, IBM came to Desk/Flex and asked it for a program that could reserve hotelers. "It was the first I had heard of it," says Tom LaBelle, president of Professional Resource Management, the company that makes Desk/Flex. "But one of the first criteria was that this system couldn't take more than an hour to learn—it was the FUD factor—when I would install a system that employees had to learn, they'd show a lot of fear, uncertainty, and doubt."

In its beginnings, Desk/Flex wasn't very user-friendly as it was just under development. It wasn't accepted into a lot of LAN systems, so companies would set up separate terminals in the lobby. "That works great in a small office with 10 or 15 people click-and-dragging their name to a location on screen. But the idea to have a couple of terminals in a lobby with over 100 people means there's a good chance you'll have people waiting in line to use the terminals," says Marina van Overbeek, workplace strategist at Cisco. Van Overbeek pushed the software developer to make an icon for the computer so that people could sit down at home and reserve a place. Now Desk/Flex works with just about any LAN or on any brand or mixed brands of PBX on one LAN or WAN.

LaBelle also wants to dispel the perception that reservation programs take 5 to 10 minutes to process a reservation. It is not a database management system using a series of macros; it is an original program written by Desk/Flex's own programmers.

Desk/Flex doesn't use a touch screen monitor as an interface because they don't work well for this kind of application and can get expensive when multiplied by many machines, says LaBelle.

Desk/Flex has enhanced its software to be more user-friendly in that they've also developed a meeting schedule system and a "Permanent Profile." Permanent Profiles assemble information about each hoteler, for example, their locker numbers, choices of desks and offices, supplies they need each time they are in the office, and whether or not they want coffee or tea. One-time requests are left on Desk/Flex's Scratch Pad File.

In 1996, LaBelle reported that there were over 200 installations of Desk/Flex across the nation and a few in Canada including Price Waterhouse, KPMG Peat Marwick, and Charles Schwab. And, as of 1997, Professional Resource Management signed an agreement with Nortel to become part of the telecom company's Preferred Partner program in which Desk/Flex will be sold and distributed.

FlexiMOVE from IBM

In 1993, IBM implemented the Workforce Mobility program to maximize its workplace usage, and out of that was born the *Mobile Office Voice Environment* (FlexiMOVE), a hoteling reservation software program the company has been selling to outside customers since 1996 (it was on, then off the market for a while because of bugs). FlexiMOVE is installed in well over 100 IBM offices around the world including Beijing, China, and Seoul, South Korea, according to Andre'a Cheatham of the Workforce Mobility Program.[5]

One of the goals for the FlexiMOVE system was that it shouldn't require end-user training. The

Figure 5.2
MCI Boston Rally Center
has a typical terminal
with hoteling software set
up in the reception area
for staff to log in and find
a space.
(Photo by Stephen
Syarto.)

panel is set up as a touch screen, or it can be used with a mouse depending on an individual's preference.

For minimum interaction, users touch their name and press the "sign in" button, and the software gives them the first available desk in the area they used the last time they signed in. The system performs an automatic "sign out" overnight. For maximum interaction, users can select their name, area, desk, and length of stay.

What's interesting about IBM's FlexiMOVE marketing package is that it sells the following benefit to potential customers: "a significant reduction in real estate costs." In addition, IBM and Gensler Associates have a strategic partnership agreement to route potential customers to each other. If IBM has a client that inquires about hoteling or FlexiMOVE, Gensler also gets a call, and vice versa.

A note on how phone forwarding works: The software assigns desks and telephones by directly activating the switching necessary to move phone numbers from location to location. Although mobile employees retain their personal phone numbers, the employee has to first sign in before the switching is activated. When an employee is not assigned to a desk, the number is rerouted to voice mail, which receives messages.

INTRANETS, EXTRANETS PROVIDE COMPANYWIDE INFORMATION ON DEMAND

An *intranet*, now a buzzword, is the virtual office's tool for disseminating proprietary information to employees and for cutting down on paperwork, binders, manuals, and other behemoth materials that take up valuable square footage. What is an *intranet?* It's a private Net. Look at it as a Web site that's only for a company's own eyes. It looks like a typical Web site on the Internet, but it's protected from anyone outside the company from logging on to it who doesn't have a company-issued password. To double protect an intranet, a company probably

Ask Your Hoteling Software Vendor the Following Basic Questions in Your RFP

- What is the grace period for sign out?
- Is there an ability to incorporate broadcast announcements?
- What are the built-in security features (encrypted authorities, passwords)?
- How does the system report?
- Does the system map other floor plans?
- How does the system

integrate with existing technology?
- Can it have a touch screen interface?
- What's the PBX integration for employee desk assignments?
- What are the backup procedures?
- Can this system be accessed remotely?
- Is this system a people finder?
- Does the system have the

ability to contact someone if he or she not at the work site?
- How long will it take to train employees to use the system?
- Does the reservation system return to a default state, and when?
- Does it accommodate guest scheduling?
- Does the vendor have on-site training?
- Can the system have

multiple facilities reservations?
- Is there a grace period for no-shows?
- What equipment is provided by the vendor?
- What is the maintenance contract?
- Can a "next location and can be reached number" be built into the locator?

Source: Tom LaBelle, Desk/Flex, 1996.

will add "*firewall*" software to create a barrier between internal and external systems.

"We are trying to point more and more of our employees to our intranet to cut down on hard copies and forms," says Walter Spevak, director of CRE, Autodesk. "It's as much of an important alternative office enabler as the laptop."

An intranet is a giant company repository for information: Employees can order supplies from an electronic catalog, reallocate investments in 401(k) plans, schedule meetings, and more. In the future, intranets will become even more sophisticated and will let employees fill out electronic forms, query corporate databases, or even have private and virtual meetings (see Cortese 1996).

According to a 1996 poll conducted by Louis Harris & Associates for American Express and the Treasury Management Association (a Bethesda, Maryland–based association with membership composed of private-sector treasury executives), out of 300 surveyed companies, 61 percent currently have or are in the process of setting up an intranet. About 78 percent of those firms already provide employees with access to the Internet, up 20 percent over the 1995 flash poll. Why? Employees use intranets for e-mail (68 percent), document sharing (55 percent), internal communications (45 percent), forms distribution (38 percent), posting of personnel policies and job openings (22 percent), access to product information (22 percent), travel bookings (7 percent), and access to policy (7 percent).

Intranet Benefits

- There is no need for employees to master multiple software programs for various platforms.
- It becomes a centralized information clearinghouse for the company.
- It provides immediate updates on disseminated information and databases.
- It reduces the amount of paper documents and the cost of producing and distributing manuals and binders.
- It can be less expensive than some popular groupware packages.

Intranet Disadvantages

- A LAN is required to set up an intranet.
- Employees won't always have access to computers.

- For it to be useful, employers must constantly update and manage their site.

Another buzzword, *extranet*, means *enhanced product realization* (EPR), which is a system that interconnects manufacturers, suppliers, dealers, customers, and other partners using the public Internet. Think of it as an electronic strategic alliance.

Extranets can access multiple corporate intranets for collaborative product development, electronic commerce, data tracking, videoconferencing, and other applications. The purpose of an extranet is to reduce manufacturing costs by using the Internet infrastructure instead of relying on proprietary information systems and dedicated telecommunications links.

InfoTEST International, an alliance of 36 U.S. corporations and government entities, came together in 1993 (then known as the NII Testbed or NIIT) and began testing in 1996 its large prototype extranet. InfoTEST is an Internet alliance with a mission to test how the Internet can be combined and leveraged with other advanced information technologies to enhance business productivity to make U.S. companies more globally competitive. Companies involved in InfoTEST include 3M, Ascend, Bay Networks, Caterpillar, DEC, Dun & Bradstreet, GCL, Hewlett-Packard, Hughes Electronics, IBM, Imation, Kmart, NCR, Sprint, and Texas Instruments, along with four laboratories and research centers, according to its Web site charter.[6]

How does an extranet reduce a company's R&D costs? It is a tool with which partners can work together to address common concerns. The mission statement says that members of an extranet can join forces and distribute information aimed at addressing a common set of challenges, which in essence spreads the cost of conducting research and development with other strategic companies.

INTEGRATED SYSTEMS DIGITAL NETWORK

ISDN. You've heard the term, now what is it? The popular joke about ISDN is that it stands for "It still does nothing." Others say ISDN is a "twisted pair on steroids." ISDN was invented more than a decade ago but the demand was low until now. ISDN offers everything DSVD does, only 5 to 10 times faster. ISDN technology enables existing twisted-pair copper wire phone lines to transmit voice and data with high accuracy at fast speeds of 64,000 to 128,000 bps. Although ISDN brings speed and power to small businesses and telecommuters, it's actually still considered to be narrowband and surprisingly enough not that much faster than a 28.8 modem.[7]

ISDN is designed and priced for mass application because it can utilize existing twisted-pair copper wire phone lines. Since 1980, ISDN has been widely used in Europe, but it is not as popular or understood in the United States due to lack of awareness and demand from consumers and businesses. Telephone companies have done little to market the services. Now, however, telephone companies in various regions across the country are seeing this service as a real source of revenue since technology-based remote work continues to evolve.

So who needs ISDN anyhow? If you still use POTS, or, plain old (analog) telephone service, with a computer and modem at home, you know that connecting to a network is not only slow, but it also means your phone line is down for the count until you are offline or not sending faxes. Or you could have a first phone line for personal calls, a second business phone line for business voice calls, and a third phone line for modem connections. You have just about everything you need for connectivity except for speed. The disadvantages of analog are many:

- It takes too long to access the office network and download files.
- Modem connections sometimes unexpectedly break off.
- You can't download large files in full because the connectivity breaks off.
- Faxing through the computer goes at a snail's pace.
- Analog phone service can't support quality video for desktop videoconferencing.

The advantages of ISDN:

- A single ISDN line supports a minimum of 8 separate devices and 64 separate telephone numbers.
- ISDN users can communicate with analog phone line users.
- It operates at multimegabit to gigabit speed transferring data starting at 64,000 or 128,000 bps.
- Group 4 fax with ISDN is 10 to 20 times faster—one page in 3 to 8 seconds as opposed to the old fax machine that processed one page per minute.
- Its speed saves on long-distance charges.
- It allows desktop videoconferencing with realistic moving images (although in his book, *The Road Ahead*, Bill Gates says the quality of motion video

is mediocre but "reasonable for routine video-conferencing," so don't expect perfection with ISDN).

Of course, there are disadvantages to ISDN, as well:

- ISDN users tend to proliferate in the Northeast and on the West Coast of the United States. Only 20 percent of other areas in the United States have ISDN, and some states such as Arkansas and Alaska don't have ISDN access at all (Frost and Sullivan, 1996 executive summary report, *U.S. Videoconferencing Systems and Services markets,* http://www.frost.com).
- It can be expensive to hook up and maintain for small amounts of information that could easily be transmitted over high-speed modems.
- Many local telephone companies don't install ISDN into residences.

ISDN technology is based on international standards maintained by the International Telecommunications Union (ITU). There are two types of ISDN service:

- The Basic Rate Interface (BRI)
- The Primary Rate Interface (PRI)

Both consist of bearer channels (called B *channels*) for voice, data, and image transmission and a separate D channel for call signaling and setup. The advantage of the separate D channel is that it allows calls to be completed in 1 to 3 seconds versus 10 to 30 seconds with analog service:

- *BRI:* Accommodates smaller users. Consists of 2 B channels. A single B channel carries transmissions of 64 kbytes/s and can be used for voice, circuit-switched data, or packed-switched data.
- *PRI:* Accommodates larger users. Consists of 23 B channels that can be combined, or "bonded," and recombined by users to accommodate variations in inbound-outbound call flow. For example, 6 B channels can be allocated for a full-motion, full-color videoconference at a particular time. The same channels can be later recombined for nighttime transmission of financial data to company locations worldwide. To combine or bond channels, you need equipment such as a mainframe, minicomputers, and PBX systems to multiplexers, video systems, and a new generation of ISDN bandwidth controllers.

The price of ISDN differs throughout the country. NYNEX, for instance, sent out a promotional package in late 1996 that quotes charges as the following:

PRICE LIST: NEW YORK STATE, 1996		
New Line Installation Charges		
Basic Telephone Service plus ISDN Basic Service		
	Business	Residential
Premises installation per line	$312	$225
Virtual service arrangement	75	75
	$387	$300
Recurring Monthly Charges Per New Line		
(3-Month Minimum)		
	Business	Residential
Line charges	$22.23	$10.10
Basic service, ISDN charges	14.00	14.00
Virtual service arrangement*	10.00	10.00
	$46.23	$34.20

*NYNEX's Virtual Service Arrangement is a charge if a customer lives outside the 3-mile area where a NYNEX central office is equipped with ISDN-switching equipment. NYNEX then provides service from the closest central office with ISDN equipment.

LOCAL AREA NETWORKS AND WIDE AREA NETWORKS

Client-servers are taking over mainframes, which has fueled the popularity of LANs and WANs. The server is a centrally located computer providing specific computer services such as data management that are used by other systems, known as *clients*. Clients draw on the resources of the server via a network, allowing remote access of networks by telecommuters and mobile and other types of remote workers. The wider the network, the more likely it is to be considered a *wide area network* or WAN.

LANs and WANs are data managers and communication vehicles, but most of the time a remote worker will need to invest in an ISDN or other kind of connection to a faster modem for access.

SWITCHED 56

When ISDN is not available, *switched* 56 (SW 56) is the next best service. It's an end-to-end, switched digital service supporting data transported at 56 kb/s. It's more expensive than ISDN, but it is available more often than ISDN.

T-1 LINES

Replace separate low-speed lines in current use with T-1 or ISDN PRI pipe to handle telecommuting traffic and other remote worker needs. A T-1 line will cost a company between $200 and $500 a month for a central site location. (ISDN PRI pipe costs between $100 and $525 a month plus the cost of a T-1 line.)

TELEPHONY AND WIRELESS PHONES

This area of telephony is changing hourly (Fig. 5.3). So it behooves facility operations to team with in-house telecommunications or MIS professionals to untangle the confusion. There's now even a new prepaid cell phone service from Omni that doesn't require an annual contract. And there's a cell phone-in-a-box from Bell Atlantic. These are just the basic cell phone services and equipment.

Nokia's 2100 series phones were one of the first to become compatible with computers and fax machines. Nokia's phones work with a cellular

Figure 5.3
The MCI Boston Rally Center has a cabinet filled with wireless radio telephones that hotelers check out when they come to the office. The phones don't work beyond a certain point in the building so there's no worry of walking phones. (Photo by Stephen Syarto.)

Plain

old telephone service, or POTS, is the common, basic phone service

Wiring for POTS Versus ISDN

delivered from the phone company to the residence in a single line with two wires. The power needed to operate POTS comes directly from the phone company and is delivered over the same two wires that carry your voice. The point at which the phone company's responsibility ends and the homeowner's begins is called the **demarcation point.** A common POTS wiring configuration is called a *daisy chain*, in which the phone cable is connected to a series of outlets in the home, one after another, terminating with the last **link** in the chain.

ISDN equipment and wiring differ from POTS. With POTS, the same electrical signals from the phone company that arrive at the demarcation point continue on to the telephone. With ISDN, an additional component called a *network termination 1* (NT1) is required between the demarc point and the ISDN terminal equipment. The NT1 converts the signal arriving on two wires to a four-wire signal. It can be a stand-alone unit or built into an ISDN telephone or other device.

Terminal equipment is the **catchall** term that refers to the communications devices you actually use. In the POTS case, it refers to a phone, fax machine, or modem-computer. With ISDN, *terminal equipment* could mean an ISDN phone, a PC with a special plug-in board to provide an ISDN interface, an ISDN fax machine, etc. A stand-alone or built-in terminal adapter is often used to convert the ISDN signal into a form usable by non-ISDN equipment.

A daisy-chain configuration is not acceptable for ISDN wiring configurations. The preferred configuration is the star arrangement in which the wiring to any individual piece of terminal equipment comes from a central point and goes directly to that terminal location. The connector normally used for ISDN services is the modular 8-position jack or plug, in which all 8 positions are equipped with pins.

In some cases, existing wiring in a home or business may be used for ISDN service. However, there is no simple way to evaluate existing wiring before using it. If there are any questions about its suitability, new wiring is recommended. The Electronic Industries Association's minimum wiring standard is 8-conductor (4 pairs) unshielded twisted-pair (UTP) category 3 or higher, 24 gauge.

The **mix** will get more confusing, according to Bill Gates. In his book, he predicts that cable companies will have technologies and strategies of their own that differ from and compete with the telephone companies. Cable companies want to be able to use their existing coaxial cable networks to compete with phone companies to provide local phone service. They have special cable modems that connect personal computers to cable networks, allowing a higher **bandwidth** than ISDN. However, phone companies will replace the copper-wire, microwave, and satellite links in their networks with fiber-optic cable so that they will have the bandwidth to carry enough bits to deliver higher-quality video. This will in turn make cable television companies increase the amount of fiber optics they use. Phone companies and cable television networks will compete with each other to be the first network provider in a neighborhood.

According to *Business Week Magazine* (Peter Coy, "Science & Technology: The Big Daddy of Data Haulers?" January 29, 1996, page 74), the article says Forrester Research predicts about 6.8 million U.S. homes will have cable modems by the year 2000.

---

phone carrier that supports both voice and data messages at a low cost of $300 for the phone.

Remember that cellular phone bills will no doubt rise over POTS phone bills when you deploy alternative and mobile workplace workers who must stay in constant communication and contact with colleagues and customers.[8]

Internet Telephony Giving Long-Distance Carriers the Jitters

The software is still in its infancy, but it's a technology about which everyone from long-distance carriers to consumers are curious. What better way to save hundreds, if not thousands, of dollars on a long-distance bill but to place a call through the Internet?

The Internet has already cut into long-distance carriers' markets. Contacting someone over the Internet regardless of where they are located is as expensive as making a local call when the online access provider is a local phone number. But with a couple of purchases, including software, a microphone, and speakers, there's no stopping an Internet user to connect long distance, voice to voice over the computer, cutting out the middle guy—the long-distance carrier.

Internet voice communications is not a mainstream way of communicating yet. However, it does have all the earmarks of becoming as popular and as easy as ham radio once the standards, software glitches, and poor sound quality issues are ironed out. There are numerous software companies experimenting with the technology including Vocaltec, Electric Magic, White Pine Software, and Netscape Navigator which offers Cooltalk software for chatting over the Internet.[9]

There are other issues, as well. In order for two parties to connect, they must arrange a time to hook up with a common host computer, search for one another, then try to connect the voice software. Sometimes, Internet telephony enthusiasts find themselves making a quick call first to arrange a connection with the other party.

The Telecommunications Act of 1996

It took 4 years of emotional negotiations, but on February 8, 1996, President Clinton signed the Telecommunications Act of 1996, a move that has reformed an entire industry from telephone companies to the Internet to cable operators. The act facilitates the development of a whole array of competitive local service providers from which to choose. Telecommunications companies may now enter new markets, long-distance carriers may not service local markets, and local carriers can provide long-distance service. In the facilities world, this means that telecommunications companies can have "forcible entry" into buildings to provide services for occupants. That means that any number of telecommunications service providers can set up house in a building regardless of space limitations, safety, and security concerns. Consumers have cause for concern, however. Since the act went into effect, it's been reported that local service providers are obstructing new entrants into markets by failing to enter into interconnection agreements. Larger national telecommunication companies are now trying to demonopolize the local markets.

What's happened is that the major companies like MCI and AT&T are scurrying to become local service providers across the country but aren't finding it easy to edge their way into various regions because local providers are doing anything they can to protect their current markets. MCI and AT&T both say that they are being denied entrance into local markets because local monopolies are sabotaging the Telecommunications Act by using delay tactics, disruption of service, and poor treatment of competitors that are trying to enter into interconnection partnership agreements with local telecommunications companies. Any real benefit to the customer will come if and when there's an end to the friction between local and long-distance companies. In addition, the act favors the use of wireless technology, and those providers will increasingly seek out more and more facilities for placement of satellites.

VIDEOCONFERENCING TECHNOLOGY AND DESIGN

Only Scott Adams, founder of the *Dilbert* empire of books and paraphernalia, could joke about something like videoconferencing. From his online newsletter, Adams suggests the following videoconference pranks:

- Arrange with everyone in the room to freeze and quit talking at the same time.
- Look directly into the camera and move your lips as if you're speaking, but make no noise.
- Have someone off-camera talk while someone of the opposite sex lip-syncs on-camera.

The joke used to be the cost of a videoconferencing set-up. Videoconferencing has been around in commercial use since the early 1970s and had slowly made its way into the fringe mainstream by 1985 when videoconferencing equipment cost $250,000 for one set-up and cost about $1000 per hour to connect. By 1992, company-owned equipment cost $10,000 and could be connected for about $15 per hour (see Churbuck, 1992). You won't have to own your own videoconferencing equipment when Kinko's videoconferencing partnership through Sprint is available for both personal and business use at about $150 per hour with as little as one day's notice.

Remember when business travel was considered a perk? With the stress of work and family balance, business travel has become more of a problem than a perk, and videoconferencing is often the solution. And saving money with videoconferencing is an attractive feature to a CFO when travel expenses and personal fatigue take a toll on company budgets and employees. According to one report from Jean Roger, CFM, ARIDO, IOC, and senior office of telephony with the information technology Department of Canadian National Railways in Montreal, one videoconferencing session in early 1996 resulted in a savings of nearly $3000. One department of the CN Railways held a videoconference connecting Montreal and the Moncton videoconferencing rooms along with a telephone audio-only line hookup to a Detroit facility. A total of 12 people met in one location for 3 hours at the cost of $415 versus $2000 in air travel alone, plus the additional cost of hotel rooms (averaging $100-plus per person), meals, additional ground transportation costs, and personal time taken for travel (see Roger 1996). The hard cost-benefits of videoconferencing are obvious: A single session paid for a quarter to a third of the cost of one facility's initial equipment expenditures. The soft cost-benefits mean that morale was higher since employees were able to forgo the stress and time of travel, spending their night in their own homes with their own families.

Mercedes-Benz U.S. uses videoconferencing to connect from the company's plant site in Tuscaloosa County, Alabama, and the company's headquarters in Stuttgart, Germany, to discuss unending details of its new vehicle designs. Although there's a 7-hour difference, the system works. On any given week, numerous 2-hour videoconferencing meetings involving the president and other members of the management team take place. In addition, about 90 percent of the engineers and professionals at

Mercedes-Benz have also used the system, which is housed in a 40-ft by 80-foot trailer on the construction site of its Alabama plant that opened in 1997.

The humble trailer set-up is flexible, however, and proves that videoconferencing facilities don't have to be encased in mahogany and marble. A tripod connected to the teleconferencing equipment lets viewers pan the construction site of its new plant. Mercedes uses ISDN for bandwidth of 128K, which is considered an economical speed and one that 85 percent of all businesses use for videoconferencing.

Now, thanks to a number of new laws and standards—as well as the marketing efforts of Kinko's—videoconferencing will start to become a more mainstream way of communication, making the technology more standardized and versatile for end users. According to a research report published July 1996 by Frost & Sullivan, the videoconferencing market in the United States, including systems and services, was $1.02 billion in 1992. It doubled to $2.94 billion in 1995 and is expected to reach $34.76 billion in 2002.

Why is all this growth expected for the videoconferencing industry?

- Development of new standards by the International Telecommunications Union, which released a second-generation standard in 1995 that renders a common platform for equipment features and interfaces. Typically, proprietary conferencing systems of different manufacturers were incompatible and could not provide collaborative interfaces to read and pass along information between two systems. As a result, video conversions suffered from line drop-outs, audio drops, and jerky pictures with time delay.
- The Telecommunications Act of 1996 means local phone markets will see price declines from competitors selling ISDN lines that are used by videoconferencing end-users.

These two reasons alone will force the market for videoconferencing systems and services to become fiercely competitive.

UNDERSTANDING THE DIFFERENCES BETWEEN GROUP VIDEOCONFERENCING SET-UPS

In an article in *Telecommuting Review* (see Reilly 1997), author Ellen Reilly discusses the videoconferencing market as she experienced it first-hand in doing research. As former president of the New York chapter of the Telecommuting Advisory Council, Reilly had an interest in seeing how far the videoconferencing market had come from when she helped a Fortune 100 company set up its videoconferencing room back in 1981. What she found impressed her.

The industry is growing, but it still has a barrier to overcome of poor consumer awareness, which perhaps Kinko's is helping to chip away. PictureTel, one of the equipment leaders in videoconferencing, says there are 100,000 video rooms worldwide. Reilly spoke with Forward Concepts, a market research firm, that quoted 25,000 videoconferencing systems were purchased in 1996. "And Kinko's estimates the use of their three videoconferencing rooms at the 52nd Street [New York City] store is 45 to 50 rentals per week, double that of 1995," says Reilly. She defines the following group videoconferencing set-ups:

- *Videowalls* are considered to be any wall-mounted screen or multiple panels other than a TV-type monitor often referred to as a *roll-about*. The larger the videowall screen, the more people can participate on screen per site. Reilly found a company, Mobile Wall One, that sells 42-inch videowall panels at $20,000 each, but she says that price is expected to be dramatically lower, at least 50 percent, by 1998.
- *Roll-abouts* are 27-or 34-inch TV-type monitors that link a maximum of three or four physical bodies per site.

DESIGNING A VIDEOCONFERENCING ENVIRONMENT

Planning and designing a videoconferencing room is not necessarily considered to be a new trick—those companies that could afford the exorbitant equipment have been videoconferencing for years. Now that technology is coming down in price and more companies opt to buy the equipment, more videoconferencing rooms are finding their way into smaller footprints (Fig. 5.4).

Not every company needs a dedicated videoconferencing facility, but when a company does add one, they should tale great care with its design. Space layout, background materials and finishes, and illumination qualities (levels, contrasts, and glare control) are all design elements that will add to the success of a videoconferencing room. Audio is a critical technological element that also affects layout and design of a room.

Even though the charge for a videoconferencing room will most likely come from the CEO, before

Figure 5.4

Videoconferencing is becoming ubiquitous in today's business world thanks to lower costs, more awareness. Here's a typical roll-about set up at an HQ Business Center. (HQ)

hiring designers and purchasing equipment, first do some preliminary homework. It's best to determine what kind of capabilities are necessary by examining potential usage by various departments within the company by conducting focus groups.

Videoconferencing sounds ideal as a cost-saving impromptu meeting enabler; however, you really have to put in a lot of preparation and planning for the site to avoid trouble down the road because of inadequate facilities. If you don't plan sufficiently, videoconferencing could be about as rewarding and clearly audible an experience as it is to order from a fast-food drive-through machine. When planning and purchasing equipment for a videoconferencing site, heed this word from the wise: Don't skimp.

PictureTel is the leader in videoconferencing equipment,[10] along with VTel, CLI, GPTBT, Sony, and other Japanese companies.

Though the cost of the technology has come down considerably, the associated costs must still be budgeted. Those include the design of the room, installation charges for equipment, wiring, extra telephone lines, cabling and power, and technical support plus upgrades in technology. (Don't forget catering services!)

Just about every videoconferencing meeting begins something like this: "Can you see me? Can you hear me?" Some designers say it's not difficult to design a videoconferencing room with good acoustics and visuals while others say the subtleties of lighting, table placement and shape, and surface materials are critical to the success of an installation.

Space Layout of a Videoconference Room

The transmitted image impacts perception, so it's critical that the location and size of the monitor produce images that are nearly lifelike in size. Ideally, a room should be set up with a dais facing a camera, located 8 feet away from the camera.

Lighting Considerations for Videoconferencing

Lighting for photography is an art, and so is lighting for videoconferencing. Lighting can't be taken for granted in a videoconferencing room because a camera has limited contrast range. It is therefore essential to have the right lighting to ensure the appropriate contrast ratio between focal element and background. If the contrast is too great or too little, the picture will be washed out during transmission. Lighting designer Chris Ripman, IESNA, and principal of Ripman Lighting Consultants in Boston, Massachusetts, offers the following suggestions for proper audiovisual lighting (see Ripman 1995):

- The correct depth of field for group shots of the room involves adequate ambient lighting in the 500- to 700-lx range for automatic sharpness.
- To achieve proper rendition of human facial features, illumination should come into the participants' faces at about a 45-degree angle in plan and section.
- Secondary sources of light to create sheen on hair and contour shoulders will add depth.
- Object-to-background luminance ratios should fall between 3:1 and 5:1.
- Full-range high-frequency dimming ballasts should be used for ambient wallwash and focal lighting.
- PAR or MR lamps should be located out of the range of participants' vision to prevent uncomfortable glare.

Audio Considerations for Videoconferencing

One of the biggest problems with videoconferencing is irritating background noise such as rumbling ducts, diffuser noise, computer fans, people milling around outside the conference room door, and passing air traffic, and street traffic. People working in environments with low-grade noise are used to the noise and tend to tune it out. Unfortunately, the background noise, along with your voice, is transmitted to the other party. Ultimately, the meeting loses its focus because of distracting noise. It pays to hire an acoustic and audiovisual consultant to deal

DEC
(DEC.) See
page 58.

**Xerox PARC/
Webster Colab**
(Photo by Floyd A.
Johnson.) See
page 60.

Ernst & Young Virginia
(Above, left and right)
(Photo by Jim Tetra.) See page 69.

TBWA/Chiat/ Day New York City
(Above)
(TBWA/Chiat/Day.) See page 74.

TBWA/Chiat/ Day Dallas
(Right)
(Photo by David Patterson Photography.) See page 76.

**IBM
Cranford, NJ**
(Peter Paige.)
See page 81.

**IBM
Virginia**
(Gensler.) See
page 85.

Avery Dennison Planning Workshop
(Above, left and right) (Gensler.) See page 106.

Kyo
(Kyo.) See page 140.

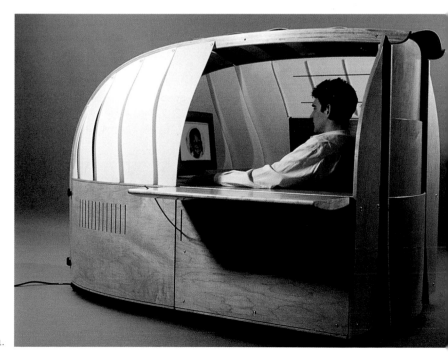

Doug Ball's New Space
(Doug Ball.) See page 141.

**Okamura's
Profice**
(Okamura.)
See page 145.

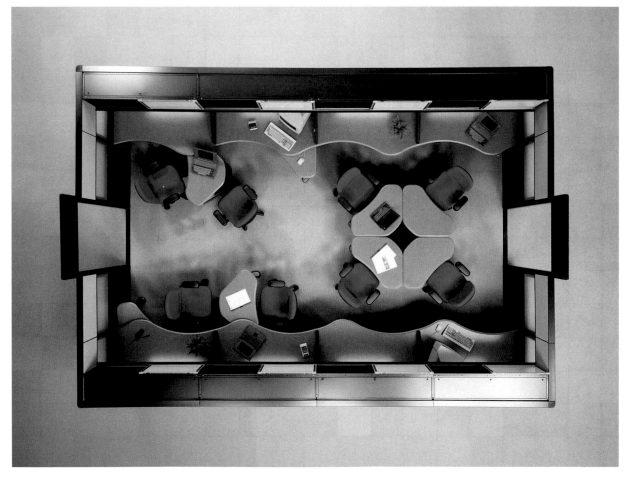

**Okamura's
Profice**
(Okamura.)
See page 146.

**Telecommuter's
Cubicle in Living
Room**
(MZS.) See page
160.

The OFFICE
(Cynthia Gurin)
See page 168.

In-House Home Office Designs
(Right and below)
(Photo by Steve Burns.) See pages 172 and 173.

with these problems. Here are three critical video-conference room acoustical pointers from Thorburn Associates, Castro Valley, California–based acoustic and audiovisual consultants:

- If there's more than one microphone used in the room, an automatic microphone mixer will limit the number of microphones active at the same time, turning on only the microphone nearest to the person speaking.
- Ceiling-mounted microphones are attractive, but voices tend to sound too distant.
- Install an acoustic echo canceler in the conference room (and surrounding rooms) to minimize "acoustic echo" in a room with open microphones and loudspeakers in full-duplex conference mode.[11] Typically, there's an unnatural half-second delay that makes people at different sites talk on top of one another.

Desktop Videoconferencing Update

Videophones haven't grabbed the consumer's attention (until 1997 with the introduction of a plug-and-play unit by a company called 8X8), but strangely enough, desktop videoconferencing has pushed the right buttons of computer enthusiasts. Now that videoconferencing standards are starting to become streamlined, it's easier to set up a platform, even for desktop videoconferencing capabilities. One product, the Color QuickCam from Connectix, connects to a computer's parallel port and doesn't require additional hardware. It captures 24-bit still or moving images and has a tiny footprint about the shape of a billiard ball. It's easy to install and inexpensive at $229 as of late 1996.

Just about the same lighting, audio, and finishes issues affect desktop videoconferencing. But when adding desktop videoconferencing to a desktop, remember that excess clutter in the background will also distract the viewer.

Training Employees for Videoconferencing Etiquette

Training employees for videoconferencing events is essential. Besides learning the technology, there are two other parts of the process that need to be relayed to employees before embarking on video-conferencing.

First, the issue of scheduling is more complex than meets the eye. Point-to-point connection is easier to schedule and pull off than multipoint videoconference sessions. Most companies with videoconferencing facilities use an automated scheduling system to account for the following items:

- Room availability, searches for simultaneous meeting times between all sites
- Room capabilities including size, type of equipment, services, and dial-in and dial-out long-distance rates and associated costs that are charged to department budgets as operational expenses
- Checklists for equipment and peripheral and administrative services
- In-room telephone numbers
- Key contacts for videoconferencing session
- An area for questions and requests
- Usage policy

Security poses another issue for videoconferencing. It's more difficult to intercept a videoconferencing session than a teleconferencing session because of the rate of code decompression. But it's still essential to request that the technology supplier offer entry and exit tones for all participants to let the sites know if other sites have joined or exited the session. Usually during a teleconference, users tend to make noise shuffling papers, clinking coffee cups or glasses, or coming in or out of the session too many times, which causes tones to go off by the second. Usually the technician intercepts to tell listeners to keep still while connected to avoid excess noise and tones. The same kind of training needs to be done before a videoconferencing session since most people are unaware of the amount of noise or confusion they are creating.

Today's technology allows only one room at a time to be shown on a screen during multipoint videoconferencing sessions. The room on the screen is usually the one making the most noise, but it in fact may not be the room that should be on the screen at the moment—it's just that excess noise was coming from that remote location.

In addition to reservation software, body language counts in a videoconferencing meeting. In fact, the convergence of people, technology, space, and furniture is quite a complex combination which requires adjustments from the participating employees. Lewis Epstein, a marketing consultant with Metro Furniture, has observed videoconference users for years as he has been gathering research to help the furniture company develop appropriate furniture and environments. He has found that the dual images of two groups on video is powerful and participants exhibit different behaviors than they would in a meeting in person. Image speaks louder than words, Epstein emphasizes—it's the little things that count like the shape of the furniture, the colors of the surfacing materials, how far away the leading presenter sits from the controls (video cameras tend to magnify positions and movements of participants, and if he or she stretches too far over to reach a knob, for example, that presenter will appear out of control of the meeting). Gentle gestures that make a person appear thoughtful and warm in person can appear fuzzy on a videoconference screen.

Epstein asks designers of videoconferencing environments to consider the following:

- How do you gauge whether or not you've emotionally reached someone during a videoconferencing session?
- How do you design an egalitarian environment in which executives are comfortable conducting a two-way meeting on video?
- How do you teach an employee to stop being self-conscious during a videoconferencing meeting?
- How do you eliminate a leader, or establish a leader, in a videoconferencing environment?

Hint: By using a rectangular table, you immediately establish a leader at the head of the table, and a half-circle table basically obliterates the tradition-al boundaries, making it unclear who is the leader of the meeting.

Some other tips for videoconferencing participants: Avoid broad gestures or abrupt motions, don't look at the ceiling, and don't wear stark white or plaid.

SUMMARY

Not only do you—as a driver of alternative workplace—have to concern yourself with the upkeep and updating of HVAC infrastructures, now you have to worry about why the hoteling software is on the fritz, whether ISDN is available for a new telecommuter working from home in the country, and whether your T-1 line should turn into a T-3 line. But you're just figuring out what POTS stands for!

Take heart, take a deep breath, and take this advice: Keep an open mind on new technologies while learning the work processes inside and out of the department or business unit embarking on alternative workplace. Knowing the work processes intimately will determine necessary on-site and off-site technologies. Plan technology infrastructures for 5 years and more, never anything less.

Confused? Now, go make a lunch date with the head of the IT department.

Finding New
Workplace Furniture
Solutions

An article on the state of the contract furniture market in *Fast Company* magazine's August/September 1996 issue started with this erroneous comment:

Grand Rapids is to office furniture what Silicon Valley is to computers—and changing just as fast.

Fishman 1996

Writer Charles Fishman's impressions of Grand Rapids differ from the design and facility professionals' impressions about how far the contract furniture industry has come in developing product to support new work processes. To the industry, Grand Rapids is to office furniture what Detroit is to automobiles—and changing just as slowly, in large part due to the huge tooling investments made to produce the products that were designed years ago. It is the nature of human beings to be adaptable, and as with cars, people tend to make due and work around the limitations of their existing and inflexible office furniture.

If we really look at the percentage of product introduced at Neocon 1997, most of it is a mix of generic furniture designed to sell volume and differs little from what was introduced at Neocon 1996—lots of ergonomic seating, panel systems with little twists here and there, traditional executive wood desks (some smaller-scaled than those of a few years back), and tables, *lots* of tables in all kinds of materials on *wheels*. "The Mart had more wheels in it than Detroit this year," was how *Officeinsight* newsletter characterized furniture found in the Chicago Merchandise Mart during Neocon 1996.

"I do think casters is a solution, but where I think the furniture industry has blown it completely is in the significance of the integration of technology," says the visionary John Duvivier, of the San Francisco–based Bottom-Duvivier design firm. "They still think about the world as desks. The world is not desks because what do you do with desks but cover them up with computers?"

Duvivier's biggest concern is the long lead time manufacturers take to introduce product. "Just think, Sun Microsystem's Java computer language didn't even exist 18 months ago, but now it's marketing that with all kinds of ancillary products that will redesign the computer world. In 6 years, Steelcase hasn't gotten Pathways out of there—we are talking about sawhorses and doors here. It isn't rocket science!" says Duvivier (see box "The Mystery Behind Steelcase's Pathways").

It's staggering to think about how long it takes to get a new furniture product out on the market because of all the manufacturing and tooling investments made for older designs. So the addition of the caster to just about every potentially movable piece of furniture is about as far as the contract furniture industry has taken products for the alternative workplace. Manufacturers say there are products supposedly in the works for 1998 and beyond that may, or may not, change the office landscape. And Haworth surprised the industry in 1995 when it introduced Crossings at Neocon, an unusual collection of mobile furniture that some say looks like a reengineered product found in the Frank Lloyd Wright Johnson Wax Administration Building built

in the 1930s. In spite of the often harsh critiques, Haworth has sold quite a bit of Crossings product. And, the company has emerged from its staid reputation as a low- to midpriced panel manufacturer to a company continuing to experiment and push the envelope on exotic products that may or may not ever make it to market (Fig. 6.1).

In 1994, Kyo made its debut at Orgatec. Kyo, a mobile modular desking system that originated from the United Kingdom, caught everyone's attention when its manufacturer, President Office Furniture, debuted the product during Neocon 1995 when it was introduced to the U.S. market. Since then, Overland Park, Kansas–based Jami has

entered into a licensing agreement with President for the manufacture and distribution of Kyo in North, South, and Central America, and promises to expand the product line that so many other companies have since tried to mimic (Fig. 6.2).

Although the industry on the whole hasn't made too many strides with the way furniture looks and acts, there are still perceptions out there about what an alternative work environment looks, feels, and acts like (Fig. 6.3). "People walk into what they think is an alternative office, and it doesn't look like a spaceship, it looks like an office," says Bruce Lanyon, real estate manager of Amdahl and head of its alternative workplace program. "I tell them it doesn't *look* different, but it *works* different."

Other industry professionals have experienced the same thing. "When I started interviewing people at Condé Nast about alternative officing, they all said, 'Oh no, not Chiat/Day!'" says Alfonso D'Elia of Manicini Duffy, discussing the planning interviews his firm conducted on a project to relocate the publishing empire to a new building in New York City's Times Square. "People don't realize how well known Chiat/Day's offices are to clients! So then I had to undo the damage done by all the negative publicity about Chiat/Day's nonterritorial offices, which I personally think are exceptional."

To undo the perceptions during client presentations, D'Elia shows clients the differences between conventional, alternative, and virtual space, helping

Figure 6.3
Doug Ball designed the Clipper in 1994, and the capsule still sells through Gilbert International's New Space division. The industry either loved it or hated it, but it's really made for intense computer workers, and many people have bought units as alternative home offices.
(Doug Ball.)

the clients to understand that an alternative office is a mix of spaces that includes conventional space, more team and activity areas, and if feasible, a virtual strategy, too. When clients begin to understand that an alternative workplace doesn't always look different from some traditional layouts, but that the way in which the space is used is very different, they become more comfortable with the concept and reality of working in an alternative work setting. In fact, many clients who make that transition to an alternative workplace reuse furniture already in inventory, sometimes supplemented with mobile tables of various shapes and sizes.

In this chapter, we will look at on-site and off-site furniture (home office solutions for the telecommuter are discussed in the next chapter) and product solutions manufacturers have begun to tinker with for use in the alternative workplace.

THE PROBLEM WITH PANELS

No one hates a cubicle more than the worker who has to suffer within its bland confines. Former Packard Bell employee-turned-millionaire cartoonist, Scott Adams, made a career out of expressing the innermost thoughts of the cubicle set (*Dilbert* is so popular it's planned to debut as a television situation comedy). Even Bob Propst, responsible for the success of Herman Miller's Action Office panel system, has contempt for the cubicle, which has turned into something very different from what he intended. "Why would anyone choose to live or work in anything other than a stimulating, revitalizing environment? But organizations get what they

deserve," Propst says in a *Fast Company* magazine article about the alarming way Corporate America has glued itself to the notion that hives of bandage-beige or grisly gray cubicles are aesthetics that make people happy and productive.

When the Quickborner Team (a German organizational efficiency consulting group) created the open-plan landscape in the 1960s, walls were torn down, straight lines of desks were eliminated to make way for random groupings of free-standing furniture that could be combined with screens or panels to define work areas. This kind of open-plan office landscape was called *Bürolandschaft*. When the open-plan landscape first appeared, panels were generously spread out far apart from each other and buffered with plants. In the late 1960s, Herman Miller introduced modular office furniture with acoustic panels, a move that allowed open plans in U.S. offices to flourish. Today, the panel system, or cubicle, of which there are hundreds of designs from numerous manufacturers, is called the "veal pen" in some circles,[1] since it shrank in size in order to accommodate more people on an office floor as Corporate America went on a hiring frenzy in the 1980s. Furniture manufacturers made fortunes on the sale of cubicles. By the mid-1990s, cubicles had taken over the nation.

At a 1996 Facility Management Symposium on alternative officing during Neocon in Chicago, the audience of facility professionals was asked about the future of panel systems. "Is the panel system dead and buried?" asked a panelist of the audience. The audience of approximately 100 facility professionals responded in unison by shaking their heads no.

The panel system is still as ubiquitous as ever. When panel systems were first introduced, they were the ultimate in flexibility—panels could be more easily reconfigured than drywall. Today, flexibility means something totally different—it generally means a piece of furniture has to be on wheels. But corporations have invested too much money in panel systems to just throw them away, so now manufacturers are trying to help their customers work around the inflexibility of panel systems. (Figs. 6.4 and 6.5).

The trouble with panel systems is that for today's needs, they are too static. There's no natural daylight streaming into the cubicle unless you have had the good fortune to snag one by a window—that is, if the perimeter is not already taken up by private offices filled by the ghosts of vice presidents who are never there anyhow. In a cubicle, there's no door

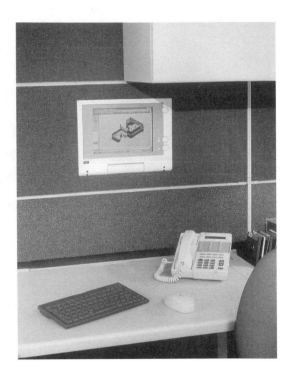

to shut if you need to tune out the loud voices of your neighbors, or if you really need to call your spouse, doctor, child, or heaven forbid, a client with a confidential problem to discuss. A cubicle with 45-inch-high panels (from the floor) is at the perfect and most comfortable height on which visitors (sometimes unwelcome) perch their elbows from a standing position. If you work with coworkers who have private offices and who get bored from being cooped up and decide to emerge for a visit with you, how do you let them know that now is the not the time to talk because you are trying to eat your lunch in peace, alone? It can get only more complicated in an alternative workplace where there's more open space and not enough etiquette training for those who are used to talking freely on the phone or meeting with people in the confines of a four-wall office. However, some workers in new workplaces report that the office is now quieter than it was before since more people are out of the office and in the field.

THE MEANING OF MOBILITY

What best characterizes a piece of furniture meant for an alternative workplace is one that is on wheels. Wheels in the office—especially the back office (shipping and receiving, factory floor, etc.)—however, aren't so new. But the advent of furniture on wheels began to evolve at a more hasty pace during the mid-1990s as work process started to seriously change in front offices (administrative areas) around the country. Furniture manufacturers began to take notice of the pulse of their customers, especially around the Silicon Valley area of California. Customers just couldn't find flexible furniture solutions for their needs. What they needed was furniture that could roll around and accommodate technology.

The first truly mobile furniture products could be found on the factory floor and in the mailroom. So the recent journey for furniture manufacturers began when they thought they were being innovative by putting wheels on office furniture (Fig. 6.6). But this is also not such a new idea. Back in 1984, Susan Szenasy, editor in chief of *Metropolis*

TVP-44LTC

Figure 6.7

Steelcase's original desks from the 1920s don't look much different from desks designed today. (Steelcase.)

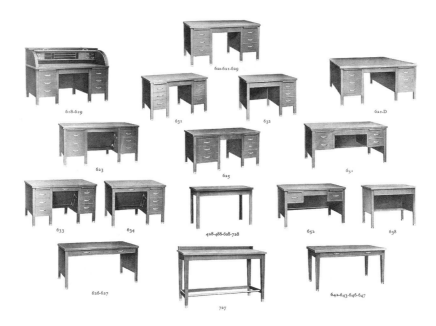

magazine, wrote a book, *Office Furniture*, in which she discussed mobile furniture for the office.

"Tables on wheels, tables that rotate, tables that can be taken apart, all express the mobility of the modern office worker." Szenasy had clearly glimpsed the future of office workers' needs even before the manufacturers could do so (see Szenasy 1984). Here are a few examples of the tables considered mobile back then: Belschner Table Group by Metro described as colorful, geometric, lightweight; Hoffmann Nesting Tables by ICF that are really end tables; the de Menil Table by Charles Gwathmey and Robert Siegel by ICF with an inlay diamond pattern; D'Urso tables by Knoll on tiny casters; the Capsule conference table by Ward Bennett for Brickel on casters; and the Lucia Mercer

Tables by Knoll, a low, stone indoor-outdoor table. In fact, the book does cite Douglas Ball's S-Drawers file cabinet made by Sunar. "The basic two-drawer pedestal file has been turned into a metal mobile unit…to roll top-secret information around the office" (Figs. 6.7 and 6.8).

MOBILITY AS ESSENTIAL FOR TEAMING

Informal teaming can be difficult to achieve if furniture doesn't move to accommodate fluid needs of teams. There are products emerging on the market to support small or large teams. However, many designers and end-users complain that although a table or chair is mobile, there are many cities in the United States (Chicago and New York, for example)

Figure 6.8

EOC's Orbit is one company's solution for the alternative office. Though the flat work surface hasn't changed much from the olden days of desk making, the question really is whether or not we even have to change the work surface. We will always need something on which to work.

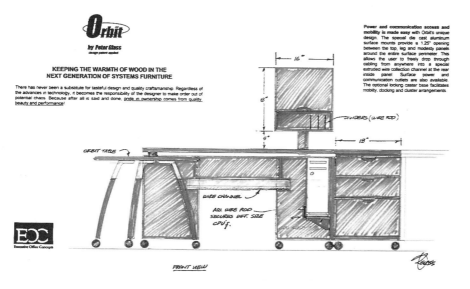

that require only hardwiring, and that mobile power cords trailing on the floor are against code making the specification of mobile furniture a moot point (Figs. 6.9 and 6.10).

A NONSYSTEM TEAM SETTING SOLUTION FROM JAPAN

When Mike Brill from BOSTI came back from his trip to Japan, he experienced first-hand how little spatial privacy Japanese workers had, and in private conversations, workers told him how difficult it was to concentrate and produce work as individuals since people were sitting so close and face-to-face with one another. What Brill was impressed with was the way the Okamura Corporation developed product to alleviate these issues. Okamura, a formidable Japanese contract furniture,[2] partition, store display, home furnishings, and industrial machinery manufacturer, has annual net sales of $1.6 billion.[3] "With sophisticated technology built in, it is technosmart and design smart, nonsystem and nonmodular; very flexible and easy for users to manipulate," he says in an article written for *Interiors* (see Brill 1996).

Okamura realized it had to develop product that would not only alleviate the stifling closeness of "island-style" office planning in Japan, but would also support the emerging global-wide work process of the self-directed team. Although teaming was popular around the world in the 1970s and 1980s in companies looking to improve the workplace, the self-managed team is the more

accepted, agile model today because it serves a company's purpose in ways that other processes may not. A self-directed team quickly comes together as a small, independent business unit that focuses on a clearly defined mission with members moving from one project to another as the need arises. The fixed workplace just wasn't working anymore in the advent of self-directed teaming, so the Japanese company decided to help its clients overcome the obstacles of the physical workplace

Figure 6.11
Okamura's Profice
alternative office
furniture has panels that
can be raised or lowered
depending on the function
the user is performing
(teaming versus heads-
down work).
(Okamura.)

that make the activity of teaming so difficult to achieve.

What began at Okamura in 1994 as informal discussions of the office of the future resulted in Profice, a furniture collection introduced in Japan in 1997, and designed to support the fluid activities of teaming. Most people will agree that a mobile furniture collection like this is quite unusual coming out of Japan, where the traditional island-style office is still prevalent. Nevertheless,

Okamura realized its more progressive clients needed something different in the physical workplace setting. Profice is a name chosen by Okamura to mean "progressive," "prompt," "productive," and "professional."

Profice isn't a system, it's a group of mobile furniture that lets the user move and adjust the height and juxtaposition of the furniture as needed (Figs. 6.11 through 6.15). Softly rounded work surfaces made from medium-density fiberboard and paint-

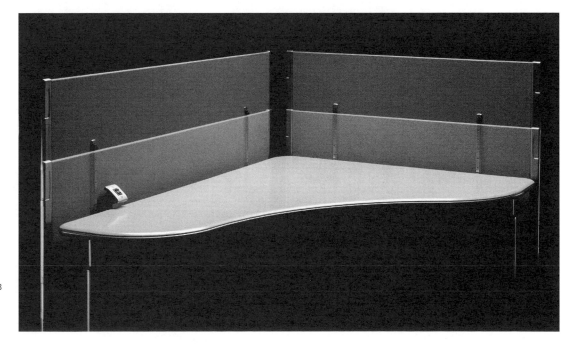

Figure 6.12
Here's a close-up of the fabric-covered steel-framed panels, which can be raised or lowered easily on a patented notched pole as high as 20 inches and as low as 8 inches from the work surface.
(Okamura.)

Figure 6.13
Profice is designed with little rolling tables (subtables) that can come together in a training or teaming environment. (Okamura.)

Figure 6.14
Profice's subtables can roll back to the individual's desk for private work. (Profice.)

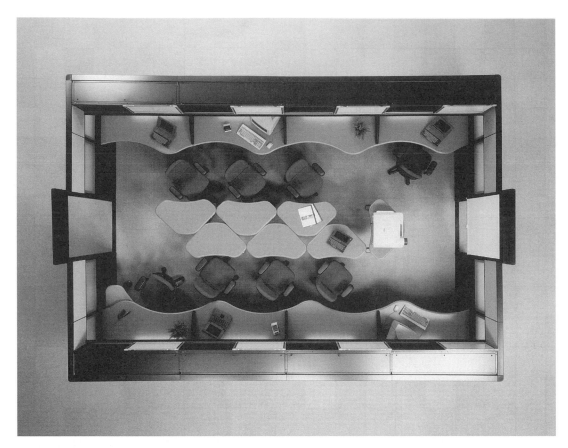

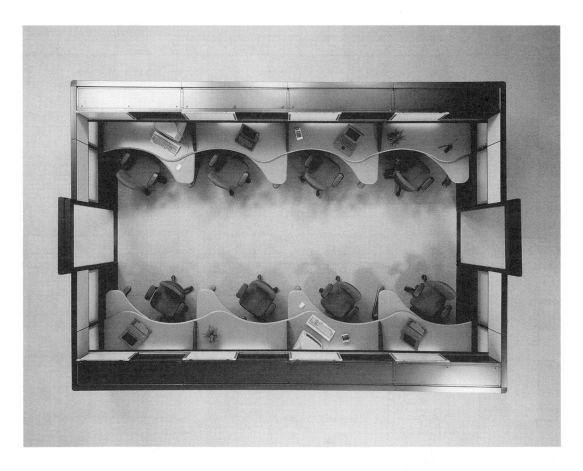

Figure 6.15

Or Profice can handle
small break-out teams
with its rolling kidney-
shaped tables. Subtables
slide under the main work
surface.
(Okamura.)

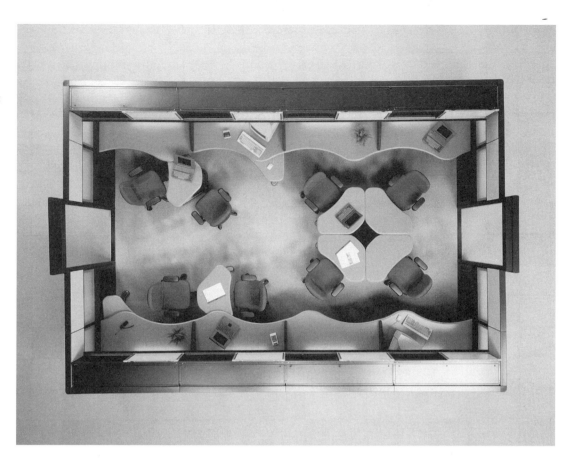

ed surfaces can be adjusted for height manually, or by the touch of a button on an optional desktop computer screen. But it's Profice's fabric-covered panels that make all the difference. The patented manual hydraulic lift mechanism easily moves the panels up and down as high as 20 inches from the work surface for maximum privacy and as low as 8 inches up from the work surface for visual contact with other team members. All of this means the user can move and adjust the furniture in seconds without the need for costly and time-consuming outside labor. Wire management still remains an issue. Even though Profice handles wire management through the use of detachable flexible tubing from tabletop to floor or wall, again, those cities that require hardwiring only will find that they really can't specify mobile furniture as it's fully intended to be used.

ON-SITE SOLUTIONS FOR THE ALTERNATIVE WORKPLACE

When Chiat/Day first designed its virtual offices in Venice, California, and New York City in the early 1990s, Laurie Coots was frustrated with the furniture on the market to support the kind of work environment she envisioned. "There weren't pieces to buy to put together what we wanted," she said. "There weren't enough choices out there to choose from." Instead, the offices in Los Angeles were filled with odds and ends—like battered tilt-a-whirls salvaged from an amusement park—that had to suffice as a private seating area. Slowly, but surely, the manufacturers began to get the hint.

Peter Drucker says in his book *Crazy Times for Crazy Organizations* (1994, Vintage Books) that Steelcase and Herman Miller may have set the world ablaze with panel systems, but that industry in Grand Rapids lost its nerve and sank into a "quicksand of commodity competition," that manufacturers never reinvented product to keep up with Corporate America's needs.

Grand Rapids, Michigan, home of the commercial furniture manufacturing market, has changed—albeit slowly—with the advent of the alternative workplace. In the early 1990s, a client would go to Grand Rapids to tour the manufacturing facility and perhaps talk a bit about what current research is in the manufacturer's pipes. But the client was there mainly for three things: to get a sneak peek of new products, see how far they could push the manufacturer to do a custom job at standard prices, and make sure the manufacturer wouldn't go out of business before the ink on the order was dry. That's all changed today.

"The type of person coming to GR today is changing," says Bob Evett, a senior consultant with Steelcase's advanced solutions group. "It used to be the real estate and facility professional only, but now they are bringing CEOs and vice presidents because now the conversations have more to do with business than they have to do with the artifact."[4]

Evett refers to the *artifact* as the physical product that prompts companies like Steelcase to spend $30 million a year on research and design. With that kind of money spent on R&D for artifacts—or products—there's bound to be keen observations of the workplace. This is the kind of information that clients are hungry to learn so they can better leverage their own properties.

THE MYSTERY BEHIND STEELCASE'S PATHWAYS

By the time you are reading this, you will have seen Phase One of Pathways, Steelcase's groundbreaking commercial furniture/environment concept. Designer John Duvivier, Bottom/Duvivier, remembers when he came up with a raft of product concepts for Steelcase that were developed around investment cost and change and have since been stripped down from the original conceptions into that of the current Pathways concept. Duvivier, who also helped Steelcase develop its Workplace Envisioning software along with the U.K.–based consulting group DEGW, is an outspoken advocate of workplace furniture innovation and has plans to start his own company to produce exactly that— innovative products. He's been continuously frustrated with the state of furniture manufacturing and design today, and he believes that even Pathways— as different as it will look—is still at best a mediocre solution to a facilities problem. "Whatever comes out this year or next is highly tooled with sophisticated capital invested, but it will be irrelevant in two years after its debut," he explains, but he keeps under wraps his own vision for furniture for the future.

Steelcase has been as tightlipped as a guard at London's royal palace about the introduction of Pathways, and Jim Hackett, CEO, admits to a certain amount of intentional spin-doctoring, as the company has managed to create drama and mystery prior to its release,[5] even though the industry is used to the manufacturer's delay in many of its

product launches. Steelcase promises that Pathways will forever change the way in which we think of offices. Pathways is an engineered product that integrates all the floor-to-ceiling interior components of an office space. Pathways is dubbed by Hackett as a "portfolio of products" in which there will be panel solutions, free-standing furniture, floors, plenums—all of the things that have to work together that typically don't since they have to be job-site modified. "Our vision is that these components are engineered so that they do work together and that the change in the cost of ownership drops dramatically because there are no redundancies or overlap," says Hackett. He also says the new chapter on panel power is ready to be written, and Pathways will address that issue, too.

Hackett is certainly not to blame for Pathways's delayed launch; in fact, when he became CEO, he's the one who put gas on the burner to resurrect and iron out the kinks in the product. It's the same problem that delayed the formal and final launch of the Personal Harbor to an industry that had already heard enough about it and was relieved that the hyperbole had finally died down. "It's fair to say that there was a dysfunction in the company in the early 1990s, and the Pathways project was shelved because of the huge capital investment needed," says Hackett. "Now that I got back onto the project, it will be less than two and a half years that Pathways will make it to market as a fully developed, engineered, and produceable product."

A NEW FURNITURE COMPANY SUPPORTING THE NEEDS OF THE ALTERNATIVE WORKER

In 1993, furniture designer Manfred Petri consulted with IBM on its nonterritorial office solution needs. From there, he became involved with similar needs at American Express, Peat Marwick, Ernst & Young, and other companies transitioning into the new workplace. Out of his research, Petri formed a company in 1995 called "Frogbench," which designed a line of furnishings for laptop users who work in nonterritorial environments (Fig. 6.16).

"We weren't going to go with any designs for the corporation at first. We were only going to work on home office design," says Petri. Frogbench will evolve its line, developing home office furniture specifically for those who work out of small, minimal spaces. "Our furniture will focus on home office workers in their late twenties and early thirties who live in a city in a small apartment with little money to invest in home office furniture."

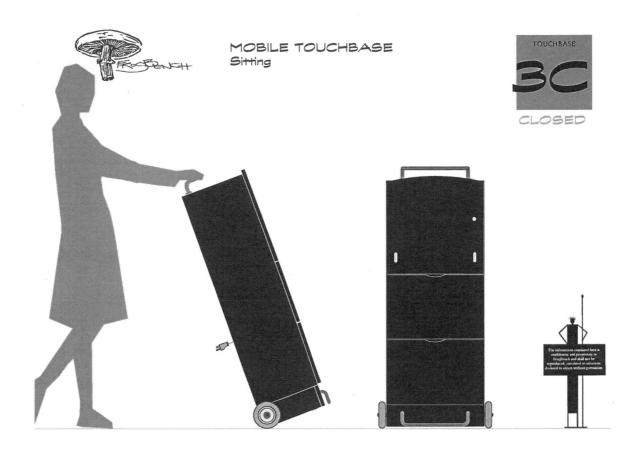

MOBILE TOUCHBASE
Sitting

TOUCHBASE
3C
CLOSED

MOBILE TOUCHBASE
Sitting

TOUCHBASE
3C
OPEN

Pendaflex
Legal /Letter
File Storage

DRAWERS REMOVED

Figure 6.16
Frogbench is an
innovative furniture
company, founded by
Manfred Petri, that
worked with all the
alternative officing
pioneers to create this
laptop unit that has now
been standardized by
IBM.
(Frogbench.)

Innovative technology to
support home officing
(Alan A. Abrahams)

Figure 6.17
Rolling pedestals are by
now a mainstream yet
practical office product
made popular by hotelers.
This one from Office
Specialty is called the
Caddi Star.
(Office Specialty.)

Frogbench is part of a program IBM put together to combat liability problems. IBM recommends certain specifications and products to its mobile and at-home workers on an intranet of which Frogbench is listed.

Petri is also involved with high-end wood case-goods producer Geiger Brickel in bringing back its home office furniture line, called "EPH," that was first introduced in 1994. John Geiger was ahead of the curve when his company was really the first to bring a contract-quality wood home office product to market, which was followed on its heels by

Steelcase's Turnstone line. "We made the same mistake everyone else did in reducing the size of a piece of contract furniture and trusting it would fit into the home," says Petri.

STORAGE AND LOCKERS: THE PAPER TRAIL

We're fervently using the Internet, intranets, voice mail, and e-mail. But we still have a love-hate relationship with our paper. Don't forget, the more printers, the more paper. The more computers online, the more Web pages that get printed out. Note that the sales of color printers under $500 surged in 1995 as 10 million units were sold, more than double the amount of units sold in 1994 (see Flynn 1996). That means we have more stuff to file.

The paper trail is here to stay for a long time, not just because of printed paper but because of faxed paper, too. In fact, if all the used fax paper sheets were placed end to end to make one continuous

Figure 6.18
Egan Visual created a
hoteling locker for the
MCI Boston Rally Center
project and brought it to
market as a standard
product in its line.
(Egan Visual.)

sheet, it would circle the globe 289, times compared to 243 times around the globe in 1995. It's estimated by paper suppliers that by 1998, the amount of fax paper used will rise to nearly 300,000 tons, up from 175,000 tons in 1996 (see *Home Office Computing* 1996).

Yet, in 1996 a *Office Trends* survey by Kennedy Research, both facility managers and interior designers expect that the offices of the future will have fewer files than they have today. Only a handful felt they would need more files in the future. The upshot is that storage needs won't disappear, but they will change. According to Kennedy's study, storage should become flexible enough to fit different types of computer items including computer disks and magnetic-media products (Figs. 6.17 through 6.19).

Paper Remains a Fact of Life*

- Each U.S. worker uses 5400 sheets of paper a year.
- Paper sales grew 5.8 percent between 1986 and 1990.
- Paper sales grew 2.5 percent from 1991 to 1994.
- Paper sales will grow 1.5 percent between 1995 and 1997.
- 30 percent of the "stuff" stored at the workplace is never used or referred to.

There's still the issue of dealing with employees' "stuff" at the workplace regardless of whether the

Figure 6.19
A survey of employees prove they want more control over their environment. (ASID.)

*Source: The Paperless Office, a seminar held during Interplan 1996

environment is traditional or alternative. For the new workplace, a bank of lockers tends to become the solution. When we think about banks of storage lockers in an alternative office, we typically picture the locker we had in high school. But go into any hospital and police station, and you will no doubt find employees using lockers to store their personal belongings. Nevertheless, despite their widespread use in some work settings, designers and their clients have had difficulties in finding products to support their needs. Take, for instance, the MCI Boston Rally Center and Chicago's O+O Software company. Both companies needed lockers to support their nonterritorial work environments (see Chap. 9 for full case studies), but they had to turn to custom work to fulfill their specifications. Out of the MCI project, however, Egan Visual caught on and brought a product to market in 1996 specifically for hoteling scenarios.

PRIVACY COMPLAINTS IN THE ALTERNATIVE WORKPLACE

E-mail posted on an America Online message board:

Subject: 3 reasons why I hate my job.

Reason 2: My cubicle neighbor snores loudly during working hours.

It's a wonder that people are so surprised by studies that show noise to be a problem with people who work in cubicles. Consider these findings:

- Background speech can cause employee output to decrease by 10 percent, and errors can increase by 12 percent.[6]
- A Steelcase/Lou Harris study concluded that the number 1 factor and the number 4 factor in increasing job performance were a quiet work environment (which enhanced concentration) and privacy in which to conduct conversation.
- It can take 15 minutes to regain concentration after one interruption (see Markhoff 1993).
- Working in a cramped environment crowded with people can take an emotional toll on employees, making them cranky and in extreme cases, can cause pathological social withdrawal, according to a study conducted by Gary Evans, Ph.D., a professor of design and environmental analysis at Cornell University, and Stephen Lepore, Ph.D., an associate professor of psychology at Carnegie Mellon University (see Segrest 1996).

Noise has always been a problem in the office, and excess sound becomes exacerbated in an alter-

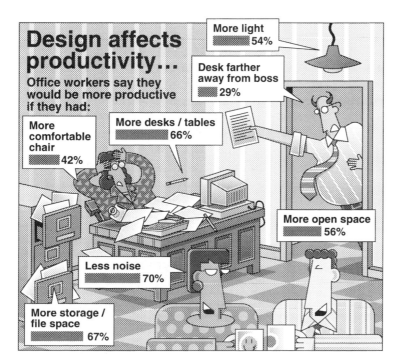

Design affects productivity...
Office workers say they would be more productive if they had:

More comfortable chair ■ 42%
More desks / tables ■ 66%
Less noise ■ 70%
More storage / file space ■ 67%
More light ■ 54%
Desk farther away from boss ■ 29%
More open space ■ 56%

native workplace, especially where universal plan, shared space, team suites, and hoteling are used.

There are two types of sounds: airborne (sound traveling through the air) and structure borne (sound traveling through the structure of a building), which includes footsteps overhead or in the vicinity and vibrations of machinery. The new types of airborne sound that occur in an alternative workplace include cell phone transmissions in the office. The popular—and wrong—perception is that a cell phone user has to speak loudly into the receiver to be heard when in fact the tiny pinholes are actually powerful microphones.

For years, structures have been blanketed with sound-attenuating materials, and cracks have been sealed with acoustical sealant. Foam-backed vinyl floor tile is also another way to dampen structure-borne noise. But air is the main medium of acoustic transmission, and the more air, the more sound, especially in alternative workplaces (see Shiner 1997).

It's easy enough to see whether or not there's a noise problem in an office—just keep your eyes open for signs such as people covering an ear in order to hear when they are on the phone, wandering to the restrooms too much, or talking to neighbors too much instead of working because they just can't concentrate.

Interestingly enough, not every alternative office is noisy. The New York City TBWA/Chiat/Day offices are actually very quiet. Even the small waiting area is hushed—quite the opposite of what you'd expect from a wild and colorful interior. When you sit on the waiting area couch, you are sitting right next to a work setting with open computer workstations made of wire—not very acoustically sound. But when you walk into the space, there are unspoken cues for visitors that tip you off to be silent—don't stare at employees and don't talk loudly to the receptionist.

To further reduce the sound problem in its mostly nonterritorial alternative office, TBWA/Chiat/Day in New York City installed colorful rubber flooring (which squeaks when brand new, according to one employee). And although employees walk around with cell phones just about glued to their ears, they have learned how to speak softly into the receiver, allowing their neighbors to concentrate while working on computers. The noisiest area, by design, is the hearth to which people naturally gravitate for socialization and a cup of coffee.

Steelcase has studied the noise issue for years, even going as far as to build a special lab in which to experiment on making the perfect panel nearly noise free. (Hint from those who work in panel systems: The panel isn't the problem; it's the open nature of the cubicle combined with loud people and chatterboxes!)

Noise continues to be a problem at Apple Computer in Cupertino, California. Its research and development complex was an open plan, but no one wanted to work there, especially engineers who relish quiet, privacy, and uninterrupted time in order to write code for computer programming. Although Apple moved in 1993 to a new complex designed with a caves and commons approach,[7] most cubicles have since turned into private offices, and some common areas have doors for not-so-common private offices (see Holbrook 1996).

THE IMPORTANCE OF SOUND MASKING IN THE NEW, MORE OPEN WORKPLACE

Antinoise technology—or at least the theory that it's possible—has been around for decades. That industry is still in its infancy, born in 1992 when a company called "Noise Cancellation" patented the rights to a microchip technology that makes it possible to produce noise-busting products that recognize sound, then generate a silencing wave. Until this technology hits the market in mainstream products, noise will continue to be abated with the typical absorption ceilings and blockers of panels and walls. Another solution, called sound masking, is a low-level background sound that covers up speech and conversation, also called white noise. It's a tool that's increasing in use, and it costs about $1.00 per square foot, according to Dynasound, makers of sound-masking devices.

OFF-SITE SOLUTIONS FOR THE MOBILE WORKER

Off-site workers comprise mobile and at-home workers, each with their own unique and special needs. The needs of the at-home worker, more likely to be referred to as the telecommuter, are addressed in the following chapter. Featured here are consummate products for the road warrior and the travel-weary business traveler.

HOTELS OF THE FUTURE, OFFICES ON THE ROAD

About 70 percent of frequent business travelers use their room as an office, according to research by Marriott Hotels. A large desk with good workspace, comfortable chair, and proper task lighting are all important to the business guest, the research shows. But just think about how difficult it can be to do work in a hotel room. There may be a desk, but the light is terrible or the phone is across the room, and the cord is too short to pull to the desk. Or it's midnight, and you need to print or fax something to someone, but the hotel's business center is closed for the night, and you don't want to leave your work at the front desk because of the risk that it will be lost. If only you had a fax, copier, larger desk, better wire management, and great lighting together in your hotel room, you'd be all set to get some serious work done.

The hospitality industry, out of its slump since the mid-1990s, recognizes that the business traveler is its bread-and-butter business and that their needs are different from the vacationing guest. A handful of the big-name hotels now act like satellite offices for guests. Hotels have had business centers for years, and they've evolved as guests' needs have increased. For instance, Doubletree Hotels added what it calls the "Business Club," 2000- to 5000-square-foot spaces that provide all the business center amenities plus free use of "minioffices," better known as Personal Harbors by Steelcase.

The Marriott is another major hospitality player in the realm of alternative officing. It started when Pacific Bell Yellow Pages directory advertising sales representatives decided to turn a local Marriott Residence Inn in Ontario, California, into a temporary office and living quarters. Why? The representatives were spending several months in one territory selling ad space before moving on to another area, and they needed temporary offices and living spaces. Pacific Bell negotiated with the Residence Inn to get a reduced rate and guaranteed occupancy of 20 rooms for five months. But not just any rooms.

Pacific Bell requested that the rooms be rewired for computers and that calls be rerouted from the hotel's phone exchange. Makeshift offices were set up in each rep's "townhouse suite" with hotel furniture plus an ergonomic chair and file cabinet provided by Pacific Bell. To add icing on the cake the hotel provided amenities such as complimentary breakfasts, in-room kitchens, and maid service (see Groves 1995).

Manufacturers Going on the Road

To address this particular segment of the market, a company called the Summerland Group, makers of The Office (see Chap. 7) for the home office, also developed a unit specifically for the needs of a hotel. The Office Traveler is a fully wired (requires only a single 100-volt electrical outlet and a phone jack for full operation), and it has a patented "lift-and-roll" mechanism. The Traveler can be relocated to other guest rooms by one person.

What makes the Traveler unique is that it is equipped as a full-service workstation. It has lighting, uninterruptible power supply and surge protector, a separate printer-specific surge protector and surge protection policy of $25,000, a pull-out keyboard desk, and a lockable laptop safe work surface.

The patent-pending Traveler is one option for hotels trying to improve service to their business travelers. Steelcase set up a division in 1994 called Steelcase—On the Road, a group of about 17 people given the charge to develop the ability to work seamlessly while in transit or while camped out at a hotel. On the Road researched how business people adapt to hotel room layouts and surroundings during a typical stay, and what the researchers found fueled the group to design a line of furniture to support the business guest's needs, developed in partnership with Marriott Hotels. What On the Road research found was that a hotel room, no matter how big or small, is voluntarily divided up by the guest into five zones: the unloading zone, the hygiene zone, the working and dining zone, the entertainment and relaxing zone, and the resting zone (see Fishman 1996). What a hotel room for the business traveler sorely needed was a way to efficiently support the working and dining zone.

Marriott's Room That Works program incorporates a special desking system, called The RoadWorks Collection. About 9000 Marriott full-service hotel rooms in U.S. and European hotels (London and Frankfurt) have installed the RoadWorks Collection by 1996, and the company hopes that thousands more rooms will have the collection by the year 2000.[8]

The RoadWorks Collection is composed of a desk within a desk—a large writing table on casters that can fit (snugly) into the smallest of hotel rooms, a task light that fits in with hotel decor, a power-database of two power outlets and a data port connection accessible at desk height, and an ergonomic chair that fits in with hotel decor (Fig. 6.20).

The RoadWorks Collection is designed to be flexible and to cross markets, working as well in a telecommuter's home office. "Companies don't want to track furniture as a capital investment, so we kept the prices of the set under $1000," says Bill

Figure 6.20
Steelcase formed a team to investigate how business travelers work in their hotel rooms. The result was RoadWorks, an evolving collection of traditional furniture—of course, on wheels—made especially for the hotel room and is now offered as home office furniture. (Steelcase.)

Gilbert of the On the Road group. "And it can be assembled in 30 minutes."

Steelcase's efforts are certainly headed in the right direction. Besides the Marriott, other hotels are helping the business traveler set up a temporary office-in-a-room in a more efficient way than ever before. The Westin's Guest Office is one such example, equipped with an ergonomically correct desk chair, glare-free task lamp, a speakerphone with data port plus an all-in-one laser printer-fax-copier machine with IBM-compatible and Macintosh printer cables. The Hyatt's amenities for business travelers include much of the same furniture and fax machines, but the printers and copiers are down the hall and available on a 24-hour basis. The Hilton is starting a smaller program in 40 of its four most popular metropolitan destinations, called Smart Desk, in which a room contains a computer, printer, and fax. At many hotels, including Westin, cell phones and laptops are commonly available for guests to rent.

THE COMFORTS OF A CAR FOR THE HARDY ROAD WARRIOR

You wouldn't buy a car without cup holders, would you? Now you can have laptop holders, too (Fig. 6.21).

The typical road warrior—business traveler—flies an average of 113,000 miles a year and drives 21,000 miles a year, according to a survey of 1225 business travelers by *USA Today* in 1993. About 28 percent of them bring computers, and 24 percent bring cell phones, the survey also said. Since that survey, you should probably double the number of people who take technology along with them on the road (Fig. 6.22).

All that technology, however, has a way of breaking. Most drivers tend to throw laptops and cell phones on the dashboard, or on the passenger seat—both dangerous places for equipment to be stored during a quick, hard stop or sharp turn. Current products, such as laptop holders from Jotto, prevent breakage and let drivers work comfortably in the car.

SUMMARY

In 1996, O'Neill Designers found they had to install custom kitchen cabinets to double as hoteling lockers for their client O+O Software, while Hoyle, Doran & Berry architects designed custom workstations and hoteling lockers for MCI's Boston Rally Center because there was nothing on the market at the time to accommodate those types of projects. As a result of these client needs, furniture manufacturers are taking a closer look at the new workplace.

Although through the early to mid-1990s it was refreshing to see drips and drabs of new furniture to support the alternative workplace, the commercial furniture industry on the whole is still pump-

Figure 6.21
There have been so many casualties involving broken laptops when they have fallen off the car seat or dashboard that Jotto designed a special laptop holder for the mobile worker. It's height adjustable and mounts to the floor for extra durability.
(Jotto.)

Figure 6.22
The Auto Exec Mobile Office is a traveling office. The nonskid surface has a compartment for 15 letter-size files. It's plastic, measures 17 inches by 16½ inches with an additional pull-out surface, weighs 12 pounds, and costs $159 through the *Reliable Home Office* catalog (see the Resources at the end of the book). It's not recommended for use in a moving vehicle.
(Mobile Office Vehicle.)

ing out traditional product—but on wheels to accommodate the demand for mobility. The fact is that end users have invested so much money in panel systems that they are looking for ways to leverage the lowly cubicle while providing flexible spaces in which to team, hotel, motel, or free-address. Herman Miller is the first to help its customers turn millions of dollars of panel systems into flexible alternative workplace furnishings with its transitional product called *Arrio* (marries free-standing mobile components with Action Office and Ethospace fixed panel systems). And Steelcase promises that Pathways will solve all sorts of office problems that stem from inflexible, existing interior infrastructures. Then there are companies in ancillary industries, such as Jotto, who are also cre-

ating a whole new line of alternative workplace products mostly for the mobile worker. Home office furniture is an entirely separate category, and the next chapter is devoted to specialized products for the telecommuter's home office.

During the mid-1990s, the products that stood out the most for alternative workplace were Steelcase's Personal Harbors and Haworth's Crossings furniture. Other notables included Kyo, Brayton's Migrations, and Egan Visual's mobile and storage products. From Japan, we look forward to the hopeful distribution in the United States of Okamura's alternative workplace products called Profice. In general, however, many new workplaces don't look different; they look like traditional offices, making use of inventoried casegoods and panels, but it's the way in which the furniture is used that makes the difference between yesterday's workplace and today's new workplace.

If there's something that can be rolled around, then sure enough some manufacturer will think of it, so look for wheels, wheels, and more wheels. There should be some significant strides in early 1998 when Steelcase introduces its much-awaited Pathways integrated officing product (still under wraps at press time although many a designer has been given a sneak preview, and the jury is still very much at large). Knoll introduced "Currents" and Teknion introduced "Ability," both mobile office furniture collections, at Neocon 1997, too—all good-looking and functional, but not radically different. After all, we do need flat work surfaces on which to work regardless of whether or not we work in an alternative office. And, look for a new type of commercial furniture company to emerge conceived and run by notable designer John Duvivier and stay tuned as Grand Rapids tries to cross the bridge into the twenty-first century.

Provisions for the Telecommuter's Home Office

Chapter

7

> If you cannot be free, be as free as you can.
>
> **Emerson**

Trend forecaster Faith Popcorn calls the home office the "hoffice," and she says in her popular 1991 book the *Popcorn Report* that it's the newest real estate development to cash in on. Popcorn is right if you look at all the home office books, articles in the popular press, magazines devoted to the subject, plus furniture and products that have come out on the market since the mid-1990s (for more information about surveys on telecommuting, see Chap. 2).

With a growing market of goods and expertise, the home office still remains a hidden design problem. It's historically been the stepchild of mid- to late-twentieth-century residential design,[1] a corner in the kitchen set up to hold a phone, answering machine, and enough work surface on which to write out a few checks to pay the bills. Today, the typical home office includes computers, printer, maybe a fax. Add mismatched files, a cheap wood door on top of the files that act as a desk, and a dining room chair with a straight ladder back. Wires and cables hang out from behind makeshift desks. Plastic milk crates (usually snatched from behind the local deli out of desperation for cheap home office storage solutions) hold everything and anything to be filed. As Bernadette Grey, the editorial director of *Home Office Computing Magazine* (see Grey 1994) said of her disastrous home office, "I have no excuse. I know better. I also know that I'm not alone. In fact, some of you are spending 50 or 60 hours a week in offices that make bus station waiting rooms look comfortable." *Home Office Computing Magazine* has recognized the problem by initiating an annual "Messiest Office" competition that attracts thousands of entries every year with one lucky person winning a home office makeover.

Home office design has become an ad hoc adventure for telecommuters, most of whom have no time to design an efficient, aesthetically pleasing space. As consumers, telecommuters are not aware of the home office furniture options they have besides what they see at the local office superstore when shopping there for odds and ends. Many telecommuters hope to grab something from the corporate office inventory as a fill-in until they get around to designing their home office. Other telecommuters are lucky enough to have companies who are taking the lead in helping the employee to set up, we hope, an efficient, ergonomic home office.

This chapter is not meant to be a "how to design a home office" essay, for there are excellent books[2] on the market (for telecommuters and small-business owners) such as *Home Office Design* by Neal Zimmerman, AIA (Wiley, 1996) and *The Complete Home Office* by Alvin Rosenbaum (Viking Studio Books, 1995) and the forthcoming book *The Practical Home Office: Real-Life Design Dilemmas and Solutions* by Marilyn Zelinsky Syarto (McGraw-Hill, 1998). In this chapter, we will explore what typical provisions employers make for telecommuters and you will find choice examples of home office furniture for telecommuters that have come out of the contract and residential furniture market.

A telecommuter, or teleworker, as we have already defined, is a corporate employee that works from home one or more days a week on a

The virtual home-office
(a modern mirage)
(Alan A. Abrahams.)

consistent basis. Companies further define a part-time telecommuter as someone who works at home one to three days a week, and a full-time telecommuter as someone who works home five days a week. Basic provisions for telecommuters include technology (networking) and furnishings. From this chapter you'll get a better idea of what companies are providing for telecommuters in the way of furniture standards. Remember, there are no pat answers, no cookie-cutter packages. Some packages are sparse, some generous, but most are starting to consider that the company has not only taken the employee out of a finely tuned, highly ergonomic environment but has also just placed its real estate burden directly onto the employee's shoulder.

Although there are formal telecommuting programs that require the telecommuter to sign an agreement (see App. F), there are armies of "closet," "underground," or "guerilla" telecommuters who receive no provisions whatsoever. Perhaps they are lucky enough to be reimbursed for phone expenses, paper, and printer ink. Closet telecommuters are employees who telecommute under the more formal definition but don't have the support from corporate executive management such as human resources. For example, one 10-person department in a particular company has two closet telecommuters. The telecommuters work at home one or more days a week on a consistent basis and fill out sign-in sheets on what projects they are working on

at home for the day. The department manager holds onto the sign-in sheets in a file just in case human resources finds out about the closet telecommuting activity and she needs to justify the fact that some of the staff telecommutes in order to complete major projects.

PROFILE OF A TYPICAL TELECOMMUTER

A typical telecommuter is a white-collar male or female who has been at his or her company for on average 2 or more years and makes in the range of $25,000 up to $75,000 and higher. The employee has a good productivity track record, is highly motivated, and is able to work by himself or herself for long stretches at a time. Most important, the employee is an excellent communicator whether it is by memo, phone, face to face, or e-mail. Those jobs best suited for telecommuting are ones with frequent phone and computer work, low face-to-face contact or interaction, or project-based jobs that need intense concentration that can be accomplished in confined areas. The typical telecommuter is also not afraid of technology, especially when he or she has to troubleshoot technical problems. Telecommuters are great adapters to environment and tend to work in unique settings.

Those white-collar knowledge workers who *cannot* typically become a telecommuter may have conflicts with time and space at home, lack willpower to stay away from the refrigerator, television, or beach, rely on or need to do their job with daily, hourly contact with coworkers, and those who need outside motivation and stimulation to be productive. There are many more people like this than there are people who will be successful, long-term telecommuters. A number of people abandon telecommuting after 6 to 18 months when they find out how difficult it can be.

Who telecommutes?

Information specialists	69 percent
Sales representatives	68 percent
Programmers	61 percent
Market research analysts	59 percent
System analysts	52 percent

Source: Cindy Hall and Web Bryant, Computing Commuting: Telecommute America Survey asked Fortune 1000 companies what types of jobs in their organizations can telecommute. *USA Today*, December 7, 1995, Business Section, page 1.

Figure 7.1

During Herman Miller's intervention study in 1996, the team saw the many ways in which real-life telecommuters make due in their home offices. For example, one telecommuter worked on a rough-hewn sawhorse and table desk. (Herman Miller.)

TELECOMMUTERS WORK...WHERE?

There are a couple of widely divergent visions the public has of where the typical telecommuter works; from the beach to a fully outfitted, professionally designed home office that many of us see in magazines and books on the subject. Where and how do telecommuters *really* work?

One furniture manufacturer, Herman Miller,[3] found out by infiltrating the homes of real corporate telecommuters. Herman Miller had already come out with a major home office furniture collection in 1994 but realized the market for this manufacturer wasn't in retail. Instead, Herman Miller decided to focus on working with its established client base—large corporations—to help them get their arms around the telecommuting issue. With that goal in mind, Herman Miller appointed Marc Lohela, director of corporate telecommuting and home office, to talk to corporate and government clients about their large-scale telecommuting needs.

It was clear that Herman Miller needed to conduct research into the telecommuting phenomena. And doing what furniture manufacturers do, it set out to find some major research to define clearly the corporate market's needs. The traditional route of questionnaires wouldn't do for this kind of research. After all, questionnaires don't tell you what it *feels* like to be a telecommuter, what it *feels* like to work at home, what it *feels* like to leave behind the corporate amenities for the comforts, or discomforts, of home. Lohela was in search of "feelings from the heart and from the gut" of what it's like to be a telecommuter. It was the *only* way to figure out how to design the right kind of home office furniture for corporate telecommuters' needs.

So from 1995 through to 1996, Herman Miller's "intervention research" project involved plucking 40 telecommuters from four companies (Fig. 7.1). "We had to go very deep and very fast, not broad and shallow," says Lohela of his strategy. Herman Miller worked with Amdahl, GTE, Atlantic Bell, and Nortel, soliciting 10 telecommuting volunteers from each company, from geographical locations and diverse professions. Lohela was able to see what it was like to telecommute from a 200-year-old farmhouse in upstate Connecticut to a 3-year-old high-rise in central Los Angeles.

"We learned really quickly that people will work in all different parts of the home—based on two factors: where they have space to allocate and where there is space to work comfortably," says Lohela. He found that participants worked out of the corners of their master bedrooms, or they'd squeeze into the corner of a family room, kitchen, or basement. What was consistent was the fact that these telecommuters cobbled together their own workspace environments, giving little thought to aesthetics, but with only one goal in mind—to get the work done in comfort.

of narrow interior doorways, long winding hallways, low ceilings, heating systems in the way, window sills and door jams that intrude on space—all issues that elude commercial interiors.

HERMAN MILLER'S INTERVENTION STUDY

You name it, telecommuters work on it (Figs. 7.2 and 7.3). Kitchen table, dining table, or a door on two sawhorses. One man in the Herman Miller study worked in the corner of his living room on his well-worn rocking recliner, his work surfaces were folding TV tables, and a large box in which his computer had been packed. To see how telecommuters work when their environments change, Herman Miller divided the group into three parts and asked the 40 telecommuters to work on other furniture the company provided at no cost.

One-third received Herman Miller commercial-grade office furniture, from panel systems to desking systems that came right out of the price book, including some Action Office panel system products. A space planner came into the homes at a cost of about $1500 for design and installation, plus another $4000 in product costs.

According to the study, participants said that the positives of having commercial-grade product in a telecommuter's home included:

- Enough storage
- Looks professional

ARCHITECTURAL IRREGULARITIES IN THE HOME OFFICE

Wherever the telecommuter made his or her home office, there was bound to be an irregular architectural element in the way. Home architecture is dramatically different than commercial architecture, but the home office furniture on the market didn't take any of that into consideration. The physical issues of getting the furniture into a residential space presented all kinds of problems. Allowing for trucks to go into residential streets was one issue. Dragging furniture up narrow back stairs was another problem. Then came the interior itself, full

Figure 7.4

Herman Miller's Beirise line (1997) is the newest generation of the company's home office furniture collection, and its refined design is based on the results of studying 40 telecommuters, their natural environments, and their needs and habits. (Herman Miller.)

- Very organized
- Lots of work surface
- Accommodates technology and wire management easily
- Lockable components
- Quality furnishings

However, they noted the downside to living with commercial-grade furniture in a home office:

- Consumes large amount of square footage
- Too officelike in look and feel
- Aesthetics not compatible with residential style
- Installation difficult
- High price
- Space planner usually necessary
- Difficult to move around, replace parts, reconfigure

One-third of the intervention participants received product purchased from local superstores labeled "home office furniture." For $399, participants received a desk to hold the computer up off the floor. And the last third of the participants received prototype furniture that Herman Miller commissioned to be designed by outside designers (Fig. 7.4). "Although telecommuters expect equity in the way they are treated, they do not want parity in terms of furnishings; they don't generally want a gray paneled workstation at the end of their living room," Lohela concluded.

OVERCOMING THE HURDLES OF HOME OFFICE FURNITURE DELIVERY

Contract furniture manufacturers like Steelcase,[4] Geiger,[5] and Herman Miller found that one major stumbling block of selling home office furniture to consumers is trying to deliver the product. The contract industry's sales, delivery, and installation infrastructure is the dealer network, and they are used to larger-scale projects and quantity jobs. Dealers aren't set up to take a single order for a residential delivery.

In the mid-1990s, Steelcase's home office furniture division, Turnstone, tried to sell midpriced product through direct-mail catalog sales, at first angering dealers who said they could sell the product to corporate end users for their telecommuting programs. Steelcase ceased its direct-mail efforts for Turnstone in 1995 because it wasn't pulling in sales. Now, Turnstone is sold only through dealers (Fig. 7.5).

What Steelcase found was that direct mail is good only for consumers who want a $39 chair and don't care what it looks like, or on the opposite side of the spectrum, for consumers who are sophisticated and know product well.

Herman Miller had its own freight and delivery problems to untangle. In an earlier beta studies of prototype executive cherry wood home office furniture, the JB Collection (no longer in production), it was reported that a truck delivering a file cabinet

Figure 7.5

Steelcase found it difficult to sell its home office furniture through a catalog. It has discontinued the entertaining, user-friendly catalog, but it still sells Turnstone product through dealers to accommodate large corporate customers who have telecommuting programs. (Steelcase.)

to a beta-site participant left the hefty box in the middle of the cul-de-sac and didn't help the homeowner take the package into the house. So the homeowner had to retrieve his hand truck from the garage to bring in the bulky box.

Herman Miller thought it had finally solved the delivery problem. It had set up an exclusive arrangement with Sears' Logistics Services. Sears does about 10,000 home deliveries every day of the year, they move 700 million pounds of freight around the states a year, and they do it exclusively for the home. Herman Miller chose this type of delivery service because it has the right sized equipment and its attitude is geared toward servicing the residential consumer. But this plan was abandoned because Herman Miller realized that delivery of Sears's products was the service's first priority, which left many end-users high and dry waiting for home office furniture deliveries. Herman Miller has since set up an arrangement with another residential goods delivery service that better understands home deliveries.

A HOME OFFICE FURNITURE DELIVERY NIGHTMARE

David Harris, purchasing representative and coordinator of furniture and equipment for over 800 telecommuters at the St. Paul Companies in St. Paul, Minnesota, shares a few unfortunate home office furniture delivery experiences. When the company first began its telecommuting program (it uses Herman Miller and HON product to furnish telecommuter home offices), Harris thought delivery and assembly of furniture to a home office would be a breeze. Telecommuters were asked to assemble their own furniture, but that plan turned out to be a disaster. Not every employee is willing, or able, to muscle a 50-pound desk into place. Nor is everyone a handyman. "Most young people didn't own tools to assemble the furniture," said Harris.

Next, Harris hired local install-and-assembly services for home office furniture deliveries. But most of the services hire high school or college kids on break who, according to Harris, were "unprofessional, unskilled, and they came to our telecommuters' homes without tools." Some didn't speak English, and most backed across lawns and damaged interior woodwork, Harris remembers.

The third plan turned out to be a charm. Harris decided it made more sense to spend the bit of extra money it took to have all the furniture delivered and assembled through the furniture manufacturer's dealers, an arrangement that works quite well for St. Paul. Harris found that the dealers provided full service and sent polite, professional, and well-trained people to his telecommuters' homes. "If they nick a wall, they fix it and it never gets back to me," Harris says.

DOES A BETTER ENVIRONMENT MAKE A MORE PRODUCTIVE TELECOMMUTER?

Although she is a major advocate of home office work, Brenda Laffin, manager of alternative officing and property services at Southern California Edison, never felt very comfortable in her old home office. Laffin and her family moved into their home when they only had one child. At the time she began to work at home full time, there were three little Laffins and no extra room to dedicate to an adequate home office space.

She was left with no choice but to work on the kitchen table, near the back door, where all the boots and knapsacks land at all hours during the day and night. Laffin's main work surfaces became the kitchen table, two folding TV tables, the top of a high-chair, and the top of a box. The TV tables, Laffin notes, were just low enough to slide underneath the kitchen table for the night.

Laffin struggled to be productive with this home office set-up. She never felt at ease—her stomach was always churning. Laffin was always wondering if an important piece of paper was lost somewhere in the kitchen. Once she redesigned her office to include the Herman Miller Beirise Collection, her working life became sane, and her children take more pride in their mom's workspace. And now the family has its kitchen table back, unencumbered by Southern California Edison paperwork.

GTE[6] documented how important the work environment really is to a telecommuter's productivity. In January 1996, an executive summary on this subject was developed and distributed at GTE. The study was conducted as a pilot program of 120 telecommuters in the Dallas, Texas, office, in conjunction with the local Department of Transportation, with the "intention of identifying salient issues relevant to the implementation of a telecommuting program." One of the several factors influencing the success or failure of this group of telecommuters was the work area adequacy and ability to work at home. The work area adequacy examined the physical features of the home work area, whether it felt large enough, felt like an office space, and had adequate equipment and comfort with the equipment in order to process work.

GTE measured the ability to work at home by the following elements: Could telecommuters talk privately at home? Could they concentrate in the home work area? And was the noise level low enough to allow them to do their work at home? GTE wanted to know whether or not telecommuters perceived the physical environment at home as a contributor to their overall job satisfaction as a remote worker.

On a scale of 1 (strongly disagree) to 7 (strongly agree), workers were asked to comment on whether the work environment and the ability to work at home contributed to their overall job satisfaction. Work area adequacy was rated somewhat higher than the ability to work at home, which points to the fact that a well-provisioned home office will enhance productivity.

FURNITURE FIT FOR A TELECOMMUTER: STANDARDS

As the demand for home offices grows in response to changing work patterns, residential and contract manufacturers are striving to address this newly important market with furniture and product design in a wide range of styles. Unfortunately, most end-users feel there is still a major void in this area. For this reason, you'll be hard-pressed to find too many companies that have strict furniture standards for telecommuters.

Laffin at SCE held off on setting up furniture standards for her HomeWork program for a couple of years until she felt comfortable with the quality and options offered in the Herman Miller Beirise Collection. In the beginning of the program, Laffin spent a lot of time evaluating home office furniture, realizing that she couldn't compare bids for any standards. "I couldn't get an apple to apple comparison; it was more like apples to oranges," she said. But Laffin was instrumental in helping Herman Miller to refine the design of its Beirise Collection to offer more sizes and finishes.

Clearly, Herman Miller and Steelcase have been the most aggressive marketers to the corporate telecommuter's needs. But most companies that have home office furniture standards for their telecommuters offer either a combination of the two collections to give users more choice in home office furniture, or a company will have a single-source contract with one of these manufacturers to supply telecommuters with home office furniture.

It doesn't matter if a home-based worker is a corporate telecommuter or an entrepreneur—most of the money that person spends on setting up a home office goes first into technology and software. Whatever money is in the budget—if there is one—goes into inexpensive home office furnishings. What home-based workers realize after a while of working in a low-grade environment is if the home office doesn't look or feel inviting, it will never be used. Whether managers like to hear it or not, the reality of avoiding the home office due to a poor set-up with little comfort and organization directly affects productivity. Even though it's difficult to satisfy management with statistical documentation of how much productivity is lost if telecommuters tend to avoid an uncomfortable home office, it's nevertheless a reality corporations should be aware of, whether they are sending people home to work on a voluntary or involuntary basis.

WHAT PROVISIONS CORPORATIONS OFFER TELECOMMUTERS FOR HOME OFFICES

Home office workers spend an average of $650 to equip their office with a desk, chair, and file cabinet, according to a 1996 study by Kennedy Research. The study says that's less than half of what it costs to outfit a traditional corporate office (it really costs on average $6000 for a workstation and chair in a corporate setting); yet the same study, says that only 40 percent of large companies pay for telecommuters' furniture expenditures. Luckily, that number is rising, and there are now corporations that do offer telecommuters and mobile workers provisions for healthy and efficient off-site work settings.

WHO PAYS FOR A TELECOMMUTER'S GAS, ELECTRICITY, AND PHONE?

Virtually no corporate telecommuting program pays for a telecommuter's gas, electric, or heating bills although it is one of the hotly debated issues among employees. In a study of 62 telecommuters in the New York City metropolitan area who worked at home 3.7 days per month, participants reported a rise in costs associated with gas, electric, and heating utilities. Air-conditioning and lighting in summer months raised their electric bills by an average of $11 a month while heat and lighting costs in the winter increased the bill by $7.95. However, this average was computed on the basis of 3.7 days a month, not 2 to 3 days a week (see Bredin 1996)!

Adding second phone lines in a telecommuter's home office can run from $100 to $200 for installation and an additional $20 a month at the basic phone rate. Installing and maintaining an ISDN is another story (discussed in Chap. 5, "Making Sense out of Alternative Workplace Technology").

Southern California Edison's Provisions

In 1996, Southern California Edison set up telecommuting programs that will impact up to 5000 peo-

ple. The most important aspect of the HomeWork program is that an employee has to give up his or her assigned office at the corporate facility.

"Because of my furniture background, I ran into a struggle and confusion with companies, especially the pioneers of alternative officing, who just gave people laptops to work at home with," says Laffin. "It may be okay with those companies that telecommuters are working on a kitchen table, but not with my company." So Laffin came up with two levels of HomeWork programs:

• *From Home*: An employee spends 2 hours or less per day on a computer on a consistent basis, which is defined as 3 days a week. This means the home worker isn't a heavy risk for carpal tunnel syndrome.
• *At Home*: An employee spends 2 or more hours per day on a computer on a consistent basis of 3 days a week.

At-Home workers are outfitted with a fully ergonomic office including adjustable keyboards, chairs, footrests, and document holders. What she found is that the cost of From Home and At Home is insignificant. So Laffin buys From-Home people keyboard trays because it's not much money and it means a lot.

In addition, Laffin suggests Herman Miller's smaller-scaled Ambi chair for home office workers. SCE has a single-source contract with Herman Miller for Beirise home office furniture, as well.

Northern Telecom (Nortel)

There are 2500 telecommuters throughout North America and the United Kingdom out of Nortel's total worldwide population of 60,000 employees. Nortel formalized its standards for telecommuters using Steelcase Turnstone and Herman Miller's Beirise Collection. Nortel offers these two collections of home office furniture to give employees a choice in style. To market Turnstone and Beirise to employees, Nortel built a miniature house in the cafeteria of its North Carolina location and on the Main Street of its new Ottawa, Canada, headquarters. Within each house are two fully operational home offices with Turnstone and Beirise furniture, complete with phone lines, ISDN, and any other technologies and products a telecommuter will typically require. Nortel has even set up a toll-free Home Base Solution Line for telecommuters to call about the status of a delivery and installation of home office furniture.

St. Paul Companies

St. Paul, an insurance company, offers both Herman Miller and HON product to its 800-plus telecommuters. Each suite of home office furniture runs the company between $1800 and $2400, according to David Harris, purchasing representative and the coordinator of the telecommuter furniture and equipment program. Employees can visit a mock-up of both furniture offerings. Fabric sample cards are also distributed to employees. Employees are discouraged from mixing and matching furniture from both Herman Miller and HON because it results in double installation costs. Though some may think HON is an odd choice for a home office furniture standards program, Harris says it is offered because it has more filing and storage options for the home office.

Tandem

Tandem deploys surplus furniture from downsized offices to the telecommuter's home. Some of the employees even take cubicles home. It's the Tandem employees' responsibility to get the furniture home and assembled.

MCI

MCI has over 800 telecommuters and is currently without a standards program. However, the national facilities division is trying to initiate a stipend program offering $500 or an agreement with the asset disposal group to make use of stale furniture inventory that would otherwise be scrapped.

BellSouth Telecommunications

BellSouth has 56,000 employees and 500 telecommuters at the moment. However, the company forecasts that by the year 2000, it will have 5000 telecommuters. BellSouth gives its telecommuters an allocation of $1500 to furnish a home office. Since the corporate offices are standardized on Steelcase, most telecommuters visit the local Steelcase dealership to pick out their furniture and ergonomic accessories.

Herman Miller

Herman Miller's Homesite Program provides telecommuting employees with a stipend of up to $1500 with which to buy furniture from the Beirise Collection, but only if they are willing to give up their workstation at the corporate facility. The furniture depreciates in value over two years.

So if an employee decides to leave the company or ceases telecommuting before the end of the two-year period, the employee reimburses Herman Miller for the remaining value of the home office furniture. After the two-year depreciation period, the employee owns the home office furniture. As an extra perk, Herman Miller also provides two hours of design service and a home office planning kit to its telecommuters.

Lucent's Provisions

Over 18 percent of Lucent's 126,000 employees worldwide work in one of three levels of telecommuting:

- *Formal:* An employee works all or part of the week in a remote location other than a Lucent facility on a regular and consistent basis during normal working hours.
- *Part-time telecommuting:* An employee works at home 2 to 3 days a week on a regular and consistent basis.
- *Casual telecommuters:* An employee works at home when he or she needs to about one to two times a month.

Formal and part-time telecommuters are required to give up their office space at the corporate facility or to share a workspace at Lucent with another telecommuter. Lucent purchases equipment for telecommuters. There is no set standards program for the furniture, and each telecommuter works with the department manager on a case-by-case basis to procure surplus furniture.

Autodesk's Provisions

The act of telecommuting comes naturally to Autodesk. It's the creation of the telecommuting policy that's been so difficult. The culture of Autodesk has included telecommuting since the day it was founded in 1982, says Walter Spevak, director of corporate real estate. Programmers have always worked from home, from a friends' place—anywhere. It's common for an Autodesk employee to telecommute even today because most workers are "telecommute-enabled" with laptops, computers at home, and Iomega Zip drives to transport information back and forth on a high-density cartridge. But what about furniture? Autodesk finally addressed this with a formal telecommuting policy that has been in place since 1996.

Currently, there is monetary assist to help offset home office set-ups in Autodesk's Kinetix division office in San Francisco. The stipend is available, but it doesn't say what explicitly it provides for the telecommuter.

Although Autodesk's telecommuting policy is flexible, Spevak sees the downside of an agreement that doesn't include furniture standards. He worries that without furniture standards, there could be inequity. "Someone will have a manager who is better able to provide furnishings and another one that will say no. We will go with this kind of agreement for a while, and it can evolve when it needs to, or it can become more specific in its provisions," says Spevak.

For now, Autodesk telecommuters are asked to complete a list of what equipment and furniture they are providing for their own home offices and what Autodesk is providing so that the company can keep a running tally.

NCR's Provisions

NCR's America's Virtual Workplace program requires its 2200 sales associates to work from home, and NCR does provide some home office furniture and equipment. During the original pilot conducted in 1994, NCR senior management suggested $1000, and Dan Accrocco, senior project manager, CRE, compromised by suggesting a $500 limit, enough to provide, at minimum, a work surface, files, and a chair. In fact, NCR wanted to continue supporting ergonomic seating and decided it would allow employees to take home the chair they had at the office.

Work surfaces posed another issue. NCR decided it wasn't going to send people home with system furniture, panels, and hang-ons. That invited too many problems: The furniture is heavy, and NCR didn't want employees to risk injury from handling it. During the original NCR pilot, the CRE division became a beta site for new and evolving Herman Miller and Steelcase home office furniture. One quarter of the 12 pilot participants settled on Herman Miller products, another quarter on Steelcase, and the other half decided to provide their own work surfaces in their home offices. NCR did, and continues to, pay for the move of existing and purchased furniture into the home office.

Tracking and retrieving furniture is not an issue. It is the least important aspect of the virtual workplace program because what the company is most interested in tracking is what associate has which computer. NCR maintains a data base correlating serial numbers and social security numbers of associates who have expensive equipment.

Perkin-Elmer's Provisions

Perkin-Elmer, makers of scientific equipment, shut down 45 sales offices during the 1990s. To compensate, it gave employees $1000 each for furniture, and the company paid separately for extra phones, phone lines, laptops, cell phones, and beepers.

RECLAMATION PROGRAMS FOR HOME OFFICE FURNITURE

Most companies say that their telecommuting programs are too new to have reclamation experience with home office furniture. However, most managers track equipment in a data base and require retrieval when an employee leaves the company. For home office furniture, however, reclamation—even for new furniture—just doesn't make sense. Companies that offer work-at-home employees excess furniture deployed from downsized offices say they won't bother to retrieve furniture because it costs too much money to recover the product, pay someone to dismantle it, ship it, refurbish it, and then store it until the inventory is reassigned. And the initial cost for brand new home office furniture set-up is so low—about $1500 (furniture only)—that most companies won't even chase down quickly depreciating first-generation home office product. For some companies, the furniture is considered a perk that reverts to employee's property. So in the end, reclamation of home office furniture is not an important issue.

PRODUCTS FOR TELECOMMUTERS

From the mundane to the creative, both contract and residential furniture manufacturers are taking Faith Popcorn's advice and cashing in on their versions of what they believe the home office worker wants and needs. Most of the challenging issues furniture manufacturers face are how to scale home office furniture down to fit into tiny crevices, rooms, and hallways that are turned into home offices, how to create a design that will integrate into a variety of home decors, and, when it gets there, how to gracefully pull the furniture into and through a house or apartment that doesn't provide a freight elevator. Examples of furniture for the home office follow in these pages.

"Office-in-a-Box" and Computer Armoires

One of the most difficult problems for a telecommuter, or any home-based worker, is finding space

Figure 7.6

Haworth's Correspondent
is an elegant fold-up
solution for the home
office worker.
(Haworth.)

for a home office. Not many people have the luxury of dedicating a 10- by 12-foot room to a home office, especially in tight urban apartments. To accommodate those needs, there has been a spate of computer armoires, including Haworth's office-in-a-box (Fig. 7.6).[7]

In the Herman Miller intervention program, some participants in the group received experimental prototypical computer armoires for their home offices. There were some important insights about this type of solution: "If you are doing serious project-oriented work at home, people won't set up in the morning and take it down at night," reported Lohela. He said that armoires are good for efficiency apartments, but that is only about 5 to 10 percent of the marketplace. From his observations, Lohela believes that people have projects that they work on in phases, and they need a place to put piles of paper. Computers pose another problem in that they are usually kept on at night for other members of the household to use, and keeping it in an armoire would interfere with that. And, in the typical armoire, the printer and fax machines are put in awkward, hard-to-reach shelves.

The Telecommuter's Ultimate Workstations

When The Office workstation won top prize during Neocon's Home Office Product Competition in 1996, sponsored by the Merchandise Mart in Chicago and *Interiors Magazine,* judges cited this piece of furniture for its ability to be a self-contained, full-service work module that actually integrated itself well into most home decors. The patent-pending unit is designed and engineered by the Summerland Group (Fig. 7.7). Made from marine plywood, it looks like an armoire on the outside and opens up to reveal a fully equipped workstation with an ergonomic chair that fits inside when the doors are closed. The office comes in five models, each with different standard and optional equipment: The CEO (the largest model measuring 28 inches deep, 72 inches wide, and 77 inches high), The Professional (48 inches wide), The Manager, The Whizzzard (in white laminate only), and The Office Traveler (for hotel rooms).

Standard equipment for The CEO, for example, includes prewired/cable-ready access for electric, phone, fax, modem, and TV/VCR; desktop lighting; a monitor lift and conceal; a wall-mounted speakerphone; cooling and exhaust controls; a desk accessory toolbar; a bulletin and white board; and an ergonomic task chair that folds and closes up inside the unit. Each unit is mobile by way of a proprietary built-in, lift-and-roll mechanism. Finishes for most models include whitewashed oak and mahogany. The CEO cost about $7000, and other models are less.

The Office was designed by Floridians Robert and Cynthia Gurin, who were "unable to find any decent home office furniture on the market." The team's design objective was to create a home office that is practical, attractive, nonintrusive, computer oriented, ergonomically responsible, user-friendly, rugged, and mobile. When the Gurins accidentally dropped a unit down a flight of stairs, it suffered only a small repairable crack in the exterior wood veneer, and they knew they had the perfect product for the serious telecommuter.

Following along the same lines is a company called Studio RTA, which has introduced a ready-to-assemble version of the full-service workstation, called the Control Tower, along with its other Tele-Commuter series of desks (Fig. 7.8). The Control

Don't Fool Around with Seating for the Home Office

Seating in the home office is just as important as it is on-site. But there are too many articles in the popular press, especially in the consumer design magazines, that show a home office with dining room chairs at the desk or some other forms of poor ergonomic seating. Employees should consider themselves lucky if their company lets them bring office chairs from the corporate facility into their home offices.

However, there's one issue that is not usually a problem in the corporate office...pets. Don't underestimate the power of pet hairs to damage the fabric of a chair brought home from the corporate office. A dog or cat will inevitably find the task chair comfortable (it is ergonomic after all), and soon, the chair will be covered in pet hair. It's not easy to pick, vacuum, wipe, or brush hair off certain types of fabrics, either. For example, a nubby or feltlike contract fabric will most likely hold onto hairs. One of the best products on the market to remove pet hairs from contract upholstery is called Gonzo Pet Hair Remover, a dry sponge that wipes up fur.

Yet another related problem is children spilling soda and juice packs onto the chair while they visit, come in to play games on the computer, or go online. At least in the corporate office, coffee stains are usually the only problem, and typically, the stained chair is switched for a cleaner version.

Figure 7.8
The TeleCommuter center from Studio RTA is also an armoirelike all-inclusive workstation that is specifically marketed to the telecommuter. (Studio RTA.)

Tower is an armoirelike corner desk on casters. Doors glide open on casters to show a 48-inch-wide and 28-inch-deep work surface designed to accommodate computer, printer, CPU, and a task chair.

THE COMPUTER MAKES A DESIGN STATEMENT

Computer manufacturers have never made the distinction of whether computers are used in the corporate office or in the home office. For example, computers have always been gray or putty in the Corporate America environment—a lasting trend that IBM began in 1981 when it introduced its first personal computer. Putty, or bandage-beige, is unobtrusive, and it fades into the woodwork. Putty is practical for a computer, however, because its color creates no "after-image" or residual color that lingers in the eye that might distract the user. Putty gray is the classic computer color, but now black has made its way into the computer world, mostly in the notebook arena. Black is an imposing and chic power color that speaks of quality and performance.

While the color of computer boxes slowly changes, so does its shape. Packard Bell offers smaller, sleeker designs such as a wedge-shaped unit that fits into the corner of a home office or on a desk and minitowers that look like furniture.

A TELECOMMUTER'S BEST TIP: TECHNOLOGY DOS AND DON'TS

Stuffing technology into a tight space—on or off site—can cause serious problems and may result in the loss of valuable stored information. Film and video professionals suggest the following tips to keep information on disk safe.

Keeping disks near computers can make retrieving information problematic. When users try to read these disks, the computer reports back that the disks are damaged or have errors, and most people have no idea why this happens. It's best to keep all audiotape and videotape a few feet away from electromagnetic sources such as TV, radio, telephones, and computer screens.

Anything that is magnetic tape-based or anything that records information such as computer disks should be kept as far away as possible from the computer screen or the system unit itself, as well as from the phone, fax, radio, TV, and electric clock, because electromagnetic waves emanating from any of these items, or even from a speaker, will erase a tape or cause dropouts and noise. And if tapes are kept near electromagnetic fields long enough, eventually they will be erased. Over the course of a few days, you'll notice problems with the disk or tape. If you keep it right on top of a TV or speaker, you'll notice an increase in noise. Even if the TV is off, eventually, it will erase the tape.

If

a company gives its telecommuters and virtual workers a

Rating Home Office Furniture for Durability and Innovation

stipend to go out and buy furniture, the company had better know what they are buying for their money. Although residential and contract manufacturers now offer home office furniture, how good is it?

Does any of it work in terms of scale, aesthetics, price, durability, distribution, and ease of assembly for home office workers and telecommuters? A brave few have explored these questions to new and evolving issues.

A team of hardy souls joined together to assemble and kick the tires of RTA (ready-to-assemble) home office furniture, and the results were published in *Home Office Computing* magazine (see Syarto 1996). Four companies that produced popular home office furniture were chosen—IKEA, Rubbermaid, Anthro, and O'Sullivan (Sauder sent a beautiful computer armoire that would have taken the team a long time to put together because of all the parts and pieces).

The results? Rubbermaid and Anthro won hands down for ease of assembly and sturdiness. But after a day of physical labor, it became clear that parity at home with RTA furniture isn't possible for the telecommuter who is used to working from a streamlined, rock-solid piece of contract furniture. The contract furniture manufacturers clearly have the upper hand when it comes to producing a sturdy product.

At the same time *Home Office Computing* was rating RTA furniture, another venture was in the making. Sensing the importance of the home office furniture segment, the Merchandise Mart in Chicago initiated a home office product competition for contract furniture manufacturers that made its debut during Neocon '95. *Interiors* magazine cosponsored the 1996 home office product competition. The panel of judges both years were journalists and designers, all of whom had had some experience with working in or designing a home office.

Based on submissions both years, it became clear that the furniture and product manufacturers need to do more research and development on the home office market's needs such as distribution, price, scale, and durability. Judges from the 1996 panel urged manufacturers to be more focused on developing innovative accessories ("You can buy most of these items at Office Depot or Staples"), desks ("Too generic"), and surface materials ("No distinction between corporate and residential home office use"). But they did spot three winners in the pack, based on the criteria of "kid-proof" durability, style, scale, function, and innovation.

The lesson here is that the home office furniture industry—whether the product comes from the contract or residential side—still has a long way to go to satisfy the corporate end-user and the telecommuter.

Keep all tapes 2 to 3 feet away. Don't put disks right on computers, don't put tapes right on top of TVs, and don't put tapes on top of speakers or amplifiers. CDs are different; they are laser, light based. Storing information on tape requires the rearranging of the electrons in the coded tape, so anything electromagnetic will disturb the order of the electrons.

Since telecommuters are responsible for all electricity, it pays to take a couple of steps to keep technology safe. If a telecommuter uses a laser printer, it should be taken into consideration that those models use a lot of power during printing. In addition, in a home that experiences hundreds of microsecond voltage surges, some over 5000 volts, many effects will be felt, from a little blip on the computer screen or dimming in the lights to a full-fledged burnout. Many of today's desktop models store data on a spinning disk called a *hard drive*, which spins at a certain rate. Whenever there's a decrease in the electricity current, the spinning slows down or speeds up, and data could be damaged, and the computer can't interpret the recorded data at warped speeds.

There are three forms of power interruption: a *voltage dip*, which occurs when motors of high-draw appliances come on (lights usually flicker); *electromagnetic interference*, which is everyday electrical activity that can scramble computer memory as mentioned above; and the *surge*, which is a rise in voltage that happens outside the house (electric company switches power from one zone to another) that can burn sensitive electronics.

To reduce the risk of corrupt data and to shield computer drives from all the above power surges, telecommuters should invest in inexpensive (average $40) surge protector strips. Inexpensive strips protect equipment from minor electrical disturbances, but for brief power interruptions, telecommuters would be wise to invest in an uninterrupted power supply device that goes for about $150 and offers a few minutes of backup power and just enough time to save and shut down the computer. Look for a UL 1449 rating (that ensures the suppression of a 6000-volt surge), an internal fuse for overwhelming surges, and a good warranty that will cover the cost of any damage a faulty suppressor caused (see Kearney 1997).

Beyond the familiar plug-in outlet surge protector strips for the home office, it's wise to invest in a "whole-house" surge protector. Doubling up on

Figure 7.9
Mark Dudka opened In-House in San Francisco when he sensed the growing importance of accessible home office design.
(Photo by Steve Burns.)

the surge protection should keep electronic equipment—including regular household appliances—from coming down unless the house is hit directly by lightning. A whole-house surge protector uses only one-half watt of electricity, which costs only about 4 cents a month. The design of whole-house surge protectors varies from a standard double circuit breaker that is easy to install to a unit mounted under the electric meter that uses a large metal oxide varistor component. These devices are sold through utility companies and require professional installation (see Dulley 1996).

THE BRANDING OF HOME OFFICE FURNITURE

Everyone jokes about the quality of superstore home office furniture. And most of us perceive furniture from a superstore as cheap, although that's not always the case. "I went shopping for a two-drawer lateral file cabinet and didn't want to spend over $100," said one telecommuter from a mid-sized publishing company. "Ha! I went to Staples and couldn't find one for under $200. Damaged and dented vertical file cabinets were on sale in my budget range, but if you touched them with a feather, they'd fall over." Frustrated, she went to the local Salvation Army store and, as luck would have it, someone had just dropped off a two-drawer HON lateral file in black. The cabinet hadn't even been tagged, but $22 later, and two cans of white spray paint that took 4 days to dry, she had in place her undamaged, undented good-quality file cabinet.

Quality and distribution of contract-quality home office furniture scaled for residential use is no doubt a problem that some retailers and superstores are trying to fix. They are also trying to fix the way they market their home office furniture, which presently leaves a lot to be desired. Most often, a

Figure 7.10

A "before" shot of a home office—it could have won *Home Office Computing's* messiest-home-office contest if it had been entered. (Photo by Steve Burns.)

consumer finds an unattractive and confusing jumble of furniture sitting on the floor off to the side of the store. This warehouse effect turns consumers off, and they walk away thinking how unappealing and cheap the furniture really is.

Office Depot, a chain of over 500 office superstores,[8] is trying to change that superstore image of utilitarian furniture. Office Depot opened two new prototype stand-alone furniture stores in 1995 and 1996 (the first was in Austin, Texas, the second was in Santa Rosa, California) called Furniture at Work with inventory catering to home office needs. The store carries what they term "famous-maker

brands" such as Gunlocke, Bernhardt, Boulevard panel systems, National Office Products, HON, Herman Miller for the Home, Bassett, Lacasse, Techline, BodyBilt, and more that are set up in vignettes around the store and sells the products for up to 60 percent off the manufacturer's list price. The store even sells desk accessories and upholstered lounge furniture from the likes of Kron. The appeal: Furniture at Work offers space planning and design services, an inventory ready for immediate shipment, and furniture assembly services.

IKEA debuted its home office furniture at InterPlan 1996 to attract larger commercial

accounts who have a telecommuting program, complemented with a major marketing blitz in 1997 targeting 1 million American Express card carriers who fit the small-business profile. The popular home furnishings retailer got into the home office market because they saw the number of home-based workers increasing steadily. IKEA realized that their products fit the right budget points, and they even include computerized space planning.

Where do you go for help for upscale home office furniture and design? Call InHouse, the small office, home office specialists. Mark Dudka, owner of InHouse, opened the retail store–design estab-lishment in San Francisco in 1996 because he saw the increasing needs of home office design in his own practice (Figs. 7.9 through 7.11).

SUMMARY

Although there's information on the broad subject of home office design, finding out what provisions employers make for telecommuters in the way of a stipend for new furniture, used inventoried furni-ture, or a standard home office furniture pro-gram…or nothing at all…is more difficult to come by. Company by company or department by department, provisions vary greatly. And the closet telecommuters whose companies don't have a formal policy must fend for themselves. This chapter summarizes some of the more well known telecommuter provisions.

Though many companies find it difficult to standardize a home office furniture program, contract furniture manufacturers are nevertheless working with their larger corporate clients, advising them on product and furniture for their work-at-home programs. This chapter has featured select examples of what's on the market now, and sure enough year by year there will be more options and outlets from which to choose. Nonetheless, the new furniture on the market beats working from a folding television tray!

Creating Policy and Applying Traditional Law in the Alternative Workplace

In 1992, during a seminar on law and alternative officing held at the International Design Center of New York, attorney Jaye Berger answered most audience questions by responding, "Laws in this area will evolve" and "There are no black-and-white answers to liability issues for telecommuters who develop carpal tunnel syndrome, but I can envision lawsuits along those lines."

Five years later, in 1997, legal experts said basically the same thing. The fact is we just don't have a lot of law yet on many of the questions that come up about remote or alternative work. Law always lags behind social changes, and it will be a number of years before we read about a specific case pertaining to telework, for example.

Granted that law is slow in keeping up with the times, but nonetheless, it's an area that anyone involved in implementing an alternative workplace program needs to be cognizant of.

It's best to have some understanding of where alternative workplace issues and the law meet. In this chapter, we will go over the basics on:

• The importance of corporate policy for telecommuting and remote work scenarios.
• Labor law [unions, wage and hour laws, workers comp, the Americans with Disabilities Act (ADA)].
• Property liability (technology, intellectual property, third-party injury, insurance).
• Zoning (for the telecommuter's and remote worker's home office).
• Taxes (for the telecommuter's and remote worker's home office).

You may think workers' comp, zoning, property insurance, unions, and security are issues only for the human resources domain; think again. Planning and design play a major role in the above categories of liability and law of off-site workplaces. As a designer and as a facility professional, you will be expected to know how zoning in residential areas affects the telecommuter and how ergonomics play a tremendous role in the prevention of workers' comp and labor union issues. In addition, and not to be taken lightly, are security and theft issues that must be dealt with in the planning and design of a telecommuter's home office. In this chapter you will find a quick overview for design and facility professionals of how traditional workplace law applies to the alternative workplace.

PREPARING ALTERNATIVE WORKPLACE POLICIES

"We are getting lots of calls now from HR and CRE professionals begging us for policies on telecommuting and alternative officing…they say 'I have to have one now, I need a policy, now!'" says Ellen Reilly, president of the Telecommuting Advisory Council New York City chapter.

Reilly, also president of Port Consulting, found there are three industry practices that exist with regard to telecommuting policies: no policy, shared employee-employer responsibility policy, and explicit corporate direction policy.

"'No policy' is a form of corporate policy," says Reilly. "This means there are no furniture specifications, funding, or installation and maintenance requirements established. The employees are totally responsible for establishing their home work environments and providing any necessary equipment." That may not be the best decision for a company sending people home to work, Reilly adds. Reilly advises that a company needs to direct the "designation of a home office area to minimize workers' compensation liability, develop ergonomic specs for the chair, desk and work area, safe file loads, assurance of safe electrical and data installation conditions, window and water locations, secured storage for printer cartridges or other hazardous materials, and minimal sharp edges."

Written policies are especially important to telecommuting programs. There is a risk that telecommuting can be regarded by employees as an entitlement rather than a privilege, which may result in an employee's suing an employer for discrimination if he or she is denied the right to telecommute (see box "Telecommuting Ruled as Reasonable Accommodation"). Companies need to create the policy and select telecommuters for work-related reasons only, carefully documenting the selection process.

Luckily, there are tried and true policies available from other companies (see App. G). A policy, however, is different than an agreement. In a policy, issues are addressed such as criteria for selection of participants for remote work. But an individual agreement addresses specific terms such as when and where a remote worker works (see App. F).

Written policies and agreements are important in any alternative officing arrangement. Experts recommend that a task force systematically go through an existing company policy document and think about each topic and how it might be different as it applies to remote work.

The first piece of advice on this complex subject of legal issues comes from someone who's been in the trenches. "When you work with legal, have ready a draft of an alternative officing agreement," says Brenda Laffin, manager of alternative officing at Southern California Edison. "Because if I asked legal to create a policy from scratch, we'd still be going through first draft revisions."

THE BASICS OF LABOR LAW AS APPLIED IN THE ALTERNATIVE WORKPLACE

Labor laws were developed from a "factory model" of labor relations where everyone worked in one location under the watchful eye of management. Those laws do not anticipate the issues that come up in telecommuting or other types of remote work.

Labor law in itself is the murkiest area of off-site alternative workplace programs. But there are other types of liability issues that arise such as theft, security, and property damage. Ask any corporation, "So, what are you doing in terms of liability," and their answer will inevitably be, "Well, we haven't had any problems so far, but when something happens, we will deal with it."

WAGE AND HOUR LAWS FOR THE ALTERNATIVE WORKPLACE

Wage and hour laws are extremely precise and can cause problems for companies that employ telecommuters and other remote workers. This area of law becomes more complex when telecommuters become involved because it is hard to keep track of their work hours at home or other remote locations. In many companies, exempt and nonexempt employees are allowed to telecommute, which further complicates the law. For example, if a nonexempt employee claims he or she worked over 40 hours a week and should receive overtime monetary compensation, there is a potential lawsuit on the employer's hands.

There are ways to avoid this situation, according to Patrick J. McCarthy, Esq., of Pitney, Hardin, Kipp & Szuch. McCarthy suggests that employers enforce methods of monitoring how the work is done at home. Paper trails are important so that employees can't claim they've worked additional hours. In addition, it should be put into the employee-supervisor agreement that the nonexempt employee should not work over 40 hours a week. It's best to check with local government because in addition to federal wage and labor laws, many states have their own regulating laws.

COMPENSATION FOR ALTERNATIVE WORKERS AND TRAVEL TIME

Traditionally, time spent commuting to and from work is not considered work time or overtime for which an employee must be compensated. Time spent traveling from job site to job site, however, is considered work time, affecting a remote or mobile worker but not a telecommuter.

SAFETY IN THE REMOTE OR HOME OFFICE WORKPLACE

Under the federal Occupational Safety and Health Administration's (OSHA) law, employers have a duty to furnish a safe workplace free from recognized hazards that pose risks of serious injury or death. Though OSHA won't go into an individual's home to evaluate whether or not it poses a risk, the "prudent employer is responsible to make sure the home office is set up correctly," advises McCarthy. However, on the flip side, McCarthy says if an employer surveys the remote home work site, the employer is open to more exposure because now "you know" the potential risks in that particular home office. Make no mistake, a home office may be considered a workplace if the employee is assigned to work from home, which would mean that the conditions must comply with OSHA standards relating to ergonomics (working in an awkward posture for more than a total of 2 hours), but possibly not to its indoor air regulations. Employers need to be cognizant of the OSHA laws and what may not even apply to the home office. "Since safety and health standards haven't in the past been drafted with the nontraditional workplace in mind, some of the current standards simply do not seem to fit the nontraditional workplace," says McCarthy.

Home Office Inspections

A number of companies say that their telecommuting policies and agreements cover the safety issues and this obliterates them from taking further responsibility or action, such as home office audits to monitor the employee's workspace. In a study of 33 companies with telecommuters conducted in 1995 by Margaret A. Klayton, Ph.D. and professor at the Mary Washington College in Fredericksburg, Virginia, researchers found that fewer than 50 percent of the companies used home inspections as a safety procedure for home-based workers. During the government's Flexiplace pilot programs, the unions agreed that telecommuters would receive 24 hours' advance notice for home inspections if there was a suspicion of hazardous or unsafe conditions in the home.

"If you have some reasonable notice and the inspection of home is limited to the work area, there are no major privacy problems there," says Robert Blackstone, chairman of labor and employment at the law firm Davis Wright Tremaine. "But that could deteriorate if an inspector starts to wander all over the house—that raises privacy concerns whether it's a public or private employee." Blackstone further explains that it's in the employer's best interest to have a written agreement signed by both the supervisor and employee that there may be, upon reasonable advanced notice, an

inspection to make sure the home office complies with written guidelines the employee has read. By having an employee sign an agreement, the company has received his or her consent, and that takes away any argument that there was an invasion of privacy upon inspection, Blackstone says.

Although it would seem that visiting and documenting the home office is the easiest solution to making sure a telecommuter's home workplace does not expose the company to any lawsuits, it can be a complicated, time-consuming, and expensive initiative.

"If you spend all these years developing corporate standards about the size of space, ergonomic issues, health and safety, and if these are elements in human resource files that influence the way in which you run your facility, are you really going to toss all that out when you send people off to work remotely?" asks Robin Morad, a veteran in the commercial furniture industry and founder of Work Now, a remote site audit company based in San Francisco. She launched her company when she realized that companies which don't pay enough attention to remote work sites expose themselves to liability issues. "You'll create a situation of have and have-nots. Even if you go as far as saying these work-at-home people are independent and it's a different grade, you're going to get in trouble—companies should proceed with due diligence," she says.

In agreement is Blackstone, who says that although the issues of telecommuting and virtual office work are two different domains ("telework is a privilege, not a condition of employment like the virtual office," he explains), there are still issues to be dealt with. "In situations where you're always working away from central office because you are a salesperson, it's then not a matter of privilege or right; you are an employee and the issue is how you are being treated, and are you being treated in some discriminatory fashion," he says. If the answer is yes, Blackstone warns, the equation changes. He says the jury or judge will look at the case differently because it is a condition of employment and the employer would have to make adjustments to reflect that.

ALTERNATIVE OFFICING/EMPLOYEES AND LABOR UNIONS

In the early 1990s, the Department of Labor in Washington set up two telecommuting pilots under its Flexiplace program, an extension of its older Flexitime program of shifting hours. Each pilot was initiated to explore pay issues, leave, workers' comp, safety, liability, privacy, and equipment and related costs inherent in a telecommuting program. What's notable about this large-scale experiment (total of 600 people volunteered) is that all the workers participating were "bargaining-unit" employees, that is, they were unionized. "The two unions were receptive to the programs," says Gail Guest, director of the Worklife Center for the Department of Human Resources in the office of the Secretary of Management and Administration in the Department of Labor. "Hammering out the pilots in terms of setting up some type of guideline was one of the easiest things we've ever accomplished with our unions."

Unions have historically had a distaste for remote work because they are concerned about exploitation and sweatshops, but at the same time, they realize remote work options are something they will have to deal with sooner than later. Unions prefer to see telecommuting and other types of alternative work as an alternative for its members to choose from, not an imposed revision of existing arrangements. In addition, if the conditions of the telecommuting program grants employees a better quality of life, unions will generally be agreeable for they exist for the health and welfare of their members. "One of the first questions is whether you have a duty to bargain with the union about the terms and conditions of telework," advises Blackstone. (Both Guest and Blackstone spoke about their experiences during a teleconference "Government and the Law Look at Telework," sponsored by TAC, December 4, 1996.) "Although I haven't seen any cases that specifically address this, I'd say most certainly that yes, this would be seen as a term or condition of employment." What that means is the employer has the duty to negotiate or bargain with the union about terms and how they would affect the bargaining unit.

Blackstone doesn't think unions in general will block negotiations. "I think it would be seen by both sides as a trial that the employees want to do, and this will push the union to be reasonable in the way in which they approach it," he says.

But union opposition to telecommuting or other off-site workplace options can occur as was the experience of the county of Los Angeles. After reaching accord with 19 unions on a telecommuting program, the local Service Employees International Union (SEIU) raised its concerns. The union said there were unresolved issues concerning workers' compensation, home office costs, and more. SEIU said that telecommuting was an issue because it affected the wages, hours, and working conditions of a significant number of employees. Fortunately, the county negotiated a successful outcome with SEIU. But negotiations did have ramifications on the content of the telecommuting policy and working hours the telecommuter was able to be available (see Kugelmass 1995). It doesn't always work out as smoothly. In a separate incident, a union argued that telecommuting is really considered to be shift work. On one hand, the unions have a point when they say a telecommuter's wages, hours, and safety are impossible to monitor. After all, one of the biggest downfalls of telecommuting is the employees' undeniable urge to overwork. Although that may drive up productivity in the short run, it encourages burnout from workaholism in the long run.

In the United Kingdom, one large white-collar union called Manufacturing, Science and Finance (MSF) has published a position paper on its view of telework. Entitled "Teleworking: A Trade Union Perspective," written by national officer Bill Walsh, the paper includes a series of negotiating guidelines for teleworking that has also been similarly adopted by the German Postal Workers' Union and the Swedish union SIF (see Bibby 1996) and include some or all of the following:

- Teleworkers should not be deemed self-employed but should remain as staff.
- Home workers should be required to visit the office periodically to avoid isolation.
- A room dedicated for home work should be required.
- Teleworkers' hours should be defined.
- All of a teleworker's computer equipment should be provided, serviced, installed, maintained, and insured by the employer.
- Employers should pay for any additional phone lines required in a teleworker's home.
- Telework should be voluntary only.

ALTERNATIVE OFFICING AND WORKERS' COMPENSATION

Guest was happy to report that during the 3-year and 2-year pilots, not one participant filed a workers' compensation claim. And Blackstone reported that by the end of 1996, there had not been one single publicized case in the courts regarding workers' compensation in the context of telecommuting or any other off-site work programs. OSHA has launched only about 400 ergonomic enforcement cases against employers in the past 10 years, citing violations of their "general duty" to maintain safe workplaces, but these cases did not deal with work being done in employees' homes. That doesn't mean it won't get worse as more people go home or out on the road to work, however.

Attempts are already being made to sue in this direction regarding *repetitive stress injuries* (RSIs) in the workplace. Since 1994, 14 cases like this have gone to jury, but only one was in favor of the plaintiffs (DEC, see below).

- In 1994, IBM was sued for repetitive stress injury by a woman who used the company's electric typewriter[1] and other IBM computer keyboards back in the 1980s, but the Supreme Court granted IBM the right to dismiss the case because the statute of limitations was up. But Blackwell, along with other lawyers, agrees that there hasn't been one case so far that is in the context of telecommuting and other forms of remote work.
- In December 1996, a federal jury in Brooklyn, New York, awarded nearly $6 million to three women who sued Digital Equipment Corporation claiming they all have RSI from the company's keyboards when they worked as secretaries. DEC said it would appeal the case, which went down in history as the largest award of its type in the United States. Then, in 1997, a federal judge threw out the verdict against DEC because new evidence showed one plaintiff's wrist injury was caused by a muscular condition in her neck, and was not related to keyboard work. A new trial has been ordered.

"There will be issues of ergonomics for telework," says Blackstone. "It will become more of a concern to the extent that someone spends a lot more time on the keyboard, more time than if they were in the office. Employers have to take steps to minimize their workers' comp exposure here."

As a side note, there's a marked increase in Social Security disability claims because of carpal tunnel syndrome. In 1960, claims totaled $576 million compared with 1996 claims, which totaled $38.7 billion (see Carey 1997).

In light of the Digital case, former Labor Secretary Robert Reich says that the Clinton administration will resume its controversial drive in 1997 to develop ergonomic standards aimed at RSI prevention, which accounts for one-third of the $60 billion in annual workers' compensation costs. OSHA was held back from any further explorations into health and safety in the workplace when Congress told the agency to stop spending money in 1996.

Blackstone says workers' comp is unique to each state and not a matter of federal law. He has seen workers' comp cases where employees hurt themselves as they are getting ready to leave home for the office. But he has not seen any cases arising in the context of organized alternative workplace programs.

But Blackstone and McCarthy both recommend to employers a few workers' comp safeguards in relation to potential fraud among telecommuters and remote workers. They suggest that policies for remote workers and agreements signed by telecommuters require immediate notice of injury to a specific and designated person. Then the company should promptly conduct an investigation.

Blackstone asks, "Is carpal tunnel from work or from writing the Great American Novel?" Although employees injured at home by work-related activities will be eligible for workers' comp, sometimes, it's just too hard to decipher the truth.

But that doesn't let the employer off the hook, says Cheryl Schneidermann, IIDA, real estate construction project manager for Sequent Computer Systems, in an interview with *Officeinsight* (December 23, 1996, issue). She says the employer does have a responsibility for cases like the Digital one. If an employee cites lost time and lost productivity, lower employee moral, increased insurance, and workers' compensation costs, plus the inability of some employers to hire replacement workers until the employee goes on permanent disability, there is a case, and it doesn't matter if it's on- or off-site.

On the bright side of workers' comp, a Towers Perrin survey found that workers' compensation dropped 13.5 percent to $2.44 per $1000 of revenue in 1995. The decrease in cost is attributed to the increased use of managed care, legislative reforms, and other efforts to control this exposure.

TELECOMMUTING AND THE ADA

Passed by Congress in 1990, the Americans with Disabilities Act mandates that employers with over 15 employees provide necessary reasonable accommodations to qualified disabled people so that they can do their jobs. As a further explanation, ADA requires employers to provide a reasonable accommodation to qualified employees with disabilities as long as the accommodation doesn't present an undue hardship in the operation of the employer's business. There are two schools of thought on disabled employees and telecommuting and remote work. Some disability rights organizations don't support telecommuting because they feel it's discriminatory or furthers isolation. Legal experts say there have been a number of court decisions in this arena that say allowing people to work at home is not necessarily a reasonable accommodation.

According to a guide called *Questions and Answers About Telecommuting for Persons with Disabilities*, researched and written in 1995 to 1996 by Dr. James Jarrett of the University of Texas in Austin, there are several programs established by employers exclusively for disabled employees. These programs, says Jarrett, were created to retain valuable employees, respond to specific medical or family situations, and comply with air-quality regulations, and a few companies reported they started their programs to increase the diversity of their workforce and comply with the ADA.

McCarthy notes one case involving ADA and telecommuting. In 1995, the *Vande Zande v. State of Wisconsin Department of Administration* case debated whether an employer must grant a disabled employee a full-time telecommuting request. A wheelchair-bound employee said her employer violated the ADA by refusing to give her a full-time job that would be done from home. Since at the time the state didn't allow employees to work at home full-time, it allowed her to work part-time and installed a computer in her home. The court ruled in favor of the employer, saying it had fulfilled its obligation to reasonably accommodate the employee on a part-time, work-at-home basis.

PROPERTY DAMAGE AND LIABILITY INSURANCE

In *Telecommute: Go to Work Without Leaving Home* by Lisa Shaw (see Shaw 1995), the author inaccurately states, "Your company is clearly liable for what happens on its own property, but whatever happens in your home office is out of its control." This is not always the case, and the subject of liability and the alternative workplace employee is far from being as cut and dry as Shaw observes.

It would be helpful if *place of employment* were clearly defined. A *place of employment* has historically meant any workplace where at least *one* of the employer's employees is working. When an employee is assigned to work from home, the home (or at least the portion used to work in at home) can be considered a *workplace* and therefore must comply with OSHA standards, according to Patrick J. McCarthy, Esq., an attorney with Pitney, Hardin, Kipp & Szuch.[2]

Home-based business owners can often get general coverage through homeowner's or business owner's policies. At the St. Paul Companies in St. Paul, Minnesota, it's suggested to telecommuting employees that they acquire a rider at their own expense on their homeowner's insurance that covers all business space in the home.

AVOIDING THIRD-PARTY INJURY

Will employers face premises-based liability for injuries to persons that occur in the home office or remote work site? Perhaps, say lawyers. With more employees working at remote sites, there is risk that children will wander into the home office where there's access to routine office products such as toner and other hazardous chemicals. A company's accident avoidance training program needs to be extended to the home and remote office.

Inform telecommuters in a written agreement that it's best to clear toys and debris from the walkways, or better yet, set up a delivery-pickup box at the curb. Suggest to telecommuters to keep children out of a home office, if possible, by locking the door to the workspace. To avoid contact with risky chemicals, insist that the telecommuter agree to

Telecommuting ruled reasonable accommodation

There are two recent examples of how telecommuting is now being ruled as a reasonable accommodation for disabled employees (see Niles 1997).

- 1997: Faircloth versus BART

  Michael Faircloth, a labor relations arbitrator for the Bay Area Rapid Transit (BART), requested that his employer allow him to telecommute one day a week because of a back injury that left him partially disabled and made his 100-mile round trip commute quite uncomfortable. BART refused his request and Faircloth sued for accommodation under the Americans with Disabilities Act (ADA). The jury awarded Faircloth $90,000 in damages.

- 1997: Hernandez versus City of Hartford

  Alma Hernandez, a health department administrative assistant for the city of Hartford, requested that her employer allow her to telecommute part-time for a variety of medical reasons related to a high-risk pregnancy. Her request was turned down, and Hernandez sued the city of Hartford, alleging that she was denied her right to a reasonable accommodation under ADA. The court ruled in Hernandez's favor that telecommuting was a reasonable accommodation.

lock up hazards. For workers who work off-site as a condition of their employment, put the same information in the company policy book.

OWNERSHIP RIGHTS AND SECURITY FOR ELECTRONIC COMMUNICATIONS

There are legal concerns that arise from the use of electronic communications that do fall under the domain of the alternative workplace. Employees who work off-site have customer lists, client data, and financial information in and around their home, in their car, in their briefcases—much of it intellectual property that companies want to keep proprietary. As part of Lucent's alternative workplace program, it is suggested that anyone participating in the telecommuting part of the program purchase a low-cost paper shredder (they run from $20 to $50) or they can always bring their garbage into the corporate facility, according to Karen Sansone, alternate work strategist at Lucent.

Large organizations often buy site licenses for software. For small companies, there is a single-use rule that says a telecommuter can legally duplicate a licensed product if it not run simultaneously by two or more users. "A telecommuter can copy a software product for home use provided that, at any time, usage alternates between the two. If software is licensed for network use by multiple users, home use of the product requires a separate, stand-alone license" (see Kugelmass 1995).

Then, there's the sticky wicket of electronic privacy. According to attorney Blackstone, e-mail written by an employee becomes company property even if it's written at home while logged on with the company password, and the federal law allows employers to monitor an employee's e-mail.

ZONING AND TAX ISSUES

Zoning and tax issues are another can of alternative workplace worms that's just waiting to be opened. According to McCarthy, "If the employer is a corporate entity, it is likely that the corporation will be found to be doing business in each state in which it has a telecommuter working."

Many alternative workplace strategists will warn others not to give remote and home-based employees any tax recommendations. But they will also add that it helps to have a basic understanding of the issues at hand and to prepare you for unanticipated questions from employees who are embarking on alternative office work. The information on the next page is intended only for general information purposes and should not be construed as legal advice or opinion. To get a basic grasp of the tax and zoning complexities as they relate to remote workers and telecommuters, the best place to begin is by ordering the following specialized publication from the IRS:

IRS Publication 587,
Business Use of Your Home,
Phone number to order: 1-800-829-1040

This IRS publication is the official booklet for unraveling the home office deduction dilemma. It's updated yearly (since 1993 when the Supreme Court case made life more difficult for the home office owner), and it covers everything from rules and requirements to tax forms. Telecommuters should realize, however, that IRS officials and accountants admit that taking a home office deduction is a red flag for an IRS auditor.

GOVERNMENT POLICY ON HOME OFFICE ZONING AND TAXES

In companies with alternative workplace programs, such Tandem Computers and NCR, their corporate policy statements suggest that any employee who works at home because the company has closed the office and doesn't have a corporate office within a certain proximity of his or her home request a letter from the company detailing the situation to assist the employee and tax advisor in determining whether or not expenses related to a home office are deductible under federal tax laws. A letter, along with other relevant information should be presented to the associate's tax advisor in order to obtain a final rendering of a tax deduction qualification. A typical letter from any company with this provision might read like this:

Dear Associate:

Under Name of Alternative Workplace Program, you have agreed to use part of your residence as a home office for the purpose of conducting activities within the scope of your employment with Company. The business use of your residence is required for the benefit and convenience of Company as your employer. In this regard, the residence business use is a condition of your employment, necessary for the proper functioning of Company's business (insert reason why) and necessary to allow you to properly perform your duties for Company (insert reason)."

Always

consult with a tax preparer or lawyer when it comes to home office tax deductions. Here are

trade or business; or, if part of the taxpayer's home is a separate structure not attached to the home that is used in conjunction with the taxpayer's trade or business.

A Thumbnail Sketch of What IRS Publication 587 Means

some quick explanations for general information purposes only about home office deductions interpreted from IRS Publication 587, "The Business Use of Your Home."

A simple set of questions taken from the IRS Publication 587 will **help** in determining if a remote worker or telecommuter can or cannot take a home office tax deduction. Again, note that these questions may change and relax slightly by 1999. Note: These questions do not apply to a remote employee who uses the home for the storage of inventory or product samples.

Definition of what the IRS means when it says:

- Regular and exclusive: If a room or other separately identifiable space in the home is the principal place of business for any trade or business in which the taxpayer engages; or, if it is a place of business to meet or deal with patients, clients, or customers in the normal course of the taxpayer's

- Principal place of business: The IRS notes that a business can be conducted in other places besides the home office. The taxpayer must determine the "relative importance" of activities performed at each business location and if the home office is where the most important activities of the business are carried out. For example, an anesthesiologist who spends most of the time at the hospital(s), a salesperson who is on the road most of the time, and a teacher who is at school carrying out the most important activities of his or her job, all cannot deduct expenses for the business use of their homes unless there is a separate structure devoted to the business.
- Separate structure: Expenses are deductible for a separate, free-standing structure such as a studio, greenhouse, unattached garage, or barn if it's used exclusively and regularly for the taxpayer's business. The structure, however, does not

need to be the taxpayer's principal place of business or where he or she meets with patients, clients, or customers.

1. Is part of the remote worker's home used in connection with a trade or business? _____
- If the answer is "no," there is no tax deduction.
- If the answer is "yes," continue to the next question.

2. Is the remote worker an employee of a corporation?_____
- If the answer is "no," jump down to question 5 and continue from there.
- If the answer is "yes," continue to the next question.

3. Does the remote worker work at home for the convenience of the employer? _____
- If the answer is "no," there is no deduction.
- If the answer is "yes," continue to the next question.

4. Does the remote worker rent part of his or her home used for business to the employer? _____
- If the answer is "no," continue to the next question.
- If the answer is "yes," there is no tax deduction.

5. Is the use of the space regular and exclusive? _____
- If the answer is "no," there is no deduction.

- If the answer is "yes," continue to the next question.

6. Is it the remote employee's principal place of business? _____
- If the answer is "no," continue to the next question.
- If the answer is "yes," there is a deduction allowed.

7. Does the remote employee meet with patients, clients, or customers in the home? _____
- If the answer is "no," continue to the next question.
- If the answer is "yes," there is a deduction allowed.

8. Is it a separate structure?___
- If the answer is "no," there is no deduction allowed.
- If the answer is "yes," there is a deduction allowed.

Even if there is no allowed deduction, an employee of a corporation may be allowed to take a depreciation deduction or elect a section 170 deduction (Election to Expense Certain Tangible Property) found on IRS tax form 4562 (Depreciation and Amortization) for furniture and equipment use in the home for work for an employer. Of course, this only applies if the remote worker or telecommuter purchased furniture and equipment for the home office out of pocket.

A telecommuter or remote home-based worker has to prove that the home office was set up for the convenience of the employer. Not all companies may agree to providing such a letter, however, because it may expose the company to further scrutiny with the government.

It seems that zoning and payroll tax issues tend to get lumped together in the case of remote work. "It's really a payroll tax issue," says alternative officing consultant and strategic facilities planner Cynthia Froggatt. "Technically, if the company buys the computer and installs it in a person's home, it's technically another local work site for the company." Froggatt shares advice a tax advisor gave her: If a large company is completely up front in the way in which they send people to work at home on a

full-time basis, then that company will have to redo their entire tax structure to add on all these taxed locations. However, she gladly adds, the electronic age will foster all kinds of new legislation to clarify the situation.

Indeed, there is hope because the IRS will be experimenting with remote work, according to John Holey, principal of Holey Associates and cofounder of @WORK. With all the budget pressure, the IRS recognizes the need to look at its own space differently and will pursue flexible environments for audit, collections, and criminal investigation departments that are now housed in district offices across the country. "The pilot project addresses workplace assessment, change management activity, and performance assessment and training issues for a remote work strategy designed to reduce costs and bring the IRS into the twenty-first century," says an @WORK profile on the project, which was initiated in 1996.

The entire government is starting to find its way into the twenty-first century when it comes to zoning and taxation of home-based and remote workers. But unfortunately, those efforts have so far been hampered when the federal and local governments began to notice home office zoning and tax issues when it became a court case in 1993. In *Commissioner v. Soliman*, the Supreme Court ruled that an anesthesiologist who saw patients in a hospital and used his home office to do paperwork couldn't deduct the office because he didn't perform his trade full-time out of that work site. That year, according to the IRS, 1.5 million people claimed deductions averaging $2000 each for home offices on their 1993 tax returns (see Nordheimer 1996).

But there was a sudden, swift change of heart about home office tax deductions in July 1997 when President Clinton signed a new budget agreement to benefit small and home-based businesses. The new home office provision expands the deduction to include any home office which is the business' sole office and that is used regularly for essential administrative or management activities. This relaxes the current ruling that states to claim a deduction for a home office, all customers of the business must physically visit the home office, and the income from the business must be generated within the office only. The expanded deduction is especially helpful to those who used to be denied the home office exemption because they had to work or visit their customers off-site. The home office rules are still complicated, and a home-based worker still has to prove the home office is the only fixed office of that particular business. The home office tax provision goes into effect January 1, 1999.

AS HOME-BASED WORK MATURES, SO DO ZONING LAWS

"I was in a focus group where a woman talked about how her neighbors complain that she gets Federal Express packages," says Cynthia Froggatt, strategic facilities planner and expert on the new workplace. "She said to her neighbors, 'Look, I don't get any more Fed Ex deliveries than the lady across the street who gets deliveries from the Home Shopping Network!'" And there you have it, the beginning of what might become a complex issue of zoning for home-based workers.

"We don't think anyone we are sending home will be heavily engaged in seeing clients, so we think that 99.99 percent of zoning issues won't come up," says Michael McGlynn, director of employee relations, human resources, at McGraw-Hill. McGlynn adds, "I get interesting tax questions. Someone asked me if he's plugged into a modem to reach a New York City site where he's manipulating all the data, but he's sitting in New Jersey, where is he working from? The IRS says until further notice that you work wherever you are physically located."

Regardless of whether someone working at home is a telecommuter or an entrepreneur, some neighbors are extremely protective of their serenity and fear that home-based businesses will disrupt the tranquillity. Most zoning laws around the country were written decades ago, allowing a laundry list of licensed professionals to work from their homes. Those home occupations included doctors, lawyers, architects, and dentists, along with miscellaneous occupations such as milliners, hairdressers, manicurists, and dance and music instructors. Numerous businesses have been shut down by towns around the country simply because home business and zoning ordinances don't list such occupations as management consultant.

Realizing that there isn't a huge demand for home-based milliners, many suburbs and cities around the country are revising, amending, or totally overturning local zoning ordinances. Depending upon how you look at it, the new laws either liberalize or prohibit home-based businesses, and they differ from town to town.

• In 1957, Chicago imposed a zoning law that would restrict any commercial businesses in residential areas. In 1995, Chicago officials, realizing that times and needs of residents had changed in 40 years, intended to overturn that law but instead merely revised it to include a host of restrictions. Telecommuters really got a break in May 1995 when officials revised zoning laws. Much to the chagrin of home-based entrepreneurs, the new home office zoning law doesn't apply to telecommuters (see Duncan 1995). The law says that home offices can measure no larger than 300 square feet, that nonresident employees are prohibited, and the number of visiting clients is limited to 10 a day (which is generous except in cases of retail establishments). The law also imposes annual licensing fees of about $125 (see Mehta 1995). Most home businesses, such as offices and artists' studios, however, won't require the special licenses, but they aren't allowed to have client or employee traffic, either (see Cleaver 1995).

- During the same time, areas around the White Plains and Westchester regions in New York were facing their own zoning battles. IBM layoffs overwhelmed areas like Scarsdale, Armonk, and other towns, forcing ex-employees to fend for themselves, many times opening their own consulting businesses and franchises. Forty-year-old zoning regulations in those towns, however, prohibited the operation of a business out of a residential home, not including the traditional home-based businesses of doctor, lawyer, dentist, or other licensed professionals. Changes in the workforce put increased pressure on planners to update outdated regulations. To encourage economic development and keep residents in place, most New York areas ravaged by IBM layoffs have expanded the number of professions permitted to operate within homes (see Hernandez 1995).

- About 50 miles away, quite another story was unfolding in Madison, Connecticut. This suburb decided to crack down on home office zoning in a most unexpected way. It got so tough there that the tax assessor was required to uncover clandestine home offices by scouring local newspapers and phone books to unearth clues to residential businesses. Why? Looking for any way to increase taxes made it necessary to ferret out home offices, audit them, and slap a tax bill and permit on them (see Nordheimer 1996).

- Blue laws still exist, but they may not necessarily be a widespread issue with which to contend. One example is in Paramus, New Jersey, where blue laws say that no one works in the borough except for "works of necessity and charity." Employers with telecommuters need to be aware that blue laws can restrict or prohibit work on weekends. Luckily, blue laws are hard to enforce when people work from their homes, and these laws don't necessarily cover the type of work telecommuters do.

Regardless of what the town's ordinance is, there's help on the way. Telluride, Colorado, the town built for telecommuters and skiers, has paved the way for other towns that look to attract new economies. Builders across the country are building into new developments that are zoned for home offices. And local chapters of such associations as the American Home-Based Business Association have popped up all over the country, ready to lobby for the home-based entrepreneurs' and telecommuters' zoning rights. Soon enough, telecommuters and other remote and home-based workers won't have to hide from the law.

SUMMARY

In 1996 and 1997 alone, suits against both IBM and Digital Equipment Corporation in relation to carpal tunnel syndrome injuries have made us painfully aware that white-collar work-related injuries don't happen only on the corporate campus; they occur wherever work happens to be that day, even if it's at the home office. But just because an employee may not work on the corporate headquarters premises at a dedicated desk with a nameplate sitting atop, the company's responsibility for safety is not relinquished to the employee.

Though laws and legislation regarding the alternative office, including the home office, tend to fall under the human resource department's domain, nevertheless, the entire alternative workplace cross-functional team that was put in place (including designer, facility, real estate, financial, marketing, and technology) should have a bare-bones understanding of the ensuing legalities for which the entire company is liable (many of these issues were discussed in this chapter). And legal should be part of that cross-functional team to help ease the program through the legal confusion.

However, nontraditional workplace programs can be a potential Pandora's Box, and companies who have programs in place generally have comprehensive written policies in place, as well. Issues that policies need to cover include labor laws, property liability, and tax and zoning issues that affect the employee and the employer. We've been hearing about health and safety issues relating to carpal tunnel syndrome. If a telecommuter, for example, is fixed to a phone and/or a keyboard daily or his or her child trips and falls over the company's computer cord resulting in injury, watch out for the potential liabilities that could arise.

Part

3

Industry:

Case Studies on Alternative Workplace Environments and Strategies

Case Studies: Companywide New Workplace Strategies

Chapter

INTRODUCTION

In the previous chapters, we've taken a look at why new workplaces emerge and what components must come together to help create an alternative workplace environment. Part 3 of this book focuses on a variety of case studies, divided into three categories: business-driven AWE case studies, interiors that support AWE, and whole buildings that use forms of AWE as a foundation for their infrastructures.

In Chapter 9, you will read about the inner workings, strategies, and objectives of seven major companies that decided to retool their work processes. We'll take a look at these companies' business-driven approaches to alternative officing. The focus is mostly on the strategic thinking behind the following alternative workplace programs:

- Amdahl—*business goal*: shift to customer-focused company
- Autodesk—*business goal*: continue to acquire companies
- an agency of the Canadian government—*business goal*: streamline costs of running agencies throughout government
- CIGNA—*business goal*: streamline for its shift in core businesses
- NCR—*business goal*: emerge from divestiture as a viable company
- Southern California Edison—*business goal*: get arms around the deregulation of the entire gas and electric industry
- Tandem Computers—*business goal*: support shift in field sales office models; streamline for Compaq's acquisition

You can find more business-driven approaches in case studies featured in Chapter 2, including VeriFone and GTE, and two more in Chapter 4, Sun Microsystems and Cisco.

WHAT IS A BUSINESS-DRIVEN AWE?

Most experts will agree that using AWE as a quick fix for anything, but especially as a sole means for real estate savings, is a big mistake that will inevitably compromise the effectiveness of an AWE program. AWE can't be a cost-driven process, but rather a business-driven process in which is rolled the issues of streamlining costs in one or more areas, including real estate.

"Companies are searching for new business models today," says John Lijewski, IIDA, principal, Perkins & Will New York, a design firm that has handled a few dozen hoteling environments for large companies. "The new business model focuses on the workplace as a tool for business. Alternative officing is an integrated strategy, and by that I mean that it's integrated with a company's business goals. A company's office environment is no longer a product, but it now becomes a process. However, the AWE strategies must match the company's original goals and business plans. If a company has a driving cause to improve distribution or manufacturing processes, then the alternative officing strategy has got to support and amplify that goal."

Each company featured in this chapter realized it had a new business model that had to be supported through updated and more focused office services and administration. Perhaps you will find a glimmer of recognition of your company's volatile issues, or your clients' frustrating dilemmas, within the following pages. And because case studies—even on AWE—can sometimes be tedious to slog through, you'll find some humor sprinkled within these pages.

Amdahl's story is a noteworthy study of how the new workplace can survive the test of time even when a company unknowingly bucks the so-called proven rules of process and implementation of reengineering the workplace.

INDUSTRY OVERVIEW

The burgeoning data processing systems, software, and services industry is more competitive today than ever. This is due to shifting technologies and customers looking for partners in their providers to help them understand how these computing environments enable them to compete in a tight, global, fast-paced market. Companies have to be more nimble and more responsive, and that means shifting from an insular, research-based company to a far-reaching, customer-focused company.

COMPANY OVERVIEW

Amdahl is a full-service information technology company with annual sales of approximately $1.5 billion. It's a supplier of data processing systems, software, and services for use across all types of computing environments. Amdahl helps companies through its products, services, and alliances to create a complex but seamless movement of information from data center to desktop back to data center. Amdahl's sales strategies fall in line with other technology companies who offer products and services in a solution-driven, enterprisewide package for customers.

In early 1996, Amdahl announced significant organizational changes to further redefine its position of its various lines of business in a competitive industry. The reorganization centralizes Amdahl's traditional IBM-compatible processor, storage, and systems maintenance operations within a single organization, called the Enterprise Computing Group.

The company's other two business units include the Antares Alliance Group, which develops and markets software for applications development and business process improvement, and the Open Enterprise Systems Group, which sells Unix system servers and systems management software for use in open, distributed computing environments. Even before the 1996 reorganization and shifting of business units, Amdahl realized it needed a new workplace that could support emerging work processes and evolving workstyles.

AMDAHL'S NEW WORKPLACE PROGRAM

Up until 1992, Amdahl offices reflected standard corporate planning, design, and function. In response to a tighter, faster-paced market, Amdahl began to rethink everything from its operations to work processes to its physical environments.

The process of how Amdahl arrived at its new workplace implementations begins back in 1992 when the facility department received a directive from the vice president of facilities located in Hartford, Connecticut, to reduce the company's portfolio and costs by 30 percent. Two teams were deployed to explore just how to do that. One group's responsibility was to look at how headquarters could be sized down while the other group's charge was to look at the field sales offices. The first group, which eventually disbanded without any solution for headquarters, was composed of about 30 people who took a more traditional approach in matching space requirements to job titles. The second, a much smaller three-person, self-directed team, came back with a two-pronged program for the reduction of field sales office occupancy costs.

This second self-directed team, headed up by Bruce Lanyon, Amdahl's real estate manager, developed two goals: to reduce space, which was a given, and to have a space reduction program positively affect employees' job satisfaction and productivity. The standard, 20-year-old-plus, 120-square-foot private offices were to be converted to a targeted new space requirement of approximately 65 square feet (6 square meters) or less per employee, and less for employees who were out of the office 50 percent of the time. "It's easy to reduce space, but if everyone quits because of that, then we aren't serving the corporation," says Lanyon.

PHASE I: FIELD OFFICES BECOME NEW ENVIRONS

The team named its program The New e/n/v/i/r/o/n/s Project (NEP) and began its

Figure 9.1

Amdahl helped its
employees embrace the
new workplace plans with
its *Participant Guide,* a
folder filled with
pertinent information on
how to transform the
workspace, including this
Owner's Manual.
(Amdahl.)

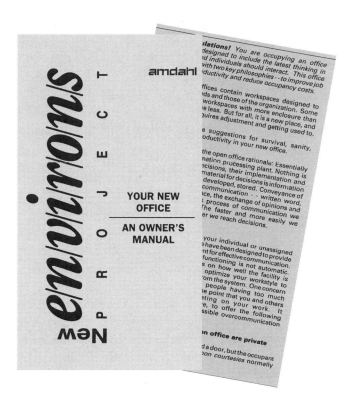

research with consultants from Cornell and BOSTI to come up with an approach to a better workspace. Like most companies, Amdahl employees in a field sales office would receive notice no more than a month before a relocation, moving boxes would arrive 2 weeks before relocating, and finally a week before a move, the employees would find out their new address. That old way of handling facility moves had to change, but that was only the tip of the iceberg. "Our research clearly showed that if you include the people who it's affecting in the solution, there's greater ownership, greater acceptance," says Lanyon. Easier said than done.

To do that, it was agreed upon that an Amdahl project manager and a senior administrative manager from the regional office would team up, go into the office, spend time with them, explain to the employees what the new workplace was about, and clarify Amdahl's goals and how NEP would meet those objectives. Then, the team would work with employees to identify their work needs and habits and eventually arrive at a solution that meets the way they do business in that particular office. Out of a total of approximately 120 field sales offices worldwide at the beginning of the program, the NEP team experimented with a handful of offices located in Montreal, Toronto, Hartford, Charlotte, Orlando, and San Ramon. To begin the workplace transformation of field sales offices, Amdahl chose to start first with the Charlotte, North Carolina, office and the Montreal office. The

results in the Charlotte office were less than desirable, but that did not discourage the NEP team from proceeding with implementing the new workplace.

CHARLOTTE: THE DEFINITIVE AMDAHL NEW WORKPLACE WAR STORY

The Charlotte field sales office was the first test office for NEP efforts. Although it was a well-designed office with a successful architectural solution with innovative use of space and technology, the project was not considered by Amdahl or by Farrington, the Atlanta-based design NEP team, to be a successful new workplace from the employees' vantage point. The lessons learned during the Charlotte pilot were invaluable in refining the process of implementing subsequent AWEs at Amdahl.

The reasons that Charlotte fell short of expectations were discovered through a postoccupancy review in which disgruntled employees said they weren't involved in the decision making during the planning and design process. There were no opportunities given to NEP to educate the management or employees about new workplace. Management in the office wasn't interested in change, but at the same time, one of the office team members chose to install a hoteling solution in spite of everyone else's wishes. In addition to that problem, that particular office employed two of the best worldwide salespeople in the organization, and they felt they were generating too much money for the company to sit in a 6-by-8-foot cubicle. As a result, there was no ownership of the new space. Lanyon says that salespeople migrated from the workstations back to the offices-conference spaces on the perimeter because they absolutely had to have their perceived status back in the form of a private office.

It was this experience that made Amdahl and Farrington extremely sensitive to the fact that they must strongly urge managers of the office to participate, become educated about the new workplace, and pay serious attention to the process of letting end-users participate in the decision-making process.

INVOLVING EMPLOYEES KEY TO MONTREAL OFFICE'S SUCCESS

The Montreal office was chosen for the pilot because it was perceived to be the most difficult one to work with at the time due to issues of low morale. Lanyon believed if an alternative workplace could make it there, it could make it anywhere.

Before Montreal was transformed into a New Environs interior, the 7000-square-foot office functioned in a very traditional way with a large reception area, drywall offices everywhere, and a secretarial station topped by in and out baskets outside every door. The secretaries were traditional—they made and fetched the coffee, filed the files, copied the copies, and faxed the faxes. Managers responsible for the different functions at Amdahl didn't talk to each other and stayed in their private offices.

By the time Lanyon and the New Environs team were done with the office, even the traditional managers were moved out from behind closed doors and were made to sit in cubicles, the reception area was eliminated because the Montreal location wasn't really one that received visitors anyway, and the staff was reeducated and taught how to use the fax and copy machines on their own and how to get their own coffee.

Facilities worked closely and diligently with the staff to find out what their traditional work processes were, what they could be if streamlined, and what tools could get them there. Everyone in this office desired a LAN and portable technology, yet everyone's equipment was different. Through discussions on how to budget for new technology, the office decided that their tradeoff would be to go into a hoteling situation, which would allow them to reduce space, which in turn would allow them to save enough money on the facilities side to fund the new wiring for LAN and to purchase identical note-

book PCs. As a result, the Montreal office spent about $100,000 on equipment in order to save about $2 million in rent during the rest of the office's lease, says Lanyon. This was done at a time when capital expenditures at Amdahl were on hold; no one could fail to see the benefits of saving that amount of money in rent due to the investment in new equipment.

Of course, the managers in the office really didn't think this new environment would work at all, regardless of the potentials offered by new technology, so they barely participated in the meetings, says Lanyon. But, in fact, the managers were at the mercy of the staff who agreed unanimously that everyone—including the managers—should move into a cubicle. "By that time, there was so much momentum that the managers were kind of stuck and had to do it," remembers Lanyon.

The hardships and lessons learned resulted in an office that was—and still is—extremely functional in spite of the fact that the size of the staff has ebbed and flowed due to downsizing, then acquisitions.

PHASE II: THE WORKPLACE PROJECT IN 1997 AND BEYOND

In 1994, the NEP team published an impressive kit called the *New Environs Project Participant Guide*, a kit for managers and employees to read that included the *Space Strategies for Existing Offices* booklet, a *Solutions* guide and *Reading* guide, *Your New Office Owner's Manual* (etiquette tips for employees), and agenda (Fig. 9.1), and survey and planning sheets for office administrators and managers.

Three years after the formalized, published NEP program, Lanyon and a multidiscipline team led by the user group have entered Phase II, a program called the "Workplace Project" in which they will want to expand and refine the original concepts.

THE WORKPLACE PROJECT PROCESS

Amdahl's new workplace program continues to evolve in spite of the fact that this mega-computer company approached its alternative workplace differently than many other companies do, proving that there's no real set formula on how to successfully pull it off. The overall philosophy that clearly drives Amdahl's new workplace efforts is that it believes there is no single solution or office standard because there are too many variables in every office.

AMDAHL BUCKS THE TRENDS

So what was so different about the way Amdahl approached its new workplace? Consider the following:

- CRE and facilities drove Phase I of the new workplace program, called The New e/n/v/i/r/o/n/s Project (NEP).
- The CEO was not called upon to champion NEP, but in Phase II, called the "Workplace Project," a senior sales executive became a champion of the process and will be sponsored by the user organization.
- In Amdahl's Montreal-based field sales office, it was the staff that drove the new workplace initiative and agreed to have reluctant managers move out of their private offices into an open plan and a hoteling scenario.
- A full integration team (HR, IT, CRE, legal, finance, etc.) was *not* set up to drive Phase I of the new workplace program, but it will be implemented in Phase II.
- Amdahl rolled out a companywide telework program in early 1997, 4 years *after* its new workplace program was developed.
- The *facilities group is driving the telework program* (a highly unusual, but fascinating, strategy).

After all, Amdahl is a great example of how new workplace is considered to be a continuous process, rather than a permanent, stagnating solution, a trap that has often resulted in the implementation of traditional office plans and layouts. But so far, Amdahl's new workplace program has been a solution for facilities issues, and the computer giant now wants to go forward with new workplace as a solution to business issues. In addition, Amdahl has acquired companies, such as the DMR Group, and the Workplace Project team needs to get to know those new companies, its cultures, and work processes.

Further yet, Amdahl has rolled out a worldwide telework program under The NEP umbrella. Interestingly enough, it is driven by the facilities group, although they admit they aren't sure yet where the real estate benefits will be since there aren't any guarantees of space reduction. Even to Lanyon, the telework portion of the Workplace Project is more of a job retention and job recruitment strategy than a facilities issue, but it only made sense that the CRE and facilities team that worked on New Environs put this piece of the puzzle together, as well. The telework program will heavily affect the entire corporate campus in addition to the sales field offices.

LEARNING TO BELIEVE IN EMPLOYEE PARTICIPATION: AMDAHL'S ON-SITE, WEEK-LONG WORKSHOP

The NEP team recognized the managers' uneasiness with the new workplace process and saw the imminent need to help them feel comfortable in buying in to a new workplace program. "Over and over we find that the most support for alternative officing seems to come from the average employee who sees this as an opportunity while mid- and high-level managers will typically offer less enthusiastic support, frequently back-pedal, or disappear from the scene if there is any discontent," says Karin Vonderach, portfolio manager, CRE at Amdahl. As far as past managerial discontent over new workplace, that thinking has since changed, and now the NEP team encourages executives to lead the charge.

The NEP's process to get managers comfortable was three-pronged and included prework, an on-site workshop, and a postoccupancy evaluation. Prework involved meeting with office management to talk about key issues and set project goals, assemble team members, and review materials to be presented to the rest of the staff.

The most important part of the equation, however, was the on-site workshop, a full week's worth of education, data gathering, analysis, and solutions for a participating sales office. Amdahl's design firm, Atlanta-based Farrington Design, was always present at these workshops, acting as unbiased facilitators to help employees aim in the right direction to develop solutions that addressed their work process needs. The presentation to the staff would be about 1½ hours, ideally to a group of under 20 people (for larger offices, staff were divided into two groups for two separate presentations). This initial meeting would introduce the NEP team and explain to the staff why they were there for a week.

The second part of the on-site workshop involved data gathering by conducting either group or individual interviews. Groups consisted of about six or less people, taking up to 1½ hours per group interview. Time was spent getting consensus answers to survey forms and following up by walking through the department's current work area to elicit comments and needs. Individual interviews took about 25 minutes per person.

When all the data were gathered, it was presented to the group in a focus-group session to verify the findings' accuracy and request affirmation of what was heard.

From the data, Farrington Design and the NEP worked together to arrive at a couple of floor plans and work process solutions from which employees would select one or two. The chosen floor plans were later modified and presented in final draft for review and employee comment.

What the NEP found was that it really didn't take much more time to handle this part of the data gathering process than it would have planning a traditional office, "listening to people screaming at you after the move on Monday morning," says Bob Skyvington, Amdahl Canada's manager of office administration, in an interview published in Farrington Design's 1995 newsletter. "If you spend the time now [to achieve ownership and buy-in], you won't spend it later."

After all was said and done, the postoccupancy survey, called the "Customer Satisfaction Survey," was given to employees 60 days after occupancy. The results were distributed to the office management.

Amdahl's Sample Interview Questions for On-Site Workshops

Here are a few sample questions (not the entire list) that the NEP team devised for on-site group or individual interviews taken from the *New Environs Project Participant Guide*. One tip: "You have to just let people dump out all the nasty things they've been holding onto for 30 years before you can get to the really positive stuff," says Frank Farrington, president of Atlanta-based Farrington Design and a facilitator of Amdahl workshops.

- What is a typical day like for you?
- How much time do you spend doing which functions of your job?
- Where are they done? How are they done? What tools do you use?

- What would be an ideal work environment?
- How has the way you work changed recently?
- What works well in the existing office, what should be kept, what doesn't work, and what should be fixed?
- How important is it for others to know that you're in the office? Is it important for others to be able to see that you're available, for you to be visually accessible to others in the office?
- How important is it to you to be able to hear what's going on around you in the office? Would you find it distracting to be able to hear conversations around you? Are there any issues of privacy and security that are important to your work?
- Do you bring customers into an office? How often? What will they do when they are in the office? Will this change?
- What are the important issues and attitudes in this office's culture that should be considered in making future changes?

Snapshot: Amdahl

Amdahl is a major supplier of large-scale mainframe computers, Unix system software and servers, data storage subsystems, data communications products, and applications development software plus professional and operational consulting services with over $1.5 billion in annual sales.

FOUNDED IN 1970
EMPLOYEES WORLDWIDE: 10,000 in 30 countries
WEB SITE: http://www.amdahl.com
HQ ADDRESS: 1250 East Arques Avenue
Post Office Box 3470
Sunnyvale, CA 94088-3470
PHONE: 408-746-6076
THE FIELD NEW ENVIRONS PROJECT TEAM: Michael Gulasch; Bruce Lanyon, real estate manager; and Karin Vonderach, portfolio manager, CRE.
FARRINGTON DESIGN NEP TEAM: Frank Farrington, AIA/IIBD, and Logan Need, Associate AIA.

Autodesk, 1993 to the Present

INDUSTRY OVERVIEW

The need to increase productivity and simplify the design process for *architectural, engineering, and construction* (AEC) professionals has driven the burgeoning *computer-aided design* (CAD) software market of which Autodesk is a leader.

COMPANY OVERVIEW

Autodesk is a leading supplier of PC and Unix-based design software and PC multimedia tools. The company's 2-D and 3-D products and data management tools are used in many industries for architectural design, mechanical design, filmmaking, videography, and geographic information systems. The fourth-largest PC software company in the world, Autodesk has 3 million customers in 118 countries.

In December 1981 Autodesk founder John Walker first formed the idea of starting a software-only company to provide software for the coming tidal wave of small computers made by large manufacturers. Walker says that when a company ceases to change at the rate demanded by the industry it exists within, it finds itself rapidly left behind. "Before long, its customers discover products of competitors that better meet their needs," he says. "As market share slips, sales fall, and earnings decline, the management of the standstill company asks, 'What's happening? We're still doing all the things we used to do.' Surely they are, but that's no longer enough." Walker says that companies with that mindset will be perceived to be relics from the past, almost "quaint," a pattern he does not intend for Autodesk to follow.

THE COMPANY CULTURE

In the early days of Autodesk, Walker—an outspoken leader—wrote status reports on the progress of the company for employees and shareholders (who were, at the time, the same group of people). In 1988, Walker became concerned primarily with software development and identifying technical directions in which the company should move, and time was slim for generating status reports. Walker relinquished his role as chairman in 1988 and has not been involved with the general management of the company since then. He has moved to

Switzerland to continue his work in software development at Autodesk's new software development center in Neuchâtel.

Autodesk, like so many other companies, has expanded with acquisitions and contracted from downsizing over the years, leaving it with a patchwork of corporate cultures. Because Autodesk is spread out all over the country and because it has been acquiring other companies, there is an interesting cross mix of cultures in each location. For example, at Autodesk's Oregon facility, development operations employees insisted on working in an open plan. When Autodesk acquired this company, there were nine people sitting in a 900-square-foot room with no walls, just folding tables and chairs. "They relished the opportunity to talk with each other all the time," says Walt Spevak, director of CRE. "When we moved them because they outgrew the space, they *absolutely wanted to be in open plan* and wouldn't even consider private offices." Engineers, Spevak found out, are not the homogeneous bunch everyone thinks they are, and designers can't pigeonhole them into standard plans.

INFORMATION TECHNOLOGY AT AUTODESK

Most Autodesk employees have three computers—a laptop and a desktop computer at home and one at the corporate office. Spevak notes the increasing use of Iomega Zip drives so that telecommuters don't have to lug their laptops or dozens of floppy disks but instead can put all their information on a cartridge that holds up to 100 MB. "It's a good technology that supports alternative officing," says Spevak. A 100MB cartridge is the equivalent of 70 floppy disks. SyQuest sells 200MB cartridges, as well.

PHYSICAL ENVIRONMENT OVERVIEW

When Spevak joined Autodesk in 1985, there were 100 employees who mostly worked wherever there was space and many times that space would be at home. Spevak worked on a folding table and chair in a hallway.

By 1992, Autodesk employees worked primarily in a closed office environment. Approximately 95

Figure 9.2
Autodesk's Kinetix
Division in San Francisco
is an example of a
hoteling environment.
(Hedrich-Blessing.)

percent of the headquarters was filled with private offices while product support and customer service remained seated in open plan. And Autodesk's e-mail dependency made it easy for everyone to stay at their desks, in their offices and never have to talk to anyone face-to-face or voice-to-voice again.

It was then that Autodesk's new CEO, Carol Barns, realized the company sorely needed to be better at internal communications and set out to change the culture companywide, in part, by refocusing the physical space.

NEW WORKPLACE PROGRAMS

To begin the daunting task of reengineering the physical space, it seemed only practical to start with the field sales offices. In 1993, Autodesk opened six sales offices of between 15 and 20 people at each location.

Field sales offices were purposely structured to the opposite of the headquarters space with 80 percent open plan and 20 percent private offices. It would be the sales offices that would become the vanguard groups that launched Autodesk into a full scale cultural shift to rid themselves of separating wall structures.

THE RESTRUCTURING OF HEADQUARTERS

In 1994, 800 Autodesk employees moved into a 15,000-square-foot corporate headquarters, and 90

percent of that building is open plan, not including corporate functions and sales and marketing. The sales offices were functioning quite well in open-plan offices, but employees at headquarters weren't having as easy a time moving into that new culture and mindset. "There certainly was no unanimity to having all that open space," says Spevak. In 1996, there were 1100 employees at headquarters, and Spevak is still counting.

POLICIES FOR THE NEW WORKPLACE

To manage Autodesk's new and emerging workstyle, a formal alternative officing task force was formed in late 1995 into 1996. The team included representatives from all the facilities plus human resources, technology, purchasing, legal, and finance—just about all the functional support departments that would be affected by an alternative officing program. Then, pilots of departments were chosen for formal alternative officing programs.

AUTODESK'S KINETIX DIVISION

The most visible results of the formal alternative office programs comes from Kinetix, one of Autodesk's divisions. In August 1996, Kinetix, the multimedia division of Autodesk, moved out of corporate headquarters to a locale closer to the heart of its business—San Francisco's Multimedia Gulch. The

Figure 9.3

Haworth's Tango
workstations and some
Crossings furniture
combine to create a
flexible new workplace
environment for this
group of software
developers at Kinetix.
(Hedrich-Blessing.)

new 25,000-square-foot space, designed by Hellmuth, Obata & Kassabaum's (HOK) San Francisco office, is 99 percent open plan, says Spevak, explaining that there is still a holdout sitting in a closed office, but that would change shortly.

Designer Laurie Goffigan, then with HOK and now with Gensler, helped Kinetix structure their workstations and space. With Spevak, Kinetix is filled with three types of workstations:

- A: There are nine A workstations that accommodate 25 employees who telecommute and who are out of the office 4 to 5 days a week (see Chap. 7 for more on Autodesk's telecommuter policy and provisions).
- B: There are 25 B workstations that measure 6- by 8-feet and are shared by 2 employees who come into the office 1 to 2 days a week.
- C: There are 60 C workstations for assigned seating for people in the office 4 to 5 days a week.

Kinetix is outfitted with Haworth Tango, not a panel system but freestanding furniture, some tac-

tical tables on wheels for conferencing table set-ups (Figs. 9.2 and 9.3). According to Spevak, employees say that Tango workstations are easy to reconfigure even when they are loaded down with computers and books.

There is also a 600-square-foot area filled with Haworth's Crossings furniture.

Snapshot: Autodesk

MANUFACTURERS OF CAD SOFTWARE (AUTOCAD) AND
 PC MULTIMEDIA TOOLS
FOUNDED IN 1982
EMPLOYEES WORLDWIDE: Over 2000
NEW WORKPLACE STRATEGIES: Telecommuting,
 open plan, teaming
WEB SITE: http://www.autodesk.com (*Author's note:*
 Autodesk has one of the best, most comprehensive Web sites out there.)
PHONE: 415-507-5000

ONE PILOT INSPIRES THE ENTIRE CANADIAN GOVERNMENT

For those who believe hoteling is an alternative space strategy only for consultants and advertising agencies, look at how a part of the Canadian government embraced the concept and implemented it within an *astounding* 46 working days to get a hoteling project up and running for 45 employees, saving the agency well over $200,000 (Canadian) that is, a year's rent.

The Canadian government, just like the U.S. government, is currently trying to save money to the tune of $70 million between 1996 and 1997 and another $80 million between 1997 and 1998. As part of a government effort to achieve this, one agency decided to try a form of hoteling.

To begin the process, the government's Real Property Services (RPS) agency surveyed 60 departments in early 1995 to find out if there was any interest in implementing AWE. About 70 percent of the departments surveyed responded, most of which said they already had employees who worked off-site on a regular basis. One public agency that became the pilot for the broader program is the Consulting and Audit Canada (CAC), which went on to initiate a hoteling strategy that has set an example for the rest of the Canadian government's agencies.

CAC is a Special Operating Agency (SOA) within Public Works and Government Services Canada (PWGSC), that provides public service management through professional consulting and audit services on a fee-for-service basis. Although the agency does not run on money from taxpayers but rather works under a revolving fund that covers all costs, the agency was attempting to reduce overhead expenditures while maintaining service to its clients. Before hoteling, CAC had already managed to cut 50 percent of its portfolio and $1.5 million of associated costs, but it needed to generate even more savings in that area. Since the nature of the business is mobile, it only made sense to focus on the further reduction of occupancy costs—most specifically, CAC realized that it could save on the rental cost of an entire floor through the introduction of a nonterritorial officing approach that dovetailed with an increased use of technology.

CAC'S HOTELING STRATEGY

In October 1995, a project team was assembled to explore hoteling for CAC. An amazing month and a half later, the hoteling project was up and running with a 3:1 ratio to accommodate 45 employees (see the sidebar "CAC's 46-Day Timeline"). The site includes an informal drop-in area, storage and filing area for personal items, and a formal meeting room. Hoteling reservations could be made on the LAN, which tracks its usage over time in order to fine-tune ratios.

The total project costs including facility redesign, technology investment, and training came to about $400,000 (Canadian dollars). The hoteling strategy will save a rental fee of $234,000 (Canadian dollars) per year, so CAC anticipates that will take 2 years for payback. The money already saved has been reinvested in new computers, telephony, and associated training. Future technology plans call for secured remote access to the LAN for mobile workers. A "follow-me" phone system from Bell Canada's PrimeLine will provide employees with seamless phoning.

CAC'S HOTELING PROCESS TIMETABLE

The first step involved organizing representatives from key departments to come together to form the CAC self-directed hoteling project team that would also report on the project to CAC's union representative on a consistent basis. The team issued an e-mail throughout the CAC to identify volunteers for the hoteling program, but the invitation was initially met with skepticism and defensiveness. It turns out that employees weren't too sure what *hoteling* really meant; they only knew they'd lose their office and phone.

As in any good AWE program, troubleshooting in the schedule is provided for, and the team made presentations to the various groups in CAC to educate them on the basics of hoteling. It was the technology packages that piqued employees' interest, especially in the Audit group. The Consulting group, however, decided to adopt a wait-and-see attitude about hoteling.

After the presentations, another questionnaire was quickly distributed that asked employees about their work process, work flow, and storage needs, and from the replies, facility design and technology strategies were determined.

HOTELING START-UP COSTS

Up-front costs of $400,000 (Canadian) will take 2 years to pay back, the team determined. The costs were categorized into three main groups: technology, professional services and training, and facility costs (see Table 9.1).

Largest Expense: Technology

Inevitably, technology cost more than the other two parts. A little over $200,000 (Canadian) was invested in new color portable computers configured with internal 14.4 modems. The CAC team emphasized that in the technology package, the costs of upgrading applications software licenses had to be folded into the moneys spent. All hoteling workstations were equipped with port replicators to connect to the LAN with keyboard, mouse, and Ethernet network adapter. PrimeLine from Canada Bell, a follow-me phone service, replaced older voice mail systems on the existing Centrex system.

Data security was a large issue. CAC consultants had modems on their workstations that were connected to the LAN. If they left their desks with the modem in auto-answer, a hacker could get into the system without a problem. To eliminate the need for desktop modems, a secure ID challenge card was installed to authenticate the user and activate a pool of modems that are located in a secured LAN room.

Before hoteling, the CAC telephony did not support remote call-forwarding. The team felt that cellular phones were too costly, so it decided on call management technology. The follow-me system means that incoming calls are answered by a greeting, then within a 4-second time frame, it tracks down the owner of the account. It still includes voice mail, all at $14.95 (Canadian) per month per employee.

Second-Largest Expense: Training and Communication

The second-largest cost was the educational program, which cost well over $100,000 (Canadian) to implement. It turned out to be the most frustrating part of the program because there were so many different levels of users and the training had to be implemented in a short time span. Most of the users had little or no experience using the Windows-based software that was preloaded into the hotelers' computers. So it made sense to give everyone a half-day private-sector, one-on-one training session that could be followed up with a training class for those that needed more help; however, that session accounted for a large chunk of the costs and time spent away from clients.

Some of the cost represents the amount of money employees would have billed for client assignments, but the time was spent on the meetings instead. The other amounts represent the money given over to experts in remote access and telephony who were contracted to educate employees.

To keep abreast of the workplace changes, employees gathered during "brown-bag" lunch sessions throughout the planning stages. Advance copies of all the communications materials were sent to unions for their information and feedback 24 hours before being formally released to employees.

Least Costly Piece of the Puzzle: Facilities

The third, less costly part of the equation was the facility management costs that totaled nearly $70,000 (Canadian). Construction and furniture expenditures were kept to a minimum, and therefore so was labor (which also minimized disruption to adjacent departments). For instance, several workstations were dismantled to make way for an informal meeting space. The rest of the workstations were reconfigured to create hoteling booths. Walls were put up to delineate storage and filing rooms, and 23 five-drawer file cabinets were purchased.

The team gave the end users a say in what necessary types of office space and support spaces they needed to be carved out for them. The site houses 45 auditors in a hoteling situation sharing 12 hotel "suites" of 120 square feet and three "booth" offices of 60 square feet. Offices can be reserved in advance either through an online LAN-based computer application or by calling the concierge. The space can accommodate up to 65 hotelers with little added construction.

Three distinct areas of the space include: the common area with soft seating and white board, the personal storage area complete with what the auditors call *tug-a-peds* (file pedestals on wheels to take to their workspace), and the booth-style offices created from parts and pieces of existing workstations.

The schedule board and informal meeting area is laid out to provide a logical walking sequence (Fig. 9.4). From the entry point, which is secured by a mag-stripe card lock system, the hotelers enter the

TABLE 9.1
CONSULTING AND AUDIT CANADA HOTELING COST ESTIMATES AS OF FEBRUARY 1996

COST TYPE (Note: Costs are figured in Canadian rates.)	QUANTITY	UNIT COST	EST. COST	TOTAL
Equipment				
Hayes modems	7	$335.72	$2,350.04	
Cubic cards	3	$3,691.67	$11,075.01	
Access control module	1	$8,666.25	$8,666.25	
Secure ID cards	25	$100.00	$2,500.00	$24,591.30
Computer and software				
AST laptops (486s)	27	$3,478.56	$93,921.12	
AST laptops (pentiums)	20	$3,573.00	$71,460.00	
Keyboards, mice, adapters				
Lotus upgrades	10	$130.00	$1,300.00	
Color monitors	14	$395.00	$5,530.00	
Security cables for PCs	47	$48.50	$2,279.50	$176,581.62
Informatics temp help				$50,083.85
GTIS consulting fees				$15,000.00
Informatics training				$14,165.00
Staff costs for billable resources				$52,648.00
Hoteling fit-up costs				
File cabinets	10	$2,320.00	$23,200.00	
Extend central filing area			$10,130.00	
Installation of PrimeLine			$1,650.00	
Hoteling misc. equipment			$508.00	
Telecom wiring			$5,020.00	
Office refits			$14,000.00	
Moving expenses			$12,986.00	
Construction of hoteling booths			$2,000.00	$69,494.00
Total estimated cost				$402,563.77

Figure 9.4 (top)
Consulting and Audit Canada pulled a hoteling environment together in 46 working days. This is the informal meeting area with a schedule board that informs hotelers where to find their offices.
(Bill Gregory/CAC.)

Figure 9.5 (bottom left)
After having coffee and checking the board, a hoteler rolls a Tug-A-Ped to a reserved office. To pull the ped, a hoteler inserts the end of the strap into the top drawer, closes the drawer and pulls the file to the assigned office.
(Bill Gregory/CAC.)

Figure 9.6 (bottom right)
This is a sample CAC booth office that measures 60 square feet but still provides ample desk space for an auditor to spread out working papers.
(Bill Gregory/CAC.)

informal meeting area where they collect coffee, review the manual schedule board to determine the office space to which they have been assigned. They can sit down and hold impromptu discussions with other staffers in an informal atmosphere.

From there, the hotelers walk into the personal storage area to retrieve personal effects and business files. Each hoteler has two drawers in a lateral file cabinet as well as a portable pedestal. The rolling tug-a-peds are pulled with a strap and handle (Fig. 9.5).

Hoteling suites and booths provide ample desk space for an auditor to spread out his or her work-

ing papers (Fig. 9.6). Each hoteler is given telephone service, called "Bell PrimeLine," that allows the flexibility of remote call forwarding to their current locations. When a call comes in, the phone switch answers the call with a personally recorded message that asks the caller to wait a few seconds while the call is being connected. The phone switch looks up the hoteler's current location and places a second call to the hoteler.

Each office or booth is equipped with a phone set and docking station to allow LAN connection. The docking station has a full-size color monitor, full-

Here

is the Consulting and Audit Canada's fast-track timeline for

CAC's 46-day timeline

the hoteling project, which was completed within 46 working days from start to finish. It was determined in October that this group would adopt a hoteling scenario for its 45 employees.

November 21, 1995
- Begin project

November 22, 1995
- Arrange meeting with union
- Finalize twelfth-floor hotel area and floor plan
- Confirm software and equipment order for auditors
- Begin to develop training plan for auditors
- Begin confirming what PrimeLine functions were necessary for auditors

November 23, 1995
- Begin finalizing informal area construction plans
- Provide communiqués to union in advance of meetings

November 24, 1995
- Order furniture for informal area
- Add union's input to communiqués

November 27, 1995
- Begin preparing training materials to be completed by 12/8/95
- Distribute formalized communiqués to staff
- Receive furniture for informal area and begin to set up

November 29, 1995
- Order PrimeLine services

November 30, 1995
- Order new business cards for staff

December 7, 1995
- Receive equipment ordered on

11/22/95
- Remove auditors out of soon-to-be hoteling area
- Install PrimeLine service

December 8, 1995
- Install software ordered 11/22/95
- Order ancillary equipment for hotel suites
- Begin PrimeLine training user orientation for staff through 12/12/95

December 11, 1995
- Conduct one-on-one training sessions for new work processes through 12/15/95

December 14, 1995
- Dismantle workstations to make room for file area

December 15, 1995
- Provide equipment to auditors installed 12/8/95 through 12/14/95

December 18, 1995
- Reconfigure workstations to hoteling booths of 60 square feet
- Reconfigure workstation for hoteling administrator

• Refit personal and central file areas
- Receive ancillary equipment for hotel suites
- Conduct any other application training sessions through 1/3/96

December 19, 1995
- Move hotel administrator into newly reconfigured workstation
- Install necessary LAN wiring
- Set up and test hotel suite equipment through 12/28/95

December 20, 1995
- Renumber hotel suites and remaining offices

December 28, 1995
- Consolidate personal and central files through 1/5/96

January 1, 1996
- Move auditors into hoteling installation

January 16, 1996
- Official ribbon cutting for CAC's completed hoteling office

size keyboard, mouse, network connector for LAN services and printing.

LESSONS FROM THE TRENCHES

To best promote the CAC pilot, an open house and ribbon-cutting ceremony was held with members of the team with guests including CAC unions and other potential government organizations that could utilize hoteling to reduce their own costs.

However, there were some hard lessons learned in the 46-day period from which the idea for the hoteling environment was born to the day of the ribbon cutting. It's unheard of to have this kind of hoteling program up and running so soon, given the technology and training issues that need to be addressed. Needless to say, that kind of extraordinary fast-track timeline does have its share of downfalls.

Some of the auditors and the team members felt the 46-day period was too little time in which to effect such a tremendous change in culture, work processes, and use of technologies. In addition,

there was initial confusion about the differences between hoteling and telecommuting—unions do not typically support telecommuting. Even the word *pilot* confused the participating employees because the program was presented to them as a permanent solution. Auditors, the volunteers of this program, said they felt undue pressure to make the hoteling work because so many cost issues for the agency were riding on the success of the program.

Snapshot: CAC

Consulting and Audit Canada is a Special Operating Agency within Public Works and Government Services Canada. The agency offers consulting and auditing services to other government agencies for a fee.

EMPLOYEES: 45
PHONE: 613-943-8385
NEW WORKPLACE STRATEGY: hoteling
CONTACT: Bill Gregory, CAC
ADDRESS: CAC, Ottawa, Canada, K1A 0S5

CIGNA, 1996 to the Present

CIGNA OVERVIEW

In 1997, CIGNA significantly changed its core business strategies. The Philadelphia-based insurer is in the process of cutting out its consumer business while expanding other markets, including property insurance. In June, CIGNA bought Healthsource, a managed-care insurer, to help itself expand into the corporate healthcare markets. In July, CIGNA announced it would sell its individual life insurance and annuity business to New York Life Insurance, while staying in the institutional life insurance market.

PHYSICAL ENVIRONMENT

Hearing the helicopter flying overhead just about every other day with the CEO in tow was a subtle reminder that the real CIGNA headquarters is in Philadelphia. Yet, it seems that the heart of CIGNA is a cluster of buildings, the anchor one built in 1958, set on a peaceful Connecticut corporate campus with ample parking, green grass, streams, ducks, and a town nearby for lunch and shopping. Most of the staff still work on the original 30- by 60-inch gray metal desks from the 1950s custom built by GF Office Furniture. It's a tough building to shift into the twenty-first century, so CRE is working with field offices to implement new ways of working, even though they are wondering why the "home office" hasn't yet embraced change.

The second issue that faces the Connecticut location is that it is spread out beyond the campus quarters into prime real estate in downtown Hartford.

Yet, costs were contained and the city planning concept was in place, so the next best thing to do was to look at facilities all across the board, consolidate, streamline, colocate, renegotiate leases for the best dollar in the best type of building...yet all of that had been accomplished, as well. Everything that could have been done within the parameters of a "classical real estate perspective" was signed, sealed, and delivered, according to the CRE division. Then along came Lynne Kelley-Lewicki, director of integrated workplace strategies at CIGNA.

NEW WORKPLACE PROGRAMS

With her background at Steelcase, Lewicki began to view real estate from a different perspective. "I'm looking at real estate and question how I move it from overhead perspective to an operational advantage...something that will make money for the organization," she explains. And so her foray into alternative officing began in 1995.

She will say right off the bat that all the alternative workplace projects include human resources, information technology, and real estate services. The type of research that this group does together investigates the long-term business strategy of the organization, how the organization works today, how it will work in the future, what technology pieces are missing, and what, if any, reengineering is going on in the corporation. Her goal with this research, information, and project work is to turn these real estate services into a turnkey operation for the company customer. "The real estate and information technology pieces are the smallest, least significant, and easiest components to change in my mind," she says.

Alternative workplace projects are in their infancy at CIGNA, but Lewicki is eager to work with clients, educating them about the benefits of new work processes that can be supported by new workplace environments.

"Usually, someone calls, tells me they have to reduce their real estate costs, but they can't move beyond that or the attitude of the manager is archaic," she says. "I'm looking to find a client who is willing to try something new, puts a lot of effort not just into managing people, but emphasizes and recognizes the creative abilities of their staff."

Lewicki came to CIGNA from Steelcase Consulting, where CIGNA was her client. Specifically, her client was the call center in Bethlehem, a project for which she was asked to come on board at CIGNA to see it through a reorganization.

Bethlehem Customer Service Center

Since June 1996, the Bethlehem Customer Service Call Center, part of the group insurance division, has operated differently than it's ever done before. "It has

Figure 9.7
CIGNA built a mock-up of an alternative office full of activity settings in a warehouse on the corporate campus. Employee group tours were given through the mock-up, beginning with a gallerylike exhibit that explains what the new workplace is all about. (Photo by MZS.)

Figure 9.8
The CIGNA mock-up includes all kinds of settings such as this teaming space with movable walls and rolling, reconfigurable conferencing tables. (Photo by MZS.)

a brand new layout, new technology, new ways of working," says Lewicki of the 150-person office. This project proves that a new workplace doesn't have to look or feel so foreign or futuristic, even though reallocating space dramatically shifts the work processes and the way staff communicates with each other.

The group came from a three-story building where they occupied one-and-a-half floors and they elected to move to one floor in another build-

ing with an upgrade to workflow imaging (scanning technology).

Lewicki usually likes to bring a consultant on board when dealing with these types of projects, someone like Fritz Steele or DEGW's Frank Duffy. But that wasn't necessary for the call center, where the employees were extremely driven, self-directed, and motivated, says Lewicki. The manager of the call center likes leading-edge projects, and was

Figure 9.9

CIGNA's CRE made the mock-up specifically in white foam core with black and beige task chairs so that employees would not be able to make any emotional decisions about the new workplace that might be based on the aesthetics of the furniture. This is a photo of a mock-cockpit office with mobile table. (Photo by MZS.)

willing to experiment a little. It was synchronicity, because the call center's lease was expiring and they were thinking of moving to workflow imaging anyhow. CRE immediately recognized this site as a prime opportunity to test and identify viable flexible options that they could take to other CIGNA departments and business units in the future." In theory, you can roll out this model to all of the other business units," says Lewicki. "But, the fact is that each division is extremely independent of one another, managers are all different, and it's critical to document our success, get matrixes in place, and present it to others."

Even studying just the employees at this call center, Lewicki's research uncovered 19 different work styles. "It's contrary to what management typically thinks about how people work," she says. "They think employees are only on the phone and the computer when the reality is that they accomplish these things all very differently." Her goal is to figure out what tools and processes they need to make their output most productive.

At the call center, one observation was that the service representatives work in teams, and within each team is a coach. For example, a team would consist of about 30 people split into several smaller specialized teams to deal with one particular client. So 6 to 8 people handling one client would sit next to a larger team of 10 to 12 people working on the same client, but for another function. But team leaders were often sprinkled throughout the floor. And, each team had different requirements in terms of furniture and technology.

CRE built in informal collaborative spaces, and purchased mobile pedestals and mobile easels and everyone is out in the open.

RETIREMENT AND INVESTMENT GROUP

From the call center, Lewicki jumped to the retirement investment services project, a large metropolitan building full of 700 people located in downtown Hartford. The project is up in the air due to some fairly dramatic organizational changes, shifting markets, varying needs.

Lewicki did not want the headway she made about alternative officing to diminish completely, however, since she already had 700 people—a captive audience—that she could educate on the new and alternative workplace options. So she took the opportunity to build a mock-up of an alternative workplace in 1996—an activity setting to be exact—and gave employees the chance to learn more about the workplace of the future (Figs. 9.7 through 9.9).

Lewicki has since taken managers through the warehouse space to get their feedback on what she put together. She has found that the mock-up has actually expedited the design process even if it isn't for an alternative space. It helps people visualize the solution to a department-specific design issue even if it doesn't result in an all-out alternative workplace solution.

LITIGATION OFFICES

"People laugh at us when we tell them we changed a litigation office into a teaming and hoteling office," she says. "Our attorneys are looking for new services, new markets, and they don't always want to sit in an office all day as a CIGNA litigation lawyer." The office is a functioning legal office, and what Lewicki found is that in order to go after new markets, attorneys need to be able to collaborate easily with one another to share information, yet, at the same time, they need privacy.

From a physical point of view, the legal office doesn't look much different than it would traditionally although the private offices are smaller. But the secretary right outside the private office door is gone, and now secretaries are clustered in two different areas throughout the space.

There is also a "lodge," which is more like a congregation area wired with outlets for data and power plugs-ins. "We asked them about their work flow pattern, and it was informal," says Lewicki. "They say 'hello' to the receptionist, check their mail, have coffee, sit in their office, go chat with others, do a little law library research, then have more coffee." What CRE wanted to do was bring together an area to encourage spontaneous information sharing among both paralegals and attorneys.

What has become popular is the "browserie," a drop-in space that is surrounded by an equipment area and plug-and-play surface.

In this particular office, some attorneys will actually telecommute, some will hotel. They are located in a unique building where they are connected by a tunnel to the courthouse that allows them to check in with the judge and come back to the office quickly and easily.

The private offices were reduced from a traditional 12- by 12-foot space to a 9- by 10-foot space. The managing attorney fought to keep his space larger, but instead of outfitting it with a traditional desk and credenza, Lewicki gave him a cockpit-style workstation so that he could also collaborate with others in his office.

Snapshot: CIGNA

CIGNA is a leading provider of healthcare, insurance, and related financial services throughout the world.

EMPLOYEES: 48,000 worldwide
HQ: One Liberty Place
1650 Market Street
Philadelphia, PA 19192-1550
PHONE: 215-761-1000
WEB SITE: http://www.cigna.com

NCR America's Virtual Workplace Program, 1994 to the Present

COMPANY OVERVIEW

Known mostly as a provider of retail and financial computer systems, NCR took on a new identity when AT&T bought it in 1991. For 5 years until the trivestiture was complete on December 31, 1996, NCR was the computing systems business unit of AT&T, but it continued to be plagued by financial woes with total net losses of $4 billion. Because of the loss, NCR is once again flying solo, but it's unwilling to go back to its troubled AT&T days. With Lars Nyberg taking over as CEO in 1995, the company is looking more streamlined than ever, and investors predict it will be the next successful turn-around story, much like IBM. By late 1996, NCR had 39,000 employees, down from 55,000 in 1991, it had stopped manufacturing PCs, and its real estate portfolio was being dramatically pared down due in part to the alternative officing strategies undertaken by its real estate organization.

Today, NCR is dedicated to providing computer products and services to customers in 130 countries. The company is also leveraging its expertise and market presence to provide computer solutions to three targeted industries—retail, financial, and communications.

THE NCR CULTURE

Historically, NCR maintained a conservative, almost stodgy approach to various business issues, including work-family trends. AT&T's influence helped to change this behavior. The merger with AT&T gave the computer giant a little bit of insight into the current trends in the family-work balance issues, which ultimately became quite an important force in shaping the NCR of today. So in 1994, NCR's corporate real estate (CRE) division collaborated with AT&T to determine the best way to begin looking at new ways of handling space and real estate. It was NCR's plan to learn from AT&T's telecommuting initiatives and expand them in practice for its own organization and pilot demonstrations.

NCR'S NEW WORKPLACE PROGRAM

During the IFMA World Workplace '96 symposium, Dan Accrocco, AIA, senior project manager with NCR's CRE division and an associate with the company since 1981, talked about the determination and gumption it takes to pull together a full-fledged alternative workplace program. Accrocco says that unusual as it may appear, NCR's CRE department drove the new workplace initiative, deciding for itself that it would become the guinea pig as a small pilot in which to educate themselves to processes of alternative workplace scenarios and to learn whether or not it was a viable option for the rest of NCR. The CRE department began by codeveloping with AT&T a five-phase process critical to implementing an alternative workplace program including a customer profile, options proposal, specifications for furniture and equipment, monitoring of activity during first 6 months, and capturing and evaluating business impacts across the board in real estate, human resources, information technology, and the business unit's goals.

Phase 1 Experiences

In 1994, Accrocco was the manager of facilities programming in the global real estate organization of AT&T Global Information Solutions (GIS, currently NCR) where he directed GIS's efforts to explore and test nontraditional officing scenarios. The CRE department, then known as the Global Real Estate organization, was spread out in two different sites on the corporate campus in Dayton. In each location, the gross square footage allowed per person was 317 and 303, well over the campus benchmark of 225 gross square feet per person. Even when CRE merged into one space, it still used 252 gross square feet per person, and they were still over what they felt it should read according to the aggressive space administrative guidelines AT&T kept for its employees. According to AT&T, associate general offices were supposed to be 155 to 175 gross square feet per person.

Working with human resources in May 1994, CRE was given a self-survey that went to 40 managers and nonmanagers to determine who, if anyone, would be interested in volunteering for this pilot. They questioned whether anyone would respond at all since part of the program mandated the loss of a dedicated workstation at the core office in order to have a dedicated home office (they would be able to sit at campus only in a hoteling cubicle). Much to everyone's surprise, 12 out of 40 participants in CRE—a mix of managerial and non-managerial employees—decided to volunteer for an alternative workplace program.

Now that the group of volunteers was set in place, CRE worked with the technology department to assess its current status of hardware and software and to see whether or not any of it was viable in a virtual workplace program. Existing technology in CRE included standard audix phone features and voice mail, LAN, Microsoft Mail, and Windows/Word/Exel version 4.0. Hardware included 386 and 486 desktop PCs and jet printers, and CRE had been budgeted already for an upgrade in software and hardware that summer.

Phase 2 Experiences

A figure of 210 gross square feet became CRE's target. The first thing the investigative team did in CRE was to analyze the "empty-office syndrome." For a 3-week period, the team went around the office at various times of the day and marked cubicles that were not occupied. The survey found that 25 percent of the time, no one was sitting in the cubicles because they were out sick, at a client's office, or traveling.

After the survey, it was recommended to managers that workstations be reduced to less than 120 square feet for managers, all managers, including vice presidents and directors. Those workstations would still be larger than the 64-square-foot cubicles normally given to CRE professionals such as real estate transaction managers, project managers, and administrative staff. The team also recommended an increase in the share of common space within the design group.

It was suggested that all CRE associates move into an open-plan, 8- by 10-foot cubicle and that the virtual team would work in a 6- by 8-foot cubicle whenever they came into the campus office. The 6 by 8 cubicle would be no more than a corner work surface and overhead bin to store materials like a phone directory, paper, pens, and a file drawer.

A Working at Home training class for everyone in CRE was held in August 1994 to explain the program and anticipated changes.

The technology was not in fact acceptable for virtual officing, so a PC upgrade plan was modified for laptop and docking ports instead of desktops for remote individuals. Remote workers received home-based phone systems including conference

Additional technology for virtual workers: Emergency 'E' Mail (Alan A. Abrahams)

calling. Two new separate business lines were installed in each participant's home office and used for stand-alone fax machines and printers dispatched to home offices.

Phase 3 Experiences

Design solutions for core office workstations were implemented. Drop-in, 48-square-foot cubicles were provided at a 1:3, office-to-virtual associate ratio. Overall space usage was figured to be 210 gross square feet (GSF) per person including the lease and facility files. Core office workstations given reconfigured with existing panel system furniture. NCR also began discussions with Herman Miller and Steelcase to see what home office furniture could be provided for remote workers by the end of 1994.

Since no one knew how to work at remote sites, training became a necessity. The AT&T School of Business (an arm of AT&T that outside vendors can tap into today—see Chap. 4) then provided the entire CRE department with training on how to work from remote sites and how nonremote workers need to function and change. Final guidelines were put into place and distributed to remote work teams prior to implementation. By October 1994, CRE had upgraded everyone's desktop computer to a 486 Globalyst, the remote team's receiving the laptop model for use with docking ports at shared hoteling stations located at the corporate campus. Remote workers could take home a monitor and

Business Unit: NCR Corporate Real Estate File: A:GISGREAO
Geographic Area: WHQ/4 Dayton, Ohio Date: 24-Jan-97

General Parameters:
Corp tax rate: 39.00%
Inflation: 3.00%
Discount rate: 4.00%
Study Period: 6

Year			1	2	3	4	5	6	7	8	Total
Months to Backfill				3							

Status Quo:

Location	GSF	Expires	Employees	GSF/Empl	Rent	Oper Exp	Bldg Serv				

Telecommuting:
Incremental Costs/(Savings)

Location	GSF	Date to Vacate	Employees	GSF/Empl	Rent/Asset S	Oper Exp	Bldg Serv	Admin Serv 1,551	Occ/Emplyee		
WHQ/4 Dayton, Ohio	(1,099)	Dec 31,1994	(12)	92	$17.00	$0.00	$0.00	$0.00	$1,555.50 /yr		
"Total Mgt Employees			39								
Percent Telecommuting			30.80%								
Rent:				(14,013)	(18,685)	(19,245)	(19,823)	(20,417)			(92,183)
Operating Expense:				0	0	0	0	0			0
Building Serv:				0	0	0	0	0			0
Base Location Cost:	0.00%			0	0	0	0	0	0	0	0
Admin Services:				0	0	0	0	0			0
Admin Serv:	0.00%			0	0	0	0	0	0	0	0
Telecom Costs:	$125.00			(13,514)	(18,018)	(18,559)	(19,115)	(19,689)			(88,894)
Total Costs Avoided:			0	(27,527)	(36,703)	(37,804)	(38,938)	(40,106)	0	0	(181,077)
Tax Shield:			0	10,736	14,314	14,743	15,186	15,641	0	0	70,620
After Tax Total			0	(16,791)	(22,389)	(23,060)	(23,752)	(24,465)	0	0	(110,457)
Discount:		1	0.97403	0.93656	0.90054	0.86591	0.83260	0.80058	0.76979	0.74018	
PV Savings:			0	0	(15,726)	(20,162)	(19,968)	(19,776)	(19,586)	0	0	(95,218)

Office Alteration Cost:	$5.99			6,584							6,584
Penalty:	$0.00				0						0
Employee Set Up:	$1,159.50			13,928	4,400	4,400					22,728
System/Phone Costs:	$175.00			18,919	25,225	25,982	26,761	27,564			124,452
Recuring Reimburses:	$0.00			0	0	0	0	0			0
Telecommute Costs:			0	39,430	29,625	30,382	26,761	27,564	0	0	153,763
Tax Shield:			0	(15,378)	(11,554)	(11,849)	(10,437)	(10,750)	0	0	(59,968)
After Tax Total			0	24,053	18,071	18,533	16,324	16,814	0	0	93,796
Discount:		1	0.97403	0.93656	0.90054	0.86591	0.83260	0.80058	0.76979	0.74018	
PV Costs:			0	0	22,527	16,274	16,048	13,592	13,461	0	0	81,901

Incremental PV:			0	0	6,800	(3,888)	(3,920)	(6,184)	(6,125)	0	0	(13,317)
PV Payback			0	0	6,800	2,913	(1,008)	(7,192)	(13,317)	(13,317)	(13,317)	
Pretax Cashflow:			0	11,903	(7,077)	(7,422)	(12,176)	(12,542)	0	0	
IRR:	61.86% Simple Payback			11,903	4,826	(2,596)	(14,772)	(27,314)	(27,314)	(27,314)	

Telecommuting:
Productivity:

Hours/day	Days/week	Hours/yr	$/hr loaded	$/yr							
0.75	3	150	$40.00	4,500							
Employee Value:				(54,054)	(55,676)	(57,346)	(59,066)	(60,838)			(286,980)
Tax Shield:			0	21,081	21,713	22,365	23,036	23,727	0	0	111,922
After Tax Total			0	(32,973)	(33,962)	(34,981)	(36,030)	(37,111)	0	0	(175,058)
Discount:		1	0.97403	0.93656	0.90054	0.86591	0.83260	0.80058	0.76979	0.74018	
PV Productivity Savings:			0	0	(30,881)	(30,584)	(30,290)	(29,999)	(29,711)	0	0	(151,465)
Total Hard/Soft Savings:			0	0	(24,081)	(34,472)	(34,210)	(36,183)	(35,835)	0	0	(164,782)
PV Payback			0	0	(24,081)	(58,553)	(92,763)	(128,947)	(164,782)	(164,782)	(164,782)	

Figure 9.10

A recent cost-benefit chart shows how NCR justifies its new workplace program. (NCR.)

keyboard. Phone service was improved, and remote workers were given fax-modem software for an initial deployment. That would be corrected later by giving remote workers stand-alone fax machines for home offices since fax-modem software applications can be limiting.

Phase 4 Experiences

At 3- and 6-month intervals from the move-in date, the team captured data to evaluate the overall space utilization. Data revealed that the new workspace plan drove down CRE's gross square footage from 300 GSF per person to 200 GSF per person. Utilization of the campus hoteling offices began to shake out, too. It turns out that the remote team visited campus for 1 to 2 days a week for no longer than 2 to 4 hours at a time.

Although remote workers were for the most part satisfied, the administrative employees were concerned about some issues and added job activity. It turns out that remote workers would call in with more administrative requests than they would have made when they were on campus (sending documents to remote locations, pulling files) and the administrative team resented the extra work. However, fewer requests were made as workers grew more comfortable with working at remote sites.

Phase 5 Experiences

At this stage, two analyses were done: One was a cost-payback for incremental costs incurred to this project over the expenses required to carry the project. It turned out that this pilot would save 20 percent of space and $14,000 in associated space costs over 5 years for just that particular slice of 40 people in the company. "We had 12 people in this pilot, but all the demographics were there to gather the information we wanted to capture," says Accrocco. Though it wasn't a large project, it was nevertheless a pilot from which CRE created the model against which to measure other business units who wished to do this type of officing.

COST-BENEFIT ANALYSIS ADVICE

Accrocco has some advice on building a cost-benefit analysis especially when it comes down to charting incremental costs. "You have to be careful not to count in newly purchased laptops for everyone in addition to new PCs for the entire organization," he warns. "The cost for the entire purchase is not what you take into account when you do the analysis for the virtual workplace. It's how much more did it cost to give laptops to the remote team versus the desktop that was going to be bought for them anyway." He suggests that each cost should be distin-

guished separately from the virtual office requirements and those of the traditional office plan that would have happened anyhow. Costs for alternative office scenarios are very specific slices of budget not to be confused with moneys dedicated to traditional budgetary requirements (Fig. 9.10).

Home office furnishings the company purchased made up a 100 percent cost addition that was incurred. Telephone lines, the telephone equipment, custom software, and the specific training were whole other areas of cost that could be fully attributed to alternative officing.

TIMELINE FOR NCR'S CRE ALTERNATIVE OFFICING PILOT

MAY 1994: CRE department surveyed for remote work volunteers.

June 1994: CRE moves into temporary location from two separate campus facilities.

August 1994: 12 participants for CRE pilot chosen.

August 1994: Working at Home training class is held for entire CRE department.

September 1994: AT&T holds Telecommute Day; CRE participants experiment.

October 1994: Remote workers begin new telecommuting and hoteling procedures.

October 1994: IT upgrades delivered and set up; training begins.

November 1994: Home office furniture ordered.

December 1994: Simultaneously, CRE relocates due to revised restack schedule. The same day as the

---

NCR's Project Phase Time Table

NCR adopted AT&T's process model, which consisted of five phases:

Phase 1: Assessment of Customer Profile
End deliverable: Customer profile including investigations of real estate portfolio, current IT system, identification of champions, team members, business unit strategies, and budgets.

Phase 2: Alternatives Proposal
End deliverable: Profile including options, impacts, cost-benefit analysis, business case development, job screening, and participant evaluations.

Phase 3: Detailed Requirements to Meet Specifications
End deliverable: Profile including furniture stacking plans, furniture and equipment inventories, deployment of inventory, procurement of systems and equipment, training and employee communications.

Phase 4: Implementation Measures
End deliverable: Data capture procedures in initial project monitoring at 3- and 6-month intervals from move date including acquisition and disposal of real estate, as well as administrative and technical support needs and costs.

Phase 5: Monitor and Evaluate Results
End deliverable: Financial evaluations including benefits for space savings, incremental savings over evaluation period, effectiveness of change management, productivity and efficiency, organizational support, and increased technical expertise.

Source: Dan Accrocco, senior project manager, NCR CRE at the World Workplace '96 symposium.

group move, the contracted mover was scheduled to relocate files, equipment, and existing furniture to home offices.

January 1995: 3-month formal assessment of the CRE pilot report is made.

April 1995: 6-month formal assessment of the CRE pilot report is made.

NCR TODAY

After analyzing the CRE pilot, NCR was ready to roll out the program to the rest of the company. At just about the same time, NCR's revenues and profits, as well as spirits, were even more depressed. In an effort to correct and turn the losses around, NCR began a sales initiative called "Return to Profitability" that would explore changes the company had to endure in order to remain solvent before the spin-off. "Eventually, Return to Profitability and the CRE initiatives were rolled into one strategy once we explained to upper management that this initiative could become an entire package involving reduced real estate and higher productivity," explains Accrocco during the IFMA 1996 conference. "We did it to survive. We were on a burning platform—it was either stay on the platform and burn or jump off and hopefully survive, so that's why several initiatives were clasped together to make us more lean and efficient."

Even now that NCR is independent once again, alternative officing remains a force in the organization, affecting 2200 sales associates across the nation, under a full-fledged formal initiative called the "America's Virtual Workplace Program." A geographically dispersed core team of people and extended partners worked with business units to kick off programs, deploy technology, and train workers on how to work from remote sites. Now that the domestic market virtual workplace initiatives are underway, NCR's CRE division plans on targeting Canada, Germany, and Australia. The company that *Business Week* hails as the next IBM has obviously inadvertently followed in Big Blue's footsteps in creating a leaner real estate portfolio that directly affects not only the bottom line but customer satisfaction.

Snapshot: NCR, Formerly a Business Unit of AT&T, Until 1997

NCR provides computer products and services to customers in all industries and in 130 countries.

FOUNDED IN 1884
EMPLOYEES WORLDWIDE: 37,900/19,000 United States
OFFICES: 1100 offices, 31 development and manufacturing locations in more than 130 locations
ALTERNATIVE WORKPLACE STRATEGIES: Dedicated home offices, hoteling
WEB SITE: www.ncr.com
HQ ADDRESS: 1700 South Patterson Boulevard, Dayton, OH 45479
PHONE: 937-445-5000
AMERICA'S VIRTUAL WORKPLACE PROGRAM TEAM: John Derkos, program manager, and Rick Hudspeth, Rick Teram, John McGinnis, Ron Campisi, Vince D'Angelo, Gary Davis, Gary Codeluppi, Deb Musson, Dan Accrocco, CRE, and Rick Chandler, WWIS. The team would especially like to thank the following champions who had enough corporate courage to be innovative: Gerald Behn, vice president, CRE; Wilson Painter, director, CRE; and Ray Carlin, senior vice president, marketing, America's Group.

Southern California Edison's New Workplace Business Strategies

INDUSTRY OVERVIEW

Most of the headlines in the popular press go to the deregulation of the telecommunications industry. But Southern California Edison (SCE) finds itself in the middle of another serious upheaval going on in another industry. Deregulation is shaking up the electric power industry, an industry used to running itself as a smug monopoly rather than as a competitively managed business. That means the way an electric company does business will change for good with the likelihood that there's no going back.

What makes it complicated is the different factions within the one industry. Major power companies have always generated most of their own electricity, sold and distributed it over their own networks, and stuck to a marked service area. Transmitting electricity over wires will most likely remain regulated since it's like owned real estate. But generating electricity is a different story since there's no monopoly on making the product from coal, natural gas, oil, nuclear power, or the natural elements. Companies won't become vertically integrated—that is, both generating and transmitting power—because there won't be incentive to do so.

If you think long-distance charges are confusing, wait for when the electric power deregulation aftermath hits your town. The charge now for electric companies becomes one of gaining customer loyalty, a marketing strategy they haven't had to do yet. There are predictions that some companies may market to consumers bundled services by packaging electricity with online or telephone services.

California and New Hampshire lead the new marketing effort, which means there's new competition among utilities companies to produce and sell electricity to consumers and businesses. The good news—electricity prices will no doubt drop. The bad news—utility companies already have profitability problems, and when electricity prices drop up to 20 percent as predicted, many companies—especially those with excess baggage in the form of nuclear power plants and all the associated expenses consumers have been paying for all along—will close down.

COMPANY OVERVIEW

"In 1998, the utility business in California will be deregulated. We are stressing to employees and management that the strict work process boundaries have to go away. We need to be more flexible and competitive…but we don't know what that means because we never had to know what that meant until now," says Brenda Laffin, SCE's manager of alternative officing and property services.

NEW WORKPLACE PROGRAMS

Laffin has worked at the company for 16 years as manager of its corporate furniture program, which includes space planning and guidelines. She's put together a comprehensive alternative officing program that will ultimately affect 17,000 employees who work in a 50,000-square-mile service territory.

In early 1996, Laffin and her team set out to put together an alternative officing business strategy. It took 9 months—a relatively short time—to put together a program that includes policies and guidelines for the eight alternative officing strategies she created for SCE. "Our definition of alternative officing is this: new approaches for how, when, and where people work," says Laffin. In fact, the tagline on many of the ancillary in-house materials she has developed for SCE says this: "Eliminating the boundaries where people work." Laffin stresses that it is not just a real estate strategy and not just a technology or just a human resources strategy. "It's like a three-legged stool—all three legs have to be there to hold up the stool" (Fig. 9.11).

A DIVERSITY OF STRATEGIES

Hoteling

In 1994, SCE implemented the Hotel Edison program, which needed further refining and led to the current model still called by the same name. To refine the program, Laffin took the model that Ernst & Young and other management consulting firms used, then tweaked it a little.

A hotel space at SCE is not a permanent office for the employee but rather is used as a supplemental

Figure 9.11

This user-friendly brochure helps Southern California Edison's at-home workers design the proper home office environment. (SCE.)

ALTERNATIVE OFFICING

Tips for Designing Your Home Office

Eliminating the boundaries where people work

Telebusiness Centers

Laffin opened accounts at shared service centers after the Northridge earthquake in 1994; however, only 12 people ever used them. The centers will still be part of the company's strategy in more remote areas where hoteling centers won't make sense to open.

There are subtle differences between the hoteling centers and the telebusiness centers. The hoteling centers are more fluid and informal spaces to drop in to work. The telebusiness center is reserved for companies to pool their resources to create a full-service working environment for employees described as "telecommuters." The groups share the expenses of real estate, equipment, supplies, and overhead. The groups commit to a fixed schedule, 1 to 2 days a week, and participation in a telebusiness center program is recorded for company compliance with the Clean Air Act.

Shared Officing

This is Laffin's "in-between solution" to get employees hooked on the idea of being virtual or mobile. It's up to the employees to work out the office schedules.

Group Offices

This scenario is based around work teams. The space morphs as the teams morph. The ratios are fairly high, up to 5:1.

Universal Plan Offices

This is extremely important to the alternative officing strategy, says Laffin. It's based on 8- by 8-foot and 10- by 15-foot single offices or two conference rooms and a door depending on the group's needs. The cost of churn at Southern California Edison is about $2600 per person. Universal planning brings that sky-high cost down to approximately $300 per person per move. "What will be more important as time goes on is not as much the *cost* of the churn but the *time* of the churn," says Laffin.

Regional Work Centers

This is a separate program that takes a look at how to leverage space typically used for the parking of customer-service trucks. Laffin is looking at the possibility of having employees take their trucks home with them so that the company can either reduce the number of service centers or expand their use.

space only. Employees use it for three reasons: to save the commute time from Los Angeles to Orange County, to hide in for doing concentrated work, and check in and out quickly between appointments. The maximum amount of time an employee can reserve a space is 2 to 3 days in a row. Today, there are seven such hotels with 6 to 15 workstations and large conference and teaming areas. They are self-sufficient and maintained by the people that frequently use the facility.

Red Carpet Hoteling

Reserved for the executives, this program incorporates a concierge and maintenance services not offered to the regular hoteling scenario above. Many of SCE departments choose to use Red Carpet Hoteling as an alternative benefit for upper management as a means to compensate them for giving up their private office. Services included banking, dry cleaning, travel arrangements, and some secretarial help. One other amenity offered for Red Carpet Hoteling but not offered in the regular hoteling program is the placement of personal items such as family pictures, artwork, and personal coffee cup once the "guest" arrives at the center.

Figure 9.12
Southern California Edison believes in keeping its alternative officing workers fully informed with a constant stream of corporate communications materials and materials that are simply designed on a desktop computer and freely distributed. (SCE.)

Alternative Officing

August 14, 1996

"Eliminating the boundaries where people work"

FP&C Project Managers operate "From" Home

Project Managers Home Offices

Five members of the FP&C Project Management team will begin operating from their home residences, eliminating the need for an office at one of SCE's corporate facilities.

Debora Tucker, John Hund, Richard Smith, Jorge Diaz and Khan Pathan are in the process of making the move home. These individuals qualify as "From Home" employees under SCE's definition of home officing.

"From Home" applies to employees who regularly spend 2 hours or less per day *in the office*, because most of their work happens with their internal SCE client base.

Furniture, technology and communication needs will be provided to these employees. Because the needs of these five individuals vary, implementation will happen on a phased basis over the next 4-8 weeks.

AO Training: technology and classroom

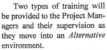

Two types of training will be provided to the Project Managers and their supervision as they move into an *Alternative* environment.

The first type of education will be *technology training*. This training will encompass teaching the PMs how to use their new printers, fax machines and back up drives; how to dial in through Sheiva to access Netscape and MS Exchange; and how to maneuver through the PC platform from one of many remote locations.

The second type of education provided will be *classroom training*. This curriculum consists of 3 days, with the

PM's attendance required at 2 of the 3 days. The first day will be training for the PMs' manager, providing refresher training on such things as performance management and communication. The second day will focus on the skills needed for the PM's to operate successfully in an AO environment, such as communication, team inclusion and personal organization. On the final day of training, the managers join the PMs to work on items such as a communication plan, and an Alternative Officing Agreement.

Alternative Officing Technology

The PMs will be provided equipment and technology in order to successfully base their work from their home residences.

They will be provided an HP855C color ink jet printer. This printer produces laser quality output in black & white or color. (This publication was produced on an HP855C.)

The PMs will also be provided with an HP700 combination fax/copier/scanner.

In addition, they will have an external drive for backing up their work, and for easy future software upgrades.

Banctec has participated in the creation of the Alternative Officing Program and is prepared for the installation and testing of all technology items in the employee's home.

For equipment repair needs, the PMs will call the Network Assistance Center (PAX 22329) and report any problem as if the equipment was located at a Edison facility. If NAC is unable to triage the situation remotely, Banctec will be notified and will respond to the employee's home (if necessary) within the next 8 work hours.

IMM rates have been established to support Home Work environments.

Voice/Data Communication

For voice communication, the PMs will each have a "phantom" PAX number. This PAX number will not exist on a physical instrument. When a call is made to the employee's PAX, it will go directly to a personal voicemail message instructing the caller that the employee will be paged immediately after a voicemail message is left. Upon being paged, the PM can use the Edison 800 number (800-600-4SCE) to return the call from any phone without incurring phone charges.

Data communications will be managed by installing a new, data conditioned phone line in the employee's home. This line will be ordered by the employee (a phone company requirement) with his/her local phone provider. The employee will submit this phone bill on their monthly Employee Expense Report.

HomeWork

Laffin built a two-tiered program for employees who work at home.

From home. An employee who works at home and spends two or fewer hours per day on a computer on a consistent basis (defined as 3 days a week) (Fig. 9-12).

At home. An employee who works at home and spends 2 or more hours per day on a computer on a consistent basis (defined as 3 days a week).

For a more detailed description of this program, see Chap. 7 on provisions for telecommuters.

TRAINING: THE KEY TO SUCCESSFUL ALTERNATIVE OFFICING

The first training sessions necessary in order to take the show on the road, so to speak, are the Shared-Services Training courses, including facilities planning and property services departments. Laffin says its like "Management 101," but it helps support services understand better the business objectives of SCE and why alternative officing plays such an important role in the overall scheme of the electric utility's future. "It's a lightweight way to bring support services up to speed about what our customer wants and needs," says Laffin. "They know they are going to have to care a whole lot more in the future than they do now about whether or not a customer's toilet is clogged up."

The second phase of training is threefold. Laffin contacted the AT&T School of Business for help in structuring a comprehensive training course for managers and employees alike on the new expectations of working in an alternative office. The course included a managers' workshop and employees' workshop with a planning workshop which a manager and employee would attend together. The following briefly outlines each.

The Employees' Workshop

The first training session is with the company employees who will be newly involved in an alternative officing program. The topics discussed include:

- How to work in an AO environment
- Managing personal performance in an AO environment
- What kinds of work habits are expected in an AO environment
- Managing personal and professional change in an AO environment
- How to work in teams
- The issues and challenges of working in an AO environment
- Preparing for Day 3 when employees come together with their supervisors

Managers' Workshop

The day after the employees go through their workshop, managers go through a workshop specially designed for their needs and concerns. That particular workshop stresses that managers play a crucial role in the implementation of alternative officing. The workshop is designed to accomplish the following:

- Describe what alternative officing is and its role at SCE.
- Identify a manager's strengths and weaknesses in making alternative officing work.
- Define a performance management process.
- Define mutual expectations, policies, procedures, and communications.
- Develop time-management strategies to make alternative officing work.
- Define strategies that can be used in a team to make alternative officing work.

The emphasis is on training managers to manage by results. The basic course is intended to show participants that managing employees in an alternative officing arrangement is no different than managing them in a traditional environment although there's a perception that it is different.

"You can't manage by face time, you can't manage by corporate citizenship, you can't manage by giving points if they are always the one filling up the copier machine with paper," emphasizes Laffin.

To get the manager to the point of accepting the fact that they have to manage by results, Laffin starts by asking the manager to self-assess their strengths and weaknesses that could help or hinder the success of an alternative officing program. The questions asked are designed to help managers flush out their fears, to let go of them, and to begin focusing on their strengths. Managers have to rate each self-assessment statement on a scale from 1 to 5, 1 being "to no degree" and 5 being "to an extensive degree." Some sample questions in the self-assessment portion of the workshop include:

- I explain how the employee's performance expectations link to department goals.
- My commitment to department and company goals is demonstrated by visible actions my team can observe.
- I let my employees or team know how they will be held accountable.

From a series of 10 questions like these, managers can begin to identify their key strengths and key challenges in making an alternative officing program work.

The managers then begin to look at some of the walls they put up as barriers to alternative officing. After identifying barriers, the managers are asked to write down preventative actions and solutions to these challenges. Again, this exercise is to help managers loosen their grip on their fear of managing remote employees. In fact, SCE prefers to say that managers are practicing remote coaching and counseling rather than managing remote. Some of the performance barriers might be:

- Employees don't know or accept what they are supposed to do.
- Employees are rewarded for not performing.
- Employees receive conflicting information.

After explaining performance management, the next important issue is planning communication with employees in alternative officing, urging managers to define their communications policies. Take beepers, for example. If a manager beeps an employee working in the middle of East Los Angeles with a "911" code, does that mean the employee should immediately stop and call, or does it mean to get to the nearest safe place, then give the manager a call? A lot of miscommunication occurs because of these little miscommunications and misconceptions between manager and employee. "Though it seem silly to have to train people on these issues, you can safely bet that the least little thing that goes wrong will be blamed on alternative officing, so it's worth it," says Laffin.

Planning Workshop

After employees and managers spend a separate day in workshops, they are brought together for the final step of alternative workplace training. Each group brings their communications plans and their performance agreements and come ready to work on the programs together. This session involves a short Meyer-Briggs test on both employee and manager to smooth out potential problems working in an alternative office. For instance, does the manager like to receive information differently than the employee likes to give information? That sort of thing can easily be ironed out.

The issues discussed and mutually agreed upon by both employee and supervisor include:

- How to plan meetings in an AO environment
- Communicating with each other in a new AO environment
- Work agreements between employee and supervisor
- Performance management plans
- Working with the changes that are bound to occur in an AO environment

SCE's Technology Lab

After 3 days of coaching on new work processes, technology becomes the next major issue to understand. The "Technology Lab" is a separate session and provides one-on-one training for new technol-ogy brought into an alternative officing program. The lab is arranged so it mirrors that of a typical work-at-home employee. The employees are taught how to work their new printers and fax machines and they are shown how to dial up remotely in order to access information. "One of the biggest messages we try to get across in this lab is that you will have to become a little bit more technologically literate," says Laffin. "You might actually have to pull a book off the shelf, read the error code, and try to figure it out yourself because there's no one over the other side of a cubicle to call over for help."

What Laffin also hopes the lab training will do is instill patience in an employee. She's had to learn the virtue of patience with technology herself—Laffin's printer sends a little error message every so often, but she took the time to learn that all she has to do is hit the reset button to put it back online without incident and without having to call in the field technicians.

Snapshot: Southern California Edison

The nation's second largest electric utility company based on the number of customers it serves: 4.2 million

ADDRESS: P.O. Box 600
Rosemead, CA 91771
PHONE: 800-655-4555
WEB SITE: http://www.sce.com/index.html
E-MAIL: corpcomm@sce.com
REAL PROPERTIES ALTERNATIVE OFFICING
STEERING COMMITTEE:
Brenda Laffin, program manager; Dan Moore, property services; Claire Spence, facilities planning and construction; Leon Machado, communications and computing services; Jeffrey Wilson, human resources; Rich Warner, occupational health and safety; Dave Falconer, corporate security; William Harn, legal; Paul Narro, facilities planning and construction; Gary Buckley, facilities planning and construction; and Les Travis, facilities planning and construction.

Tandem Computers, 1993 to the Present

COMPANY OVERVIEW

On December 10, 1996, three Antarctic explorers embarked on a 1300-kilometer journey as part of the Tandem One Step Beyond South Pole Challenge program. Tandem Computers' goal was to follow explorers to the South Pole armed with satellite and Web technology to link the historic walk to anyone around the world who wanted to share in the experience of the Antarctic expedition. Schools from around the world participated in the project, bringing an awareness of not only the South Pole to children but of the abilities of technology to bring together information in a virtual environment. It's one of the ways Tandem is showing the world that it supports and believes in the power of technology. Tandem knows all about the power of technology as it began to see the possibilities 3 years before the Antarctic exploration when it embarked on its own in-house journey—the expedition toward the office-of-the-future.

Even before formal AWE programs took place at Tandem, the company's CRE department was busy gathering research and data on new work processes and supporting environments. But it wasn't until 1993 when Tandem's business and financial models began to dramatically change, that senior management realized it needed to finally take a hard look at what its real estate was costing the company in both dollars and productivity.

As the Tandem product evolved and subsequently became smaller in size, so did a new way of selling become necessary. The once huge mainframe computer systems were showcased in a glass-fronted, raised-floor computer room and were the focal point in their sales offices. Customers coming into the offices would immediately see what Tandem sold, and the entire sales presentation took place in that office. As the industry matured, customers and potential customers wanted solutions for their businesses. This drove the Tandem sales staff to team up and specialize in computer applications such as financial, retail, commercial, and telecommunications. The Tandem specialists often found themselves supporting sales efforts elsewhere in the United States, leaning toward a line of business management, further supporting the fact that peo-

ple in the sales organization were out of the office a majority of the time.

After the space utilization evaluations, Tandem decided it could easily reduce the portfolio of its U.S. field sales offices now that it was using the line-of-business mode, downsizing the actual 450 square footage allocated per employee down to a more reasonable 150 to 200 square feet per person using more uniform office footprints over oddly shaped office space. CRE knew that all this could be done in such a way that Tandem could stay in "class A" locations and still have a program to affect sales, revenue, and productivity in the most positive way.

Although senior management now saw the advantages of AWE, it wanted the assurance that the implementation of an AWE at Tandem would be slow and sure with more than adequate communication to employees as to why the workplace was changing and what they should expect to take place. Considered to be one of the best companies to work for in the United States according to author Robert Levering in his 1993 book *100 Best Companies to Work for in America*, senior management did not want to tread all over its corporate culture that for years had relied on Tandem's employee-driven policies and expectations.

NEW WORKPLACE PROGRAMS

Careful in their approach to studying the new workplace, CRE chose a site in 1993 and began to study what it then called the "Office of the Future." At the same time, Tandem teamed up with Michael Brill of BOSTI to arrive at a new office design through the process of top management interviews, site visits, space utilization studies, and in-house meetings with a team comprised of CRE, HR, MIS finance, and Telecom.

Coinciding with the time frame in which BOSTI was brought on board to gather research, Tandem had several field relocations under way: one was in Itasca, Illinois, and another was in Atlanta. Both projects incorporated some of the new ideas, such as free address, drop in offices, shared offices, hoteling, and caves and commons, in fact, just

Figure 9.13

Itasca was one of the first Tandem virtual workplaces designed by the Environments Group. (Environments Group.)

al sites, where there are already a handful of refined Business Centers.

But what Tandem did find out through its Office of the Future explorations at Itasca, with the help of The Environments Group (one of the numerous design firms with which Tandem currently consults) are the potential pitfalls of the alternative workplace. The task groups expressed concern to The Environments Group about implementing any of the Office of the Future solutions on a permanent basis for the following reasons:

- *Territoriality:* Unwillingness to forgo dedicated work spaces
- *Technology support:* Concern related to Tandem's commitment to technology implementation
- *Facility resource use:* Need for access to facility-related personal resources such as project files and meeting spaces
- *Security at client sites:* Some customers do not allow portable computers in and out of the site
- *Remote management:* Difficulty managing remote employees; no opportunity for interaction
- *Culture:* Concern about degradation of Tandem's favorable corporate culture with everyone out of office
- *Mentoring:* Concern over ability to integrate new employees into the corporate culture and to teach a mobile workforce
- *Administrative costs:* Absence of a central authority in the facility and administrative functions such as workstation set-up and file management

Further research in the Itasca and subsequent field office sites, using BOSTI's bedcheck method of determining actual patterns of office utilization, confirmed that there were many categories of employees (common to all of Tandem's sales offices) who were out of the office 70 percent of the time (Fig. 9.13). That group were called "runners," and it was this group of employees that was identified as those who could easily work from a shared, nondedicated workspace with ratios of 3:1, if the appropriate technology for phone forwarding were put in place. Employees who were based at the office a majority of the time were called "sitters," and they would remain in dedicated workstations with a 1:1 ratio.

THE BUSINESS CENTER MODEL

In early 1994, the research derived from the Office of the Future evolved into a more permanent AWE strategy called the "Business Center," which took

about every alternative workplace solution known, but neither of the sites was considered to be permanent as an alternative workplace.

Using the input from programming meetings at Itasca, vision sessions with representatives in the field, and the input from Atlanta, Tandem was able to address the concerns that employees expressed in converting to a new real estate model.

In early 1994, when the BOSTI study was complete, Tandem abandoned the term "Office of the Future" and moved into a newer, more permanent phase—one to call their own—coined the Business Center. Although the Itasca interior was alternative in its implementation, Tandem doesn't consider that space the first beta Business Center model.

As of 1997, Tandem has experienced many changes, one being that it's been acquired by Compaq Computers. Nevertheless, the Business Center concept thrives. So far, 25 U.S. field sales locations have been transformed into a Business Center and another 10 will be implemented in 1997 and 1998. The Tandem new workplace team will now move its reach overseas to its internation-

15 months to roll out across all the U.S. sales field offices. Between 1995 and 1996, 17 Tandem sites across the country went through either the preliminary design phase, final building selection, site search, or evaluation of option stage to get to the ultimate goal of a completed Business Center.

The Business Center initiative was born using the Business Center real estate model supplied by collaboration between BOSTI and the CRE, and it is based solely on that particular office's headcount of runners and sitters. The Business Center model forecasts a rentable square footage that can support the number of employees in the office and the functions or tasks spaces associated in that particular location. The Tandem model provides sizes and suggests quantities of support rooms, such as conference, workrooms, "big rooms," equipment galleries (i.e., mail, copy, printer), cockpit offices, and managers' and administrative offices based on headcount. The model's standard for cockpit offices (used for runners at a 3:1 ratio—three persons to one cockpit office) is 6- by 8-feet and a manager's office (used for sitters at a 1:1 ratio) is 10- by 12-feet. However, these larger managers' offices are also considered temporal spaces, that is, spaces that are used for meeting rooms when managers are out of the office. Although it may be more expensive to build hard-walled cockpit offices rather to reconfigure mobile furniture or to use universal open-plan workstations, Tandem took a leap of faith with a fairly secure estimation of what its future business plans would shake out to be.

What is so clearly wonderful about the Business Center model is that it has within one envelope a variety of multitask rooms with usage patterns that end up blurring the lines between what space is used for which activity. The Business Center breaks from the notion that one space is but for one function. Interestingly enough, the Business Center model was implemented at Tandem before it shifted its selling method from a geographical sales model to the line-of-business sales model previously described. Even though Tandem's sales model switched in form, few changes were made to the original Business Center model, which proves how inherently flexible the concept really is.

Now that there is a Business Center model on paper for easy sales office conversions, the new task for design firms involved with Tandem Business Center initiatives is to fine-tune how that particular office "spends" its space. It may be that the office in Cincinnati needs another workroom and prefers to have a small break area rather than a lunch room.

Local offices use the model, but they are involved in how the standard elements of the Business Center are designed. Working directly with the Tandem project manager and outside design professional, the local offices use the square-footage model and are involved in how the standard elements of the Business Center are designed (Fig. 9.14). They work directly with the architect or designer on the work flow, colors and materials selections, functional requirements of each space, and the issues that surface as the project progresses into construction. In this way, the local offices assume ownership for their work environment.

It doesn't matter how big or small a particular Tandem office is; there is a Business Center model to which individual locations can adapt (Fig. 9.15). There's a model for offices the size of 1 to 10 people, one for 10 to 20 people, and one for 20 to 30 people (Fig. 9.16). Any office larger than 80 people can ask CRE to adjust the model to fit the headcount. Adjustments are easy since the models are calculated on an Excel spreadsheet programmed so that the CRE inputs headcount and then it immediately calculates the quantity and area necessary for cockpits and sitting spaces, sizes of conference rooms and work lounges, and the gross square footage and the square footage per person. It has simple metrics that the CRE can use to keep track of each office.

Another key element in making Tandem's alternative workplace solution successful is the consistency of technology in every Business Center. No matter what the Business Center looks like, the employee knows that the telephone, data, fax, and copier all work the same way. Information for Business Center models now includes detailed listings of all equipment, phone switch, and network services.

As of late 1997, Tandem didn't have a standard for home office furniture used by Business Center employees. Its human resources department was just beginning to handle the issues of liability.

LESSON 1 FROM THE TRENCHES: EMOTIONS RUN HIGH

"Tandem's salespeople travel a lot, so we thought that just about everyone was familiar with what a Business Center looked like," says Ernest J. Piccone, director, real estate, corporate real estate, and site services. "Well, in fact, that's true for most people, but there's still a value to having a meeting about the Business Center, answer questions, and hold

Figure 9.14

Here's an example of a cockpit office developed by BOSTI and implemented in all of Tandem's Business Centers. This is in Cincinnati. (Environments Group.)

hands to get them to think about how this new way of working fits into their own lives."

The emotional issue for salespeople at Tandem was, "I don't have a home," says Piccone. When they get past the point where they realize that the Business Center is a fact of life for Tandem, the emotions dissolve. What helps to break down the emotional walls employees put up when faced with AWE is to show them that the new space is extremely pleasing aesthetically and, that there will always be enough room for them to work. "It takes about three months after a Business Center is up and running before they realize they can control acoustics, dim the lighting, and the environment is quiet," says Piccone. "Then it all goes well after that point."

Tandem owes a great deal of the success in keeping its corporate culture intact during implementation of the Business Center initiative to the Business Center Handbook, which spent a significant time developing. The guide, which is distributed to every office, reviews the processes used in developing the Business Center, discusses model concepts, and highlights the new work processes that will grow from the new work environment.

Tandem also recommends the use of the Business Center Initiative Continuous Improvement Survey, a sort of in-house, postoccupancy evaluation form, filled out by employees to get a satisfaction level reading on their whether or not the physical workplace has affected their productivity, use of technology, and relationships with managers and coworkers. The survey also asks them how much time they spend in each of the various activity settings in the Business Center such as the cockpit office, big room, work lounge, or dedicated office.

LESSON 2 FROM THE TRENCHES: TECHNOLOGY

When Tandem began to roll out the Business Centers, a key technology element, called the *mobile office business environment* (MOBE), was presented to the

Figure 9.15
This is a generic floor plan for a Business Center for 25 people that Tandem asks its design consultants to use as a template.
(Tandem.)

Figure 9.16
This is a generic floor plan for a Business Center for 46 people that Tandem asks its design consultants to use as a template. Note that although the number of staff has nearly doubled, the square footage has not expanded twice as much because of the hoteling environment.
(Tandem.)

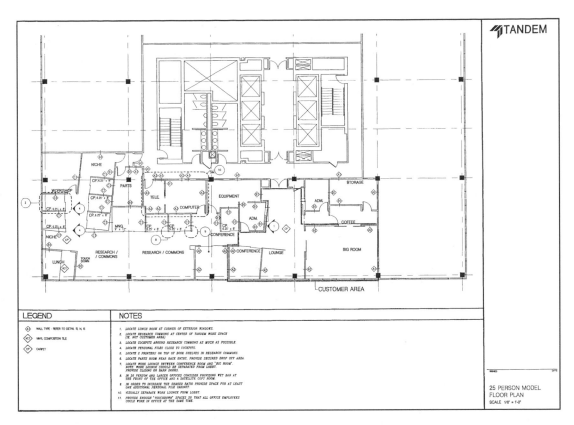

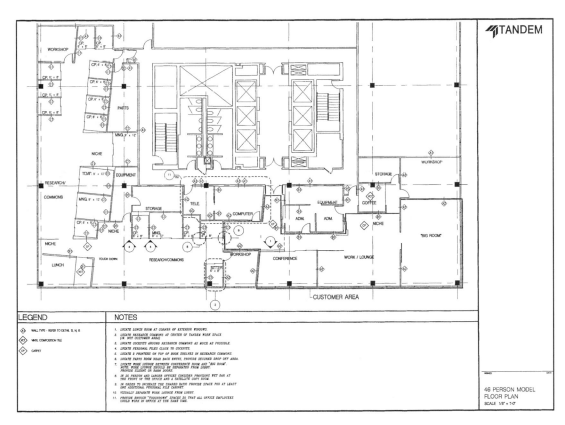

field organization. MOBE allowed Tandem employees with portable tools to dial into Tandem's LAN and WAN so that they could work from anywhere. With the roll-out of MOBE, Tandem found that although most offices had LAN, there was no consistency between offices and no way to create the WAN until all the LANs conformed. Tandem people knew the Tandem network but not the differences in LAN/WAN operations. Field support staff had to be quickly trained.

MOBE incorporates Tandem software, including boilerplate proposals, templates, current pricing, and remote mail all bundled together on a portable laptop. Training for MOBE includes a class, and upon completion, employees receive a coupon for a free Macintosh Powerbook loaded with MOBE—a move that turned out to be quite an incentive to learning how to work from remote sites.

At the time of the Business Center roll-out, technology for mobile follow-me phone service wasn't available, and Tandem's phone provider was not able to forward as many phones as necessary on a daily basis. However, they were lucky enough to find a software program called DeskFlex, produced by Professional Resources Management, which is easily run on a Tandem PC, allowing the user to log on and assign their phone number to a particular workplace. Around midnight, the software clears all the phones so that there's no confusion the next day.

"Convert technology first to make sure it works perfectly before you roll it out—don't do it at the same time," warns Piccone.

TAKING TANDEM'S BUSINESS CENTER MODEL GLOBAL

Tandem in the United States had the highest occupancy costs of any division of the worldwide computer company, but thanks to AWE and the Business Center model, that's no longer true. Up until now, only the U.S. offices were mandated to convert over to the Business Center model, but now the CRE team is looking across the Atlantic Ocean at the potential implementation of Business Centers in Europe (there are 35 Tandem offices in Europe). But because corporate real estate is already so efficient in parts of Europe, Asia, and Japan, there may not be much opportunity for implementation of the U.S. Business Center model, says Piccone. There are, however, opportunities for a Business Center in

Moscow when Tandem switches over from selling through distributors to direct selling.

As with any global project, cultural norms will have to be taken into consideration. "The United Kingdom will be easy to talk to about Business Centers since it tends to mirror the United States, and they are very openminded," says Piccone. "Germany will be a little more complex because of its stringent workplace regulations. But in Europe, workers are used to working in open space and in teams, although there's still the issue of some senior managers who, because of custom and tradition, have large private offices and conference rooms." With that in mind, it will be more important for CRE to "hold hands" with offices overseas that convert to Business Centers, the next phase of AWE for this progressive computer company.

TANDEM'S ANNUAL DESIGN BRAINSTORMING SESSION

Tandem is known for its diversity in the design teams it uses around the country. From Stevens & Wilkinson, Farrington Design, Staffelbach Designs, Holey Associates, to The Environments Group, each Business Center has its own flavor, its own design imprint, thanks to the talent of the firms with which CRE works.

To celebrate Tandem's best practices and best designs, it orchestrates an annual 2-day brainstorming meeting with all of its design consultants, CRE, technical support divisions, and more who join in on the cross-functional teams. The fall of 1996 marked the second annual meeting, and Tandem should be applauded for sponsoring this event because it brings together an inordinate amount of design talent to share the wealth of their knowledge with each another under one roof.

In the following paragraphs two design firms with two different but equally successful points of view are discussed.

Staffelbach's Design Process, Baltimore, 1996

Since 1991, Staffelbach Designs has worked with Tandem CRE and site services (CRESS) to provide design services during the development, implementation, and evolution of the Business Center model (Fig. 9.17).

For the Baltimore Business Center model, Tandem CRESS identified the need to relocate this

Figure 9.17

Staffelbach Designs has
worked with Tandem on
Business Centers since
1991. This firm designed
the Baltimore office in
1996.
(Staffelbach.)

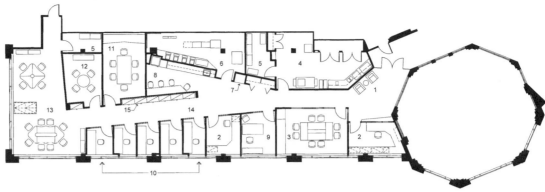

1   LOBBY/WORK LOUNGE
2   ADMINISTRATION OFFICE
3   BIG ROOM
4   EQUIPMENT/GALLEY
5   STORAGE
6   SERVER/TELECOM ROOM
7   RSVP STATION
8   BREAK ROOM
9   MANAGER OFFICE
10 COCKPIT OFFICES
11 WORKSHOP
12 CONFERENCE
13 RESEARCH COMMONS
14 COMMONS
15 LOCKERS

BALTIMORE BUSINESS CENTER
TANDEM COMPUTERS, INC.
STAFFELBACH DESIGNS AND ASSOCIATES INC

office from existing leasing space. Tandem CRESS determined that the number and type of employees who would work in the office, and the programming model was used to provide a preliminary determination of lease space area required. This model incorporates a ratio of office space to employees for each type of staff and lists standard support spaces based on the Business Center model.

Staffelbach Designs presented the space plan studies to the staff in Baltimore, and through roundtable discussion the requirements of the particular office were determined and the various merits and deficiencies of the Business Center model were identified.

The design elements of the Baltimore Business Center include the following:

- *Lobby-work lounge:* Serves visitors and employees for reading or informal communications.
- *Administration offices and managers' offices:* Dedicated workspaces for staff members who are considered "sitters" in the Business Center model.
- *Big room:* The largest flexible meeting space and a place to meet with clients and visitors. The table can be configured in different shapes to accommodate any situation. A millwork unit along one wall houses a large-screen television and VCR. A counter with power and data connections hangs on another wall.

- *The equipment galley:* Houses the equipment everyone uses such as the copier, printers, fax, mail equipment, and shredder.
- *Break room:* Another space for informal gatherings enhanced with architectural elements and color. There's a counter for meals and full power-data connectivity so that the room can be used for individual and group work.
- *RSVP station:* Adjacent to the break room, this small station allows staff to reserve a cockpit office and instructs the software to which office his or her telephone calls should be routed.
- *Cockpit offices:* Nondedicated work areas with full-height walls, glass doors, and windows to maximize visual connection with other office areas. They are fitted with a work counter, full data and power connectivity, indirect ambient lighting, task lighting, acoustical panels, white boards, a glass door, and a side light. The visual connection between the cockpit offices and the other areas is tempered with translucent patterned glass in the windows.
- *Lockers:* Located across from the cockpit offices, these storage spaces are for employees who share these workstations.
- *Workshop and conference room:* Meeting and work areas with full data and power connections. The room is sized to allow for future conversion to an office if needed.

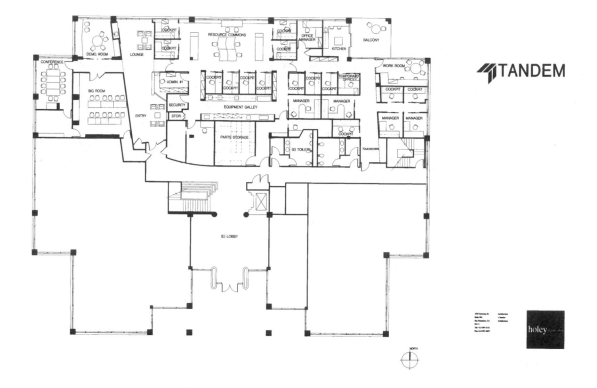

TANDEM

Figure 9.18
Holey Associates is another firm that Tandem consults with to design its Business Centers. This floor plan is from the Seattle office. (Holey.)

• *Research commons*: Reference library and work area for individuals and small groups. Tables in this area can be combined in different shapes and have built-in data and power connections.

Holey's design process, Seattle, 1997

Tandem hired Holey Associates to design the 6700-square-foot Seattle Business Center for 39 sales and service employees. The project incorporates the original guidelines of the BOSTI real estate model and refines it with respect to the footprint of the Seattle building. In addition, this design helped Tandem to reduce its original Seattle office space by 40 percent (Figs. 9.18 and 9.19). The fluid environment allows workers to select from a variety of concentrative and collaborative work environments. The strategic planning and analysis of the business functions resulted in a design that addressed the specific ways Tandem workers require smooth transition from a traditional way of working into radically changed work processes (Fig. 9.20).

The design features of this office includes the following:

Individual Workspaces for Concentrative Tasks

• *Nonterritorial cockpit spaces*: The offices are reserved by "runners" on an as-needed basis and available

on a reservation system. The 6- by 8-foot offices are classic cockpit style with enclosed hard walls and sliding glass doors. Most cockpit spaces open out onto a resource commons area, and still more cockpits are located away from the collaborative resource commons area to provide additional privacy.

• *Dedicated manager spaces*: Enclosed hard-wall offices for sitters who are at the office on a daily basis are slightly larger than the cockpit offices and measure 8- by 8-feet with sliding glass doors.

Collaborative Workspaces with Plural Functions

• *Resource commons space*: A versatile area for collaboration among mobile workers. Key resources and information manuals are located here, bringing workers into the space. With over half of the cockpit offices opening out onto this space, it also easily becomes a space for impromptu meetings and conversations. This area is also used for lunch, plus this space has the most access to outdoor views and natural light to draw people into it.

• *Conference room*: This space allows for collaborative meetings for up to 12 people.

Figure 9.19

Here's a photo of the interior of the Seattle Business Center, employing Steelcase's Activity Tables. (Photo by Donna Day.)

- *Big room:* The room has easily reconfigurable furniture for functions such as training, conferencing, and meeting tasks.

- *Lounge and lobby:* These two adjacent areas together form a large space that also doubles for impromptu gatherings. It also serves as a breakout area for training sessions and meetings held in the big room.

- *Break room at balcony:* This break-out area capitalizes on the exterior balcony with an outside table that accommodates a group meeting, informal lunch meeting, or an individual worker seeking a quiet place to work outside.

- *Touchdown spaces:* This space allows for short-term users to plug laptops in, retrieve e-mail, and do quick phone work.

Support Spaces

- *Equipment galley:* Houses printers, copiers, servers, and databases. Functions as a mail room, as well.
- *Personal lockers:* Runners store personal belongings near cockpits. Lockers consist of a 3- by 6-inch lateral drawer and a shelf of the same size, both of which can be locked.

Holey Associates created the guidelines, based on this design, for a standard package to be rolled out for over 50 Tandem Business Centers throughout the United States.

Snapshot: Tandem

A supplier of computer processing systems for banking, stock exchange, and telecommunication

Business Center *Etiquette*

Phones

UPDATE YOUR VOICEMAIL daily. Include the day and date in your outgoing message. If you are in meetings, traveling, or on vacation, update your message accordingly. • Encourage use of your direct line instead of asking callers to go through the main number • Discourage callers from dialing "0" • Refer callers to a location or number where you can be reached when out of the office. • Don't use voicemail as a filing system; delete messages regularly. • Keep the volume on your speaker phone turned down so other employees will not be disturbed.

Common Areas

WHEN YOU'VE FINISHED using workspaces and common areas, be sure to **WRAP-UP** before you leave:

Wipe off tables and white boards

Return equipment and chairs to their proper places

Accidents happen, but don't leave them unattended; report them

Pitch out trash

Used any supplies? Replace them or have them ordered

Problems with equipment? Report them for repair

Hallways and work areas: Be considerate to others; keep the noise down! Speak softly and turn down speaker phones. • Meeting rooms: When your guests leave, WRAP-UP before you go. Schedule meeting rooms according to your business center's scheduling procedure. • Break room: Clean up after yourself, wash your own dishes, and notify staff when supplies are low. • Library/research commons: Keep documents and manuals in order so other employees can find what they need. Always WRAP-UP before you leave.

Little Things

REFILL COPY PAPER, staples, and fax paper when they run out. Replace toner in laser printers and copiers. • If equipment breaks, don't walk away. Either fix it or notify someone who can. • Be considerate of other employees; ask before you borrow something, and always return it in the same condition. • If you borrow an extra chair from a cockpit or common area, return it where you found it when your guest leaves.

R.S.V.P.

THE R.S.V.P. SYSTEM not only signs you in to the phone system, it also tracks availability of workspaces as "in use" or "open." If you don't use the system, other employees and visitors will walk in on you. RSVP prevents inconvenience and conflict. • Always sign in and out. • Visitors—including Tandem employees from other offices—should also sign in and out.

RUNNERS ARE EMPLOYEES who do not have assigned workspaces (Tandem defines "runners" according to job code). Almost all workspaces within the business center are not assigned. These workspaces include cockpits, "touch-down stations," workshops, common areas, and meeting rooms. • **COCKPITS ARE NEVER ASSIGNED.** All cockpits are available to anyone who uses the business center, on a first-come, first-serve basis. This includes all Tandem employees and visitors. • Never leave items, whether personal or work-related, in cockpits or other workspaces. This includes equipment, post-it-notes, manuals, documents, and posters. • Always sign in and sign out of workspaces. • Supplies such as staplers, scissors, and tape dispensers are available in each cockpit. Do not take these supplies; leave them for other employees and visitors to use. • Always WRAP-UP before you leave.

Workspaces

SITTERS ARE EMPLOYEES who have assigned workspaces (Tandem defines "sitters" according to job code). • Always keep your assigned work area neat. • Only your nameplate should be visible on the outside of your cubicle. No art work, decorations, or documents should be posted or stacked above or beyond your cubicle walls.

Remember . . .

BUSINESS CENTER ETIQUETTE is nothing more than common sense and common courtesy. Your business center is not just a place; it's a way of doing business. Sharing space and resources is a big part of this new office environment.

If you have any suggestions or concerns about the Eastern Region's Business Centers, please call the **Business Center Hotline** at 617-558-3492. Your comments and questions are welcome.

Tandem Computers Incorporated, April 1995. For additional copies contact Janie Johns, Loc-53, 901-278-8333 or Johns_Janie@Memphis

operations. For example, over 80 percent of all ATMs run on Tandem servers. Two-thirds of the world's credit card transactions go through Tandem servers.

$2.3 BILLION COMPANY

FOUNDED IN 1974

ACQUIRED BY COMPAQ COMPUTERS IN 1997

EMPLOYEES WORLDWIDE: 8500

ALTERNATIVE WORKPLACE STRATEGIES: Business center concept

WEB SITE: http://www.tandem.com

HQ ADDRESS: 10400 North Tantau Avenue Cupertino, CA 95014

PHONE: 408-285-3200

CRE TEAM FOR BUSINESS CENTERS: Ernest J. Piccone, director, real estate, CRE and site services; Candice McLaren, IIDA, project manager, CRE and site services; Bob Bechen, AIA, project manager, CRE and construction; and Jacquie Salerno, real estate portfolio manager.

Case Studies: Design That Supports the New Workplace

Chapter

10

INTRODUCTION

We've looked at companywide, business-driven alternative workplace strategies. Now, we'll focus on the interior designs of 11 workplaces. Keep in mind that in many alternative workplaces, there's little notable distinction from what a traditional office might look like; instead, the distinction is in the way the office space is used by employees.

However, alternative workplaces should have a higher level of finish and design than a traditional office. "If you're taking away a permanent space from employees, you have to produce a better workspace for them. If you don't achieve that balance, you compromise the alternative officing strategy," says John Lijewski, principal, Perkins & Will New York.

As you browse through these case studies, keep in mind that the cost of designing and building out an alternative workplace environment is comparable to—or slightly lower than—the cost of a conventional work environment. Perceptions of cost are all over the map—some people perceive that designing an alternative workplace environment costs twice as much as traditional space while others perceive that an alternative workplace costs less than 50 percent of the cost of a conventional office. A reality check: wiring up with appropriate technology to support new workstyles is what really takes up a chunk of the cost of an alternative workplace program.

To set the record straight, Lijewski compares the associated costs of building out a conventional office space versus a hoteling environment. Using as a model a hoteling project Perkins & Will completed for a major accounting firm, Lijewski says a conventional build out would have cost the client $65 a square foot (for 70,000 square feet of conventional space to house 341 people), and for hoteling, the costs went up slightly to $88 a square foot (for 41,000 square feet of hoteling space for the same number of employees) because the client wanted millwork in private offices and conference rooms. Lijewski says it costs an estimated $36 a square foot to furnish a conventional office, and for hoteling it cost the client about $28 a square foot.

But as you can see, hoteling configurations don't cost too much more than conventional build outs. In fact, Perkins & Will saved its client 29 percent in overall costs (including design fees), since it would have cost the client $9.8 million to go with a conventional office space and in actuality, it cost them $7 million for a hoteling environment—a 29 percent savings for the client.

Each of the following companies provided their employees with high-quality alternative workplace interiors to support shifting workstyles:

Axiom Business Consulting—management consulting firm
BBDO West—ad agency
Benevia—consumer goods
Deloitte & Touche—independent major accounting firm
Fallon/McElligott/Duffy—ad agency
Gould Evans Goodman—design firm
Hotwired—online provider
KPMG Peat Marwick—accounting firm, merged with Ernst & Young in October 1997
MCI—telecommunications company in the throes of a potential merger as of late 1997
O+O Software—business software applications
Steelcase—contract furniture manufacturer

AXIOM BUSINESS CONSULTING, SAN FRANCISCO, 1995

PROJECT BY HOLEY ASSOCIATES
NONTERRITORIAL

COMPANY BACKGROUND

Although much has been written about the design of Axiom's San Francisco office, not much has been said about how the company arrived at the design.

Axiom, a $15 million subsidiary of Cambridge Technology Partners, is an international management consulting company that assists clients with reengineering and other transformation projects. *Inc. Magazine* rated it among its top 100 fastest-growing companies in 1996. Its focus on business renewal is underscored by its new offices located in a 16-foot-high loft space in the South of Market area of San Francisco, also known as "Multimedia Gulch."

BEFORE: THE OLD WORKPLACE

Axiom's headquarters is an old warehouse in Multimedia Gulch that was once the headquarters of a jewelry company. Its old ceilings reach to heights of 12 and 16 feet. But the workspaces were

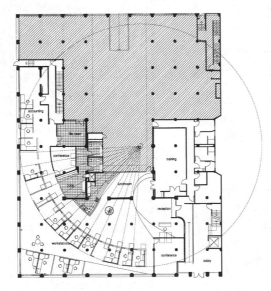

Figure 10.1
The curving wall is the distinctive design element in this nonterritorial office at Axiom Management Consultants in San Francisco. The wall is wired with data and voice outlets so that a consultant can wheel a table up to the wall and plug in.
(Charles McGrath for Holey Associates.)

AXIOM

traditional 8- by 8-foot assigned cubicles, with some shared private offices here and there. The problem was that about 80 percent of the 65 consultants at Axiom were out of the office 75 percent of the time, leaving most of the space empty and unused. The president of the company saw this great waste of space and supported the idea of a new workplace that would seriously address their real estate issue. He felt that it was time to stop wasting money and create an environment that did not have any empty offices.

AFTER: THE NEW WORKPLACE

The majority of the headquarters is composed of nonterritorial offices for traveling consultants. There are no private hard-wall offices in the entire facility; the open plan reduced barriers to communication (Figs. 10.1 and 10.2).

There are a number of types of places in which to work. One is a 6- by 8-foot workstation, and another is a 6-foot-wide touchdown space, which is more like a telephone shelf with a plug for laptop connectivity. The space will accommodate 95 consultants if and when they are ever in at the same time.

The major design element is the central curving wall partition with nonterritorial offices on one side to provide computer hook-up. Soft seating and work tables can be placed anywhere around the wall, as well.

Acoustical problems began to get out of hand after the nonterritorial offices were put in place. Too many loud people on the cellular phones and too many people having loud conversations upset the librarylike atmosphere in which other consultants wanted to work. To counteract the loud behavior, the company has trained staff on the protocols of nonterritorial office living.

WHAT HOLEY ASSOCIATES LEARNED

The ratios set for the space are 4:1, but John Holey, Holey Associates, felt an aggressive ratio of 12:1 would work well at Axiom today. There are more workstations than they need because the company

Figure 10.2
This old warehouse is full of natural light and soothing colors. This full view of Axiom's nonterritorial office space shows a mix of heads-down workstations. In addition, there is soft seating around the inside windows. Mobile tables can be wheeled to any spot.
(Photo by Charles McGrath for Holey Associates.)

didn't grow as quickly as it expected. "It's empty much of the time, and that kind of constant, empty space affects the well-being of the corporate culture," says Holey. "We learned that the less people come together to share experiences with the little time they use to come into the office, the more there needs to be a sort of physical tightness that needs to happen to push people together and have them be closer and face to face with one another."

Holey also learned that seating becomes a more important element in a nonterritorial office than it does in a traditional office where the permanent user of the chair has already set the chair at the preferred height and angle. In a nontraditional office, there are too many different types of people who use the same chair, so it's critical to spec-

ify one that is comfortable and easy to adjust for everyone.

Snapshot: Axiom

FOUNDED IN 1988
EMPLOYEES: 130
ADDRESS: 539 Bryant Street
San Francisco, CA 94107
PHONE: 415-546-6800
WEB SITE: http://www.axiom.com
PROJECT: 10,000-square-foot ground floor, 8000-square-foot second floor
DESIGN TEAM: John E. Holey, Linda Herman, Leandro Sensible, and Rob Wooding

BBDO WEST, LOS ANGELES, CALIFORNIA, 1996

PROJECT BY BECKSON DESIGN ASSOCIATES (BDA)

OPEN PLAN, FLATTENED HIERARCHY

COMPANY BACKGROUND

At BBDO West, most employees are in one day and out the next. It has nothing to do with downsizing. It has everything to do with face-to-face client contact. BBDO West, whose parent is Omnicom, one of the largest marketing communications companies in the world and owner of other ad agencies including TBWA/Chiat/Day, has recognized how different the ad agency business has become since the 1980s (Fig. 10.3).

BEFORE: THE OLD WORKPLACE

But BBDO West management still wanted to create the kind of organization that had identity, a place where over 200 people felt as if they belonged to a piece of the whole, that there was a home to go to, an office to be in—but pared down, on a budget, and all within two floors totaling 49000 square feet.

Gray granite, gray carpeting, gray flannel walls, engraved logos in granite—all connoted more of a traditional law office than it did a West Coast adver-

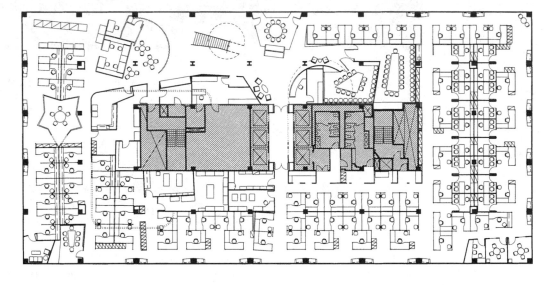

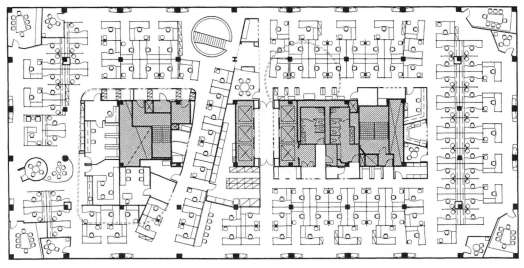

Figure 10.3
The open plan of BBDO West shows a distinct lack of private office space. Prior to this floorplan, BBDO was housed in a traditional, stuffy, very 1980s-style hierarchical space decked in granite and gray flannel walls.
(Photo by Tom Bonner.)

Figure 10.4
Proof in the pudding.
David Lubars, president
of BBDO West, sits in
this open workstation.
The only difference from
the others' stations is that
Lubars's is 2 feet larger.
(Photo by Tom Bonner.)

tising agency. No longer did the corporate trap-
pings, all packed together under the roof of a "big
black box" office building, serve their needs or
reflect the highly creative agency atmosphere of
BBDO West. Everyone was housed in offices, so they
wanted to create space where all employees were
on an equal playing field and interacting, a better
environment in which to foster interoffice communication and allow for what they termed "information osmosis." As BBDO West's president David
Lubars says in an article about the space in *Interior
Design* (see Cohen 1996), "At our old space, people
were having too many meetings. They would talk a
lot about what they were going to do, but they
spent too little time actually doing it."

AFTER: THE NEW WORKPLACE

To begin, BBDO and BDA decided it was best to
drop the old standard of the private office arranged
by department. The other mandates: no drywall, no
traditional panel systems. Everyone, including the
CEO, would sit in equal, custom, open workstations
grouped more efficiently by client core teams in
workstations that measured 80 square feet. The only

exception would be Lubars's area because his workstation is two feet larger than others (Fig. 10.4).

The other exception would be the media buying
offices. Although they would measure 80 square
feet, as well, there would be a door to close when
they were on the phone—which is constantly—hav
ing intense conversations that shouldn't be heard.

There would be work rooms, war rooms, and
phone rooms available for others. However, no one
would be assigned to individual panel workstations
because people might begin to feel that those were
permanent places.

All the architectural elements would be reduced
to their rawest natural states without decoration,
including the exposed columns, decking, ductwork, and conduit. *Interior Design* writer Cohen wrote
that the "most often-heard comment is 'When will
this project be finished?'"

ERECTOR SET WORKSTATIONS

The design team, Steven Heisler, Ed Gabor, and
Michael Beckson, custom designed the workstations for BBDO West. Intended to be a kit of parts,
the workstations can be easily reconfigured and

moved because they are made up of an Erector set of building components. The framework is made of galvanized steel bars used in the construction industry but more commonly recognized as the sticks on top of which traffic stop signs are found. A variety of parts are available to snap into the frames such as magnetic writing surfaces and chalkboard and are made of a variety of materials such as metal or perforated metal. The cost to build the workstations came to $11 per square foot.

Snapshot: BBDO West

Advertising agency

EMPLOYEES, LOS ANGELES: 200
ADDRESS: 10960 West Wilshire Blvd.
  Westwood, CA 90024
WEB SITE: http://www.bbdo.com
PROJECT: 49,000-square-feet, bilevel facility
DESIGN TEAM: Michael Beckson, Ed Gabor, and
  Steven Heisler

BENEVIA, MERCHANDISE MART, CHICAGO, ILLINOIS, 1996

PROJECT BY THE ENVIRONMENTS GROUP
UNIVERSAL PLAN

COMPANY BACKGROUND

In 1995, the consumer products operation of the NutraSweet Company and Searle merged to become Benevia—in Latin, *bene* means good, and *via* means way. Benevia is a leader in the consumer alternative sweetener market, with sweetener brands sold in more than 100 countries and found in over 5000 products. In addition to sweeteners, Benevia also markets chocolate bars, chocolate drink mixes, powdered soft drinks, and food supplements in various European and Latin American countries.

BEFORE: THE OLD WORKPLACE

Nick Rosa, the energetic president of Benevia, felt strongly that the tabletop division (the group that sells NutraSweet packets, tablets, and liquid to retail and hospitality outlets) needed its own identity. At the time, the company's headquarters were located in a 1980s Class A office building in Deerfield, Illinois, with interiors designed by John Saladino. Rosa felt this group needed to be closer to a culturally diverse part of Chicago. He also wanted to be in the position to attract employees who were young, creative, and hip.

AFTER: THE NEW WORKPLACE

In the 1980s, it would be a move most corporations would think of as backward in progression. But for the 1990s, Benevia's move was a smart one. Rosa had his heart set on finding a concrete loft building in downtown Chicago, but there were none to be found with all the amenities a company like Benevia would still require such as access to transportation, building security, and state-of-the-art mechanical and electrical wiring. In Chicago, most loft spaces are on alley ways or in river neighborhoods, far from the heart of the city. Rosa turned to the mammoth landmark, the Merchandise Mart, with spaces large enough to treat as if they were lofts. So be it, a quarter of the ninth floor of the Mart would become Benevia's new home (Figs. 10.5 through 10.8).

"It's down in the southeast corner where Arconis and Reff used to be," says Cary Johnson of The Environments Group, the design firm for Benevia. "You get off the elevator, look down the hall, and you see this painted drywall protrusion coming out of the line-up of old, abandoned showrooms, and you say, 'What IS that?'"

"Benevia's approach to their facility promotes interaction and collaboration; everybody, including Nick, is assigned to an open plan workstation," Johnson says. The space is designed to foster a culture of open and honest communication. "Already we're seeing a difference in the way we work—less

Figure 10.5
There are virtually no dedicated private offices at the new Benevia offices, and everyone, including the CEO, sits in an open-plan cubicle.

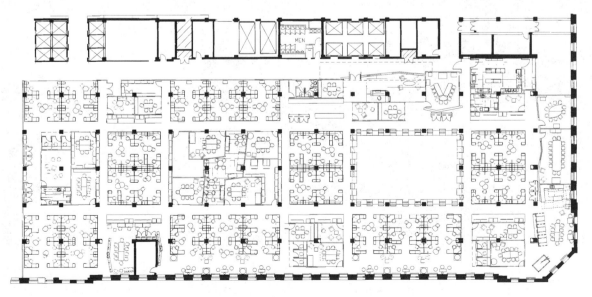

Benevia
The Merchandise Mart

9th Floor – South East Corner
Furniture Plan

A6-9

Figure 10.6 (left)
No one would ever guess that this is the inside of the Merchandise Mart in Chicago. It looks more like a loft in downtown Tribeca, New York, just the look that Benevia was after to attract young talent to its growing consumer marketing division. (Photo by Steve Hall at Hedrich Blessing.)

Figure 10.7 (below)
This space at Benevia holds 135 people with the help of universal planning. Workstations are assigned, and private offices must be reserved. Note the mix of recycled workstations, Haworth's Crossings mobile shelving units, and Herman Miller's Aeron chairs. (Photo by Steve Hall at Hedrich Blessing.)

Figure 10.8 (right-hand page)
These unusual drop-in spaces at Benevia are outfitted with Wilkhahn's Stitz chairs—the right seat for an impromptu meeting or to fire off a quick round of e-mail. (Photo by Steve Hall at Hedrich Blessing.)

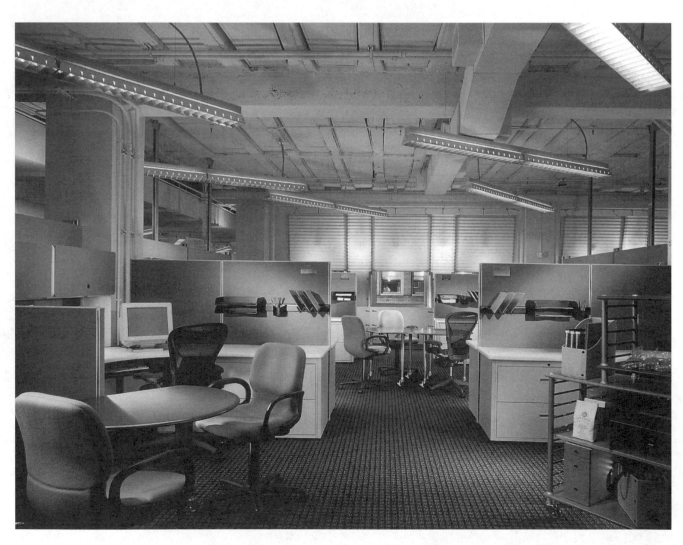

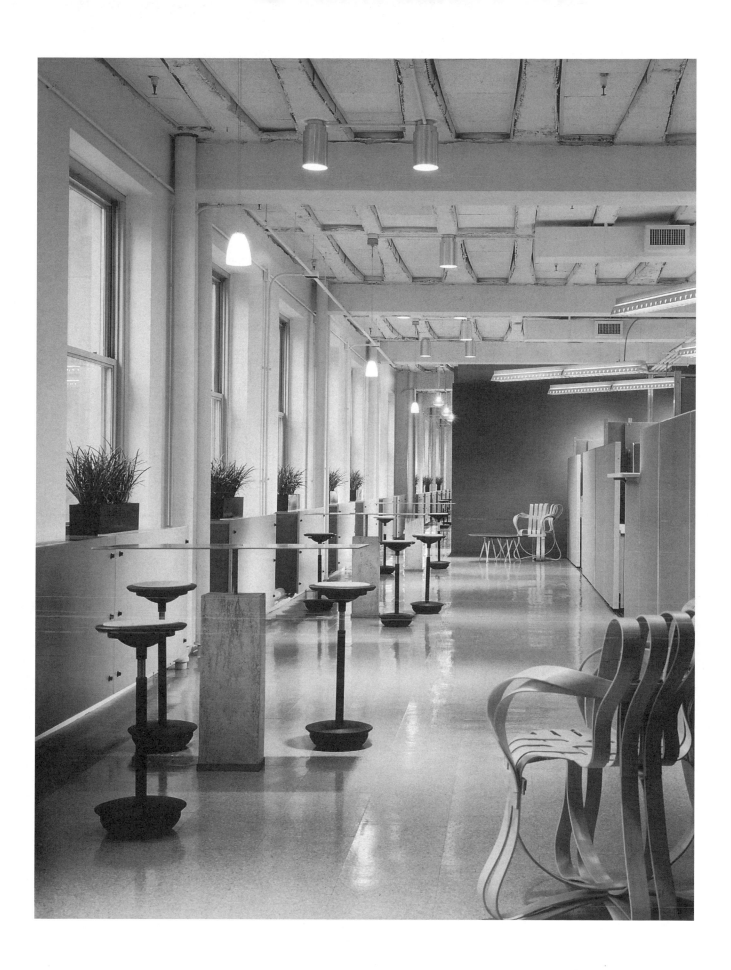

formality, more collaboration, faster decision making," says Rosa.

The space is really considered to be universally planned to hold 135 people. No station is different from the other, and most all have wireless phones with which they can make a personal call by walking into a private area set up for such occasions.

It wasn't a problem at all to bring the proper cable distribution and a T-1 line up into the Mart. "Even though the Mart is old, it was overdesigned mechanically and electrically, and it is superior to speculative buildings from the 1970s and 1980s," says Johnson about the vintage space.

THE LANGUAGE OF BENEVIA'S WORKSPACE

- Bays are support spaces.
- The Recreation Bay has pool tables and diner banquets.
- The Telebay is a call center for customer service.
- The General Store is for product display. The Resource Bay is an electronic library with terminals.
- The Team Bay is for the sales department.
- The Alley is for food and beverage service.
- The Collaborative Bays are the four corners of the floor plate to be used for teaming.

Snapshot: Benevia

Makers of consumer products such as NutraSweet

ADDRESS: Merchandise Mart, 200 WTC, Chicago, IL 60654

WEB SITE: http://www.monsanto.com/MonPub/BusinessUnits/Benevia/

PROJECT SUMMARY:
20,000 square feet, Chicago Merchandise Mart

DESIGNER: The Environments Group

DELOITTE & TOUCHE, NEW YORK CITY, 1996

PROJECT BY THE HILLIER GROUP
HOTELING, SHARED SPACE, TEAMING

INDUSTRY BACKGROUND

Although the public sees accounting firms as backward, nonprogressive bean counters who sit in dark rooms lit by only a bare bulb, donning green eyeshades pulled over their heads, this caricature is far from the truth of how major accounting firms are run today. Accounting firms are ahead of the curve today when it comes to workplace reengineering and new workplace design. In an effort to challenge themselves to be more efficient, they have adopted alternative workplace environments to support the new work processes that have taken over the accounting world.

COMPANY BACKGROUND

Classified ad excerpt from Deloitte & Touche as seen in the March 9, 1997, edition of *The New York Times*:

> "Motelling Coordinator—As the primary contact to the consulting staff, you will reserve, set up, and personalize their office space, files, and phones…with the ultimate goal of efficiently managing the daily facilities usage."

Deloitte & Touche nationally has used all kinds of alternative officing options in many of its offices across the country. The consulting division began to use hoteling as a way to absorb growth for several years longer than a traditional layout would, which meant that there would be considerably fewer remodeling costs, as well.

The company's foray into hoteling began in 1993 when the San Francisco consulting office projected a growth that would require the addition of one

Figure 10.9
Wood-filled partner offices at Deloitte & Touche in New York City are still around the perimeter, but they have been reduced from 200 to 400 square feet down to one uniform size of 150 square feet. It was either squeeze into existing office space or lay off staff, so smaller offices were the readily accepted choice. Black drawers are removable from millwork for mobility of paperwork and files.
(Photo by Jeff Goldberg.)

floor of 16,000 usable square feet. To counteract the need to take on more space for a group of employees who never used their offices anyhow, Deloitte & Touche worked out a space in which there were four types of areas: setting for private, solitary work; teaming; short-term use; and a space for informal gatherings. "At that time, we didn't know about the terms *hearth* and *commons*, *drop-in offices, touchdown spaces*, or *temporal offices*," says Richard Lane, head of national facilities at Deloitte & Touche. The consulting office was designed to accommodate a total population of 96 people in 44 workstations, 20 offices, and 10 team rooms. Today, Lane says that space handles over 150 people with the same number of workstations, offices, and team rooms, and there's still room to grow. In other words, says Lane, hoteling handled 100 percent of the growth of the San Francisco office staff by hoteling, saving $1 million over the remainder of that 7-year lease.

Though Deloitte & Touch first used alternative officing tactics as a way to reduce long-term expense of rent, there are other important reasons that the company continues to consider alternative forms of the workplace. For one, the traditional office layout no longer reflected what they did in the office, most notably because consulting, audit, tax, and compliance service employees spent more time with their clients than in their offices. CRE also felt that "the ideal space is not always a larger space," says Lane.

Today, management has mandated that every Deloitte & Touche office explore alternative officing options before additional space is leased or a relocation occurs (Fig. 10.9).

BEFORE: THE OLD WORKPLACE, NEW YORK

Each Deloitte & Touche office handles its reengineering in a different way. New York is no different. In November 1991, Deloitte & Touche were planning to consolidate its merged divisions Deloitte Haskins & Sells and Touche Ross. Though the merger happened in 1989, Deloitte Haskins & Sells was located downtown in the World Trade Center while Touche Ross was located in midtown. Although other Deloitte & Touche offices had already consolidated physical spaces, the New York City office needed to wait for long-term leases to expire before making a move. The New York City office had limited facilities for the 400,000 square feet it was seeking for consolidation, so it took a full year more to decide that everyone would move down to the World Trade Center where one division was already located.

From April through July 1993, the Hillier Group went about doing programming studies, focus groups, and one-on-one interviews to get ready for the consolidation. In June 1993, the fateful World Trade Center bomb went off, which meant that Deloitte & Touche had to scurry to find a new space. For months, consultants were working at their clients' offices full time in situations in which 12 people were packed tightly into a 10- by 10-foot conference room. In December 1993, it signed a lease in the World Financial Center, which gave the company a clean slate on which to draw up a new workspace.

THE CORPORATE CULTURE OF AN ACCOUNTING OFFICE

One of the most fascinating nuances of the culture of an accounting firm as big as Deloitte & Touche is this notion of "how they sit." "In my first meeting with the general managing partner, one of his objectives and priorities was to change how they 'sat,'" says Barbara Hillier of the Hillier Group. "This project became about how they 'sat,' which would be the foundation of how this firm would ultimately be able to change its work processes."

Traditionally, the audit division of the company has been a huge part of the business, generating 55 percent of the business; tax came second, generating 30 percent of the business; and consulting third, contributing 15 to 20 percent of the revenues. Typically, audit was grouped together and sat apart from the tax group, which sat apart from the consulting group. A strong sense of kinship was felt among the members of each group, and the groups were secure in their own identities.

"The tax professionals in particular felt they would lose their identity if we asked them to split up the way they sat," says Dorothy Alpert of Deloitte & Touche, New York. "That's exactly what we wanted. We wanted to go to market as an industry group so that if we sat down with a client, they wouldn't know the difference between who was audit, tax, or consulting. We wanted to be a united team."

What the New York office wanted to do instead was group industry specialists together instead of grouping disciplines together. A group of specialists familiar with the securities industry made up of audit, tax, and consulting would sit together. A group of specialists familiar with the banking industry made up of the same components of audit, tax, and consulting would sit together in a different area.

AFTER: THE NEW WORKPLACE, NEW YORK

Through tragedy came an opportunity for Deloitte & Touche to start fresh. Deloitte & Touche's New York City space now accommodates over 1000 employees in 400,000 square feet total spread out over nine floors.

Overall, the floors tend to look traditional because of their woodwork, wood doors, and custom-designed woodwork walls and cabinets, not to mention the wood desks and chairs that grace the private partners' and senior managers' offices (Fig. 10.9).

Partner offices located on the perimeter have been pared down to 150 square feet from the previous standard of 200 to 400 square feet. Even the senior partners share conferencing space and maintain small offices that are only slightly larger than 150 square feet just to accommodate the floor plate. Senior managers share offices at a ratio of 2:1. They have different furniture than partner offices, but the size of the offices remains the same, and some junior senior managers have workstations that measure 150 square feet. Partners and managers share conferencing facilities, which are 135-square-foot suites with formal conference tables.

Accountants and auditors were used to sharing workstations with one another, so hoteling wasn't a big culture shock for them as much as it was for the tax and consulting departments. About 600 accounting and auditing staff share 75 desks, at a ratio of 8:1, almost double what they worked with before.

Yet another cultural change Deloitte & Touche is emphasizing is the shift from the paper-strewn office to the paperless office. If a memo comes out in paper form, it's sent back with a big note on it that says, "please send out electronically." Deloitte and Touche forecasts that the entire operation will be paperless by the year 2000.

Snapshot: Deloitte & Touche National

Deloitte & Touche LLP, one of the nation's leading professional service firms, provides accounting, tax management, and consulting services through 17,300 employees in more than 100 cities. Deloitte & Touche is a member of Deloitte & Touche Tohmatsu International, a global leader in professional services, with 56,600 people in offices in 122 countries.

EMPLOYEES, NEW YORK OFFICE: 1000—plus
NEW YORK ADDRESS: Two World Financial Center
New York, NY 10281-1414
NATIONAL WEB SITE: http://www.dttus.com
NATIONAL HQ: 10 Westport Road
Wilton, CT 06897

Project Summary

ARCHITECTURE AND INTERIOR DESIGN FIRM: The Hillier Group
DESIGN TEAM: Barbara A. Hillier, AIA; Gerald F. X. Geier II, AIA; Richard Ashworth; Karen Bann; Sonja Bijelic; Marty Bloomenthal; Greg Burke; Paul Heflin;, Stephen Laurie; Nancy McKendrick; Jeffrey H. Mooney; Christopher Reed; Robert Ritger; David Sandefer; and Jennifer Teitel

FALLON/MCELLIGOTT/DUFFY, INC., MINNEAPOLIS, MINNESOTA, 1994
PROJECT BY PERKINS & WILL/WHEELER
FREE-ADDRESS

COMPANY BACKGROUND

The Minneapolis-based advertising agency Fallon/McElligott/Duffy (FMD), known for its spunky, highly original campaigns for Timex and BMW, seems to have found a strong voice in the crowded world of creatives. So strong, in fact, that it resigned its McDonald's Arch Delux account at the end of January 1997 because it felt it was constrained in the creative freedom it needed to manage the campaign. It's a highly unusual move for an agency to make, even though it quit to free itself to pursue another fast-food account.

How Fallon became so strong is no secret. It carved out a niche for itself as being one of the most creative agencies outside of New York City, a city to which it seems most of the advertising talent

flocks. Now that Fallon has become a symbol of a successful ad agency from the Midwest, it is bringing its talent into New York, and it has opened a creative outpost in New York City called Fallon McElligott Berlin. The freshly minted New York City office—mostly open plan—is a step to achieving its goal to become a large, global, independent ad agency.

BEFORE: THE OLD WORKPLACE

Today, most ad agencies recognize that creative people work best in situations that allow freedom to come and go—to interact or to work solo on any given project. Understanding this approach, Perkins & Will/Wheeler, formerly known as the Wheeler Group, the firm that designed the project, helped the agency to articulate the philosophy by reconfiguring some of its existing offices into a flexible and experimental free-address environment that maximizes creative output (Figs. 10.10 and 10.11).

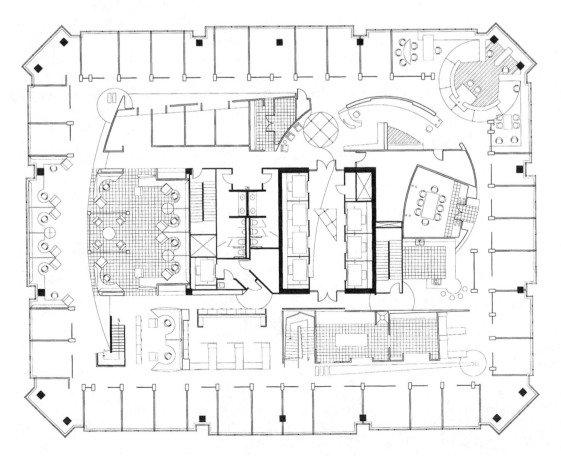

Figure 10.10
Fallon/McElligott/Duffy experimented with one of its floors and turned it into a free-address environment. (Wheeler.)

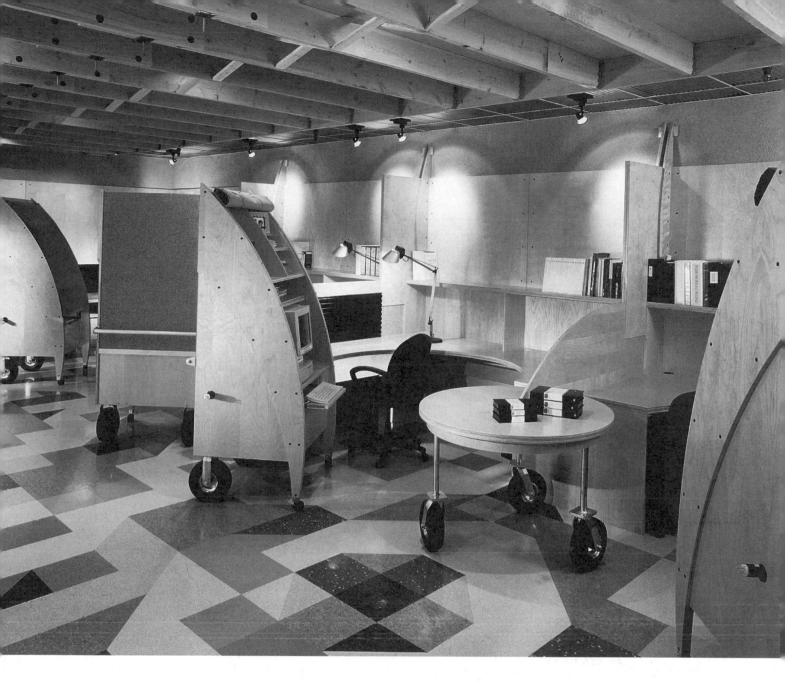

Figure 10.11
The experiment with mobility at Fallon/ McElligott/Duffy resulted in problems with acoustics and lack of privacy. But there's a lesson in furniture design here: There are no sharp edges or corners, and the cockpit-style desks offer more work surface. (Photo by Dana Wheelock.)

In undertaking the renovation, FMD looked to Chiat/Day and drew on that agency's bravery in building its new workplace to support new work processes. FMD wanted to make better use of space allocated to employees who work away from the office 3 or 4 days a week. (Joe Duffy, president and creative director of the agency, is a firm believer in client collaboration, that "it's better to work within our clients' walls than our own.") The firm also envisioned adding to its 300-person base staff as its account list grew, but it did not want to lease additional space in the building.

The environment of the Minneapolis office was fairly traditional, renovated by the Wheeler Group in the early 1990s when FMD moved into a 32-story building, taking six floors totaling 99,000 square feet.

Cognizant of the need to ease staff into alternative officing, the Wheeler Group's principal-in-charge, James Young, ASID, CID, and interior designer Amy Kleppe, crafted a multiphase experimental program in which employees could partake and that would ultimately affect the way the agency worked. Luckily, employees already had a handle on the alternative office vernacular because many had collaborated with Chiat/Day on a project for Coca-Cola, experiencing first-hand the ups and downs of its well-established virtual offices.

AFTER: THE NEW WORKPLACE

FMD's 30-person planning department would be the "guinea pigs" of the alternative officing experiment on the 30th floor because they had the most

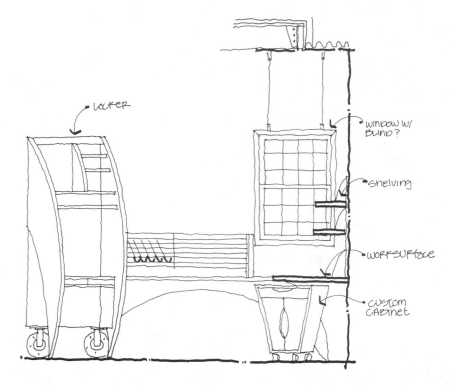

Figure 10.12

Twenty-eight rolling birch lockers were built for Fallon/McElligott/Duffy at a low cost of $1200 each. The lockers have a 4- to 6-week lead time to acquire versus the 12- to 16-week lead time that standard furniture manufacturers need. (Wheeler.)

locker

window w/ blind?

shelving

worksurface

custom cabinet

interaction with different parts of the agency. Subsequently, various agency departments would also experiment in this space, the broadcast production department among others. One 18,000-square-foot floor became a free-address environment, where employees who are mostly out of the office do not have permanent or assigned offices or desks but instead store materials in furniture that can be rolled over to any stretch of workspace.

The award-winning design (it won Best Large Office in *Interiors* magazine's annual design competition in 1995) is deconstructive in theme, using commonplace materials in unusual ways. Parts of the exposed ceiling feature steel trusses dressed in fire insulation and mechanical ductwork. Other areas of the ceiling feature birch beams that match birch furniture. Bright color was brought into the space with randomly placed, multicolored vinyl tile.

Mobile lockers became one of the most important design elements of this project. Employees were given the chance to root around in prototypes of custom mobile furniture for a couple of weeks before making the final design decision. The unusual shaped locker measures 50 inches wide, 28 inches deep, and 66 inches high, deftly designed to use every square inch to hold personal items, files, electronic equipment, power raceway, marker or tack board, and a sliding work surface, all which can be covered by a canvas shade (Fig. 10.12).

With the first phase completed, the planning department will move out of the 30th floor soon to be replaced by the broadcast department to continue the ongoing experiment. Depending on departmental needs, other parts of the agency will eventually move into the free-address space on the 30th floor. The concept of flexible office space is now flowing through to other parts of the agency. The Wheeler Group just completed the 29th floor for FMD's 40-person creative group, designed as a modified free-address environment in which less of the furniture is mobile but where there's a menu to choose from of open or closed offices. Never an industry to cling to tradition, the ad agency business is one of the first to welcome the challenges and the freedom provided by new officing design.

Snapshot: Fallon/McElligott/Duffy

Advertising agency

EMPLOYEES: 300+

ADDRESS: 901 Marquette Avenue
 Minneapolis, MN 55402

PHONE: 612-332-2445

PROJECT SUMMARY: 18,000 square-foot floor
 turned into free-addressing environment

DESIGN TEAM: James E. Young, ASID, CID; Amy L.
 Kleppe; and Sara Nigon

CUSTOM FURNITURE CONSULTANTS: Artiflex
 Millwork

MILLWORK: Osvold Millwork

GOULD EVANS GOODMAN, KANSAS CITY, MISSOURI, 1996

PROJECT BY GOULD EVANS GOODMAN
TEAMING AND SEMI-ACTIVITY SETTING

COMPANY BACKGROUND

Gould Evans Goodman doesn't specialize in any one discipline. Instead, this design firm, founded in 1974, is a multidisciplinary company practicing architecture, interior design, landscape architecture, urban planning, and accessibility design. The firm has offices in Kansas City, Missouri; Lawrence, Kansas; Tampa, Florida; Philadelphia, Pennsylvania; and Phoenix, Arizona.

BEFORE: THE OLD WORKPLACE

Ten years after Gould Evans Associates (the original name) began doing business, the firm opened up a Kansas City office that measured 100 square feet and housed two employees. Too cramped for comfort, the firm soon graduated to a disjointed office of 3000 square feet spread out over three floors, which connected the 130 employees by elevators. As the firm continued to grow at an average rate of 46 percent a year, it grabbed odd bits of office space in the same building as it became available in order to keep up with additional employees. Soon the design firm was working in 16,000 square feet of irregular space (Figs. 10.13 through 10.17).

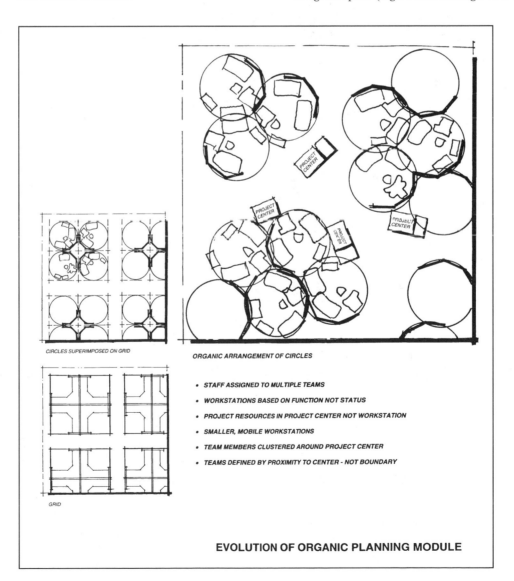

CIRCLES SUPERIMPOSED ON GRID

ORGANIC ARRANGEMENT OF CIRCLES

- STAFF ASSIGNED TO MULTIPLE TEAMS
- WORKSTATIONS BASED ON FUNCTION NOT STATUS
- PROJECT RESOURCES IN PROJECT CENTER NOT WORKSTATION
- SMALLER, MOBILE WORKSTATIONS
- TEAM MEMBERS CLUSTERED AROUND PROJECT CENTER
- TEAMS DEFINED BY PROXIMITY TO CENTER - NOT BOUNDARY

GRID

EVOLUTION OF ORGANIC PLANNING MODULE

Figure 10.13
The evolution of Gould Evans Goodman's open-plan project centers starts with thumbnail sketches with circles superimposed on a grid. (Gould Evans Goodman Associates.)

Figure 10.14
This sketch shows how many times people moved in and out of teams within a 10-month period of time. Mobile furniture is the only type of product that makes sense with this kind of churn. (Gould Evans Goodman.)

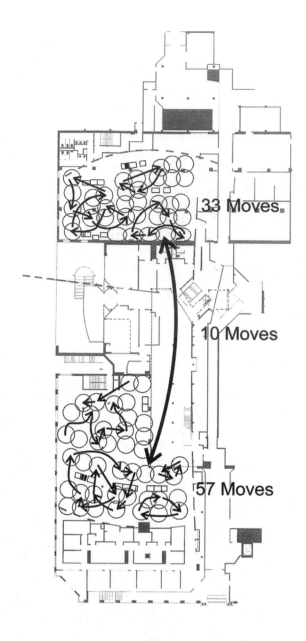

33 Moves

10 Moves

57 Moves

STAFF MOVES 12.95 to 10.96

In 1990, the search began for suitable space. It took 3 years, and along the way came a lot of soul-searching and self-analysis of the firm's goals. The analysis clearly pointed to reducing the high average of annual churn and the need for enhanced in-house communication. Employees relocated as much as 8 to 10 times a year because of evolving and disbanding project teams. Working with traditional furniture required time, labor, and money to reconfigure. A new workplace was clearly in order.

AFTER: THE NEW WORKPLACE

In 1991, the firm found an abandoned shopping center and decided to convert it to an office com-

plex. The leased 32,000-square-foot area was spread out over three adjacent buildings and included two retail outlets in the first two buildings and a bakery in the third. Significant demolition resulted in 40-foot-high ceilings in one building, 15-foot-high ceilings in another building, and lower ceilings in the third building.

Office planning came next. One of the biggest challenges was to reduce the churn that was inherent in this firm's operations, as it is in any teaming situation. In any design office, teaming is essential, and to support Gould Evans Goodman's teaming approach, the interior would be defined by groups called "project centers." It was planned that groups would rally around the project center in the middle

Figure 10.15
This enlarged furniture plan of a section filled with mobile Crossings furniture is reminiscent of the famous Quickborner Team's office landscape floor plan, Bürolandschaft, from Germany in the 1960s. (Gould Evans Goodman Associates.)

Figure 10.16 (below)
The anatomy of a "project center" using Haworth's Crossings' mobile cabinets and vertical fence screens. (Gould Evans Goodman Associates.)

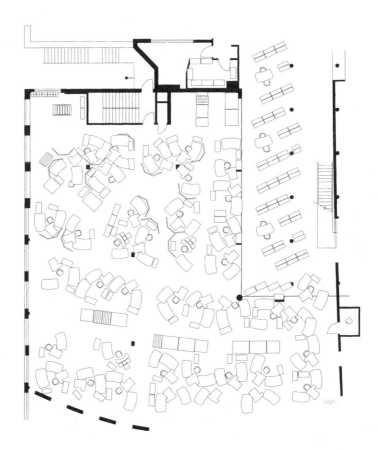

ENLARGED FURNITURE PLAN

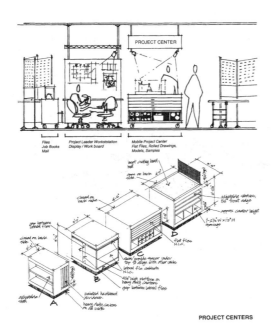

PROJECT CENTERS

of which the team leader sits. As projects come and go, these teaming and project centers would shift, teams would be redeployed, and furniture would be moved about the space.

Furniture turned out to be the missing piece of the puzzle at first. Karen Gould, interior designer, knew mobile furniture was the only way this concept was going to work, but there was nothing on

Figure 10.17

An open office teaming area is a project center. This is the first phase of Crossings furniture: Haworth has since introduced a few new phases to the line to help it integrate better with existing furniture. (Gould Evans Goodman Associates.)

the market at the time to support this work process. Out of the blue, a Haworth salesperson called on her to tell her about some experimental furniture on wheels that was about to be introduced at Neocon 1995. The furniture line was Crossings, and Gould and Haworth ended up working together, using the Gould Evans Goodman offices as a beta test site to further refine the Crossings product.

The office offers a host of other environments for employees including solitude nooks, quiet enclosed areas to work in seclusion or make private phone calls; break-out areas for informal meetings located adjacent to the project teams; conference rooms in a variety of sizes to hold from 5 to 50 people; and a charrette room where interactive design workshops are held with the firm's clients.

Snapshot: Gould Evans Goodman

Architecture, interior design, landscape architecture, urban planning, and disability planning

EMPLOYEES, KANSAS CITY OFFICE: 150
ADDRESS: 4041 Mill Street
Kansas City, MO 64111-3008

HOTWIRED, A DIVISION OF WIRED VENTURES, SAN FRANCISCO, CALIFORNIA, 1996

PROJECTS BY HOLEY ASSOCIATES
OPEN-PLAN AND ACTIVITY SETTINGS

COMPANY BACKGROUND

If you are a Netizen of the United States, proceed to Wired Ventures, Inc., a company dedicated to giving cyberholics their monthly, daily, and now hourly shot of news from a world that lives beyond the computer screen, is the creator of HotWired, Wired News, HotBot, and Talk.com, launched the HotWired Network in 1994. The HotWired Network develops news and entertainment sites on the Web that contain colorful screens full of original content on digital business, politics, travel, arts, technology, media, and more with column names like Netizen (a column on the wrongdoings of the media), Webmonkey, and Brain Tennis. HotWired Network unveiled Wired News, a digital news service to deliver up-to-the-minute, online news. To give you an indication of how many people it takes to put out an electronic newspaper, Wired News has a dedicated news staff of 20 and an overall creative team of 80 employees.

BEFORE: THE OLD WORKPLACE

Though it's hard to think that a new-media company actually had a workplace history, from 1995 until 1996, HotWired employees lived on top of one another in a 15,000-square-foot space. It got pretty uncomfortable trying to put out its daily electronic newspaper. They realized it was time to move. What this group really wanted to do was move into Multimedia Gulch south of Market Street in San Francisco. They picked an old coffee warehouse with 44,000 square feet of space in which they

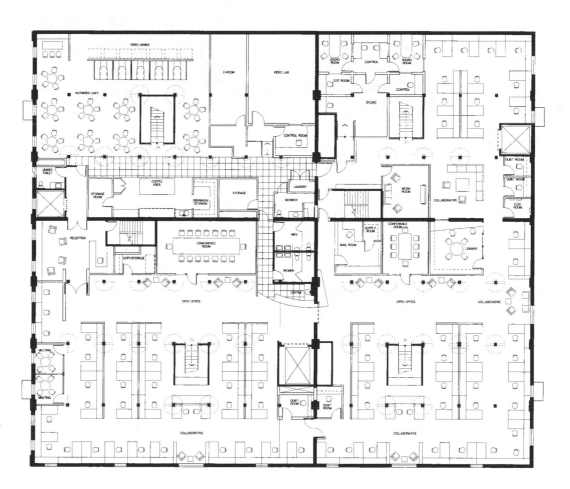

Figure 10.18
The HotWired Café is on the fourth floor of the new space, but there are plenty of other spaces to which an employee can escape for a few moments away from the mania of new media.
(Photo by Chun Y. Lai.)

could create, produce, and distribute in one place an intangible product they call an *online magazine*.

AFTER: THE NEW WORKPLACE

John Holey, principal of Holey Associates, was familiar with the culture of Wired Ventures. Holey had designed *Wired* magazine's offices a couple of years earlier, so he believed he was already familiar with the culture and thinking of the company. "When we were given the project, HotWired, we were told to think of green hair and pierced everything," says Holey of his initial talks about HotWired's new space. But what he observed was a group of employees that was still young, but was maturing as a staff and—most interestingly—as an industry.

Holey began to see something take shape that he had only a glimpse of during the work he did with Apple and the *Wired* project he did in the early 1990s. "If you're a young technonerd at *Wired* or HotWired and can only afford to rent a room in a flophouse with a bunch of other technonerds, when you get into the office, you're grateful to have sofas and a place to hang out and eat," Holey says. "The office then becomes a great place to hang out and work all night. HotWired is more of this office-home environment, and I think we'll see more of these office-home types of workplaces in the new-media industry." Look for more of that within Wired Ventures, a place where there's a story about a staffer who even brought a bunk bed into the office and lived there for months to stay on deadline.

Holey used the *Wired* space as a loose model from which to design the HotWired environment because the method of communication is similar. What's different about the two worlds is the way in

space into another are more complex, calling for more collaboration," explains Holey.

Inevitably, a few people wanted private offices. To remedy that, Holey designed numerous private spaces that would be accessible to all employees who needed a closed door once in a while for a conversation. Everyone was comfortable with that arrangement, and the president of HotWired sits out in the open and Holey insists it will stay like that.

"They didn't spend a whole lot of money on finishes," says Holey. "But what they did was spend a whole lot of time thinking about how the space would work for them." The HotWired space consists of 10 different types of environments, more than enough places to satisfy 130 employees and large enough to accommodate up to 200 people. There are library research centers, conference and meeting rooms, touchdown spaces with white boards, and informal seating scattered throughout the hallways for groups of people to have quick conversations. The spaces around the stairways have printers, so those areas naturally lure passers-by into a circle to talk.

The HotWired Café is a place to serve food, but it also becomes a conferencing space, and a sanctuary, says Holey. As in the *Wired* space, HotWired serves breakfast, lunch, and dinner to keep employees at work (Figs. 10.18 through 10.20).

Snapshot: HotWired (Wired Ventures)

Produces online newspaper and news service
Launched in 1994

ADDRESS: c/o Wired, 520 3rd St., 4th Floor
San Francisco, CA 94107
PHONE: 415-276-5000
WEB SITE: www.wired.com/news/

which they collaborate. One organization is designing a paper product, the other is designing an intangible product. "On the paper side, people work individually for longer spans of time than in the online environment where time frames are shorter and linkages that take a product from one

KPMG PEAT MARWICK, RADNOR, PENNSYLVANIA, 1995
PROJECT BY TOM MCHUGH
HOTELING

INDUSTRY BACKGROUND

As you saw in Chap. 2, pioneers Andersen Consulting and Ernst & Young show that management consulting firms are leaders in using hoteling strategies.

Up until a few years ago, management consulting firms were better known as The Big Six accounting firms: Arthur Anderson & Company (under which Andersen Consulting and Arthur Andersen are separate entities); Coopers & Lybrand; Deloitte & Touche; Ernst & Young; KPMG Peat Marwick; and Price Waterhouse. This industry has evolved quickly in just a short time. Now, the industry leaders have separated consulting operations from auditing and tax practices. Collectively, the Big Six firms say that consulting accounts for between 25 and 50 percent of their total revenue. Consultants help companies

cut costs and increase profits, boost efficiency, and install new computer network systems.

There are three scenarios specific to these newly evolved management consulting firms in which hoteling can be used effectively:

1. *Camped at clients:* Consultants are at their clients' offices 70 to 80 percent or more of the time, leaving their primary offices at corporate headquarters empty.
2. *Changing "how they sit:"* Typically tax specialists sat together, audit specialists sat in another group, and consultants grouped themselves together. No longer the case, disciplines are expected to sit differently according to industry groups. For instance, at Deloitte & Touche in New York, one group might be securities and banking in which there would be an audit, tax, and consultant specialist.
3. *"On the beach:"* Consultants are in between client projects, but they still need a place to come into at the corporate office.

Figure 10.21
The floor plan for Peat Marwick shows the delineation of universal offices, short-term hoteling (or moteling), storage kiosks, and conference rooms (see legend).
(Tom McHugh.)

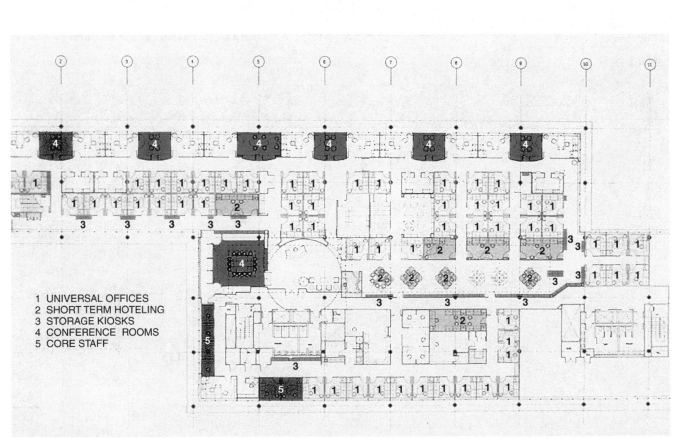

1 UNIVERSAL OFFICES
2 SHORT TERM HOTELING
3 STORAGE KIOSKS
4 CONFERENCE ROOMS
5 CORE STAFF

Figure 10.22
This Peat Marwick
interior won a bronze
award under
environmental design in
the 1995 *Business Week*
Annual Design Awards.
Here's an example of a
reservable office with a
pocket door.
(Photo by Tom Crane.)

Another trend specific to the majors: women who complain that they hit the glass ceiling. And they say it gets worse if a woman has a family. Many female accountants and management consultants that work at the majors firms say the demands of the profession haven't changed to accommodate the balance of work and family. There is some movement in this area. For example, a female partner at Price Waterhouse works in the office 4 days a week and in her Westchester home once a week. With all the merger activity, hopefully the work/life balance in accounting firms won't be forgotten about. Alternative workplace strategies that some of the firms are implementing, such as telecommuting, should also loosen up partner attitudes.

The interesting thing about management consulting firms is that they are now getting into helping their clients use alternative workplace concepts. Look at Arthur Andersen, a consulting company that doesn't like to expose its own alternative officing strategies but nevertheless, has a business publications print ad campaign with the following copy: "Find out how Arthur Andersen can help build teamwork and knock down walls that keep your people from being inventive, more confident—and reaching your company's goals." More copy is accompanied by a photograph of an employee climbing the walls, helplessly trapped within the confines of a tiny office or found under overwhelming piles of paperwork.

COMPANY BACKGROUND

Clearly, KPMG Peat Marwick and Deloitte & Touche are second-generation alternative workplace leaders. Not even a half a mile from the spic-and-span, but antiquated, train station in Radnor, Pennsylvania, is a corporate park, where KPMG Peat Marwick is but one tenant in the mix. It's quite a busy train station with interstate and reverse commuters making the trek from their jobs. But those that work at Peat Marwick may not always take the train to and from Radnor on a daily basis. They may not even make it in to the office once a month. They may be hotelers (Figs. 10.21 through 10.23).

BEFORE: THE OLD WORKPLACE

In 1992, KPMG Peat Marwick faced an operations dilemma. Although the information technology consulting practice occupied 40,000 square feet in two locations in suburban Pennsylvania, there were insufficient seats, workstations, and offices. Why? The staff had grown 40 percent the year before.

There was a paradox to the overcrowding scenario, however. On any given day, 75 percent to as much as

85 percent of the offices were vacant. Like any consulting firm, the action was always taking place at the clients' offices. Even with dedicated offices sitting as empty shells most of the time, other consultants in for the day or week couldn't use a vacant office because they were cluttered with papers and stuff.

Furthermore, large conference rooms were set up in the boardroom style with inflexible seating and inadequate audiovisual and computer display equipment. Small conference rooms did not contain the audiovisual equipment, marker boards, or support for desktop computers necessary for small groups assembled to work on projects.

It was clear that the partners had grown frustrated with this empty space syndrome, and they knew what had to be done. Peat Marwick decided to consolidate offices in a convenient geographic location in a facility that would support the firm's image of a leading-edge technology consultancy, even if it meant reinventing the manner in which work was performed. It's not that they didn't want to start *saving* money by doing this…they wanted to stop *wasting* money, says Joni Casta, director of administration at Peat Marwick in Radnor. Why not? Their competitors were doing the same thing simultaneously if not earlier in the game.

AFTER: THE NEW WORKPLACE

Even before the company formally became a hoteling environment, Casta immediately saw the benefits of hoteling and tells this story to nonbelievers in unconventional workstyles. The company couldn't extend the lease on the old space and had no choice but to move into its incomplete hoteling space the second week of December 1993. Within the first month, they experienced an unexpected 40 percent rate of growth, hiring as many as five consultants a week. Casta was hoteling at a ratio of about 8:1 for a while, more than doubling the intended 3:1 and 4:1 ratios. Though it would seem that this kind of situation would lead to great chaos, there was little inconvenience, according to Casta, who attributes the smooth transition to hoteling.

THE UNIVERSAL OFFICE

The initial step in the hoteling program was to reduce the standard 10- by 13-foot office size to a universal size of 10 by 10 feet for hotelers. A 2:1 ratio of employees per office was set. To ensure the maximum visual and acoustical privacy, individual offices were drywall constructed, some demountable, and outfitted with systems furniture. Systems furniture was chosen for the private offices because it provides the versatility and flexibility required to accommodate a broad cross section of employees. Height-adjustable work surfaces and highly ergonomic seating are critical to the hoteling program, as well.

Many of the universal offices are on the perimeter, a few in the core. Each office is simple, private, and clean, outfitted with a Knoll system and adjustable boomerang table. Offices have two white boards that flip over and become tack boards. Housekeeping provides each guest with a drawer filled with office supplies (except for scissors, which are too expensive to risk being taken off premises) and a mobile pedestal.

The 10 partners' permanent offices were reduced to 150 square feet from 225 square feet, but shared conference rooms were placed between offices to give the impression of larger suites. An unadorned, but healthy size veneer wood desk, credenza, and overhead shelving fill the offices. Partners' offices are allowed to be used for other hotelers when partners are traveling.

MANAGING A HOTELING PROGRAM

Casta set out to develop internal hoteling procedures to tame a corporate culture while containing costs, starting with the "housekeeping" staff that supports hoteling procedures. Casta's housekeeping and concierge staff of four is composed of mail room, copy center, and human resource personnel.

Casta tapped into her existing staff for house-keeping tasks for several reasons. First, she realized that housekeeping tasks take up only a few hours a week and wouldn't justify a full-time position. Casta allows housekeeping staff to take turns, and some prefer to come in over the weekends to set up for extra overtime pay. The staff has procedures down to a science, and they have reduced the initial 7 hours a week of housekeeping down to almost a third of that time.

To keep the idea of hoteling novel, the house-keeping staff has adopted hotel lingo, and they go as far as leaving a daily mint on each guest's desk.

PACK RATS AND STORAGE

By far, Casta's biggest challenge was paper. It wasn't as simple as ordering more file cabinets. Historically, she says, consultants are known for being pack rats, saving proposals and paperwork from years ago. Sure enough, the biggest complaint about hoteling from employees was their fear of losing storage space for the stuff they so haphazardly accumulated.

Since each employee was programmed to get a four-drawer cabinet topped by a small storage box, it was necessary for consultants to rid themselves of 3 years' worth of paperwork and other items. Casta insisted they condense 3 years' of work down to 3 manageable months. She threw Pack & Purge Nights with pizza to encourage new habits. In addition, employees can send storage to two off-site storage facilities, take things home, share reference materials in the communal library, or simply throw things out.

Though employees stay in an office anywhere from 1 day to 1 month, they are moved to another office if they have gone over the maximum 30-day reservation. Casta explains that if employees stay any longer than 30 days, they begin to pick up their old pack-rat habits again.

Most corridors are lined with vertical storage for hotelers. Four horizontal drawers topped by a small cabinet with two doors provides the same amount of storage for each employee. Each locker has a

name and number for identification. Employees are free to store personal items in storage totes that can be brought into the reserved office. The facility's central storage area is located near the atrium. Files are stored in movable totes that are loaded into pushcarts and then transported to and from the universal offices by housekeeping staff.

ATRIUM FOR MOTELING

Within the atrium are clusters of short-term moteling workstations composed simply of a work surface, computer, and phone. These stations are available without a reservation for those needing a space for a couple of hours between appointments.

TEAMING AREAS

Universal teaming areas for project teams are reserved by groups that need to be together for several weeks or more. Some of the universal offices have removable walls to create larger team space when necessary.

SIGNAGE

Hoteling scenarios demand effective signage in order to determine worker location. A movable and changeable signage system was developed to accommodate hotelers. Every workstation is numbered, and a name slot is provided for each office so that an employee's name can be inserted when he or she arrives in the morning.

Snapshot: KPMG Peat Marwick

RADNOR ADDRESS: Suite 500
One Radnor Corporate Center
100 Matsonford Road
Radnor, PA 19087
WEB SITE: http://www.us.kpmg.com/
TOTAL FLOOR AREA PHASE I: 27,500 square feet
NUMBER OF FLOORS: Phase I-1
TOTAL STAFF SIZE: 130 hotelers, 40 administrative, 10 partners
CLIENT PROJECT TEAM: Jose Suarez, director of architecture and construction, KPMG Peat Marwick, and Joni Casta, director of administration, KPMG Peat Marwick

MCI BOSTON RALLY CENTER, BOSTON, MASSACHUSETTS, 1996

PROJECT BY HOYLE, DORAN & BERRY ARCHITECTS

HOTELING, VIRTUAL, NONTERRITORIAL

COMPANY BACKGROUND

In 1997, a commercial about a telecommuter who wears bunny slippers while collaborating on computer screen with a conference room full of men in suits and who doesn't shower until midmorning caught everyone's attention. With that commercial alone, MCI has single-handedly brought the art of telecommuting into more homes, boiling it down into a simple 30-second, slice-of-life television bit that tugs at the heartstrings of most overworked Americans.

MCI's motto is this: "In five years, 50 percent of MCI's revenue will be in businesses we are not yet in at this moment." Don't doubt them. It's said that if MCI were an animal, it would be a pit bull. Full of young and brash employees, this company founded in 1968 surprised everyone when it announced its planned merger with a more staid British Telecom in 1997. British Telecom said in October 1996 that it planned to buy 80 percent of the Washington-based MCI that it did not already

Figure 10.24
The floor plan of the MCI Boston Rally Center, a hoteling office that has stayed a hoteling office since it opened in 1996 because it works for everyone despite internal issues and a pending merger.
(HDB.)

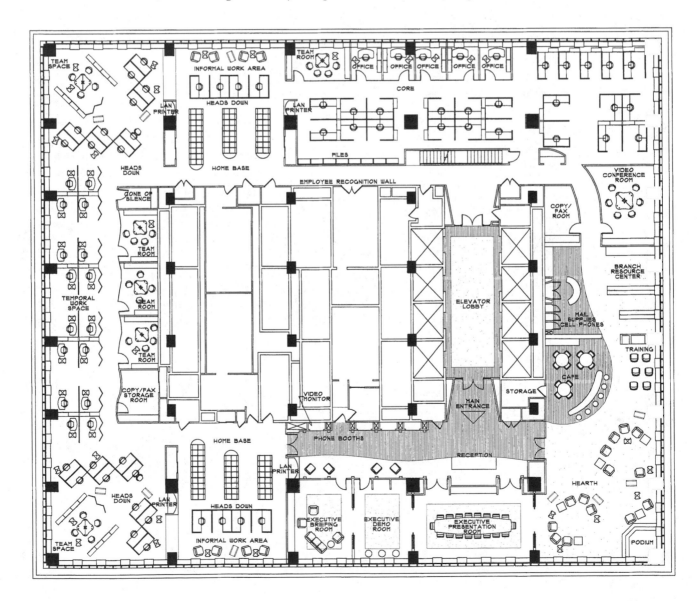

Figure 10.25
Designer Ethan Anthony
had to design a custom
locker because there
wasn't any product on the
market at the time to
support the project. Since
then, Egan Visual has
introduced a line item
based on this design.
(Photo by Steve Syarto.)

own. As of late 1997, MCI, WorldCom, and BT were still hashing out acquisition issues. It was the first of many megamerger announcements after the deregulation of the industry in February 1996.

MCI is already the second-largest, long-distance telecommunications company in the United States after AT&T. Its core business is long-distance service, but it has branched out into all other areas of telephony, including wireless technology, paging, and Internet services.

BEFORE: THE OLD WORKPLACE, BOSTON

The old MCI Boston offices were typically traditional. High-end conference rooms along with generic, plain-vanilla offices made for a mediocre office that employees hesitated to bring clients into for a tour.

AFTER: THE NEW WORKPLACE, BOSTON

Starting in 1995, MCI rolled out its plan for complete field automation, deploying computer, software, and networking technology to more than 5000 of its U.S. sales and service employees (Figs 10.24 through 10.29).

The next phase of the field automation strategy was to convert all field offices over to a virtual workplace, based on the model Hoyle, Doran & Berry Architects (HDB) designed for the Boston office called the "MCI Boston Rally Center." The new workplace is called a "Rally Center" to express the centralized and collaborative nature of the environment. The Rally Center was to be the first of many such offices to open around the country, but much of the initiative has since been put aside or modified due to numerous internal shifts. In addition, all the champions of the MCI Boston Rally Center, including former branch director Susan Beckmann, have since left the company.

Nevertheless, the Boston Rally Center remains a virtual office, occupying 24,500 rentable square feet in the class A Prudential Towers in downtown Boston. The Rally Center is 35 percent smaller than the previous offices. The space accommodates 118 employees, 93 of whom are mobile (sales reps who come and go as they need to) and 25 dedicated employees (administrative staff and a few managers) who are in the office daily. The office can accommodate a growth of up to 140 mobile employees given the flexibility of the space.

There's a sign-in system in the reception area for MCI staff to reserve an office space for the day or week and route their phones to the appropriate line, as well. MCI's call management system also equips employees with a single telephone number that can be programmed to follow them to a stationary phone, cellular phone, or networkMCI Pager. Employees can also check out cell phones at the Resource/Supply area for use throughout the office during their stay.

After signing in, employees have the freedom to use the following workspaces:

The Hearth

Much like a living room at home, the hearth space is the heart of the MCI Boston Rally Center. It is a place in which employees can gather for community meetings. This area has lots of little black Herman Miller "scooters" on wheels on which people place their laptop while working near a window, the place to which most hotelers migrate.

THE CAFÉ

Next to the hearth, the café has voice and data lines on top of the bar to plug into while enjoying a cup of coffee.

Heads Down

These spaces for individual quiet work are numerous and spread out all over the floor. There are lots

Figure 10.26
These folding translucent screens are used everywhere in the MCI Boston Rally Center open-space plan. (Photo by Steve Syarto.)

Figure 10.27
A real working hoteling office in action at MCI Boston Rally Center. Baskets full of folders and personal items are rolled to a workstation. (Photo by Steve Syarto.)

of translucent screens employees use to cocoon themselves into a workspace. There are also some hoteled offices available in which there are Crossings tables on wheels.

Cone of Silence

There's only one cone of silence, and it's a completely private and enclosed space with audio privacy for confidential meetings or phone work.

Team Rooms

Numerous team rooms are set up for collaborative meetings with plug-and-play devices in the middle of each table.

Home Base

The storage lockers for the virtual workers made some employees feel like they were in high school again. But on the upside, having such limited space for storage forced employees to throw out big binders, 95 percent of which had not been updated within the past year. MCI filled nine huge laundry hampers with empty binders, then donated them to local schools.

LIST OF MCI BOSTON RALLY CENTER DESIGN AND TECHNOLOGY ELEMENTS

Seats

Total	134
Temporal	109
Dedicated	25
Team room	24
Heads down	44
Informal	22
Cone of silence	1
Café seats	
Bar	6
Tables	12
Total lockers	104
Total work surfaces	69
Growth capacity	138

Connections

Analog lines	200
Digital lines	160
ISDN lines	2
LAN	72

Employees

Temporal	93
Dedicated	25

SHORT SUPPLY OF FURNITURE TO MEET VIRTUAL OFFICE NEEDS

Contract furniture manufacturer Egan Visual became involved in the project once designer Ethan Anthony of HDB realized there just wasn't any product to support the interior he and his client envisioned for the Rally Center.

First, a home-base workplace hoteling unit—a locker—was created, designed by Anthony and Egan Visual. The lockable units gang together, providing users with space to lock personal items and supplies. Inside the locker is room for a mobile basket in which users can transfer files and other items to their reserved desk. The unit has double, lockable doors with identifying signage.

TECHNOLOGY FOR THE VIRTUAL OFFICE

Employees use an IBM ThinkPad 755CD laptop in conjunction with client-server software in the MCI network to store and share information.

Phones can be checked out from a cabinet near the supply center. "The phones were my biggest fear about moving into the Rally Center—what a management nightmare," says Robert Mitchell, Rally Center branch manager. "But the reality is that the phones are really radio transceivers, and they work only wherever there are transceivers on the floors of MCI, so the phones don't work outside the building."

LESSONS LEARNED FROM IMPLEMENTING A VIRTUAL OFFICE

- *Robert Mitchell, branch manager, MCI Boston Rally Center:* "In December 1995, a couple of people left because the transition made them uncomfortable. What I've learned is that 30 percent of the employees will be upset before the move, 30 percent will be upset during the move, and 30 percent will be upset after the move."
- *Ethan Anthony, Hoyle, Doran & Berry Architects:* "My personal belief is that certain firms have hyped the little experience they do have to make it appear they are heavyweights in virtual office design when a visit to the sites usually reveals nothing other than a different color palette or a sea of ordinary unassigned cubicles."
- *Diane Jarry, facilities manager, MCI Boston Rally Center:* "We tried to stress to furniture manufacturers how important this project would be, but no one wanted to be flexible enough in giving MCI what we truly needed to support work. We had to rely on custom furniture."

Figures 10.28 and 10.29
The MCI café is next to the hearth, a way to do casual work while greeting others or eating. Everywhere you go on the floor, there's a pop-up plug ready to connect you to a phone or laptop. (Photos by Steve Syarto.)

• *Laura Woznitski, former MCI project manager from facilities in Atlanta involved in the Rally Center:* "In hindsight, I suggest hiring a consultant-facilitator, a voice of reason, who knows how to handle senior management and who knows how to keep on top of them so that they will be heavily involved with the day-to-day business of implementing a virtual office."

Snapshot: MCI Boston Rally Center

MCI is a provider of long-distance service (core business), wireless communications, global telecommunications, Internet software and access, business software, paging, and more.

EMPLOYEES: over 50,000
HQ located in Washington, D.C.
BOSTON RALLY CENTER ADDRESS:
800 Boylston Street
Boston, MA 02199
WEB SITE: http://www.mci.com
PROJECT TEAM, MCI BOSTON RALLY CENTER: Ethan Anthony, Hoyle, Doran & Berry Architects; Diane F. Jarry, facilities manager; Susan Beckmann, former branch manager; and Robert Mitchell, branch business manager, Northeast Region.

O+O SOFTWARE, INC., NAPERVILLE, ILLINOIS, 1996

PROJECT BY ODI

DESKLESS OFFICE, NONTERRITORIAL

COMPANY BACKGROUND

If you ever visit O+O Software in Naperville, Illinois, don't wear jeans. And definitely don't wear sneakers. Business attire is the dress code here with its office in Tonbridge (near London) the exception, a place where it's the norm to work barefoot as evidenced by the staff photos. The Naperville office is not *that* kind of a software company, and there are no dress-down Fridays here. It is, however, the kind of a software development company that works in an environment unique to others. They don't have a café—or even a bike rack—in the reception area, there are no pooltables or basketball hoops in the main office space, no music blaring. What they do have is an open environment that looks like a hybrid of an upscale gentlemen's club and an elegant den at home—minus the cigars and brandy snifters (Figs. 10.30 through 10.32).

But talk to a couple of the employees. One is a college graduate who "doesn't know any better" about how other offices operate so he's enjoying himself. "He thinks it's cool to work here," says James Pierce, CEO of one of his employees, a software programmer. Another employee, one who has an impressive background of software development, loves the way he can take his radio phone and walk around the office while making calls. Making a software program developer comfortable and happy is half the battle in an industry in which your best friend is your computer screen. But talk to one woman who interviewed at O+O for an administrative position, and she graciously turned the job down because it was clear that she felt uncomfortable in this type of collaborative environment.

O+O, founded by James O. Pierce in 1993, are the creators of the O+O Business System, a software package for corporations designed to encourage reengineering of fundamental business processes— that is, management systems. The software is built to help a company reengineer common business processes into a more logical and productive flow of information in administrative areas such as human resources, payroll, fixed assets, accounts receivable, and more. O+O supplies to its clients online documentation, help, and training so that the user can learn and correct simultaneously, not unlike what the commercial online services provide.

Pierce, the CEO, began his first software company over 20 years ago. That firm, Cyborg Systems, was also geared toward payroll, human resources, and fixed assets. There were many years when he worked at home. "I was always comfortable working at home. It was always quiet," says Pierce about his personal workstyle, which involved sitting in a recliner in his family room. "When working at home, I realized I was most comfortable looking down at the computer screen while I was working—like reading a book. Sometimes I'd just leave the monitor on the floor and it was fine with me, but then I graduated to a coffee table, and that was the perfect height."

BEFORE: THE OLD WORKPLACE

It was exactly that comfort level Pierce wanted to emulate in the company's new 9000-square-foot office when the company leased the space during 1993. But it wasn't so easy. Pierce wanted the interiors to have some of the high-end aesthetic qualities—traditional materials like wood and leather— that could be found in an established law firm, but have it read like a teaming environment at the same time.

The building that the software company moved into was previously a single-tenant building. The space was a warren of cubicles that the prior insurance claim processing company tenant had left behind. When the Pierces said that they wanted the cubicles removed and the walls torn down, the building managers were baffled. "No one ever wants to tear walls down, they usually want to put them up," says Pierce.

O'Neil Designers, Inc. (ODI), in Naperville helped O+O pull it off. ODI realized this company could not function in a standard private office and cubicle environment. What came out of the project

Figure 10.30

Notice the simplicity of the O+O floor plan—it has no desks! (Photo by David Clifton.)

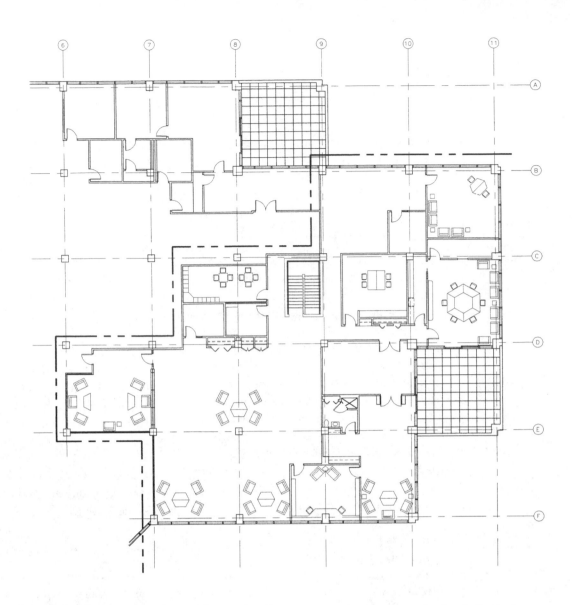

is a semihoteling, semiteaming workspace that fits the culture of this company like a glove.

AFTER: THE NEW WORKPLACE

"For someone that's coming in and wants to learn about the company fast, this is a far better style than any other one because you sit with everyone else and have the chance to question everyone else because they are right there with you," says CEO Pierce. "They sit in a group for 4 months, and after that, they have all the expertise they need. This way, they don't have to constantly run from cubicle to cubicle asking questions."

While the quasi-hoteling-teaming space was under construction, programmers worked in a temporary space in which they experimented with the new workstyle that would be waiting for them. Employees worked on top of boxes to get an idea of what it would be like to work with lower monitors.

Not everyone takes to this kind of style, however. In the beginning, one programmer wanted to move out of his group and work by himself. "If everyone said they wanted to work in a different way, the whole thing would fall apart," says Pierce. But an exception was made, and the employee has a dedicated office in the back of the space, but Pierce insists it's because his job required quiet and solitude, independent of a group.

THE DESKLESS OFFICE

Finding the right furniture solutions to support this workstyle took about 2 years, in part, because of the determination and fastidious direction from Mary Pierce, O+O's managing director. "People thought programmers wanted cubicles," says Pierce of the preconceived notions people have about the way programmers like to work. "We talked to standard manufacturers when we moved into the space, and

they couldn't think outside the box. They were used
to supplying customers their way, so we had a difficult time finding what we were looking for." (It's
interesting to note that today, Mary Pierce says that
numerous manufacturers are calling for tours of
O+O.) Even the building management was bowled
over when the company moved in and the Pierces
started requesting that the walls be torn down and
the cubicles left by the prior insurance company
tenant be moved out.

ODI began its long search in 1994 for vendors
that were willing to work with the unusual specifications the Pierce's required. What was so simple to
the Pierces seemed to baffle many manufacturers.
All the Pierces wanted were low tables strong
enough to hold computer monitors and comfortable lounge chairs that looked tailored and profes-

sional. The U.K. office found there were more furniture solutions in Europe, and that office changed
their office style before the U.S. office.

Finally, the right seating manufacturer surfaced,
in Canada. Arconis (see Resources) took an order
for 32 chairs. Employees are assigned a chair that
they can move around at will in and out of teams.
The arms are oversized at 14 inches wide for a reason. "We wanted a place where someone could sit
down and look over someone's shoulder to work
on a project," says Mary Pierce. "You can sit on this
arm and it doesn't interfere with someone else's
work space."

Programmers pull up chairs (with added gliders)
to surround a coffee-table-height table on which
everyone puts their monitors. Keyboards are relegated to the armrests or laps of programmers. For those

Figure 10.32
The lockers at O+O are actually custom oak kitchen cabinets stained to look mahogany and are located in the break room.
(Photo by David Clifton.)

programmers who need more of a desk, O+O keeps a supply of inexpensive kidney-shaped, 13- by-31-inch cherry Levenger Lap Desks (contact them at 800-544-0800) in the programming area. Although Davis, manufacturer of the tables, thought that cutting down legs would ruin the integrity of the product, the client fought hard, convincing them that it was okay to give them a shorter table. The height of most tables is 18½ inches—the typical height of most residential coffee tables—and other tables at O+O are lower yet for piling magazines and books (employees determined the best heights for the tables using boxes). The tables are square, rectangular tables from Davis, called *Connect Tables*, and have legs that screw in and out. O+O has an inventory of different-height legs that can be used for a variety of applications including conferencing.

There are, however, a couple of offices with actual desks in which sit Mary Pierce and the vice president of finance. But Jim Pierce's office, left empty by him most of the day since he spends time working in his teams, still looks like a den. A few of the seats surround a round coffee table, all enveloped by walls of mahogany.

VISIONS OF A PAPERLESS OFFICE: STORAGE

Virtually no papers are brought into the programming and teaming areas. Although employees do have lockers that are customized from upscale kitchen cabinets, no baskets or carts are used to wheel papers or other items around the office.

TECHNOLOGY

O+O spent about $50,000 for additional networking, wiring, and receptacle placement in just about every nook and cranny of the office. The only thing missing from Connect Tables is wire management, say the Pierces. Wires get tucked under tables and chairs so no one trips over them. Radio phones are used for mobility within the office.

"We want people to rethink work," says CEO Pierce. "When a client or prospect comes to our offices, we want them to see that as a company, we don't take things for granted, we are willing to be daring and work from the ground up to solve a problem."

Snapshot: O+O Software, Inc.

Manufacturers of software

FOUNDED IN 1993
EMPLOYEES WORLDWIDE: 20+ in the United States, the United Kingdom, and Australia
ADDRESS: 1717 Park Street
Naperville, Illinois 60653
E-MAIL: opluso_inc_jop@msn.com
SIZE: 9000 square feet, one floor
DESIGN TEAM: ODI, Inc., Elaine Barkoulis, Leslie Blasco, Ginger Frued, Mike Madl, Cindy O'Neil, Tammie Rudner, and Paul Seral
CLIENT TEAM: James Pierce and Mary Pierce
LOCKERS: A. M. Keuchmann, Inc., seating Arconas, tables Davis and NuCraft

THE STEELCASE LEADERSHIP COMMUNITY, GRAND RAPIDS, MICHIGAN, 1995

PROJECT BY IN-HOUSE STEELCASE DESIGN AND FACILITIES TEAM

CAVES AND COMMONS

COMPANY BACKGROUND

Ask anyone who works for Steelcase what's required reading, and they will no doubt say that Peter Senge's *The Fifth Discipline* used to be at the top of the list. The *Fifth Discipline* (and its workbook) study the art and practice of what Senge terms the "learning organization," an "organization that is continually expanding its capacity to create its future," explains the author. What Senge means is that if a company and its employees don't continually learn about itself, it cannot re-create itself and will stagnate and die. The book's mass of text may be daunting, but it is well worth reading to find out that becoming a learning organization is actually easy to say, and easy to do, if a company is run and staffed by a collective of open minds. Perhaps its a company like Steelcase, run by young Turk Jim Hackett, that is on its way to becoming a model right out of the pages of Senge's book.

But is Grand Rapids any place for a learning organization? This tri-city area, home to the commercial furnishings industry, includes Grand Rapids, New Zealand, and Holland, Michigan, and are not towns known for their high cost of living, exorbitant housing, or commercial leasing costs or roads that look like parking lots during rush hour. In fact, the area is an hour's plane ride away from Chicago, it has attainable housing, lots of warehousing space, relatively clean air even though it has a heavy furniture manufacturing industry, and wide open roads to travel to and from home and work. This area of the country is not one in dire need of alternative officing to reduce occupancy costs or contribute to cleaner air. So, what's there to learn from here?

It is precisely this part of the country, thanks to Steelcase, that is experimenting with the alternative workplace. And very well it should be learning from its own new workplace experiments since it sells furniture and products marketed to the design and facility professional for new workplaces that result from new work processes. In fact, Steelcase has had a telecommuting program in place for a few years and is now expanding on that effort to include a serious study in teaming involving Hackett and other senior executives who gave up their dynasties of oversized offices for Personal

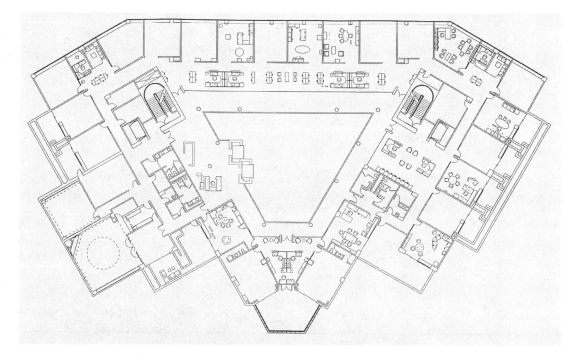

Figure 10.33

Before: The executive floor at Steelcase looked like this before moving down to the ground floor. Many of the vast executive offices were filled with a different style of a high-end furniture collection from Stow Davis. (Steelcase.)

Figure 10.34

The floor plan of the Steelcase Leadership Community packs in quite a few activity settings. The middle section is the core of the set-up, a control room in which there is videoconferencing, projection monitors, and 32 ports for laptop connections.

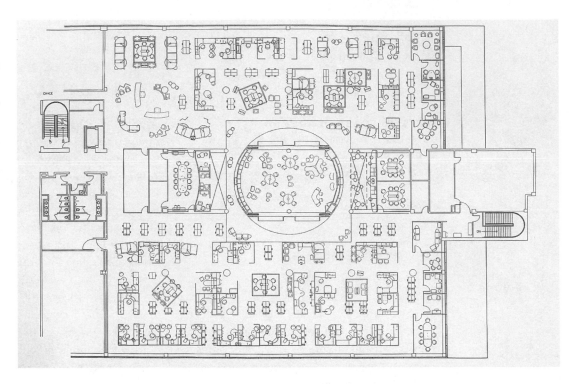

Harbors. The newly minted Steelcase Leadership Community is an exercise in walking one's talk, practicing what one preaches. Teaming has overtaken Steelcase from the top down.

Steelcase has always managed to surprise its audience with big introductions of long-overdue product—Turnstone, Personal Harbors, and, the much awaited, nearly 6-years in the making, integrated platform and technology plug-and-play mobile component product called Pathways designed with IDEO that the company says redefines the commercial furniture industry—if it works. This is the company with the dramatic and expensive television commercials and print ads to trade show booths that show any product. Nevertheless, the design and facility community continues to turn to Steelcase for its extensive research in not only the physical workspace design but occupational behaviors, spatial relationships, and conceptual ideas about the office of the future. All this is taking place under a big pyramid built in 1989.

Enter Hackett, the former head of Steelcase's brand of home office furniture, known as Turnstone, and CEO of Steelcase, Inc., since December 1994. Young, spunky, and completely likable (what's not to like about a CEO of a major company whose favorite movie is *Ghostbusters*), this is one CEO who you could see actually forgoing the banalities of the lush corner office in favor of real communication and flexibility in the workplace.

Hackett's broader-based workplace philosophies started in 1993 when he was named president of Turnstone, a division that did not have the luxury of starting up in the executive suite. Instead, it was housed off-campus in a half-finished warehouse with no furniture, no carpet, just a lot of cement-floored, fluorescent-fixture-lit rooms with a bunch of prototypes.

"While working for Turnstone, my intuition told me that technology and the growth of teams were going to alter the work settings forever," says Hackett of his experiences at Turnstone. "I saw myself as a senior person being much more effective by buying into the landscape instead of sitting atop it, hoping that it would work." Hackett says that the start-up Turnstone facility had yet another characteristic that wasn't as obvious to the casual observer. Turnstone was organized physically by process, not by hierarchy, because a process-driven environment was clearly the only way to get work done (Figs. 10.33 through 10.35).

THE CORPORATE CULTURE

It was always the joke in the A&D community circles that a Steelcase employee never smiles, never laughs, and sleeps in a suit. That has since changed since Hackett came on-board as CEO. "There's no softer pillow than a clear conscience," Hackett likes to quote from a favorite book called *The Power of*

Figure 10.35
When Jim Hackett of Steelcase shows a fellow CEO his modest 48-square-foot Personal Harbor workspace, he gets strange reactions. He's been called the "Dilbert of CEOs." People also tend to apologize to him for the amount of space they work in. All Hackett wants to do is educate CEOs that they don't need 700-square-foot offices (his old office) in order to be efficient. (Steelcase.)

Ethical Management by Norman Vincent Peal. Instead of following the rules and fitting into this past rigid culture, however, Steelcase's culture now values the sharpening of an employee's goals and experimenting with ways to achieve them. Hackett says he "lives or dies" by his promise to never downsize the company to bring costs in line but swears that through growth and rationalizing, the business will become more profitable. Experimentation at Steelcase is now key to that objective, and it's a way of work life that has hit the furniture company's executive row hard.

BEFORE: THE OLD WORKPLACE

Executive row at Steelcase or anyplace USA had not changed much over the years. However, most executives work differently to gain a competitive advan-

tage in a complex, global job market that requires broadened leadership roles. This shift has caused leadership to become less tactical (concerned only for the product) and more strategic (concerned for the holistic nature of a company that includes customers, employees, and community).

To achieve this shift in its own company's executive row, Steelcase needed to take the executives out of their isolating, albeit huge, private offices and bring all them all into a single, interactive space to facilitate information sharing and giving that would result in gaining a competitive advantage. As it stood, Steelcase executives spent about 80 percent of their time managing their divisions and departments and only 20 percent of their time developing corporate strategic direction as a team. Hackett's goal was to reverse that proportion by leveraging and pooling each executive's wealth of knowledge and wisdom. To Hackett, teaming is a better way to manage complexity, but it needed a physical environment that would support these efforts by integrating technology and workplace, and at the same time, assimilating reams of intricate data.

AFTER—THE NEW WORKPLACE

In an experiment in executive workspace that brings to mind the same type of trial that Alcoa's CEO Paul O'Neill and his team are going through now (see Chap. 2), the Steelcase Leadership Community should be the impetus for dramatic lessons, ideas, and shifts in mindsets that will, it is hoped, soon spill over into their corporate customers' executive suites.

A NASA-like control center is the focal point of the Leadership Community. There are five 100-inch screens, 32 ports for laptops, a VCR that automatically adapts to foreign-language video formats, and documentation cameras—a concept from Xerox's PARC. A ticker-tape type of dashboard device means that executives collectively and collaboratively interpret ongoing and updated, real-time information on the company's performance. Since Steelcase is a privately held company, this ticker tape doesn't show stock prices; rather, it measures products sold, orders fulfilled, and customers served. This control center is surrounded by a range of work settings and supported by a radio-frequency phone system to let team members travel from floor to floor and still remain connected.

Today, there are four private offices, down from the 20-plus private offices from the old days at Steelcase." We haven't abandoned privacy," says Hackett. "We endorse privacy and the enclave structure." Upstairs where the executives resided before is a chairman's office and two other offices for board members so that when they visit, they can sit in familiar surroundings. Hackett's old office is now used for ceremony only. It's still in place, but he uses it only three to four times a year for meetings with partners from Asia. In fact, it's been converted to a dining facility for guests. "Now they get to sit on top of the business," says Hackett.

Snapshot: Steelcase Leadership Community

Manufacturers of commercial furniture and ancillary products; providers of facility consulting services.

ADDRESS: 901 44th Street S.
Grand Rapids, MI 49508
PHONE: 616-247-2710
WEB SITE: http://www.steelcase.com
LEADERSHIP COMMUNITY PROJECT TEAM: Barb Constant, Frank Graziano, Barb Groat, James Hackett, Peter Jeff, William Keller, James Lawler, Matthew Mead, Rick Rummler, Fritz Steele, Mark VonDerHeide, and Dan Wiljanen

Kinetix Interior
(Hedrich-Blessing.)
See page 195.

CAC Booth Office
(Bill Gregory/CAC.)
See page 199.

**Cigna
Mock-Up 1**
(Photo by MZS.)
See page 202.

**Cigna
Mock-Up 2**
(Photo by MZS.)
See page 203.

**Tandem
Cockpit
Office**
(Environments
Group.) See
page 218.

**Seattle
Business
Center**
(Photo by
Donna Day.)
See page 223.

**BBDO West
Interior**
(Photo by Tom
Bonner.) See page
229.

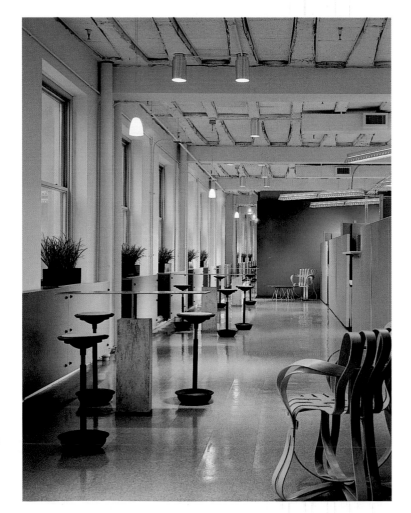

**Benevia Drop-In
Space**
(Photo by Steve
Hall at Hedrich
Blessing.) See
page 233.

Deloitte & Touche NYC
(Above, left)
(Photo by Jeff Goldberg.)
See page 235.

FMD Free-Address
(Above, right)
(Photo by Dana
Wheelock.) See page 239.

**Gould Evans Goodman
Interior**
(Gould Evans Goodman
Associates.) See page
243.

The HotWired Interior
(Photo by Chun Y. Lai.)
See page 245.

Home Base
(Photo by Steve Syarto.) See page 252.

MCI Interior
(Photo by Steve Syarto.) See page 253.

MCI Boston Rally Center Interior
(Photo by Steve Syarto.) See page 253.

MCI Cafe
(Photo by Steve Syarto.) See page 255.

0+0 Interior
(Photo by David
Clifton.) See page 258.

0+0 Hoteling Lockers
(Steelcase.) See page
259.

**Jim
Hackett's
Office**
(Steelcase.)
See page
262.

**Lobby of 76
Products**
(Photo by
Toshi Yoshihi.)
See page 267.

Building a New Workplace from Scratch

Chapter

11

BUILDING A NEW WORKPLACE FROM SCRATCH

As we saw in Chapter 1, trophy buildings have fallen out of favor throughout much of Corporate America. Since the 1980s, larger companies continue to shy away from committing to sprawling corporate campuses even if they think they'll be needing more space in which to grow. And many of the single-tenant buildings built on speculation in the 1980s have since emptied out, and are being remodeled and remarketed for multitenant use. Other palace-size office buildings that can't attract a single tenant are often recycled into residential or retail properties.

But this doesn't mean the building of new headquarters has stopped cold. Alcoa built a newer, smaller building in Pittsburgh, I.B.M. has done the same in Armonk, New York, the Swiss Bank's new corporate campus is located in Stamford, Connecticut, and Hoffmann-La Roche built a "green" building on its New Jersey campus based on universal planning.

There are a number of buildings that are under construction or newly renovated, but most of them have shifted gears when it comes to planning and designing the interior. There's something different about these headquarters from those princely buildings that sprang up throughout the 1980s.

Today's headquarters are built using direct input from workers; the building's entire physical envi-

ronment supports new work processes and they are wired to provide enough technology infrastructure to allow for growth for at least the next 10 years.

Still other companies are experimenting by taking a floor of their headquarters and creating an alternative workspace just to see if the rest of the building ought to go in that direction. For example, the 1.3 million-square-foot General Motors building, originally designed by Albert Kahn in 1920 and built to be the largest office complex in the world, is a historical, albeit a trophy, building. Albert Kahn Associates built a prototype wing 4A of the building, a 7500-square-foot alternative office area featuring mobile furniture, teaming environments, and hoteling spaces designed in contemporary stainless steel and birch wood.

Regardless whether an alternative workplace takes up one floor, one wing, or 1 million square feet, these buildings are shaping up to be the new models for headquarters for today's, and tomorrow's, new workstyles.

Pfizer's renovation of one of their buildings in New York City, 76 Products' state-of-the-art building in Costa Mesa, California, and the renovated building at 55 Broad Street, the New York Information and Technology Center, will be featured in this chapter.

76 Products' Headquarters: Costa Mesa, California, 1996

Oil company Unocal was founded in 1891 and has remained a staid, traditional company for over 100 years. Today, it's trying to adapt to a changing world marked by lower demand for petroleum and tough price competition. The company has experienced a fall-off in revenue of about 35 percent since 1990, and as a result, it has cut more than 4000 jobs, according to *The Los Angeles Times* (see Miller).

To deal with these pressures, Unocal bundled together its refining and marketing operations in 1994 into a new subsidiary called 76 Products Company, run by Larry Higby, a marketing specialist from outside the industry who had worked at the White House during the Nixon years.

Higby was given the green light to build a new home for 76 Products, but many financial analysts say that it's typical of a company to tidy up and streamline operations right before a sale. They were right, and in 1997 Unocal signed the papers selling 76 Products to Tosco in Stamford, Connecticut.

The sale is credited to Larry Higby, president of 76 Products Company, for increasing sales and production, operating safety, and overall system efficiency. Higby noted that this performance was one of the reasons for Tosco's interest.

Even in 1994, however, Higby's views on the workplace were no doubt radical (not too radical since he evidently still works in a large, rather posh private office) for the Unocal culture. He came on board with the intention of creating an environment in which employees could practice "free interchange, free thought" all in an effort to boost morale, increase efficiencies, and have a little fun with new technologies.

76 PRODUCTS BEFORE: PHYSICAL SPACE FOR OLD WORKSTYLE PATTERNS

Before the Costa Mesa headquarters was built, employees were scattered in eight Unocal locations throughout Southern California. Most of the employees moved from Unocal Center, an old, 12-story building built in 1958 in downtown Los Angeles. The award-winning building has withstood the test of earthquakes, but it had become a relic of a trophy building with escalators instead of elevators and 100-foot-long hallways dotted with doors that had bland nameplates for identification.

Most employees left behind coveted private offices with window views for the new universal floor plan evident throughout the newly built headquarters. Before the move, 75 percent of employees worked in private offices, and 25 percent were working in an open plan. After the move, those percentages were reversed.

Although 76 Products was created to be a profit team made up of various departments such as accounting, analysis, sales, construction (of gas stations), and real estate, each individual was in a private office with closed doors, not supporting or communicating with one another. "Physical barriers were preventing people from talking to each other," says Nancy Levy of IA, the firm that designed the headquarters. "They played sneaker-net rather than using the computer—running down the hall everytime they needed to talk to someone."

Only 700 employees of 76 Products moved into the new space while 2800 others won't be joining the Costa Mesa group, and the parent company, Unocal, decided to keep its El Segundo headquarters.

76 PRODUCTS' CORPORATE CULTURE

Employees at Unocal are long-term professionals who grew up in the oil business. In IA's research, it found that managers spent less than 30 percent of their time in their private offices while lower-level employees spent over 70 percent of their time at their desks. Employees of Unocal were not e-mail dependent; many of them, in fact, never opened their e-mail because they were afraid of the technology, says *The Los Angeles Times* article. But they were also slow to answer voice mail, and that kind of communication problem was costing the company millions of dollars in lost business. Traders who buy and sell fuel sit in an open trading room so they can handle transactions on the spot. When millions of gallons of fuel need to exchange hands with petroleum brokers, and every cent counts, a refinery can't wait for an accountant to respond to voice mail 3 hours after the urgent call. Communication between these various departments became a key issue in the design of the new building.

Figure 11.1
It looks like a party, but it's really the lobby floor of 76 Products' headquarters in Costa Mesa, California. (Photo by Toshi Yoshihi.)

WORK PROCESSES BOGGING DOWN EMPLOYEES

Nancy Levy, principal with the Los Angeles office of IA, the firm that originally renovated the building, worked with Higby on traditional programming until one day they began to discuss the interviews she conducted with the managers. Higby asked Levy how it was going, to which she responded, "Everyone is *really* tired. They don't have the energy to work anymore, and they are nervous because

they've lost a lot of friends from the reorganization." Levy said there was just *too much* change going on for the employees, many of whom had worked at Unocal for nearly 30 years.

"I told him it was the first time in my experience in strategic programming that I couldn't find a link between the way the different groups worked with one another," she said. "There seemed to be a disconnect between departments." Accounting groups

Figure 11.2
76 Products is wired for
10 years out and will
have to stay connected
via videoconferencing
with its new parent
company, Tosco, in
Connecticut.
(Photo by Toshi Yoshihi.)

were running the numbers to trade oil, but they
had no way to update traders within critical seconds. Help desks took 3 to 4 days to return employees' distress calls over failed software. No one, said
Levy, could figure out what department they should
sit near because no one seemed to relate their work
or projects to one another. Right then and there,
Higby realized the traditional ways of doing things
just didn't work anymore.

Levy's statistics showed that people spent 5 hours
a week on average waiting in line for the fax
machine. "Those are the kind of statistics that
helped convince the board of directors that these
people needed fax modems to be more productive," Levy says.

76 PRODUCTS AFTER: PHYSICAL SPACE FOR NEW WORKSTYLE PATTERNS

The 12-story, 215,000-square-foot building that
the company was moving into was a mere 9 years
old, having been built in the mid-1980s to house a
litany of companies that came and left. Bank of
America was the last tenant before Unocal. Though
the bones of the building were in great condition,
the interior was traditional, cells of offices with
outdated technology infrastructure. It took more
than $15 million to bring the building up to speed
for the 700 employees of 76 Products. The new
space is filled with some Steelcase but mostly
Herman Miller workstations.

AN EMERGING CORPORATE CULTURE

Higby wanted to create a building to which people
would be excited to come work. His aim was to
create informal and formal collaboration between
employees, and he decided that food would be the
incentive with which to accomplish that goal.

The ground floor of the building (Fig. 11.1) has
fast-food outlets (there are no vending-machines
on any of the floors), and the design of the "food
court" has a purpose. To get food, employees walk
through a room with booths and tables that looks
like a restaurant and that is called the "Club Room."

The Club Room has electrical outlets and high-
speed data connections for laptops, which make it an
ideal meeting ground for impromptu conferencing.

In the day-to-day universally planned work
floors, employees sit in cubicles that have reconfigurable tables on wheels. Because managers infrequently used their offices, the small number of private offices in the new headquarters were moved to
the center of the building to clear the views and
window space for the other employees who spend
most of their time at their desks.

Quiet rooms dot each floor for private time that
employees can't get in a cubicle.

76 PRODUCTS' NEW TECHNOLOGY AND WORK PROCESSES

Levy said that many employees were unaware of the
technology they had in their old offices. So while

they were in the process of moving, management educated all the employees to ensure that everyone knew how to use the $4 million worth of technology put in place in Costa Mesa.

The second floor of the building houses all the technology. The massive and powerful computer network is built upon a foundation of fiber-optic cables that even lets employees place lunch orders to the ground floor through their desktop computers. The fiber-optic cables shoot up through the spine of the building to the top floor. When an employee moves to a different desk or office, the information technology department simply drags, by mouse, an employee's files, access codes, and software to a new desk.

76 Products is aiming for a paperless office, as well, and hopes the technology will get them to where other companies seem to fail to go. Since moving into the building, most of the paper files are being stored electronically. In addition, employees are asked to rely on internal fax modems rather than on free-standing fax machines.

Since many employees of 76 Products are scattered about, the company relies on videoconferencing to keep communications going even at a distance. Although Higby sits in a private office, he has desktop videoconferencing capabilities (Fig. 11.2).

Snapshot: 76 Products

Unocal, an oil company, created a division in 1994 called "76 Products" under which bundled its marketing, refining, and transportation businesses. In 1997, 76 Products was sold to Tosco in Stamford, Connecticut. Assets include 1300 retail outlets (gas stations mostly in California), oceangoing vessels, refineries and pipelines, and associated outlets.

EMPLOYEES: 700 employees in Costa Mesa plus nearly 3000 employees global
HQ: 20307 Bear Valley Road
Apple Valley, CA 92308-5107
PHONE: 619-247-8799
WEB SITE: http://www.76products.com

The New York Information Technology Center, New York City: 1997 Work-In-Progress

The ghost of fictional Wall Street executive Sherman McCoy haunts the byways of Wall Street. Masters of the Universe no longer walk the halls of one particular building they left behind when things went bust in the financial district, a true bonfire of the vanities en mass, just as author Tom Wolff imagined it would be.

Perhaps those former egos lie dormant in downtown Manhattan despite today's bull market, but rising from the ashes in the financial district is a spirit of place. Downtown isn't dead, yet…perhaps it never will be, thanks to New York City's downtown revitalization plan. It's a long road ahead for the compact, dreary area whose buildings were left shell-shocked and empty—about 35 10-story-high "antique skyscraper" buildings built in the late 1960s through the 1970s and left one-third empty after the October 1987 crash. But Phase 1 of New York City's plan to make a home for new-media companies is taking place right smack in the middle of Wall Street. The New York Information Technology Center, an older building shunned for years for its perceived obsolescence, has now turned into a magnet for new-media companies (Fig. 11.3).

It was synchronicity for Rudin Management, a New York City developer who saw the need to reawaken Wall Street. The developer had a total of 36 properties—22 residential and 14 commercial—and they were gearing up for the demand for increased bandwidth they were sure their tenants would want in the advent of the digital revolution. And then came an offer from New York City. Could the Rudins take on a building on Wall Street, fix it up, help the downtown area come alive again in a new and different way than it had been in the past? Could the Rudins clear the path for this emerging industry called "new media" to find its way downtown and make a home on the southern tip of Manhattan, an area that had for years catered only to bulls and bears? Instinctively the Rudin family knew what those new-media companies needed — and needed badly—lots of technology embedded into bargain-basement-priced working environments. Within 48 hours of the offer, William Rudin, president of Rudin, said yes to what seemed like mission impossible: Take an empty, obsolete, class A building and reconfigure it as an incubation home to new-media companies.

Figure 11.3
Wall Street never looked this hip and happening. The former building of failed junk bond company Drexel Burnham Lambert is now called the New York Information Technology Center at 55 Broad Street, Rudin Management's home for small- and big-name new-media companies. (Photo by Maryanne Russell.)

Figure 11.4
Fox & Fowle Architects is shaping up the building for tenants that demand top-notch state-of-art technology, starting with this computerized version of 55 Broad Street's newfangled lobby with a videowall that acts as an advertising and communications vehicle for tenants. Each tenant's Web site shows up on the screen throughout the day. A cybercafé is planned for the lobby, as well. It's the first visual clue that this building is no longer your typical Wall Street office building.
(Fox & Fowle Architects.)

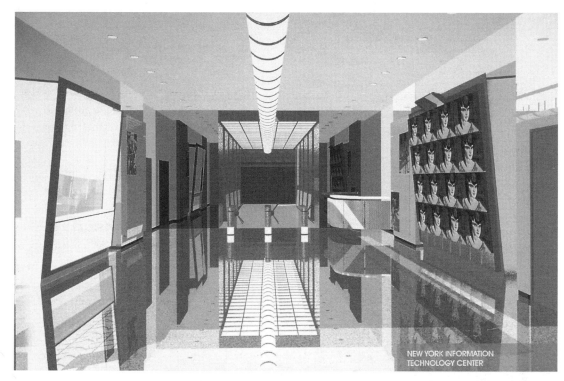

Figure 11.5
Many of 55 Broad Street's new-media tenants don't have the money to set up their own videoconferencing facility, but they can rent out the one being built on the fourth floor. Its top-notch facilities include numerous conferencing areas, as well.
(Fox & Fowle Architects.)

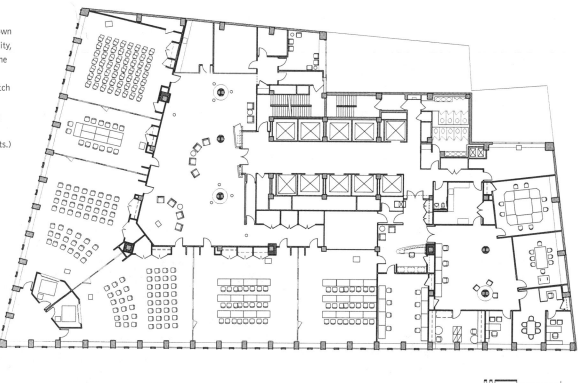

FROM NEW MONEY TO NEW MEDIA

Conditions were never as right as they were in 1995 when the Rudins took charge of the 400,000-square-foot, 30-story building originally built in 1966 but abandoned since its sole tenant, the ill-fated junk-bond company Drexell Burnham Lambert, went belly up in 1991. With the help of city and state tenant tax-incentive packages and $15 million capital investments both from private and government sources, Rudin turned 55 Broad Street into an affordable haven in the heart of Wall Street built for entrepreneurial providers of Internet services and multimedia software developers.

The converted building is wired up with fiber optics, high-speed copper wire, ISDN, and T-1 lines so that tenants can just plug in and work, saving each business the estimated $40,000 it would take to install this kind of connectivity on their own if they rented a loft elsewhere. In fact, that's where a lot of the tenants just came from. "My old office was my apartment where I had a 28.8 connection and a basic phone line," says Daniel Herschlag, president of Intercom Online who came to 55 Broad for its technology bandwidth and redundancies all at a reduced rate. Need to Know (N2K), the building's first tenant, also had a team of employees working from apartments. "Technology hook-ups always caused problems. In Brooklyn, if anyone even knew what a T-1 line was, it would take 4 months to hook it up, and, it was always a hassle to deal with the phone companies," says J. J. Rosen, the online music and entertainment company's president. Most of the original tenants aren't well established yet but rather, are small upstarts coming out of apartments or lofts and some directly from college dorm rooms, all of whom are looking to rent an average of 1500 square feet.

The New York Information Technology Center is a shining knight in glass and steel armor to new-media tenants. There are real savings at 55 Broad Street. Real estate tax abatements, commercial rent tax exemptions, energy cost savings…but is all of this too good to be true? There really is a hitch: a lease hitch, what else? To qualify for the tax initiatives, companies with 50 or fewer employees must sign a minimum 5-year lease (all the savings are ushered in during the first 5 years of the lease), and companies with over 50 employees are required to sign a minimum 10-year lease.

The tenant list has grown since 55 Broad opened in 1995. At the end of 1996, it had 48 tenants, up from 27 a few months earlier. As of 1996, the building was already 50 percent committed, and in 1977, approached full occupancy when Ernst & Young's Advanced Development Center leased 48,000 square feet. Low-cost leases run $14 per square foot to the mid-$20s in the tower where the views are better. Tenants range from the Plaid Brothers Software company and N2K to larger companies like IBM and Sun Microsystems who are working on Internet projects at that location. What once started out as only a birthing center for new-media upstarts has turned into a breeding ground for any company large and small—established or not—that's considered to be part of the information technology industry.

THE HARD DRIVE FOR HARD-WALL OFFICES AT 55 BROAD STREET

The architects at Fox & Fowle, the firm on the project, had an astonishing observation about the tenants' office space. "We expected to see a lot more open, shared spaces in the offices at 55 Broad Street," says Don Erwin, senior associate at Fox & Fowle. "Many tenants want private offices with doors!" In fact, all the original tenants were given a $35-a-square-foot build-out allowance, and some maximized the drywall possibilities. J. J. Rosen, the president of N2K has a very traditional, private corner office furnished with a U-shaped executive wooden desk, located down the end of one hall. Erwin says that some of the new-media businesses opened their doors at 55 Broad Street with a folding table and chair in a couple hundred square feet. "Now they are coming back to us asking for a full floor and looking at mahogany reception desks," he says. "After they spend 18 months establishing themselves and focusing on the business, they tend to hit pay dirt; then they invest in furniture and finishes the second go around."

THE LOBBY AND VIDEOCONFERENCING ROOM

Under construction, with Fox & Fowle as the project architect, is a massive videoconferencing facility and a cybercafé in the lobby. "The video display wall in the lobby is not for decoration. It's an advertising and communications tool for the building's tenants," says Erwin (Figs. 11.4 and 11.5).

TECHNOLOGY AT 55 BROAD STREET

"We've equipped our tenants with broad bandbrushes, easels, chisels, and hammers for them to create digital products that push the envelope," so eloquently describes the technology package at 55 Broad Street by John Gilbert, Rudin's chief operating officer, until he hits us with a reality check. "We now look at telecommunications delivery as simply another service we as building owners can provide to our tenants—no different than air-conditioning or security."

"At 55 Broad, we find that whole offices tend to turn off their lights. They just use the ambient light from under the door because they are spending all day and night looking at an illuminated screen," says Erwin.

Snapshot: New York Information Technology Center, New York City

TENANTS: Information technology, including new-media, companies
OPENED: 1995
WEB SITE: http://www.55broadst.com
ADDRESS: 55 Broad Street, New York, NY 10004
PHONE: 212-407-2400 (Rudin Management)

Pfizer Headquarters, New York City: 1997, Work-In-Progress

The world's top 10 pharmaceutical firms each spend about $1 billion a year on research. Pfizer, Inc., the world's sixth-largest drug and health care company, spent $1.7 billion on research in 1996 and expects to invest $2 billion in research in 1997.

In 1995, Pfizer introduced about half a dozen new products including the blood pressure medication Norvasc, which now has annual sales of about $1.8 billion, and the antifungal agent Diflucan, selling at nearly $1 billion a year. In 1996, Aricept for Alzheimer's disease, Lipitor for lowering cholesterol, and Trovafloxacin, an antibiotic, were on the dockets for launch in 1996. Dofetilide, a drug to control serious heart arhythmias, and Ziprasidone, a drug to control schizophrenia, are both scheduled to roll out in 1999. By the year 2000, Pfizer will be ready to launch Candoxatril, a compound for congestive heart failure, Voriconazole, which attacks a life-threatening fungus, and Eletriptan, which controls migraine headaches.

What do all these drug introductions have to do with the new workplace? Quite a bit. Because if the product teams are not supported by their physical environment or by appropriate technology, the downtime or longer lead time caused by poor planning and design can cost this company billions of dollars in revenue and profit.

"As our research and development teams form, break down, regroup again and again, we need to be able to pack people up and move them overnight to wherever their new team location is," says Donna Rose, senior project engineer in facilities at Pfizer. "The days of taking an A office, breaking it into two B offices, taking two B offices and breaking them into three C offices, and vice versa are over. We don't have time to do that anymore."

It's not just any product team, however; it's the restructuring of the International Pharmaceuticals Group at Pfizer that is causing the renovation of the Pfizer headquarters in New York City. This is the group that has led Pfizer in its phenomenal growth, introducing products that have been widely embraced by over 150 countries around the world.

PFIZER BEFORE: THE PHYSICAL SPACE

The International Pharmaceuticals Group was always a team in spirit, but they weren't as much of a team in the physical sense. Over 260 people in the group were scattered in three buildings across town, which made for some hair-raising delays when it came to communication and collaboration. For the first time in the company's history, this group had an opportunity to come together under one roof, to consolidate in one spot, in the Pfizer headquarters.

The group warmly embraced the chance to consolidate, but the task was easier said than done for Pfizer's headquarters is an amalgam of buildings side by side. Pfizer owns two buildings and rents space from another building. One of the buildings was built in 1905 as a depot for trolleys. Of course, this building is next door to the main headquarters space that was built in the 1960s.

The 1905 building was termed the "nasty building" by many employees because it had considerable physical drawbacks compared to the newer building next door. The windows were small and "ugly," and the floor-to-ceiling height was rather low with columns spaced close together on each floor. It required total renovation in order to comfortably house the International Pharmaceuticals Group. However, the building was already gutted because it was originally part of another project that was stopped midway through the process. The building was then reallocated as the new home for the pharmaceuticals group.

Before starting construction on the already gutted space, Pfizer decided to do it right and first do a little internal soul searching on exactly what would make the pharmaceuticals group happy and continually prosperous. Before finding a designer for the project, Pfizer wrote down a matrix of performance goals that could be supported by the physical space. For example, one goal was to increase the collaboration and interaction between departments. The designer was then asked to give them a physical environment to support those goals.

Pfizer set up a competition in which three design firms participated. But the competition wasn't held to find a *design* approach; it was held to find a *conceptual* approach. No programming, no planning—just concept. Brennan Beer Gorman Monk/Interiors of New York City won the competition.

PFIZER DURING: PROGRAMMING THAT LED TO A UNIVERSAL PLAN

Brennan Beer Gorman Monk's original, winning concept was to create an atrium with connecting staircases for increased and overlapping visual interaction and to bring more natural light into the old building. Three floors of 90 people was the original density programmed into the space that would also hold 120 people per floor. That was before the International Pharmaceuticals Group grew from 260 to 300 people in 1996.

It became clear that this group was composed of complex teams and that employee interaction in the planning and programming process was necessary for the success of this project. Brennan Beer Gorman Monk initiated two questionnaires: one that was distributed to everyone in the International Pharmaceuticals Group and one to the department heads. Though Bill Whistler of Brennan Beer Gorman Monk says its atypical to send out a questionnaire to everyone involved in the reengineering of space, it nonetheless signals to everyone that this is a different kind of project and that management is sincerely interested in obtaining their input.

After the questionnaires were collected, the design team followed up with interviews with department heads. Out of the massive amount of information the design team had to synthesize, one thing stood out with crystal clarity: It was unanimous that the priority was to give product teams whatever they needed to do their jobs. The product teams, in essence, drove Pfizer's explosive growth.

"Each product has a team of about 10 to 20 people," explains Whistler. "The teams think up the product, create it, and interact with the other groups that deal with the FDA and with the research groups, manufacturing, promotion, and marketing. Then there's the maintenance of the product. So, how do you support such complex teams?"

As the staff grew, the project grew and changed at the same time. During this growth period, Whistler took the rare opportunity to sit in on the team meetings in the International Pharmaceuticals Group to see how they interacted and how he and his design team could best design a physical space to support their work processes. "I found that some of the team for drug A and some of the team for drug B will be working simultaneously on a team for drug C," says Whistler. "So I ask again, how do you support the constant creation and reformation of teams?"

Whistler took the opportunity to sit in on numerous team meetings to see how they interact with one another in order to develop a design. During those meetings he had a chance to test some of the design team's ideas out on the employees. But as the staff continued to grow, the designs continued to evolve.

PFIZER AFTER: THE NEW WORKPLACE TO COME

Whistler developed a plan to account for continuous growth. He also noted that too much energy was being wasted on employees' worrying about whether or not they would get a B or C office, a problem many companies experience. At the same time, though there were different titles, everyone, regardless of their titles, needed nearly the same amenities. They needed meeting spaces, and they needed storage spaces for research and books.

A universal module of a 12-foot, 6-inch, by 12-foot, 6-inch, office was developed as the standard office size including a cockpit desk and choice of storage unit (bookshelves or filing space). There will be a distinction between wood furniture and metal furniture, but it's easy to move the wood suite of furniture in and the metal suite of furniture out or vice versa. Changes can be made in a day if necessary.

A mock-up of the office and the workstations to be placed on the window walls were built, and computer renditions were shown throughout a succession of six presentations that Whistler made over a period of three mornings. Each session lasted 45 minutes, after which everyone voted on color scheme, glass selection (the chosen glass will be stained for a muted color effect), and furniture specifications. Votes were tallied, and the results were published in the ongoing newsletter that is distributed to the company every 6 weeks or so to update employees on the project's timetable.

"This is a renovation project where everyone in the group is involved throughout the lengthy time frame," says Whistler. "Normally, it's a negative experience for a company, but we are providing a space that everyone truly believes will be superior to the old space. They know they've been involved with the process, so there will be no shock value when it comes time for move-in" (Figs. 11.6a and b).

PFIZER TECHNOLOGY AND WORK PROCESSES

When the Blizzard of '96 hit the East Coast in January, Pfizer employees were prepared. They took home their laptops on Friday evening in anticipation of a problem commuting into the office on

Figure 11.6a and b
Brennan Beer Gorman Monk/Interiors gave 260 Pfizer employees a presentation of what their universal offices and workstations could look like and asked them to vote for their preferred configurations. Every private office will have a 9-foot wide, 7-foot-high, storage wall with their choice of components: file, bookcase, or storage drawer. No more churn headaches for the product development groups at Pfizer.
(Brennan Beer Gorman Monk/Interiors.)

Monday morning. Sure enough, the building had to be shut down for 2 days, but Pfizer employees were up and humming along on their computers, checking e-mail and sending e-mail.

That sums up the new work processes at Pfizer. Global companies don't believe in geographical or time restrictions on accessing and receiving information. Global companies are 24-hour-a-day com-

panies. To that effect, information and documentation at Pfizer is online now with an emphasis on going paperless. It used to be that if an employee needed to know about a paid invoice, he or she would call the accounting department and wait for an answer. Now, accounting is online and accessible to everyone. The responsibility, however, has shifted to the inquiring employee to find out whether or not a bill has been paid, but at least it's done at a faster, more efficient pace. "More and more bits and pieces of my time are spent tracking down information that would have ordinarily been given to someone else to check on," says Donna Rose in facilities. "We're doing much of the same work we did 5 years ago, but with fewer people and a lot faster."

At Pfizer, more and more pieces of equipment that were stand-alone are now being integrated into everyone's computer. Today, communicating by phone is a last resort for most Pfizer employees because they are dependent upon their laptops. In fact, since 1995, the information technology department reports that it has rarely ordered anything but a laptop computer. The smaller, the lighter, the better, say Pfizer employees. With less physical and psychological baggage resulting from a new and improved workplace comes the free-dom to develop more life-saving, life-enhancing products.

Snapshot: Pfizer, Inc.

Pfizer is a research-based, health-care company with global operations. It's the world's sixth-largest drug and health-care company, and it spent $1.7 billion on research in 1996, and it expects to invest about $2 billion on research and development in 1997. In 1996, the company reported sales of more than $11 billion.

EMPLOYEES: 35,000 worldwide
ADDRESS: 235 E. 42nd Street, New York, NY
 10017-5755
PHONE: 212-573-2323
WEB SITE: http://www.pfizer.com

Sample Cost-Benefit Analysis
for a Telework Center from
the Employer's Point of View

Appendix

A

SAMPLE COST-BENEFIT ANALYSIS FOR A TELEWORK CENTER
(At the end of first year of telecommuting)

Assumptions Average annual salary is $26,000
                     Telecommuting days per week 1.5

Cost to employer per telecommuter

Direct costs	One-time costs	Recurring annual costs	Notes
Additional training	$150		Both telecommuter and supervisor trained
Telecommunications			
New installations	$505		ISDN phone line (2 B+D and interface card)
Services		$912	Depends on need for telecommunications and local tariff structure
Computers	$960		Telecommuter uses company laptop and docking station
Moving costs			
Computer equipment	$20		Move from central facility to telework center
Renovation/installation	$50		Some employee-specific materials such as lock boxes
Facilities leasing		$1,440	Varies telecenter to telecenter
Furniture purchases and leasing	0	0	Included in lease costs
Insurance	0	0	Included in lease costs
Equipment purchase and rental costs		0	Included in lease costs
Performance evaluation	$700		Varies depending on level of detail required
Total direct costs	$2,385	$2,352	
Telecommuters' direct benefits			
Increased employee effectiveness		$3,120	Average 12% relative to non-commuters at 1.5 days per week
Decreased sick leave		$226	2 days per year reduction in 230-workday year

Direct costs	One-time costs	Recurring annual costs	Notes
Increased organizational effectiveness		$520	Average 2%
Decreased turnover rate		$1,300	Equivalent to 5% of salary in search and training costs avoided
Reduced parking requirements		$360	30% reduction in monthly space requirements for non-car-poolers
Office space savings		$3,240	150 SF at $6 per month SF proportionally reclaimed
Total direct benefits		$8,766	
Indirect benefits			
Decreased air pollution			Put own number here for compliance with AQ compliance
Increased competitiveness			Put own number here for effect on productivity
Total indirect benefits			
Annual net benefits	($2,385)	$6,414	
First-year net benefits		$4,029	

Source: Jack M. Niles, JALA International (e-mail: jala@ix.netcom.com) in Los Angeles, June 1996 figures.

Client Questionnaire for Use As an Alternative Workplace Readiness Test

Appendix

The following is the thought process through which the design firm GHK brings their clients to determine if alternative workplace strategies are necessary or appropriate for the company. The questionnaire is divided into three categories: outsourcing, remote officing, and rethinking space.

SCORING COLUMN

	YES	NO

OUTSOURCING

1. Have management or shareholders developed an interest in or developed a mandate to outsource noncore business activities?
2. Are there noncore business activities that could be candidates for off-site outsourcing?
3. Are there noncore business activities that could be candidates for on-site outsourcing?
4. Is the local workforce fully employed and unable to provide people power for continued corporate growth?
5. Is there a freeze on hiring?

REMOTE OFFICING

1. Do you have individuals or a group who enjoy challenge who could participate in a pilot program?
2. Do you have team leaders and supervisors who could support remote workers?
3. Are there employees hiding in their offices or workspaces who could spend less time in their offices and more time on-site with clients and customers?
4. Are you radically changing or expanding your use of technology?
5. Do you have employees or new candidates who are asking to work at home, from satellite offices?
6. Does your company monitor its productivity, and do these studies indicate a need for change?
7. Does your company have a desire to improve air quality, the flow of traffic, or parking congestion by reducing the number of employees commuting to your facility?
8. Are you seeking a new or expanded workforce, and are the usual sources drying up?
9. Are you willing to make the investment of time and money on an experimental effort?
10. Do a significant number of employees commute in excess of 1 hour each way on a daily basis?

RETHINKING SPACE

1. Are you now or have you recently reengineered work processes or reorganized and restructured your company?
2. Do changing corporate values indicate the abandonment of a hierarchical environment in favor of a more empowered workforce?

3. Are you radically changing or expanding your use of technology, for example, in computers, phones, and networks?

4. Do you move people frequently, that is, in excess of 30 percent of your workforce in a year?

5. Do you reconfigure more than 30 percent of your offices or workstations every year?

6. Are you considering external sources to provide you with services and outsourcing that would create vacant space in your facility?

7. Are you planning on making any changes in the built environment to comply with ADA legislation or other state and local codes?

8. Are you downsizing or upsizing at a rate of 10 percent or more per year?

9. Do you have leases at term or expiring, or are you planning on relocation or renovation of existing facilities?

10. Are you currently out of space, or will you be soon, but your lease doesn't terminate for 2 or more years?

11. Are you under a mandate to cut costs to optimize or shrink your real estate portfolio?

12. Is there a freeze on taking more space?

13. Do any of your employees travel with absences of 3 weeks or more at any one time?

14. Do any of the departments in your organization have 65 percent or more of their staff doing work away from their workstations such as in a computer lab, a client's office, or on sales calls?

15. Does your company support flextime or job sharing?

16. Do any of your employees spend less than 65 to 85 percent of their time in the office?

17. Does your strategic plan call for more interactive and collaborative work processes?

18. Are reward systems in your company based on team success rather than individual achievement?

19. Do any of your employees spend 60 minutes a day walking up and down, back and forth, to printers, copiers, mailrooms, and fax machines?

20. Are there amenities currently accessible to a few individuals that could be better utilized if they were accessible to many individuals such as private spaces for phone calls, specialized computer terminals, and space for team meetings?

21. Do employees engage in spontaneous conversations and meetings?

22. Are employees missing deadlines or budgets because of barriers to productive work?

If you have answered "yes" to 3 or more questions in the "outsourcing" section, your company is a candidate for outsourcing.

If you answered "yes" to 5 or more questions in the "remote officing" section, your company is a candidate for a remote work program.

For the "rethinking space" section, score your answers the following way: If you answered "yes" to at least 10 questions in that section, and 5 or more of them can be found in questions 1 through 8, then your company may be a candidate for universal planning. If you answered "yes" to 11 or more questions in that section, and at least 7 of them can be found in questions 9 through 17, then your company may be a candidate for a hoteling program. If you answered "yes" to at least 13 questions in this section with 6 or more of them found in questions 16 through 23, your company may be a candidate for team settings.

Source: GHK. World Workplace 1996, authors of the questionnaire: Cheryl Duvall and Marilyn Farrow.

Sample Housekeeping and Reservation Sheet for Hoteling

C

TO MAKE RESERVATIONS

1. Call extension XXXX, and leave message:
   - Length of stay
   - Computer equipment needed
   - Working with anyone
   - Special requirements (totes from locker, etc.)

AFTER RESERVATION IS MADE

1. I will look for availability.
2. I will try and put you closest to your secretary and/or locker and/or anyone you are working with.
3. I will then call you with your room number and length of stay (to reconfirm).
4. I will fill out forms and hand them to housekeeping, who will then take care of making sure that your room is set up and ready for you to work in.
5. All secretaries and receptionists will receive the hoteling office schedule for the day
6. I will place the daily schedule on the BBS (which you can retrieve easily by holding down the option key and clicking twice on the file).
7. A voice mail will be placed by 9:00 a.m. if you do not arrive in the office. If we do not hear from you by 9:30 a.m., your whole reservation will be canceled. This does not just mean that day; it includes whatever you have scheduled (1 week, 2 weeks, etc.), just like the airlines when you miss a segment of your flight.
8. If you are going to be out of the office for a day (or more), I may need to hotel someone in the office on those days. We will try not to disturb your stuff when this happens, but you should be aware of this when you leave for that day and, as much as possible, organize your materials prior to departure.

CLEANUP

1. The office phone is deprogrammed.
2. All totes are put back into your locker.
3. Nameplates are replaced.

SET-UP

1. Totes from your locker are brought into the office for you (when requested).
2. All mail.
3. Fresh set of supplies (scissors are not included).

Source: This is an actual hoteling procedures sheet found in each office from a major Big Six accounting firm that prefers not to be named.

Sample Telecommuter's Home Office Inspection Guidelines and Employee Checklist (written for employee use)

The following information is provided to assist you in setting up your home office for telecommuting. It should be used as a guide to familiarize you with the many hazards that can be found in a home office workspace. If you suspect that something in your home office is hazardous but are not sure, contact your telecommuting coordinator.

FLOORS

Check for the following to ensure safety of your home office space:

Torn carpet
Electrical or telephone cords in walkways
Open file cabinet drawers that could trip
    someone

FURNITURE AND ERGONOMICS

Take time to become familiar with the term *ergonomics*, which refers to the applied science of fitting the physical surroundings to the human being. For you, the telecommuter, ergonomics will mean having the best possible furniture in which to do your work comfortably and safely. Learn what works best for you by talking to your facility manager, and be sure to outfit your home office in the most ergonomic way possible to ensure your safety and comfort.

ELECTRICAL SAFETY

If you have set up a home office, it's likely that there is an addition to the household of equipment (computers, fax machines, copiers, etc.) or appliances (coffeemakers, hot plates, radios, clocks, televisions, heaters, etc.). There are three hazards related to electricity: shocks, burns, and fire. All three can be avoided if you take care to check for the following hazards.

Electrical Outlets

Look for:

• Cracked or broken outlets
• Outlets without covers
• Signs of arcing or burns around the outlets
• Excess heat coming from the outlets
• Mild electrical shocks when you touch the outlet surface

As a general rule for grounding, if an appliance comes with a three-prong plug, it should be internally grounded. The ground pin should not be broken off, nor should the device be used ungrounded via an adapter or extension cord. Large appliances such as refrigerators, computers, and copiers, as well as heating devices such as coffeepots and hot plates should also be grounded.

If your home office is in a basement, garage, or near a water source, the following is critical to note. You should have a *ground fault circuit interrruptor* (GFCI) because it trips faster and sooner than a circuit breaker to prevent shock, and it is required anywhere within 4 feet of a sink that is located in a basement, kitchen, or garage. If an appliance gets wet, the GFCI acts fast to cut the breaker.

Electrical Cords

Look for:

• Frayed or damaged insulation
• Defective plugs
• Exposed wires

Extension cords must be monitored so that they don't cause any problems. Do not use one that is thin, old, and dried out. Use a newer extension cord that has a grounded plug. Use an extension cord that has a thicker gauge of wire to handle a large load of electricity. The gauge of wire should be as thick or thicker than the primary cord(s) so that there is enough width to handle the electrical load.

A major cause of fire is overloaded electrical circuits. This usually occurs through the use of multiple-outlet adapters or extension cords with a multiple-outlet connector. Limit the number of devices connected to any outlet to the number of receptacles provided by the outlet. If additional outlets are needed, they should be properly installed by a qualified electrician.

Make sure to buy an appropriate surge protector, and ask your local electrical store to suggest the best one for the amount of amps used in your home.

FIRE PROTECTION

Be sure to have in your house near to your home office work area the following:

Fire Extinguisher

- Permanently mount the extinguisher.
- Make sure the extinguisher is clearly accessible and not obstructed by furniture.
- Never place a fire extinguisher more than 75 feet away from your office.
- Inspect the extinguisher annually, and attach a tag showing the inspection date.
- Check to see if it is full; the gauge's arrow will point straight up if full.
- Examine the hose and nozzle for damage.
- Check for surface dents, which could mean that it has been used or tampered with.

SMOKE DETECTOR

The most important thing to remember about your smoke detector is to replace the battery yearly whether it needs to be changed or not, but also check it monthly to make sure it's working. As a general rule, one smoke detector should be placed on every level of a house. Place a smoke detector in the hallway outside your home office area, but don't place it too close to the kitchen where kitchen smoke can set it off. Don't place the detector on the ceiling where it meets the top of the wall; place it in an open area on the ceiling.

ALARM SYSTEM

Apartment buildings over one story in height are generally expected to have an approved fire alarm notification system that is clearly marked and visible.

SPRINKLER SYSTEMS

If you work in an apartment building, check your automatic sprinkler system. Check to see that the sprinkler heads have not been painted over. Don't pile anything high up near the sprinkler heads, which would prevent the water from spraying. Do not hang anything from the sprinkler heads.

FURNITURE

Furniture and draperies are not fireproof, but they may be fire resistant if they are made from adequate materials.

STORAGE

Don't store items on top of tall cabinets for many reasons. If you attempt to climb up on a piece of furniture to get the items down, you may fall and injure yourself. Items in storage can fall from shelves and injure you or someone else in your office. If you place items too high, they may interfere with lighting fixtures or sprinkler heads. Maintain a clearance of 18 inches from the ceiling.

If you have tall file cabinets, don't leave bottom drawers empty because doing so could cause the entire cabinet to tip over when heavy upper drawers are pulled out.

Always store away scissors, razor blades, or any other sharp implements so that no one gets hurt while in your home office.

APPLIANCES

Fans, coffeepots, radiators, and similar appliances need to be watched if used in your home office. Portable heaters can be considered a substantial hazard and are prohibited from use in your home office during the working hours that you and your supervisor have established. If you work in an older home that has radiators for heat, don't place flammable articles on or near them. Do not let electrical cords touch the radiators, either.

Coffeepots can be considered hazardous, too. If you choose to use a coffeepot in your home office during established working hours, keep an eye on it because it can overheat and start a fire. *Be sure to turn it off at the end of your working day.* Never use immersion-type water heaters for coffee or tea in your home office space. Even small hot plates to warm your coffee cup can be hazardous if papers are allowed to touch the appliance when it's turned on.

SAMPLE TELECOMMUTING EMPLOYEE SAFETY CHECKLIST

To employee: Please fill out and return to your telecommuting coordinator.

Name:

Title:

Department:

Remote work address:

Remote work phone number:

E-mail address:

The following checklist is designed to assess the overall safety of your telecommuting home office:

1. Are there any steps you must climb to reach your home office?
2. If there are more than four steps, do you have handrails for support?
3. Do you know where your circuit breakers are?
4. Do you know how to use your circuit breaker?
5. Are the circuit breakers clearly marked in opened and closed positions?
6. Did you check your home office area for frayed cords and wires?
7. Are there any exposed live wires in your home office?
8. Are other electrical cords, phone cords, and extension cords out of the way, secured under a baseboard or under a desk?
9. Do you have a fire extinguisher?
10. Is it easily accessible?
11. When was it last inspected, or is it new?
12. If you live in an apartment, do you have a sprinkler system?
13. Do you have a smoke detector near your home office?
14. Do you believe you have an easy escape from your home office in case of fire?
15. Do you have a portable heater in your home office?
16. Do you have a coffeemaker in your home office?
17. Do you have a heating plate in your home office?
18. Are there any loose casters on your chair?
19. Are file cabinets arranged so that open drawers will not obstruct anyone walking by?
20. Can you secure or lock your home office area so that children cannot access the space, equipment, appliances, or information?
21. Are floor surfaces clean, dry, and level?
22. If you have a carpet, is it loose enough that you may slip and fall when you walk on it?
23. Are your carpet's seams frayed or worn?
24. How many light sources do you have in your home office?
25. Can you easily read the text on your computer screen?
26. Do you feel this lighting is adequate?
27. Do you have an ergonomic task chair at your desk?
28. Do you know how to adjust it?
29. Is your back adequately supported?
30. Is there enough leg room under your desk?
31. Do you have glare on your computer screen?
32. Do you have to strain your neck to look up at the screen?
33. Is your keyboard located directly on your desk surface and is this comfortable for you?
34. Is your keyboard located on an adjustable, attached tray?
35. When you are using your keyboard, are your forearms resting at your sides and nearly parallel with the floor?
36. Are your wrists straight when you are using the keyboard?
37. Do you have to strain your arm to use the mouse?
38. Additional comments and concerns?

Telecommuter's signature   Date

_____

Supervisor's signature   Date

_____

Telecommuter coordinator's signature Date

_____

Telecommuter coordinator's comments:

Source: This Appendix has been adapted from the current U.S. Department of Labor's National Council of Field Labor Locals Flexible Workplace Program Work Agreement.

Appendix

E

NAME: _____

TITLE: _____

DEPARTMENT: _____

SUPERVISOR: _____

Describe what you do.

How long have you been in your current position?

Have you ever worked at home before while in this position?

If yes, describe why, when, and how often, and what you worked on while at home.

Explain why you would like to participate in the telecommuting program.

What element(s) of your job can you do at home?

Explain why you would prefer doing this job function(s) at home.

What prevents you from performing this job function or functions at the office?

How many times per week do you suggest you meet with your supervisor if you are a telecommuter?

How many days a week do you want to telecommute?

One day a week

Two days a week

Three days a week

Once every two weeks

Once a month

Do you feel you are self-motivated and self-disciplined enough to work at home? Why or why not?

Will you schedule, organize, and plan tasks to do at home? How far in advance? Describe.

How will you track your productivity as a telecommuter?

How will you make yourself accessible to your supervisor, coworkers, and customers or clients when you telecommute?

Do you think you will tend to work too much overtime as a telecommuter?

Will you miss the social and face-to-face interaction of the main office if you work at home as a telecommuter?

In what part of your home do you want to set up a home office for telecommuting purposes?

Do you mind absorbing any related costs to remodeling or furnishing a home office?

Check off below what equipment and services you need and what you currently have at home.

Equipment or Service	Need	Have
Computer		
Printer		
Modem		
Additional phone line		
Software		
Typewriter		
Desk		
Storage and filing space		
Ergonomic desk chair		
Ergonomic computer and keyboard accessories		
Fax machine		
Voice mail		
Other (please specify)		

Describe briefly the kinds of work you would do as a telecommuter (check as many as apply):

Writing _____

Data entry _____

Administrative _____

Reading _____

Research _____

Phone work _____

Planning _____

Client visits _____

Other (please specify) _____

Are there any family distractions or obligations that will make working at home difficult?

Yes   No

Do you consider yourself a suitable candidate for telecommuting?

Yes   No

Supervisor's comments:

SAMPLE 1

This agreement is a composite of three agreements in use by major companies in the United States who have asked not to be identified by name.

Name of telecommuter:

Department:

I have read and understand the attached Telecommuting Policy and agree to the duties, obligations, responsibilities, and conditions for telecommuters expressed in that document in addition to my normal duties, obligations, and responsibilities as a [company name] employee.

I agree to work at home ## days per week/month/every 2 weeks.

My telecommuting work hours will be:

My home office is located:

I agree to incur any costs in furnishing my home office with the following ergonomic items:

I agree to incur any costs in furnishing my home office with the following storage items:

I agree to have [company name] install and pay for a phone line for the following use:

I agree to protect company assets, information, trade secrets, software, and other company-owned items in the following way:

Here is a list of company-provided assets for my work as a telecommuter:

Description   ID NUMBER

I understand that telecommuting is voluntary and I may stop telecommuting, at will, at any time. I also understand that the company may, at will, change any or all of the conditions under which I am permitted to telecommute or withdraw permission to let me telecommute. I also understand that the company has the right to inspect at any time during working hours and for any reason pertinent to company business my work-at-home conditions to ensure proper maintenance of company-owned property and work-site conformance with safety standards.

I understand the company will not be held liable for damages to my personal or real estate property during the course of performance of work duties or while using company-owned equipment in my home or car. I also understand the company is not held liable for any personal or real estate property damages if I hold business or client meetings at my house during the agreed-to days and hours I telecommute.

I agree to be fiscally responsible to service and maintain any furnishings or equipment that are not provided by the company in order for me to continue being productive for the company. I also understand that the company will not be responsible for operating costs, home maintenance, or any other incidental cost whatsoever (i.e., utilities, personal residential phone bills, home and auto insurance).

I agree to let the company know in a timely fashion of any service or maintenance necessary for any company-provided furnishings or equipment.

I agree to meet with my supervisor to receive and discuss assignments to be done in my home office and to review completed work as necessary or appropriate.

Telecommuter's remote work location address:

Street:

City:

State:

Zip code:

Residence phone number:

Second or business phone number (if applicable):

E-mail address:

In an emergency, contact:

Directions to my remote work location (attach map if necessary):

A photo of my home office space is attached.   yes   no

Comments and special instructions:

Date   Employee signature:

                        Employee title:

Date   Supervisor signature:

SAMPLE 2: TELECOMMUTING AGREEMENT, NONEXEMPT VERSION

The following agreement has been reproduced word for word as it is used by a major publishing company. It is reprinted here with the publisher's permission, although this Fortune 500 company prefers to not be identified by name.

Dear _____

I am very pleased that you have chosen to take part in the telecommuting pilot program. This program is part of a corporatewide effort to develop new strategies that will help us work better and more effectively. Your participation will provide valuable feedback that will assist us in designing a more formal telecommuting program.

In order to help familiarize you with how the telecommuting pilot program will work, the following is provided to clarify your duties and responsibilities regarding your employment from a site other than [the company name's] office as a_____and the installation of certain equipment to enable you to perform your employment duties. As we have discussed, the duration of this telecommuting assignment is from_____to_____, unless earlier terminated or extended by [the company]. Upon termination of the telecommuting pilot program, you may be required to report to a [company's name] office.

Please be aware that while telecommuting, you will be responsible for maintaining the security and confidentiality of all company information in your possession, as well as any materials, manuals, and supplies provided to you. For your reference, a copy of [the company's] Code of Business Ethics and Affirmation Statement are attached to this memorandum. Please familiarize yourself with the code, and sign the affirmation statement and return it to me. As a reminder, all company materials and information must be maintained in a secure location and be protected from disclosure to unauthorized parties.

As we have discussed, if the equipment installed at your work location is leased or owned by [the company's name], you may not sell, rent, or use it for purposes other than performance of your work without prior written permission. Although [the company's name] will provide or arrange for routine maintenance of the equipment, you will be responsible for the cost of any repairs caused by misuse or abuse of the equipment. Repairs and maintenance will be performed by [the company's name] or by a service representative under contract by the company. Please remember that you are to notify me promptly of any problems experienced with the equipment or of any damage to the equipment.

To foster concentration and to ensure a safe work environment, it is recommended that you set up a separate workspace at your work location. It may be necessary for you to provide access to your work location and equipment, on advance notice, to your manager or other authorized persons for purposes of equipment maintenance and work-related meetings. In the event you cease employment with [the company's name] or your telecommuting assignment is discontinued, all company property must be returned to [the company's name], or access must be provided to a representative of [the company's name] to retrieve company property.

[The company's name] will reimburse you for all company-related calls made from and charged to your personal line, as well as modem online time for company-related business upon submission of your telephone bill. You will not, however, be reimbursed for any portion of the monthly service charge. In addition, [the company's name] will furnish you with all miscellaneous stationery and supplies such as paper and pens.

It is important that all network access procedures be followed and that all necessary steps to protect the integrity of the company systems be taken. Accordingly, network access will be limited to those times and systems authorized by [the company's name]. Any attempt to gain access to restricted systems or in any other way compromise security procedures and confidential information will subject you to termination. It is important that you remember to sign off the "system" and/or lock the computer when it is not in use, and please be sure that no unauthorized person is permitted to view the "system" while in operation.

Except to the extent caused by negligence or willful misconduct, [the company's name] insurance will be primary for all liabilities, expenses, and losses resulting from any accident, injury, or damage that is caused by the malfunction of the equipment or that arises out of the conduct of company business at your work location. Your insurance will be primary for any other claims.

During the period that you telecommute, you are expected to work_____(fill in the employee's normal work hours under this agreement) hours per week. Further, it is expected you will be telecommuting_____(insert days of the week the employee will be telecommuting). Your hours are_____to_____to ensure you are readily available by phone during this time. If your position is eligible for overtime and you need to work more than the number of hours noted above, you must obtain my advance approval. As you are benefiting from the flexibility of telecommuting, you will not be paid additional premium pay for work on the sixth or seventh workday if such hours are within your normal work hours. If you are eligible for overtime, you will receive premium pay only for work in excess of forty hours, or as required by local law (managers should check to be sure this state's legislation does not call for premium pay for time worked in excess of 8 hours daily) per week.

You are to alert me immediately if you are sick and unable to work, plan to take time off the job, or plan to change your normal work schedule. Work hours and exceptions (sick, vacation, holidays, etc.) are to be reported weekly using the Time Sheet for Telecommuting Employees, which must be submitted to me no later than_____on alternate Fridays. Regardless of the hours you work, you will not be paid any shift premium or meal reimbursements.

As we discussed, on occasion it will be necessary for you to attend meetings, project reviews, etc., in the office.

This telecommuting pilot program may be terminated or extended by [the company's name] at any time and is not intended to change your status as an employee "at will."

Please sign below, indicating that you understand and will adhere to the requirements of this telecommuting assignment.

If you have any questions regarding the contents of this memorandum or any aspect of the telecommuting pilot program, please feel free to contact me or [*insert name of human resources contact*]. I strongly believe that this telecommuting pilot will be a mutually beneficial arrangement and look forward to working with you to ensure its success.

Sincerely,

_____

(Manager's Name)

_____   _____

Signed   Date

cc: Human resources representative
    Next level of management
    Employee relations or telecommuting program contact person

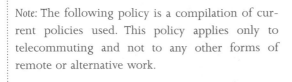

Sample Text Template for Telecommuting Policy

Note: The following policy is a compilation of current policies used. This policy applies only to telecommuting and not to any other forms of remote or alternative work.

A Telecommuting Policy Provides the Following:

- A statement of commitment to telecommuting in the form of a president's letter or even one sentence from someone representing company senior management
- A definition of telecommuting for your company, which can run from a single paragraph or to a more elaborate definition that breaks out types of telecommuters [Some companies have two or more tiers of telecommuter types such as full time, part time, virtual, or mobile, depending upon frequency.]
- How telecommuting candidates are chosen
- How an employee can determine if he or she wants to pursue telecommuting
- The terms and conditions of employment of a telecommuter [management]
- Performance and evaluations measurements [management]
- Equipment and furniture provisions for telecommuters [setting up home office]
- Workspace parameters and safety policy for telecommuters [setting up home office]
- Child-care parameters [setting up home office]
- Tax and zoning implications [optional under setting up home office]
- Telecommuting agreement [If program is voluntary, it must be clearly emphasized here.] [See App. F for sample template.]

DRAFT LETTER FROM THE PRESIDENT OF THE COMPANY

[Company] encourages you to think about the concept of telecommuting. Telecommuting is a flexible work option that can offer you a better quality of life, balance between work and family, and higher productivity and morale; it also supports our corporate concern for a cleaner, healthier environment. Telecommuting may not be appropriate for all of you; some jobs have responsibilities that are difficult to carry out at home. If you feel you have responsibilities that can be handled while working at home, read the following policy to further determine whether or not telecommuting is for you. If you have worked in the same department for a minimum of 6 months, have an excellent performance record, and wish to telecommute, I strongly encourage you to talk to your supervisor to determine if it is a viable option. Good luck!

CONTENTS: SAMPLE TELECOMMUTING POLICY HANDBOOK

I. WHAT IS TELECOMMUTING?

Telecommuting is an exciting and alternative way to work. It means that you can eliminate your commute and work at home one or more days a week. Telecommuters work from home with as little as a pencil, pad of paper, and phone or with sophisticated computer equipment and a second phone line. Telecommuting is a tool that offers you a greater quality of life while enhancing your productivity at work.

The advantages of telecommuting are many. What's in it for you?

- You eliminate the grind of your daily commute to and from the office.

- You eliminate the cost of your daily commute.
- You can create your own comfortable work environment. No one is watching you work. You can wear comfortable, casual clothes. You can listen to music while you work. You won't have to worry about disruptions from coworkers. You don't have to listen to loud office noise when you work at home.
- You can save money by not going out to lunch.

II. DETERMINING WHETHER OR NOT YOU WANT TO CONSIDER TELECOMMUTING

If you choose to pursue the path of becoming a telecommuter, you may encounter some concerns that telecommuters from other companies have faced. There are some questions you should ask yourself before you decide you would like to telecommute:

1. If you telecommuted, would you feel left "out of the loop" at the office?
2. Do you feel you would become invisible to coworkers if you telecommuted?
3. Do you feel your supervisor would forget about you or pass you over for promotions or raises if you telecommuted?
4. Do you feel you have enough space at home to telecommute?
5. Do you feel disciplined enough to work at home and complete your projects and responsibilities?
6. Do you make decisions quickly on your own?
7. Can you deal with slightly higher heating, electricity, and water bills that you would incur if you worked at home?
8. Can you afford to purchase your own home office furniture?
9. Can you separate yourself from the demands of family and nearby friends if you were to work at home?
10. Do you realize that telecommuting from here is not a substitute for child or elder care?

III. EMPLOYEE SELECTION GUIDELINES

Not all jobs are appropriate for telecommuting. If you can answer yes to the following questions, your job may be appropriate for telecommuting. After you answer these questions, you and your supervisor can work together to identify whether your position is an appropriate one for which you can telecommute.

Can you and your supervisor measure productivity in terms of the number of projects or objectives completed?

Do you require little face-to-face communication with staff or customers?

Can you conduct your job easily with electronic communication?

Does your job require little supervision?

Can you carry your office with you? Can you work without constant access to corporate office offline files or equipment?

Does your job involve "thinking tasks" such as writing, research, programming, or analyzing?

IV. GUIDELINES FOR MANAGEMENT OF TELECOMMUTERS

Terms and Conditions of Employment of a Telecommuter

A telecommuter is responsible for the following:

- Training courses provided by company in all technology
- Attending telecommuting program orientation with manager
- Working a standard 37.5-hour week
- Proposing work schedules for managerial agreement   (A normal work schedule is assumed to be between 9:00 a.m. to 5:00 p.m., Monday through Friday, unless reviewed and approved by mutual signatures to be different by both manager and telecommuter. Note that exempt employees may be required to work beyond the customary 40 hours per week to ensure completion of a job.)
- Timekeeping regarding attendance hours even on telecommuting days

Managing the Telecommuter

Managers who used to rely on observation to determine employee performance now need to learn the following skills, in addition to attending the telecommuting program orientation with the employee:

- Setting goals
- Managing by results
- Providing definitive feedback
- Using excellent listening skills
- Providing an atmosphere of mutual trust
- Making performance and evaluation measurements

In addition, the manager of a telecommuter must have an open, positive attitude toward telecommuting plus an innovative and flexible approach to managing staff members. Managers of telecommuters have the obligation to treat the employee equitably and fairly and make sure all work is recognized.

V. GUIDELINES FOR SETTING UP A HOME OFFICE

Equipment Provisions for Telecommuters

Each telecommuter is provided with the appropriate computer, phone equipment, and peripherals to set up a productive home office environment. The company provides the following equipment for telecommuters (list customized by company):

- Make of computer
- Make and speed of modem
- Type of software
- Make of fax machine
- Make of shredder

If you need other equipment, please talk to your supervisor for approval. All telecommuters must fill out an inventory form listing any company equipment that is dispatched to the home office and any personal equipment they have of their own in the home office. If you are chosen to be a telecommuter, the company will dispatch, deliver, and install equipment to your home office at no cost.

In the event that your job assignment no longer necessitates or requires home office equipment or services or it's discovered that the equipment and services are being abused in any way, the company has the right to remove or discontinue the use of such equipment. The company does not assume any liability for loss, damage, or wear of employee-owned equipment, but it will maintain company-owned equipment when necessary.

Telecommuters can take home a reasonable amount of office supplies such as pens, pencils, paper, paper clips, and computer disks and will be reimbursed for other supplies of a practical nature deemed necessary by them and their manager to do their job from home.

The company will also reimburse you for 100 percent of all business-related phone calls while telecommuting.

The company won't, however, reimburse or pay for costs associated with running a house such as electricity, heat, water, or basic monthly charges you would pay if you weren't telecommuting.

Furniture Provisions for Telecommuters

Special furniture that the company has approved for telecommuting home offices includes [list customized by company]:

- Make and measurements of work surface
- Make of ergonomic chair (mandatory)
- Make and measurement of file
- Make of task light
- Make of options such as keyboard and document holder.

In addition, the company will set up the following [list customized by company]:

- Voice and data line in house
- Installation of ISDN

The company will order, deliver, and install the furniture configuration to your door at no charge. If you prefer to work on another setup, discuss it with your supervisor for his or her approval. You are responsible for the appropriate maintenance of your home office furniture.

Workspace Parameters

Telecommuters must be able to provide for themselves a space in the home in which to work during agreed-upon hours. A dedicated room with a door is highly recommended in order to keep work and home separate. If you don't have an extra room, find an area in which you feel most comfortable working and one in which you won't have to move your work after hours. You may decide where to locate the workstation provided to you by the company. Any costs related to remodeling or redecorating must be absorbed by you, however. In addition, find a location that is far away from sources of noise such as conversation and traffic. For this reason, a kitchen or family room is not necessarily the best place in which to set up your home office.

As a telecommuter, you will also be responsible for locking your office door or using file and storage drawers for locking up harmful equipment and tools such as ink for printers, toner, letter openers, scissors, and other items considered dangerous and harmful upon handling.

[Option for companies that are not giving employees home office furniture]

Ergonomic Necessities

Just because you are going to work from home doesn't mean you have to give up the ergonomic tools you became used to working with at the corporate office. Take these recommendations into consideration:

- Work on a glare-free surface with rounded corners at a proper height.
- Don't keep your keyboard too high. It should be positioned as close as possible to your lap so that you are typing with your hands parallel to your lap, and not angled up.
- Make sure your monitor is not too high. It should be positioned so that you are looking directly into the monitor without looking up straining your neck.
- Don't sit in the most cushioned chair available. Find a chair with a harder seat than you think is possible to work on. You will be surprised at how much it will make a difference in your comfort level. It's strongly recommended that you spend your money wisely on a good-quality ergonomic chair that is height adjustable with a flexing back that moves with your body.
- Glare from the monitor will make you squint, and you'll find yourself uncomfortable. To avoid discomfort, don't position the monitor directly under a window because sunlight will cause glare on the face of the monitor and make it hard to work.

Child- and Elder-Care Parameters

Although you have the opportunity to see and interact with your children and elders, you may tend to take care of them for longer hours since you don't have to spend time commuting to and from work. Please understand that telecommuting is *never a substitute for child care. Please continue your current child- and elder-care arrangements should you be allowed to telecommute.*

Information Security Parameters

Information is a valuable company asset, and the telecommuter is responsible for protecting it from being seen, taken, modified, or destroyed by unauthorized parties. The company suggests a shredder be used in the home office; however, the shredder should be locked up when not in use so that it does not pose any harm to others.

Inspecting Home Offices

A telecommuter has the responsibility to maintain his or her home office in a safe condition free from hazards. The employee agrees that upon 24-hour advance notice, a company representative reserves the right to visit your home and inspect only and specifically your workspace to ensure that it is safe and free from danger.

Tax and Zoning Implications

Talk to your accountant about possible home office deductions. Zoning can be complicated, but most towns don't allow manufacturing business to be conducted in residential areas.

A Note About Family Life

You will need to "train" your family about your new telecommuting position because it changes everyone's lifestyle and family patterns on a daily level. Consider the following:

- Discuss the changes in your schedule with your children, and make them realize that when you are in the home office area, it's important that they let you work.
- Discuss the changes with neighbors, and let them know that just because you work at home, you aren't available for visits.
- Discuss the changes with other family members who may wrongly assume that just because you are telecommuting, you will have time to do all of their chores and more.
- If you feel isolated from others when you telecommute, find an office buddy whom you feel free to call.

Glossary

This glossary contains language and terms most closely related to the understanding, planning, designing, and management of today's new workplaces and new workstyles.

activity setting: An environment that provides a variety of work settings to fit diverse individual or group activities, that is, an area that includes, for example, a lounge, a worksurface/area, or a conference.

ADSL (asymmetric digital subscriber line): Wiring that allows simultaneous high-speed video, data, and voice communications over regular phone lines.

alternative officing: Catch-all term to describe different workplace strategies that have changed the design of the workplace and how people work.

analog: Nondigital information or signal that is gathered, stored, and reproduced each time it's needed, but becomes imprecise after numerous transmissions.

ATM (asynchronous transfer mode): An outgrowth of ISDN that offers faster switching; ATM is still under development as of 1997.

bandwidth: The amount of information, usually measured in bits per second for digital circuits or hertz for analog circuits, that can be transmitted in a given amount of time; copper wiring carries narrow bandwidth, and fiber optics carry wider bandwidths. The greater the bandwidth, the faster the rate of data transmission.

baud rate: Speed of a modem.

bed check: Unannounced survey taken place in an office to determine how many hours, days, or weeks a person uses an office; used to determine new workplace strategies and floor plans.

benchmarking: Formal way to gather, input, and analyze competitive data of best practices to improve company work processes.

bit: A tiny piece of computer information; the basic signaling unit in all digital transmission systems.

bonus room: A term home builders now use to refer to a flexible room off the garage or in the basement, usually wired and designed with built-ins set up for home office use.

bps (bits per second): The proper unit with which to measure the speed of a modem.

broadband: Allows several networks to coexist on a single cable and doesn't interfere with traffic from other networks.

Bürolandschaft: German term for open office landscaping.

byte: A piece of computer information made up of bits.

cable management: A part of the workstation in which cabling is laid and routed, usually at the work surface.

caster: Wheel of hard or soft plastic used to increase a piece of furniture's mobility.

category 5 cable: A new and standardized data cabling specified for most newer computer networks. Data cabling is now prewired to each office for turnkey LAN and WAN networks. Cat 5 is small in diameter, consisting of 4 pairs of unshielded twisted pair (UTP) of copper wire covered by an outer jacket. Cat 5 transmits over 155 million bits of data per second at a low cost.

caves and commons: Environment that integrates settings for individual work and teamwork.

cellular office: European term to mean a traditional long corridor on which both sides are lined with enclosed private offices.

champion: A committed high-ranking corporate executive who sponsors the implementation of a company's successful alternative workplace program.

change management: Process of supporting a company's cultural transformation.

churn: Relocation of an individual or group of individuals resulting in a change to the physical work environment; costs money, time, and labor; alternative officing tactics reduce churn issues.

client–server: A computer with tremendous information storage capacity is called a *server* on which numerous *clients* (other computers) rely for connections to retrieve stored information.

club: Combination of shared group and individual work settings.

cockpit offices: Small, hard-walled offices with L-shaped desks anchored by small tables for impromptu roundtable meetings.

coevolution: Strategic planning term to mean the collaboration between direct competitors, customers, and suppliers to create new markets, businesses, and industries.

combioffice: Scandinavian term for activity setting.

commons: A place in the corporate headquarters that supports shared activities. It is the center of office life and fosters idea gathering and socializing. The space can be a quiet lounge or an eat-in area for team breaks and conferences.

contract work: See *outsourcing.*

cordless office: European term meaning an office with wireless technology.

corporate culture: A complex collection of oftentimes unspoken beliefs and behaviors of a company's employee population.

cross-functional team: A support group of various disciplines within a company formed to cover all aspects and to mutually develop a cohesive alternative workplace program.

CT (computer–telephony integration): A link between computers and telecommunications enabling computers to tap the power of networks and call processing applications.

concierge: A person who receives office reservations from an employee, oftentimes the receptionist or office manager. Special software allows an employee to make reservations electronically.

cone of silence: Small office provided for hoteling or nonterritorial workers who need maximum privacy for heads-down work.

den: Informal teaming area.

desktop videoconferencing: Two parties can simultaneously see and hear each other on the desktop computer using special software and cameras. Simultaneous document sharing is available through this technology.

digital: Nonanalog electronic information or signal converted into binary numbers made up of bits, fed to and stored in computers as long strings of bits.

digital record storage: The technology with which scanners digitize and store a photo or other document onto the computer, which can be called up onto the screen.

distance learning: Interactive video and audio technologies that allow students to attend classes and training sessions regardless of where they are physically located in the world.

digital network: A LAN and/or WAN.

distributed work: See *outsourcing*.

downsizing: Term for massive layoffs in Corporate America; most popular during early and mid 1990s.

drop-in offices: See *moteling*.

dumb terminal: A CRT limited in technology with only word-processing capability.

DVSD (digital simultaneous voice data): Voice and data transmitted over one phone line, not as fast as ISDN.

e-mail: Electronic (paperless) messages or mail sent from computer screen to computer screen and accessed while online.

executive suite: New definition: Fully equipped office or conference space rentable by the hour or day found in a multiuse building. Old definition: Oversized office.

extranet: An intranet cross-indexed and used by only a company's staff, vendors, and customers.

fiber optics: High-bandwidth transmission medium allowing data to be transmitted by modulating a light wave through special glass or plastic cable rather than transmitting electromagnetic pulses (from copper wiring). Has low levels of loss or interference in signals, with high quality retained over long distances.

flexiwork: Any arrangement that a corporation has with its employees that allows them to take advantage of one or more concepts such as telecommuting, 4-day workweeks, flextime, or hoteling.

flextime: A flexible arrangement that a corporation makes with employees that allows them to come in early so they can leave early, or come in later so they can leave later.

fractal office: German term that, when simplified, means "office full of teaming areas."

free address: No reservations needed for employees. An individual's work is stored in mobile furniture that can be docked into any empty workspace.

group address: See *team suite*.

groupware: Software that supports concurrent use of objects by multiple LAN users.

guesting: An arrangement between two unrelated companies that allows for mutual use of space at each other's facilities.

guest office: A traditional term used to describe a full-service nondedicated office or two that a company would keep empty for use by a visitor.

Hawthorne effect: Improvements in worker productivity resulting from perceived management interest in employees, coined from experiments done at Western Electric's Hawthorne factory by Mayo and Roesthlisberger between 1927 and 1932.

hearth: A comfortable, homelike place in the corporate headquarters set up like a breakfast nook but with technology and bulletin boards, for informal working or idea-exchanging gatherings.

help desk: A technical support center set up by the corporate headquarters that allows virtual office workers to contact for help with hardware, software, or other technical difficulties.

hive: European term to mean full floors of cubicles.

hoffice: Term used by futurist Faith Popcorn to define the integration of home and office.

home office: New definition: A home in the office. The old definition: The corporate headquarters.

hot-desking: Taken from U.S. Navy term "hot bunking" to describe ship beds slept in by numerous sailors on different shifts, means unassigned desk or office space used by numerous workers.

hoteling: Reserved space at a corporate location for remote workers. A concept whereby employees who use the corporate office a couple of days a week call a company concierge ahead of arrival to reserve an office. Offices are designed alike with basic systems furniture, white boards, supplies, and equipment. Employees who hotel often keep their personal belongings and other paperwork in a centralized locker area or in mobile storage units that can be brought into the reserved office.

hoteling software: Software specially designed to help employees choose which work setting or office they need to reserve for a duration of time.

independent contractor: A definition the IRS grapples with, but in general, a specialist paid by the job, who supplies his own tools and equipment for trade or business use, and can work for more than one company at a time without being officially on staff.

information age: Describes the time in history, beginning in the 1980s, in which vast amounts of information handled and distributed by various modes of technology defines economies, lifestyles, and values of a society.

information technology (IT): A range of computer-based technologies.

information worker: White-collar knowledge worker.

intellectual property: The amount of highly valued and intangible understanding, knowledge, and analytical skills a professional worker has gathered through experience and learning.

Internet: The most important development in the communication industry since the television; some say it is the CB radio of the 1990s. The Internet is a global network of computers that have the ability to communicate with each other.

Internet migrant: Jargon for a person who is new to the Internet community.

intranet: A Web site that is proprietary to a company, accessible only to employees with a password.

intranaut: Jargon for a person who explores the Internet.

ISDN (integrated services digital network): A set of standards for transmission of simultaneous voice, data, and video information over fewer channels. Common ISDN systems provide one data and two voice circuits over a traditional twisted-pair copper wire or fiber-optic cable transferring voice and data starting at 64,000 or 128,000 bps, 5 to 10 times faster than DSVD.

JIT (just in time): Term coined by Andersen Worldwide, taken from the manufacturing community, to mean offices assigned to employee on a temporary as-needed basis.

kilobits: A per second unit of measure for data transfer rates.

kilobyte: A unit of size measurement for computer information.

knowledge worker: Any worker involved with the use of information rather than manufacturing of a product. See *information worker*.

LAN (local area network): A network of connected computers within a single building or campus of buildings. A system links together to form a network, usually with a wiring-based cabling scheme. LANs connect PCs and other equipment, enabling users to communicate and share resources (data storage and printing, for example) and other networks.

landing site: Another term for drop-in office.

lean office: European term for nonterritorial office.

megabyte: Unit of disk-storage space or memory measurement: 1000K in a megabyte.

modem: A small desktop device allowing computers to communicate with each other via telephone lines.

modified standards: Spatial and furniture goals of office and common space that improve productivity and efficiencies and support organizational objectives.

mobile office: Working remote, away from a corporate campus, in a car, hotel, or airplane with the aid of technology.

moteling: A concept whereby people visit the corporate office a couple of hours a week or less. They do not need a prior reservation for an office but instead, come in and pick a small carrel in which to do some quick work.

niche: Small cut-outs in hallways designed to support impromptu meetings, sometimes set up with perches—an elbow-height railing for leaning or to place papers, a white board, and/or some seats.

Noise Reduction Coefficient (NRC): Rating of the sound absorbancy of a material. Important consideration in open-plan offices.

Nomadic career: Refers to the career pattern of an independent contractor; see *portfolio career.*

nomadic work: Mobile work done on the road; see *road warrior.*

nonterritorial offices: Workspace without assigned desks or offices; no reservations needed.

notebook: New definition: A laptop computer. Old definition: Pad of paper.

oasis: See *hearth.*

occupancy study: See *bed check.*

officing: A term used to define any kind of work done in an office, wherever the office may be.

online: When a computer is hooked up to LAN, WAN, or the Internet via a modem or other more powerful transmission lines such as T-1 and T-3 wires.

open-plan office: Antithesis of cellular office. Floor layout with office workers segregated by nothing more than low paneled cubicles.

outsourcing: When a company contracts out to another specialized company or person the job functions that were once handled by existing staff.

packet: Unit of information by which a network communicates with one another; each packet contains the identities of the sending and receiving stations, error control information, a request for services, information on how to handle the request, and the data to be transferred.

Perch: Elbow height railings and/or seating placed in hallways of office buildings to encourage ad hoc, impromptu discussions like those that take place "at the water cooler."

periodic residents: Employees who come into the corporate headquarters infrequently and make use of hoteling, moteling, or telecommuting systems.

pocket office: A compact home office space, usually in a closet.

portfolio career: Contemporary term describing the short-term projects an independent contractor works on to develop his or her specialty.

postoccupancy evaluation (POE): Measurement by facility manager and/or design team of the actual performance of a redesigned or newly designed facility; rarely done because of client's time constrictions and client's fear of employee complaints.

POTS: Plain old telephone service.

push technology: Delivery of customized Internet content to users computer screen.

Quickborner team: German team that developed the *Bürolandschaft* concept.

remote work centers: See *telework centers.*

Red Carpet Club or Office: Original definition means a mix of task-specific work settings available on an as-needed basis such as carrels, work lounges, meeting spaces, phone booths, commons, and shared services set up like an airport club for frequent fliers. Today, it has evolved to mean an enhanced hoteling environment with higher grade of amenities or more activity settings in a corporate office.

road warrior: Mobile worker who spends little time in the corporate or home office but rather works on the road.

router: A software or hardware connection between two or more networks that permits traffic to be routed from one network to the other.

satellite office: See *telework center.*

scanner: Equipment that takes a picture of a piece of paper and displays it on computer screen (photo can be stored in computer as well).

search engines: A search service found on the World Wide Web designed to help the user quickly find a list of topic-specific documents and information on the Internet.

shared space: When two or more staff employees share a single, assigned workspace simultaneously or on different shifts or schedules.

SOHO (small office home office): A market niche carved out by manufacturers and service providers.

sound masking: Constant, broadband, low-level background sound that masks conversational distractions and unwanted noise; similar to the sound of an HVAC system air diffuser; also known as "white noise"; typically set at a sound level of NC 40 (48 dBA, dBA ±2 dB).

switches: Sophisticated computers that route millions of simultaneous streams of data from one track to another.

T-1 line: Wiring that allows 1.5 Mbits to pass at once. Used by companies who frequently access Internet, intranets, and extranets.

T-3 line: Wiring that allows 25 Mbits to pass at once.

Taylorism: Named after Frederick W. Taylor's scientific management experiments in the early 1900s in which he measured efficiency of tasks and workers' movements.

teaming areas: Small meeting areas immediately adjacent to individual workspaces designed for brief or impromptu meetings between departments or business unit staff members.

team suite: A dedicated room where a team "lives" while working on a project; some team suites have small individual touchdown workspaces and lockers for storage.

teamwork: Members from different disciplines in a company collaborate to achieve specific short-term goals.

telecenter: See *telework center.*

teleconferencing: Audioconference over phone connecting one to hundreds of people at a time.

telecommuter: Any employee who works at home either during the formal workweek, or after hours, linking to the corporate office via computer.

telecommuting: A term coined by Jack Nilles, it means using technology that enables an employee to work outside the traditional workplace—at home, on the road, or at a satellite office.

telecottages: European term for telework center.

telephony: A generic term used to describe any kind of voice telecommunications, over phone lines, computer, or wireless means.

teleport center: See *telework center.*

telework: Work that can be done over the computer or telephone at a location other than the corporate office. See *telecommuting.*

telework center: A mixed-purpose complex that incorporates on-site remote workers from different companies that have leased or rented square footage. Support equipment and administrative services are shared. Teleconferencing, Internet access, and other telephony services available. Facilities usually located on fringes of an urban area or in a suburb.

temporal office: Private office used by a manager and transformed into a conference room or teaming room when uninhabited.

thin client: A computer terminal that has been stripped down to be a simple box used primarily for Internet surfing.

touchdown spaces: Nondedicated small carrels designed for individuals who come into the headquarters for a couple of hours a week and need a work surface for some quick phone or computer work. Used in moteling environments.

uninterrupted power supply (UPS): A device installed by a power company that automatically provides battery-generated power to a single computer system for about 15 minutes; also protects the computer from power spikes and surges, kicking in automatically for a few milliseconds as needed.

Unitel: European term for activity settings.

universal plan offices: One-size-fits-all standard office or open-plan workstations, means people—not walls—move; streamlines standards and dissolves hierarchical space allocations and instead is based on floor-plate grid.

videoconferencing: Holding a meeting in two or more locations that are connected visually and with audio via a large-screen computer that usually allows all parties to remain in view.

virtual company: A company whose employees operate continuously through traditional barriers of time and distance, mostly reliant on technology for communication.

virtual office: A concept by which people work productively anywhere, any time, at a beach, in the car, at home, or at any preferred location via technology.

virtual reality: Computer-generated simulation of a reality; most commonly experienced for entertainment through wearing virtual reality goggles hooked up to a computer.

voice mail: An automatic answering machine networked throughout a corporation.

WAN: Wide area network. Two or more LANs in separate geographical locations connected by a remote link.

war room: see *team suite.*

Web master: Person responsible for designing and maintaining content of a Web site.

white board: An often mobile, white, washable or electronic board used in war rooms, team rooms, private offices, hearths, etc., for document sharing.

white-space opportunity: Strategic planning term to mean areas of potential growth that often fall between the cracks because they don't naturally match skills of existing business units.

wireless networks: Cellular phone systems that allow users to connect with the Internet and other computer systems without plugging into an outlet.

workplace: Any setting in which work is done.

workstation: In the furniture world it means desk, and in the computer world, it means the physical computer unit.

World Wide Web (WWW): A popular part of the Internet that allows access to hypertext documents, graphics, text, sound, and video databases created and maintained by an unlimited number of individuals, organizations, publications, and other groups that cover every conceivable subject.

World Wide Web browser: A piece of software, usually supplied by an online provider or purchased separately, that allows the user to access from the computer the World Wide Web part of the Internet.

Zoning laws: Local regulations restricting certain residential or commercial areas to certain uses.

Notes

CHAPTER 1

1. The term *officing* was coined by workplace design consultant Duncan Sutherland, Jr., to describe the way in which we make our work in an office, much like the word *manufacturing* describes the making of objects.

2. From a talk Gere Piscasso gave at the International Society of Facility Executives Symposium at the Merchandise Mart in Chicago, June 1996.

3. The *alt. office Journal* is a quarterly published by Miller Freeman.

4. Before 1996, there was a fifth condition, called "Unfolding Legislature," which centered on the Clean Air Act Amendments of 1990. Because the act was amended and put on hold, it has naturally taken a back seat for the time being and folded itself into issues of real estate and urban planning since some communitites do take it seriously enough to initiate grassroots movements, as you will read about in that section.

5. Take any numerical surveys about Internet use with a grain of salt. It's nearly impossible to gather accurate details about how many people access the Internet for a variety of reasons. Many surveys count Internet users via the number of "hits" a Web site has—that means the number of people that called up the page or site. Counting hits is done with the use of a "cookie," an imbedded electronic device that tracks a visit to a site. But built-in America Online (AOL) browsers don't support cookies (see glossary), and AOL is the largest online service with millions of subscribers (see Wildstrom 1996).

6. GVU surveys are located at http://www-survey.cc.gatech.edu/.

7. Of 245 CEOs and senior executives surveyed by Doremus & Co., an ad agency, only one-fifth of these business leaders have a computer on their desks (see Lublin 1996).

8. This particular *Tonight Show* aired November 27, 1996.

9. There's even a cybercafé association Web site at www.cyberiacafe.net/cyberia/guide/ccafe.htm.

10. See Chap. 2 under Xerox PARC's Portable Office section.

11. Berube was the organizer of IFI's "Office of the Future" 1996 forum in Bombay.

12. Prices come directly from Optima Offices' advertisement in *The New York Times*' 3 March 1996 issue on page 10 in the Real Estate Section.

13. InfoZone (http://infozone.telluride.co.us/InfoZone.html), a program of the Telluride Institute and run by director Richard Lowenberg (rl@infozone.org) explores telecommunity networking and learning. The institute is constantly working with wireless internetworking systems and cable modem providers to set up testbeds within the community.

14. Don't look for many cooperative apartments in New York City to switch over to live/work. About 70 percent of all coops don't allow home offices. Read more about zoning issues in Chap. 8.

15. In 1996, New York City almost went as far as revoking rent stabilization laws that prevent landlords from jacking up rents to exorbitant prices. Abolishing the rent stabilization law would have driven thousands of New Yorkers out of the city because they would no longer be able to afford living there.

16. For more on 55 Broad Street, see the case study in Part 3, Chap. 11.

17. The OTA was formed in 1972 as an analytical arm of Congress to help legislative policymakers anticipate plans for the consequences of technological changes and to examine the ways in which technology affects people's lives.

18. The more things change, the more they stay the same. We're facing the same issues as we did 200 years ago when the industrial revolution came to America, taking craftswork out of the home and into the factory where it took fewer people to do the job. Then the notion of efficiency through streamlining became popular in the late 1800s when Frederick Winslow Taylor began studying how individual tasks were preformed at a mill at which he worked. He found a connection between the way a workstation was arranged and the efficiency of the worker. Taylorism was born in the factory and has since moved through the office as quality and reengineering efforts, and now downsized companies are expected to practice a form of corporate Taylorism.

19. The New York New Media Associations Web site is http://www.nynma.org.

20. This speech came from Julin's state of the industry speech during BOMA International's 89th Annual Convention in June 1996.

21. Manpower has a total of 1100 offices in the United States and Canada.

22. The shrinking workforce is upon us as 44 million Generation Xers make their way into the job market. By all accounts, that's a small number of available workers considering that there are 77 million baby-boomers in the job market today (see Mann 1996).

23. Davidow and Malone explain that the term *virtual* has evolved over the years to mean many different things to various cultures and industries (see Davidow 1992).

24. Career women who waited to have children increase their chances of having twins. Those who take fertility drugs enhance chances of becoming pregnant but often have multiple births. According to the National Center for Health Statistics, the number of "supertwin" births (triplets and more) jumped 23 percent between 1991 and 1993 (see Martin 1996).

25. Catalyst, founded in 1962 after Schwartz had spent a decade at home raising her children, focused in its early years on lobbying employers to allow women to combine family and part-time work. The organization pioneered several job-sharing pilot projects in which two women shared a full-time job. It also undertook studies on family issues in the workplace.

CHAPTER 2

1. There's another notable term worth mentioning here. In 1995, the Hillier Group coined the term "appropriate officing" for its alternative workplace strategies on the basis that the word "appropriate" is more meaningful to the planning and design process than the word "alternative."

2. Telecommuting in itself is an extremely flexible component of the alternative workplace and can be used with hoteling and other concepts.

3. Much of the language here was coined by Mike Brill, BOSTI. Language like *Red Carpet Club*, *hoteling*, *caves and commons*, and *hearth* are a few of the words that Brill used in his research to describe unfolding work settings.

4. Hoffman gave an audioconference speech about Alcoa on December 12, 1995, sponsored by the Telecommuting Advisory Council.

5. Reilly outlined GTE's telecommuting ventures during a speech she gave at a Telecommuting Advisory Council seminar in 1996.

6. See Chap. 1 for more information about the virtual company.

7. Even a virtual company like VeriFone has some real properties like its manufacturing facility in Bangalore, India. Although Tyabji considers his IBM laptop his office, the company does have a headquarters in Redwood City, California, where he maintains an office, as well. For more information on the company, Verifone's Web site is http://www.verifone.com.

8. *Guerilla telecommuters* are employees who informally telecommute without the explicit approval of their human resource department.

9. It should be noted that these results were taken from facility professionals who may not be aware of the informal telecommuting or hoteling that goes on within many companies but are never reported to human resources or facilities. As with any survey, this one, too, should be taken with a grain of salt.

CHAPTER 3

1. Sims spoke about alternative officing at a seminar at Interplan 1996.

2. For two decades, we've been searching for ways to pull power down from the ceiling using a UL–approved device. Haworth's Irrigator, USG's Treescape, and IDEO's homemade solution may be the solution.

3. Xerox PARC's Colab was not the first of its kind to study team support. Douglas Englebart, a Stanford Research Insitute computer scientist and inventor of the first computer mouse in the early 1960s, built a "time-sharing" prototype computer system in 1960 to support structured information sharing in the electronic community. The concept was well ahead of its time and met with little enthusiasm. However, in 1980, Engelbart's system was finished as a product called AUGMENT, distributed through McDonnell Douglas (see Schrage 1990 and Wizards 1996).

4. Today, Xerox sells the LiveBoard Interactive Meeting System through its company called LiveWorks, Inc. LiveBoard, the product that grew out of Colab's experiments in the 1980s, connects up to 31 remote groups and displays networked information in real time on a 67-inch screen. Special conferencing software, called MeetingDesk, allows individuals to participate using desktop PCs.

5. Andersen Consulting is the "global management and technology consulting organization whose mission is to help clients change to be more successful, linking strategy, people, processes and technology." Arthur Andersen is the global accounting, tax, economic, and financial and business consulting firm that has recently established a practice it calls the "Real Estate Transformation Services group" to "interpret the emerging impact of technology on real estate," according to its Web site.

6. To manage its tremendous worldwide portfolio of over 10 million square feet (1 million square meters), Andersen Worldwide developed in conjunction with DEGW its proprietary Global Real Estate Management Strategy (GREMS) space analysis guidelines for use by Andersen's managing partners around the world.

7. After moving into the building, the agency sold it and leased the space for which it became famous.

8. In 1991, American Express launched the Hearth Program, a change management and training arm for the company's virtual worker community, headed up by Yee Jao, project leader, travel automation development and support. In October 1996, American Express eliminated the department and Jao's position.

9. Tiani went on to become the director of new business development, responsible for leading Amex's entry into a $20 billion commerical market, which will be served by a new corporate card product.

10. To keep costs down and tight schedules from being extended, IBM opted to use existing furniture in the Cranford facility. All-steel panel systems with panel heights of 42 inches configured the 6- by 8-foot stations.

11. See more on federal government alternative workplace programs in Chap. 2 under "Telecenters."

CHAPTER 4

1. Walsh spoke in October 1996 at a conference called Form & Function, an event sponsored by IFMA's New York chapter and initiated by Stacey Goldman, director of design for Sony Theaters, who envisioned the forum to help members of the facilities and design communities understand one another's boundaries and perspectives, to build a better relationship between facility managers and designers, and to increase awareness and appreciation for each profession's role.

2. Consulting firm DEGW facilitated the strategy and produced the Building Guidelines for the use of Andersen's managing partners around the world.

3. Unfortunately, since so many companies aren't making home office furniture purchases for telecommuters, war stories point to the fact that when it comes to initiating a telecommuting program, facility professionals detach themselves from the initiative because they feel it's just an HR and legal issue.

4. Hammer defined *reengineering* as the "radical redesign of business processes for dramatic improvement."

5. Greenwell Goetz Architects of Washington, D.C., is the interior architect for the Mobil project.

6. Strategic planning guru Adrian J. Slywotsky coined the term and wrote a book called *Value Migration*.

7. In 1996, JavaStation cost $750 for the basic model and under $1000 for one that includes a keyboard, mouse, and monitor.

8. Harmon-Vaughan spoke about benchmarking at World Workplace '96 conference.

9. Learn more on methods from The International Benchmarking Clearinghouse in Houston (123 North Post Oak Lane, Houston, Texas, at 713-685-4666).

10. See Chap. 9 for a full case study on CAC.

11. Questionnaires were mailed to all active North American IFMA members, and the data are based on the first 2200 usable questionnaires returned by the end of 1995.

12. Okidata is a division of Oki America, Inc., with sister divisions Oki Telecom and Oki Semiconductor. Oki America is a wholly-owned subsidiary of Japanese telecommunications and technology leader Oki Electric Industry Co., Ltd.

13. A term The Hillier Group trademarked to mean AWE.

14. There's a second school of thought on the alternative workplace and churn. Other industry professionals view AWE as a way to achieve 0 percent churn since there is nothing being moved except the person. For example, Brenda Laffin from Southern California Edison says that the cost of her company's churn is about $2600 per person per move, but with universal planning, churn is down to $300 to $500 per person. "What will be more important as time goes on is not so much the cost of the churn but the time of the churn," she says. Michael Brill of BOSTI believes the more work we do in spaces our companies don't own (airline clubs, home offices, online), the less churn from within the company facilities departments will have to deal with.

15. For a more in-depth dialog about workplace performance, visit the Walsh Brothers' Web site, created by Redman, at http://www.walshbros.com.
16. IMD is the International Institute for Management Development located in Lausanne, Switzerland. Strebel's article is based on part of his book *New Personal Compacts: The Missing Link in Change Management*, published by the Harvard Business School press.

CHAPTER 5

1. According to Infonetics, a network technology research firm in San Jose, California.
2. Based on a 1995 survey of 200 small companies by Impulse Research in Los Angeles.
3. For more information on technology consultants, refer to the Resources section in the back of the book.
4. Frame relay can cost as little as $125 a month according to a reference in the *Ascend Resource Guide: Telecommuting Network Planning Guide*. Ascend is a remote networking technology company in Alameda, California.
5. For more information, see the Resources section in the back of the book.
6. InfoTEST's Web site can be found at http://www.infotest.com.
7. It takes a minute and a half to download a page at 28.8 modem speed—with ISDN, it should take half a minute.
8. Consider the phone bill from the city of New York. Its phone bill jumped nearly 20 percent in 1997 although there were 20,000 fewer workers on the payroll, according to an article in *The New York Post*, May 21, 1996, by David Seifman (page 2). The reason? The staff that remained in the office needed to make more use of computers, modems, Internet connections, fax machines, and cell phones for constant communication with field workers.
9. The software doesn't work with America Online or other online service providers. A full and direct Internet service provider is necessary. In addition, some intranets have firewalls that inadvertently block Internet voice communications (see Cushman 1996).
10. In 1994, PicTel had 49 percent of the group systems unit market share.
11. Full-duplex conference mode is tricky—it means that one videoconference site doesn't have to wait for the other room to stop talking before speaking back. Unfortunately, the result is often that there are too many electronic audio signals going back and forth in each direction, and the sound mimics that of a public address system in a stadium.

CHAPTER 6

1. In his book *Generation X*, author Douglas Coupland briefly talks about the way he disdains cubicles.
2. Okamura collaborates in sales and product development with Howe Furniture for tables and Haworth for panel systems, plus a variety of other companies overseas such as Castelli S.P.A. in Italy for seating systems.
3. Per Okamura's 1996 annual report and based on its translation from yen into U.S. dollars at the rate of 106.35 yen to $1, the exchange rate on March 31, 1996.
4. Evett explains that an artifact is a tangible product manufactured for the workplace.
5. As of late 1997, Steelcase could still not commit to a time when Pathways would be released, nor would they release any visual images of the new product.
6. This statistic comes from a study done on clerical efficiency by C. M. Mackenzie and R. K. Mackenzie of the Heriot-Watt University, and it was reported in a sales promotion item from Dynasound, makers of sound-masking devices.
7. Four firms designed the Apple complex: Backen Arrigoni and Ross; Gensler; Holey Associates; and Studios.

8. Marriott is also looking at the opportunity for in-room teleconferencing capabilities.

CHAPTER 7

1. Luckily a spate of home office design books were published for the consumer market in 1995 and 1996, a list of which can be found at the back of this book. At the same time, the mass media became acutely aware of the need to publish more information on the home office. From *Popular Mechanics* to *Business Week* to *Country Decorator Magazine*, articles on designing the home office proliferated in an attempt to address entrepreneurial readers, further educating a public who never thought much about the importance of ergonomics in the home. Packard Bell introduced a TV commercial for a new computer in December 1996 with the tag line, "Wouldn't you rather be at home," targeting the telecommuter and home-based worker. MCI followed suit with its "Confessions of a Telecommuter" ad campaign depicting the joys of working at home in pajamas and fuzzy slippers.
2. There's also an excellent, comprehensive and fun direct-mail catalog on the market for the home office called *Reliable Home Office*. It even sells a miniwatercooler so telecommuters won't have to feel so removed from the corporate campus. (See the Resources section at the back of this book for more details.)
3. Herman Miller had been making residential furnishings from the 1920s through the 1950s until it set its sights on the burgeoning office furniture market. So it was fitting when Herman Miller introduced its first line of home office furniture in 1994 that was sold through an exclusive retail arrangement with the Crate & Barrel store.
4. In 1994 Steelcase debuted its Turnstone home office product to be purchased through a direct-mail catalog.
5. Geiger was really the first contract furniture manufacturer to introduce a home furniture line in 1994. Geiger also tried to sell the program, called EPH, through an 800 direct phone line. EPH was soon abandoned after it had sold a few hundred units. As of 1998, it will revisit the home office furniture market again with new and refined products.
6. GTE had an ad hoc telecommuting program until 1996 when it became formal throughout the company based on a company-wide memo from the CEO. See Chap. 2 for more detail under the telecommuting mini-case study.
7. The first "office-in-a-box" and computer armoire concepts can be traced back in history. The computer armoire is clearly derived from writing cabinets with doors from the twentieth century. But the office-in-a-box concept is quite interesting, dating back to the early 1800s when Giovanni Socci designed and built a mechanical desk with a chair on a retractable plinth that when closed, looked like an oval commode (see Linley 1996). The Box System by Pierluigi Molinary, manufactured by Asnaghi Rinaldo & Figli, was introduced into the United States in 1970 as a low-cost unit from Italy designed to bring modern design to a wider audience. The low cabinets had sliding plastic shutter doors. Inside were shelves, drawers, and a fold-down desk that resembled a wall-mounted ironing board (see Mang Karl).
8. In 1996, Office Depot and Staples initiated a merge, but the deal fell through in 1997.

CHAPTER 8

1. For those who wonder why carpal tunnel syndrome injuries were less frequent when everyone typed on typewriters versus keyboards, there is an explanation. Some experts say manual typewriters did not allow typists to work fingers as fast, and repetitive action was stopped with carriage return and paper replacement movements.
2. McCarthy gave a speech on law and the nontraditional workplace at the Strategic Research Institute's Telecommuting Plan workshop in July 1995.

References

CHAPTER 1

Abel, Judy. 1996. Sisters: The New Generation Gap. *The New York Post.* 6 August, 47.

Ayensu, Edward S., Michael Marshall, and Philip Whitfield. 1982. *The Timetable of Technology.* New York: Hearst Books.

Charles, Eleanor. 1995. For Duracell, a $70 Million, Self-Sufficient HQ. *The New York Times.* 17 December, Real Estate Section.

Coupland, Douglas. 1991. *Generation X.* New York: St. Martin's Press.

Courter, Sheila A. 1996. Big Companies Keep on Firing People But Hire Almost as Many, Study Finds. *The Wall Street Journal.* 21 October, B7.

Coy, Peter. 1997. Help! I'm a Prisoner in a Shrinking Cubicle. *Business Week.* 4 August, 40.

Davidow, William H., and Michael S. Malone. 1992. The Virtual Corporation. *Harper Business.* 4–5.

Davidson, John. 1996. My Mother's Keeper. *Self Magazine.* February, 154–157, 170–171.

Denitto, Emily. 1996. More Apartments Designed with Home Work in Mind. *Crain's Business New York.* 4 March.

Deutsch, Claudia H. 1996. A Short Move, but to a Whole Different Mindset. *The New York Times.* 11 February, 12.

Dobrzynski, Judith. 1995. Women Less Optimistic About Work, Poll Says. *The New York Times.* 12 September.

Downs, Hugh, and Craig Leake. 1991. Is This A Life? 20/20 ABC News. 14 June. Show Transcript 1125.

Duff, Christina. 1996. More Than Friends: The Tie That Binds Is Glittering Anew. *The Wall Street Journal.* 3 April, 1.

Egan, Timothy. 1996. A Temp Force to be Reckoned With. *The New York Times.* 20 May, 1.

———. 1996. Urban Sprawl Strains Western States. *The New York Times.* 29 December, 1, 20.

Gabriel, Trip. 1996. Decoding TV's Cool New World of "Screen-Agers." *The New York Times.* 15 November, D1.

———. 1996. The Meteoric Rise of Web Site Designers. *The New York Times.* 12 February, D1, D7.

Gates, Bill. 1995. *The Road Ahead.* New York: Viking.

———. 1997. Bill Gates Predicts What's Ahead in '97. *The New York Post.* 2 January, 24.

Goldberg, Carey. 1995. Choosing the Joys of a Simplified Life. *The New York Times.* 21 September, C1-C9.

Hafner, Katie, and Matthew Lyon. 1996. *Where Wizards Stay Up Late: The Origins of the Internet.* New York: Simon & Schuster.

Hales, Dianne, and Robert Hales. 1996. You Can Beat Stress on the Job. *Parade Magazine.* 17 March, 24–25.

Hall, Cindy, and Sam Ward. 1996. Snapshots. *USA Today.*

Handy, Charles. 1995. Trust and the Virtual Organization. *Harvard Biz Review.* May/June, 40–50.

Herring, Hubert B. 1995. Buy a Cellular Phone? Never! Well, OK., Maybe: One Man's Path Through a Maze of Service Plans. *Money & Business.* 5 November, 8.

Herszenhorn, David. 1995. Fewer Secretaries on Hand to Celebrate Their Day. *The New York Times.* 23 April, 15.

Holusha, John. 1996. To Attract Small Tenants, Landlords Prebuild Offices. *The New York Times.* 14 July, 11.

Keating, John. 1992. The Long Day's Journey. *New York Newsday.* 31 March, 54–55.

Kelly, Katy. 1997. Mountaintop Office Keeps Skiers in Touch. *USA Today.* 21 February, 1A–2A.

Kirk, Margaret O. 1996. The Virtual Office Bumps Into Some Very Real Limits. *The New York Times.* 3 March, Section 3–10.

Koretz, Gene. 1996. An Update on Downsizing. *Business Week.* 25 November, 30.

Lohr, Steve. 1996. Though Upbeat on the Economy, People Still Fear for Their Jobs. *The New York Times.* 29 December, A1, A22.

Lublin, Joann S. 1996. Computer Illiterates Still Roam Executive Suites. *The Wall Street Journal.* 24 June, B1, B10.

Lupton, Ellen. 1993. *Mechanical Brides.* New York: Princeton Architectural Press.

Magnell, Denise. 1996. Flex Appeal. *Connecticut Post,* 12 May, A1, A11.

Mann, Armistead & Epperson Investment Bankers and Advisors. 1996. The Changing Face of Office Work: Implications for Business Furnishings. *Furnishings Digest.* Richmond, Va.

Martin, Antoinette. 1996. Multiple Births: A Wake-Up Call. *The New York Times.* 8 February, C1, C4.

Murphy, H. Lee. Business Architecture Today: Buildings Now Are Cheaper, Smaller, Purely Functional. 20 March 1995. America On-Line. Available from *Today's News,* Crain's Chicago Business.

Murray, Kathleen. 1996. The Childless Feel Left Out When Parents Get a Lift. *The New York Times.* 1 December, D12.

Safire, William. 1996. Downsized. *The New York Times Magazine.* 26 May, 12.

Schachner Chanen, Jill. 1997. In Chicago's Loop. Offices Are Converted to Condos. *The New York Times.* 27 July, Section 9, p. 7.

Schiesel, Seth. 1997. Lucent Is Set to Buy Leader in Voice Mail. *The New York Times.* 18 July, D1.

Schellhardt, Timothy D. 1996. Downsized Workers: Jobs Are Available (But It's a Secret). *The Wall Street Journal.* 21 October, 1.

Shellenbarger, Sue. 1996. Work & Family. *The Wall Street Journal.* 31 January, B1.

———. 1996. Insurance Firm Cracks Tight Labor Market with Flexible Hours. *The Wall Street Journal.* 13 November, B1.

Shuster, Scott. 1996. Outsourcing! *Business Week.* 9 September, 115–118.

Smolowe, Jill. 1996. The Stalled Revolution. *Time Magazine.* 6 May, 63.

Spy. 1996. Galzheimers. *Fast Company.* October/November, 176.

Steinhauer, Jennifer. 1996. It's Cool, It's Hip. Will Baby Busters Buy It? *The New York Times.* 16 September, D1.

Stone, Andrea. 1996. Not Boomers, Not Xers, They Are Tweeners. *USA Today.* 22–24 March, 1.

Swaney, Chriss. 1997. For a City's Icons, a Shrinking Hometown Presence. *The New York Times.* 5 January, Real Estate Section, 9.

Uchitelle, Louis. 1996. The Business Buzz: Growth Is Good. *The New York Times.* 18 June, D1.

———. 1996. More Downsized Workers Returning to Jobs As Rentals. *The New York Times*. 8 December, 1, 34.

Verity, John W., and Paul C. Judge. 1996. Making Computers Disappear. *Business Week*. 24 June, 118–119.

Vizard, Mary McAleer. 1994. Marketing Opulent Waifs Abandoned by Austerity. *The New York Times*. 23 January, 15.

———. 1995. Rules Restricting Home Offices Are Reconsidered. *The New York Times*. 9 April, 11.

Wilde, Anna D. 1995. It's a New Generation of Business Travelers. *The New York Times*. 12 November, Section 3-1.

CHAPTER 2

Denitto, Emily. 1996. Companies Design Space Squeeze. *Crain's New York Business*. 25 November, 14

Hamilton, Joan, Stephen Baker, and Bill Vlasic. 1996. The New Workplace. *Business Week*. 29 April, 107–117.

McDonnell, Sharon. 1995. Telecommuting trend bypassing New York. *Crain's New York Business*. 30 January, 26

Taylor, William. 1996. At Verifone, It's a Dog's Life (and They Love It). *Fast Company*. February/March, 115–121.

U.S. General Services Administration, Office of Workplace Initiatives. 1994. *Federal Interagency Telecommuting Centers*. Interim Report. December.

CHAPTER 3

Birnbach, Lisa. 1988. *Going to Work*. New York: Villard Books.

Cohen, Edie. 1996. Andersen Consulting Project. *Interior Design Magazine*, November.

Crain, Rance. 1995. IBM's Mobile Work Force Virtual Success A Year Later. *Crain's New York Business*. 13 February, 11.

Groves, Martha. 1995. The New Nomads of Corporate America. *The Los Angeles Times*, 17 March, 1.

Noble, Barbara Presley. 1995. AT&T Pushes for Telecommuting. *The New York Times*. 10 July, 30.

Olson, Margrethe H. 1989. *Technological Support for Work Group Collaboration*. Hillsdale, NJ: Lawrence Erlbaum Associates.

Schellhardt, Timothy. 1992. Marketplace: Managing. *The Wall Street Journal*. 22 July, B1.

Schrage, Michael. 1990. *Shared Minds: The New Technologies of Collaboration*. New York: Random House. *Building Collaborative Architectures*, page 164.

Tetlow, Karin. 1987. Readout on Office Automation: A Prototype Space for Computer Supported Sessions. *Interiors Magazine*. October, 49.

CHAPTER 4

Burroughs, Marilyn S., and Ronald A. Gunn. 1996. Work Spaces That Work: Designing High-Performance Offices. *The Futurist*. March–April, 19–24.

Byrne, John A. 1996. Strategic Planning: After a Decade of Gritty Downsizing, Big Thinkers Are Back in Corporate Vogue. *Business Week*. 26 August, 46–52.

Denitto, Emily. 1996. Brokers Do Home Work. *Crain's New York Business*. 18 March, 12.

Frank, John F. 1995. IBM Mobile Workforce Thrives. *The Total Quality Review*. July/August, 1–6.

Gross, Daniel. 1996. Nailing Some Business. *Crain's New York Business*. 15 April, 19, 20.

Haas, Nancy. 1996. Grab Something to Eat…It's Free! *Fast Company*. February/March, 97.

Jennings, William C. 1996. Viewpoint: A Corporate Conscience Must Start at the Top. *The New York Times*. 29 December, Money & Business, D14.

Snyder, David Pearce. 1996. The Revolution in the Workplace: What's Happening to Our Jobs? *The Futurist*. March–April, 8–13.

Strebel, Paul. 1996. Why Do Employees Resist Change? *Harvard Business Review*. May/June, 86.

CHAPTER 5

Churbuck, David C., and Jeffrey S. Young. 1992. The Virtual Workplace. *Forbes*. 23 November.

Cortese, Amy. 1996. Here Comes the Intranet. *Business Week*. 26 February, 76–84.

Cushman, John H., Jr. 1996. Calling Long Distance, on a PC and the Internet. *The New York Times*. 19 May, 8.

Deutsch, Claudia H. 1993. Using Fiber Optics to Attract—or Keep—Tenants. *The New York Times*. 31 October, 13.

Reilly, Ellen. 1997. Life-Size Videowalls Let You "Meet" Face to Face. *Telecommuting Review*. January, 11–15.

Ripman, Christopher Hugh. 1995. Virtually Face-to-Face: Tools and Techniques for Lighting Videoconference Spaces. *LD+A*. April, 49–52.

Roger, Jean. 1996. Virtual Presence Meets User-Friendly: Humanizing Videoconference Technology. *FM Journal*. September–October, 40–45.

Sullivan, Nick. 1997. The Magic 8 Ball on 1997. *Home Office Computing Magazine*. January, 148.

CHAPTER 6

Brill, Michael. 1996. Shaping Work's Future in Japan. *Interiors*. September, 162.

Fishman, Charles. 1996. We've Seen the Future of Work, and It Works, But Very Differently. *Fast Company*. August/September, 53–62.

Flynn, Laurie. 1996. Is the Black and White Printer a Goner? *The New York Times*. 20 May, Business Day 1.

Groves, Martha. 1995. The New Nomads of Corporate America. *The Los Angeles Times*. 17 March, A1, A18, A19.

Holbrook, Dana. 1996. Is There a Quiet Place in the Alternative Office? *Architectural Record*. November, 54–57.

Home Office Computing. 1996. Up Front: Fax Facts. 26 December.

Markoff, John. 1993. Where the Cubicle Is Dead. *The New York Times*. 25 April. 7.

Segrest, Susan A. 1996. Self-Discovery News: Privacy Counts. *New Woman*. July, 52.

Shiner, Allen H. 1997. Sound Advice: Acoustical Tips to Assure Success and Avoid Surprises. *Perspective*. Winter, 33–36.

Szenasy, Susan. 1984. *Office Furniture*. New York: A Quarto Book by Facts on File.

CHAPTER 7

Bredin, Alice. 1996. *Virtual Office Survival Handbook*. New York: John Wiley & Sons. Chap. 3, p. 29.

Dulley, James. 1996. Home Energy. *Connecticut Post*. 1 December, H5.

Grey, Bernadette. 1994. The Front Page. *Home Office Computing*. May, 8.

Kearney, Alan J. 1997. Suppressing the Surge. *Today's Homeowner*. February, 50.

Linley, David. 1996. *Extraordinary Furniture*. New York: Harry N. Abrams, Incorporated.

Mang, Karl. Date unknown. *History of Modern Furniture*. New York: Harry N. Abrams, Incorporated.

Syarto, Marilyn Zelinsky. 1996. No Frills Furniture: It's Cheap, But Is It Easy? *Home Office Computing*. January, 58–61.

CHAPTER 8

Bibby, Andrew. 1996. Teleworking and Flexible Work Contracts: How the Trade Unions Are Responding. *Flexible Working Journal*. February, 10–14.

Carey, Anne R., and Web Bryant. 1997. Social Security Disability Rise. *USA Today.* 3 March, p. 1.

Cleaver, Joanne. 1995. Home-Based Law Bunts on Details. *Crain's Small Business.* June, *America Online Newstand.*

Duncan, Laura. 1995. Home-Based Biz License Fizzles. *Crain's Small Business.* September, *America Online Newstand.*

Hernandez, Raymond. 1995. Making It Easier to Do Business at Home. *The New York Times.* 20 March, Metro Section.

Kugelmass, Joel. 1996. *Telecommuting: A Manager's Guide to Understanding Flexible Work.* New York: Lexington Books, pp. 132, 162.

Mehta, Stephanie N. 1995. Chicago Targets Home Offices. *The Wall Street Journal.* 3 April, 2.

Niles, Jack. 1997. Telecommuting as a "Reasonable Accommodation" Under ADA. *Telecommuting Review.* July, 1–2.

Nordheimer, Jon. 1996. You Work at Home. Does the Town Board Care? *The New York Times.* 14 July, Section 3, 1.

Shaw, Lisa. 1996. *Telecommute: Go to Work Without Leaving Home.* New York: John Wiley & Sons, p. 132.

CHAPTER 10

Cohen, Edie Lee. 1996. Beckson Design. *Interior Design Magazine.* July, 77.

CHAPTER 11

Miller, Greg. 1996. Anatomy of a Corporate Transplant. 28 January. D1, D6-D7.

Resources

DESIGN FIRMS

@WORK
2 South Park, 3rd Floor
San Francisco, CA 94107
Phone: 415-537-0999
Fax: 415-537-0953
E-mail: mail@holeyassociates.com

Beckson Design Associates
933 North La Brea Avenue, Suite 300
Los Angeles, CA 90038
Phone: 213-874-6144
Fax: 213-874-6148

Bottom & Duvivier
2603 Broadway Street
Redwood City, CA 94063
Phone: 415-361-1209

Brennan Beer Gorman
Monk/Interiors
515 Madison Avenue
New York, NY 10022
Phone: 212-888-7667

The Environments Group
Suite 315
303 East Wacker Drive
Chicago, IL 60601
Phone: 312-644-5080

Farrington Design Group
Suite 300
3391 Peachtree Road NE
Atlanta, GA 30326
Phone: 404-261-6626

Fox & Fowle Architects
22 West 19th Street
New York, NY 10011
Phone: 212-627-1700

Gensler Associates
Suite 500
One Rockefeller Plaza
New York, NY 10020
Phone: 212-492-1400

Gould Evans Goodman
4041 Mill Street
Kansas City, MO 64111
Phone: 816-931-6655

Greenwell Goetz Architects
1310 G Street N.W.
Washington, DC 20005
Phone: 202-682-0700

Griswold, Heckel & Kelly Associates, Inc.
55 West Wacker Drive
Chicago, IL 60601-1611
Phone: 312-263-6605

The Hillier Group
500 Alexander Park CN 23
Princeton, NJ 08543-0023
Phone: 609-452-8888
Web site: http://www.hillier.com

HLW International
115 Fifth Avenue
New York, NY 10003
Phone: 212-353-4600

Helmuth, Obata & Kassabaum, Inc.
One Metropolitan Square
211 North Broadway
St. Louis, MO 63102-2733
Phone: 314-421-2000
Web site: http://www.hok.com

Holey Associates
2 South Park
3rd Floor
San Francisco, CA 94107
Phone: 415-537-0999
Fax: 415-537-0953
E-mail: mail@holeyassociates.com

Hoyle, Doran, and Berry Architects
38 Newbury Street
Boston, MA 02116
Phone: 617-424-6200
Fax: 617-424-7762

IA (Interior Architects)
Suite 1100
550 South Hope Street
Los Angeles, CA 90071
Phone: 213-623-2164

In-House
343 Vermont Street
San Francisco, CA 94103
Phone: 415-554-1950

Leo A Daly
911 Wilshire Boulevard
Los Angeles, CA 90017-3451
Phone: 213-629-0100

Robert Luchetti Associates
14 Arrow Street
Cambridge, MA 02138
Phone: 617-492-6611
Fax: 617-492-8441

Mancini Duffy
Two World Trade Center
New York, NY 10048
Phone: 212-938-1260

Tom McHugh, AIA
762 North 25th Street
Philadelphia, PA 19130
Phone: 215-232-2044

O'Neil Designers, Inc.
999 East Touhy Avenue
Des Plaines, IL 60018-2738
Phone: 847-299-7700

Osburn Design
Suite 208
200 Kansas Street
San Francisco, CA 94103
Phone: 415-487-2333
E-mail: osburns@aol.com

Perkins & Will/The Wheeler Group
701 Fourth Avenue South
Minneapolis, MN 55415
Phone: 612-339-1102

Perkins & Will
330 North Wabash Avenue
Chicago, IL 60611
Phone: 312-755-4601

Skidmore, Owings & Merrill
220 East 42nd Street
New York, NY 10017
Phone: 212-309-9534

Staffelbach Designs and Associates, Inc.
2525 Carlisle
Dallas, TX 75201-1397
Phone: 214-747-2511

The Switzer Group
535 Fifth Avenue
New York, NY 10017
Phone: 212-922-1313
E-mail:
102344.2475@Compuserve.com

STUDIOS
885 Third Avenue
New York, NY 10022-4082
Phone: 212-230-3291
Fax: 212-772-6956

Sverdrup Facilities
400 South Fourth Street
St. Louis, MO 63102-1825
Phone: 314-552-8191
E-mail: rogersks@sverdrup.com

Thompson, Ventulett, Stainback &
Associates, Inc.
2700 Promenade Two
1230 Peachtree Street NE
Atlanta, GA 30309-3591
Phone: 404-888-6600

STRATEGIC PLANNING CONSULTANTS

DEGW N.Y.
315 Hudson Street
New York, NY 10013
Phone: 212-633-4799
Fax: 212-633-4760
E-mail: alaing@degw.co.uk

The Buffalo Organization for Social
and Technological Innovation
Michael Brill
1479 Hertel Avenue
Buffalo, NY 14216
Phone: 716-837-7120
Fax: 716-837-7123

Cornell University—IWSP Program
E. 213 MUR Hall
Ithaca, NY 14853
Prof. Frank Becker
Phone: 607-255-1950
Fax: 607-255-3542
E-mail: fdb2@cornell.edu
Web site: http://iwsp.human.cornell.edu

Facility Technics
505 17th Street
Oakland, CA 94612
Phone: 510-763-7200

Froggatt Consulting
11 West 95th Street
New York, NY 10025
Phone: 212-749-4989
E-mail: c.froggatt@worldnet.att.net

TELECENTER SOURCES

Charles County Community College
Mitchell Road
Post Office Box 910
La Plata, MD 20646-0910
Phone: 301-934-2251
(Government telecenters in
Maryland)

Telework Centers of America
One Independence Plaza
280 Highway 35
Red Bank, NJ 07701
Phone: 908-842-4958

RESEARCH ARMS

IDC/Link
Suite 1420
Two Park Avenue
New York, NY 10016
Phone: 212-726-0900

LEGAL COUNCIL

Clean Air Act Compliance Information
(New York State only)
Phone: 800-882-9721

Robert Blackstone
Davis, Wright Tremaine
1501 4th Avenue #2600
Seattle, WA 98101
Phone: 206-628-7610

Patrick J. McCarthy, Esq.
Pitney, Hardin, Kipp & Szuch
P.O. Box 1945
Morristown, NJ 07962-1945
Phone: 201-966-6300

BEHAVIORAL CONSULTANTS AND CHANGE MANAGEMENT CONSULTANTS

Kaizen Consulting Group
Specialty: Change management
Suite 501
Two Berkeley Street
Toronto, Ont. M5A 2W3
Phone: 416-947-9416
E-mail: 74130,2154@compuserve.com

Progressive Strategies
Specialty: Change management
Suite 7
7319 Beverly Boulevard
Los Angeles, CA 90036
Phone: 213-525-1651

Realty Kinetics
Specialty: Change management
610 Smithfield Street
Pittsburgh, PA 15222
Phone: 412-391-1010
E-mail: sander@rkinetics.com

The Portsmouth Consulting Group
Fritz Steele
Specialty: Organizational behavior
151 Longwood Avenue
Brookline, MA 02146
Phone: 617-738-0843

Dr. Ronald Goodrich
Specialty: Psychologist for work-
place issues
Workspace Research Group
Phone: 212-562-3637

Gladys Foxe, CSW
Specialty: Psychodynamic factors of
working at home
133 West 72nd Street
New York, NY 10023
Phone: 212-721-4649

Working Spaces
Specialty: Training employees to
solve workspace and performance
problems
1228 Montgomery Street
San Francisco, CA 94133
Phone: 415-421-6139

MANUFACTURERS

Arconas
580 Orwell Street
Mississauga, ON Canada L5A 3V7
Phone: 905-272-0727

Brayton
255 Swathmore Avenue
High Point, NC 27264
Phone: 800-627-6770
Web site:
http://www.4brayton.com &
http://www.2Migrations.com

Cauffiel Industries
3171 North Republic Boulevard
Toledo, OH 43615-1515
Phone: 419-843-6285

Dynasound
6439 Atlantic Boulevard
Norcross, GA 30071
Phone: 770-242-8176

Egan Visual
  300 Hanlan Road
  Woodbridge, Ont.
  Canada, L4L 3P6
  Phone: 905-851-2826

Executive Office Concepts
  1705 Anderson Avenue
  Compton, CA 90220
  Phone: 800-421-5927
  E-mail: eoc@earthlink.net
  Web site: http://www.furniture-
  office.com/eoc

Frogbench
  Manfred Petri
  3589 Spencer
  Marietta, GA 30066
  Phone: 800-899-FROG

Gilbert International/New Space
  459 South Calhoun Street
  Fort Worth, TX 76104
  Phone: 817-921-5331

Haworth
  One Haworth Center
  Holland, MI 49423-9576
  Phone: 800-344-2600
  Web site: http://www.haworth-
  furn.com

Herman Miller
  855 East Main Road
  Zeeland, MI 49464
  Phone: 800-851-1196
  Web site: http://www.herman-
  miller.com

Advantage/InstaDoor
  365 East Middlefield Road
  Mountain View, CA 94043
  Phone: 800-642-3876
  Web site: http://www.ADVOS.com

Jotto Laptop Desk/Assembled
  Products Corp.
  115 East Linden
  Rogers, AR 72756
  Phone: 800-548-3373

Knoll
  105 Wooster Street
  New York, NY 10012
  Phone: 212-343-4000
  Fax: 212-343-4180
  Web site: http://www.knoll.com/

Levenger Lap Desk
  420 Commerce Drive
  Delray Beach, FL 33445
  Phone: 800-544-0880

Mobile Office Vehicle
  6143 28th Street SE
  Grand Rapids, MI 49546
  Phone: 800-373-9635

Office Specialty
  67 Toll Road
  Holland Landing, Ont.
  Canada L9N 1H2
  Phone: 905-836-7676

Okamura Corporation
  Overseas Sales Department
  Kokusai Shin-Akasaka
  Minatoku, Tokyo, 107 Japan
  Phone: 81-3-5561-4085
  Fax: 81-3-5561-4086
  Web site: http://www.toppan.-
  co.jp/okamura

Precision/Kyo
  1140 Merchandise Mart
  Chicago, IL 60654
  Phone: 312-644-0482

Skools Inc./Kin-der-link
  Suite 15A
  40 Fifth Avenue
  New York, NY 10011
  Phone: 800-545-4474

Steelcase, Inc.
  901 44th St., SE
  Grand Rapids, MI 49508
  Phone: 800-333-9939
  Web site:
  http://www.steelcase.com/

Studio RTA
  2067 East 55th Street
  Vernon, CA 90058
  Phone: 213-583-8882

Summerland Group
  Third Street and East Shore Drive
  Post Office Box 912
  Summerland Key, FL 33042-0912
  Phone: 305-745-4303
  Web site: http://www.the-
  office.com/the-
  office/research.products

Teknion
  901 Lincoln Drive West
  Marlton, NJ 08053
  Phone: 609-596-7608
  Fax: 609-596-8088
  Web site: http://www.tekus.com

Transwall
  Brandywine Industrial Park
  1220 Wilson Drive
  Post Office Box 1748
  West Chester, PA 19380
  Phone: 610-429-1400

WallTalkers/NuVu
  Suite 700
  5050 Newport Drive
  Rolling Meadows, IL 60008
  Phone: 800-820-9255
  Web site:
  http://www.walltalkers.com
  Home office product catalog:
  Reliable Home Office
  Phone: 1-800-869-6000

VIDEOCONFERENCING

Kinkos
  255 West Stanley Avenue
  Ventura, CA 93002-8000
  Phone: 805-652-4000 or 800-743-
  Copy

HQ Business Centers
  601 California Street
  San Francisco, CA 94108
  Phone: 415-433-8200
  Web site: http://www.hqny.com

VIDEOCONFERENCING EQUIPMENT

VPI
  Contact: 212-432-8900

Teleport
  Contact: 937-836-9995

Mobile Wall One
  Contact: 212-679-5590

TELECOM AND TECHNOLOGY SOURCES

US West Home Office Consulting
Center
  Suite 400
  3550 North Central Avenue
  Phoenix, AZ 85012
  Phone: 800-898-9675

HOTELING SOFTWARE VENDORS

Professional Resource Management's DeskFlex
   Suite 3-5
   50 North Brockway Street
   Palatine, IL 60067
   Phone: 847-359-3990
   E-mail: DESKFLEX@aol.com

Andre'a Jackson-Cheatham
   IBM FlexiMOVE
   999 Waterside Drive, 19th Floor
   Norfolk, VA 23510
   Phone: 804-446-6408
   Fax: 804-446-6288
   E-mail:
   Cheatham@VNET.IBM.COM

TECHNOLOGY AND TELECOMMUTING CONSULTANTS

AT&T School of Business Centers
   7 Schoolhouse Road
   Somerset, NJ 08875
   Phone: 908-302-5400

Alternative Work Environments' OfficeLYNX
   Specialty: Helps companies set up alternative workplace programs
   The Clock Tower
   1001 Washington Street
   Conshohocken, PA 19428
   Phone: 610-940-5886
   E-mail for AWE:
   russells@awelynx.com
   E-mail for Virtual Resources: sfoxo-hara@aol.com

Bell Atlantic
   Specialty: Training seminars on new workplace technology
   Bell Atlantic Professional Services
   104 Carnegie Center
   Princeton, NJ 08543
   Phone: 800-242-7675
   Web site: http://bell-atl.com/baprof

OfficeVisions Consulting
   Specialty: Futurevisioneering through research, assessment, and education on complex technologies
   112 Monterey Drive
   Brick, NJ 08723
   Phone: 908-920-5187
   E-mail: kruk@chelsea.ios.com

Costello, Maione, Schuch
   Specialty: Home workplace technology, teleconferencing, and audio/video
   1120 Old Country Road
   Plainview, NY 11803
   Phone: 516-933-0747
   E-mail: 70313.3256@compuserve.com
   Web site: http://www.usa.net/icia/cms

Now Work
   Specialty: Works with facility managers to set up and maintain remote work sites
   1173 Grizzly Peak Boulevard
   Berkeley, CA 94708-1740
   Phone: 510-649-8759
   E-mail: rbnmoorad@aol.com

InteleWorks, Inc.
   Specialty: Advises on corporate telecommuting programs
   Suite 200
   4168 Valley Brook Road
   Snellville, GA 30278-4223
   Phone: 404-979-9459

The Synergy Group
   Specialty: Telecommuting services and technology training
   477 Tappan Road
   Northvale, NJ 07647
   Phone: 800-972-8836
   Fax: 201-784-8127

Port Strategic Consulting
   Specialty: Set up telecommuting programs
   155 East 38th Street
   New York, NY 10016
   Phone: 212-661-7111
   Fax: 212-661-9545
   E-mail: EMReilly@aol.com

WorkAnywhere, Inc.
   Specialty: Works with telecommuters to plan space; works with companies to plan telecommuting programs
   12 Stuyvesant Oval/12D
   New York, NY 10009-2215
   Phone: 212-982-5028
   E-mail: BredinA@aol.com

ASSOCIATIONS RELATED TO THE NEW WORKPLACE

International Facility Management Association (IFMA)
   Suite 1100
   One East Greenway Plaza
   Houston, TX 77047-0194
   Phone: 713-623-4362

International Telework Association (formerly known as the Telecommuting Advisory Council)
   204 East Street NE
   Washington, DC 20002
   Phone: 202-547-6157
   Web site: http://www.telecommute.org/

International Society of Facilities Executives
   336 Main Street, E28-100
   Cambridge, MA 02142-1014
   Phone: 617-253-7252
   E-mail: ISFE@MIT.EDU

International Development Research Council
   Suite 150
   35 Technology Park
   Norcross, GA 30092
   Phone: 770-446-8955
   Web site: http://www.idrc.org

EXPOSITIONS, CONFERENCES, AND TRADE SHOWS RELATED TO THE NEW WORKPLACE

Telecommuting and Home Office Exposition and Conference
   Contact: 800-393-THOE
   E-mail: mdolaher@mha.com
   Web site: http://www.mha.com/thoe

ComNet
   Largest telecommunications and computer networking trade shows
   Contact: 617-440-2756
   Web site: http://www.mha.com/comnet/s

alt.office
   Trade show focusing on alternative office environments, launched 1997
   Contact: 212-615-2649
   Web site: http://www.altoffice.com

Telecommute
   Phone: 800-854-0056
   E-mail: 75464.1777@compuserve.com
   Web site: http://www.gilgordon.com

PUBLICATIONS WITH A FOCUS ON THE NEW WORKPLACE

alt.office Journal
   One Penn Plaza
   New York, NY 10110-1198
   Contact: 212-615-2605 or 2717
   Web site: http://www.altoffice.com

Business@Home
610 SW Broadway, Suite 200
Portland, OR 97205
Phone: 503-223-0304
Fax: 503-221-6544
Web site: http://www.gohome.com

Business Week
1221 Avenue of the Americas
New York, NY 10020
Phone: 212-512-2000

Fast Company
Suite 401
77 North Washington Street
Boston, MA 02114-1927
Phone: 617-973-0312
E-mail: loop@fastcompany.com
Web site: http://www.fastcompany.com

Home Office Computing Magazine
730 Broadway
New York, NY 10003
Phone: 800-288-7812
Web site: On America On-Line,
Keyword hoc

Shift: The Journal for the Evolving
Workplace
P.O. Box 638
Highland Park, IL 60035
Phone: 847-831-0300
Fax: 847-564-1199
E-mail:
shifteditor@shiftchange.com

Telecommuting Review
10 Donner Court
Monmouth Junction, NJ 08852
Phone: 732-329-2266
Fax: 732-329-2703
E-mail: gil@gilgordon.com
Web site: http://
www.gilgordon.com/

Workplace
(a publication dedicated to developing the workplace of tomorrow
and today)
Suite 252
255 North Market Street
San Jose, CA 95110-2409
Phone: 408-999-6630

BOOKS ON TELECOMMUTING AND THE HOME OFFICE

For a complete list of every book published on the subject, visit this web site:
http://www.gilgordon.com/gga/amazon.html

Telecommuting: A Manager's Guide to Flexible Work Arrangements
By Joel Kugelmass. Lexington Books, New York, 1995

Home Office Design
By Neal Zimmerman, AIA. John Wiley & Sons, New York, 1996

The Home Office and Small Business Answer Book
By Janet Attard. Henry Holt, New York, 1993

The Virtual Office Survival Handbook
By Alice Bredin. John Wiley & Sons, New York, 1996

The Complete Home Office
By Alvin Rosenbaum. Viking Studio Books, New York, 1995

Telecommute: Go to Work Without Leaving Home
By Lisa Shaw. John Wiley & Sons, New York, 1996

Home Sweet Office
By Jeff Meade. Peterson's, Princeton, NJ, 1993

Making the Most of Work Spaces
By Lorrie Mack, Rizzoli, New York, 1995

Teleworking Explained
By M. Gray, N. Hodson, and G. Gordon, John Wiley & Sons, New York, 1993.

The State of Arizona Program Coordinator Handbook
Call: 602-542-3647

The Telecommuter's Handbook: How to Work for a Salary Without Ever Leaving the House
By Brad and Debra Schepp, McGraw-Hill, New York, 1995

The Home Office Book
By Donna Paula, Artisan, New York, 1996

BOOKS ON THE NEW WORKPLACE

The Telecommuters Advisor
By June Langhoff, Aegis Publishing, Newport, RI, 1996

Manual of Remote Working
By Kevin Curran and Geoff Williams, Gower Publishing, 1997

The Virtual Office: Ten Case Studies
By Anita Dennis, American Institute of Certified Public Accountants, 1997

The Demise of the Office
By Erik Veldhoen and Bart Piepers Veldhoen Facility Consultants BV.PO Box 4500
NL-6202 SB Maastricht
Phone: (31).(0)43.363.89.89, 1995

Workplace by Design
By Franklin Becker and Fritz Steele. Jossey-Bass, San Francisco, 1995

Workspace Strategies
By Dr. Jacqueline C. Vischer. Chapman & Hall, New York, 1996

The New Office
By Karin Tetlow. PBC International, Glen Cove, NY, 1996

Managing the Reinvented Workplace
By William Sims and Franklin Becker, Cornell University, and Michael Joroff, MIT
IDRC's Corporate Real Estate 2000 Project through IDRC and IFMA, Atlanta, GA, 1996

Creating Workplaces Where People Can Think
By Phyl Smith and Lynn Kearny. Jossey-Bass, San Francisco, 1994

VIDEOS ON THE NEW WORKPLACE

The Virtual Office: Wherever Work Needs To Be
By Gil Gordon Associates c/o United Training Media, 1996, 800-424-0364—Code #399. Comes with handbook.

Index

About the Author

Marilyn Zelinsky is the former editor of *Interiors* magazine and has written for several other national publications including *Home Office Computing Magazine*. She has reported extensively on product design, and, is a specialist on the subject of alternative work environment planning and design. She is a member of the National Telecommuting Advisory Council. Now a full-time home-based worker herself, she judged the first annual home-office products competition at NEOCON in 1995, and, she coordinated the second competition in 1996. Marilyn is currently writing a second book about home office design solutions.